S0-AIN-950

THE LOEB CLASSICAL LIBRARY

FOUNDED BY JAMES LOEB 1911

EDITED BY

JEFFREY HENDERSON

EDITOR EMERITUS

G. P. GOOLD

XENOPHON

III

LCL 90

XENOPHON

ANABASIS

WITH AN ENGLISH TRANSLATION BY
CARLETON L. BROWNSON

REVISED BY JOHN DILLERY

HARVARD UNIVERSITY PRESS
CAMBRIDGE, MASSACHUSETTS
LONDON, ENGLAND

Copyright © 1998 by the President and Fellows
of Harvard College
All rights reserved

First published 1922
Reprinted six times
Revised Edition 1998
Reprinted with corrections 2001

LOEB CLASSICAL LIBRARY® is a registered trademark
of the President and Fellows of Harvard College

ISBN 0-674-99101-X

Composed in ZephGreek and ZephText by
Technologies 'N Typography, Merrimac, Massachusetts.
Printed in Great Britain by St Edmundsbury Press Ltd,
Bury St Edmunds, Suffolk, on acid-free paper.
Bound by Hunter & Foulis Ltd, Edinburgh, Scotland.

CONTENTS

REVISED EDITION, 1998

For this Revised Edition of Xenophon's *Anabasis,* John Dillery has extensively revised the text in accordance with current scholarship, made consequent revisions as well as corrections throughout Carleton L. Brownson's translation, supplied updated notes, and provided a new Introduction.

INTRODUCTION

The *Anabasis* is Xenophon's account of the march of ten thousand Greek soldiers through much of the western portion of the Persian empire. Mercenaries hired by a rebellious Achaemenid prince, Cyrus the Younger, they followed him to the great battle of Cunaxa, fought near Babylon in the summer of 401 BC. There Cyrus fell in the effort to wrest the throne of Persia from his brother, Artaxerxes II, and the Ten Thousand (as they were later called), without their leader and employer, had to make their own way back to the Greek world. Along the way their generals were captured (and later executed), and the Ten Thousand were forced to choose new leaders. Xenophon emerged as the ideal replacement, and guided the men through difficult terrain, food shortages, and sometimes hostile peoples to reach the relative safety of the northwest coast of Asia Minor.

For many decades the language, style, and content of the *Anabasis* made it the recommended text for learners of Attic Greek. At the same time scholarly attention was addressed mainly to its stylistic and linguistic features. More recent studies have redressed this balance by greater

Note. I would like to thank Professor Zeph Stewart for his generous and invaluable advice about this introduction.

concentration on the work's importance as a historical source and as a work of literature. The *Anabasis* tells us a great deal about the inner workings of the Persian empire at the end of the fifth century, about relations between the Greeks and the Persians, and more generally about the experience of one of the earliest mercenary armies in the West, a type of army that was to be seen with greater frequency in the years to come. It also provides us with more reliable information about the life of Xenophon himself than any other document surviving from antiquity. The *Anabasis* is first and foremost a memoir written by a military man about his earlier career. But it is also a work of biography, containing, most notably, a famous obituary of Cyrus, as well as brief character sketches of the captured generals. Indeed, as with so many of Xenophon's works, the *Anabasis* defies generic categorization: not entirely a history nor a travelogue, the work combines elements of both.

Xenophon

Xenophon was a man of unusually wide experience who lived for more than seventy years. He seems to have known personally, to varying degrees of familiarity, several of the men who shaped the political and intellectual landscape of the last years of the fifth century and the first half of the fourth: among them, Socrates, Cyrus the Younger, and Agesilaus of Sparta. He was both a professional soldier and a writer. In his corpus we find works we can style philosophy as well as history: indeed, in antiquity he was considered first a philosopher, and secondly a historian. He lived in an age of change and was, as an exile from his native Athens who also had an intimate knowledge of Sparta, in

an intermediary or interstitial position: from his vantage point he could draw on experiences few others had, and provide unique insights into the world in which he lived. All his works demonstrate a mind that was at one moment very much a product of its time, yet also capable of radically new understandings. The *Anabasis* is particularly illustrative in this regard.

The *Anabasis* tells us more about Xenophon than any other document from antiquity; but with that said, we do not know very much. Indeed, passages from this work are at the heart of three disputed points regarding his life: the year of his birth, and consequently his age; the precise circumstances surrounding his exile from Athens (the date and cause); and the exact nature of Xenophon's relationship with Socrates. Although all these issues remain unresolved, the *Anabasis* does provide repeated confirmation of perhaps the most important fact about his career: Xenophon was a military man, and military thinking is at the center of how he understood his world.

As with many authors from antiquity, we do not know precisely when Xenophon was born. All that can be said with certainty is that the year of his birth was probably between 430 and 425.[1] At 3.1.25 he implies that his youth might discourage some from appointing him leader of a unit once commanded by his Boeotian friend Proxenus; we learn in Proxenus' obituary that he was about 30 when he died (2.6.20). Hence modern scholars have reasoned that Xenophon was probably younger than Proxenus, putting him in his late twenties in 401, which sets his year of birth

---

[1] Dates are BC unless otherwise specified; all references without title are to the *Anabasis*.

in 428. A passage that has been overlooked in this discussion, and one that complicates the standard view of Xenophon's age, is the Thracian chief Seuthes' offer to Xenophon to take as wives each other's daughters (7.2.38). For Seuthes to imagine that Xenophon had a daughter of roughly marriageable age (which, of course, could be as early as twelve or thirteen), he could not have been quite as young as 3.1.25 implies.

Another major question concerning Xenophon's life that is touched on in the *Anabasis* is his exile from Athens. At 5.3.4ff. we learn about two dedications he made from booty acquired with the mercenary army, one to Apollo at Delphi, and the other to Artemis of Ephesus. In reporting how he managed the second dedication he mentions his exile from his native city (5.3.6–7). The problem centers on the precise phrasing of "when Xenophon was in exile," and in particular the exact time that is indicated.[2] Whatever the correct reading may be, most scholars conclude that 5.3.7 suggests that Xenophon was banished either shortly before or after the battle of Coronea (394). It seems most likely

---

[2] The manuscripts transmit a variety of readings. The three major ones are ἐπεὶ δ᾽ ἔφυγε, ἐπεὶ δ᾽ ἔφευγε, and ἐπειδὴ δ᾽ ἔφευγε. It is the readings with imperfect verb form that have been accepted in modern critical editions: Marchant (OCT) and Masqueray (Budé) print ἐπειδὴ δ᾽ ἔφευγε; Hude/Peters (Teubner) ἐπεὶ δ᾽ ἔφευγε. It needs to be pointed out, however, that the two main families of manuscripts are judged to be of equal value: see the introductory statement about the text. See also C. Tuplin, "Xenophon's Exile Again," in *Homo Viator: Classical Essays for John Bramble*, M. Whitby, P. Hardie, M. Whitby eds. (Bristol 1987) 62 and n.15.

that his participation in Agesilaus' march back to Greece from Asia Minor (spring-summer 394), combined with his earlier service with Cyrus, a friend of Sparta and enemy of Athens, were both causes for the banishment.

The *Anabasis* also contains an important passage that relates to the issue of the relationship between Xenophon and Socrates: the famous story at 3.1.4–8 of Xenophon's consultation at Delphi regarding service with Cyrus, and Socrates' advice on the matter. There we are told that his friend Proxenus had written him a letter inviting him to join the other mercenaries in Cyrus the Younger's army. Without explaining why, Xenophon reports that he then showed the letter to Socrates "the Athenian." At this point Socrates expresses his worry that support for Cyrus would lead to suspicion at home; further, he recommends that Xenophon consult the oracle of Apollo at Delphi. Xenophon goes to Delphi and asks to which god he should sacrifice and pray in order that he might fare well on his intended journey and return home in safety. Having received his answer Xenophon returns to Athens and tells Socrates the response he had been given; Socrates scolds Xenophon for not first asking whether he should go on the journey at all. But, since the god had responded positively, Socrates recommends that Xenophon follow the advice of the oracle.

This story reflects a close relationship between Xenophon and Socrates. Xenophon has no reservations about taking his problem to the philosopher; Socrates, for his part, is concerned that the young man will excite hostility at home. Socrates' scolding of Xenophon for not asking the primary question—should I go on the expedition—sug-

gests almost a father/son relationship. Although Xenophon implies here and elsewhere a close bond between himself and Socrates, it is widely believed that while he was more than just an acquaintance of Socrates, they were not intimate. Whatever the precise nature of the connection, Xenophon thought of himself as a follower of Socrates; and like other associates of Socrates, he may have played some role in the government of the Thirty Tyrants, perhaps as a member of the 3000 enrolled citizens.

The precise year of Xenophon's death, as with his birth, is not known. The last datable event alluded to in his *Hellenica* is from some time between 357/6 and 353. And we know from his last work, the *Poroi* or *Revenues*, that he lived to see the end of the Social War between Athens and its allies (355).[3] Hence, a date for Xenophon's death in the late 350s seems most probable.

Anabasis: Formal Issues

At the beginning of Book Three of his *Hellenica* Xenophon provides a succinct summary of the *Anabasis:* "As to how Cyrus collected an army and with this army made the march up country (ἀνέβη) against his brother, how the battle [of Cunaxa] was fought, how Cyrus was slain, and how after that the Greeks effected their return in safety to the sea—all this has been written by Themistogenes the Syracusan" (*Hell.* 3.1.1–2, Brownson trans. LCL). The ref-

---

[3] *Hell.* 6.4.37 refers to the Thessalian king Tisiphonus being in power; his reign is known from Diodorus to extend from 357/6 to 353 (Diod. 16.14.1, 35.1).

erence to Themistogenes is remarkable. The only other ancient authority also to mention Themistogenes is the *Suda*, and its entry is dubious and looks as if it has been constructed out of the passage from the *Hellenica*. Plutarch, for one, believed that Xenophon was attributing his own work to a fictional Themistogenes in order "to win greater credence for his narrative by referring to himself in the third person" (*Moralia* 345e). While there was probably not a Themistogenes the Syracusan, there were two and possibly three other accounts of the journey of the Ten Thousand. We know from Xenophon himself that Ctesias also dealt with it in his history of Persia which went down to 397, for he mentions Ctesias' version of Cunaxa in his own treatment of the battle (1.8.26–7 = *FGH* 688 F 21). Additionally, another veteran of the march, Sophaenetus, also wrote a Κύρου Ἀνάβασις, as we can tell from a number of geographical references preserved in the sixth century AD writer Stephanus of Byzantium (*FGH* 109 FF 1–4). The suggestion has been made that Xenophon wrote his *Anabasis* in part as a response to Sophaenetus' account. Later, in the first century, Diodorus of Sicily also wrote about the Ten Thousand. His source (Ephorus, fourth century) was manifestly drawing on material different from what Xenophon provides; further, to judge from Diodorus' narrative, this earlier version did not even mention Xenophon. If Sophaenetus is the text in question, he evidently did not think Xenophon's role in the army was important, and Xenophon may have wanted to counter this assessment. Ephorus' source is uncertain. It has recently been argued that he was using not Sophaenetus but the unknown author of a continuation of Thucydides' history of

the Peloponnesian war, the so-called Oxyrhynchus historian.[4] However the question of the source for Diodorus/Ephorus might be resolved, it remains that Xenophon's *Anabasis* was not the only history of the events it recounts, and that Xenophon may have been motivated to write his version in response to another.

The title *Anabasis* means a journey up-country or inland, referring to the march of Cyrus the Younger and his army from the coast of Asia Minor to the Tigris-Euphrates river valley where the decisive battle of Cunaxa was fought. Xenophon uses this term to describe the beginning of Cyrus' march in his summary of the *Anabasis* in the *Hellenica*, quoted above. Inasmuch as this phase of the march covers only the first two books of the text, some have thought that the work would be better called a *katabasis* or "journey back," or perhaps also *parabasis* for the "journey along" the Black Sea to Byzantium, following a division of the march that was observed by ancient writers. *Anabasis,* however, is the title used by Diogenes Laertius in his list of the works of Xenophon (2.56).

The dating of the composition of the *Anabasis* is problematic, as is the case with most of Xenophon's works. An early examination of the change in particle usage in the works of Xenophon suggested the *Anabasis* came from the middle period of his literary career.[5] Few would now

[4] H. D. Westlake, "Diodorus and the Expedition of Cyrus," *Phoenix* 41 (1987) 241–54.

[5] W. Dittenberger, "Sprachliche Kriterien für die Chronologie der platonischen Dialoge," *Hermes* 16 (1881) 331. Cf. J. Hatzfeld, "Notes sur la composition des *Helléniques*," *RPh* 4 (1930) 113–17

endorse the precise chronology that emerged from this and similar studies. All that can be said with confidence is that the *Anabasis* was written late in Xenophon's life, not earlier. This suggestion suits the view that it is in part an *apologia* or response to other accounts of the same events. Further, many have argued on the basis of Xenophon's description of his estate at Scillus (5.3.7–13) that when he wrote up his version of the March of the Ten Thousand, he had lost this property as a result of the first Theban invasion of the Peloponnese following the battle of Leuctra, that is, after 371: the passage is thought to have a nostalgic or even wistful outlook that makes sense if it concerns something that Xenophon no longer possessed. This argument, however, is highly speculative.

The *Anabasis* has no real precursors. It is true that in the fifth century, travel literature was not uncommon, a genre that combines biography, autobiography, and ethnography—elements that are also to be found in the *Anabasis*.[6] Indeed, passages that have often bored and confused its readers find an explanation if we remember that this work was written when gazetteers were also popular. Xenophon frequently mentions distances between stopping points on the march inland; he may have derived

and 209–26, and M. MacLaren, "On the Composition of Xenophon's *Hellenica*," *AJP* 55 (1934) 121–39 and 249–62.

[6] Scylax of Caryanda, mentioned in Herodotus (4.44.1; cf. Aristotle, *Pol.* 1332b), included autobiographic information in the account of his nautical explorations, and probably also penned a biography of Heraclides, tyrant of Mylasa. Ion of Chios wrote an account of his visits to famous people and places in the *Epidemiai* or *Hypomnemata*.

these from a written description of the Persian road system, perhaps from Ctesias' history of the Persian empire.[7] The repeated description of cities and other communities as inhabited, flourishing, great, and the like (1.2.6–7, 10–14, 20; 1.4.1; 1.5.4; 2.4.13; 3.4.7; 4.7.19; 6.4.6), almost certainly comes from geographical literature.[8] But these details provide only a superficial link between the *Anabasis* and other literature from the period.

The obituaries Xenophon provides for Cyrus (1.9) and the captured generals of the Ten Thousand (2.6) offer a better clue to the orientation of the *Anabasis*. These are clearly biographies. The latter group of portraits has been linked to the description of the heroes in Euripides' *Suppliants* (860ff.).[9] They were surely planned as a set, contrasting good and bad forms of leadership: the Spartan Clearchus is presented as an energetic and capable leader who was too severe; Proxenus the Boeotian is the opposite, a "soldiers' man" who lacked the necessary discipline; Menon was altogether worthless, interested in his own ad-

---

[7] G. Cawkwell, *Xenophon: The Persian Expedition* (Harmondsworth 1972) 21–22. Cyrus did not take the famous Royal Road inland; cf. Herodotus 8.98 and Xenophon, *Cyr.* 6.17–18.

[8] H. R. Immerwahr, "*Ergon*: History as a Monument in Herodotus and Thucydides," *AJP* 81 (1960) 264 and n.7, and the bibliography cited there. Note also L. Geysels, "Πόλις οἰκουμένη dans l'Anabase de Xénophon," *Les études classiques* 42 (1974) 29–38. The phrase "great and flourishing" was relatively common: cf. Aristophanes, *Birds* 37. It had a long life: it is in Dexippus *FGH* 100 F 3, and was spoofed by Lucian, *Hist. Conscr.* 31.

[9] A. Momigliano, *The Development of Greek Biography* (Cambridge Mass. 1971; exp. ed. 1993) 49 and 57; cf. C. Collard, *Euripides Supplices* vol. 2 (Groningen 1975) 445.

vancement and wealth, and proving to be a completely unreliable and deceitful commander with a lurid past. It is telling that Ctesias' characterization of Menon is not so negatively drawn (*FGH* 688 F 27–28); further, Menon does not appear to be the reprobate Xenophon considers him in the Platonic dialogue that bears his name.[10]

The ideal leader is Cyrus. In the obituary Xenophon traces his life from childhood in the Persian court to his death at Cunaxa. Focus is directed primarily on his ability to generate loyalty among his followers, to cultivate good soldiers, to outdo his friends in kindness and the giving of rewards and outdo his enemies in exacting punishment and revenge. In many ways Cyrus is the ideal Greek: he is expert at helping his friends and hurting his enemies. When earlier in the *Anabasis* Cyrus complains that his own native troops are vastly inferior to the Greeks under his command, he also confesses that rather than all the material goods he possesses he would prefer to have the freedom that makes excellent soldiers (1.7.3–4); Herodotus could not have put the difference between Greek and barbarian better (Cyrus even uses the term *barbaros* in the passage). In Xenophon's understanding, Cyrus has the mentality of a Greek, and a particularly insightful and generous one at that.

Xenophon's interest in ideal leadership is found throughout his corpus. In the *Hellenica* he provides miniature portraits of successful and unsuccessful commanders similar to those at *Anabasis* 2.6: the paired studies of Iphicrates and Mnasippus (*Hell*. 6.2.4–32), and the two estimations of Teleutias' leadership (*Hell*. 5.1.3–4, 5.3.3–7) espe-

[10] Cawkwell, *Persian Expedition* 25, 135 n.12.

11

cially come to mind. In all of these passages Xenophon implies that one of the functions of history ought to be the education of future military commanders in the art of leadership.[11] The obituary of Cyrus, on the other hand, is similar to Xenophon's encomium of the Spartan king Agesilaus, perhaps influenced by Isocrates' *Evagoras*. The *Agesilaus* also moves from a narrative of the life of its subject to a more general summation of his virtues.

The closest parallel to the portrait of Cyrus is the *Cyropaedia*, Xenophon's fictional account of the education of Cyrus the Great, Cyrus the Younger's ancestor and the founder of the Achaemenid dynasty. The linking of the two men as representatives of the ideal leader is suggested by Xenophon himself at the beginning of the obituary: the younger Cyrus was the man "who was the most kingly and the most worthy to rule of all the Persians who have been born since Cyrus the Elder" (2.9.1).[12] What made the second man a good leader is precisely what forms the subject of the work devoted to the first: education and royal character. Clearly the influence of Socrates is to be felt in all of Xenophon's experiments in moral-didactic biography; and to the extent that this is true, he was participating in the

[11] Cf. H. R. Breitenbach, *Historiographische Anschauungsformen Xenophons* (Freiburg in der Schweiz 1950); P. J. Rahn, "Xenophon's Developing Historiography," *TAPA* 102 (1971) 497-508.

[12] This tendency to associate the two Cyruses, which appears elsewhere in the literature of the period (e.g. Antisthenes), may be linked to Persian sympathizers of the younger Cyrus: on the fashioning of his tomb after Cyrus the Great's, see Boyce *HZ* 210 and n.3.

newly emerging genre of biography that found its first real impetus and inspiration in the person of Socrates.

The autobiographical elements of the *Anabasis* are also significant. The work is the first representative we have of what later the Romans would call *commentarii*, or memoirs, often written by military men documenting their campaigns—including Alexander's generals Ptolemy, Aristobulus, and Nearchus, and later the Achaean general Aratus of Sicyon. As Momigliano noted, throughout the *Anabasis* Xenophon presents events "with a strongly subjective approach." Indeed, at one point in the narrative, after the generals have been treacherously seized by Tissaphernes, it is because of Xenophon's exhortations that the army avoids a complete breakdown of morale and recovers its fighting spirit. What is more, Xenophon's decision to take charge of this desperate situation and rebuild the confidence of the army is presented as an internal dialogue with himself (3.1.11ff.). His own inspiration comes in the form of a dream sent from Zeus. As Xenophon presents it, there would have been no return march of the Ten Thousand without divine intervention and his own initiative. One is left to wonder how instrumental Xenophon really was in rebuilding the army's confidence. Yet, assuming that there were others who knew the events being described—veterans of the march—how far could he deviate from the truth?

This autobiographical tendency doubtless stems in part from the apologetic purpose of the text. But more than this, the autobiographic is also connected to Xenophon's propensity to view the actions of the army primarily through the lens of the individual commander. Throughout much of the middle portion of the *Anabasis*, from the

march from Cunaxa until the arrival at the Black Sea, the actions of the army are reduced to the actions of the unit leaders: when the Ten Thousand march through the territory of the Carduchi, it is "Xenophon" and "Cheirisophus" who rush to each other's support and secure the passage of the army through mountainous terrain (4.2.26), even though whole units of men are in question. On another occasion, an important pass through the land of the Taochi is gained when what appears to be a handful of individuals, in rivalry with one another, hold a contest to see who can get to a strategically placed village before the others (4.7.10–12). Almost completely absent is any mention of the common foot soldiers. To be sure, part of the reason for this manner of presentation is that it is standard military parlance. However, taking the narrative of Thucydides as a point of comparison, we do not find there the same exclusive focus on the commander. Thucydides' account often moves forward by alternating sections of collective activity with narrative driven by the thoughts and actions of leaders: "commander narrative."[13] But his text is a careful blending of the two modes of presentation. By contrast, there are moments in the *Anabasis*, especially in Books 3 to 5, when one completely loses sight of the larger army of soldiers. Commanders are presented not simply as a shorthand for the thoughts and actions of the army as a whole; they are individuals achieving personal fame or censure. At the height of its operational success, then, the Ten Thousand become a heroic warrior band, and the narrative centers on the achievements of a few leaders, much as in

[13] W. R. Connor, *Thucydides* (Princeton 1984) 54–55.

Homer the description of the action is confined primarily to the heroes.[14] This feature of the presentation may help to explain some of the epic resonances that are to be found in the text, such as the dream sent from Zeus.[15]

Xenophon's conception of the army as a band of warriors is no doubt to be connected to an interest in finding paradigms of good leadership; yet there is more to this trend than the didactic. As can also be seen from the presentation of important events in the *Hellenica*, Xenophon understood the past as primarily the actions of individual persons, specifically charismatic leaders, not necessarily states or armies, and in this he was not unique. The role of the individual in historical writing was to become increasingly important as the fourth century proceeded, from Theopompus' *Philippika* to the accounts of Alexander's conquests.

[14] Cf. J. G. Howie, "The Major *aristeia* in Homer and Xenophon," *Papers of the Leeds International Latin Seminar* 9 (1996) 197–217, which examines primarily the *Cyropaedia* and Homer. For other Homeric connections as they relate specifically to the *Anabasis*, see M. Lossau, "Xenophons Odyssee," *Antike und Abendland* 36 (1990) 47–52, and A. Dalby, "Greeks Abroad: Social Organization and Food among the Ten Thousand," *JHS* 112 (1992) 16–30.

[15] Note also Clearchus' speech to his troops at 1.3.6, which has been connected to Andromache's famous appeal to Hector (*Iliad* 6.429–30). Odysseus is explicitly mentioned at 5.1.2; the Lotus Eaters at 3.2.25. Xenophon urges his men forward against the Colchians, noting that "if it were possible, we ought to devour them raw" (4.8.14), a statement both shocking and Homeric: see *Iliad* 4.34–5, 22.346–7 and 24.212–13. Cf. *Hell.* 3.3.6.

XENOPHON

The Anabasis and Political History

It is important for the reader of the *Anabasis* to have some acquaintance with the history and governance of the Persian empire. To begin with, it must always be remembered that the work takes as its starting point the revolt of a Persian prince against his brother the King. Cyrus the Younger's rebellion against his brother Artaxerxes, however, was not the first dynastic conflict between Achaemenids. Indeed, with the exception of Cambyses' assumption of the throne of his father Cyrus the Great, all of the Achaemenid royal successions were attended by conflict between princes.[16] What Cyrus attempted was not at all novel in the court of the Persians.

The *Anabasis* reveals a good knowledge of the administrative organization of the Achaemenid empire; other of Xenophon's works are also illuminating is this regard (e.g. *Oec.* 4.4, *Cyr.* 8.6). What he knew about Persian government he learned from knowledgeable informants: although Xenophon may well have acquired some basic facts about the Achaemenid empire through autopsy, we can tell from a passage in the *Anabasis* that he did not know Persian (4.5.34), and hence had to rely on others for more detailed information.

The most important figure in the Persian government was of course the Great King. Immediately below him were the administrators of large areas of the empire: the satraps and native rulers. Although ultimately subject to

[16] For the Achaemenid succession down to Cyrus the Younger, see esp. A. Kuhrt, *The Ancient Near East* vol. II (London and New York 1995) 664–73.

the authority of the King, and responsible for payment of tribute to him, the satraps were largely autonomous: they had control over their own armies, had their own elaborate retinue, and could even conduct foreign policy on their own.[17] The native rulers, left in charge of their lands by grant from the throne, seem to have been semi-independent in much the same way as the satraps.[18] Satraps were not necessarily the same as high-level military officers (what the Greeks call generals, στρατηγοί), though functionally they often were.[19] There were also important limits on the independence of the satrap. While satraps could conduct foreign policy, they could not deviate from, or fail to carry out, the wishes of the King without risking dire consequences.[20] While the satrap was free to raise the tribute in whatever manner he wished, if his methods became objectionable to the King, the satrap had to make changes.[21] The King kept track of the affairs of his subordinates through the "royal scribe" assigned to each satrap as well as by an informal chain of informants; there was in addition a senior official at the royal court known as the

[17] Army and tribute: see, e.g., 1.1.8; satrap's court: see, e.g., 1.5.15, and 1.9.31; foreign policy: see esp. Cyrus as executor of the King's plans at *Hell.* 1.4.3.

[18] Note the case of Syennesis: 1.8.21ff.

[19] A. Andrewes, *A Historical Commentary on Thucydides* vol. V (Oxford 1981) 14, discussing Pharnabazus' remarks at *Hell.* 4.1.37.

[20] At *Hell.* 4.8.16 Tiribazus worries that he should not change the policy of the King without consulting with him first. Cf. the treatment of Tissaphernes at *Hell.* 3.4.25.

[21] For problems with tribute collection, see the famous letter from Darius to Gadatas, ML no.12.

King's Eye, responsible for what might be called internal security.[22] Occasionally special representatives from the King would also intervene in satrapal business, and sometimes satraps were given authority over other satrapies when the need arose. Furthermore, royal judges administered law throughout the realm for the monarch.[23] Central control was also exercised when the King visited his *paradeisoi* or country residences throughout the empire.[24]

For the most part, however, power was decentralized in the Achaemenid realm. This held true even within each individual satrapy. Hyparchs, or district governors, stood in relation to the satraps in much the same way the satraps stood in relation to the Great King: they too had their own armies, and could accumulate vast sums of money in their treasuries.[25] Other regional executive officers were also found: at one point in the *Anabasis*, Cheirisophus and Xeno-

[22] Cf C. Tuplin, "The Administration of the Achaemenid Empire," in *Coinage and Administration in the Athenian and Persian Empires*, Ian Carradice ed. (Oxford 1987) 120.

[23] In the early years of Cyrus the Great's rule there was a "governor of the land" (*sakin mati*) in Babylonia, later replaced by a satrap "of Babylonia and Beyond the River." See Tuplin, in Carradice, *Coinage and Administration* 114. On royal judges, see Tuplin 119–20.

[24] *Paradeisos* (paradise) is an Iranian word: P. Chantraine, *Dictionnaire étymologique de la langue grecque* vol. II (Paris 1984) 857.

[25] Note the case of Belesys (1.4.10, 7.8.25): M. W. Stolper, "The Babylonian Enterprise of Belesys," in P. Briant ed., *Dans les pas des Dix-Mille* (Toulouse 1995) = *Pallas* 43, 217–238. See also the case of Mania, hyparch of Dardanus in the satrapy of Pharnabazus: *Hell.* 3.1.10ff.

phon hold extensive negotiations with a *komarch*, or village leader (4.5.10ff); his powers, it seems, are surprisingly broad. In general, the *Anabasis* gives the impression of a highly fragmented empire in which there are several autonomous regions.

This administrative structure was designed, above all else, to facilitate and maintain the extraction of wealth from the various lands of the empire. It is clear from both documentary and literary evidence that the satraps and their subordinates collected tribute for the King; and if they fell into arrears, they had to do their best to make up the funds owing (1.1.8).[26] Tribute ($\delta a \sigma \mu \acute{o} s$) was paid most often in silver. However, tribute could also be paid in kind, specifically for the maintenance of the King's own person and household. At 4.5.24, for example, we learn that a village in Armenia pays a royal *dasmos* of 17 horses.[27] Importantly, these payments in kind could also be made to satraps and other officials of high rank: at 3.4.31, Xenophon tells of barley, wine, and feed for horses being set aside for the satrap of the region.[28] In the *Hellenica* (3.1.16) there is also a passing reference to the hereditary possession of cities, and consequently presumably also of the rights to the revenue collection associated with them.

Cyrus the Younger's own position in relation to his father Darius II and his brother Artaxerxes II was complex. We know from 1.9.7 that he was sent out in 407 by his

[26] Cf. Thucydides 8.5.5; Ps. Aristotle, *Oec*. 1348a.

[27] Cf. Herodotus 3.91.2, 90.3, 92.1.

[28] Cf. Parysatis, 1.4.9. Thucydides reports the famous case of Themistocles: he was given Magnesia for his bread, Lampsacus for his wine, and Myus for his meat (1.138.5).

father as satrap of Lydia, Great Phrygia, and Cappadocia; we learn from the same passage that in addition to holding this satrapy, he was made commander "of all those who were compelled to muster in the plain of the Castolus River" (cf. 1.1.2 and *Hell*. 1.4.3).[29] The two jobs were not the same. Cyrus was to replace Tissaphernes as the King's personal representative in his negotiations with the Greeks and specifically the Spartans. Often the individuals sent out to deal with the situation in western Asia Minor had very specific instructions from the King. Hence, Cyrus' command was technically an extraordinary one with far-reaching powers. In addition to his large satrapy (Tissaphernes' seemed to be reduced to Caria), other satraps were answerable to him (Pharnabazus, satrap of northwest Asia Minor: cf. *Hell*. 1.4.5). This command, given at the expense of Tissaphernes, may well account for the latter's hostility toward Cyrus.

As we learn at the beginning of the *Anabasis*, when Darius II felt that his death was imminent, he sent for Cyrus. After the death of the old King and the establishment of Artaxerxes II on the throne, Tissaphernes is reported as scheming against Cyrus, suggesting to Artaxerxes that his brother was plotting to usurp the throne. Arrested, Cyrus is saved only by his mother's pleadings, and is restored to his post—though now truncated, inasmuch as the Ionian cities, which had been his before (*Hell*. 2.1.4), then had to revolt from Tissaphernes in order to join his side (1.1.6–8). At least as Xenophon presents it, Artaxerxes' treatment of Cyrus is the cause of the latter's rebellion.

---

[29] Cf. Herodotus 5.102.2.

Given the history of dynastic dispute among the Achaemenids, this account is surely not the whole story.

More to the point, the structure of Achaemenid imperial administration helps to explain how the attempt of Cyrus could have begun in the first place, and why the Ten Thousand succeeded in surviving even though they seemed to be facing such great obstacles. The autonomy granted satraps and other officials meant that they were often in conflict with one another. We have already noted Cyrus' replacement of Tissaphernes in the West and the conflict it no doubt caused. In the *Hellenica* (3.1.5) we see even more clearly two satraps at odds with one another: Tissaphernes and Pharnabazus.[30] Furthermore, as Cyrus did, satraps would also on occasion revolt from the King.[31] Cyrus succeeds in disguising the creation of his army because his brother believes that he is at war with Tissaphernes (1.1.8): this suggests that the mustering of armies was well within the competence of satraps such as Cyrus, and further, that conflicts between satraps were to be expected. The independence enjoyed by Cyrus in the satrapal system permitted him to create the army of the Ten Thousand.

That the Ten Thousand were not destroyed by Persian forces is also explained by the nature of the Achaemenid realm. Significant areas of the empire were not under the control of the Persians: in a speech in the *Anabasis* Xeno-

[30] Cf. Thucydides 8.6.1–2.

[31] E.g., Pissuthnes, satrap of Lydia, and his son Amorges: Ctesias, *FGH* 688 F 15.53; Thucydides 8.5.5, 19.2, 28.2–5, 54.3. Also the famous Satraps' Revolt: see esp. Nepos, *Life of Datames;* Diodorus 15.90–3. Note also Herodotus 9.113 for Masistes and Bactria.

phon mentions the independence of Mysia, Pisidia, and Lycaonia (3.2.23). Some regions would have felt little if any Persian presence. In addition, the Ten Thousand were not regarded by the Persians as a serious threat, despite what later Greek propaganda said about them.[32]

Another issue connected with Achaemenid rule (and specifically dynastic conflict) that we also see—however fleetingly—in the pages of the *Anabasis* is the importance of royal women. Clearly Parysatis, the mother of both Cyrus the Younger and Artaxerxes, is a woman of considerable power: indeed, she almost succeeds in helping Cyrus usurp the throne. Further, Epyaxa, a Cilician queen, gives Cyrus a vast sum of money to help pay for his army (1.2.12). It is of course true that Greek historians tend to focus on "harem politics," and attribute to Persian women a great deal of influence at court because they wish to characterize Persian culture as effeminate and ruled in some sense by women. However, documentary evidence such as the Persepolis Fortification Tablets suggests that women were in fact very powerful figures.

While the *Anabasis* is in the main an account of the Ten Thousand, the Persians, and their subject peoples through whose territory the Greeks must march, the work also contains important information regarding the relationship between Persia and Sparta. It is therefore useful to recall the history of Persian and Spartan relations leading up to the revolt of Cyrus as well as immediately afterwards. In the winter of 413/12, a little more than a year after Athens and Sparta had resumed hostilities—the beginning of the "Ionian" phase of the Peloponnesian war—Darius II had

[32] Cawkwell, *Persian Expedition* 28.

demanded that his western satraps, Tissaphernes and Pharnabazus, pay the tributes due from the Greek cities of Asia. From the summer of 412 to the spring of 411 Tissaphernes conducted a series of negotiations with the Spartans, until the Spartans acknowledged the King's right of control over the Greeks of Asia Minor in return for Persian help, both monetary and material (ships), in raising and maintaining a fleet to fight the Athenians. Darius was in a delicate position: while he probably saw Athens as his main enemy, inasmuch as they were in possession of what he regarded as his (the Greek cities of Asia), he did not want to ally openly with Sparta; rather, as can be seen in Tissaphernes' planning, at first both sides were to be supported in the hope that they would destroy each other.[33]

In 410 Tissaphernes claimed that he was following the King's orders to fight the Athenians (*Hell*. 1.1.9), and in 407 the position of Persia in the Peloponnesian war became unambiguous. Darius was now openly behind the Spartans against Athens: it is at this time that Cyrus was sent to take up the Lydian satrapy (replacing Tissaphernes, who was now in charge of Caria only) as well as the command of the forces "that muster on the plain of the Castolus." Shortly thereafter (406), the Spartans sent out Lysander as supreme commander, and he complained to Cyrus of Tissaphernes' leadership and encouraged the prince to become more involved in the war against Athens; this Cyrus promised to do, offering a vast sum of money (500 talents), and more if needed, to help with the costs of the war (*Hell*. 1.5.2–3). The friendship between the two men formed the

[33] Thucydides 8.18, 37, 43, 48, 58.

cornerstone of Persian and Spartan policy in the region (cf. *Hell*. 1.5.6, 2.1.13–15, and *Oec*. 4.20–25).

When Cyrus revolted, Sparta was put into an awkward position. On the testimony of the *Hellenica*, Sparta seemed openly to back Cyrus' claim to the throne (see esp. *Hell*. 3.1.1–2). To judge from the *Anabasis*, however, the Spartans did not enthusiastically support the effort, indeed were later hostile to the Greeks who had been in Cyrus' service: the Ten Thousand are declared outlaws by the Spartans (6.6.9), and a Spartan general puts a price on Xenophon's head (7.6.43). And, in fact, earlier the Ten Thousand had almost sacked a Spartan controlled city: Byzantium (7.1.7–17). The Spartans, and Lysander in particular, had profited enormously from the friendship of Cyrus. On the other hand, open support for him would have brought them into conflict with Artaxerxes II. It may well be that, under the influence of Lysander's policy, Sparta did back Cyrus, but had to do so covertly.[34] Later, in the autumn of 400, with Athens defeated, the Spartans repudiated their agreement with the King and declared war on Persia under the banner of restoring freedom to the Greeks of Asia Minor.[35] In the spring of 399, we learn in

[34] See, e.g., P. Cartledge, *Agesilaos and the Crisis of Sparta* (Baltimore 1987) 352–3, and D. M. Lewis, *Sparta and Persia* (Leiden 1977) 138. Spartan help included ships: see *Hell*. 3.1.1.

[35] Some historians believe that this was the Spartans' primary aim: thus, Lewis, *Sparta and Persia* esp.144ff. Others see the campaign as an example of Spartan imperialism: see, e.g., H.W. Parke, "The Development of the Second Spartan Empire," *JHS* 50 (1930) 37–79, and R. Seager and C. Tuplin, "The Freedom of the Greeks of Asia Minor: On the Origins of a Concept and the

the *Anabasis* (7.8.24), the remnants of the Ten Thousand were incorporated into the Spartan army operating in Asia Minor under Thibron.

The Anabasis and Social and Intellectual History

As precursors to the Ten Thousand we find Greeks in the employ of satraps in the early years of the Peloponnesian War: Pissuthnes sends seven hundred mercenaries (ἐπί-κουροι) to the anti-Athenian faction on Samos and later also provides Notium with men described as Arcadian and barbarian mercenaries. His son Amorges can field a force of mercenaries drawn primarily from the Peloponnese.[36] As the composition of the Ten Thousand also suggests, the northern Peloponnese (Arcadia, Achaea) was a popular area for the recruitment of professional soldiers (1.1.6, 6.2.10).

With the Ten Thousand, however, we enter into a new era in mercenary warfare. Earlier, Greek professional soldiers had served mostly in small units, often as the elite or guard units of tyrants and foreign rulers. The mercenaries in Cyrus the Younger's army, by contrast, constituted the largest collection up to that time of such troops from the Greek world. Furthermore, even after the death of their employer, and later the capture of their commanders, they remained together, campaigning successfully for almost

Creation of a Slogan," *JHS* 100 (1980) 141–157. A. Andrewes takes an agnostic position: "Spartan Imperialism?" in *Imperialism in the Ancient World*, P. Garnsey and C. Whittaker eds. (Cambridge 1978) 91–102 and 301–6.

[36] Thucydides 1.115.4, 3.34.2, 8.28.4.

two years before being absorbed into the Spartan army (summer 401 to spring 399). This fact alone suggests that they managed to develop a high degree of group identity, even if toward the end of the march they experienced desertions and division in the ranks. Indeed, while serving in the Spartan army in Asia under king Agesilaus in 395, the Ten Thousand, who had been known as the "Cyreans," were still recognizable as a distinct contingent—now as the "Dercylideans."[37]

Both the size and unity of the Ten Thousand anticipate emerging trends in mercenary warfare. Large professional armies became quite common in the fourth century. This was due in part to the development of tactics involving *peltasts* or light-armed troops; many mercenaries were of this type. On numerous occasions the *peltast* proved himself superior to the hoplite, the traditional, heavily armed soldier in the Greek world.[38] Secondly, city-states became more reliant on mercenaries and less on their own citizen armies. The causes of this development are difficult to determine; in part it was surely the result of the change in tactics just mentioned. Additionally, there was an increase in the numbers of available soldiers at the end of the fifth century, at the end of the Peloponnesian war. At Sparta there was a significant decline in the number of adult full citizens, necessitating greater reliance on merce-

[37] *Hell.Oxy.* 21.2; they took their name from a Spartan commander, Dercylidas, who had assumed command of the army after Thibron (*Hell.* 3.1.8).

[38] See esp. the battle of Lechaeum near Corinth in 390 (*Hell.* 4.5.10–19). Cf. J. K. Anderson, *Military Theory and Practice in the Age of Xenophon* (Berkeley and Los Angeles 1970) Ch.VII.

nary troops as well as other types of soldiers (*perioikoi*, *neodamodeis* etc.). Finally, more states were involved in military operations than before; hence there was a greater demand for professional soldiers and a greater supply of them. But whatever the reasons may have been, by the second quarter of the fourth century the widespread presence of mercenary forces in the Greek world can be documented in a number of texts. Aeneas the Tactician, an exact contemporary of Xenophon, assumes that mercenaries will be found in every city; Xenophon himself refers to mercenary commanders as regular participants in sacrifices while the Spartan army was on campaign.[39]

The presence of mercenaries throughout the Greek world, as well as large numbers of demobilized soldiers, evidently caused significant social problems at the end of the fifth century and into the fourth. Aeneas can imagine a city taken over by its mercenaries (10.12.2); the orator Isocrates suggests that bands of indigent soldiers were roaming around the Greek world attacking whomever they met (*Phil.* 120). The issue of renegade mercenaries was connected to deeper social problems: although the remarks of Aeneas and Isocrates seem exaggerated, they suggest that there was widespread fear of social discord and its exploitation by opportunistic professional soldiers. As a solution to this problem some advocated colonizing parts of the Persian empire with these troublesome soldiers: in the *Philippus*, Isocrates recommends combining the wandering mercenaries into an army, attacking the Persian empire, and detaching a portion of the King's realm from his control where these same professional soldiers could

---

[39] Aen.Tact., e.g., 10.10.7, 10.12–13. Xenophon, *Lac.*13.4.

be settled. In this way Greece would be rendered safe both from the threat of the Persians and from their own mercenaries (*Phil*. 121–23).

Isocrates' twin goals, the removal of strife from the Greek world and the conquest of Persia, were the chief elements of what modern scholars have termed panhellenism. The *Anabasis* gives us several views of this difficult and notoriously slippery concept. Two standard topoi are found in it that suggest the characteristic subservience of the Persians, and hence their weakness: soldiers in the King's army are driven into battle "under the lash" (3.4.26; cf. Herodotus 7.22, 56 and 223); and the practice of obeisance (*proskynesis*) is attacked by Xenophon himself in one of his speeches (3.2.13).[40] Even Cyrus, of course a barbarian himself, is made to lament the weakness of his native troops in comparison with the Greeks (1.7.3–4). Further, it is Cyrus who observes that while the Persian empire may seem large and populous, it is really just a paper tiger that will fall if someone attacks it quickly (1.5.9).

Others shared Cyrus' observation that the Persian empire was ripe for conquest; and for them the Ten Thousand offered proof of this evaluation. In his *Panegyricus*, published about twenty years after the events of the *Anabasis*, Isocrates refers explicitly to their march: although the whole of Asia opposed them, and despite the loss of Cyrus and later their generals, the Ten Thousand (or, according to Isocrates, Six Thousand) succeeded in marching

[40] Cf. A. Momigliano, "Persian Empire and Greek Freedom," in *The Idea of Freedom: Essays in Honour of Isaiah Berlin*, Alan Ryun ed. (Oxford 1979) 145–6.

through the Persian empire and thereby exposed the "soft-ness" (μαλακία) of the Persians. Isocrates argues that if poor men unable to survive in their own lands were able to accomplish this much, a capable general at the head of good soldiers could achieve significantly more (*Pan*. 146–50). Later authors, being in a position to make comparisons with the forces of Philip and Alexander, saw the Ten Thousand in very similar terms: precursors of the Macedonian army that was to bring to reality the panhellenic plans of men such as Isocrates.[41]

The *Anabasis*' treatment of panhellenism, however, is far from simple. In the same speech in which he decries *proskynesis*, Xenophon complicates the view that the success of the Ten Thousand will be a uniformly positive achievement. In drawing notice to the autonomous regions of the Persian empire, Xenophon suggests that the King would be happy to provide one of these semi-independent peoples (the Mysians) with guides so that they might leave his land. He further observes that if the King would be willing to so accommodate the Mysians, he would be more than willing to make room for the Ten Thousand. However, Xenophon fears that the good living of Asia, in particular the Persian and Median women, will make the soldiers forget their homeward way, just as the Lotus Eaters made Odysseus' men forget. He recommends that the Ten Thousand return to Greece in order to show that the poverty in which they live at home is voluntary—that they can always live abroad in luxury, but choose not to (3.2.24–6).

This passage must be read very carefully against the

41 E.g. Polybius 3.6.10–12, Arrian, *An.* 1.12.3–4.

views of men like Isocrates. On the one hand we see quite clearly the weakness of the Persian empire and the settlement of Greece's poor in the East. Additionally, the suggestion that the Greeks are willingly poor is related to the crucial difference between Hellenic freedom and Persian servitude. But despite these clear indications of the passage's alignment with the central tenets of panhellenism, Xenophon's words preclude a simple interpretation. While the threat of permanent settlement will frighten the King into aiding the Greeks in their return, settlement in the East is characterized as a threat also to the Greeks: the Greeks will be seduced by the good living of the Persians and decide to settle in Asia. There is a suggestion here that the Greeks will in some way lose their identity, that in losing their desire to return home they will lose their Greekness. At least in this passage, then, the most ambitious panhellenic project of defeating the barbarian and colonizing his land is also conceived of as anti-hellenic insofar as it entails the obliteration of Greekness itself.

The ambiguity of panhellenism is also explored later in the work, after the Ten Thousand have reached the Black Sea. At a place called Cotyora, Xenophon has a remarkable vision. Noting the excellent condition of the army as well as the fact that it is at that time encamped in a remote, yet ideal spot, he forms the idea of founding a city, one that he feels will add territory and power to Greece (5.6.15–16). This plan is unmistakably akin to the Isocratean scheme of settling mercenary soldiers in Asia. However, as we learn in the narrative that follows, his vision remains a fantasy: his hope for founding a city is revealed to the men, and while some approve of the idea, most object (5.6.17–

18). Still later in the *Anabasis* Xenophon again hopes to settle the army at a site halfway between Heraclea and Byzantium; the place, Port Calpe, is described in utopian terms (perfect harbor, excellent natural resources, prosperous villages) and furthermore "suitable for settling ten thousand men." But, as at Cotyora, the men do not go along with the plan (6.4.3–8).[42]

One of the most interesting questions we can ask regarding the *Anabasis* is why Xenophon chose to include these unfulfilled visions. It is important to remember that the *Anabasis* is a work of reminiscence. It was completed late in the author's life when he was revising many of his earlier views. In such a context, it makes sense that these panhellenic visions should be presented as unrealized. For Xenophon, then, the Ten Thousand had become a utopia. It is probably no accident that in Book 5, before Xenophon shows us his vision at Cotyora, he also gives us a detailed and touching description of life on his estate at Scillus near Olympia after his return to Greece. If this passage was written after he had lost this property (likely, but still a matter of speculation), then Scillus can be understood as another utopia: a lost ideal, but, unlike Cotyora and Port Calpe, one Xenophon actually saw come to reality for a time.

In Xenophon's narrative the Ten Thousand started out as a mercenary army in the service of Cyrus the Younger and ended up as one fighting for the Thracian chieftain Seuthes before finally being absorbed by the Spartan

---

[42] Arrian remembered Xenophon's description of Port Calpe in his own *Periplus Maris Euxini* (Roos) 12.5.

forces which were campaigning in Asia Minor. In between, however, they underwent a two-stage evolution.[43] When unity of action and common goals (i.e. survival and the return home) were uppermost in the soldiers' minds, the Ten Thousand worked well, surmounting the numerous obstacles presented by food shortages, hostile peoples, and difficult terrain. The success of this period, one that saw the Ten Thousand move from Cunaxa to the coast of the Black Sea (Books 3 and 4), was due in large measure to the initiative and bravery of its commanders; indeed, the fact that it was an army on the move is sometimes lost in this portion of the *Anabasis*, because, as noted above, the individual commander, and Xenophon in particular, takes over as the focus of the narrative: here we see the Ten Thousand as warrior band. After their famous sighting of the sea (θάλαττα θάλαττα 4.7.24), and arrival at Trapezus, their unity disintegrates as soldiers become more concerned with accumulating wealth: the failed raiding expedition of Clearatus (5.7.14–16) is paradigmatic. Significantly, it is in this period that the Ten Thousand most resemble a city, with assemblies of the men, and the generals acting as magistrates and probouleutic advisers; ethnic divisiveness also makes itself felt at this juncture, with the Achaeans and Arcadians splitting off from the army (6.2.9ff). Thus Xenophon has his utopian visions precisely when the community of the Ten Thousand begins to fall apart through divisiveness and lack of discipline.

[43] For the division of the Ten Thousand into four phases, see esp. G. B. Nussbaum, *The Ten Thousand: A Study in Social Organization and Action in Xenophon's Anabasis* (Leiden 1967).

It is illuminating to compare Xenophon's utopias at Cotyora and Port Calpe to the description of the encampment
of another army in which he served. We learn in the *Hellenica* that in the spring of 395 king Agesilaus of Sparta
began to drill his army, which included elements of the Ten
Thousand, at Ephesus in Asia Minor. Xenophon describes
the scene as one that also featured an ideal, well-run army,
a sight he describes as inspirational, a place "full of good
hope" (*Hell*. 3.4.16–18).[44] What we see with great clarity at
Ephesus, but which is also implied for the Ten Thousand
on the Black Sea, is the order of the army. This army, and
the Ten Thousand, are both forces composed of highly
trained, complementary parts that work together. *Taxis*,
the principle of order and ordering, was central to Xenophon's understanding of success in human affairs: as Is-
chomachus declares in the *Oeconomicus*, "nothing is as
useful or as good for human beings as order" (8.3). From
the same passage we learn that order is a perceptibly beautiful thing; it permits all human endeavor to realize the
good it is designed to achieve. One senses, however, that
it is the army that Xenophon thinks best represents the
good that is achieved through *taxis*. This privileging of the
army as the best model of order, and hence human excellence, no doubt derives from Xenophon's long career as a

----

[44] This passage is also found, with small differences, at *Ages.*
1.25–7; see also 4.8.27–8 and *Lac.* 12.5. Polybius remembered
the Ephesus passage in his own description of Scipio's preparations in New Carthage (Polybius 10.20.7); the phrase "workshop
of war" (πολέμου ἐργαστήριον) became proverbial: Athenaeus
10.421 B.

military man. Additionally, by this time the inherently political aspect of the army had become a popular concept.[45]

We can tell from a number of Xenophon's works that his last years were painful ones in which he was forced to revise many of his earlier views. He had lost his estate at Scillus, so lovingly described in the *Anabasis*, after the first Theban invasion of the Peloponnese (370). Less than ten years later he lost his son Gryllus, who fell in a skirmish preliminary to the battle of Mantinea. His exile from Athens had been revoked, but it is not likely that he returned. In the *Cyropaedia* (8.8) as well as in his *Constitution of the Spartans* (14) Xenophon states that societies he had regarded as exemplary he now regarded as having degenerated from their earlier glory; some would even add the final chapter of the *Anabasis* to this group of palinodes.[46] Late in his life, when he was writing (or rewriting) several of the important works in his corpus, Xenophon came to believe that many of his most cherished beliefs about what contributed to successful community life were wrong. While no doubt initially discouraged, he did not give up trying to make sense of the world around him, and in so doing, gained an insight that transcended his times. All these events made Xenophon ponder the nature of power and the mutability of human fortune. More than anything else, though, it was the self-destruction of Sparta, brought about

[45] E.g. Alcaeus 112 (Voigt), Herodotus 8.61.2, and Thucydides 7.77.7.

[46] C. H. Grayson, "Did Xenophon Intend To Write History?" in *The Ancient Historian and His Materials*, B. Levick ed. (Westmead 1975) 34–5.

chiefly because of the leadership of his personal friend
Agesilaus, that forced him to revise much of his thinking
about what constituted good government and good leadership. It was at this time that he wrote the bulk of the
Hellenica; it was about this time, too, that he put the finish-
ing touches on the *Anabasis*. His utopian visions at Cotyora
and Port Calpe were in part shaped by this late spirit of
revision and pessimism.

Text, Translation, and Annotation

The manuscripts of the *Anabasis* divide into two main
families, f and c. The chief representatives of f are F =
Vaticanus 1335 (10th–11th century AD) and M = Mar-
cianus 590 (12th–13th); of c, C = Parisinus 1640 (9th–10th).
Beginning with L. Dindorf's Leipzig edition of 1825, most
modern editors favored the readings of c against f. For his
Loeb edition, C. L. Brownson followed this practice. Indeed, he referred throughout his apparatus to the "better"
and "inferior" MSS.[47] Additionally, he was heavily in-
debted to the conjectures of W. Gemoll (2nd ed. 1909). C.
Hude's Teubner text of 1931 was more cautious in its approach, treating Gemoll's readings more critically, and further, on the basis of papyri, being more balanced in its
reliance on the main MS families: "papyri enim modo ab
altera, modo ab altera familia stant, ut nomina meliorum
deteriorumve usu tradita relinquenda sint" (p.vii). J. Pe-

---

[47] Cf. H. Erbse, "Überlieferungsgeschichte der griechischen
klassichen und hellenistischen Literatur," in *Geschichte der Text-
überlieferung* vol.1 (Zürich 1961) 271–2.

ters, in his revision of Hude (1971), updated the text in much the same spirit.

In recent years, papyrological studies of the textual tradition of the *Anabasis* have continued to underscore the need not to favor one reading over another on the basis of affiliation with a particular MS family. In particular, it was the conclusion of A. H. R. E. Paap, *The Xenophon Papyri = Pap. Lugd. Bat.* vol.18 (Leiden 1970) 11, that "the choice between the variants in the manuscript tradition of the *Anabasis* as a whole is to be based exclusively on their merit, whether they occur in c or in f. There is no room for the traditional preference for c."[48] This conclusion confirms the statements of earlier scholars who had urged a similar view.[49]

In this revision of Brownson's text, this more balanced understanding of the MS tradition of the *Anabasis* has been followed. In the main the text is that of Hude/Peters; however, I have not infrequently opted for other readings. Brownson's text has therefore been altered at several points, in many cases leading to the acceptance of readings that had not been followed because of his rigid adherence to the presumed superiority of c. This correction of Brown-

[48] A complete list of Xenophon papyri is now available in J. Dillery and T. Gagos, "P.Mich. Inv. 4922: Xenophon and an Unknown Christian Text with an Appendix of All Xenophon Papyri," *ZPE* 93 (1992) 187–89, with corrections by M. E. van Rossum-Steenbeek, "Four Notes on the List of Xenophon Papyri," *ZPE* 99 (1993) 17.

[49] So, e.g., A.W. Persson, *Zur Textgeschichte Xenophons* = Lunds Universitets Årrskrift 10.2 (Lund and Leipzig 1915) 162–3; H. Erbse, "Xenophons Anabasis," *Gymnasium* 73 (1966) 491.

son's text has necessitated extensive changes in the translation. Additionally, where Brownson felt that elaborate defense was needed in his critical apparatus, it has often been possible to streamline the note or remove it entirely.

In general I have tried to update Brownson's translation throughout, as well as to remove errors. The notes have been thoroughly revised, though many remain as they were first written; and many new ones have been added. They are aimed at helping the reader see connections between the *Anabasis* and other of Xenophon's works; even more importantly, it is hoped that they will show how the *Anabasis* has a great deal to tell us about the Persian empire, and specifically Greek-Persian relations at the end of the fifth century, both areas where much more is known now than was the case in Brownson's day.

BIBLIOGRAPHY

Principal Modern Editions

1825 *Xenophontis Expeditio Cyri*. 1st ed., L. Dindorf, Leipzig: Teubner.

1904 *Xenophontis Opera Omnia*. vol. 3, E. C. Marchant, Oxford: Oxford University Press.

1909 *Xenophontis Expeditio Cyri*. 2nd ed., W. Gemoll, Leipzig: Teubner.

1930–31 *Xénophon Anabase*. 2 vols., P. Masqueray, Paris: Budé.

1931/1972 *Xenophon Expeditio Cyri*. C. Hude, corrected J. Peters, Leipzig: Teubner.

Selected Studies

Anderson, J. K. (1974) *Xenophon*, London: Duckworth.

Austin, M. M. and P. Vidal-Naquet (1977) *Economic and Social History of Ancient Greece*, Berkeley and Los Angeles: University of California Press.

Breitenbach, H. R. (1967) "Xenophon," *RE* 9A part 2: 1569–2052.

Briant, P. (1996) *Histoire de l'empire perse de Cyrus à Alexandre* 2 vols. = *Achaemenid History* 10, Leiden: Nederlands Instituut voor het Nabije Oosten.

Briant, P. ed. (1995), *Dans les pas des Dix-Mille* = *Pallas* 43.

BIBLIOGRAPHY

Cawkwell, G. (1972) Introduction and notes to *Xenophon: The Persian Expedition*, translation of the *Anabasis* by R. Warner, Harmondsworth: Penguin Books.

Dalby, A. (1992) "Greeks Abroad: Social Organisation and Food among the Ten Thousand," *JHS* 112: 16–30.

Delebecque, E.(1957) *Essai sur la vie de Xénophon*, Paris: C. Klincksieck.

Dillery, J. (1995) *Xenophon and the History of His Times*, London and New York: Routledge.

Erbse, H. (1966) "Xenophons Anabasis," *Gymnasium* 73: 485–505.

Fornara, C. W. (1983) *The Nature of History in Ancient Greece and Rome*, Berkeley and Los Angeles: University of California Press.

Kuhrt, A. (1995) *The Ancient Near East* 2 vols., London and New York: Routledge.

Lendle, O. (1995) *Kommentar zu Xenophons Anabasis*, Darmstadt: Wissenschaftliche Buchgesellschaft.

Lewis, D. M. (1977) *Sparta and Persia*, Leiden: E. J. Brill.

Luce, T. J. (1997) *The Greek Historians*, London and New York: Routledge.

Marincola, J. (1997) *Authority and Tradition in Ancient Historiography*, Cambridge: Cambridge University Press.

Nickel, R. (1979) *Xenophon*, Darmstadt: Wissenschaftliche Buchgesellschaft.

Nussbaum, G. B. (1967) *The Ten Thousand A Study in - Social Organisation and Action in Xenophon's Anabasis*, Leiden: E. J. Brill.

Perlman, S. (1976/1977) "The Ten Thousand: A Chapter in the Military, Social and Economic History of the

Fourth Century," *Rivista storica dell'Antichità* 6/7: 241–284.

Roy, J. (1967) "The Mercenaries of Cyrus," *Historia* 16: 287–323.

Roy, J. (1968) "Xenophon's Evidence for the *Anabasis*," *Athenaeum* 46: 37–46.

Tuplin, C. (1987) "The Administration of the Achaemenid Empire," in *Coinage and Administration in the Athenian and Persian Empires*, I. Carradice ed., Oxford: British Archaeological Reports series 343: 109–66.

Tuplin, C. (1991) "Modern and Ancient Travellers in the Achaemenid Empire: Byron's Road to Oxiana and Xenophon's *Anabasis*," *Achaemenid History* 7: 37–57.

ABBREVIATIONS

Works of Xenophon

Ages. = Agesilaus
Ap. = Apologia Socratis
Cyr. = Cyropaedia
Hell. = Hellenica
Hipp. = Hipparchicus

Lac. = Constitution of the
   Spartans
Mem. = Memorabilia
Oec. = Oeconomicus
Smp. = Symposium

Journals and Reference Works

AJP = *American Journal of Philology.*

Boyce HZ = M. Boyce (1982) *A History of Zoroastrianism* vol.2, Leiden and Cologne: E. J. Brill.

Briant Histoire = P. Briant (1996) *Histoire de l'empire perse de Cyrus à Alexandre* 2 vols. = Achaemenid History 10, Leiden: Nederlands Instituut voor het Nabije Oosten.

CAH = *Cambridge Ancient History* (1928–), Cambridge: Cambridge University Press.

CQ = *Classical Quarterly.*

DB = R. Schmitt ed. (1991) *The Bisitun Inscriptions of Darius the Great, Old Persian Text = Corpus Inscriptionum Iranicarum* part I vol. 10, London: Lund Humphries.

DK =   H. Diels and W. Kranz eds. (1951–1952)
            Die Fragmente der Vorsokratiker (6 ed.),
            Berlin: Weidmann.

FGH =   F. Jacoby ed. (1923–1958) *Die Fragmente
            der griechischen Historiker*, Berlin and
            Leiden: E. J. Brill.

IG =   *Inscriptiones Graecae* (1873–) Berlin: de
            Gruyter.

JHS =   *Journal of Hellenic Studies.*

LIMC =   *Lexicon Iconographicum Mythologiae
            Classicae* (1981–), Zürich: Artemis Verlag.

LSJ =   H.G. Liddell and R. Scott, with H. Stuart
            Jones (1996) *A Greek-English Lexicon*,
            with a revised Supplement (9 ed.),
            Oxford: Oxford University Press.

ML =   R. Meiggs and D. Lewis (1989) *A
            Selection of Greek Historical Inscriptions*,
            Oxford: Oxford University Press.

OGIS =   W. Dittenberger ed. (1903) *Orientis
            Graeci Inscriptiones Selectae*, Leipzig:
            Hirzel.

PMG =   D. L. Page (1962) *Poetae Melici Graeci*,
            Oxford: Oxford University Press.

RE =   A. Pauly, G. Wissowa, W. Kroll et al. eds.
            (1893–1980) *Real-Encyclopädie der
            classischen Altertumswissenschaft*,
            Stuttgart: Alfred Druckenmüller.

RPh =   *Revue de Philologie.*

TAPA =   *Transactions of the American Philological
            Association.*

ZPE =   *Zeitschrift für Papyrologie und
            Epigraphik.*

ANABASIS

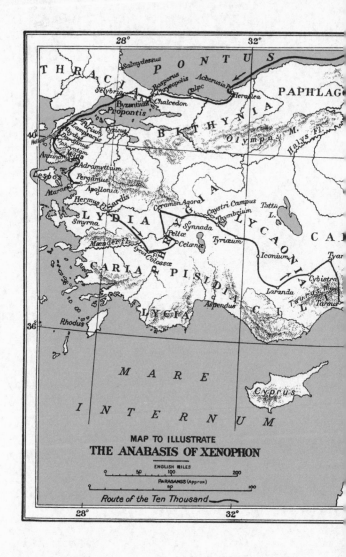

MAP TO ILLUSTRATE
THE ANABASIS OF XENOPHON

ENGLISH MILES

PARASANGS (Approx)

Route of the Ten Thousand

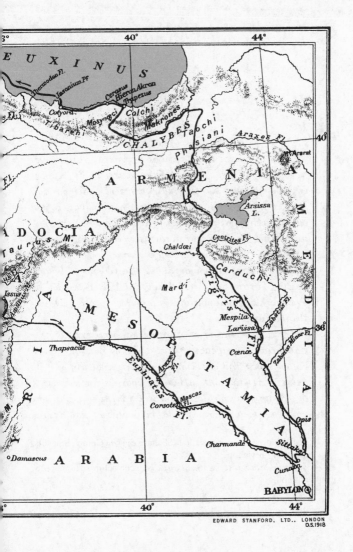

A

I. Δαρείου καὶ Παρυσάτιδος γίγνονται παῖδες δύο,
πρεσβύτερος μὲν Ἀρταξέρξης, νεώτερος δὲ Κῦρος·
ἐπεὶ δὲ ἠσθένει Δαρεῖος καὶ ὑπώπτευε τελευτὴν τοῦ
2 βίου, ἐβούλετο τὼ παῖδε ἀμφοτέρω παρεῖναι. ὁ μὲν
οὖν πρεσβύτερος παρὼν ἐτύγχανε· Κῦρον δὲ μεταπέμπεται ἀπὸ τῆς ἀρχῆς ἧς αὐτὸν σατράπην ἐποίησε, καὶ
στρατηγὸν δὲ αὐτὸν ἀπέδειξε πάντων ὅσοι εἰς Καστωλοῦ πεδίον ἀθροίζονται. ἀναβαίνει οὖν ὁ Κῦρος
λαβὼν Τισσαφέρνην ὡς φίλον καὶ τῶν Ἑλλήνων δὲ
ἔχων ὁπλίτας τριακοσίους,[1] ἄρχοντα δὲ αὐτῶν Ξενίαν
Παρράσιον.
3   Ἐπεὶ δὲ ἐτελεύτησε Δαρεῖος καὶ κατέστη εἰς τὴν
βασιλείαν Ἀρταξέρξης, Τισσαφέρνης διαβάλλει τὸν
Κῦρον πρὸς τὸν ἀδελφὸν ὡς ἐπιβουλεύοι αὐτῷ. ὁ δὲ
πείθεταί τε καὶ συλλαμβάνει[2] Κῦρον ὡς ἀποκτενῶν· ἡ
δὲ μήτηρ ἐξαιτησαμένη αὐτὸν ἀποπέμπει πάλιν ἐπὶ
4 τὴν ἀρχήν. ὁ δ᾽ ὡς ἀπῆλθε κινδυνεύσας καὶ ἀτιμα-

---

[1] Before τριακοσίους the MSS. have ἀνέβη: Gemoll brackets,
following Bisschop.
[2] συλλαμβάνει MSS.: λαμβάνει corrector of one MS,
Gemoll.

BOOK I

I. Darius and Parysatis had two sons born to them, of whom the elder was Artaxerxes and the younger Cyrus. Now when Darius lay sick and suspected that the end of his life was near, he wished to have both his sons with him. The elder, as it chanced, was with him already; but Cyrus he summoned from the province over which he had made him satrap, and he had also appointed him commander of all the forces that muster in the plain of Castolus.[1] Cyrus accordingly went up[2] to his father, taking with him Tissaphernes as a friend and accompanied by three hundred Greek hoplites,[3] under the command of Xenias of Parrhasia.

When Darius had died and Artaxerxes had become established as king, Tissaphernes falsely accused Cyrus to his brother of plotting against him. And Artaxerxes, believing the accusation, arrested Cyrus, with the intention of putting him to death; his mother, however, made intercession for him, and sent him back again to his province. Now when Cyrus had thus returned, after his danger and dis-

---

[1] Castolus was the mustering place for all the Persian forces of western Asia Minor. See also I. ix. 7, *Hell.* I. iv. 4, Hdt. V. cii. 1.

[2] See Introduction.   [3] *i.e.* heavy-armed infantrymen, the regular "troops of the line" in Greek warfare. In this instance, of course, they are serving Cyrus as a bodyguard.

XENOPHON

σθείς, βουλεύεται ὅπως μήποτε ἔτι ἔσται ἐπὶ τῷ
ἀδελφῷ, ἀλλ', ἢν δύνηται, βασιλεύσει ἀντ' ἐκείνου.
Παρύσατις μὲν δὴ ἡ μήτηρ ὑπῆρχε τῷ Κύρῳ, φιλοῦσα
5 αὐτὸν μᾶλλον ἢ τὸν βασιλεύοντα Ἀρταξέρξην. ὅστις
δ' ἀφικνοῖτο τῶν παρὰ βασιλέως πρὸς αὐτὸν πάντας
οὕτω διατιθεὶς ἀπεπέμπετο ὥστε αὐτῷ μᾶλλον φίλους
εἶναι ἢ βασιλεῖ. καὶ τῶν παρ' ἑαυτῷ δὲ βαρβάρων
ἐπεμελεῖτο ὡς πολεμεῖν τε ἱκανοὶ εἴησαν καὶ εὐνοϊκῶς
6 ἔχοιεν αὐτῷ. τὴν δὲ Ἑλληνικὴν δύναμιν ἤθροιζεν ὡς
μάλιστα ἐδύνατο ἐπικρυπτόμενος, ὅπως ὅτι ἀπαρα-
σκευότατον λάβοι βασιλέα.

Ὧδε οὖν ἐποιεῖτο τὴν συλλογήν. ὁπόσας εἶχε φυλακὰς ἐν ταῖς πόλεσι παρήγγειλε τοῖς φρουράρχοις
ἑκάστοις λαμβάνειν ἄνδρας Πελοποννησίους ὅτι πλείστους καὶ βελτίστους, ὡς ἐπιβουλεύοντος Τισσαφέρνους ταῖς πόλεσι. καὶ γὰρ ἦσαν αἱ Ἰωνικαὶ πόλεις
Τισσαφέρνους τὸ ἀρχαῖον ἐκ βασιλέως δεδομέναι,
τότε δὲ ἀφειστήκεσαν πρὸς Κῦρον πᾶσαι πλὴν Μιλή-
7 του· ἐν Μιλήτῳ δὲ Τισσαφέρνης προαισθόμενος τὰ
αὐτὰ ταῦτα βουλευομένους, ἀποστῆναι πρὸς Κῦρον,
τοὺς μὲν αὐτῶν ἀπέκτεινε, τοὺς δ' ἐξέβαλεν. ὁ δὲ
Κῦρος ὑπολαβὼν τοὺς φεύγοντας συλλέξας στράτευμα ἐπολιόρκει Μίλητον καὶ κατὰ γῆν καὶ κατὰ
θάλατταν καὶ ἐπειρᾶτο κατάγειν τοὺς ἐκπεπτωκότας.
καὶ αὕτη αὖ ἄλλη πρόφασις ἦν αὐτῷ τοῦ ἀθροίζειν

grace, he set about planning that he might never again be in the power of his brother, but, if possible, might be king in his stead. He had, in the first place, the support of Parysatis, his mother, for she loved him better than the son who was king, Artaxerxes. Again, when any of the King's court came to visit him, he treated them all in such a way that when he sent them back they were more devoted to him than to the King. He also took care that the barbarians[4] of his own province should be capable soldiers and should feel kindly toward him. Lastly, as regards his Greek force, he proceeded to collect it with the utmost secrecy, so that he might take the King as completely unprepared as possible.

It was in the following way, then, that he gathered this force: In the first place, he sent orders to the commanders of all the garrisons he had in the cities to enlist as many Peloponnesian soldiers of the best sort as they severally could, on the plea that Tissaphernes had designs upon their cities. For, in fact, the Ionian cities had originally belonged to Tissaphernes, by gift of the King,[5] but at that time all of them except Miletus had revolted and gone over to Cyrus. The people of Miletus also were planning to do the very same thing, namely, to go over to Cyrus, but Tissaphernes, finding out about it in time, put some of them to death and banished others. Cyrus thereupon took the exiles under his protection, collected an army, and laid siege to Miletus both by land and by sea, and endeavoured to restore the exiles to their city; and this, again, made him another pre-

---

[4] "Barbarians" translates βάρβαροι, which was the name the Greeks gave to all peoples who were not Greeks.

[5] See Introduction.

8 στράτευμα. πρὸς δὲ βασιλέα πέμπων ἠξίου ἀδελφὸς
ὢν αὐτοῦ δοθῆναι οἷ ταύτας τὰς πόλεις μᾶλλον ἢ
Τισσαφέρνην ἄρχειν αὐτῶν, καὶ ἡ μήτηρ συνέπραττεν
αὐτῷ ταῦτα· ὥστε βασιλεὺς τὴν μὲν πρὸς ἑαυτὸν
ἐπιβουλὴν οὐκ ᾐσθάνετο, Τισσαφέρνει δὲ ἐνόμιζε
πολεμοῦντα αὐτὸν ἀμφὶ τὰ στρατεύματα δαπανᾶν·
ὥστε οὐδὲν ἤχθετο αὐτῶν πολεμούντων. καὶ γὰρ ὁ
Κῦρος ἀπέπεμπε τοὺς γιγνομένους δασμοὺς βασιλεῖ
ἐκ τῶν πόλεων ὧν Τισσαφέρνους[3] ἐτύγχανεν ἔχων.

9 Ἄλλο δὲ στράτευμα αὐτῷ συνελέγετο ἐν Χερρονήσῳ τῇ κατ᾽ ἀντιπέρας Ἀβύδου τόνδε τὸν τρόπον.
Κλέαρχος Λακεδαιμόνιος φυγὰς ἦν· τούτῳ συγγενό-
μενος ὁ Κῦρος ἠγάσθη τε αὐτὸν καὶ δίδωσιν αὐτῷ
μυρίους δαρεικούς. ὁ δὲ λαβὼν τὸ χρυσίον στράτευμα
συνέλεξεν ἀπὸ τούτων τῶν χρημάτων καὶ ἐπολέμει ἐκ
Χερρονήσου ὁρμώμενος τοῖς Θραξὶ τοῖς ὑπὲρ Ἑλλήσποντον οἰκοῦσι καὶ ὠφέλει τοὺς Ἕλληνας· ὥστε καὶ
χρήματα συνεβάλλοντο αὐτῷ εἰς τὴν τροφὴν τῶν
στρατιωτῶν αἱ Ἑλλησποντιακαὶ πόλεις ἑκοῦσαι.
τοῦτο δ᾽ αὖ οὕτω τρεφόμενον ἐλάνθανεν αὐτῷ τὸ
στράτευμα.

10 Ἀρίστιππος δὲ ὁ Θετταλὸς ξένος ὢν ἐτύγχανεν
αὐτῷ, καὶ πιεζόμενος ὑπὸ τῶν οἴκοι ἀντιστασιωτῶν

---

[3] Τισσαφέρνης Mar., following Krüger: Τισσαφέρνης MSS.:
Τισσαφέρνης ἔτι Gem.

text for gathering an army. Meanwhile he sent to the King and urged, on the ground that he was his brother, that these Ionian cities should be given to him instead of remaining under the rule of Tissaphernes, and his mother cooperated with him in this. The result was that the King failed to perceive the plot against himself, but believed that Cyrus was spending money on his troops because he was at war with Tissaphernes. Consequently he was not at all displeased at their being at war, the less so because Cyrus regularly remitted to the King the tribute which came in from the cities he chanced to have that belonged to Tissaphernes.

Still another army was being collected for him in the Chersonese which is opposite Abydus, in the following manner: Clearchus[6] was a Lacedaemonian exile; Cyrus, making his acquaintance, came to admire him, and gave him ten thousand darics.[7] And Clearchus, taking the gold, collected an army by means of this money, and using the Chersonese as a base of operations, proceeded to make war upon the Thracians who dwell beyond the Hellespont, thereby aiding the Greeks.[8] Consequently, the Hellespontine cities of their own free will sent Clearchus contributions of money for the support of his troops. So it was that this army also was being secretly maintained for Cyrus.

Again, Aristippus the Thessalian chanced to be a friend of Cyrus, and since he was hard pressed by his political

[6] For the reason for his banishment see II. vi. 2–4.

[7] The daric was a Persian gold coin, weighing 8.3g. Briant, *Histoire* I, 420. It was worth about 25 or 26 Attic drachmas.

[8] *i.e.* the Greeks on the European side of the Hellespont, who suffered from the incursions of their Thracian neighbours.

ἔρχεται πρὸς τὸν Κῦρον καὶ αἰτεῖται αὐτὸν εἰς δισχιλίους ξένους καὶ τριῶν μηνῶν μισθόν, ὡς οὕτως
περιγενόμενος ἄν τῶν ἀντιστασιωτῶν. ὁ δὲ Κῦρος
δίδωσιν αὐτῷ εἰς τετρακισχιλίους καὶ ἔξ μηνῶν μισθόν, καὶ δεῖται αὐτοῦ μὴ πρόσθεν καταλῦσαι πρὸς
τοὺς ἀντιστασιώτας πρὶν ἂν αὐτῷ συμβουλεύσηται.
οὕτω δὲ αὖ τὸ ἐν Θετταλίᾳ ἐλάνθανεν αὐτῷ τρεφόμενον
στράτευμα.

11   Πρόξενον δὲ τὸν Βοιώτιον ξένον ὄντα ἐκέλευσε
λαβόντα ἄνδρας ὅτι πλείστους παραγενέσθαι, ὡς ἐς
Πισίδας βουλόμενος στρατεύεσθαι, ὡς πράγματα
παρεχόντων τῶν Πισιδῶν τῇ ἑαυτοῦ χώρᾳ. Σοφαίνετον
δὲ τὸν Στυμφάλιον καὶ Σωκράτη τὸν Ἀχαιόν, ξένους
ὄντας καὶ τούτους, ἐκέλευσεν ἄνδρας λαβόντας ἐλθεῖν
ὅτι πλείστους, ὡς πολεμήσων Τισσαφέρνει σὺν τοῖς
φυγάσι τοῖς Μιλησίων. καὶ ἐποίουν οὕτως οὗτοι.

II. Ἐπεὶ δ' ἐδόκει αὐτῷ ἤδη πορεύεσθαι ἄνω, τὴν
μὲν πρόφασιν ἐποιεῖτο ὡς Πισίδας βουλόμενος ἐκ-
βαλεῖν παντάπασιν ἐκ τῆς χώρας· καὶ ἀθροίζει ὡς ἐπὶ
τούτους τό τε βαρβαρικὸν καὶ τὸ Ἑλληνικόν. ἐνταῦθα
καὶ παραγγέλλει τῷ τε Κλεάρχῳ λαβόντι ἥκειν ὅσον
ἦν αὐτῷ στράτευμα, καὶ τῷ Ἀριστίππῳ συναλλαγέντι
πρὸς τοὺς οἴκοι ἀποπέμψαι πρὸς ἑαυτὸν ὃ εἶχε
στράτευμα· καὶ Ξενίᾳ τῷ Ἀρκάδι, ὃς αὐτῷ προειστήκει τοῦ ἐν ταῖς πόλεσι ξενικοῦ, ἥκειν παραγγέλλει
λαβόντα τοὺς ἄλλους πλὴν ὁπόσοι ἱκανοὶ εἴησαν τὰς

opponents at home, he came to Cyrus and asked him for three months' pay for two thousand mercenaries, urging that in this way he should get the better of his opponents. And Cyrus gave him six months' pay for four thousand, and requested him not to come to terms with his opponents until he had consulted with him. Thus the army in Thessaly, again, was being secretly maintained for him.

Furthermore, Cyrus directed Proxenus the Boeotian, who was a friend of his, to come to him with as many men as he could get, saying that he wished to undertake a campaign against the Pisidians, because, as he said, they were causing trouble to his province. He also directed Sophaenetus the Stymphalian[9] and Socrates the Achaean, who were likewise friends of his, to come with as many men as they could get, saying that he intended to make war upon Tissaphernes with the aid of the Milesian exiles; and they proceeded to carry out his directions.

II. When he thought the time had come to begin his upward march, the pretext he offered was that he wished to drive the Pisidians out of his land entirely, and it was avowedly against them that he set about collecting both his barbarian and his Greek troops. At that time he also sent word to Clearchus to come to him with the entire army which he had, and to Aristippus to effect a reconciliation with his adversaries at home and send him the army which he had; and he sent word to Xenias the Arcadian, who commanded for him the mercenary force in the cities,[10] to come with his troops, leaving behind only so many as were necessary to garrison the citadels. He likewise

---

[9] *FGH* 109. He also wrote an account of the Ten Thousand.
[10] See i. 6.

2 ἀκροπόλεις φυλάττειν. ἐκάλεσε δὲ καὶ τοὺς Μίλητον
πολιορκοῦντας, καὶ τοὺς φυγάδας ἐκέλευσε σὺν αὐτῷ
στρατεύεσθαι, ὑποσχόμενος αὐτοῖς, εἰ καλῶς κατα-
πράξειεν ἐφ᾽ ἃ ἐστρατεύετο, μὴ πρόσθεν παύσεσθαι[4]
πρὶν αὐτοὺς καταγάγοι οἴκαδε. οἱ δὲ ἡδέως ἐπείθοντο·
ἐπίστευον γὰρ αὐτῷ· καὶ λαβόντες τὰ ὅπλα παρῆσαν
εἰς Σάρδεις.

3 Ξενίας μὲν δὴ τοὺς ἐκ τῶν πόλεων λαβὼν παρ-
εγένετο εἰς Σάρδεις ὁπλίτας εἰς τετρακισχιλίους, Πρόξενος δὲ παρῆν ἔχων ὁπλίτας μὲν εἰς πεντακοσίους
καὶ χιλίους, γυμνῆτας δὲ πεντακοσίους, Σοφαίνετος
δὲ ὁ Στυμφάλιος ὁπλίτας ἔχων χιλίους,[5] Σωκράτης δὲ
ὁ Ἀχαιὸς ὁπλίτας ἔχων ὡς πεντακοσίους, Πασίων
δὲ ὁ Μεγαρεὺς τριακοσίους μὲν ὁπλίτας, τριακοσίους
δὲ πελταστὰς ἔχων παρεγένετο· ἦν δὲ καὶ οὗτος καὶ
ὁ Σωκράτης τῶν ἀμφὶ Μίλητον στρατευομένων. οὗτοι
μὲν εἰς Σάρδεις αὐτῷ ἀφίκοντο.

4 Τισσαφέρνης δὲ κατανοήσας ταῦτα, καὶ μείζονα
ἡγησάμενος εἶναι ἢ ὡς ἐπὶ Πισίδας τὴν παρασκευήν,
πορεύεται ὡς βασιλέα ᾗ ἐδύνατο τάχιστα ἱππέας ἔχων
5 ὡς πεντακοσίους. καὶ βασιλεὺς μὲν δὴ ἐπεὶ ἤκουσε
Τισσαφέρνους τὸν Κύρου στόλον, ἀντιπαρεσκευάζετο.

Κῦρος δὲ ἔχων οὓς εἴρηκα ὡρμᾶτο ἀπὸ Σάρδεων·
καὶ ἐξελαύνει διὰ τῆς Λυδίας σταθμοὺς τρεῖς παρα-

---

[4] παύσεσθαι some MSS., Hude/Peters, Mar.: παύσασθαι
most MSS., Gem.   [5] Σοφαίνετος … χιλίους MSS.: Gem.
brackets, following Dindorf.

summoned the troops which were besieging Miletus, and urged the Milesian exiles to take the field with him, promising them that, if he should successfully accomplish the object for which he was taking the field, he would not stop until he had restored them to their homes. And they gladly obeyed—for they trusted him—and presented themselves, under arms, at Sardis.

Xenias, then, arrived at Sardis with the troops from the cities, who were hoplites to the number of four thousand; Proxenus was there with hoplites to the number of fifteen hundred, and five hundred light-armed troops; Sophaenetus the Stymphalian with a thousand hoplites; Socrates the Achaean with about five hundred hoplites; and Pasion the Megarian arrived with three hundred hoplites and three hundred peltasts.[11] The last-named, and Socrates also, belonged to the force that had been engaged in besieging Miletus. All these came to Cyrus at Sardis.

Meanwhile Tissaphernes had taken note of these proceedings and come to the conclusion that Cyrus' preparations were too extensive to be against the Pisidians; he accordingly made his way to the King as quickly as he could, with about five hundred horsemen. And when the King heard from Tissaphernes about Cyrus' array, he set about making counter-preparations.

Cyrus was now setting forth from Sardis with the troops I have mentioned; and he marched through Lydia three

[11] Peltasts differed from ordinary light-armed troops (cf. $\gamma\nu\mu$-$\nu\hat{\eta}\tau\alpha\varsigma$ above) only in the fact that they carried a small, light shield, the $\pi\acute{\epsilon}\lambda\tau\eta$—whence their name.

σάγγας εἴκοσι καὶ δύο ἐπὶ τὸν Μαίανδρον ποταμόν.
τούτου τὸ εὖρος δύο πλέθρα· γέφυρα δὲ ἐπῆν ἐζευγ-
6 μένη πλοίοις ἑπτά.[6] τοῦτον διαβὰς ἐξελαύνει διὰ Φρυγίας σταθμὸν ἕνα παρασάγγας ὀκτὼ εἰς Κολοσσάς,
πόλιν οἰκουμένην [καὶ] εὐδαίμονα καὶ μεγάλην. ἐνταῦθα ἔμεινεν ἡμέρας ἑπτά· καὶ ἦκε Μένων ὁ Θετταλὸς
ὁπλίτας ἔχων χιλίους καὶ πελταστὰς πεντακοσίους,
7 Δόλοπας καὶ Αἰνιᾶνας καὶ Ὀλυνθίους. ἐντεῦθεν ἐξελαύνει σταθμοὺς τρεῖς παρασάγγας εἴκοσιν εἰς Κε-
λαινάς, τῆς Φρυγίας πόλιν οἰκουμένην, μεγάλην καὶ
εὐδαίμονα. ἐνταῦθα Κύρῳ βασίλεια ἦν καὶ παράδεισος μέγας ἀγρίων θηρίων πλήρης, ἃ ἐκεῖνος ἐθή-
ρευεν ἀπὸ ἵππου, ὁπότε γυμνάσαι βούλοιτο ἑαυτόν τε
καὶ τοὺς ἵππους. διὰ μέσου δὲ τοῦ παραδείσου ῥεῖ ὁ
Μαίανδρος ποταμός· αἱ δὲ πηγαὶ αὐτοῦ εἰσιν ἐκ τῶν
8 βασιλείων· ῥεῖ δὲ καὶ διὰ τῆς Κελαινῶν πόλεως. ἔστι
δὲ καὶ μεγάλου βασιλέως βασίλεια ἐν Κελαιναῖς
ἐρυμνὰ ἐπὶ ταῖς πηγαῖς τοῦ Μαρσύου ποταμοῦ ὑπὸ
τῇ ἀκροπόλει· ῥεῖ δὲ καὶ οὗτος διὰ τῆς πόλεως καὶ
ἐμβάλλει εἰς τὸν Μαίανδρον· τοῦ δὲ Μαρσύου τὸ εὖρός
ἐστιν εἴκοσι καὶ πέντε ποδῶν. ἐνταῦθα λέγεται Ἀπόλλων ἐκδεῖραι Μαρσύαν νικήσας ἐρίζοντά οἱ περὶ

6 ἐπῆν ἐζευγμένη ... ἑπτά Hude/Peters: ἐπεζευγμένη MSS.
ἑπτά ἐπεζευγμένη Gem., following Hug.

---

12 σταθμός = lit. a stopping-place, hence a day's journey.
13 A Persian measure of distance, equivalent to 30 Greek
stadia, or about 3.3 English miles.

stages,[12] a distance of twenty-two parasangs,[13] to the Maeander river. The width of this river was two plethra,[14] and there was a bridge over it made of seven boats. After crossing the Maeander he marched through Phrygia one stage, a distance of eight parasangs, to Colossae, an inhabited city, prosperous and large.[15] There he remained seven days; and Menon[16] the Thessalian arrived, with a thousand hoplites and five hundred peltasts, consisting of Dolopians, Aenianians, and Olynthians. Thence he marched three stages, twenty parasangs, to Celaenae, an inhabited city of Phrygia, large and prosperous. There Cyrus had a palace and a large park full of wild animals, which he used to hunt on horseback whenever he wished to give himself and his horses exercise. Through the middle of this park flows the Maeander river; its sources are beneath the palace, and it flows through the city of Celaenae also. There is likewise a palace of the Great King[17] in Celaenae, strongly fortified and situated at the foot of the Acropolis over the sources of the Marsyas river; the Marsyas also flows through the city, and empties into the Maeander, and its width is twenty-five feet. It was here, according to the story, that Apollo flayed Marsyas,[18] after having defeated him in a

[14] The plethrum = about 97 English feet.

[15] The phrase is formulaic; cf. ii. 10–14, 20; iv. 1; v. 4; II. iv. 13; III. iv. 7; IV. vii. 19; VI. iv. 6. For "prosperous and large," cf. Aristophanes, *Birds* 37. See L. Geysels, *Les études classiques* 42 (1944) 29–38.

[16] Who had been sent by Aristippus (see §1 above).

[17] A title often given by the Greeks to the king of Persia.

[18] Marsyas, a Phrygian satyr, was so proud of his skill with the flute that he presumed to challenge Apollo, god of music and master of the lyre. Cf. Hdt. VII. xxvi. 3.

σοφίας, καὶ τὸ δέρμα κρεμάσαι ἐν τῷ ἄντρῳ ὅθεν αἱ
πηγαί· διὰ δὲ τοῦτο ὁ ποταμὸς καλεῖται Μαρσύας.
9 ἐνταῦθα Ξέρξης, ὅτε ἐκ τῆς Ἑλλάδος ἡττηθεὶς τῇ
μάχῃ ἀπεχώρει, λέγεται οἰκοδομῆσαι ταῦτά τε τὰ
βασίλεια καὶ τὴν Κελαινῶν ἀκρόπολιν. ἐνταῦθα ἔμεινε
Κῦρος ἡμέρας τριάκοντα· καὶ ἧκε Κλέαρχος ὁ Λακεδαιμόνιος φυγὰς ἔχων ὁπλίτας χιλίους καὶ πελταστὰς
Θρᾷκας ὀκτακοσίους καὶ τοξότας Κρῆτας διακοσίους.
ἅμα δὲ καὶ Σῶσις παρῆν ὁ Συρακόσιος ἔχων ὁπλίτας
τριακοσίους, καὶ Σοφαίνετος ὁ Ἀρκὰς[7] ἔχων ὁπλίτας
χιλίους. καὶ ἐνταῦθα Κῦρος ἐξέτασιν καὶ ἀριθμὸν τῶν
Ἑλλήνων ἐποίησεν ἐν τῷ παραδείσῳ, καὶ ἐγένοντο οἱ
σύμπαντες ὁπλῖται μὲν μύριοι καὶ χίλιοι, πελτασταὶ
δὲ ἀμφὶ τοὺς δισχιλίους.

10 Ἐντεῦθεν ἐξελαύνει σταθμοὺς δύο παρασάγγας
δέκα εἰς Πέλτας, πόλιν οἰκουμένην. ἐνταῦθ᾽ ἔμεινεν
ἡμέρας τρεῖς· ἐν αἷς Ξενίας ὁ Ἀρκὰς τὰ Λύκαια ἔθυσε
καὶ ἀγῶνα ἔθηκε· τὰ δὲ ἆθλα ἦσαν στλεγγίδες χρυ-
σαῖ· ἐθεώρει δὲ τὸν ἀγῶνα καὶ Κῦρος. ἐντεῦθεν ἐξελαύνει σταθμοὺς δύο παρασάγγας δώδεκα ἐς Κερά-
μων ἀγοράν, πόλιν οἰκουμένην, ἐσχάτην πρὸς τῇ
11 Μυσίᾳ χώρᾳ. ἐντεῦθεν ἐξελαύνει σταθμοὺς τρεῖς
παρασάγγας τριάκοντα εἰς Καΰστρου πεδίον, πόλιν

---

[7] Σοφαίνετος ὁ Ἀρκὰς some MSS. Gem., Hude/Peters, Mar.:
other MSS. Ἀρκάδας· Ἀγίας ὁ Ἀρκὰς Köchly.

[19] Battle of Salamis, in 480.

contest of musical skill; he hung up his skin in the cave
from which the sources issue, and it is for this reason that
the river is called Marsyas. It was here also, report has it,
that Xerxes, when he was on his retreat from Greece after
losing the famous battle,[19] built the palace just mentioned
and likewise the citadel of Celaenae. Here Cyrus remained
thirty days; and Clearchus, the Lacedaemonian exile, arrived, with a thousand hoplites, eight hundred Thracian
peltasts, and two hundred Cretan bowmen. At the same
time came also Sosis the Syracusan with three hundred
hoplites and Sophaenetus the Arcadian with a thousand
hoplites. And here Cyrus held a review and made an enumeration of the Greeks in the park, and they amounted all
told to eleven thousand hoplites and about two thousand
peltasts.[20]

Thence he marched two stages, ten parasangs, to
Peltae, an inhabited city. There he remained three days,
during which time Xenias the Arcadian celebrated the
Lycaean[21] festival with sacrifice and held games; the prizes
were golden strigils, and Cyrus himself was one of those
who watched the games. Thence he marched two stages,
twelve parasangs, to the inhabited city of Ceramon-
agora,[22] the last Phrygian city as one goes toward Mysia.
Thence he marched three stages, thirty parasangs, to
Caÿstru-pedion[23] an inhabited city. There he remained five

[20] Here used in the general sense, *i.e.*, to include all kinds of
light-armed troops; cf. note on §3 above. Xenophon here uses
round numbers. The exact totals, according to the figures previously given, are 10,600 hoplites and 2,300 light-armed troops.

[21] In honour of Lycaean Zeus, i.e. Zeus of Mt. Lycaeus, in
Arcadia.   [22] Or Tilemarket.   [23] Or C asterfield.

XENOPHON

οἰκουμένην. ἐνταῦθ᾽ ἔμεινεν ἡμέρας πέντε· καὶ τοῖς
στρατιώταις ὠφείλετο μισθὸς πλέον ἢ τριῶν μηνῶν,
καὶ πολλάκις ἰόντες ἐπὶ τὰς θύρας ἀπῄτουν. ὁ δὲ
ἐλπίδας λέγων διῆγε καὶ δῆλος ἦν ἀνιώμενος· οὐ γὰρ
ἦν πρὸς τοῦ Κύρου τρόπου ἔχοντα μὴ ἀποδιδόναι.

12 ἐνταῦθα ἀφικνεῖται Ἔπυαξα ἡ Συεννέσιος γυνὴ τοῦ
Κιλίκων βασιλέως παρὰ Κῦρον· καὶ ἐλέγετο Κύρῳ
δοῦναι χρήματα πολλά. τῇ δ᾽ οὖν στρατιᾷ τότε ἀπέδωκε Κῦρος μισθὸν τεττάρων μηνῶν. εἶχε δὲ ἡ
Κίλισσα φυλακὴν περὶ αὐτὴν Κίλικας καὶ Ἀσπεν-
δίους· ἐλέγετο δὲ καὶ συγγενέσθαι Κῦρον τῇ Κιλίσσῃ.

13 Ἐντεῦθεν ἐξελαύνει σταθμοὺς δύο παρασάγγας
δέκα εἰς Θύμβριον, πόλιν οἰκουμένην. ἐνταῦθα ἦν
παρὰ τὴν ὁδὸν κρήνη ἡ Μίδου καλουμένη τοῦ Φρυγῶν
βασιλέως, ἐφ᾽ ᾗ λέγεται Μίδας τὸν Σάτυρον θηρεῦσαι

14 οἴνῳ κεράσας αὐτήν. ἐντεῦθεν ἐξελαύνει σταθμοὺς δύο
παρασάγγας δέκα εἰς Τυριάειον, πόλιν οἰκουμένην.
ἐνταῦθα ἔμεινεν ἡμέρας τρεῖς. καὶ λέγεται δεηθῆναι ἡ
Κίλισσα Κύρου ἐπιδεῖξαι τὸ στράτευμα αὐτῇ· βουλόμενος οὖν ἐπιδεῖξαι ἐξέτασιν ποιεῖται ἐν τῷ πεδίῳ τῶν

15 Ἑλλήνων καὶ τῶν βαρβάρων. ἐκέλευσε δὲ τοὺς Ἕλληνας ὡς νόμος αὐτοῖς εἰς μάχην οὕτω ταχθῆναι καὶ
στῆναι, συντάξαι δ᾽ ἕκαστον τοὺς ἑαυτοῦ. ἐτάχθησαν
οὖν ἐπὶ τεττάρων· εἶχε δὲ τὸ μὲν δεξιὸν Μένων καὶ οἱ

---

24 "King" in name, but in fact a dependent of the king of
Persia. Syennesis was seeking, as the narrative indicates, to keep

days. At this time he was owing the soldiers more than
three months' pay, and they went again and again to his
headquarters and demanded what was due them. He all
the while expressed hopes, and was manifestly troubled;
for it was not Cyrus' way to withhold payment when he had
money. At this juncture arrived Epyaxa, the wife of Syennesis, the king[24] of the Cilicians, coming to visit Cyrus, and
the story was that she gave him a large sum of money; at
any rate, Cyrus paid the troops at that time four months'
wages. The Cilician queen was attended by a body-guard
of Cilicians and Aspendians; and people said that Cyrus
had intimate relations with the queen.

Thence he marched two stages, ten parasangs, to the
inhabited city of Thymbrium. There, alongside the road,
was the so-called spring of Midas, the king of the Phrygians, at which Midas, according to the story, caught the
satyr by mixing wine with the water of the spring.[25] Thence
he marched two stages, ten parasangs, to Tyriaeum, an
inhabited city. There he remained three days. And the
Cilician queen, as the report ran, asked Cyrus to exhibit
his army to her; such an exhibition was what he desired to
make, and accordingly he held a review of the Greeks and
the barbarians on the plain. He ordered the Greeks to form
their lines and take their positions just as they were accustomed to do for battle, each general marshalling his own
men. So they formed the line four deep, Menon and his

on good terms with both Cyrus and Artaxerxes, secretly aiding the
former, while still making a show of resistance (see §21 below) to
his march. "Syennesis" was in fact the native title for the ruler of
Cilicia.   [25] This story is also told by one of Xenophon's con-
temporaries, Theopompus of Chios, *FGH* 115 F 75.

σὺν αὐτῷ, τὸ δὲ εὐώνυμον Κλέαρχος καὶ οἱ ἐκείνου, τὸ
16 δὲ μέσον οἱ ἄλλοι στρατηγοί. ἐθεώρει οὖν ὁ Κῦρος
πρῶτον μὲν τοὺς βαρβάρους· οἱ δὲ παρήλαυνον τεταγμένοι κατ᾽ ἴλας καὶ κατὰ τάξεις· εἶτα δὲ τοὺς
Ἕλληνας, παρελαύνων ἐφ᾽ ἅρματος καὶ ἡ Κίλισσα
ἐφ᾽ ἁρμαμάξης. εἶχον δὲ πάντες κράνη χαλκᾶ καὶ
χιτῶνας φοινικοῦς καὶ κνημῖδας καὶ τὰς ἀσπίδας
17 ἐκκεκαλυμμένας. ἐπειδὴ δὲ πάντας παρήλασε, στήσας
τὸ ἅρμα πρὸ τῆς φάλαγγος μέσης, πέμψας Πίγρητα
τὸν ἑρμηνέα παρὰ τοὺς στρατηγοὺς τῶν Ἑλλήνων
ἐκέλευσε προβαλέσθαι τὰ ὅπλα καὶ ἐπιχωρῆσαι ὅλην
τὴν φάλαγγα. οἱ δὲ ταῦτα προεῖπαν τοῖς στρατιώταις·
καὶ ἐπεὶ ἐσάλπιγξε, προβαλόμενοι τὰ ὅπλα ἐπῇσαν.
ἐκ δὲ τούτου θᾶττον προϊόντων σὺν κραυγῇ ἀπὸ τοῦ
αὐτομάτου δρόμος ἐγένετο τοῖς στρατιώταις ἐπὶ τὰς
σκηνάς, τῶν βαρβάρων φόβος πολύς τε καὶ ἄλλοις,
18 καὶ ἡ Κίλισσα ἔφυγεν[8] ἐπὶ τῆς ἁρμαμάξης καὶ οἱ ἐκ
τῆς ἀγορᾶς καταλιπόντες τὰ ὤνια ἔφυγον. οἱ δὲ
Ἕλληνες σὺν γέλωτι ἐπὶ τὰς σκηνὰς ἦλθον. ἡ δὲ
Κίλισσα ἰδοῦσα τὴν λαμπρότητα καὶ τὴν τάξιν τοῦ
στρατεύματος ἐθαύμασε. Κῦρος δὲ ἥσθη τὸν ἐκ τῶν
Ἑλλήνων εἰς τοὺς βαρβάρους φόβον ἰδών.
19   Ἐντεῦθεν ἐξελαύνει σταθμοὺς τρεῖς παρασάγγας
εἴκοσιν εἰς Ἰκόνιον, τῆς Φρυγίας πόλιν ἐσχάτην. ἐν-

---

[8] τῶν βαρβάρων ... πολύς τε καὶ ἄλλοις καὶ ἡ, Persson,
followed by Peters: τῶν δὲ ... καὶ ἥ τε MSS. Hude.

troops occupying the right wing, Clearchus and his troops
the left, and the other generals the centre. Cyrus inspected
the barbarians first, and they marched past with their cavalry formed in troops and their infantry in companies; then
he inspected the Greeks, driving past them in a chariot,
the Cilician queen in a carriage. And the Greeks all had
helmets of bronze, crimson tunics, and greaves, and carried their shields uncovered. When he had driven past
them all, he halted his chariot in front of the centre of the
phalanx, and sending his interpreter Pigres to the generals
of the Greeks, gave orders that the troops should advance
arms and the phalanx move forward in a body. The generals transmitted these orders to the soldiers, and when the
trumpet sounded, they advanced arms and charged. And
then, as they went on faster and faster, at length with a
shout the troops broke into a run of their own accord, in
the direction of the camp. As for the barbarians and the
others, they were terribly frightened; the Cilician queen
took to flight in her carriage, and the people in the market[26]
left their wares behind and took to their heels; while the
Greeks with a roar of laughter came up to their camp. Now
the Cilician queen was filled with admiration at beholding
the brilliant appearance and the order of the Greek army;
and Cyrus was delighted to see the terror with which the
Greeks inspired the barbarians.

Thence he marched three stages, twenty parasangs, to
Iconium, the last city of Phrygia. There he remained three

---

[26] Greek troops were not supplied with rations, but bought
their provisions from day to day from merchants who accompanied the army. The commander's duty ended with "providing a
market" ($\dot{\alpha}\gamma o\rho\dot{\alpha}\nu\ \pi\alpha\rho\acute{\epsilon}\chi\epsilon\iota\nu$).

ταῦθα ἔμεινε τρεῖς ἡμέρας. ἐντεῦθεν ἐξελαύνει διὰ τῆς
Λυκαονίας σταθμοὺς πέντε παρασάγγας τριάκοντα.
ταύτην τὴν χώραν ἐπέτρεψε διαρπάσαι τοῖς Ἕλλησιν
20 ὡς πολεμίαν οὖσαν. ἐντεῦθεν Κῦρος τὴν Κίλισσαν εἰς
τὴν Κιλικίαν ἀποπέμπει τὴν ταχίστην ὁδόν· καὶ συνέπεμψεν αὐτῇ στρατιώτας οὓς Μένων εἶχε καὶ αὐτόν.
Κῦρος δὲ μετὰ τῶν ἄλλων ἐξελαύνει διὰ Καππαδοκίας
σταθμοὺς τέτταρας παρασάγγας εἴκοσι καὶ πέντε
πρὸς Δάνα, πόλιν οἰκουμένην, μεγάλην καὶ εὐδαίμονα.
ἐνταῦθα ἔμειναν ἡμέρας τρεῖς· ἐν ᾧ Κῦρος ἀπέκτεινεν
ἄνδρα Πέρσην Μεγαφέρνη, φοινικιστὴν βασίλειον,
καὶ ἕτερόν τινα τῶν ὑπάρχων δυνάστην, αἰτιασάμενος
ἐπιβουλεύειν αὐτῷ.

21 Ἐντεῦθεν ἐπειρῶντο εἰσβάλλειν εἰς τὴν Κιλικίαν·
ἡ δὲ εἰσβολὴ ἦν ὁδὸς ἁμαξιτὸς ὀρθία ἰσχυρῶς καὶ
ἀμήχανος εἰσελθεῖν στρατεύματι, εἴ τις ἐκώλυεν.
ἐλέγετο δὲ καὶ Συέννεσις εἶναι ἐπὶ τῶν ἄκρων φυλάττων τὴν εἰσβολήν· διὸ ἔμεινεν ἡμέραν ἐν τῷ πεδίῳ. τῇ
δὲ ὑστεραίᾳ ἧκεν ἄγγελος λέγων ὅτι λελοιπὼς εἴη
Συέννεσις τὰ ἄκρα, ἐπεὶ ᾔσθετο ὅτι τό τε Μένωνος
στράτευμα ἤδη ἐν Κιλικίᾳ εἴη εἴσω τῶν ὀρέων, καὶ
ὅτι τριήρεις ἤκουε περιπλεούσας ἀπ᾽ Ἰωνίας εἰς
Κιλικίαν Τάμων ἔχοντα τὰς Λακεδαιμονίων καὶ αὐτοῦ
22 Κύρου. Κῦρος δ᾽ οὖν ἀνέβη ἐπὶ τὰ ὄρη οὐδενὸς κωλύ-

---

27 In leaving Phrygia Cyrus was passing beyond the limits of
his own satrapy.   28 For the title φοινικιστὴς βασίλειος, see
Briant, *Histoire* I, 644 and LSJ Supp. (rev.) sv.

days. Thence he marched through Lycaonia five stages, thirty parasangs. This country he gave over to the Greeks to plunder, on the ground that it was hostile territory.[27] From there Cyrus sent the Cilician queen back to Cilicia by the shortest route, and he sent some of Menon's troops to escort her, Menon himself commanding them. With the rest of the army Cyrus marched through Cappadocia four stages, twenty-five parasangs, to Dana, an inhabited city, large and prosperous. There they remained three days; and during that time Cyrus put to death a Persian named Megaphernes, who was a royal secretary,[28] and another dignitary among his subordinates, on the charge that they were plotting against him.

From there they made ready to try to enter Cilicia. Now the entrance was by a wagon-road, exceedingly steep and impracticable for an army to pass if there was anybody to oppose it; and in fact, as report ran, Syennesis was upon the heights, guarding the entrance; therefore Cyrus remained for a day in the plain. On the following day, however, a messenger came with word that Syennesis had abandoned the heights, because he had learned that Menon's army was already in Cilicia, on his own side of the mountains, and because, further, he was getting reports that triremes belonging to the Lacedaemonians[29] and to Cyrus himself were sailing around from Ionia to Cilicia under the command of Tamos. At any rate Cyrus climbed the mountains without meeting any opposition, and saw

[29] Cyrus had asked the Lacedaemonians "to show themselves as good friends to him as he had been to them in their war against Athens" (*Hell.* II. i. 1). The aid they now rendered (see also iv. 2–3) was in response to that request.

οντος, καὶ εἶδε τὰς σκηνὰς οὗ οἱ Κίλικες ἐφύλαττον.
ἐντεῦθεν δὲ κατέβαινεν εἰς πεδίον μέγα καὶ καλόν,
ἐπίρρυτον, καὶ δένδρων παντοδαπῶν σύμπλεων καὶ
ἀμπέλων·[9] πολὺ δὲ καὶ σήσαμον καὶ μελίνην καὶ
κέγχρον καὶ πυροὺς καὶ κριθὰς φέρει. ὄρος δ᾽ αὐτὸ
περιεῖχεν ὀχυρὸν καὶ ὑψηλὸν πάντῃ ἐκ θαλάττης εἰς
23 θάλατταν. καταβὰς δὲ διὰ τούτου τοῦ πεδίου ἤλασε
σταθμοὺς τέτταρας παρασάγγας πέντε καὶ εἴκοσιν εἰς
Ταρσούς, τῆς Κιλικίας πόλιν μεγάλην καὶ εὐδαίμονα.
ἐνταῦθα ἦσαν τὰ Συεννέσιος βασίλεια τοῦ Κιλίκων
βασιλέως· διὰ μέσου δὲ τῆς πόλεως ῥεῖ ποταμὸς
24 Κύδνος ὄνομα, εὖρος δύο πλέθρων. ταύτην τὴν πόλιν
ἐξέλιπον οἱ ἐνοικοῦντες μετὰ Συεννέσιος εἰς χωρίον
ὀχυρὸν ἐπὶ τὰ ὄρη πλὴν οἱ τὰ καπηλεῖα ἔχοντες·
ἔμειναν δὲ καὶ οἱ παρὰ τὴν θάλατταν οἰκοῦντες ἐν
Σόλοις καὶ ἐν Ἰσσοῖς.

25 Ἔπυαξα δὲ ἡ Συεννέσιος γυνὴ προτέρα Κύρου
πέντε ἡμέραις εἰς Ταρσοὺς ἀφίκετο· ἐν δὲ τῇ ὑπερβολῇ τῶν ὀρέων τῇ εἰς τὸ πεδίον δύο λόχοι τοῦ
Μένωνος στρατεύματος ἀπώλοντο· οἱ μὲν ἔφασαν
ἁρπάζοντάς τι κατακοπῆναι ὑπὸ τῶν Κιλίκων, οἱ δὲ
ὑπολειφθέντας καὶ οὐ δυναμένους εὑρεῖν τὸ ἄλλο
στράτευμα οὐδὲ τὰς ὁδοὺς εἶτα πλανωμένους ἀπολέ-
26 σθαι· ἦσαν δ᾽ οὖν οὗτοι ἑκατὸν ὁπλῖται. οἱ δ᾽ ἄλλοι
ἐπεὶ ἧκον, τήν τε πόλιν τοὺς Ταρσοὺς διήρπασαν, διὰ
τὸν ὄλεθρον τῶν συστρατιωτῶν ὀργιζόμενοι, καὶ τὰ

the camp where the Cilicians had been keeping guard. Thence he descended to a large and beautiful plain, well-watered and full of trees of all sorts and vines; it produces an abundance of sesame, millet, panic, wheat, and barley, and it is surrounded on every side, from sea to sea, by a lofty and formidable range of mountains. After descending he marched through this plain four stages, twenty-five parasangs, to Tarsus, a large and prosperous city of Cilicia. There the palace of Syennesis, the king of the Cilicians, was situated; and through the middle of the city flows a river named the Cydnus, two plethra in width. The inhabitants of this city had abandoned it and fled, with Syennesis, to a stronghold upon the mountains—all of them, at least, except the tavern-keepers; and there remained also those who dwelt on the seacoast, in Soli and Issus.

Now Epyaxa, the wife of Syennesis, had reached Tarsus five days ahead of Cyrus, but in the course of her passage over the mountains to the plain two companies of Menon's army[30] had been lost. Some said that they had been cut to pieces by the Cilicians while engaged in a bit of plundering; another story was that they had been left behind, and, unable to find the rest of army or the roads, had thus wandered about and perished; at any rate, they numbered a hundred hoplites. And when the rest of Menon's troops reached Tarsus, in their anger over the loss of their comrades they plundered thoroughly, not only the city, but also

[30] Cf. §20, above.

[9] Castiglioni reads πεδίον μέγα καὶ καλὸν καὶ ἐπίρρυτον, δένδρων ... σύμπλεων.

βασίλεια τὰ ἐν αὐτῇ. Κῦρος δ᾽ ἐπεὶ εἰσήλασεν εἰς τὴν
πόλιν, μετεπέμπετο τὸν Συέννεσιν πρὸς ἑαυτόν· ὁ δ᾽
οὔτε πρότερον οὐδενί πω κρείττονι ἑαυτοῦ εἰς χεῖρας
ἐλθεῖν ἔφη οὔτε τότε Κύρῳ ἰέναι ἤθελε, πρὶν ἡ γυνὴ

27 αὐτὸν ἔπεισε καὶ πίστεις ἔλαβε. μετὰ δὲ ταῦτα ἐπεὶ
συνεγένοντο ἀλλήλοις, Συέννεσις μὲν ἔδωκε Κύρῳ
χρήματα πολλὰ εἰς τὴν στρατιάν, Κῦρος δὲ ἐκείνῳ
δῶρα ἃ νομίζεται παρὰ βασιλεῖ τίμια, ἵππον χρυσο-
χάλινον καὶ στρεπτὸν χρυσοῦν καὶ ψέλια καὶ ἀκινά-
κην χρυσοῦν καὶ στολὴν Περσικήν, καὶ τὴν χώραν
μηκέτι ἁρπάζεσθαι· τὰ δὲ ἡρπασμένα ἀνδράποδα, ἤν
που ἐντυγχάνωσιν, ἀπολαμβάνειν.

III. Ἐνταῦθα ἔμεινε ὁ Κῦρος καὶ ἡ στρατιὰ ἡμέρας
εἴκοσιν· οἱ γὰρ στρατιῶται οὐκ ἔφασαν ἰέναι τοῦ
πρόσω· ὑπώπτευον γὰρ ἤδη ἐπὶ βασιλέα ἰέναι· μισθω-
θῆναι δὲ οὐκ ἐπὶ τούτῳ ἔφασαν. πρῶτος δὲ Κλέαρχος
τοὺς αὑτοῦ στρατιώτας ἐβιάζετο ἰέναι· οἱ δ᾽ αὐτόν τε
ἔβαλλον καὶ τὰ ὑποζύγια τὰ ἐκείνου, ἐπεὶ ἄρξαιντο

2 προϊέναι. Κλέαρχος δὲ τότε μὲν μικρὸν ἐξέφυγε μὴ
καταπετρωθῆναι, ὕστερον δ᾽ ἐπεὶ ἔγνω ὅτι οὐ δυνήσεται βιάσασθαι, συνήγαγεν ἐκκλησίαν τῶν αὑτοῦ
στρατιωτῶν. καὶ πρῶτον μὲν ἐδάκρυε πολὺν χρόνον
ἑστώς· οἱ δὲ ὁρῶντες ἐθαύμαζον καὶ ἐσιώπων· εἶτα δὲ
ἔλεξε τοιάδε.

3 Ἄνδρες στρατιῶται, μὴ θαυμάζετε ὅτι χαλεπῶς

the palace that was in it. As for Cyrus, after he had marched into the city he more than once summoned Syennesis to his presence; but Syennesis said that he had never yet put himself in the hands of anyone who was more powerful than he was, and he would not now put himself in the hands of Cyrus until his wife had won him over and he had received pledges. When the two men finally met one another, Syennesis gave Cyrus a large sum of money for his army, while Cyrus gave him gifts which are regarded at court[31] as tokens of honour—a horse with a gold-mounted bridle, a gold necklace and bracelets, a gold dagger and a Persian robe—promising him, further, that his land should not be plundered any more and that they might take back the slaves that had been seized in case they should chance upon them anywhere.

III. Cyrus and his army remained here at Tarsus twenty days, for the soldiers refused to go any farther; for they suspected by this time that they were going against the King, and they said they had not been hired for that. Clearchus was the first to try to force his men to go on, but they pelted him and his pack-animals with stones as often as they began to go forward. At that time Clearchus narrowly escaped being stoned to death; but afterwards, when he realized that he could not accomplish anything by force, he called a meeting of his own troops. And first he stood and wept for a long time, while his men watched him in wonder and were silent; then he spoke as follows:

"Fellow soldiers, do not wonder that I am distressed at

[31] *i.e.* such gifts as could be bestowed only by the Persian king. Cyrus is already assuming royal prerogatives. See Briant, *Histoire* I, 317.

φέρω τοῖς παροῦσι πράγμασιν. ἐμοὶ γὰρ ξένος Κῦρος
ἐγένετο καί με φεύγοντα ἐκ τῆς πατρίδος τά τε ἄλλα
ἐτίμησε καὶ μυρίους ἔδωκε δαρεικούς· οὓς ἐγὼ λαβὼν
οὐκ εἰς τὸ ἴδιον κατεθέμην ἐμοὶ οὐδὲ καθηδυπάθησα,
4 ἀλλ᾽ εἰς ὑμᾶς ἐδαπάνων. καὶ πρῶτον μὲν πρὸς τοὺς
Θρᾷκας ἐπολέμησα, καὶ ὑπὲρ τῆς Ἑλλάδος ἐτιμωρού-
μην μεθ᾽ ὑμῶν, ἐκ τῆς Χερρονήσου αὐτοὺς ἐξελαύνων
βουλομένους ἀφαιρεῖσθαι τοὺς ἐνοικοῦντας Ἕλληνας
τὴν γῆν. ἐπειδὴ δὲ Κῦρος ἐκάλει, λαβὼν ὑμᾶς ἐπο-
ρευόμην, ἵνα εἴ τι δέοιτο ὠφελοίην αὐτὸν ἀνθ᾽ ὧν εὖ
5 ἔπαθον ὑπ᾽ ἐκείνου. ἐπεὶ δὲ ὑμεῖς οὐ βούλεσθε συμπορεύεσθαι, ἀνάγκη δή μοι ἢ ὑμᾶς προδόντα τῇ
Κύρου φιλίᾳ χρῆσθαι ἢ πρὸς ἐκεῖνον ψευσάμενον μεθ᾽
ὑμῶν εἶναι. εἰ μὲν δὴ δίκαια ποιήσω οὐκ οἶδα, αἱρήσο-
μαι δ᾽ οὖν ὑμᾶς καὶ σὺν ὑμῖν ὅ τι ἂν δέῃ πείσομαι.
καὶ οὔποτε ἐρεῖ οὐδεὶς ὡς ἐγὼ Ἕλληνας ἀγαγὼν εἰς
τοὺς βαρβάρους, προδοὺς τοὺς Ἕλληνας τὴν τῶν
6 βαρβάρων φιλίαν εἱλόμην, ἀλλ᾽ ἐπεὶ ὑμεῖς ἐμοὶ οὐκ
ἐθέλετε πείθεσθαι οὐδὲ ἕπεσθαι[10] ἐγὼ σὺν ὑμῖν ἕψομαι
καὶ ὅ τι ἂν δέῃ πείσομαι. νομίζω γὰρ ὑμᾶς ἐμοὶ εἶναι
καὶ πατρίδα καὶ φίλους καὶ συμμάχους, καὶ σὺν ὑμῖν
μὲν ἂν οἶμαι εἶναι τίμιος ὅπου ἂν ὦ, ὑμῶν δὲ ἔρημος
ὢν οὐκ ἂν ἱκανὸς οἶμαι εἶναι οὔτ᾽ ἂν φίλον ὠφελῆσαι
οὔτ᾽ ἂν ἐχθρὸν ἀλέξασθαι. ὡς ἐμοῦ οὖν ἰόντος ὅπῃ ἂν
καὶ ὑμεῖς οὕτω τὴν γνώμην ἔχετε.
7   Ταῦτα εἶπεν· οἱ δὲ στρατιῶται οἵ τε αὐτοῦ ἐκείνου

the present situation. For Cyrus became my friend and not only honoured me, an exile from my fatherland, in various ways, but gave me ten thousand darics. And I, receiving this money, did not lay it up for my own personal use or squander it in pleasure, but I proceeded to expend it on you. First I went to war with the Thracians, and for the sake of Greece I inflicted punishment upon them with your aid, driving them out of the Chersonese when they wanted to deprive the Greeks who dwelt there of their land. Then when Cyrus' summons came, I took you with me and set out, in order that, if he had need of me, I might give him aid in return for the benefits I had received from him. But you now do not wish to continue the march with me; so it seems that I must either desert you and continue to enjoy Cyrus' friendship, or prove false to him and remain with you. Whether I shall be doing what is right, I know not, but at any rate I shall choose you and with you shall suffer whatever I must. And never shall any man say that I, after leading Greeks into the land of the barbarians, betrayed the Greeks and chose the friendship of the barbarians; nay, since you do not care to obey me nor follow, I shall follow with you and suffer whatever I must. For I consider that you are to me both fatherland and friends and allies; with you I think I shall be honoured wherever I may be, bereft of you I do not think I shall be able either to aid a friend or to ward off a foe. Be sure, therefore, that wherever you go, I shall go also."

Such were his words. And the soldiers—not only his

---

10 οὐκ ἐθέλετε, most MSS.: one MS. οὐ θέλετε. οὐδὲ ἔπεσθαι some MSS.: others omit.

καὶ οἱ ἄλλοι ταῦτα ἀκούσαντες ὅτι οὐ φαίη παρὰ
βασιλέα πορεύεσθαι ἐπήνεσαν· παρὰ δὲ Ξενίου καὶ
Πασίωνος πλείους ἢ δισχίλιοι λαβόντες τὰ ὅπλα καὶ
τὰ σκευοφόρα ἐστρατοπεδεύσαντο παρὰ Κλεάρχῳ.
8 Κῦρος δὲ τούτοις ἀπορῶν τε καὶ λυπούμενος μετεπέμπετο τὸν Κλέαρχον· ὁ δὲ ἰέναι μὲν οὐκ ἤθελε, λάθρᾳ
δὲ τῶν στρατιωτῶν πέμπων αὐτῷ ἄγγελον ἔλεγε θαρρεῖν ὡς καταστησομένων τούτων εἰς τὸ δέον. μεταπέμ-
πεσθαι δ᾽ ἐκέλευεν αὐτόν· αὐτὸς δ᾽ οὐκ ἔφη ἰέναι.

9 Μετὰ δὲ ταῦτα συναγαγὼν τούς θ᾽ ἑαυτοῦ στρατιώτας καὶ τοὺς προσελθόντας αὐτῷ καὶ τῶν ἄλλων
τὸν βουλόμενον, ἔλεξε τοιάδε. Ἄνδρες στρατιῶται, τὰ
μὲν δὴ Κύρου δῆλον ὅτι οὕτως ἔχει πρὸς ἡμᾶς ὥσπερ
τὰ ἡμέτερα πρὸς ἐκεῖνον· οὔτε γὰρ ἡμεῖς ἐκείνου ἔτι
στρατιῶται, ἐπεί γε οὐ συνεπόμεθα αὐτῷ, οὔτε ἐκεῖνος
ἔτι ἡμῖν μισθοδότης. ὅτι μέντοι ἀδικεῖσθαι νομίζει ὑφ᾽
10 ἡμῶν οἶδα· ὥστε καὶ μεταπεμπομένου αὐτοῦ οὐκ ἐθέλω
ἐλθεῖν, τὸ μὲν μέγιστον αἰσχυνόμενος ὅτι σύνοιδα
ἐμαυτῷ πάντα ἐψευσμένος αὐτόν, ἔπειτα καὶ δεδιὼς
μὴ λαβών με δίκην ἐπιθῇ ὧν νομίζει ὑπ᾽ ἐμοῦ ἠδικῆ-
11 σθαι. ἐμοὶ οὖν δοκεῖ οὐχ ὥρα εἶναι ἡμῖν καθεύδειν
οὐδ᾽ ἀμελεῖν ἡμῶν αὐτῶν, ἀλλὰ βουλεύεσθαι ὅ τι χρὴ
ποιεῖν ἐκ τούτων. καὶ ἕως γε μένομεν αὐτοῦ σκεπτέον
μοι δοκεῖ εἶναι ὅπως ὡς[11] ἀσφαλέστατα μένουμεν, εἴ
τε ἤδη δοκεῖ ἀπιέναι, ὅπως ὡς ἀσφαλέστατα ἄπιμεν,

[11] After ὅπως, in this line and the next, Cobet has inserted ὡς,
followed by Gem., Hude/Peters.

own men, but the rest also—when they heard that he said he would not go on to the King's capital, commended him; and more than two thousand of the troops under Xenias and Pasion took their arms and their baggage train and encamped with Clearchus. But Cyrus, perplexed and distressed by this situation, sent repeatedly for Clearchus. Clearchus refused to go to him, but without the knowledge of the soldiers he sent a messenger and told him not to be discouraged, because, he said, this matter would be settled in the right way. He directed Cyrus, however, to keep on sending for him though he himself, he said, would refuse to go.

After this Clearchus gathered together his own soldiers, those who had come over to him, and any others who wanted to be present, and spoke as follows: "Fellow soldiers, it is clear that the relation of Cyrus to us is precisely the same as ours to him; that is, we are no longer his soldiers, since we decline to follow him, and likewise he is no longer our paymaster. I know, however, that he considers himself wronged by us. Therefore, although he keeps sending for me, I decline to go, chiefly, it is true, from a feeling of shame, because I am conscious that I have proved utterly false to him, but, besides that, from fear that he may seize me and inflict punishment upon me for the wrongs he thinks he has suffered at my hands. In my opinion, therefore, it is no time for us to be sleeping or unconcerned about ourselves; we should rather be considering what course we ought to follow under the present circumstances. And so long as we remain here we must consider, I think, how we will remain most safely; or, again, if we count it best to depart at once, how we will depart most

73

καὶ ὅπως τὰ ἐπιτήδεια ἕξομεν· ἄνευ γὰρ τούτων οὔτε
12 στρατηγοῦ οὔτε ἰδιώτου ὄφελος οὐδέν. ὁ δ᾽ ἀνὴρ πολλοῦ μὲν ἄξιος ᾧ ἂν φίλος ᾖ, χαλεπώτατος δ᾽ ἐχθρὸς
ᾧ ἂν πολέμιος ᾖ, ἔχει δὲ δύναμιν καὶ πεζὴν καὶ
ἱππικὴν καὶ ναυτικὴν ἣν πάντες ὁμοίως ὁρῶμέν τε καὶ
ἐπιστάμεθα· καὶ γὰρ οὐδὲ πόρρω δοκοῦμέν μοι αὐτοῦ
καθῆσθαι. ὥστε ὥρα λέγειν ὅ τι τις γιγνώσκει ἄριστον εἶναι. ταῦτα εἰπὼν ἐπαύσατο.

13   Ἐκ δὲ τούτου ἀνίσταντο οἱ μὲν ἐκ τοῦ αὐτομάτου,
λέξοντες ἃ ἐγίγνωσκον, οἱ δὲ καὶ ὑπ᾽ ἐκείνου ἐγκέλευ-
στοι, ἐπιδεικνύντες οἵα εἴη ἡ ἀπορία ἄνευ τῆς Κύρου
14 γνώμης καὶ μένειν καὶ ἀπιέναι. εἷς δὲ δὴ εἶπε προσ-
ποιούμενος σπεύδειν ὡς τάχιστα πορεύεσθαι εἰς τὴν
Ἑλλάδα στρατηγοὺς μὲν ἑλέσθαι ἄλλους ὡς τάχιστα,
εἰ μὴ βούλεται Κλέαρχος ἀπάγειν· τὰ δ᾽ ἐπιτήδει᾽
ἀγοράζεσθαι—ἡ δ᾽ ἀγορὰ ἦν ἐν τῷ βαρβαρικῷ στρατεύματι—καὶ συσκευάζεσθαι· ἐλθόντας δὲ Κῦρον
αἰτεῖν πλοῖα, ὡς ἀποπλέοιεν· ἐὰν δὲ μὴ διδῷ ταῦτα,
ἡγεμόνα αἰτεῖν Κῦρον ὅστις διὰ φιλίας τῆς χώρας
ἀπάξει· ἐὰν δὲ μηδὲ ἡγεμόνα διδῷ, συντάττεσθαι τὴν
ταχίστην, πέμψαι δὲ καὶ προκαταληψομένους τὰ
ἄκρα, ὅπως μὴ φθάσωσι μήτε Κῦρος μήτε οἱ Κίλικες
καταλαβόντες, ὧν πολλοὺς καὶ πολλὰ χρήματα ἔχομεν ἀνηρπακότες. οὗτος μὲν τοιαῦτα εἶπε.

15   Μετὰ δὲ τοῦτον Κλέαρχος εἶπε τοσοῦτον· Ὡς μὲν
στρατηγήσοντα ἐμὲ ταύτην τὴν στρατηγίαν μηδεὶς
ὑμῶν λεγέτω· πολλὰ γὰρ ἐνορῶ δι᾽ ἃ ἐμοὶ τοῦτο οὐ

safely and how we will secure provisions—for without provisions neither general nor private is of any use. And remember that while this Cyrus is a valuable friend when he is your friend, he is a most dangerous foe when he is your enemy; furthermore, he has an armament—infantry and cavalry and fleet—which we all alike see and know about; for I take it that our camp is not very far away from him. It is time, then, to propose whatever plan anyone of you deems best." With these words he ceased speaking.

Thereupon various speakers arose, some of their own accord to express the opinions they held, but others at the instigation of Clearchus to make clear the difficulty of either remaining or departing without the consent of Cyrus. One man in particular, pretending to be in a hurry to proceed back to Greece with all speed, proposed that they should choose other generals as quickly as possible, in case Clearchus did not wish to lead them back; secondly, that they should buy provisions—the market was in the barbarian army!—and pack up their baggage; then, to go to Cyrus and ask for vessels to sail away in; and if he would not give them vessels, to ask him for a guide to lead them homeward through a country that was friendly; and if he would not give them a guide, either, to form in line of battle with all speed and likewise to send a force to occupy the mountain heights in advance, in order that neither Cyrus nor the Cilicians should forestall them—"and we have in our possession," he said, "many of these Cilicians and much of their property that we have seized as plunder." Such were the words of this speaker.

After him Clearchus said merely this: "Let no one among you speak of me as the man who is to hold this command, for I see many reasons why I should not do so;

ποιητέον· ὡς δὲ τῷ ἀνδρὶ ὃν ἂν ἕλησθε πείσομαι ᾗ
δυνατὸν μάλιστα, ἵνα εἰδῆτε ὅτι καὶ ἄρχεσθαι ἐπί-
16 σταμαι ὥς τις καὶ ἄλλος μάλιστα ἀνθρώπων. μετὰ
τοῦτον ἄλλος ἀνέστη, ἐπιδεικνὺς μὲν τὴν εὐήθειαν τοῦ
τὰ πλοῖα αἰτεῖν κελεύοντος, ὥσπερ πάλιν τὸν στόλον
Κύρου ποιουμένου, ἐπιδεικνὺς δὲ ὡς εὔηθες εἴη ἡγεμόνα αἰτεῖν παρὰ τούτου ᾧ λυμαινόμεθα τὴν πρᾶξιν.
εἰ δὲ καὶ τῷ ἡγεμόνι πιστεύσομεν ὃν ἂν Κῦρος διδῷ,
τί κωλύει καὶ τὰ ἄκρα ἡμῖν κελεύειν Κῦρον προκατα-
17 λαμβάνειν; ἐγὼ γὰρ ὀκνοίην μὲν ἂν εἰς τὰ πλοῖα
ἐμβαίνειν ἃ ἡμῖν δοίη, μὴ ἡμᾶς αὐταῖς ταῖς τριήρεσι
καταδύσῃ, φοβοίμην δ' ἂν τῷ ἡγεμόνι ᾧ δοίη ἕπεσθαι,
μὴ ἡμᾶς ἀγάγῃ ὅθεν οὐκ ἔσται ἐξελθεῖν· βουλοίμην δ'
ἂν ἄκοντος ἀπιὼν Κύρου λαθεῖν αὐτὸν ἀπελθών· ὃ οὐ
18 δυνατόν ἐστιν. ἀλλ' ἐγώ φημι ταῦτα μὲν φλυαρίας
εἶναι· δοκεῖ δέ μοι ἄνδρας ἐλθόντας πρὸς Κῦρον
οἵτινες ἐπιτήδειοι σὺν Κλεάρχῳ ἐρωτᾶν ἐκεῖνον τί
βούλεται ἡμῖν χρῆσθαι· κἂν μὲν ἡ πρᾶξις ᾖ παρα-
πλησία οἷάπερ καὶ πρόσθεν ἐχρῆτο τοῖς ξένοις, ἕπεσθαι καὶ ἡμᾶς καὶ μὴ κακίους εἶναι τῶν πρόσθεν
19 τούτῳ συναναβάντων· ἐὰν δὲ μείζων ἡ πρᾶξις τῆς
πρόσθεν φαίνηται καὶ ἐπιπονωτέρα καὶ ἐπικινδυνο-
τέρα, ἀξιοῦν ἢ πείσαντα ἡμᾶς ἄγειν ἢ πεισθέντα πρὸς
φιλίαν ἀφιέναι· οὕτω γὰρ καὶ ἑπόμενοι ἂν φίλοι αὐτῷ
καὶ πρόθυμοι ἐποίμεθα καὶ ἀπιόντες ἀσφαλῶς ἂν

---

32 As described in i. 2,
33 i.e., in the form of extra pay.

say rather that I shall obey to the best of my ability the man whom you choose, in order that you may know that I understand as well as any other person in the world how to be a subordinate also." After he had spoken another man arose to point out the foolishness of the speaker who had urged them to ask for vessels, just as if Cyrus were going home again, and to point out also how foolish it was to ask for a guide "from this man whose enterprise we are ruining. Indeed, if we propose to trust the guide that Cyrus gives us, what is to hinder us from directing Cyrus also to occupy the heights for us in advance? For my part, I should hesitate to embark on the vessels that he might give us, for fear of his sinking us with his own ships, and I should be afraid to follow the guide that he might give, for fear of his leading us to a place from which it will not be possible to escape; my choice would be, in going off without Cyrus' consent, to go off without his knowledge—and that is not possible. Now in my own opinion the plans just proposed are nonsense; rather, I think we should send to Cyrus men of the proper sort, along with Clearchus, to ask him what use he wishes to make of us; and if his enterprise is like the sort of one in which he employed mercenaries before,[32] I think that we also should follow him and not be more cowardly than those who went up with him on the former occasion; if, however, his enterprise is found to be greater and more laborious and more dangerous than the former one, we ought to demand that he should either offer sufficient persuasion[33] and lead us on with him, or yield to our persuasion and let us go home in friendship; for in this way, if we should follow him, we should follow as friends and zealous supporters, and if we should go back, we should go back in safety. I propose, further, that our represen-

ἀπίοιμεν· ὅ τι δ' ἂν πρὸς ταῦτα λέγῃ ἀπαγγεῖλαι
δεῦρο· ἡμᾶς δ' ἀκούσαντας πρὸς ταῦτα βουλεύεσθαι.

20 Ἔδοξε ταῦτα, καὶ ἄνδρας ἑλόμενοι σὺν Κλεάρχῳ
πέμπουσιν οἳ ἠρώτων Κῦρον τὰ δόξαντα τῇ στρατιᾷ.
ὁ δ' ἀπεκρίνατο ὅτι ἀκούοι Ἀβροκόμαν ἐχθρὸν ἄνδρα
ἐπὶ τῷ Εὐφράτῃ ποταμῷ εἶναι, ἀπέχοντα δώδεκα
σταθμούς· πρὸς τοῦτον οὖν ἔφη βούλεσθαι ἐλθεῖν· κἂν
μὲν ᾖ ἐκεῖ, τὴν δίκην ἔφη χρῄζειν ἐπιθεῖναι αὐτῷ, ἢν
21 δὲ φύγῃ, ἡμεῖς ἐκεῖ πρὸς ταῦτα βουλευσόμεθα. ἀκούσαντες δὲ ταῦτα οἱ αἱρετοὶ ἀγγέλλουσι τοῖς στρα-
τιώταις· τοῖς δὲ ὑποψία μὲν ἦν ὅτι ἄγει πρὸς βασιλέα,
ὅμως δὲ ἐδόκει ἕπεσθαι. προσαιτοῦσι δὲ μισθόν· ὁ δὲ
Κῦρος ὑπισχνεῖται ἡμιόλιον πᾶσι δώσειν οὗ πρότερον
ἔφερον, ἀντὶ δαρεικοῦ τρία ἡμιδαρεικὰ τοῦ μηνὸς τῷ
στρατιώτῃ· ὅτι δὲ ἐπὶ βασιλέα ἄγοι οὐδὲ ἐνταῦθα
ἤκουσεν οὐδεὶς ἐν γε τῷ φανερῷ.

IV. Ἐντεῦθεν ἐξελαύνει σταθμοὺς δύο παρασάγγας
δέκα ἐπὶ τὸν Ψάρον ποταμόν, οὗ ἦν τὸ εὖρος τρία
πλέθρα. ἐντεῦθεν ἐξελαύνει σταθμὸν ἕνα παρασάγγας
πέντε ἐπὶ τὸν Πύραμον ποταμόν, οὗ τὸ εὖρος στάδιον.
ἐντεῦθεν ἐξελαύνει σταθμοὺς δύο παρασάγγας πεντεκαίδεκα εἰς Ἰσσούς, τῆς Κιλικίας ἐσχάτην πόλιν ἐπὶ
2 τῇ θαλάττῃ οἰκουμένην, μεγάλην καὶ εὐδαίμονα. ἐνταῦθα ἔμειναν ἡμέρας τρεῖς· καὶ Κύρῳ παρῆσαν αἱ
ἐκ Πελοποννήσου νῆες τριάκοντα καὶ πέντε καὶ ἐπ'
αὐταῖς ναύαρχος Πυθαγόρας Λακεδαιμόνιος. ἡγεῖτο

tatives should report back to us whatever reply he may make, and that we after hearing it should deliberate about the matter."

This plan was adopted, and they chose representatives and sent them with Clearchus; and they proceeded to put to Cyrus the questions resolved upon by the army. He replied that he had heard that Abrocomas, a foe of his, was at the Euphrates river, twelve stages distant. It was against him therefore, he said, that he desired to march. And if he were there, he wished to inflict due punishment upon him; "but if he has fled," he continued, "we will deliberate about the matter then and there." Upon hearing this reply the deputies reported it to the soldiers, and they, while suspecting that Cyrus was leading them against the King, nevertheless thought it best to follow him. They asked, however, for more pay, and Cyrus promised to give them all half as much again as they had been receiving before, namely, a daric and a half a month to each man instead of a daric; but as regards the suspicion that he was leading them against the King, no one heard it expressed even then—at any rate, not openly.

IV. Thence he marched two stages, ten parasangs, to the Psarus river, the width of which was three plethra. From there he marched one stage, five parasangs, to the Pyramus river, the width of which was a stadium.[34] From there he marched two stages, fifteen parasangs, to Issus, the last city in Cilicia, a place situated on the sea, and large and prosperous. There they remained three days; and the ships from Peloponnesus[35] arrived to meet Cyrus, thirty-five in number, with Pythagoras the Lacedaemonian as admiral in

[34] The stadium = 582½ English feet.   [35] See ii. 21.

δ᾽ αὐταῖς Τάμως Αἰγύπτιος ἐξ Ἐφέσου, ἔχων ναῦς
ἑτέρας Κύρου πέντε καὶ εἴκοσιν, αἷς ἐπολιόρκει Μίλητον ὅτε Τισσαφέρνει φίλη ἦν, καὶ συνεπολέμει Κύρῳ
3 πρὸς αὐτόν.[12] παρῆν δὲ καὶ Χειρίσοφος Λακεδαιμόνιος
ἐπὶ τῶν νεῶν, μετάπεμπτος ὑπὸ Κύρου, ἑπτακοσίους
ἔχων ὁπλίτας, ὧν ἐστρατήγει παρὰ Κύρῳ. αἱ δὲ νῆες
ὥρμουν παρὰ τὴν Κύρου σκηνήν. ἐνταῦθα καὶ οἱ παρὰ
Ἀβροκόμα μισθοφόροι Ἕλληνες ἀποστάντες ἦλθον
παρὰ Κῦρον τετρακόσιοι ὁπλῖται καὶ συνεστρατεύ-
οντο ἐπὶ βασιλέα.
4   Ἐντεῦθεν ἐξελαύνει σταθμὸν ἕνα παρασάγγας
πέντε ἐπὶ πύλας τῆς Κιλικίας καὶ τῆς Συρίας. ἦσαν δὲ
ταῦτα δύο τείχη, καὶ τὸ μὲν ἔσωθεν ⟨τὸ⟩[13] πρὸ τῆς
Κιλικίας Συέννεσις εἶχε καὶ Κιλίκων φυλακή, τὸ δὲ
ἔξω τὸ πρὸ τῆς Συρίας βασιλέως ἐλέγετο φυλακὴ
φυλάττειν. διὰ μέσου δὲ ῥεῖ τούτων ποταμὸς Κάρσος
ὄνομα, εὖρος πλέθρου. ἅπαν δὲ τὸ μέσον τῶν τειχῶν
ἦσαν στάδιοι τρεῖς· καὶ παρελθεῖν οὐκ ἦν βίᾳ· ἦν γὰρ
ἡ πάροδος στενὴ καὶ τὰ τείχη εἰς τὴν θάλατταν
καθήκοντα, ὑπερθεν δ᾽ ἦσαν πέτραι ἠλίβατοι· ἐπὶ δὲ
5 τοῖς τείχεσιν ἀμφοτέροις ἐφειστήκεσαν πύλαι. ταύτης
ἕνεκα τῆς παρόδου Κῦρος τὰς ναῦς μετεπέμψατο, ὅπως

[12] ὅτε ... αὐτόν: condemned by Cobet, whom many edd. follow.   [13] τὸ Vossius.

---

[36] See i. 7.
[37] See note on ii. 21. These seven hundred hoplites under

command of them. They had been guided from Ephesus to Issus by Tamos the Egyptian, who was at the head of another fleet of twenty-five ships belonging to Cyrus— these latter being the ships with which Tamos had besieged Miletus, at the time when it was friendly to Tissaphernes,[36] and had supported Cyrus in his war upon Tissaphernes. Cheirisophus the Lacedaemonian also arrived with this fleet, coming in response to Cyrus' summons,[37] together with seven hundred hoplites, over whom he continued to hold command in the army of Cyrus. And the ships lay at anchor alongside Cyrus' tent. It was at Issus also that the Greek mercenaries who had been in the service of Abrocomas—four hundred hoplites—joined Cyrus, after deserting Abrocomas, and so bore a share in his expedition against the King.

Thence he marched one stage, five parasangs, to the Gates between Cilicia and Syria. These Gates consisted of two walls; the one on the hither, or Cilician, side was held by Syennesis and a garrison of Cilicians, while the one on the farther, the Syrian, side was reported to be guarded by a garrison of the King's troops. And in the space between these walls flows a river named the Carsus, a plethrum in width. The entire distance from one wall to the other was three stadia; and it was not possible to effect a passage by force, for the pass was narrow, the walls reached down to the sea, and above the pass were precipitous rocks, while, besides, gates stood upon both the walls. It was because of this pass that Cyrus had sent for the fleet, in order that he

Cheirisophus had been sent by the Lacedaemonian authorities to aid Cyrus, and were the only troops in his army which stood in any official connection with any Greek state.

81

ὁπλίτας ἀποβιβάσειεν εἴσω καὶ ἔξω τῶν πυλῶν, καὶ
βιασάμενοι τοὺς πολεμίους παρέλθοιεν εἰ φυλάττοιεν
ἐπὶ ταῖς Συρίαις πύλαις, ὅπερ ᾤετο ποιήσειν ὁ Κῦρος
τὸν Ἀβροκόμαν, ἔχοντα πολὺ στράτευμα. Ἀβροκόμας δὲ οὐ τοῦτ' ἐποίησεν, ἀλλ' ἐπεὶ ἤκουσε Κῦρον ἐν
Κιλικίᾳ ὄντα, ἀναστρέψας ἐκ Φοινίκης παρὰ βασιλέα
ἀπήλαυνεν, ἔχων, ὡς ἐλέγετο, τριάκοντα μυριάδας
στρατιᾶς.

6   Ἐντεῦθεν ἐξελαύνει διὰ Συρίας σταθμὸν ἕνα παρασάγγας πέντε εἰς Μυρίανδον, πόλιν οἰκουμένην ὑπὸ
Φοινίκων ἐπὶ τῇ θαλάττῃ· ἐμπόριον δ' ἦν τὸ χωρίον
7 καὶ ὥρμουν αὐτόθι ὁλκάδες πολλαί. ἐνταῦθα ἔμεινεν
ἡμέρας ἑπτά· καὶ Ξενίας ὁ Ἀρκὰς καὶ Πασίων ὁ
Μεγαρεὺς ἐμβάντες εἰς πλοῖον καὶ τὰ πλείστου ἄξια
ἐνθέμενοι ἀπέπλευσαν, ὡς μὲν τοῖς πλείστοις ἐδόκουν
φιλοτιμηθέντες ὅτι τοὺς στρατιώτας αὐτῶν τοὺς παρὰ
Κλέαρχον ἀπελθόντας ὡς ἀπιόντας εἰς τὴν Ἑλλάδα
πάλιν καὶ οὐ πρὸς βασιλέα εἴα Κῦρος τὸν Κλέαρχον
ἔχειν. ἐπεὶ δ' ἦσαν ἀφανεῖς, διῆλθε λόγος ὅτι διώκοι
αὐτοὺς Κῦρος τριήρεσι· καὶ οἱ μὲν ηὔχοντο ὡς δειλοὺς
ὄντας αὐτοὺς ληφθῆναι, οἱ δ' ᾤκτιρον εἰ ἁλώσοιντο.

8   Κῦρος δὲ συγκαλέσας τοὺς στρατηγοὺς εἶπεν·
Ἀπολελοίπασιν ἡμᾶς Ξενίας καὶ Πασίων. ἀλλ' εὖ γε
μέντοι ἐπιστάσθων ὅτι οὔτε ἀποδεδράκασιν· οἶδα γὰρ
ὅπη οἴχονται· οὔτε ἀποπεφεύγασιν· ἔχω γὰρ τριήρεις
ὥστε ἑλεῖν τὸ ἐκείνων πλοῖον· ἀλλὰ μὰ τοὺς θεοὺς οὐκ

---

[38] Of which Abrocomas was satrap.   [39] See iii. 7.

might disembark hoplites between and beyond the walls, and thus they might dislodge the enemy and pass through, if they should be keeping guard at the Syrian Gates—and that was precisely what Cyrus supposed Abrocomas would do, for he had a large army. Abrocomas, however, did not do so, but as soon as he heard that Cyrus was in Cilicia, he turned about in his journey from Phoenicia[38] and marched off to join the King, with an army, so the report ran, of three hundred thousand men.

Thence Cyrus marched one stage, five parasangs, to Myriandus, a city on the sea coast, inhabited by Phoenicians; it was a trading place, and many merchant ships were lying at anchor there. There he remained seven days; and Xenias the Arcadian and Pasion the Megarian embarked upon a ship, put on board their most valuable effects, and sailed away; they were moved to do this, as most people thought, by a feeling of jealous pride, because their soldiers had gone over to Clearchus[39] with the intention of going back to Greece again instead of proceeding against the King, and Cyrus had allowed Clearchus to keep them. After they had disappeared, a report went round that Cyrus was pursuing them with warships; and while some people prayed that they might be captured, because, as they said, they were cowards, yet others felt pity for them if they should be caught.

Cyrus, however, called the generals together and said: "Xenias and Pasion have deserted us. But let them, nevertheless, know full well that they have not escaped from me—either by stealth, for I know in what direction they have gone, or by speed, for I have men-of-war with which I can overtake their craft. But for my part, I swear by the

ἔγωγε αὐτοὺς διώξω, οὐδ' ἐρεῖ οὐδεὶς ὡς ἐγὼ ἕως μὲν
ἂν παρῇ τις χρῶμαι, ἐπειδὰν δὲ ἀπιέναι βούληται,
συλλαβὼν καὶ αὐτοὺς κακῶς ποιῶ καὶ τὰ χρήματα
ἀποσυλῶ. ἀλλὰ ἴτωσαν,[14] εἰδότες ὅτι κακίους εἰσὶ περὶ
ἡμᾶς ἢ ἡμεῖς περὶ ἐκείνους. καίτοι ἔχω γε αὐτῶν καὶ
τέκνα καὶ γυναῖκας ἐν Τράλλεσι φρουρούμενα· ἀλλ'
οὐδὲ τούτων στερήσονται, ἀλλ' ἀπολήψονται τῆς
9 πρόσθεν ἕνεκα περὶ ἐμὲ ἀρετῆς. καὶ ὁ μὲν ταῦτα εἶπεν·
οἱ δὲ Ἕλληνες, εἴ τις καὶ ἀθυμότερος ἦν πρὸς τὴν
ἀνάβασιν, ἀκούοντες τὴν Κύρου ἀρετὴν ἥδιον καὶ
προθυμότερον συνεπορεύοντο.

Μετὰ ταῦτα Κῦρος ἐξελαύνει σταθμοὺς τέτταρας
παρασάγγας εἴκοσιν ἐπὶ τὸν Χάλον ποταμόν, ὄντα τὸ
εὖρος πλέθρου, πλήρη δ' ἰχθύων μεγάλων καὶ πραέων,
οὓς οἱ Σύροι θεοὺς ἐνόμιζον καὶ ἀδικεῖν οὐκ εἴων, οὐδὲ
τὰς περιστεράς. αἱ δὲ κῶμαι ἐν αἷς ἐσκήνουν Παρυ-
10 σάτιδος ἦσαν εἰς ζώνην δεδομέναι. ἐντεῦθεν ἐξελαύνει
σταθμοὺς πέντε παρασάγγας τριάκοντα ἐπὶ τὰς
πηγὰς τοῦ Δάρδατος ποταμοῦ, οὗ τὸ εὖρος πλέθρου.
ἐνταῦθα ἦσαν τὰ Βελέσυος βασίλεια τοῦ Συρίας
ἄρξαντος, καὶ παράδεισος πάνυ μέγας καὶ καλός,
ἔχων πάντα ὅσα ὧραι φύουσι. Κῦρος δ' αὐτὸν ἐξέκοψε
11 καὶ τὰ βασίλεια κατέκαυσεν. ἐντεῦθεν ἐξελαύνει σταθμοὺς τρεῖς παρασάγγας πεντεκαίδεκα ἐπὶ τὸν Εὐφράτην ποταμόν, ὄντα τὸ εὖρος τεττάρων σταδίων· καὶ

---

14 ἴτωσαν Hude/Peters, Mar., following Bornemann: ἰέτ-
ωσαν MSS.: ἴτων Gem.

gods that I shall not pursue them, nor shall anyone say about me that I use a man so long as he is with me and then, when he wants to leave me, seize him and maltreat him and despoil him of his possessions. Nay, let them go, with the knowledge that their behaviour toward us is worse than ours toward them. To be sure, I have their wives and children under guard in Tralles,[40] but I shall not deprive them of these, either, for they shall receive them back because of their former excellence in my service." Such were his words; as for the Greeks, even those who had been somewhat despondent in regard to the upward march, when they heard of the magnanimity of Cyrus they continued on their way with greater satisfaction and eagerness.

After this Cyrus marched four stages, twenty parasangs, to the Chalus river, which is a plethrum in width and full of large, tame fish; these fish the Syrians regarded as gods, and they would not allow anyone to harm them, or the doves, either.[41] And the villages in which the troops encamped belonged to Parysatis, for they had been given her for girdlemoney.[42] From there Cyrus marched five stages, thirty parasangs, to the sources of the Dardas river, the width of which is a plethrum. There was the palace of Belesys, the late ruler of Syria, and a very large and beautiful park containing all the products of the seasons. But Cyrus cut down the park and burned up the palace. Thence he marched three stages, fifteen parasangs, to the Euphrates river, the width of which was four stadia; and on

[40] A city in Caria.   [41] According to the legend, the Syrian goddess Derceto had been transformed into a fish, and her daughter, Semiramis, into a dove. Cf. Diodorus II. iv. 2ff.

[42] Cf. II. iv. 27. See Intro.; also Briant, *Histoire* I, 475.

πόλις αὐτόθι ᾠκεῖτο μεγάλη καὶ εὐδαίμων Θάψακος
ὄνομα. ἐνταῦθα ἔμειναν ἡμέρας πέντε· καὶ Κῦρος
μεταπεμψάμενος τοὺς στρατηγοὺς τῶν Ἑλλήνων
ἔλεγεν ὅτι ἡ ὁδὸς ἔσοιτο πρὸς βασιλέα μέγαν εἰς
Βαβυλῶνα· καὶ κελεύει αὐτοὺς λέγειν ταῦτα τοῖς στρα-
12 τιώταις καὶ ἀναπείθειν ἕπεσθαι. οἱ δὲ ποιήσαντες
ἐκκλησίαν ἀπήγγελλον ταῦτα· οἱ δὲ στρατιῶται ἐχαλέπαινον τοῖς στρατηγοῖς, καὶ ἔφασαν αὐτοὺς πάλαι
ταῦτ᾽ εἰδότας κρύπτειν, καὶ οὐκ ἔφασαν ἰέναι, ἐὰν μή
τις αὐτοῖς χρήματα διδῷ, ὥσπερ τοῖς προτέροις μετὰ
Κύρου ἀναβᾶσι παρὰ τὸν πατέρα τοῦ Κύρου, καὶ
ταῦτα οὐκ ἐπὶ μάχην ἰόντων, ἀλλὰ καλοῦντος τοῦ
13 πατρὸς Κῦρον. ταῦτα οἱ στρατηγοὶ Κύρῳ ἀπήγγελ-
λον· ὁ δ᾽ ὑπέσχετο ἀνδρὶ ἑκάστῳ δώσειν πέντε ἀργυρίου μνᾶς, ἐπὰν εἰς Βαβυλῶνα ἥκωσι, καὶ τὸν μισθὸν
ἐντελῆ μέχρι ἂν καταστήσῃ τοὺς Ἕλληνας εἰς Ἰωνίαν
πάλιν. τὸ μὲν δὴ πολὺ τοῦ Ἑλληνικοῦ οὕτως ἐπείσθη.

Μένων δὲ πρὶν δῆλον εἶναι τί ποιήσουσιν οἱ ἄλλοι
στρατιῶται, πότερον ἕψονται Κύρῳ ἢ οὔ, συνέλεξε τὸ
αὑτοῦ στράτευμα χωρὶς τῶν ἄλλων καὶ ἔλεξε τάδε.
14 Ἄνδρες, ἐάν μοι πεισθῆτε, οὔτε κινδυνεύσαντες οὔτε
πονήσαντες τῶν ἄλλων πλέον προτιμήσεσθε στρα-

---

43 Most probably Jerablus: see P. A. Brunt in Arrian (Loeb
Classical Library), I, 486.

44 The troops are not now asking for additional pay, as at Tarsus (iii. 21), but for a special donation. See below.

the river was situated a large and prosperous city named Thapsacus.[43] There they remained five days. And Cyrus summoned the generals of the Greeks and told them that the march was to be to Babylon, against the Great King; he directed them, accordingly, to explain this to the soldiers and try to persuade them to follow. So the generals called an assembly and made this announcement; and the soldiers were angry with the generals, and said that they had known about this for a long time, but had been keeping it from the troops; furthermore, they refused to go on unless they were given money,[44] as were the men who made the journey with Cyrus before,[45] when he went to visit his father; they had received the donation, even though they marched, not to battle, but merely because Cyrus' father summoned him. All these things the generals reported back to Cyrus, and he promised that he would give every man five minas[46] in silver when they reached Babylon and their pay in full until he brought the Greeks back to Ionia again.[47] By these promises the greater part of the Greek army was persuaded.

But as for Menon, before it was clear what the rest of the soldiers would do, that is, whether they would follow Cyrus or not, he gathered together his own troops apart from the others and spoke as follows: "Soldiers, if you will obey me, you will, without either danger or toil, be honoured by Cyrus above and beyond the rest of the

[45] See i. 2.   [46] The Attic mina was equivalent to 100 drachmas, pay for several months.

[47] Mercenaries were usually expected to make their own way home after a campaign had ended and did not receive pay for the time consumed by the homeward journey.

τιωτῶν ὑπὸ Κύρου. τί οὖν κελεύω ποιῆσαι; νῦν δεῖται
Κῦρος ἕπεσθαι τοὺς Ἕλληνας ἐπὶ βασιλέα· ἐγὼ οὖν
φημι ὑμᾶς χρῆναι διαβῆναι τὸν Εὐφράτην ποταμὸν
πρὶν δῆλον εἶναι ὅ τι οἱ ἄλλοι Ἕλληνες ἀποκρινοῦνται
15 Κύρῳ. ἢν μὲν γὰρ ψηφίσωνται ἕπεσθαι, ὑμεῖς δόξετε
αἴτιοι εἶναι ἄρξαντες τοῦ διαβαίνειν, καὶ ὡς προθ-
υμοτάτοις οὖσιν ὑμῖν χάριν εἴσεται Κῦρος καὶ ἀπο-
δώσει· ἐπίσταται δ' εἴ τις καὶ ἄλλος· ἢν δὲ ἀποψηφί-
σωνται οἱ ἄλλοι, ἄπιμεν μὲν ἅπαντες τοὔμπαλιν, ὑμῖν
δὲ ὡς μόνοις πειθομένοις πιστοτάτοις χρήσεται καὶ
εἰς φρούρια καὶ εἰς λοχαγίας, καὶ ἄλλου οὗτινος ἂν
16 δέησθε οἶδα ὅτι ὡς φίλου[15] τεύξεσθε Κύρου. ἀκούσαντες ταῦτα ἐπείθοντο καὶ διέβησαν πρὶν τοὺς ἄλλους
ἀποκρίνασθαι. Κῦρος δ' ἐπεὶ ἤσθετο διαβεβηκότας,
ἤσθη τε καὶ τῷ στρατεύματι πέμψας Γλοῦν εἶπεν·
Ἐγὼ μέν, ὦ ἄνδρες, ἤδη ὑμᾶς ἐπαινῶ· ὅπως δὲ καὶ
ὑμεῖς ἐμὲ ἐπαινέσετε ἐμοὶ μελήσει, ἢ μηκέτι με Κῦρον
17 νομίζετε. οἱ μὲν δὴ στρατιῶται ἐν ἐλπίσι μεγάλαις
ὄντες ηὔχοντο αὐτὸν εὐτυχῆσαι, Μένωνι δὲ καὶ δῶρα
ἐλέγετο πέμψαι μεγαλοπρεπῶς. ταῦτα δὲ ποιήσας
διέβαινε· συνείπετο δὲ καὶ τὸ ἄλλο στράτευμα αὐτῷ
ἅπαν. καὶ τῶν διαβαινόντων τὸν ποταμὸν οὐδεὶς
18 ἐβρέχθη ἀνωτέρω τῶν μαστῶν ὑπὸ τοῦ ποταμοῦ. οἱ
δὲ Θαψακηνοὶ ἔλεγον ὅτι οὐπώποθ' οὗτος ὁ ποταμὸς
διαβατὸς γένοιτο πεζῇ εἰ μὴ τότε, ἀλλὰ πλοίοις, ἃ

---

[15] φίλου Bisschop, followed by Gem., Hude/Peters: φίλοι
MSS.

troops. What, then, do I direct you to do? At this moment Cyrus is begging the Greeks to follow him against the King; my own plan, then, is that you should cross the Euphrates river before it is clear what answer the rest of the Greeks will make to Cyrus. For if they vote to follow him, it is you who will get the credit for that decision because you began the crossing, and Cyrus will not only feel grateful to you, regarding you as the most zealous in his cause, but he will return the favour—and he knows how to do that if any man does; on the other hand, if the rest vote not to follow him, we shall all go back together, but you, as the only ones who were obedient, are the men he will employ being the most reliable, not only for garrison duty,[48] but for captaincies; and whatever else you may desire, I know that you will secure it from Cyrus, on the grounds that he is your friend." Upon hearing these words the soldiers were persuaded, and made the crossing before the rest gave their answer. When Cyrus learned that they had crossed, he was delighted and sent Glus to the troops with this message: "Soldiers, today I commend you; but I shall see to it that you also shall have cause to commend me, else count me no longer Cyrus." So Menon's troops cherished high hopes and prayed that he might be successful, while to Menon himself Cyrus was said to have sent magnificent gifts besides. After so doing Cyrus proceeded to cross the river, and the rest of the army followed him, to the last man. And in the crossing no one got wet above the breast by the water. The people of Thapsacus said that this river had never been passable on foot except at this time, but only

---

[48] *i.e.* easy service.

τότε Ἀβροκόμας προϊὼν κατέκαυσεν, ἵνα μὴ Κῦρος διαβῇ. ἐδόκει δὴ θεῖον εἶναι καὶ σαφῶς ὑποχωρῆσαι τὸν ποταμὸν Κύρῳ ὡς βασιλεύσοντι.

19   Ἐντεῦθεν ἐξελαύνει διὰ τῆς Συρίας σταθμοὺς ἐννέα παρασάγγας πεντήκοντα· καὶ ἀφικνοῦνται πρὸς τὸν Ἀράξην ποταμόν. ἐνταῦθα ἦσαν κῶμαι πολλαὶ μεσταὶ σίτου καὶ οἴνου. ἐνταῦθα ἔμειναν ἡμέρας τρεῖς καὶ ἐπεσιτίσαντο.

V. Ἐντεῦθεν ἐξελαύνει διὰ τῆς Ἀραβίας τὸν Εὐφράτην ποταμὸν ἐν δεξιᾷ ἔχων σταθμοὺς ἐρήμους πέντε παρασάγγας τριάκοντα καὶ πέντε. ἐν τούτῳ δὲ τῷ τόπῳ ἦν μὲν ἡ γῆ πεδίον ἅπαν ὁμαλὲς ὥσπερ θάλαττα, ἀψινθίου δὲ πλῆρες· εἰ δέ τι καὶ ἄλλο ἐνῆν ὕλης ἢ καλάμου, ἅπαντα ἦσαν εὐώδη ὥσπερ ἀρώ-
2 ματα· δένδρον δ' οὐδὲν ἐνῆν, θηρία δὲ παντοῖα, πλεῖστοι μὲν ὄνοι ἄγριοι, πολλαὶ δὲ στρουθοὶ αἱ μεγάλαι· ἐνῆσαν δὲ καὶ ὠτίδες καὶ δορκάδες. ταῦτα δὲ τὰ θηρία οἱ ἱππεῖς ἐνίοτε ἐδίωκον. καὶ οἱ μὲν ὄνοι, ἐπεί τις διώκοι, προδραμόντες ἕστασαν· πολὺ γὰρ τῶν ἵππων ἔτρεχον θᾶττον· καὶ πάλιν, ἐπεὶ πλησιάζοιεν οἱ ἵπποι, ταὐτὸν ἐποίουν, καὶ οὐκ ἦν λαβεῖν, εἰ μὴ διαστάντες οἱ ἱππεῖς θηρῷεν διαδεχόμενοι. τὰ δὲ κρέα τῶν ἁλισκομένων ἦν παραπλήσια τοῖς ἐλαφείοις,
3 ἁπαλώτερα δέ. στρουθὸν δὲ οὐδεὶς ἔλαβεν· οἱ δὲ διώξαντες τῶν ἱππέων ταχὺ ἐπαύοντο· πολὺ γὰρ ἀπέσπα φεύγουσα, τοῖς μὲν ποσὶ δρόμῳ, ταῖς δὲ πτέρυξιν αἴρουσα, ὥσπερ ἱστίῳ χρωμένη. τὰς δὲ ὠτίδας ἄν τις ταχὺ ἀνιστῇ ἔστι λαμβάνειν· πέτονται

by boats; and these Abrocomas had now burned, as he marched on ahead of Cyrus, in order to prevent him from crossing. It seemed, accordingly, that here was a divine intervention, and that the river had plainly retired before Cyrus because he was destined to be king.[49]

Thence he marched through Syria nine stages, fifty parasangs, and they arrived at the Araxes river. There they found many villages full of grain and wine, and there they remained for three days and provisioned the army.

V. Thence he marched through Arabia, keeping the Euphrates on the right, five stages through desert country, thirty-five parasangs. In this region the ground was an unbroken plain, as level as the sea, and full of wormwood; and whatever else there was on the plain by way of shrub or reed, was always fragrant, like spices; trees there were none, but wild animals of all sorts, vast numbers of wild asses and many ostriches, besides bustards and gazelles. These animals were sometimes chased by the horsemen. As for the asses, whenever one chased them, they would run on ahead and stop—for they ran much faster than the horses—and then, when the horses came near, they would do the same thing again, and it was impossible to catch them unless the horsemen posted themselves at intervals and hunted them in relays. The flesh of those that were captured was like venison, but more tender. But no ostrich was captured by anyone, and any horseman who chased one speedily desisted; for it would distance him at once in its flight, not merely plying its feet, but hoisting its wings and using them like a sail. The bustards, on the other hand,

[49] Cf. Alexander and the retreat of the Pamphylian sea: Arrian, *An*. I. xxvi. 2 and Callisthenes, *FGH* 124 F 31.

τε γὰρ βραχὺ ὥσπερ οἱ πέρδικες καὶ ταχὺ ἀπαγο-
ρεύουσι. τὰ δὲ κρέα αὐτῶν ἥδιστα ἦν.

4 Πορευόμενοι δὲ διὰ ταύτης τῆς χώρας ἀφικνοῦνται
ἐπὶ τὸν Μάσκαν ποταμόν, τὸ εὖρος πλεθριαῖον. ἐνταῦθα ἦν πόλις ἐρήμη, μεγάλη, ὄνομα δ᾿ αὐτῇ Κορ-
σωτή· περιερρεῖτο δ᾿ αὕτη ὑπὸ τοῦ Μάσκα κύκλῳ.

5 ἐνταῦθ᾿ ἔμειναν ἡμέρας τρεῖς καὶ ἐπεσιτίσαντο. ἐντεῦθεν ἐξελαύνει σταθμοὺς ἐρήμους τρεῖς καὶ δέκα
παρασάγγας ἐνενήκοντα τὸν Εὐφράτην ποταμὸν ἐν
δεξιᾷ ἔχων, καὶ ἀφικνεῖται ἐπὶ Πύλας. ἐν τούτοις τοῖς
σταθμοῖς πολλὰ τῶν ὑποζυγίων ἀπώλετο ὑπὸ λιμοῦ·
οὐ γὰρ ἦν χόρτος οὐδὲ ἄλλο οὐδὲν δένδρον, ἀλλὰ ψιλὴ
ἦν ἅπασα ἡ χώρα· οἱ δὲ ἐνοικοῦντες ὄνους ἀλέτας
παρὰ τὸν ποταμὸν ὀρύττοντες καὶ ποιοῦντες εἰς Βαβυλῶνα ἦγον καὶ ἐπώλουν καὶ ἀνταγοράζοντες σῖτον

6 ἔζων. τὸ δὲ στράτευμα ὁ σῖτος ἐπέλιπε, καὶ πρίασθαι
οὐκ ἦν εἰ μὴ ἐν τῇ Λυδίᾳ ἀγορᾷ ἐν τῷ Κύρου βαρβαρικῷ, τὴν καπίθην ἀλεύρων ἢ ἀλφίτων τεττάρων
σίγλων. ὁ δὲ σίγλος δύναται ἑπτὰ ὀβολοὺς καὶ ἡμιω-
βέλιον Ἀττικούς· ἡ δὲ καπίθη δύο χοίνικας Ἀττικὰς
ἐχώρει. κρέα οὖν ἐσθίοντες οἱ στρατιῶται διεγίγνοντο.

7 ἦν δὲ τούτων τῶν σταθμῶν οὓς πάνυ μακροὺς ἤλαυνεν,
ὁπότε ἢ πρὸς ὕδωρ βούλοιτο διατελέσαι ἢ πρὸς χιλόν.

---

50 "The Gates." The precise location of this place is not
known: V. Manfredi, *La Strada dei Diecimila* (Milan, 1986)
132–3.

51 The Lydians were famous as merchants: Hdt. I. clv. 4.

52 See ii. 18 and the note thereon, and iii. 14.

can be caught if one is quick in starting them up, for they fly only a short distance, like partridges, and soon tire; and their flesh was delicious.

Marching on through this region they arrived at the Mascas river, which is a plethrum in width. There, in the desert, was a large city named Corsote, completely surrounded by the Mascas. There they remained three days and provisioned the army. Thence Cyrus marched thirteen stages through desert country, ninety parasangs, keeping the Euphrates river on the right, and arrived at Pylae.[50] In the course of these stages many of the baggage animals died of hunger, for there was no fodder and, in fact, no growing thing of any kind, but the land was absolutely bare; and the people who dwelt here made a living by quarrying mill-stones along the river banks, then fashioning them and taking them to Babylon, where they sold them and bought grain in exchange. As for the troops, their supply of grain gave out, and it was not possible to buy any except in the Lydian[51] market attached to the barbarian army of Cyrus,[52] at the price of four *sigli* for a *capithē* of wheat flour or barley meal. The *siglus* is worth seven and one-half Attic obols, and the *capithē* had the capacity of two Attic choenices.[53] The soldiers therefore managed to subsist by eating meat.[54] And Cyrus sometimes made these stages through the desert very long, whenever he wanted to reach water or fresh fodder.

[53] There were six obols in an Attic drachma. The choenix = about 1 quart. The prices stated were about fifty times normal prices at Athens.   [54] The Greeks of Xenophon's time ate comparatively little meat under any circumstances, but in the Arabian desert a diet of meat constituted a real hardship.

Καὶ δή ποτε στενοχωρίας καὶ πηλοῦ φανέντος ταῖς
ἁμάξαις δυσπορεύτου ἐπέστη ὁ Κῦρος σὺν τοῖς περὶ
αὐτὸν ἀρίστοις καὶ εὐδαιμονεστάτοις καὶ ἔταξε Γλοῦν
καὶ Πίγρητα λαβόντας τοῦ βαρβαρικοῦ στρατοῦ
8 συνεκβιβάζειν τὰς ἁμάξας. ἐπεὶ δ' ἐδόκουν αὐτῷ σχο-
λαίως ποιεῖν, ὥσπερ ὀργῇ ἐκέλευσε τοὺς περὶ αὐτὸν
Πέρσας τοὺς κρατίστους συνεπισπεῦσαι τὰς ἁμάξας.
ἔνθα δὴ μέρος τι τῆς εὐταξίας ἦν θεάσασθαι. ῥίψαντες
γὰρ τοὺς πορφυροῦς κάνδυς ὅπου ἔτυχεν ἕκαστος
ἑστηκώς, ἵεντο ὥσπερ ἂν δράμοι τις περὶ νίκης καὶ
μάλα κατὰ πρανοῦς γηλόφου, ἔχοντες τούτους τε τοὺς
πολυτελεῖς χιτῶνας καὶ τὰς ποικίλας ἀναξυρίδας,
ἔνιοι δὲ καὶ στρεπτοὺς περὶ τοῖς τραχήλοις καὶ ψέλια
περὶ ταῖς χερσίν· εὐθὺς δὲ σὺν τούτοις εἰσπηδήσαντες
εἰς τὸν πηλὸν θᾶττον ἢ ὥς τις ἂν ᾤετο μετεώρους
9 ἐξεκόμισαν τὰς ἁμάξας. τὸ δὲ σύμπαν δῆλος ἦν
Κῦρος ὡς σπεύδων πᾶσαν τὴν ὁδὸν καὶ οὐ διατρίβων
ὅπου μὴ ἐπισιτισμοῦ ἕνεκα ἤ τινος ἄλλου ἀναγκαίου
ἐκαθέζετο, νομίζων, ὅσῳ θᾶττον ἔλθοι, τοσούτῳ
ἀπαρασκευοτέρῳ βασιλεῖ μαχεῖσθαι, ὅσῳ δὲ σχο-
λαίτερον, τοσούτῳ πλέον συναγείρεσθαι βασιλεῖ
στράτευμα. καὶ συνιδεῖν δ' ἦν τῷ προσέχοντι τὸν νοῦν
ἡ βασιλέως ἀρχὴ πλήθει μὲν χώρας καὶ ἀνθρώπων
ἰσχυρὰ οὖσα, τοῖς δὲ μήκεσι τῶν ὁδῶν καὶ τῷ δι-
εσπάσθαι τὰς δυνάμεις ἀσθενής, εἴ τις διὰ ταχέων
τὸν πόλεμον ποιοῖτο.

10   Πέραν δὲ τοῦ Εὐφράτου ποταμοῦ κατὰ τοὺς ἐρήμους σταθμοὺς ἦν πόλις εὐδαίμων καὶ μεγάλη, ὄνομα

Once in particular, when they came upon a narrow, muddy place which was hard for the wagons to get through, Cyrus halted with his train of nobles and dignitaries and ordered Glus and Pigres to take some of the barbarian troops and help to pull the wagons out. But it seemed to him that they took their time with the work; accordingly, as if in anger, he directed the Persian nobles who accompanied him to take a hand in hurrying on the wagons. And then one might have beheld a sample of good discipline: they each threw off their purple cloaks where they chanced to be standing, and rushed, as a man would run to win a victory, down a most exceedingly steep hill, wearing these costly tunics and coloured trousers, some of them, indeed, with necklaces around their necks and bracelets on their arms; and leaping at once, with all this finery, into the mud, they lifted the wagons high and dry and brought them out more quickly than one would have thought possible. In general, it was clear that Cyrus was in haste throughout the whole journey and was making no delays, except where he halted to procure provisions or for some other necessary purpose; his thought was that the faster he went, the more unprepared the King would be to fight with him, while, on the other hand, the slower he went, the greater would be the army that was gathering for the King. Furthermore, one who observed closely could see at a glance that while the King's empire was strong in its extent of territory and number of inhabitants, it was weak by reason of the greatness of the distances and the scattered condition of its forces, in case one should be swift in making his attack upon it.

Across the Euphrates river in the course of these desert marches was a large and prosperous city named Char-

δὲ Χαρμάνδη· ἐκ ταύτης οἱ στρατιῶται ἠγόραζον τὰ
ἐπιτήδεια, σχεδίαις διαβαίνοντες ὧδε. διφθέρας ἃς
εἶχον σκεπάσματα ἐπίμπλασαν χόρτου κούφου, εἶτα
συνῆγον καὶ συνέσπων, ὡς μὴ ἅπτεσθαι τῆς κάρφης
τὸ ὕδωρ· ἐπὶ τούτων διέβαινον καὶ ἐλάμβανον τὰ
ἐπιτήδεια, οἶνόν τε ἐκ τῆς βαλάνου πεποιημένον τῆς
ἀπὸ τοῦ φοίνικος καὶ σῖτον μελίνης· τοῦτο γὰρ ἦν ἐν
τῇ χώρᾳ πλεῖστον.

11 Ἀμφιλεξάντων δέ τι ἐνταῦθα τῶν τέ του Μένωνος
στρατιωτῶν καὶ τῶν τοῦ Κλεάρχου ὁ Κλέαρχος κρίνας
ἀδικεῖν τὸν τοῦ Μένωνος πληγὰς ἐνέβαλεν· ὁ δὲ ἐλθὼν
πρὸς τὸ ἑαυτοῦ στράτευμα ἔλεγεν· ἀκούσαντες δ᾽ οἱ
στρατιῶται ἐχαλέπαινον καὶ ὠργίζοντο ἰσχυρῶς τῷ
12 Κλεάρχῳ. τῇ δὲ αὐτῇ ἡμέρᾳ Κλέαρχος ἐλθὼν ἐπὶ τὴν
διάβασιν τοῦ ποταμοῦ καὶ ἐκεῖ κατασκεψάμενος τὴν
ἀγορὰν ἀφιππεύει ἐπὶ τὴν ἑαυτοῦ σκηνὴν διὰ τοῦ
Μένωνος στρατεύματος σὺν ὀλίγοις τοῖς περὶ αὐτόν·
Κῦρος δὲ οὔπω ἧκεν, ἀλλ᾽ ἔτι προσήλαυνε· τῶν δὲ
Μένωνος στρατιωτῶν ξύλα σχίζων τις ὡς εἶδε Κλέαρχον διελαύνοντα, ἵησι τῇ ἀξίνῃ· καὶ οὗτος μὲν αὐτοῦ
ἥμαρτεν· ἄλλος δὲ λίθῳ καὶ ἄλλος, εἶτα πολλοί,
13 κραυγῆς γενομένης. ὁ δὲ καταφεύγει εἰς τὸ ἑαυτοῦ
στράτευμα, καὶ εὐθὺς παραγγέλλει εἰς τὰ ὅπλα· καὶ
τοὺς μὲν ὁπλίτας αὐτοῦ ἐκέλευσε μεῖναι τὰς ἀσπίδας
πρὸς τὰ γόνατα θέντας, αὐτὸς δὲ λαβὼν τοὺς Θρᾷκας
καὶ τοὺς ἱππέας οἳ ἦσαν αὐτῷ ἐν τῷ στρατεύματι
πλείους ἢ τετταράκοντα, τούτων δὲ οἱ πλεῖστοι Θρᾷκες, ἤλαυνεν ἐπὶ τοὺς Μένωνος, ὥστ᾽ ἐκείνους ἐκπε-

mande, and here the soldiers made purchases of provisions, crossing the river on rafts in the following way: they took skins which they had for tent covers, filled them with hay, and then brought the edges together and sewed them up, so that the water could not touch the hay; on these they would cross and get provisions—wine made from the date of the palm tree and bread made of millet, for this grain was very abundant in the country.

There, when one of Menon's men got into dispute with the men of Clearchus' contingent, Clearchus, deciding that Menon's man was in the wrong, gave him a flogging. The man then went to his own army and told about it, and when his comrades heard of the matter, they took it hard and were exceedingly angry with Clearchus. On the same day Clearchus, after going to the place where they crossed the river and there inspecting the market, was riding back to his own tent through Menon's army, having only a few men with him; and Cyrus had not yet arrived, but was still on the march toward the place; and one of Menon's soldiers who was splitting wood threw his axe at Clearchus when he saw him riding through the camp. Now this man missed him, but another threw a stone at him, and still another, and then, after an outcry had been raised, many. Clearchus escaped to his own army and at once called his troops to arms; he ordered his hoplites to remain where they were, resting their shields against their knees,[55] while he himself with the Thracians[56] and the horsemen, of which he had in his army more than forty, most of them Thracians, advanced upon Menon's troops; the result was that these

[55] i.e. in readiness to support him in case of need.
[56] See ii. 9.

πλῆχθαι καὶ αὐτὸν Μένωνα, καὶ τρέχειν ἐπὶ τὰ ὅπλα·

14 οἱ δὲ καὶ ἔστασαν ἀποροῦντες τῷ πράγματι. ὁ δὲ Πρόξενος—ἔτυχε γὰρ ὕστερος προσιὼν καὶ τάξις αὐτῷ ἑπομένη τῶν ὁπλιτῶν—εὐθὺς οὖν εἰς τὸ μέσον ἀμφοτέρων ἄγων ἔθετο τὰ ὅπλα καὶ ἐδεῖτο τοῦ Κλεάρχου μὴ ποιεῖν ταῦτα. ὁ δ᾽ ἐχαλέπαινεν ὅτι [αὐτοῦ] ὀλίγου δεήσαντος καταλευσθῆναι πράως λέγοι τὸ αὑτοῦ πάθος, ἐκέλευσέ τε αὐτὸν ἐκ τοῦ μέσου ἐξίστα-

15 σθαι. ἐν τούτῳ δ᾽ ἐπῄει καὶ Κῦρος καὶ ἐπύθετο τὸ πρᾶγμα· εὐθὺς δ᾽ ἔλαβε τὰ παλτὰ εἰς τὰς χεῖρας καὶ σὺν τοῖς παροῦσι τῶν πιστῶν ἧκεν ἐλαύνων εἰς τὸ

16 μέσον, καὶ λέγει τάδε. Κλέαρχε καὶ Πρόξενε καὶ οἱ ἄλλοι οἱ παρόντες Ἕλληνες, οὐκ ἴστε ὅ τι ποιεῖτε. εἰ γάρ τινα ἀλλήλοις μάχην συνάψετε, νομίζετε ἐν τῇδε τῇ ἡμέρᾳ ἐμέ τε κατακεκόψεσθαι καὶ ὑμᾶς οὐ πολὺ ἐμοῦ ὕστερον· κακῶς γὰρ τῶν ἡμετέρων ἐχόντων πάντες οὗτοι οὓς ὁρᾶτε βάρβαροι πολεμιώτεροι ἡμῖν

17 ἔσονται τῶν παρὰ βασιλεῖ ὄντων. ἀκούσας ταῦτα ὁ Κλέαρχος ἐν ἑαυτῷ ἐγένετο· καὶ παυσάμενοι ἀμφό-τεροι κατὰ χώραν ἔθεντο τὰ ὅπλα.

VI. Ἐντεῦθεν προϊόντων ἐφαίνετο ἴχνη ἵππων καὶ κόπρος. ἠκάζετο δ᾽ εἶναι ὁ στίβος ὡς δισχιλίων ἵππων. οὗτοι προϊόντες ἔκαιον καὶ χιλὸν καὶ εἴ τι ἄλλο χρήσιμον ἦν. Ὀρόντας δὲ Πέρσης ἀνὴρ γένει τε προσήκων βασιλεῖ καὶ τὰ πολέμια λεγόμενος ἐν τοῖς ἀρίστοις Περσῶν ἐπιβουλεύει Κύρῳ καὶ πρόσθεν

and Menon himself were thoroughly frightened and ran
to their arms, though there were some who stood stock-
still, nonplussed by the situation. But Proxenus—for he
chanced to be now coming up, later than the others, with
a battalion of hoplites following him—straightway led his
troops into the space between the two parties, halted them
under arms, and began to beg Clearchus not to proceed
with his attack. Clearchus, however, was angry, because,
when he had barely escaped being stoned to death,
Proxenus was talking lightly of his grievance, and he ordered him to remove himself from between them. At this
moment Cyrus also came up and learned about the situation, and he immediately took his spears in his hands and,
attended by such of his counsellors as were present, came
riding into the intervening space and spoke as follows:
"Clearchus, and Proxenus, and all you other Greeks who
are here, you know not what you are doing. For as certainly
as you come to fighting with one another, you may be sure
that on this very day I shall be instantly cut to pieces and
yourselves not long after me; for once let ill fortune overtake us, and all these barbarians whom you see will be
more hostile to us than are those who stand with the King."
On hearing these words Clearchus came to his senses, and
both parties ceased from their quarrel and returned to
their quarters.

VI. As they went on from there, they kept seeing tracks
of horses and horses' dung. To all appearances it was the
trail of about two thousand horses, and the horsemen as
they proceeded were burning up fodder and everything
else that was of any use. At this time Orontas, a Persian,
who was related to the King by birth and was reckoned
among the best of the Persians in matters of war, devised

2 πολεμήσας, καταλλαγεὶς δέ. οὗτος Κύρῳ εἶπεν, εἰ
αὐτῷ δοίη ἱππέας χιλίους, ὅτι τοὺς προκατακαίοντας
ἱππέας ἢ κατακάνοι ἂν ἐνεδρεύσας ἢ ζῶντας πολλοὺς
αὐτῶν ἕλοι καὶ κωλύσειε τοῦ καίειν ἐπιόντας, καὶ
ποιήσειεν ὥστε μήποτε δύνασθαι αὐτοὺς ἰδόντας τὸ
Κύρου στράτευμα βασιλεῖ διαγγεῖλαι. τῷ δὲ Κύρῳ
ἀκούσαντι ταῦτα ἐδόκει ὠφέλιμα εἶναι, καὶ ἐκέλευεν
αὐτὸν λαμβάνειν μέρος παρ᾽ ἑκάστου τῶν ἡγεμόνων.

3 ὁ δ᾽ Ὀρόντας νομίσας ἑτοίμους εἶναι αὐτῷ τοὺς ἱππέας γράφει ἐπιστολὴν παρὰ βασιλέα ὅτι ἥξοι ἔχων
ἱππέας ὡς ἂν δύνηται πλείστους· ἀλλὰ φράσαι τοῖς
αὐτοῦ ἱππεῦσιν ἐκέλευεν ὡς φίλιον αὐτὸν ὑποδέχε-
σθαι. ἐνῆν δὲ ἐν τῇ ἐπιστολῇ καὶ τῆς πρόσθεν φιλίας
ὑπομνήματα καὶ πίστεως. ταύτην τὴν ἐπιστολὴν δίδωσι πιστῷ ἀνδρί, ὡς ᾤετο· ὁ δὲ λαβὼν Κύρῳ δίδω-

4 σιν. ἀναγνοὺς δὲ αὐτὴν ὁ Κῦρος συλλαμβάνει Ὀρόνταν, καὶ συγκαλεῖ εἰς τὴν ἑαυτοῦ σκηνὴν Πέρσας τοὺς
ἀρίστους τῶν περὶ αὐτὸν ἑπτά, καὶ τοὺς τῶν Ἑλλήνων
στρατηγοὺς ἐκέλευεν ὁπλίτας ἀγαγεῖν, τούτους δὲ
θέσθαι τὰ ὅπλα περὶ τὴν αὐτοῦ σκηνήν. οἱ δὲ ταῦτα
ἐποίησαν, ἀγαγόντες ὡς τρισχιλίους ὁπλίτας.

5 Κλέαρχον δὲ καὶ εἴσω παρεκάλεσε σύμβουλον, ὅς
γε καὶ αὐτῷ καὶ τοῖς ἄλλοις ἐδόκει προτιμηθῆναι
μάλιστα τῶν Ἑλλήνων. ἐπεὶ δ᾽ ἐξῆλθεν, ἐξήγγειλε
τοῖς φίλοις τὴν κρίσιν τοῦ Ὀρόντα ὡς ἐγένετο· οὐ γὰρ

a plot against Cyrus—in fact, he had made war upon him
before this, but had become his friend again. He now said
to Cyrus that if he would give him a thousand horsemen,
he would either ambush and kill these horsemen who were
burning ahead of him, or he would capture many of them
alive and put a stop to their burning as they advanced; and
he would see to it that they should never be able to behold
Cyrus' army and get to the King with their report. When
Cyrus heard this plan, it seemed to him to be an expedient
one, and he directed Orontas to get a detachment from
each one of the cavalry commanders. Then Orontas, thinking that his horsemen were assured him, wrote a letter to
the King saying that he would come to him with as many
horsemen as he could get; and he urged the King to direct
his own cavalry to receive him as a friend. The letter also
contained reminders of his former friendship and fidelity.
This letter he gave to a man whom he supposed to be
faithful to him; but this man took it and gave it to Cyrus.
When Cyrus had read it, he had Orontas arrested, and
summoned to his tent seven of the noblest Persians among
his attendants,[57] while he ordered the Greek generals to
bring up hoplites and bid them station themselves under
arms around his tent. And the generals obeyed the order,
bringing with them about three thousand hoplites.

Clearchus was also invited into the tent as a counsellor,
for both Cyrus and the other Persians regarded him as the
man who was honoured above the rest of the Greeks. And
when he came out, he reported to his friends how Orontas'
trial was conducted—for it was no secret. He said that

[57] A Persian dynast's inner circle of advisors; see Briant,
Histoire I, 322–4.

6 ἀπόρρητον ἦν. ἔφη δὲ Κῦρον ἄρχειν τοῦ λόγου ὧδε.
Παρεκάλεσα ὑμᾶς, ἄνδρες φίλοι, ὅπως σὺν ὑμῖν
βουλευόμενος ὅ τι δίκαιόν ἐστι καὶ πρὸς θεῶν καὶ
πρὸς ἀνθρώπων, τοῦτο πράξω περὶ Ὀρόντα τουτουί.
τοῦτον γὰρ πρῶτον μὲν ὁ ἐμὸς πατὴρ ἔδωκεν ὑπήκοον
εἶναι ἐμοί· ἐπεὶ δὲ ταχθείς, ὡς ἔφη αὐτός, ὑπὸ τοῦ
ἐμοῦ ἀδελφοῦ οὗτος ἐπολέμησεν ἐμοὶ ἔχων τὴν ἐν
Σάρδεσιν ἀκρόπολιν, καὶ ἐγὼ αὐτὸν προσπολεμῶν
ἐποίησα ὥστε δόξαι τούτῳ τοῦ πρὸς ἐμὲ πολέμου
7 παύσασθαι, καὶ δεξιὰν ἔλαβον καὶ ἔδωκα.   Μετὰ
ταῦτα, ἔφη, ὦ Ὀρόντα, ἔστιν ὅ τι σε ἠδίκησα; ἀπεκρίνατο ὅτι οὔ. πάλιν δὲ ὁ Κῦρος ἠρώτα· Οὐκοῦν ὕστερον,
ὡς αὐτὸς σὺ ὁμολογεῖς, οὐδὲν ὑπ' ἐμοῦ ἀδικούμενος
ἀποστὰς εἰς Μυσοὺς κακῶς ἐποίεις τὴν ἐμὴν χώραν
ὅ τι ἐδύνω; ἔφη ὁ Ὀρόντας. Οὐκοῦν, ἔφη ὁ Κῦρος,
ὁπότ' αὖ ἔγνως τὴν σεαυτοῦ δύναμιν, ἐλθὼν ἐπὶ τὸν
τῆς Ἀρτέμιδος βωμὸν μεταμέλειν τέ σοι ἔφησθα καὶ
πείσας ἐμὲ πιστὰ πάλιν ἔδωκάς μοι καὶ ἔλαβες παρ'
8 ἐμοῦ; καὶ ταῦθ' ὡμολόγει ὁ Ὀρόντας. Τί οὖν, ἔφη ὁ
Κῦρος, ἀδικηθεὶς ὑπ' ἐμοῦ νῦν τὸ τρίτον ἐπιβουλεύων
μοι φανερὸς γέγονας; εἰπόντος δὲ τοῦ Ὀρόντα ὅτι
οὐδὲν ἀδικηθείς, ἠρώτησεν ὁ Κῦρος αὐτόν· Ὁμολογεῖς
οὖν περὶ ἐμὲ ἄδικος γεγενῆσθαι; Ἦ γὰρ ἀνάγκη, ἔφη
Ὀρόντας. ἐκ τούτου πάλιν ἠρώτησεν ὁ Κῦρος· Ἔτι
οὖν ἂν γένοιο τῷ ἐμῷ ἀδελφῷ πολέμιος, ἐμοὶ δὲ φίλος
καὶ πιστός; ὁ δὲ ἀπεκρίνατο ὅτι οὐδ' εἰ γενοίμην, ὦ
9 Κῦρε, σοί γ' ἄν ποτε ἔτι δόξαιμι. πρὸς ταῦτα Κῦρος
εἶπε τοῖς παροῦσιν· Ὁ μὲν ἀνὴρ τοιαῦτα μὲν πεποίηκε,

Cyrus began the conference in this way: "My friends, I have invited you here in order that I may consult with you and then take such action in the case of Orontas here as is right in the sight of gods and men. This man was given me at first by my father, to be my subject; then, at the bidding, as he himself said, of my brother, this man levied war upon me, holding the citadel of Sardis, and I, by the war I waged against him, made him count it best to cease from warring upon me, and I received and gave the hand-clasp of friendship. Since that," he said, "Orontas, have I done you any wrong?" "No," Orontas answered. Cyrus went on questioning him: "Did you not afterwards, although, as you yourself admit, you had suffered no wrong at my hands, desert me for the Mysians, and do all the harm you could to my territory?" "Yes," said Orontas. "Did you not," Cyrus said, "when once more you had learned the slightness of your own power, go to the altar of Artemis and say you were sorry, and did you not, after prevailing upon me to pardon you, again give me pledges and receive pledges from me?" This also Orontas admitted. "What wrong, then," said Cyrus, "have you suffered at my hands, that you now for the third time have been found plotting against me?" When Orontas replied," None," Cyrus asked him: "Do you admit, then, that you have proved yourself a doer of wrong toward me? " "I cannot choose but do so," said Orontas. Thereupon Cyrus asked again: "Then could you henceforth prove yourself a foe to my brother and a faithful friend to me?" "Even if I should do so, Cyrus," he replied, "you could never after this believe it of me." Then Cyrus said to those who were present: "Such have been this man's

τοιαῦτα δὲ λέγει· ὑμῶν δὲ σὺ πρῶτος, ὦ Κλέαρχε,
ἀπόφηναι γνώμην ὅ τι σοι δοκεῖ. Κλέαρχος δὲ εἶπε
τάδε. Συμβουλεύω ἐγὼ τὸν ἄνδρα τοῦτον ἐκποδὼν
ποιεῖσθαι ὡς τάχιστα, ὡς μηκέτι δέῃ τοῦτον φυλάττεσθαι, ἀλλὰ σχολὴ ᾖ ἡμῖν, τὸ κατὰ τοῦτον εἶναι,
10 τοὺς ἐθελοντὰς φίλους, τούτους εὖ ποιεῖν. ταύτῃ δὲ τῇ
γνώμῃ ἔφη καὶ τοὺς ἄλλους προσθέσθαι.

Μετὰ ταῦτα κελεύοντος Κύρου ἔλαβον τῆς ζώνης
τὸν Ὀρόνταν ἐπὶ θανάτῳ ἅπαντες ἀναστάντες καὶ οἱ
συγγενεῖς· εἶτα δὲ ἐξῆγον αὐτὸν οἷς προσετάχθη. ἐπεὶ
δὲ εἶδον αὐτὸν οἵπερ πρόσθεν προσεκύνουν, καὶ τότε
προσεκύνησαν, καίπερ εἰδότες ὅτι ἐπὶ θάνατον ἄγοιτο.
11 ἐπεὶ δὲ εἰς τὴν Ἀρταπάτα σκηνὴν εἰσήχθη τοῦ πιστο-
τάτου τῶν Κύρου σκηπτούχων, μετὰ ταῦτα οὔτε ζῶντα
Ὀρόνταν οὔτε τεθνηκότα οὐδεὶς εἶδε πώποτε, οὐδὲ
ὅπως ἀπέθανεν οὐδεὶς εἰδὼς ἔλεγεν· ἤκαζον δὲ ἄλλοι
ἄλλως· τάφος δὲ οὐδεὶς πώποτε αὐτοῦ ἐφάνη.

VII. Ἐντεῦθεν ἐξελαύνει διὰ τῆς Βαβυλωνίας
σταθμοὺς τρεῖς παρασάγγας δώδεκα. ἐν δὲ τῷ τρίτῳ
σταθμῷ Κῦρος ἐξέτασιν ποιεῖται τῶν Ἑλλήνων καὶ
τῶν βαρβάρων ἐν τῷ πεδίῳ περὶ μέσας νύκτας· ἐδόκει
γὰρ εἰς τὴν ἐπιοῦσαν ἔω ἥξειν βασιλέα σὺν τῷ
στρατεύματι μαχούμενον· καὶ ἐκέλευε Κλέαρχον μὲν
τοῦ δεξιοῦ κέρως ἡγεῖσθαι, Μένωνα δὲ τὸν Θετταλὸν
2 τοῦ εὐωνύμου, αὐτὸς δὲ τοὺς ἑαυτοῦ διέταξε. μετὰ δὲ
τὴν ἐξέτασιν ἅμα τῇ ἐπιούσῃ ἡμέρᾳ ἥκοντες
αὐτόμολοι παρὰ μεγάλου βασιλέως ἀπήγγελλον
Κύρῳ περὶ τῆς βασιλέως στρατιᾶς.

deeds, such are now his words; and now, Clearchus, be the first of my counsellors to express the opinion you hold." And Clearchus said: "My advice is to put this man out of the way as speedily as possible, so that we may no longer have to be on our guard against the fellow, but may be left free, so far as concerns him, to requite with benefits those who are willingly friends." In this opinion Clearchus said that the others also concurred.

After this, at the bidding of Cyrus, every man of them arose, even Orontas' kinsmen, and took him by the girdle, as a sign that he was condemned to death; and then those to whom the duty was assigned led him out. And when the men who in former days were wont to do him homage saw him, they made their obeisance even then, although they knew that he was being led forth to death. Now after he had been conducted into the tent of Artapates, the most faithful of Cyrus' chamberlains, from that moment no man ever saw Orontas living or dead, nor could anyone say from actual knowledge how he was put to death—it was all conjectures, of one sort and another; and no grave of his was ever seen.

VII. From there Cyrus marched through Babylonia three stages, twelve parasangs. On the third stage he held a review of the Greeks and the barbarians on the plain at about midnight; for he thought that at the next dawn the King would come with his army to do battle; and he ordered Clearchus to act as commander of the right wing and Menon the Thessalian of the left, while he himself marshalled his own troops. On the morning following the review, at daybreak, there came deserters from the great King and brought reports to Cyrus about his army.

105

Κῦρος δὲ συγκαλέσας τοὺς στρατηγοὺς καὶ λοχαγοὺς τῶν Ἑλλήνων συνεβουλεύετό τε πῶς ἂν τὴν
μάχην ποιοῖτο καὶ αὐτὸς παρῄνει θαρρύνων τοιάδε.
3 Ὦ ἄνδρες Ἕλληνες, οὐκ ἀνθρώπων ἀπορῶν βαρβάρων[16] συμμάχους ὑμᾶς ἄγω, ἀλλὰ νομίζων ἀμείνονας
καὶ κρείττους πολλῶν βαρβάρων ὑμᾶς εἶναι, διὰ τοῦτο
προσέλαβον. ὅπως οὖν ἔσεσθε ἄνδρες ἄξιοι τῆς ἐλευ-
θερίας ἧς κέκτησθε καὶ ἧς ὑμᾶς ἐγὼ εὐδαιμονίζω. εὖ
γὰρ ἴστε ὅτι τὴν ἐλευθερίαν ἑλοίμην ἂν ἀντὶ ὧν ἔχω
4 πάντων καὶ ἄλλων πολλαπλασίων. ὅπως δὲ καὶ εἰδῆτε
εἰς οἷον ἔρχεσθε ἀγῶνα, ἐγὼ ὑμᾶς εἰδὼς διδάξω. τὸ
μὲν γὰρ πλῆθος πολὺ καὶ κραυγῇ πολλῇ ἐπίασιν· ἂν
δὲ ταῦτα ἀνάσχησθε, τἆλλα καὶ αἰσχύνεσθαί μοι
δοκῶ οἵους ἡμῖν γνώσεσθε τοὺς ἐν τῇ χώρᾳ ὄντας
ἀνθρώπους. ὑμῶν δε ἀνδρῶν ὄντων καὶ εὖ τῶν ἐμῶν
γενομένων, ἐγὼ ὑμῶν τὸν μὲν οἴκαδε βουλόμενον
ἀπιέναι τοῖς οἴκοι ζηλωτὸν ποιήσω ἀπελθεῖν, πολλοὺς
δὲ οἶμαι ποιήσειν τὰ παρ' ἐμοὶ ἑλέσθαι ἀντὶ τῶν οἴκοι.
5 Ἐνταῦθα Γαυλίτης παρὼν φυγὰς Σάμιος, πιστὸς
δὲ Κύρῳ, εἶπε· Καὶ μήν, ὦ Κῦρε, λέγουσί τινες ὅτι
πολλὰ ὑπισχνεῖ νῦν διὰ τὸ ἐν τοιούτῳ εἶναι τοῦ
κινδύνου προσιόντος, ἂν δὲ εὖ γένηταί τι, οὐ μεμνή-
σεσθαί σέ φασιν· ἔνιοι δὲ οὐδ' εἰ μεμνῇό τε καὶ
βούλοιο δύνασθαι ἂν ἀποδοῦναι ὅσα ὑπισχνεῖ. ἀκού-
6 σας ταῦτα ἔλεξεν ὁ Κῦρος· Ἀλλ' ἔστι μὲν ἡμῖν, ὦ

---

[16] βαρβάρων MSS: Gem. Hude/Peters bracket, following
Bisschop.

At this time Cyrus called together the generals and captains of the Greeks, and not only took counsel with them as to how he should fight the battle, but, for his own part, exhorted and encouraged them as follows: "Men of Greece, it is not because I have not barbarians enough that I have brought you hither to fight for me; but because I believe that you are braver and stronger than many barbarians, for this reason I took you also. Be sure, therefore, to be men worthy of the freedom you possess, upon the possession of which I congratulate you. For you may be certain that freedom is the thing I should choose in preference to all that I have and many times more. And now, in order that you may know what sort of a contest it is into which you are going, I who do know will tell you. Our enemies have great numbers and they will come on with a great outcry; for the rest, however, if you can hold out against these things, I am ashamed, I assure you, to think what sorry fellows you will find the people of our country to be. But if you be men and if my undertaking turn out well, I shall make anyone among you who wishes to return home an object of envy to his friends at home upon his return, while I shall cause many of you, I imagine, to choose life with me in preference to life at home."

Hereupon Gaulites, a Samian exile who was there and was in the confidence of Cyrus, said: "And yet, Cyrus, there are those who say that your promises are big now because you are in such a critical situation—for the danger is upon you—but that if any good fortune befall, you will fail to remember them; and some say that even if you should - remember and have the will, you would not have the means to make good all your promises." Upon hearing these words Cyrus said: "Well, gentlemen, my father's realm ex-

ἄνδρες, ἡ ἀρχὴ ἡ πατρῴα πρὸς μὲν μεσημβρίαν μέχρι
οὗ διὰ καῦμα οὐ δύνανται οἰκεῖν ἄνθρωποι, πρὸς δὲ
ἄρκτον μέχρι οὗ διὰ χειμῶνα· τὰ δ᾽ ἐν μέσῳ τούτων

7 ἄπαντα σατραπεύουσιν οἱ τοῦ ἐμοῦ ἀδελφοῦ φίλοι. ἢν
δ᾽ ἡμεῖς νικήσωμεν, ἡμᾶς δεῖ τοὺς ἡμετέρους φίλους
τούτων ἐγκρατεῖς ποιῆσαι. ὥστε οὐ τοῦτο δέδοικα, μὴ
οὐκ ἔχω ὅ τι δῶ ἑκάστῳ τῶν φίλων, ἂν εὖ γένηται,
ἀλλὰ μὴ οὐκ ἔχω ἱκανοὺς οἷς δῶ. ὑμῶν δὲ τῶν Ἑλλή-

8 νων καὶ στέφανον ἑκάστῳ χρυσοῦν δώσω. οἱ δὲ ταῦτα
ἀκούσαντες αὐτοί τε ἦσαν πολὺ προθυμότεροι καὶ τοῖς
ἄλλοις ἐξήγγελλον. εἰσῇσαν δὲ παρ᾽ αὐτὸν καὶ[17] τῶν
ἄλλων Ἑλλήνων τινὲς ἀξιοῦντες εἰδέναι τί σφίσιν
ἔσται, ἐὰν κρατήσωσιν. ὁ δὲ ἐμπιμπλὰς ἁπάντων τὴν

9 γνώμην ἀπέπεμπε. παρεκελεύοντο δὲ αὐτῷ πάντες
ὅσοιπερ διελέγοντο μὴ μάχεσθαι, ἀλλ᾽ ὄπισθεν ἑαυτῶν τάττεσθαι. ἐν δὲ τῷ καιρῷ τούτῳ Κλέαρχος ὧδέ
πως ἤρετο τὸν Κῦρον· Οἴει γάρ σοι μαχεῖσθαι, ὦ
Κῦρε, τὸν ἀδελφόν; Νὴ Δί᾽, ἔφη ὁ Κῦρος, εἴπερ γε
Δαρείου καὶ Παρυσάτιδός ἐστι παῖς, ἐμὸς δὲ ἀδελφός,
οὐκ ἀμαχεὶ ταῦτ᾽ ἐγὼ λήψομαι.

10   Ἐνταῦθα δὴ ἐν τῇ ἐξοπλισίᾳ ἀριθμὸς ἐγένετο τῶν
μὲν Ἑλλήνων ἀσπὶς μυρία καὶ τετρακόσια, πελτασταὶ
δὲ δισχίλιοι καὶ πεντακόσιοι, τῶν δὲ μετὰ Κύρου
βαρβάρων δέκα μυριάδες καὶ ἅρματα δρεπανηφόρα

---

[17] Before καὶ the MSS. have οἵ τε στρατηγοί: Gem.,
Hude/Peters bracket, following Weiske.

tends toward the south to a region where men cannot dwell
by reason of the heat, and to the north to a region where
they cannot dwell by reason of the cold; and all that lies
between these limits my brother's friends rule as satraps.
Now if we win the victory, we must put our friends in
control of these provinces. I fear, therefore, not that I shall
not have enough to give to each of my friends, if success
attends us, but that I shall not have enough friends to give
to. And as for you men of Greece, I shall give each one of
you a wreath of gold besides." When they heard these
words, the officers were far more eager themselves and
carried the news away with them to the other Greeks. Then
some of the others also sought Cyrus' presence, demanding to know what they should have, in case of victory; and
he satisfied the expectations of every one of them before
dismissing them. Now all alike who conversed with him
urged him not to take part in the fighting, but to station
himself in their rear. Taking this opportunity Clearchus
asked Cyrus a question like this: "But do you think, Cyrus,
that your brother will fight with you?" "Yes, by Zeus," said
Cyrus, "if he is really a son of Darius and Parysatis and a
brother of mine, I shall not win this realm without fighting
for it."

At this time, when the troops were marshalled under
arms,[58] the number of the Greeks was found to be ten
thousand four hundred hoplites, and two thousand five
hundred peltasts,[59] while the number of the barbarians

---

[58] *i.e.* in the review mentioned in § 1.   [59] There is a dis-
crepancy, as yet unexplained, between these numbers and those
previously given. cf. ii. 9 and note; also ii. and iv. 3.

11 ἀμφὶ τὰ εἴκοσι. τῶν δὲ πολεμίων ἐλέγοντο εἶναι ἑκατὸν καὶ εἴκοσι μυριάδες καὶ ἅρματα δρεπανηφόρα
διακόσια. ἄλλοι δὲ ἦσαν ἑξακισχίλιοι ἱππεῖς, ὧν
Ἀρταγέρσης ἦρχεν· οὗτοι δὲ πρὸ αὐτοῦ βασιλέως
12 τεταγμένοι ἦσαν. τοῦ δὲ βασιλέως στρατεύματος
ἦσαν ἄρχοντες[18] τέτταρες, τριάκοντα μυριάδων ἕκαστος, Ἀβροκόμας, Τισσαφέρνης, Γωβρύας, Ἀρβάκης.
τούτων δὲ παρεγένοντο ἐν τῇ μάχῃ ἐνενήκοντα μυριάδες καὶ ἅρματα δρεπανηφόρα ἑκατὸν καὶ πεντήκοντα·
Ἀβροκόμας δὲ ὑστέρησε τῆς μάχης ἡμέραις πέντε, ἐκ
13 Φοινίκης ἐλαύνων. ταῦτα δὲ ἤγγελλον πρὸς Κῦρον οἱ
αὐτομολήσαντες παρὰ μεγάλου βασιλέως[19] πρὸ τῆς
μάχης, καὶ μετὰ τὴν μάχην οἱ ὕστερον ἐλήφθησαν
τῶν πολεμίων ταὐτὰ ἤγγελλον.

14 Ἐντεῦθεν δὲ Κῦρος ἐξελαύνει σταθμὸν ἕνα παρασάγγας τρεῖς συντεταγμένῳ τῷ στρατεύματι παντὶ
καὶ τῷ Ἑλληνικῷ καὶ τῷ βαρβαρικῷ· ᾤετο γὰρ ταύτῃ
τῇ ἡμέρᾳ μαχεῖσθαι βασιλέα· κατὰ γὰρ μέσον τὸν
σταθμὸν τοῦτον τάφρος ἦν ὀρυκτὴ βαθεῖα, τὸ μὲν
εὖρος ὄργυιαι πέντε, τὸ δὲ βάθος ὄργυιαι τρεῖς.
15 παρετέτατο δὲ ἡ τάφρος ἄνω διὰ τοῦ πεδίου ἐπὶ

---

[18] After ἄρχοντες the MSS. have καὶ στρατηγοὶ καὶ
ἡγεμόνες: Gem., Hude/Peters, bracket, following Weiske.
[19] παρὰ ... βασιλέως: Immediately before this phrase the
MSS. have ἐκ τῶν πολεμίων : Hude/Peters, Mar. bracket, following Kiehl.

under Cyrus was one hundred thousand and there were about twenty scythe-bearing chariots. The enemy it was reported, numbered one million two hundred thousand,[60] and had two hundred scythe-bearing chariots; besides, there was a troop of six thousand horsemen, under the command of Artagerses, which was stationed in front of the King himself. And the King's army had four commanders, each at the head of three hundred thousand men, namely, Abrocomas, Tissaphernes, Gobryas, and Arbaces. But of the forces just enumerated only nine hundred thousand, with one hundred and fifty scythe-bearing chariots, were present at the battle for Abrocomas, marching from Phoenicia, arrived five days too late for the engagement. Such were the reports brought to Cyrus by those who deserted from the Great King before the battle, and after the battle identical reports were made by the prisoners taken thereafter.

From there Cyrus marched one stage, three parasangs, with his whole army, Greek and barbarian alike, drawn up in line of battle; for he supposed that on that day the King would come to an engagement; for about midway of this day's march there was a deep trench, five fathoms[61] in width and three fathoms in depth. This trench extended up through the plain for a distance of twelve parasangs,

---

[60] The number is grossly overstated. Ctesias, the King's Greek physician (see viii. 26), is said by Plutarch to have given it as 400,000 (*Artax*. XIII.3 = FGH 688 F 22).

[61] ὄργυα = the reach of the outstretched arms (cf. ὀρέγω), or, as an exact unit of measurement, 6 Greek feet = 5 ft. 10 in. English measure.

δώδεκα παρασάγγας μέχρι τοῦ Μηδίας τείχους.[20] ἦν
δὲ παρὰ τὸν Εὐφράτην πάροδος στενὴ μεταξὺ τοῦ
ποταμοῦ καὶ τῆς τάφρου ὡς εἴκοσι ποδῶν τὸ εὖρος·
16 ταύτην δὲ τὴν τάφρον βασιλεὺς ποιεῖ μέγας ἀντὶ
ἐρύματος, ἐπειδὴ πυνθάνεται Κῦρον προσελαύνοντα.
ταύτην δὴ τὴν πάροδον Κῦρός τε καὶ ἡ στρατιὰ
17 παρῆλθε καὶ ἐγένοντο εἴσω τῆς τάφρου. ταύτῃ μὲν οὖν
τῇ ἡμέρᾳ οὐκ ἐμαχέσατο βασιλεύς, ἀλλ᾽ ὑποχωρούν-
των φανερὰ ἦσαν καὶ ἵππων καὶ ἀνθρώπων ἴχνη
18 πολλά. ἐνταῦθα Κῦρος Σιλανὸν καλέσας τὸν Ἀμπρακιώτην μάντιν ἔδωκεν αὐτῷ δαρεικοὺς τρισχιλίους
ὅτι τῇ ἑνδεκάτῃ ἀπ᾽ ἐκείνης ἡμέρᾳ πρότερον θυόμενος
εἶπεν αὐτῷ ὅτι βασιλεὺς οὐ μαχεῖται δέκα ἡμερῶν,
Κῦρος δ᾽ εἶπεν· Οὐκ ἄρα ἔτι μαχεῖται, εἰ ἐν ταύταις οὐ
μαχεῖται ταῖς ἡμέραις· ἐὰν δ᾽ ἀληθεύσῃς, ὑπ-
ισχνοῦμαί σοι δέκα τάλαντα. τοῦτο τὸ χρυσίον τότε
19 ἀπέδωκεν, ἐπεὶ παρῆλθον αἱ δέκα ἡμέραι. ἐπεὶ δ᾽ ἐπὶ
τῇ τάφρῳ οὐκ ἐκώλυε βασιλεὺς τὸ Κύρου στράτευμα

---

[20] After Μηδίας τείχους the MSS. proceed as follows: ἔνθα
αἱ διώρυχες, ἀπὸ τοῦ Τίγρητος ποταμοῦ ῥέουσαι· εἰσὶ δὲ
τέτταρες, τὸ μὲν εὖρος πλεθριαῖαι, βαθεῖαι δὲ ἰσχυρῶς, καὶ
πλοῖα πλεῖ ἐν αὐταῖς σιταγωγά· εἰσβάλλουσι δὲ εἰς τὸν Εὐφράτην, διαλείπουσι δ᾽ ἑκάστη παρασάγγην, γέφυραι δ᾽
ἔπεισιν. [Here also are the canals, which flow from the Tigris
river; they are four in number, each a plethrum wide and exceedingly deep, and grain-carrying ships ply in them; they empty into
the Euphrates and are a parasang apart, and there are bridges over
them.] This passage is regarded by edd. generally as an interpolation.

reaching to the wall of Media,[62] and alongside the Euphrates there was a narrow passage, not more than about twenty feet in width, between the river and the trench; and the trench[63] had been constructed by the Great King as a means of defence when he learned that Cyrus was marching against him. Accordingly Cyrus and his army went through by the passage just mentioned, and so found themselves on the inner side of the trench. Now on that day the King did not offer battle, but tracks of both horses and men in retreat were to be seen in great numbers. Then Cyrus summoned Silanus, his Ambraciot soothsayer, and gave him three thousand darics; for on the eleventh day before this, while sacrificing, he had told Cyrus that the King would not fight within ten days, and Cyrus had said: "Then he will not fight at all, if he will not fight within ten days; however, if your prediction proves true, I promise you ten talents."[64] So it was this money that he then paid over, the ten days having passed. But since the King did not appear at the trench and try to prevent the passage of Cyrus' army,

[62] Described by Xenophon in II. iv. 12. Xenophon's description of the geography of Babylonia is problematic. Most importantly the precise location of Cunaxa, where the decisive battle is fought (Plutarch, *Artax.* 8), is not known. See Manfredi, *La Strada* 130–39. On the Median Wall, see Briant, *Histoire* II, 912 and 1014 with bibliography.

[63] It would seem that the rapid approach of Cyrus had prevented the King from completing the trench.

[64] Hence 10 (Attic) talents = 3,000 (Persian) darics. A talent was 60 minas, and therefore a mina was counted equivalent to 5 darics. See above i. 9 and n.

διαβαίνειν, ἔδοξε καὶ Κύρῳ καὶ τοῖς ἄλλοις ἀπεγνω-
κέναι τοῦ μάχεσθαι· ὥστε τῇ ὑστεραίᾳ Κῦρος ἐπορεύ-
20 ετο ἠμελημένως μᾶλλον. τῇ δὲ τρίτῃ ἐπί τε τοῦ ἅρματος καθήμενος τὴν πορείαν ἐποιεῖτο καὶ ὀλίγους ἐν
τάξει ἔχων πρὸ αὑτοῦ, τὸ δὲ πολὺ αὐτῷ ἀνατεταραγ-
μένον ἐπορεύετο καὶ τῶν ὅπλων τοῖς στρατιώταις
πολλὰ ἐπὶ ἁμαξῶν ἤγοντο καὶ ὑποζυγίων.

VIII. Καὶ ἤδη τε ἦν ἀμφὶ ἀγορὰν πλήθουσαν καὶ
πλησίον ἦν ὁ σταθμὸς ἔνθα ἔμελλε καταλύσειν, ἡνίκα
Πατηγύας, ἀνὴρ Πέρσης τῶν ἀμφὶ Κῦρον πιστῶν,
προφαίνεται ἐλαύνων ἀνὰ κράτος ἱδρῶντι τῷ ἵππῳ,
καὶ εὐθὺς πᾶσιν οἷς ἐνετύγχανεν ἐβόα καὶ βαρβαρι-
κῶς καὶ ἑλληνικῶς ὅτι βασιλεὺς σὺν στρατεύματι
πολλῷ προσέρχεται ὡς εἰς μάχην παρεσκευασμένος.
2 ἔνθα δὴ πολὺς τάραχος ἐγένετο· αὐτίκα γὰρ ἐδόκουν
οἱ Ἕλληνες καὶ πάντες δὲ ἀτάκτοις σφίσιν ἐπιπεσεῖ-
3 σθαι· Κῦρός τε καταπηδήσας ἀπὸ τοῦ ἅρματος τὸν
θώρακα ἐνέδυ καὶ ἀναβὰς ἐπὶ τὸν ἵππον τὰ παλτὰ εἰς
τὰς χεῖρας ἔλαβε, τοῖς τε ἄλλοις πᾶσι παρήγγελλεν
ἐξοπλίζεσθαι καὶ καθίστασθαι εἰς τὴν ἑαυτοῦ τάξιν
4 ἕκαστον. ἔνθα δὴ σὺν πολλῇ σπουδῇ καθίσταντο,
Κλέαρχος μὲν τὰ δεξιὰ τοῦ κέρατος ἔχων πρὸς τῷ
Εὐφράτῃ ποταμῷ, Πρόξενος δὲ ἐχόμενος, οἱ δ' ἄλλοι
μετὰ τοῦτον, Μένων δὲ καὶ τὸ στράτευμα τὸ εὐώνυμον

---

65 *i.e.* the middle of the morning.

66 *i.e.* the Greek army as a whole constituted the right wing of
Cyrus' entire army, his Persian troops forming the centre and the

both Cyrus and the rest concluded that he had given up the idea of fighting. Hence on the following day Cyrus proceeded more carelessly; and on the third day he was making the march seated in his chariot and with only a small body of troops drawn up in line in front of him, while the greater part of the army was proceeding in disorder and many of the soldiers' arms and accoutrements were being carried in wagons and on pack-animals.

VIII. It was now about full-market time[65] and the stopping-place where Cyrus was intending to halt had been almost reached, when Pategyas, a Persian, one of Cyrus' trusted advisors, came into sight, riding at full speed, with his horse in a sweat, and at once shouted out to everyone he met, in the barbarian tongue and in Greek, that the King was approaching with a large army, all ready for battle. Then ensued great confusion; for the thought of the Greeks, and of all the rest in fact, was that he would fall upon them immediately, while they were in disorder; and Cyrus leaped down from his chariot, put on his breastplate, and then, mounting his horse, took his spears in his hands and passed the word to all the others to arm themselves and get into their places, every man of them. Thereupon they proceeded in great haste to take their places, Clearchus occupying the right end of the Greek wing,[66] close to the Euphrates river, Proxenus next to him, and the others beyond Proxenus, while Menon and his army took the left

left wing. Clearchus and Menon, then occupy the right and left wings, respectively, of the Greek contingent. Xenophon's description of the battle of Cunaxa and its preliminaries is beset with difficulties: see G. Cawkwell, Intro. to *Xenophon, The Persian Expedition* (Harmondsworth, 1972) 38–43.

5 κέρας ἔσχε τοῦ Ἑλληνικοῦ. τοῦ δὲ βαρβαρικοῦ ἱππεῖς
μὲν Παφλαγόνες εἰς χιλίους παρὰ Κλέαρχον ἔστησαν
ἐν τῷ δεξιῷ καὶ τὸ Ἑλληνικὸν πελταστικόν, ἐν δὲ τῷ
εὐωνύμῳ Ἀριαῖός τε ὁ Κύρου ὕπαρχος καὶ τὸ ἄλλο
6 βαρβαρικόν, Κῦρος δὲ καὶ οἱ ἱππεῖς τούτου ὅσον
ἑξακόσιοι κατὰ τὸ μέσον,[21] ὡπλισμένοι θώραξι μὲν
αὐτοὶ καὶ παραμηριδίοις καὶ κράνεσι πάντες πλὴν
Κύρου· Κῦρος δὲ ψιλὴν ἔχων τὴν κεφαλὴν εἰς τὴν
7 μάχην καθίστατο.[22] οἱ δ᾽ ἵπποι πάντες οἱ μετὰ Κύρου[23]
εἶχον καὶ προμετωπίδια καὶ προστερνίδια· εἶχον δὲ
καὶ μαχαίρας οἱ ἱππεῖς Ἑλληνικάς.

8 Καὶ ἤδη τε ἦν μέσον ἡμέρας καὶ οὔπω καταφανεῖς
ἦσαν οἱ πολέμιοι· ἡνίκα δὲ δείλη ἐγίγνετο, ἐφάνη
κονιορτὸς ὥσπερ νεφέλη λευκή, χρόνῳ δὲ συχνῷ ὕστερον ὥσπερ μελανία τις ἐν τῷ πεδίῳ ἐπὶ πολύ. ὅτε δὲ
ἐγγύτερον ἐγίγνοντο, τάχα δὴ καὶ χαλκός τις
ἤστραπτε καὶ αἱ λόγχαι καὶ αἱ τάξεις καταφανεῖς
9 ἐγίγνοντο. καὶ ἦσαν ἱππεῖς μὲν λευκοθώρακες ἐπὶ τοῦ
εὐωνύμου τῶν πολεμίων· Τισσαφέρνης ἐλέγετο τούτων
ἄρχειν· ἐχόμενοι δὲ τούτων γερροφόροι, ἐχόμενοι δὲ
ὁπλῖται σὺν ποδήρεσι ξυλίναις ἀσπίσιν. Αἰγύπτιοι δ᾽
οὗτοι ἐλέγοντο εἶναι. ἄλλοι δ᾽ ἱππεῖς, ἄλλοι τοξόται.
πάντες δ᾽ οὗτοι κατὰ ἔθνη ἐν πλαισίῳ πλήρει

---

[21] κατὰ τὸ μέσον inserted by Leunclavius, whom Gem.,
Hude/Peters, Mar. follow.
[22] After καθίστατο the MSS. have λέγεται δὲ καὶ τοὺς
ἄλλους Πέρσας ψιλαῖς ταῖς κεφαλαῖς ἐν τῷ πολέμῳ διακινδυνεύειν. [In fact, it is said of the Persians in general that they

116

end of the Greek wing. As for the barbarians, Paphlagonian horsemen to the number of a thousand took station beside Clearchus on the right wing, as did the Greek peltasts, on the left was Ariaeus, Cyrus' lieutenant, with the rest of the barbarian army, and in the centre Cyrus and his horsemen, about six hundred in number. These troopers were armed with breastplates and thigh-pieces and, all of them except Cyrus, with helmets—Cyrus, however, went into the battle with his head unprotected—and all the horses in the squadron with Cyrus had frontlets and breast-pieces; and the men carried, besides their other weapons, Greek sabres.

And now it was midday, and the enemy were not yet in sight; but when afternoon was coming on, there was seen a rising dust, which appeared at first like a white cloud, but some time later like a kind of blackness in the plain, extending over a great distance. As the enemy came nearer and nearer, there were presently flashes of bronze here and there, and spears and the hostile ranks began to come into sight. There were horsemen in white cuirasses on the left wing of the enemy, under the command, it was reported, of Tissaphernes; next to them were troops with wicker shields and, farther on, hoplites with wooden shields which reached to their feet, these latter being Egyptians, people said; and then more horsemen and more bowmen. All these troops were marching in national divisions, each

---

venture all the perils of war with their heads unprotected.] This passage is bracketed by almost all edd., following Wyttenbach.

[23] οἱ μετὰ Κύρου MSS: Gem. and Mar. bracket, following Schenkl.

10 ἀνθρώπων ἕκαστον τὸ ἔθνος ἐπορεύετο. πρὸ δὲ αὐτῶν
ἅρματα διαλείποντα συχνὸν ἀπ' ἀλλήλων τὰ δὴ δρεπανηφόρα καλούμενα· εἶχον δὲ τὰ δρέπανα ἐκ τῶν
ἀξόνων εἰς πλάγιον ἀποτεταμένα καὶ ὑπὸ τοῖς δίφροις
εἰς γῆν βλέποντα, ὡς διακόπτειν ὅτῳ ἐντυγχάνοιεν. ἡ
δὲ γνώμη ἦν ὡς εἰς τὰς τάξεις τῶν Ἑλλήνων ἐλθόντων
11 καὶ διακοψόντων. ὃ μέντοι Κῦρος εἶπεν ὅτε καλέσας
παρεκελεύετο τοῖς Ἕλλησι τὴν κραυγὴν τῶν βαρβάρων ἀνέχεσθαι, ἐψεύσθη τοῦτο· οὐ γὰρ κραυγῇ ἀλλὰ
σιγῇ ὡς ἀνυστὸν καὶ ἡσυχῇ ἐν ἴσῳ καὶ βραδέως
προσῇσαν.

12 Καὶ ἐν τούτῳ Κῦρος παρελαύνων αὐτὸς σὺν Πί-
γρητι τῷ ἑρμηνεῖ καὶ ἄλλοις τρισὶν ἢ τέτταρσι τῷ
Κλεάρχῳ ἐβόα ἄγειν τὸ στράτευμα κατὰ μέσον τὸ
τῶν πολεμίων, ὅτι ἐκεῖ βασιλεὺς εἴη· κἂν τοῦτ', ἔφη,
13 νικῶμεν, πάνθ' ἡμῖν πεποίηται. ὁρῶν δὲ ὁ Κλέαρχος
τὸ μέσον στῖφος καὶ ἀκούων Κύρου ἔξω ὄντα τοῦ[24]
εὐωνύμου βασιλέα—τοσοῦτον γὰρ πλήθει περιῆν
βασιλεὺς ὥστε μέσον τῶν ἑαυτοῦ ἔχων τοῦ Κύρου
εὐωνύμου ἔξω ἦν—ἀλλ' ὅμως ὁ Κλέαρχος οὐκ ἤθελεν
ἀποσπάσαι ἀπὸ τοῦ ποταμοῦ τὸ δεξιὸν κέρας,
φοβούμενος μὴ κυκλωθείη ἑκατέρωθεν, τῷ δὲ Κύρῳ
ἀπεκρίνατο ὅτι αὐτῷ μέλοι ὅπως καλῶς ἔχοι.

14 Καὶ ἐν τούτῳ τῷ καιρῷ τὸ μὲν βαρβαρικὸν στράτευμα ὁμαλῶς προῄει, τὸ δὲ Ἑλληνικὸν ἔτι ἐν τῷ αὐτῷ

---

[24] After τοῦ the MSS. have Ἑλληνικοῦ: Gem., Hude/Peters
bracket, following Hertlein.

nation in a solid square. In front of them were the so-called scythe-bearing chariots, at some distance from one another; and the scythes they carried reached out sideways from the axles and were also set under the chariot bodies, pointing towards the ground, so as to cut to pieces whatever they met; the intention, then, was that they should drive into the ranks of the Greeks as they advanced with the intention of splitting the opposing line. As for the statement, however, which Cyrus made when he called the Greeks together and urged them to hold out against the shouting of the barbarians, he proved to be mistaken in this point; for they came on, not with shouting, but in the utmost silence and quietness, with equal step and slowly.

At this moment Cyrus rode along the line, attended only by Pigres, his interpreter, and three or four others, and shouted to Clearchus to lead his army against the enemy's centre, for the reason that the King was stationed there; "and if," he said, "we are victorious there, our whole task is accomplished." Clearchus, however, since he saw the compact body at the enemy's centre and heard from Cyrus that the King was beyond his left wing (for the King was so superior in numbers that, although occupying the centre of his own line, he was beyond Cyrus' left wing), was unwilling to draw the right wing away from the river, for fear that he might be turned on both flanks; and he told Cyrus, in reply, that he was taking care to make everything go well.

At this critical time the King's army was advancing evenly, while the Greek force, still remaining in the same

μένον συνετάττετο ἐκ τῶν ἔτι προσιόντων. καὶ ὁ Κῦρος
παρελαύνων οὐ πάνυ πρὸς αὐτῷ τῷ στρατεύματι κατ-
εθεᾶτο ἑκατέρωσε ἀποβλέπων εἴς τε τοὺς πολεμίους
15 καὶ τοὺς φίλους. ἰδὼν δὲ αὐτὸν ἀπὸ τοῦ Ἑλληνικοῦ
Ξενοφῶν Ἀθηναῖος, ὑπελάσας ὡς συναντῆσαι ἤρετο
εἴ τι παραγγέλλοι· ὁ δ' ἐπιστήσας εἶπε καὶ λέγειν
ἐκέλευε πᾶσιν ὅτι καὶ τὰ ἱερὰ καλὰ καὶ τὰ σφάγια
16 καλά. ταῦτα δὲ λέγων θορύβου ἤκουσε διὰ τῶν τάξεων
ἰόντος, καὶ ἤρετο τίς ὁ θόρυβος εἴη. ὁ δὲ εἶπεν[25] ὅτι
τὸ σύνθημα παρέρχεται δεύτερον ἤδη. καὶ ὃς ἐθαύμασε τίς παραγγέλλει καὶ ἤρετο ὅ τι εἴη τὸ σύνθημα.
17 ὁ δ' ἀπεκρίνατο· Ζεὺς σωτὴρ καὶ νίκη. ὁ δὲ Κῦρος
ἀκούσας Ἀλλὰ δέχομαί τε, ἔφη, καὶ τοῦτο ἔστω. ταῦτα
δ' εἰπὼν εἰς τὴν αὑτοῦ χώραν ἀπήλαυνε.

Καὶ οὐκέτι τρία ἢ τέτταρα στάδια διειχέτην τὼ
φάλαγγε ἀπ' ἀλλήλων ἡνίκα ἐπαιάνιζόν τε οἱ Ἕλ-
18 ληνες καὶ ἤρχοντο ἀντίοι ἰέναι τοῖς πολεμίοις. ὡς δὲ
πορευομένων ἐξεκύμαινέ τι τῆς φάλαγγος, τὸ ὑπολει-
πόμενον ἤρξατο δρόμῳ θεῖν· καὶ ἅμα ἐφθέγξαντο
πάντες οἷόνπερ τῷ Ἐννυαλίῳ ἐλελίζουσι, καὶ πάντες δὲ
ἔθεον. λέγουσι δέ τινες ὡς καὶ ταῖς ἀσπίσι πρὸς τὰ
19 δόρατα ἐδούπησαν φόβον ποιοῦντες τοῖς ἵπποις. πρὶν
δὲ τόξευμα ἐξικνεῖσθαι ἐγκλίνουσιν οἱ βάρβαροι καὶ
φεύγουσι. καὶ ἐνταῦθα δὴ ἐδίωκον μὲν κατὰ κράτος οἱ
Ἕλληνες, ἐβόων δὲ ἀλλήλοις μὴ θεῖν δρόμῳ, ἀλλ' ἐν

[25] Before εἶπεν the MSS. have Κλέαρχος: Gem., Hude/
Peters, and Mar. bracket, following Bornemann.

place, was forming its line from those who were still coming up. And Cyrus, riding along at some distance from his army, was making a survey, looking in either direction, both at his enemies and his friends. Then Xenophon,[67] an Athenian, seeing him from the Greek army, approached so as to meet him and asked if he had any orders to give; and Cyrus pulled up his horse and bade Xenophon tell everybody that the sacrificial victims and omens were all favourable. While saying this he heard a noise running through the ranks, and asked what the noise was. Xenophon replied that the watchword was now passing along for the second time.[68] And Cyrus wondered who had given it out, and asked what the watchword was. Xenophon replied "Zeus Saviour and Victory." And upon hearing this Cyrus said, "Well, I accept it, and so let it be." After he had said these words he rode back to his own position.

At length the opposing lines were not three or four stadia apart, and then the Greeks struck up the paean and began to advance against the enemy. And when, as they proceeded, a part of the phalanx billowed out, those who were thus left behind began to run; at the same moment they all set up the sort of war-cry which they raise to Enyalius,[69] and all alike began running. It is also reported that some of them clashed their shields against their spears, thereby frightening the enemy's horses. And before an arrow reached them, the barbarians broke and fled. Thereupon the Greeks pursued with all their might, but shouted meanwhile to one another not to run at a headlong pace,

[67] The author. He always speaks of himself in the third person.
[68] *i.e.* back again, from the last man to the first.
[69] *i.e.* Ares.

20 τάξει ἕπεσθαι. τὰ δ' ἅρματα ἐφέροντο τὰ μὲν δι' αὐτῶν
τῶν πολεμίων, τὰ δὲ καὶ διὰ τῶν Ἑλλήνων κενὰ
ἡνιόχων. οἱ δ' ἐπεὶ προΐδοιεν, διίσταντο· ἔστι δ' ὅστις
καὶ κατελήφθη ὥσπερ ἐν ἱπποδρόμῳ ἐκπλαγείς· καὶ
οὐδὲν μέντοι οὐδὲ τοῦτον παθεῖν ἔφασαν, οὐδ' ἄλλος
δὲ τῶν Ἑλλήνων ἐν ταύτῃ τῇ μάχῃ ἔπαθεν οὐδεὶς
οὐδέν, πλὴν ἐπὶ τῷ εὐωνύμῳ τοξευθῆναί τις ἐλέγετο.

21 Κῦρος δ' ὁρῶν τοὺς Ἕλληνας νικῶντας τὸ καθ'
αὑτοὺς καὶ διώκοντας, ἡδόμενος καὶ προσκυνούμενος
ἤδη ὡς βασιλεὺς ὑπὸ τῶν ἀμφ' αὐτόν, οὐδ' ὣς ἐξήχθη
διώκειν, ἀλλὰ συνεσπειραμένην ἔχων τὴν τῶν σὺν
ἑαυτῷ ἑξακοσίων ἱππέων τάξιν ἐπεμελεῖτο ὅ τι ποιήσει
βασιλεύς. καὶ γὰρ ᾔδει αὐτὸν ὅτι μέσον ἔχοι τοῦ
22 Περσικοῦ στρατεύματος. καὶ πάντες δ' οἱ τῶν βαρβάρων ἄρχοντες μέσον ἔχοντες τὸ αὑτῶν ἡγοῦνται, νομίζοντες οὕτω καὶ ἐν ἀσφαλεστάτῳ εἶναι, ἢν ᾖ ἡ ἰσχὺς
αὐτῶν ἑκατέρωθεν, καὶ εἴ τι παραγγεῖλαι χρῄζοιεν,
23 ἡμίσει ἂν χρόνῳ αἰσθάνεσθαι τὸ στράτευμα. καὶ
βασιλεὺς δὴ τότε μέσον ἔχων τῆς αὑτοῦ στρατιᾶς
ὅμως ἔξω ἐγένετο τοῦ Κύρου εὐωνύμου κέρατος. ἐπεὶ
δὲ οὐδεὶς αὐτῷ ἐμάχετο ἐκ τοῦ ἀντίου οὐδὲ τοῖς αὑτοῦ
τεταγμένοις ἔμπροσθεν, ἐπέκαμπτεν ὡς εἰς κύκλωσιν.
24 Ἔνθα δὴ Κῦρος δείσας μὴ ὄπισθεν γενόμενος
κατακόψῃ τὸ Ἑλληνικὸν ἐλαύνει ἀντίος· καὶ ἐμβαλὼν
σὺν τοῖς ἑξακοσίοις νικᾷ τοὺς πρὸ βασιλέως τεταγ-

but to keep their ranks in the pursuit. As for the enemy's chariots, some of them plunged through the lines of their own troops, others, however, through the Greek lines, but without charioteers. And whenever the Greeks saw them coming, they would open a gap for their passage; one fellow, to be sure, was caught, like a befuddled man on a race-course, yet it was said that even he was not hurt in the least, nor, for that matter, did any other single man among the Greeks get any hurt whatever in this battle, save that some one on the left wing was reported to have been hit by an arrow.

When Cyrus saw that the Greeks were victorious over the division opposite them and were in pursuit, although he was pleased and was already being saluted with homage as King by his attendants, he nevertheless was not induced to join the pursuit, but, keeping in close formation the six hundred horsemen of his troop, he was watching to see what the King would do. For he knew that the King held the centre of the Persian army; in fact, all the generals of the barbarians hold their own centre when they are in command, for they think that this is the safest position, namely, with their forces on either side of them, and also that if they want to pass along an order, the army will get it in half the time; so in this instance the King held the centre of the army under his command, but still he found himself beyond the left wing of Cyrus. Since, then, there was no one in his front to give battle to him or to the troops drawn up before him, he proceeded to wheel round his line with the intention of encircling the enemy.

Thereupon Cyrus, seized with fear lest he might get in the rear of the Greek troops and cut them to pieces, charged to meet him; and attacking with his six hundred,

μένους καὶ εἰς φυγὴν ἔτρεψε τοὺς ἑξακισχιλίους, καὶ
ἀποκτεῖναι λέγεται αὐτὸς τῇ ἑαυτοῦ χειρὶ Ἀρταγέρ-
25 σην τὸν ἄρχοντα αὐτῶν. ὡς δ' ἡ τροπὴ ἐγένετο, δια-
σπείρονται καὶ οἱ Κύρου ἑξακόσιοι εἰς τὸ διώκειν
ὁρμήσαντες, πλὴν πάνυ ὀλίγοι ἀμφ' αὐτὸν κατελείφ-
26 θησαν, σχεδὸν οἱ ὁμοτράπεζοι καλούμενοι. σὺν τούτοις δὲ ὢν καθορᾷ βασιλέα καὶ τὸ ἀμφ' ἐκεῖνον
στῖφος· καὶ εὐθὺς οὐκ ἠνέσχετο, ἀλλ' εἰπών, Τὸν
ἄνδρα ὁρῶ, ἵετο ἐπ' αὐτὸν καὶ παίει κατὰ τὸ στέρνον
καὶ τιτρώσκει διὰ τοῦ θώρακος, ὥς φησι Κτησίας ὁ
ἰατρός, καὶ ἰάσασθαι αὐτὸς τὸ τραῦμά φησι.

27 Παίοντα δ' αὐτὸν ἀκοντίζει τις παλτῷ ὑπὸ τὸν
ὀφθαλμὸν βιαίως· καὶ ἐνταῦθα μαχόμενοι καὶ βασιλεὺς καὶ Κῦρος καὶ οἱ ἀμφ' αὐτοὺς ὑπὲρ ἑκατέρου,
ὁπόσοι μὲν τῶν ἀμφὶ βασιλέα ἀπέθανον Κτησίας
λέγει· παρ' ἐκείνῳ γὰρ ἦν· Κῦρος δὲ αὐτός τε ἀπέθανε
καὶ ὀκτὼ οἱ ἄριστοι τῶν περὶ αὐτὸν ἔκειντο ἐπ' αὐτῷ.
28 Ἀρταπάτης δ' ὁ πιστότατος αὐτῷ τῶν σκηπτούχων
θεράπων λέγεται, ἐπειδὴ πεπτωκότα εἶδε Κῦρον, κατα-
29 πηδήσας ἀπὸ τοῦ ἵππου περιπεσεῖν αὐτῷ. καὶ οἱ μέν
φασι βασιλέα κελεῦσαί τινα ἐπισφάξαι αὐτὸν Κύρῳ,
οἱ δ' ἑαυτὸν ἐπισφάξασθαι σπασάμενον τὸν ἀκινάκην·
εἶχε γὰρ χρυσοῦν· καὶ στρεπτὸν δ' ἐφόρει καὶ ψέλια
καὶ τἄλλα ὥσπερ οἱ ἄριστοι Περσῶν· ἐτετίμητο γαρ
ὑπὸ Κύρου δι' εὔνοιάν τε καὶ πιστότητα.

he was victorious over the forces stationed in front of the King and put to flight the six thousand,[70] slaying with his own hand, it is said, their commander Artagerses. But when they turned to flight, Cyrus' six hundred, setting out in pursuit, became scattered also, and only a very few were left about him, chiefly his so-called table companions. While attended by these only, he caught sight of the King and the compact body around him; and on the instant he lost control of himself and, with the cry "I see the man," rushed upon him and struck him in the breast and wounded him through his breastplate—as Ctesias[71] the physician says, adding also that he himself healed the wound.

While Cyrus was delivering his stroke, however, some one hit him a hard blow under the eye with a javelin; and then followed a struggle between the King and Cyrus and the attendants who supported each of them. The number that fell on the King's side is stated by Ctesias, who was with him; on the other side, Cyrus himself was killed and eight of the noblest of his attendants lay dead upon him. Of Artapates, the one among Cyrus' chamberlains who was his most faithful follower, it is told that when he saw Cyrus fallen, he leaped down from his horse and threw his arms about him. And one report is that the King ordered someone to slay him upon the body of Cyrus, while others say that he drew his dagger and slew himself with his own hand; for he had a dagger of gold, and he also wore a necklace and bracelets and all the other ornaments that the noblest Persians wear; for he had been honoured by Cyrus because of his affection and fidelity.

[70] See vii. 11.   [71] *FGH* 688 F 21.

IX. Κῦρος μὲν οὖν οὕτως ἐτελεύτησεν, ἀνὴρ ὢν Περσῶν τῶν μετὰ Κῦρον τὸν ἀρχαῖον γενομένων βασιλικώτατός τε καὶ ἄρχειν ἀξιώτατος, ὡς παρὰ πάντων ὁμολογεῖται τῶν Κύρου δοκούντων ἐν πείρᾳ

2 γενέσθαι. πρῶτον μὲν γὰρ ἔτι παῖς ὢν ὅτ᾽ ἐπαιδεύετο καὶ σὺν τῷ ἀδελφῷ καὶ σὺν τοῖς ἄλλοις παισί, πάντων

3 πάντα κράτιστος ἐνομίζετο. πάντες γὰρ οἱ τῶν ἀρίστων Περσῶν παῖδες ἐπὶ ταῖς βασιλέως θύραις παιδεύονται· ἔνθα πολλὴν μὲν σωφροσύνην καταμάθοι ἄν τις, αἰσχρὸν δ᾽ οὐδὲν οὔτ᾽ ἀκοῦσαι οὔτ᾽ ἰδεῖν ἔστι.

4 θεῶνται δ᾽ οἱ παῖδες καὶ τιμωμένους ὑπὸ βασιλέως καὶ ἀκούουσι, καὶ ἄλλους ἀτιμαζομένους· ὥστε εὐθὺς παῖδες ὄντες μανθάνουσιν ἄρχειν τε καὶ ἄρχεσθαι.

5 ἔνθα Κῦρος αἰδημονέστατος μὲν πρῶτον τῶν ἡλικιωτῶν ἐδόκει εἶναι, τοῖς τε πρεσβυτέροις καὶ τῶν ἑαυτοῦ ὑποδεεστέρων μᾶλλον πείθεσθαι, ἔπειτα δὲ φιλιππότατος καὶ τοῖς ἵπποις ἄριστα χρῆσθαι· ἔκρινον δ᾽ αὐτὸν καὶ τῶν εἰς τὸν πόλεμον ἔργων, τοξικῆς τε καὶ ἀκοντίσεως, φιλομαθέστατον εἶναι καὶ μελετηρότατον.

6 ἐπεὶ δὲ τῇ ἡλικίᾳ ἔπρεπε, καὶ φιλοθηρότατος ἦν καὶ πρὸς τὰ θηρία μέντοι φιλοκινδυνότατος. καὶ ἄρκτον ποτὲ ἐπιφερομένην οὐκ ἔτρεσεν, ἀλλὰ συμπεσὼν κατεσπάσθη ἀπὸ τοῦ ἵππου, καὶ τὰ μὲν ἔπαθεν, ὧν καὶ τὰς ὠτειλὰς φανερὰς²⁶ εἶχεν, τέλος δὲ κατέκανε· καὶ τὸν πρῶτον μέντοι βοηθήσαντα πολλοῖς μακαριστὸν ἐποίησεν.

²⁶ φανερὰς some MSS. omit.

IX. In this way, then, Cyrus came to his end, a man who was the most kingly and the most worthy to rule of all the Persians who have been born since Cyrus the Elder, as all agree who are reputed to have known Cyrus intimately.[72] For firstly, while he was still a boy and was being educated with his brother and the other boys, he was regarded as the best of them all in all respects. For all the sons of the noblest Persians are educated at the King's court. There one may learn discretion and self-control in full measure, and nothing that is base can be either heard or seen. The boys have before their eyes the spectacle of men honoured by the King and of others dishonoured; they likewise hear of them; and so from earliest boyhood they are learning how to rule and how to submit to rule. Here, then, Cyrus was reputed to be, in the first place, the most modest of his fellows, and even more obedient to his elders than were his inferiors in rank; secondly, the most devoted to horses and the most skilful in managing horses; he was also adjudged the most eager to learn, and the most diligent in practising military accomplishments, alike the use of the bow and of the javelin. Then, when he was of suitable age, he was the fondest of hunting and, more than that, the fondest of incurring danger in his pursuit of wild animals. On one occasion, when a bear charged upon him, he did not take to flight, but grappled with her and was dragged from his horse; he received some injuries, the scars of which he retained visible to all, but in the end he killed the bear; and, furthermore, the man who was the first to come to his assistance he made an object of envy to many.

[72] For the obituary of Cyrus see Intro.

7 Ἐπεὶ δὲ κατεπέμφθη ὑπὸ τοῦ πατρὸς σατράπης
Λυδίας τε καὶ Φρυγίας τῆς μεγάλης καὶ Καππαδοκίας, στρατηγὸς δὲ καὶ πάντων ἀπεδείχθη οἷς καθήκει
εἰς Καστωλοῦ πεδίον ἀθροίζεσθαι, πρῶτον μὲν ἐπ-
έδειξεν αὐτὸν ὅτι περὶ πλείστου ποιοῖτο, εἴ τῳ σπεί-
σαιτο καὶ εἴ τῳ συνθοῖτο καὶ εἴ τῳ ὑπόσχοιτό τι,
8 μηδὲν ψεύδεσθαι. καὶ γὰρ οὖν ἐπίστευον μὲν αὐτῷ αἱ
πόλεις ἐπιτρεπόμεναι, ἐπίστευον δ' οἱ ἄνδρες· καὶ εἴ
τις πολέμιος ἐγένετο, σπεισαμένου Κύρου ἐπίστευε
9 μηδὲν ἂν παρὰ τὰς σπονδὰς παθεῖν· τοιγαροῦν ἐπεὶ
Τισσαφέρνει ἐπολέμησε, πᾶσαι αἱ πόλεις ἑκοῦσαι
Κῦρον εἵλοντο ἀντὶ Τισσαφέρνους πλὴν Μιλησίων·
οὗτοι δὲ ὅτι οὐκ ἤθελε τοὺς φεύγοντας προέσθαι
10 ἐφοβοῦντο αὐτόν. καὶ γὰρ ἔργῳ ἐπεδείκνυτο καὶ
ἔλεγεν ὅτι οὐκ ἄν ποτε προοῖτο, ἐπεὶ ἅπαξ φίλος
αὐτοῖς ἐγένετο, οὐδ' εἰ ἔτι μὲν μείους γένοιντο, ἔτι δὲ
κάκιον πράξειαν.

11 Φανερὸς δ' ἦν καὶ εἴ τίς τι ἀγαθὸν ἢ κακὸν ποιήσειεν αὐτόν, νικᾶν πειρώμενος· καὶ εὐχὴν δέ τινες
αὐτοῦ ἐξέφερον ὡς εὔχοιτο τοσοῦτον χρόνον ζῆν ἔστε
νικῴη καὶ τοὺς εὖ καὶ τοὺς κακῶς ποιοῦντας ἀλεξόμε-
12 νος. καὶ γὰρ οὖν πλεῖστοι δὴ αὐτῷ ἑνί γε ἀνδρὶ τῶν
ἐφ' ἡμῶν ἐπεθύμησαν καὶ χρήματα καὶ πόλεις καὶ τὰ
13 ἑαυτῶν σώματα προέσθαι. οὐ μὲν δὴ οὐδὲ τοῦτ' ἄν τις
εἴποι ὡς τοὺς κακούργους καὶ ἀδίκους εἴα καταγελᾶν,

---

[73] See i. 6 *fin.*   [74] See i. 7 and ii. 2.

Again, when he was sent down by his father to be satrap of Lydia, Greater Phrygia, and Cappadocia and was also appointed commander of all the troops whose duty it is to muster in the plain of Castolus, he showed, in the first place, that he counted it of the utmost importance, when he concluded a treaty or compact with anyone or made anyone any promise, under no circumstances to prove false to his word. It was for this reason, then, that the cities trusted him and put themselves under his protection,[73] and that individuals also trusted him; and if anyone had been an enemy, when Cyrus made a treaty with him he trusted that he would suffer no harm in violation of that treaty. Consequently, when he came to hostilities with Tissaphernes, all the cities of their own accord chose Cyrus rather than Tissaphernes, with the exception of Miletus;[74] and the reason why the Milesians feared him was, that he would not prove false to the exiles from their city. For he showed repeatedly, by deed as well as by word, that he would never abandon them when once he had come to be their friend, not even if they should become still fewer in number and should meet with still worse misfortune.

It was manifest also that whenever a man conferred any benefit upon Cyrus or did him any harm, he always strove to outdo him; in fact, some people used to report it as a prayer of his that he might live long enough to outdo both those who benefited and those who injured him, returning like for like. Hence it was that he had a greater following than any other one man of our time of friends who eagerly desired to entrust to him both treasure and cities and their very bodies. Yet, on the other hand, none could say that he permitted malefactors and wicked men to laugh at him; on

ἀλλ' ἀφειδέστατα πάντων ἐτιμωρεῖτο· πολλάκις δ' ἦν
ἰδεῖν παρὰ τὰς στειβομένας ὁδοὺς καὶ ποδῶν καὶ
χειρῶν καὶ ὀφθαλμῶν στερομένους ἀνθρώπους· ὥστ'
ἐν τῇ Κύρου ἀρχῇ ἐγένετο καὶ Ἕλληνι καὶ βαρβάρῳ
μηδὲν ἀδικοῦντι ἀδεῶς πορεύεσθαι ὅποι τις ἤθελεν,
ἔχοντι ὅ τι προχωροίη.

14   Τούς γε μέντοι ἀγαθοὺς εἰς πόλεμον ὡμολόγητο
διαφερόντως τιμᾶν. καὶ πρῶτον μὲν ἦν αὐτῷ πόλεμος
πρὸς Πισίδας καὶ Μυσούς· στρατευόμενος οὖν καὶ
αὐτὸς εἰς ταύτας τὰς χώρας, οὓς ἑώρα ἐθέλοντας
κινδυνεύειν, τούτους καὶ ἄρχοντας ἐποίει ἧς κατεστρέ-
15 φετο χώρας, ἔπειτα δὲ καὶ ἄλλοις δώροις ἐτίμα· ὥστε
φαίνεσθαι τοὺς μὲν ἀγαθοὺς εὐδαιμονεστάτους, τοὺς
δὲ κακοὺς δούλους τούτων ἀξιοῦσθαι[27] εἶναι. τοιγαροῦν πολλὴ ἦν ἀφθονία αὐτῷ τῶν ἐθελόντων κινδυνεύ-
16 ειν, ὅπου τις οἴοιτο Κῦρον αἰσθήσεσθαι. εἴς γε μὴν
δικαιοσύνην εἴ τις αὐτῷ φανερὸς γένοιτο ἐπιδείκνυ-
σθαι βουλόμενος, περὶ παντὸς ἐποιεῖτο τούτους
πλουσιωτέρως ποιεῖν τῶν ἐκ τοῦ ἀδίκου φιλοκερ-
17 δούντων. καὶ γὰρ οὖν ἄλλα τε πολλὰ δικαίως αὐτῷ
διεχειρίζετο καὶ στρατεύματι ἀληθινῷ ἐχρήσατο. καὶ
γὰρ στρατηγοὶ καὶ λοχαγοί, οἳ χρημάτων ἕνεκα πρὸς
ἐκεῖνον ἔπλευσαν, ἔγνωσαν κερδαλεώτερον εἶναι
18 Κύρῳ καλῶς ἄρχειν[28] ἢ τὸ κατὰ μῆνα κέρδος. ἀλλὰ

---

[27] The text is uncertain: Hude/Peters, Mar. follow, though
doubtfully, the MSS. reading ἀξιοῦσθαι: Gem., following
Schenkl, has ἀξίως.

the contrary, he was merciless to the last degree in punishing them, and one might often see along the travelled roads people who had lost feet or hands or eyes; thus in Cyrus' province it became possible for either Greek or barbarian, provided he were guilty of no wrongdoing, to travel fearlessly wherever be wished, carrying with him whatever it was to his interest to have.

But it was the brave in war, as all agree, whom he honoured especially. For example, he was once at war with the Pisidians and Mysians and commanded in person an expedition into their territories;[75] and whomsoever in his army he found willing to meet dangers, these men he would not only appoint as rulers of the territory he was subduing, but would honour thereafter with other gifts also. Thus the brave were seen to be most prosperous, while cowards were deemed fit to be their slaves. Consequently Cyrus had men in great abundance who were willing to meet danger wherever they thought that he would observe them. As for uprightness, if a man showed that he desired to distinguish himself in that quality, Cyrus considered it all important to enable such an one to live in greater opulence than those who were greedy of unjust gain. Hence he not only had many and various functions performed for him with fidelity, but, in particular, he secured the services of an army worthy of the name. For generals and captains who came overseas to serve him for the sake of money judged that loyal obedience to Cyrus was worth more to

[75] Cf. II. v. 13, III. ii. 23.

---

28 Constantinian excerpta read ἄρχειν: πειθαρχεῖν MSS.

μὴν εἴ τίς γέ τι αὐτῷ προστάξαντι καλῶς ὑπηρετή-
σειεν, οὐδενὶ πώποτε ἀχάριστον εἴασε τὴν προθυμίαν.
τοιγαροῦν κράτιστοι δὴ ὑπηρέται παντὸς ἔργου Κύρῳ
ἐλέχθησαν γενέσθαι.

19 Εἰ δέ τινα ὁρῴη δεινὸν ὄντα οἰκονόμον ἐκ τοῦ
δικαίου καὶ κατασκευάζοντά τε ἧς ἄρχοι χώρας καὶ
προσόδους ποιοῦντα, οὐδένα ἂν πώποτε ἀφείλετο, ἀλλ'
ἀεὶ πλείω προσεδίδου· ὥστε καὶ ἡδέως ἐπόνουν καὶ
θαρραλέως ἐκτῶντο καὶ ὃ ἐπέπατο αὖ τις ἥκιστα
Κῦρον ἔκρυπτεν· οὐ γὰρ φθονῶν τοῖς φανερῶς πλου-
τοῦσιν ἐφαίνετο, ἀλλὰ πειρώμενος χρῆσθαι τοῖς τῶν
ἀποκρυπτομένων χρήμασι.

20 Φίλους γε μήν, ὅσους ποιήσαιτο καὶ εὔνους γνοίη
ὄντας καὶ ἱκανοὺς κρίνειε συνεργοὺς εἶναι ὅ τι τυγχά-
νοι βουλόμενος κατεργάζεσθαι, ὁμολογεῖται πρὸς
21 πάντων κράτιστος δὴ γενέσθαι θεραπεύειν. καὶ γὰρ
αὐτὸ τοῦτο οὗπερ αὐτὸς ἕνεκα φίλων ᾤετο δεῖσθαι, ὡς
συνεργοὺς ἔχοι, καὶ αὐτὸς ἐπειρᾶτο συνεργὸς τοῖς
φίλοις κράτιστος εἶναι τούτου ὅτου ἕκαστον αἰσθά-
22 νοιτο ἐπιθυμοῦντα. δῶρα δὲ πλεῖστα μὲν οἶμαι εἷς γε
ἀνὴρ ἐλάμβανε διὰ πολλά· ταῦτα δὲ πάντων δὴ
23 μάλιστα τοῖς φίλοις διεδίδου, πρὸς τοὺς τρόπους
ἑκάστου σκοπῶν καὶ ὅτου μάλιστα ὁρῴη ἕκαστον
δεόμενον. καὶ ὅσα τῷ σώματι αὐτοῦ κόσμον πέμποι
τις ἢ ὡς εἰς πόλεμον ἢ ὡς εἰς καλλωπισμόν, καὶ περὶ
τούτων λέγειν αὐτὸν ἔφασαν ὅτι τὸ μὲν ἑαυτοῦ σῶμα
οὐκ ἂν δύναιτο τούτοις πᾶσι κοσμηθῆναι, φίλους δὲ

them than their mere monthly pay. Again, so surely as a man performed with credit any service that he assigned him, Cyrus never let his zeal go unrewarded. In consequence, he was said to have gained the very best supporters for every undertaking.

Furthermore, whenever he saw that a man was a skilful and just administrator, not only organizing well the country over which he ruled, but producing revenues, he would never deprive such a man of territory, but would always give him more besides. The result was that they toiled with pleasure and grew wealthy with confidence, and, likewise no one would conceal from Cyrus the store which he had acquired; for it was clear that he did not envy those who were frankly and openly rich, but strove to make use of the possessions of such as tried to conceal their wealth.

As to friends, all agree that he showed himself pre-eminent in his attentions to all the friends that he made and found devoted to him and adjudged to be competent co-workers in whatever he might be wishing to accomplish. For, just as the precise object for which he thought he needed friends himself was that he might have co-workers, so he tried on his own part to be a most vigorous co-worker with his friends to secure that which he found each one of them desired. Again, he received more gifts, I presume, than any other one man, and for many reasons; and surely he of all men distributed gifts most generously among his friends, with an eye to the tastes of each one and to whatever particular need he noted in each case. As for all the gifts which people sent him to wear upon his person, whether intended for war or merely for show, it is reported that he said of them that his own person could not be adorned with all these things, but that in his opinion

XENOPHON

καλῶς κεκοσμημένους μέγιστον κόσμον ἀνδρὶ νομί-
24 ζοι. καὶ τὸ μὲν τὰ μεγάλα νικᾶν τοὺς φίλους εὖ
ποιοῦντα οὐδὲν θαυμαστόν, ἐπειδή γε καὶ δυνατώτερος
ἦν· τὸ δὲ τῇ ἐπιμελείᾳ περιεῖναι τῶν φίλων καὶ τῷ
προθυμεῖσθαι χαρίζεσθαι, ταῦτα ἔμοιγε μᾶλλον δοκεῖ
25 ἀγαστὰ εἶναι. Κῦρος γὰρ ἔπεμπε βίκους οἴνου
ἡμιδεεῖς πολλάκις ὁπότε πάνυ ἡδὺν λάβοι, λέγων ὅτι
οὔπω δὴ πολλοῦ χρόνου τούτου ἡδίονι οἴνῳ ἐπιτύχοι·
τοῦτον οὖν σοὶ ἔπεμψε καὶ δεῖταί σου τήμερον τοῦτον
26 ἐκπιεῖν σὺν οἷς μάλιστα φιλεῖς. πολλάκις δὲ χῆνας
ἡμιβρώτους ἔπεμπε καὶ ἄρτων ἡμίσεα καὶ ἄλλα
τοιαῦτα, ἐπιλέγειν κελεύων τὸν φέροντα· Τούτοις ἥσθη
27 Κῦρος· βούλεται οὖν καὶ σὲ τούτων γεύσασθαι. ὅπου
δὲ χιλὸς σπάνιος πάνυ εἴη, αὐτὸς δ' ἐδύνατο παρασκευάσασθαι διὰ τὸ πολλοὺς ἔχειν ὑπηρέτας καὶ διὰ
τὴν ἐπιμέλειαν, διαπέμπων ἐκέλευε τοὺς φίλους τοῖς
τὰ ἑαυτῶν σώματα ἄγουσιν ἵπποις ἐμβάλλειν τοῦτον
τὸν χιλόν, ὡς μὴ πεινῶντες τοὺς ἑαυτοῦ φίλους
28 ἄγωσιν. εἰ δὲ δή ποτε πορεύοιτο καὶ πλεῖστοι μέλλοιεν
ὄψεσθαι, προσκαλῶν τοὺς φίλους ἐσπουδαιολογεῖτο,
ὡς δηλοίη οὓς τιμᾷ. ὥστε ἔγωγε, ἐξ ὧν ἀκούω, οὐδένα
κρίνω ὑπὸ πλειόνων πεφιλῆσθαι οὔτε Ἑλλήνων οὔτε
29 βαρβάρων. τεκμήριον δὲ τούτου καὶ τόδε· παρὰ μὲν
Κύρου δούλου ὄντος οὐδεὶς ἀπῄει πρὸς βασιλέα, πλὴν

76 A term habitually applied by the Greeks to the subjects of
an absolute monarch, especially those of the Persian king. But see,

friends nobly adorned were a man's greatest ornament. To be sure, the fact that he outdid his friends in the greatness of the benefits he conferred is nothing surprising, for the manifest reason that he had greater means than they; but that he surpassed them in solicitude and in eagerness to do favours, this in my opinion is more admirable. For example, when Cyrus got some particularly good wine, he would often send the half-emptied jar to a friend with the message: "Cyrus says that he has not chanced upon better wine than this for a long time; so he sends it to you, and asks you to drink it up today in company with the friends you love best." So he would often send halves of geese and of loaves and so forth, instructing the bearer to add the message: "Cyrus enjoyed this, and therefore wants you also to take a taste of it." And wherever fodder was exceedingly scarce and he was able to get it for his own use because of the large number of his servants and because of his good planning, he would distribute this fodder among his friends and tell them to give it to the horses that carried their own bodies, that they might not be hungry while carrying his friends. And whenever he was on the march and was likely to be seen by very many people, he would call his friends to him and engage them in earnest conversation, in order to show whom he honoured. Hence, as I at least conclude from what comes to my ears, no man, Greek or barbarian, has ever been loved by a greater number of people. Here is a fact to confirm that conclusion: although Cyrus was a slave,[76] no one deserted him to join the King, save that

e.g., the famous Letter of Darius, ML no. 12.4, and cf. I. vi. 6. The Persian term that is here translated δοῦλος is *bandaka*. See Briant, *Histoire* I, 336.

Ὀρόντας ἐπεχείρησε· καὶ οὗτος δὴ ὃν ᾤετο πιστόν οἱ
εἶναι ταχὺ αὐτὸν ηὗρε Κύρῳ φιλαίτερον ἢ ἑαυτῷ·
παρὰ δὲ βασιλέως πολλοὶ πρὸς Κῦρον ἀπῆλθον, ἐπεὶ
πολέμιοι ἀλλήλοις ἐγένοντο, καὶ οὗτοι μέντοι οἱ
μάλιστα αὐτοὺς ἀγάμενοι,[29] νομίζοντες παρὰ Κύρῳ
ὄντες ἀγαθοὶ ἀξιωτέρας ἂν τιμῆς τυγχάνειν ἢ παρὰ
30 βασιλεῖ. μέγα δὲ τεκμήριον καὶ τὸ ἐν τῇ τελευτῇ τοῦ
βίου αὐτῷ γενόμενον ὅτι καὶ αὐτὸς ἦν ἀγαθὸς καὶ
κρίνειν ὀρθῶς ἐδύνατο τοὺς πιστοὺς καὶ εὔνους καὶ
31 βεβαίους. ἀποθνήσκοντος γὰρ αὐτοῦ πάντες οἱ περὶ
αὐτὸν φίλοι καὶ συντράπεζοι ἀπέθανον μαχόμενοι
ὑπὲρ Κύρου πλὴν Ἀριαίου· οὗτος δὲ τεταγμένος
ἐτύγχανεν ἐπὶ τῷ εὐωνύμῳ τοῦ ἱππικοῦ ἄρχων· ὡς δ'
ᾔσθετο Κῦρον πεπτωκότα, ἔφυγεν ἔχων καὶ τὸ
στράτευμα πᾶν οὗ ἡγεῖτο.

X. Ἐνταῦθα δὴ Κύρου ἀποτέμνεται ἡ κεφαλὴ καὶ ἡ
χεὶρ ἡ δεξιά. βασιλεὺς δὲ διώκων εἰσπίπτει εἰς τὸ
Κύρειον στρατόπεδον· καὶ οἱ μὲν μετὰ Ἀριαίου οὐκέτι
ἵστανται, ἀλλὰ φεύγουσι διὰ τοῦ αὐτῶν στρατοπέδου
εἰς τὸν σταθμὸν ἔνθεν ὡρμῶντο· τέτταρες δ' ἐλέγοντο
2 παρασάγγαι εἶναι τῆς ὁδοῦ. βασιλεὺς δὲ καὶ οἱ σὺν
αὐτῷ τά τε ἄλλα πολλὰ διαρπάζουσι καὶ τὴν Φωκαΐδα
τὴν Κύρου παλλακίδα τὴν σοφὴν καὶ καλὴν λεγο-
3 μένην εἶναι λαμβάνει. ἡ δὲ Μιλησία ἡ νεωτέρα[30]

---

[29] αὐτοὺς ἀγάμενοι Hude/Peters: ὑπ' αὐτοῦ ἀγαπώμενοι
MSS. Cf. Xen., Ap. V.

Orontas attempted to do so (and he, mark you, speedily found out that the man he imagined was faithful to him, was more devoted to Cyrus than to him); on the other hand, many went over from the King to Cyrus after the two had become enemies (these being, moreover, the men who especially possessed self-respect), because they thought that if they were deserving, they would gain a worthier reward with Cyrus than with the King. Furthermore, what happened to Cyrus at the end of his life is a strong indication that he was a true man himself and that he knew how to judge those who were faithful, devoted, and constant. When he died, namely, all his bodyguard of friends and table companions died fighting in his defence, with the exception of Ariaeus; he, it chanced, was stationed on the left wing at the head of the cavalry, and when he learned that Cyrus had fallen, he took to flight with the whole army that he commanded.

X. Then the head of Cyrus and his right hand were cut off. But the King, pursuing Ariaeus, burst into the camp of Cyrus; and Ariaeus and his men no longer stood their ground, but fled through their own camp to the stopping-place from which they had set out, a distance, it was said, of four parasangs. So the King and his troops proceeded to secure plunder of various sorts in abundance, while in particular he captured the Phocaean woman, Cyrus' concubine, who, by all accounts, was clever and beautiful. The Milesian woman, however, the younger one, after being

---

30 ἡ νεωτέρα Hude/Peters, Mar. with some MSS.: other MSS. read ἦν νεωτέρα ἥ, which words, with Μιλησία, Gem. brackets, following Lincke.

ληφθεῖσα ὑπὸ τῶν ἀμφὶ βασιλέα ἐκφεύγει γυμνὴ
πρὸς τῶν Ἑλλήνων οἳ ἔτυχον ἐν τοῖς σκευοφόροις
ὅπλα ἔχοντες καὶ ἀντιταχθέντες πολλοὺς μὲν τῶν
ἁρπαζόντων ἀπέκτειναν, οἱ δὲ καὶ αὐτῶν ἀπέθανον· οὐ
μὴν ἔφυγόν γε, ἀλλὰ καὶ ταύτην ἔσωσαν καὶ τἆλλα,
ὁπόσα ἐντὸς αὐτῶν καὶ χρήματα καὶ ἄνθρωποι ἐγένοντο, πάντα ἔσωσαν.

4   Ἐνταῦθα διέσχον ἀλλήλων βασιλεύς τε καὶ οἱ
Ἕλληνες ὡς τριάκοντα στάδια, οἱ μὲν διώκοντες τοὺς
καθ᾽ αὑτοὺς ὡς πάντας νικῶντες, οἱ δ᾽ ἁρπάζοντες ὡς
5   ἤδη πάντες νικῶντες. ἐπεὶ δ᾽ ᾔσθοντο οἱ μὲν Ἕλληνες
ὅτι βασιλεὺς σὺν τῷ στρατεύματι ἐν τοῖς σκευοφόροις
εἴη, βασιλεὺς δ᾽ αὖ ἤκουσε Τισσαφέρνους ὅτι οἱ
Ἕλληνες νικῷεν τὸ καθ᾽ αὑτοὺς καὶ εἰς τὸ πρόσθεν
οἴχονται διώκοντες, ἐνταῦθα δὴ βασιλεὺς μὲν ἀθροίζει
τε τοὺς ἑαυτοῦ καὶ συντάττεται, ὁ δὲ Κλέαρχος ἐβουλεύετο Πρόξενον καλέσας, πλησιαίτατος γὰρ ἦν, εἰ
πέμποιέν τινας ἢ πάντες ἴοιεν ἐπὶ τὸ στρατόπεδον
6   ἀρήξοντες. ἐν τούτῳ καὶ βασιλεὺς δῆλος ἦν προσιὼν
πάλιν, ὡς ἐδόκει, ὄπισθεν. καὶ οἱ μὲν Ἕλληνες στραφέντες παρεσκευάζοντο ὡς ταύτῃ προσιόντος καὶ
δεξόμενοι, ὁ δὲ [βασιλεὺς] ταύτῃ μὲν οὐκ ἦγεν, ᾗ δὲ

---

77 The Greeks had advanced straight forward from their position on the right wing and the King straight forward from *his*
centre (which was beyond the left wing of Cyrus' entire, *i.e.* Greek
and barbarian, army); hence the two had passed by one another
at a considerable distance. The question now was, whether the

seized by the King's men made her escape, lightly clad, to some Greeks who had chanced to be standing guard amid the baggage train and, forming themselves in line against the enemy, had killed many of the plunderers, although some of their own number had been killed also; nevertheless, they did not take to flight, but they saved this woman and, furthermore, whatever else came within their lines, whether persons or property, they saved all alike.

At this time the King and the Greeks were distant from one another about thirty stadia, the Greeks pursuing the troops in their front, in the belief that they were victorious over all the enemy, the King and his followers plundering, in the belief that they were all victorious already. When, however, the Greeks learned that the King and his forces were in their baggage train, and the King, on the other hand, heard from Tissaphernes that the Greeks were victorious over the division opposite them and had gone on ahead in pursuit, then the King proceeded to gather his troops together and form them in line of battle, and Clearchus called Proxenus (for he was nearest him in the line) and took counsel with him as to whether they should send a detachment or go in full force to the camp, for the purpose of lending aid. Meanwhile the Greeks saw the King advancing again, as it seemed, from their rear, and they accordingly countermarched and made ready to meet his attack in case he should advance in that direction;[77] the King, however, did not do so, but returned by the same route he had followed before, when he passed outside of

King on his return march would move obliquely, so as to meet the Greeks, or would follow the same route by which he advanced, thus keeping clear of them again.

παρῆλθεν ἔξω τοῦ εὐωνύμου κέρατος ταύτῃ καὶ ἀπ-
ῆγεν, ἀναλαβὼν καὶ τοὺς ἐν τῇ μάχῃ πρὸς[31] τοὺς
Ἕλληνας αὐτομολήσαντας καὶ Τισσαφέρνη καὶ τοὺς
7 σὺν αὐτῷ. ὁ γὰρ Τισσαφέρνης ἐν τῇ πρώτῃ συνόδῳ
οὐκ ἔφυγεν, ἀλλὰ διήλασε παρὰ τὸν ποταμὸν κατὰ
τοὺς Ἕλληνας πελταστάς· διελαύνων δὲ κατέκανε μὲν
οὐδένα, διαστάντες δ᾽ οἱ Ἕλληνες ἔπαιον καὶ ἠκόντιζον αὐτούς· Ἐπισθένης δὲ Ἀμφιπολίτης ἦρχε τῶν
8 πελταστῶν καὶ ἐλέγετο φρόνιμος γενέσθαι. ὁ δ᾽ οὖν
Τισσαφέρνης ὡς μεῖον ἔχων ἀπηλλάγη, πάλιν μὲν
οὐκ ἀναστρέφει, εἰς δὲ τὸ στρατόπεδον ἀφικόμενος τὸ
τῶν Ἑλλήνων ἐκεῖ συντυγχάνει βασιλεῖ, καὶ ὁμοῦ δὴ
πάλιν συνταξάμενοι ἐπορεύοντο.

9 Ἐπεὶ δ᾽ ἦσαν κατὰ τὸ εὐώνυμον τῶν Ἑλλήνων
κέρας, ἔδεισαν οἱ Ἕλληνες μὴ προσάγοιεν πρὸς τὸ
κέρας καὶ περιπτύξαντες ἀμφοτέρωθεν αὐτοὺς κατα-
κόψειαν· καὶ ἐδόκει αὐτοὺς ἀναπτύσσειν τὸ κέρας καὶ
10 ποιήσασθαι ὄπισθεν τὸν ποταμόν. ἐν ᾧ δὲ ταῦτα
ἐβουλεύοντο, καὶ δὴ βασιλεὺς παραμειψάμενος εἰς τὸ
αὐτὸ σχῆμα κατέστησεν ἀντίαν τὴν φάλαγγα ὥσπερ

---

[31] πρὸς some MSS., Mar.: κατὰ other MSS., Gem.: Gem.,
however, following Schenkl, brackets κατὰ . . . Ἕλληνας.

---

[78] See viii. 4–5.

[79] The fronts of the two armies—which were facing in opposite directions, and each in the direction opposite to that which it
took in the first encounter—were in approximately the same
straight line. Xenophon means by "the left wing" that which had
been the left wing in the original formation; it was now the right.

Cyrus' left wing, and in his return picked up not only those
who had deserted to the Greeks during the battle, but
also Tissaphernes and his troops. For Tissaphernes had not
taken to flight in the first encounter, but had charged along
the river through the Greek peltasts;[78] he did not kill anyone in his passage, but the Greeks, after opening a gap
for his men proceeded to deal blows and throw javelins
upon them as they went through. The commander of the
Greek peltasts was Episthenes of Amphipolis, and it was
said that be proved himself a sagacious man. At any rate,
after Tissaphernes had thus come off with the worst of it,
he did not wheel round again, but went on to the camp of
the Greeks and there fell in with the King; so it was that,
after forming their lines once more, they were proceeding
together.

When they were over against the left wing of the
Greeks,[79] the latter conceived the fear that they might advance against that wing and, by outflanking them on both
sides, cut them to pieces; it seemed best, then, that they
draw the wing back and get the river in their rear.[80]
But while they were taking counsel about this matter, the
King, had already changed his line of battle to the same
form as theirs and brought it into position opposite them,
just as when he had met them for battle the first time.[81]

[80] The Greek line was now, as in the beginning, at right angles
to the Euphrates. The movement here described would (if executed) have made it parallel to the river, the latter serving as a
defence in the rear.   [81] Xenophon seems to mean that the
King now moved to the right until his flank (like that of the
Greeks—see the preceding notes) rested upon the Euphrates.
The two armies, therefore, were again squarely facing one another, though with positions relatively reversed.

τὸ πρῶτον μαχούμενος συνῄει. ὡς δὲ εἶδον οἱ Ἕλληνες
ἐγγύς τε ὄντας καὶ παρατεταγμένους, αὖθις παιανίσαντες ἐπῇσαν πολὺ ἔτι προθυμότερον ἢ τὸ πρόσθεν.
11 οἱ δ᾽ αὖ βάρβαροι οὐκ ἐδέχοντο, ἀλλὰ ἐκ πλέονος ἢ
τὸ πρόσθεν ἔφευγον· οἱ δ᾽ ἐπεδίωκον μέχρι κώμης
12 τινός· ἐνταῦθα δ᾽ ἔστησαν οἱ Ἕλληνες· ὑπὲρ γὰρ τῆς
κώμης γήλοφος ἦν, ἐφ᾽ οὗ ἀνεστράφησαν οἱ ἀμφὶ
βασιλέα, πεζοὶ μὲν οὐκέτι, τῶν δὲ ἱππέων ὁ λόφος
ἐνεπλήσθη, ὥστε τὸ ποιούμενον μὴ γιγνώσκειν. καὶ
τὸ βασίλειον σημεῖον ὁρᾶν ἔφασαν ἀετόν τινα χρυ-
13 σοῦν ἐπὶ πέλτῃ [ἐπὶ ξύλου][32] ἀνατεταμένον. ἐπεὶ δὲ
καὶ ἐνταῦθ᾽ ἐχώρουν οἱ Ἕλληνες, λείπουσι δὴ καὶ τὸν
λόφον οἱ ἱππεῖς· οὐ μὴν ἔτι ἀθρόοι ἀλλ᾽ ἄλλοι ἄλλο-
θεν· ἐψιλοῦτο δ᾽ ὁ λόφος τῶν ἱππέων· τέλος δὲ καὶ
14 πάντες ἀπεχώρησαν. ὁ οὖν Κλέαρχος οὐκ ἀνεβίβαζεν
ἐπὶ τὸν λόφον, ἀλλ᾽ ὑπ᾽ αὐτὸν στήσας τὸ στράτευμα
πέμπει Λύκιον τὸν Συρακόσιον καὶ ἄλλον ἐπὶ τὸν
λόφον καὶ κελεύει κατιδόντας τὰ ὑπὲρ τοῦ λόφου τί
15 ἐστιν ἀπαγγεῖλαι. καὶ ὁ Λύκιος ἤλασέ τε καὶ ἰδὼν
ἀπαγγέλλει ὅτι φεύγουσιν ἀνὰ κράτος. σχεδὸν δ᾽ ὅτε
ταῦτα ἦν καὶ ἥλιος ἐδύετο.
16   Ἐνταῦθα δ᾽ ἔστησαν οἱ Ἕλληνες καὶ θέμενοι τὰ
ὅπλα ἀνεπαύοντο· καὶ ἅμα μὲν ἐθαύμαζον ὅτι οὐδαμοῦ
Κῦρος φαίνοιτο οὐδ᾽ ἄλλος ἀπ᾽ αὐτοῦ οὐδεὶς παρείη·
οὐ γὰρ ᾔδεσαν αὐτὸν τεθνηκότα, ἀλλ᾽ ἤκαζον ἢ διώ-

---

[32] ἐπὶ ξύλου MSS.: Hude/Peters, Gem. bracket, following
Cobet: Mar. regards as corrupt.

And when the Greeks saw that the enemy were near them and in battle-order, they again struck up the paean and advanced to the attack yet more eagerly than before; and the barbarians once again failed to await the attack, but took to flight when at a greater distance from the Greeks than they were the first time. The Greeks pursued as far as a certain village, and there they halted; for above the village was a hill, upon which the King and his followers rallied; and they were not now footsoldiers, but the hill was covered with horsemen, so that the Greeks could not perceive what was going on. They did see, they said, the royal standard, a kind of golden eagle on a shield, raised aloft upon a pole.[82] But when at this point also the Greeks resumed their forward movement, the horsemen at once proceeded to leave the hill; they did not keep together, however, as they went, but scattered in different directions; so the hill became gradually cleared of the horsemen, till at last they were all gone. Clearchus, accordingly, did not lead the army up the hill, but halted at its foot and sent Lycius the Syracusan and another man to the summit, directing them to observe what was beyond the hill and report back to him. And Lycius, after riding up and looking, brought back word that the enemy were in headlong flight. At about this time the sun set.

Then the Greeks halted, grounded arms, and proceeded to rest themselves. At the same time they wondered that Cyrus was nowhere to be seen and that no one else had come to them from him; for they did not know

[82] See Boyce *HZ* 287–8; the bird was more likely a falcon.

κοντα οἴχεσθαι ἢ καταληψόμενόν τι προεληλακέναι·
17 καὶ αὐτοὶ ἐβουλεύοντο εἰ αὐτοῦ μείναντες τὰ σκευοφόρα ἐνταῦθα ἄγοιντο ἢ ἀπίοιεν ἐπὶ τὸ στρατόπεδον.
ἔδοξεν οὖν αὐτοῖς ἀπιέναι· καὶ ἀφικνοῦνται ἀμφὶ
18 δορπηστὸν ἐπὶ τὰς σκηνάς. ταύτης μὲν τῆς ἡμέρας
τοῦτο τὸ τέλος ἐγένετο. καταλαμβάνουσι δὲ τῶν τε
ἄλλων χρημάτων τὰ πλεῖστα διηρπασμένα καὶ εἴ τι
σιτίον ἢ ποτὸν ἦν, καὶ τὰς ἁμάξας μεστὰς ἀλεύρων
καὶ οἴνου, ἃς παρεσκευάσατο Κῦρος, ἵνα εἴ ποτε
σφόδρα τὸ στράτευμα λάβοι ἔνδεια, διαδιδοίη τοῖς
Ἕλλησιν—ἦσαν δ᾽ αὗται τετρακόσιαι, ὡς ἐλέγοντο,
ἅμαξαι—καὶ ταύτας τότε οἱ σὺν βασιλεῖ διήρπασαν.
19 ὥστε ἄδειπνοι ἦσαν οἱ πλεῖστοι τῶν Ἑλλήνων· ἦσαν
δὲ καὶ ἀνάριστοι· πρὶν γὰρ δὴ καταλῦσαι τὸ
στράτευμα πρὸς ἄριστον βασιλεὺς ἐφάνη. ταύτην μὲν
οὖν τὴν νύκτα οὕτω διεγένοντο.

that he was dead, but conjectured that he had either gone off in pursuit or pushed on to occupy some point. So they took counsel for themselves as to whether they should remain where they were and bring the baggage train thither, or return to their camp. The decision was to return, and they reached their tents about supper-time. Such was the conclusion of this day. They found most of their property pillaged, in particular whatever there was to eat or drink, and as for the wagons loaded with flour and wine which Cyrus had provided in order that, if ever serious need should overtake the army, he might have supplies to distribute among the Greeks (and there were four hundred of these wagons, it was said), these also the King and his men had now pillaged. The result was that most of the Greeks had no dinner; and they had had no breakfast, either, for the King had appeared before the time when the army was to halt for breakfast. Thus it was, then that they got through this night.

B

2   I.[1] Ἅμα δὲ τῇ ἡμέρᾳ συνελθόντες οἱ στρατηγοὶ
ἐθαύμαζον ὅτι Κῦρος οὔτε ἄλλον πέμποι σημανοῦντα
ὅ τι χρὴ ποιεῖν οὔτε αὐτὸς φαίνοιτο. ἔδοξεν οὖν αὐτοῖς
συσκευασαμένοις ἃ εἶχον καὶ ἐξοπλισαμένοις προ-
3   ϊέναι εἰς τὸ πρόσθεν ἕως Κύρῳ συμμείξειαν. ἤδη δὲ ἐν
ὁρμῇ ὄντων ἅμ' ἡλίῳ ἀνίσχοντι ἦλθε Προκλῆς ὁ
Τευθρανίας ἄρχων, γεγονὼς ἀπὸ Δαμαράτου τοῦ Λάκωνος, καὶ Γλοῦς ὁ Τάμω. οὗτοι ἔλεγον ὅτι Κῦρος μὲν
τέθνηκεν, Ἀριαῖος δὲ πεφευγὼς ἐν τῷ σταθμῷ εἴη μετὰ
τῶν ἄλλων βαρβάρων ὅθεν τῇ προτεραίᾳ ὡρμῶντο,
καὶ λέγοι ὅτι ταύτην μὲν τὴν ἡμέραν περιμείνειεν ἂν

---

[1] The MSS. here prefix the following summary of the preceding narrative: ὡς μὲν οὖν ἠθροίσθη Κύρῳ τὸ Ἑλληνικὸν ὅτε
ἐπὶ τὸν ἀδελφὸν Ἀρταξέρξην ἐστρατεύετο, καὶ ὅσα ἐν τῇ
ἀνόδῳ ἐπράχθη καὶ ὡς ἡ μάχη ἐγένετο καὶ ὡς Κῦρος
ἐτελεύτησε καὶ ὡς ἐπὶ τὸ στρατόπεδον ἐλθόντες οἱ Ἕλληνες
ἐκοιμήθησαν οἰόμενοι τὰ πάντα νικᾶν καὶ Κῦρον ζῆν, ἐν τῷ
πρόσθεν λόγῳ δεδήλωται. A like introduction is prefixed to each
of the following books except the sixth. All these summaries must
have been the work of a late editor. Cf. Chariton, *Callirhoe* V. 1–2.

---

[1] Summary (see note to text): The preceding narrative has
described how a Greek force was collected for Cyrus at the time

146

BOOK II

1.[1] At daybreak the generals came together, and they wondered that Cyrus neither sent anyone else to tell them what to do nor appeared himself. They resolved, accordingly, to pack up what they had, arm themselves, and push forward until they should join forces with Cyrus. When they were on the point of setting out, and just as the sun was rising, came Procles, the ruler of Teuthrania, a descendant of Damaratus,[2] the Laconian, and with him Glus, the son of Tamos. They reported that Cyrus was dead, and that Ariaeus had fled and was now, along with the rest of the barbarians, at the stopping-place from which they had set out on the preceding day; further, Ariaeus sent word that he was that day waiting for the Greeks, on the chance that they intended to join them, but on the next day, so he said,

[1] when he was planning an expedition against his brother Artaxerxes, what events took place during the upward march, how the battle was fought, how Cyrus met his death, and how the Greeks returned to their camp and lay down to rest, supposing that they were victorious at all points and that Cyrus was alive.

[2] A king of Sparta who was deposed in 491 B.C., fled to Persia, and afterwards accompanied Xerxes in his expedition against Greece. Teuthrania (in western Asia Minor) made part of the territory given him by Xerxes as a reward for this service. See D. Lewis, *Sparta and Persia* (Leiden, 1977) 54 and n. 30.

αὐτούς, εἰ μέλλοιεν ἥκειν, τῇ δὲ ἄλλῃ ἀπιέναι φαίη ἐπὶ
4 Ἰωνίας, ὅθενπερ ἦλθε. ταῦτα ἀκούσαντες οἱ στρατηγοὶ καὶ οἱ ἄλλοι Ἕλληνες πυνθανόμενοι βαρέως
ἔφερον. Κλέαρχος δὲ τάδε εἶπεν. Ἀλλ᾽ ὤφελε μὲν
Κῦρος ζῆν· ἐπεὶ δὲ τετελεύτηκεν, ἀπαγγέλλετε Ἀριαίῳ
ὅτι ἡμεῖς γε νικῶμεν βασιλέα καί, ὡς ὁρᾶτε, οὐδεὶς
ἔτι ἡμῖν μάχεται, καὶ εἰ μὴ ὑμεῖς ἤλθετε, ἐπορευόμεθα
ἂν ἐπὶ βασιλέα. ἐπαγγελλόμεθα δὲ Ἀριαίῳ, ἐὰν
ἐνθάδε ἔλθῃ, εἰς τὸν θρόνον τὸν βασίλειον καθιεῖν
αὐτόν· τῶν γὰρ μάχην νικώντων καὶ τὸ ἄρχειν ἐστί.
5 ταῦτ᾽ εἰπὼν ἀποστέλλει τοὺς ἀγγέλους καὶ σὺν αὐτοῖς
Χειρίσοφον τὸν Λάκωνα καὶ Μένωνα τὸν Θετταλόν·
καὶ γὰρ αὐτὸς Μένων ἐβούλετο· ἦν γὰρ φίλος καὶ
ξένος Ἀριαίου.

6   Οἱ μὲν ᾤχοντο, Κλέαρχος δὲ περιέμενε· τὸ δὲ
στράτευμα ἐπορίζετο σῖτον ὅπως ἐδύνατο ἐκ τῶν ὑποζυγίων κόπτοντες τοὺς βοῦς καὶ ὄνους· ξύλοις δὲ
ἐχρῶντο μικρὸν προϊόντες ἀπὸ τῆς φάλαγγος οὗ ἡ
μάχη ἐγένετο τοῖς τε οἰστοῖς πολλοῖς οὖσιν, οὓς
ἠνάγκαζον οἱ Ἕλληνες ἐκβάλλειν τοὺς αὐτομολοῦντας
παρὰ βασιλέως, καὶ τοῖς γέρροις καὶ ταῖς ξυλίναις
7 ἀσπίσι ταῖς Αἰγυπτίαις· πολλαὶ δὲ καὶ πέλται καὶ
ἅμαξαι ἦσαν φέρεσθαι ἔρημοι· οἷς πᾶσι χρώμενοι
κρέα ἕψοντες ἤσθιον ἐκείνην τὴν ἡμέραν.

Καὶ ἤδη τε ἦν περὶ πλήθουσαν ἀγορὰν καὶ ἔρχονται παρὰ βασιλέως καὶ Τισσαφέρνους κήρυκες οἱ μὲν
ἄλλοι βάρβαροι, ἦν δ᾽ αὐτῶν Φαλῖνος εἷς Ἕλλην, ὃς

he would set out on the return journey for Ionia, whence
he had come. The generals upon hearing this message, and
the rest of the Greeks as they learned of it, were greatly
distressed. Clearchus, however, said: "Well, would that
Cyrus were alive! but since he is dead, carry back word to
Ariaeus that, for our part, we have defeated the King, that
we have no enemy left, as you see, to fight with, and that
if you had not come, we should now be marching against
the King. And we promise Ariaeus that, if he will come
here, we will set him upon the royal throne; for to those
who are victorious in battle belongs also the right to rule."
With these words he sent back the messengers, sending
with them Cheirisophus the Laconian and Menon the
Thessalian; for this was Menon's own wish, inasmuch as he
was an intimate and guest-friend of Ariaeus.

So they went off, and Clearchus awaited their return;
meanwhile the troops provided themselves with food as
best they could, by slaughtering oxen and asses of the baggage train. As for fuel, they went forward a short distance
from their line to the place where the battle was fought
and used for that purpose not only the arrows, many in
number, which the Greeks had compelled all who deserted
from the King to throw away, but also the wicker shields
and the wooden Egyptian shields; there were likewise
many light shields and wagons that they could carry off, all
of them abandoned. These various things, then, they used
for fuel, and so boiled meat and lived on it for that day.[3]

And now it was about full-market time[4] and heralds
arrived from the King and Tissaphernes, all of them barbarians except one, a Greek named Phalinus, who, as it

---

[3] See note on I. v. 6.   [4] See note on I. viii. 1.

ἐτύγχανε παρὰ Τισσαφέρνει ὢν καὶ ἐντίμως ἔχων· καὶ
γὰρ προσεποιεῖτο ἐπιστήμων εἶναι τῶν ἀμφὶ τάξεις
8 τε καὶ ὁπλομαχίαν. οὗτοι δὲ προσελθόντες καὶ
καλέσαντες τοὺς τῶν Ἑλλήνων ἄρχοντας λέγουσιν ὅτι
βασιλεὺς κελεύει τοὺς Ἕλληνας, ἐπεὶ νικῶν τυγχάνει
καὶ Κῦρον ἀπέκτονε, παραδόντας τὰ ὅπλα ἰόντας ἐπὶ
βασιλέως θύρας εὑρίσκεσθαι ἄν τι δύνωνται ἀγαθόν.
9 ταῦτα μὲν εἶπον οἱ βασιλέως κήρυκες· οἱ δὲ Ἕλληνες
βαρέως μὲν ἤκουσαν, ὅμως δὲ Κλέαρχος τοσοῦτον
εἶπεν, ὅτι οὐ τῶν νικώντων εἴη τὰ ὅπλα παραδιδόναι·
ἀλλ᾽, ἔφη, ὑμεῖς μέν, ὦ ἄνδρες στρατηγοί, τούτοις
ἀποκρίνασθε ὅ τι κάλλιστόν τε καὶ ἄριστον ἔχετε· ἐγὼ
δὲ αὐτίκα ἥξω. ἐκάλεσε γάρ τις αὐτὸν τῶν ὑπηρετῶν,
ὅπως ἴδοι τὰ ἱερὰ ἐξηρημένα· ἔτυχε γὰρ θυόμενος.
10 Ἔνθα δὴ ἀπεκρίνατο Κλεάνωρ ὁ Ἀρκάς, πρεσβύτατος ὤν, ὅτι πρόσθεν ἂν ἀποθάνοιεν ἢ τὰ ὅπλα
παραδοῖεν. Πρόξενος δὲ ὁ Θηβαῖος, Ἀλλ᾽ ἐγώ, ἔφη, ὦ
Φαλῖνε, θαυμάζω πότερα ὡς κρατῶν βασιλεὺς αἰτεῖ
τὰ ὅπλα ἢ ὡς διὰ φιλίαν δῶρα. εἰ μὲν γὰρ ὡς κρατῶν,
τί δεῖ αὐτὸν αἰτεῖν ἀλλ᾽ οὐ λαβεῖν ἐλθόντα; εἰ δὲ
πείσας βούλεται λαβεῖν, λεγέτω τί ἔσται τοῖς στρα-
11 τιώταις, ἐὰν αὐτῷ ταῦτα χαρίσωνται. πρὸς ταῦτα
Φαλῖνος εἶπε· Βασιλεὺς νικᾶν ἡγεῖται, ἐπεὶ Κῦρον
ἀπέκτεινε. τίς γὰρ αὐτῷ ἔστιν ὅστις τῆς ἀρχῆς

---

5 Member of a growing class of military experts. Cf VII. i. 33.
6 These words recall the famous answer which Leonidas at

chanced, was with Tissaphernes and was held in honour by
him; for this Phalinus professed to be an expert in tactics
and the handling of heavy infantry.[5] When these heralds
came up, they called for the leaders of the Greeks and said
that the King, since victory had fallen to him and he had
slain Cyrus, directed the Greeks to give up their arms, go
to the King's court, and seek for themselves whatever favour they might be able to get. Such was the message of
the King's heralds. The Greeks received it with anger, but
nevertheless Clearchus said as much as this, that it was
not victors who gave up their arms; "However," he continued, "do you, my fellow generals, give these men whatever answer you can that is best and most honourable, and
I will return immediately." For one of his servants had
summoned him to see the vital organs that had been taken
out of a sacrificial victim, for Clearchus chanced to be
engaged in sacrificing.

Then Cleanor the Arcadian, being the eldest of the
generals, made answer that they would die sooner than
give up their arms. And Proxenus the Theban said: "For
my part, Phalinus, I wonder whether the King is asking for
our arms on the assumption that he is victorious or simply
as gifts, on the assumption that we are his friends. For if
he asks for them as victor, why need he ask for them,
instead of coming and taking them?[6] But if he desires to
get them by persuasion, let him set forth what the soldiers
will receive in case they do him this favour." In reply to this
Phalinus said: "The King believes that he is victor because
he has slain Cyrus. For who is there now who is contending

Thermopylae made to the same demand: μολὼν λαβέ, "Come
and take them," Plutarch, *Mor.* 225D.

ἀντιποιεῖται; νομίζει δὲ καὶ ὑμᾶς αὐτοῦ εἶναι, ἔχων ἐν
μέσῃ τῇ αὐτοῦ χώρᾳ καὶ ποταμῶν ἐντὸς ἀδιαβάτων
καὶ πλῆθος ἀνθρώπων ἐφ' ὑμᾶς δυνάμενος ἀγαγεῖν,
ὅσον οὐδ' εἰ παρέχοι ὑμῖν δύναισθε ἂν ἀποκτεῖναι.

12 μετὰ τοῦτον Ξενοφῶν[2] Ἀθηναῖος εἶπεν· Ὦ Φαλῖνε,
νῦν, ὡς σὺ ὁρᾷς, ἡμῖν οὐδὲν ἔστιν ἀγαθὸν ἄλλο εἰ μὴ
ὅπλα καὶ ἀρετή. ὅπλα μὲν οὖν ἔχοντες οἰόμεθα ἂν καὶ
τῇ ἀρετῇ χρῆσθαι, παραδόντες δ' ἂν ταῦτα καὶ τῶν
σωμάτων στερηθῆναι. μὴ οὖν οἴου τὰ μόνα ἀγαθὰ
ἡμῖν ὄντα ὑμῖν παραδώσειν, ἀλλὰ σὺν τούτοις καὶ

13 περὶ τῶν ὑμετέρων ἀγαθῶν μαχούμεθα. ἀκούσας δὲ
ταῦτα ὁ Φαλῖνος ἐγέλασε καὶ εἶπεν· Ἀλλὰ φιλοσόφῳ
μὲν ἔοικας, ὦ νεανίσκε, καὶ λέγεις οὐκ ἀχάριστα· ἴσθι
μέντοι ἀνόητος ὤν, εἰ οἴει τὴν ὑμετέραν ἀρετὴν περι-

14 γενέσθαι ἂν τῆς βασιλέως δυνάμεως. ἄλλους δέ τινας
ἔφασαν λέγειν ὑπομαλακιζομένους ὡς καὶ Κύρῳ
πιστοὶ ἐγένοντο καὶ βασιλεῖ γ' ἂν πολλοῦ ἄξιοι
γένοιντο, εἰ βούλοιτο φίλος γενέσθαι· καὶ εἴτε ἄλλο
τι θέλοι χρῆσθαι εἴτ' ἐπ' Αἴγυπτον στρατεύειν, συγ-
καταστρέψαιντ' ἂν αὐτῷ.

15 Ἐν τούτῳ Κλέαρχος ἧκε, καὶ ἠρώτησεν εἰ ἤδη
ἀποκεκριμένοι εἶεν. Φαλῖνος δὲ ὑπολαβὼν εἶπεν·
Οὗτοι μέν, ὦ Κλέαρχε, ἄλλος ἄλλα λέγει· σὺ δ' ἡμῖν

16 εἰπὲ τί λέγεις. ὁ δ' εἶπεν. Ἐγώ σε, ὦ Φαλῖνε, ἄσμενος

---

[2] Some MSS. read Θεόπομπος here.

against him for his realm? Further, he believes that you also are his because he has you in the middle of his country, enclosed by impassable rivers, and because he can bring against you a multitude of men so great that you could not slay them even if he were to put them in your hands." Then Xenophon, an Athenian, said: "Phalinus, at this moment, as you see for yourself, we have no other possession save arms and valour. Now if we keep our arms, we imagine that we can make use of our valour also, but if we give them up, that we shall likewise be deprived of our lives. Do not suppose, therefore, that we shall give up to you the only possessions that we have; rather, with these we shall do battle against you for your possessions as well." When he heard this, Phalinus laughed and said: "Why, you talk like a philosopher, young man, and what you say is quite pretty; be sure, however, that you are a fool if you imagine that your valour could prove superior to the King's might." There were some others, so the story goes, who weakened a little, and said that, just as they had proved themselves faithful to Cyrus, so they might prove valuable to the King also if he should wish to become their friend; he might want to employ them for various purposes, perhaps for a campaign against Egypt, which they should be glad to assist him in subduing.[7]

At this time Clearchus returned, and asked whether they had yet given an answer. And Phalinus broke in and said: "These people, Clearchus, all say different things; but tell us what your own opinion is." Clearchus replied: "I myself, Phalinus, was glad to see you, and, I presume, all

[7] Persian control of Egypt at this time was tenuous at best: see J. Ray, *CAH*[2] IV, 284. Cf. II. v. 13.

ἑόρακα, οἶμαι δὲ καὶ οἱ ἄλλοι πάντες οὗτοι· σύ τε γὰρ
Ἕλλην εἶ καὶ ἡμεῖς τοσοῦτοι ὄντες ὅσους σὺ ὁρᾷς· ἐν
τοιούτοις δὲ ὄντες πράγμασι συμβουλευόμεθά σοι τί
17 χρὴ ποιεῖν περὶ ὧν λέγεις. σὺ οὖν πρὸς θεῶν συμ-
βούλευσον ἡμῖν ὅ τι σοι δοκεῖ κάλλιστον καὶ ἄριστον
εἶναι, καὶ ὅ σοι τιμὴν οἴσει εἰς τὸν ἔπειτα χρόνον
λεγόμενον,[3] ὅτι Φαλῖνός ποτε πεμφθεὶς παρὰ βασιλέως κελεύσων τοὺς Ἕλληνας τὰ ὅπλα παραδοῦναι
συμβουλευομένοις συνεβούλευσεν αὐτοῖς τάδε. οἶσθα
δὲ ὅτι ἀνάγκη λέγεσθαι ἐν τῇ Ἑλλάδι ἃ ἂν συμ-
18 βουλεύσῃς. ὁ δὲ Κλέαρχος ταῦτα ὑπήγετο βουλόμενος
καὶ αὐτὸν τὸν παρὰ βασιλέως πρεσβεύοντα συμ-
βουλεῦσαι μὴ παραδοῦναι τὰ ὅπλα, ὅπως εὐέλπιδες
μᾶλλον εἶεν οἱ Ἕλληνες. Φαλῖνος δὲ ὑποστρέψας
19 παρὰ τὴν δόξαν αὐτοῦ εἶπεν· Ἐγώ, εἰ μὲν τῶν μυρίων
ἐλπίδων μία τις ὑμῖν ἐστι σωθῆναι πολεμοῦντας
βασιλεῖ, συμβουλεύω μὴ παραδιδόναι τὰ ὅπλα· εἰ δέ
τοι μηδεμία σωτηρίας ἐστὶν ἐλπὶς ἄκοντος βασιλέως,
20 συμβουλεύω σῴζεσθαι ὑμῖν ὅπῃ δυνατόν. Κλέαρχος
δὲ πρὸς ταῦτα εἶπεν. Ἀλλὰ ταῦτα μὲν δὴ σὺ λέγεις·
παρ᾽ ἡμῶν δὲ ἀπάγγελλε τάδε, ὅτι ἡμεῖς οἰόμεθα, εἰ
μὲν δέοι βασιλεῖ φίλους εἶναι, πλείονος ἂν ἄξιοι εἶναι
φίλοι ἔχοντες τὰ ὅπλα ἢ παραδόντες ἄλλῳ, εἰ δὲ δέοι
πολεμεῖν, ἄμεινον ἂν πολεμεῖν ἔχοντες τὰ ὅπλα ἢ
21 ἄλλῳ παραδόντες. ὁ δὲ Φαλῖνος εἶπε· Ταῦτα μὲν δὴ
ἀπαγγελοῦμεν· ἀλλὰ καὶ τάδε ὑμῖν εἰπεῖν ἐκέλευσε

---

[3] λεγόμενον Cob., Mar., edd.: ἀναλεγόμενον MSS.: ἀναγ-
γελλόμενον Gem.: Hude/Peters despair.

these others were, too; for you are a Greek and so are we, whose numbers you can observe for yourself. Now since we are in such a situation, we ask you to advise us as to what we ought to do about the matter you mention. Do you, then, in the sight of the gods, give us whatever advice you think is best and most honourable, advice which will bring you honour in future time when it is reported in this way: 'Once on a time Phalinus, when he was sent by the King to order the Greeks to surrender their arms, gave them, when they sought his counsel, the following advice.' And you know that any advice you may give will certainly be reported in Greece." Now Clearchus was making this crafty suggestion in the hope that the very man who was acting as the King's ambassador might advise them not to give up their arms, and that thus the Greeks might be made more hopeful. But, contrary to his expectation, Phalinus also made a crafty turn, and said: "For my part, if you have one chance in ten thousand of saving yourselves by carrying on war against the King, I advise you not to give up your arms; but if you have no hope of deliverance without the King's consent, I advise you to save yourselves in what way you can." In reply to this Clearchus said: "Well, that is what you say; but as our answer carry back this word, that in our view if we are to be friends of the King, we should be more valuable friends if we keep our arms than if we give them up to someone else, and if we are to wage war with him, we should wage war better if we keep our arms than if we give them up to someone else." And Phalinus said: "That answer then, we will carry back; but the King

βασιλεύς, ὅτι μένουσι μὲν ὑμῖν αὐτοῦ σπονδαὶ εἴησαν, προϊοῦσι δὲ καὶ ἀπιοῦσι πόλεμος. εἴπατε οὖν καὶ
περὶ τούτου πότερα μενεῖτε καὶ σπονδαί εἰσιν ἢ ὡς
πολέμου ὄντος παρ' ὑμῶν ἀπαγγελῶ. Κλέαρχος δ'

22 ἔλεξεν· Ἀπάγγελλε τοίνυν καὶ περὶ τούτου ὅτι καὶ ἡμῖν
ταὐτὰ δοκεῖ ἅπερ καὶ βασιλεῖ. Τί οὖν ταῦτά ἐστιν;
ἔφη ὁ Φαλῖνος. ἀπεκρίνατο⁴ Κλέαρχος· Ἢν μὲν μένω-
μεν, σπονδαί, ἀπιοῦσι δὲ καὶ προϊοῦσι πόλεμος. ὁ δὲ
πάλιν ἠρώτησε· Σπονδὰς ἢ πόλεμον ἀπαγγελῶ;

23 Κλέαρχος δὲ ταῦτα πάλιν ἀπεκρίνατο· Σπονδαὶ μὲν
μένουσιν, ἀπιοῦσι δὲ ἢ προϊοῦσι πόλεμος. ὅ τι δὲ
ποιήσοι οὐ διεσήμανε.

II. Φαλῖνος μὲν δὴ ᾤχετο καὶ οἱ σὺν αὐτῷ. οἱ δὲ
παρὰ Ἀριαίου ἧκον Προκλῆς καὶ Χειρίσοφος· Μένων
δὲ αὐτοῦ ἔμεινε παρὰ Ἀριαίῳ· οὗτοι δὲ ἔλεγον ὅτι
πολλοὺς φαίη ὁ Ἀριαῖος εἶναι Πέρσας ἑαυτοῦ βελτίους, οὓς οὐκ ἂν ἀνασχέσθαι αὐτοῦ βασιλεύοντος·
ἀλλ' εἰ βούλεσθε συναπιέναι, ἥκειν ἤδη κελεύει τῆς

2 νυκτός. εἰ δὲ μή, αὔριον πρῲ ἀπιέναι φησίν. ὁ δὲ
Κλέαρχος εἶπεν· Ἀλλ' οὕτω χρὴ ποιεῖν· ἐὰν μὲν
ἥκωμεν, ὥσπερ λέγετε· εἰ δὲ μή, πράττετε ὁποῖον ἂν
τι ὑμῖν οἴησθε μάλιστα συμφέρειν. ὅ τι δὲ ποιήσοι
οὐδὲ τούτοις εἶπε.

3 Μετὰ ταῦτα ἤδη ἡλίου δύνοντος συγκαλέσας τοὺς
στρατηγοὺς καὶ λοχαγοὺς ἔλεξε τοιάδε. Ἐμοί, ὦ
ἄνδρες, θυομένῳ ἰέναι ἐπὶ βασιλέα οὐκ ἐγίγνετο τὰ

bade us tell you this also, that if you remain where you are, you have a truce, if you advance or retire, war. Inform us, therefore, on this point as well: shall you remain and is there a truce, or shall I report from you that there is war?" Clearchus replied: "Report, then, on this point that our view is precisely the same as the King's." "What, then, is that? " said Phalinus. Clearchus replied, "If we remain, a truce, if we retire or advance, war." And Phalinus asked again, "Shall I report truce or war?" And Clearchus again made the same reply, "Truce if we remain, if we retire or advance, war." What he meant to do, however, he did not indicate.

II. So Phalinus and his companions departed. But the messengers from Ariaeus arrived—Procles and Cheirisophus only, for Menon stayed behind with Ariaeus; they reported that Ariaeus said there were many Persians of higher rank than himself and they would not tolerate his being king. " But," the messengers continued, "if you wish to make the return journey with him, he bids you come at once, during the night; otherwise, he says he will set out tomorrow morning." And Clearchus said: "Well, let it be this way: if we come, even as you propose; if we do not, follow whatever course you may think most advantageous to yourselves." But what he meant to do, he did not tell them, either.

After this, when the sun was already setting, he called together the generals and captains and spoke as follows: "When I sacrificed, gentlemen, the omens did not result

---

4 ἀπεκρίνατο some MSS., Hude/Peters Mar.: ἀπεκρίθη ὁ other MSS., Gem.

ἱερά. καὶ εἰκότως ἄρα οὐκ ἐγίγνετο· ὡς γὰρ ἐγὼ νῦν
πυνθάνομαι, ἐν μέσῳ ἡμῶν καὶ βασιλέως ὁ Τίγρης
ποταμός ἐστι ναυσίπορος, ὃν οὐκ ἂν δυναίμεθα ἄνευ
πλοίων διαβῆναι· πλοῖα δὲ ἡμεῖς οὐκ ἔχομεν. οὐ μὲν
δὴ αὐτοῦ γε μένειν οἷόν τε· τὰ γὰρ ἐπιτήδεια οὐκ ἔστιν
ἔχειν· ἰέναι δὲ παρὰ τοὺς Κύρου φίλους πάνυ καλὰ
4 ἡμῖν τὰ ἱερὰ ἦν. ὧδε οὖν χρὴ ποιεῖν· ἀπιόντας δειπνεῖν
ὅ τι τις ἔχει· ἐπειδὰν δὲ σημήνῃ τῷ κέρατι ὡς ἀναπαύεσθαι, συσκευάζεσθε· ἐπειδὰν δὲ τὸ δεύτερον,
ἀνατίθεσθε ἐπὶ τὰ ὑποζύγια· ἐπὶ δὲ τῷ τρίτῳ ἔπεσθε
τῷ ἡγουμένῳ, τὰ μὲν ὑποζύγια ἔχοντες πρὸς τοῦ
5 ποταμοῦ, τὰ δὲ ὅπλα ἔξω. ταῦτ' ἀκούσαντες οἱ
στρατηγοὶ καὶ λοχαγοὶ ἀπῆλθον καὶ ἐποίουν οὕτω.
6 καὶ τὸ λοιπὸν ὁ μὲν ἦρχεν, οἱ δὲ ἐπείθοντο, οὐχ
ἑλόμενοι, ἀλλὰ ὁρῶντες ὅτι μόνος ἐφρόνει οἷα δεῖ τὸν
ἄρχοντα, οἱ δ' ἄλλοι ἄπειροι ἦσαν.[5]
7 Ἐντεῦθεν ἐπεὶ σκότος ἐγένετο Μιλτοκύθης μὲν ὁ
Θρᾷξ ἔχων τούς τε ἱππέας τοὺς μεθ' ἑαυτοῦ εἰς τετταράκοντα καὶ τῶν πεζῶν Θρᾳκῶν ὡς τριακοσίους
8 ηὐτομόλησε πρὸς βασιλέα. Κλέαρχος δὲ τοῖς ἄλλοις
ἡγεῖτο κατὰ τὰ παρηγγελμένα, οἱ δ' εἵποντο· καὶ

---

[5] §6 in the MSS. reads ἀριθμὸς τῆς ὁδοῦ ἣν ἦλθον ἐξ
Ἐφέσου τῆς Ἰωνίας μέχρι τῆς μάχης σταθμοὶ τρεῖς καὶ
ἐνενήκοντα, παρασάγγαι πέντε καὶ τριάκοντα καὶ πεντακόσιοι, στάδιοι πεντήκοντα καὶ ἑξακισχίλιοι καὶ μύριοι·
ἀπὸ δὲ τῆς μάχης ἐλέγοντο εἶναι εἰς Βαβυλῶνα στάδιοι
ἑξήκοντα καὶ τριακόσιοι. This passage is regarded by edd.
generally as an interpolation.

favourably for proceeding against the King. And with good reason, it proves, they were not favourable; for, as I now ascertain, between us and the King is the Tigris, a navigable river, which we could not cross without boats—and boats we have none. On the other hand, it is not possible for us to stay where we are, for we cannot get provisions; but the omens were extremely favourable for our going to join the friends of Cyrus. This, then, is what you are to do: go away and dine on whatever you severally have; when the horn gives the signal for going to rest, pack up; when the second signal is given, load your baggage upon the beasts of burden; and at the third signal follow the van, keeping the beasts of burden on the side next to the river and the hoplites outside." Upon hearing these words the generals and captains went away and proceeded to do as Clearchus had directed. And thenceforth he commanded and they obeyed, not that they had chosen him, but because they saw that he alone possessed the wisdom which a commander should have, while the rest were without experience.[8]

Afterwards, when darkness had come on, Miltocythes the Thracian, with the horsemen under his command, forty in number, and about three hundred Thracian footsoldiers, deserted to the King. But Clearchus put himself at the head of the rest of the troops, following out the plan of his previous orders, and they followed; and they reached the

[8] §6 (see note to text): The length of the journey they had made from Ephesus, in Ionia, to the battlefield was ninety-three stages, five hundred and thirty-five parasangs, or sixteen thousand and fifty stadia; and the distance from the battlefield to Babylon was said to be three hundred and sixty stadia.

ἀφικνοῦνται εἰς τὸν πρῶτον σταθμὸν παρ' Ἀριαῖον
καὶ τὴν ἐκείνου στρατιὰν ἀμφὶ μέσας νύκτας· καὶ ἐν
τάξει θέμενοι τὰ ὅπλα συνῆλθον οἱ στρατηγοὶ καὶ
λοχαγοὶ τῶν Ἑλλήνων παρ' Ἀριαῖον· καὶ ὤμοσαν οἵ
τε Ἕλληνες καὶ ὁ Ἀριαῖος καὶ τῶν σὺν αὐτῷ οἱ
κράτιστοι μήτε προδώσειν ἀλλήλους σύμμαχοί τε
ἔσεσθαι· οἱ δὲ βάρβαροι προσώμοσαν καὶ ἡγήσεσθαι
9 ἀδόλως. ταῦτα δὲ ὤμοσαν, σφάξαντες ταῦρον καὶ
λύκον καὶ κάπρον καὶ κριὸν εἰς ἀσπίδα, οἱ μὲν
Ἕλληνες βάπτοντες ξίφος, οἱ δὲ βάρβαροι λόγχην.
10 ἐπεὶ δὲ τὰ πιστὰ ἐγένετο, εἶπεν ὁ Κλέαρχος· Ἄγε δή,
ὦ Ἀριαῖε, ἐπείπερ ὁ αὐτὸς ἡμῖν στόλος ἐστὶ καὶ ὑμῖν,
εἰπὲ τίνα γνώμην ἔχεις περὶ τῆς πορείας, πότερον
ἄπιμεν ἥνπερ ἤλθομεν ἢ ἄλλην τινὰ ἐννενοηκέναι
11 δοκεῖς ὁδὸν κρείττω. ὁ δὲ εἶπεν· Ἣν μὲν ἤλθομεν
ἀπιόντες παντελῶς ἂν ὑπὸ λιμοῦ ἀπολοίμεθα· ὑπάρχει
γὰρ νῦν ἡμῖν οὐδὲν τῶν ἐπιτηδείων. ἑπτακαίδεκα γὰρ
σταθμῶν τῶν ἐγγυτάτω οὐδὲ δεῦρο ἰόντες ἐκ τῆς
χώρας οὐδὲν εἴχομεν λαμβάνειν· ἔνθα δέ τι ἦν, ἡμεῖς
διαπορευόμενοι κατεδαπανήσαμεν. νῦν δ' ἐπινοοῦμεν
πορεύεσθαι μακροτέραν μέν, τῶν δ' ἐπιτηδείων οὐκ
12 ἀπορήσομεν. πορευτέον δ' ἡμῖν τοὺς πρώτους σταθμοὺς ὡς ἂν δυνώμεθα μακροτάτους, ἵνα ὡς πλεῖστον
ἀποσπασθῶμεν τοῦ βασιλικοῦ στρατεύματος· ἢν γὰρ
ἅπαξ δύο ἢ τριῶν ἡμερῶν ὁδὸν ἀπόσχωμεν, οὐκέτι μὴ
δυνήσεται βασιλεὺς ἡμᾶς καταλαβεῖν. ὀλίγῳ μὲν γὰρ
στρατεύματι οὐ τολμήσει ἐφέπεσθαι· πολὺν δ' ἔχων
στόλον οὐ δυνήσεται ταχέως πορεύεσθαι· ἴσως δὲ καὶ

first stopping-place,[9] and there joined Ariaeus and his army, at about midnight. Then, while they halted under arms in line of battle, the generals and captains had a meeting with Ariaeus; and the two parties—the Greek officers, and Ariaeus together with the highest in rank of his followers—made oath that they would not betray each other and that they would be allies, while the barbarians took an additional pledge to lead the way without treachery. These oaths they sealed by sacrificing a bull, a wolf, a boar, and a ram over a shield, the Greeks dipping a sword in the blood and the barbarians a lance. After the pledges had been given, Clearchus said: "And now, Ariaeus, since you are to make the same journey as we, tell us what view you hold in regard to the route—shall we return by the same way we came, or do you think you have discovered another way that is better?" Ariaeus replied: "If we should return by the way we came, we should perish utterly from starvation, for we now have no provisions whatever. For even on our way hither we were not able to get anything from the country during the last seventeen stages; and where there was anything, we consumed it entirely on our march through. Now, accordingly, we intend to take a route that is longer, to be sure, but one where we shall not lack provisions. And we must make our first marches as long as we can, in order that we be separated as far as possible from the King's army; for if we once get a two or three days' journey away from the King, he will not then be able to overtake us. For he will not dare to pursue us with a small army, and with a large array he will not find it possible to march rapidly; and perhaps, furthermore, he will lack pro-

[9] See i. 3.

τῶν ἐπιτηδείων σπανιεῖ. ταύτην, ἔφη, τὴν γνώμην ἔχω
ἔγωγε.

13 Ἦν δὲ αὕτη ἡ στρατηγία οὐδὲν ἄλλο δυναμένη
ἀποδρᾶναι ἢ ἀποφυγεῖν· ἡ δὲ τύχη ἐστρατήγησε
κάλλιον. ἐπεὶ γὰρ ἡμέρα ἐγένετο, ἐπορεύοντο ἐν δεξιᾷ
ἔχοντες τὸν ἥλιον, λογιζόμενοι ἥξειν ἅμα ἡλίῳ δύνον-
τι εἰς κώμας τῆς Βαβυλωνίας χώρας· καὶ τοῦτο μὲν
14 οὐκ ἐψεύσθησαν. ἔτι δὲ ἀμφὶ δείλην ἔδοξαν πολεμίους
ὁρᾶν ἱππέας· καὶ τῶν τε Ἑλλήνων οἳ μὴ ἔτυχον ἐν
ταῖς τάξεσιν ὄντες εἰς τὰς τάξεις ἔθεον, καὶ Ἀριαῖος,
ἐτύγχανε γὰρ ἐφ᾽ ἁμάξης πορευόμενος διότι ἐτέτρωτο,
15 καταβὰς ἐθωρακίζετο καὶ οἱ σὺν αὐτῷ. ἐν ᾧ δὲ ὡπλί-
ζοντο ἧκον λέγοντες οἱ προπεμφθέντες σκοποὶ ὅτι οὐχ
ἱππεῖς εἰσιν, ἀλλ᾽ ὑποζύγια νέμοιντο. καὶ εὐθὺς ἔγνωσαν πάντες ὅτι ἐγγύς που ἐστρατοπεδεύετο βασιλεύς·
καὶ γὰρ καπνὸς ἐφαίνετο ἐν κώμαις οὐ πρόσω.

16 Κλέαρχος δὲ ἐπὶ μὲν τοὺς πολεμίους οὐκ ἦγεν· ᾔδει
γὰρ καὶ ἀπειρηκότας τοὺς στρατιώτας καὶ ἀσίτους
ὄντας· ἤδη δὲ καὶ ὀψὲ ἦν· οὐ μέντοι οὐδὲ ἀπέκλινε,
φυλαττόμενος μὴ δοκοίη φεύγειν, ἀλλ᾽ εὐθύωρον ἄγων
ἅμα τῷ ἡλίῳ δυομένῳ εἰς τὰς ἐγγυτάτω κώμας τοὺς
πρώτους ἔχων κατεσκήνωσεν, ἐξ ὧν διήρπαστο ὑπὸ
τοῦ βασιλικοῦ στρατεύματος καὶ αὐτὰ τὰ ἀπὸ τῶν
17 οἰκιῶν ξύλα. οἱ μὲν οὖν πρῶτοι ὅμως τρόπῳ τινὶ
ἐστρατοπεδεύσαντο, οἱ δὲ ὕστεροι σκοταῖοι προσιόντες ὡς ἐτύγχανον ἕκαστοι ηὐλίζοντο, καὶ κραυγὴν
πολλὴν ἐποίουν καλοῦντες ἀλλήλους, ὥστε καὶ τοὺς
πολεμίους ἀκούειν· ὥστε οἱ μὲν ἐγγύτατα τῶν πολε-

visions. This," said he, "is the view which I hold, for my part."

This plan of campaign meant nothing else than effecting an escape, either by stealth or by speed; but fortune planned better. For when day came, they set out on the march, keeping the sun on their right and calculating that at sunset they would reach villages in Babylonia—and in this they were not disappointed. But while it was still afternoon they thought that they saw horsemen of the enemy; and such of the Greeks as chanced not to be in the lines proceeded to run to the lines, while Ariaeus, who was making the journey in a wagon because he was wounded, got down and put on his breastplate, and his attendants followed his example. While they were arming themselves, however, the scouts who had been sent ahead returned with the report that it was not horsemen, but pack animals grazing. Straightway everybody realized that the King was encamping somewhere in the neighbourhood—in fact, smoke was seen in villages not far away.

Clearchus, however, would not advance against the enemy, for he knew that his troops were not only tired out, but without food, and, besides, it was already late; still, he would not turn aside, either, for he was taking care to avoid the appearance of flight, but leading the army straight ahead he encamped with the van at sunset in the nearest villages, from which the King's army had plundered even the very timbers of the houses. The van nevertheless encamped after a fashion, but the men who were further back, coming up in the dark, had to bivouac each as best they could, and they made a great uproar with calling one another, so that the enemy also heard it; the result was that

18 μίων καὶ ἔφυγον ἐκ τῶν σκηνωμάτων. δῆλον δὲ τοῦτο
τῇ ὑστεραίᾳ ἐγένετο· οὔτε γὰρ ὑποζύγιον ἔτ᾽ οὐδὲν
ἐφάνη οὔτε στρατόπεδον οὔτε καπνὸς οὐδαμοῦ πλησίον. ἐξεπλάγη δέ, ὡς ἔοικε, καὶ βασιλεὺς τῇ ἐφόδῳ
τοῦ στρατεύματος. ἐδήλωσε δὲ τοῦτο οἷς τῇ ὑστεραίᾳ
19 ἔπραττε. προϊούσης μέντοι τῆς νυκτὸς ταύτης καὶ τοῖς
Ἕλλησι φόβος ἐμπίπτει, καὶ θόρυβος καὶ δοῦπος ἦν
20 οἷον εἰκὸς φόβου ἐμπεσόντος γενέσθαι. Κλέαρχος δὲ
Τολμίδην Ἠλεῖον, ὃν ἐτύγχανεν ἔχων παρ᾽ ἑαυτῷ
κήρυκα ἄριστον τῶν τότε, τοῦτον ἀνειπεῖν ἐκέλευσε
σιγὴν κατακηρύξαντα ὅτι προαγορεύουσιν οἱ ἄρχοντες, ὃς ἂν τὸν ἀφέντα τὸν ὄνον εἰς τὰ ὅπλα μηνύσῃ,
21 ὅτι λήψεται μισθὸν τάλαντον ἀργυρίου. ἐπεὶ δὲ ταῦτα
ἐκηρύχθη, ἔγνωσαν οἱ στρατιῶται ὅτι κενὸς ὁ φόβος
εἴη καὶ οἱ ἄρχοντες σῷ. ἅμα δὲ ὄρθρῳ παρήγγειλεν ὁ
Κλέαρχος εἰς τάξιν τὰ ὅπλα τίθεσθαι τοὺς Ἕλληνας
ᾗπερ εἶχον ὅτε ἦν ἡ μάχη.

III. Ὁ δὲ δὴ ἔγραψα ὅτι βασιλεὺς ἐξεπλάγη τῇ
ἐφόδῳ, τῇδε δῆλον ἦν. τῇ μὲν γὰρ πρόσθεν ἡμέρᾳ
πέμπων τὰ ὅπλα παραδιδόναι ἐκέλευε, τότε δὲ ἅμα
2 ἡλίῳ ἀνατέλλοντι κήρυκας ἔπεμψε περὶ σπονδῶν. οἱ δ᾽
ἐπεὶ ἦλθον πρὸς τοὺς προφύλακας, ἐζήτουν τοὺς
ἄρχοντας. ἐπειδὴ δὲ ἀπήγγειλαν οἱ προφύλακες, Κλέαρχος τυχὼν τότε τὰς τάξεις ἐπισκοπῶν εἶπε τοῖς
προφύλαξι κελεύειν τοὺς κήρυκας περιμένειν ἄχρι ἂν
3 σχολάσῃ. ἐπεὶ δὲ κατέστησε τὸ στράτευμα ὥστε
καλῶς ἔχειν ὁρᾶσθαι πάντη φάλαγγα πυκνήν, τῶν δὲ

the nearest of the enemy actually took to flight from their quarters. This became clear on the following day, for not a pack animal was any more to be seen nor camp nor smoke anywhere near. Even the King, so it seems, was terrified by the approach of the army. He made this evident by what he did the next day. However, as the night went on a panic fell upon the Greeks also, and there was confusion and din of the sort that may be expected when panic has seized an army. Clearchus, however, directed Tolmides the Elean, who chanced to be with him as herald and was the best herald of his time, to make this proclamation, after he had ordered silence: "The commanders give public notice that whoever informs on the man who let the ass loose among the arms shall receive a reward of a talent of silver." When this proclamation had been made, the soldiers realized that their fears were groundless and their commanders safe. And at dawn Clearchus ordered the Greeks to get under arms in line of battle just as they were when the battle took place.

III. The fact which I just stated, that the King was terrified by the approach of the Greeks, was made clear in the following way: although on the day before he had sent and ordered them to give up their arms, he now, at sunrise, sent heralds to negotiate a truce. When these heralds reached the pickets, they asked for the commanders. And when the pickets reported, Clearchus, who chanced at the time to be inspecting the ranks, told the pickets to direct the heralds to wait till he should be at leisure. Then after he had arranged the army so that it should present a fine appearance from every side as a compact phalanx, with

ἀόπλων[6] δὲ μηδένα καταφανῆ εἶναι, ἐκάλεσε τοὺς
ἀγγέλους, καὶ αὐτός τε προῆλθε τούς τε εὐοπλοτάτους
ἔχων καὶ εὐειδεστάτους τῶν αὑτοῦ στρατιωτῶν καὶ
4 τοῖς ἄλλοις στρατηγοῖς ταῦτα ἔφρασεν. ἐπεὶ δὲ ἦν
πρὸς τοῖς ἀγγέλοις, ἀνηρώτα τί βούλοιντο. οἱ δ᾽ ἔλεγον ὅτι περὶ σπονδῶν ἥκοιεν ἄνδρες οἵτινες ἱκανοὶ
ἔσονται τά τε παρὰ βασιλέως τοῖς Ἕλλησιν ἀπαγ-
5 γεῖλαι καὶ τὰ παρὰ τῶν Ἑλλήνων βασιλεῖ. ὁ δὲ
ἀπεκρίνατο· Ἀπαγγέλλετε τοίνυν αὐτῷ ὅτι μάχης δεῖ
πρῶτον· ἄριστον γὰρ οὐκ ἔστιν οὐδ᾽ ὁ τολμήσων περὶ
σπονδῶν λέγειν τοῖς Ἕλλησι μὴ πορίσας ἄριστον.
6 ταῦτα ἀκούσαντες οἱ ἄγγελοι ἀπήλαυνον, καὶ ἧκον
ταχύ· ᾧ καὶ δῆλον ἦν ὅτι ἐγγύς που βασιλεὺς ἦν ἢ
ἄλλος τις ᾧ ἐπετέτακτο ταῦτα πράττειν· ἔλεγον δὲ ὅτι
εἰκότα δοκοῖεν λέγειν βασιλεῖ, καὶ ἥκοιεν ἡγεμόνας
ἔχοντες οἳ αὐτούς, ἐὰν σπονδαὶ γένωνται, ἄξουσιν
7 ἔνθεν ἕξουσι τὰ ἐπιτήδεια. ὁ δὲ ἠρώτα εἰ αὐτοῖς τοῖς
ἀνδράσι σπένδοιτο [τοῖς] ἰοῦσι καὶ ἀπιοῦσιν, ἢ καὶ
τοῖς ἄλλοις ἔσοιντο σπονδαί. οἱ δέ, Ἅπασιν, ἔφασαν,
8 μέχρι ἂν βασιλεῖ τὰ παρ᾽ ὑμῶν διαγγελθῇ. ἐπεὶ δὲ
ταῦτα εἶπαν, μεταστησάμενος αὐτοὺς ὁ Κλέαρχος
ἐβουλεύετο· καὶ ἐδόκει τὰς σπονδὰς ποιεῖσθαι καὶ καθ᾽
9 ἡσυχίαν ἐλθεῖν τε ἐπὶ τὰ ἐπιτήδεια καὶ λαβεῖν. ὁ δὲ
Κλέαρχος εἶπε· Δοκεῖ μὲν κἀμοὶ ταῦτα· οὐ μέντοι ταχύ
γε ἀπαγγελῶ, ἀλλὰ διατρίψω ἔστ᾽ ἂν ὀκνήσωσιν οἱ
ἄγγελοι μὴ ἀποδόξῃ ἡμῖν τὰς σπονδὰς ποιήσασθαι·

---

[6] τῶν δὲ ἀόπλων some MSS.: others ἐκ τῶν ὅπλων δὲ.

no one of those without armor to be seen, he summoned the messengers; and he himself came forward with the best armed and best looking of his own troops and told the other generals to do likewise. Once face to face with the messengers, he inquired what they wanted. They replied that they had come to negotiate for a truce, and were empowered to report the King's proposals to the Greeks and the Greeks' proposals to the King. And Clearchus answered: "Report to him, then, that we must have a battle first; for we have had no breakfast, and there is no man alive who will dare to talk to Greeks about a truce unless he provides them with a breakfast." Upon hearing these words the messengers rode away, but were speedily back again, which made it evident that the King, or someone else who had been charged with carrying on these negotiations, was somewhere near. They stated that what the Greeks said seemed to the King reasonable, and that they had now brought guides with them who would lead the Greeks, in case a truce should be concluded, to a place where they could get provisions. Thereupon Clearchus asked whether he was making a truce merely with the men who were coming and going, or whether the truce would bind the others also. "Every man of them," they replied, "until your message is carried to the King." When they had said this, Clearchus had them retire and took counsel about the matter; and it was thought best to conclude the truce speedily, so that they could go and get the provisions without being molested. And Clearchus said: "I, too, agree with this view; nevertheless, I shall not so report at once, but I shall delay until the messengers get fearful of our

οἶμαί γε μέντοι, ἔφη, καὶ τοῖς ἡμετέροις στρατιώταις
τὸν αὐτὸν φόβον παρέσεσθαι. ἐπεὶ δὲ ἐδόκει καιρὸς
εἶναι, ἀπήγγελλεν ὅτι σπένδοιτο, καὶ εὐθὺς ἡγεῖσθαι
ἐκέλευε πρὸς τἀπιτήδεια.

10   Καὶ οἱ μὲν ἡγοῦντο, Κλέαρχος μέντοι ἐπορεύετο
τὰς μὲν σπονδὰς ποιησάμενος, τὸ δὲ στράτευμα ἔχων
ἐν τάξει, καὶ αὐτὸς ὠπισθοφυλάκει. καὶ ἐνετύγχανον
τάφροις καὶ αὐλῶσιν ὕδατος πλήρεσιν, ὡς μὴ δύνασθαι διαβαίνειν ἄνευ γεφυρῶν· ἀλλ᾽ ἐποιοῦντο δια-
βάσεις ἐκ τῶν φοινίκων οἳ ἦσαν ἐκπεπτωκότες, τοὺς
11 δὲ καὶ ἐξέκοπτον. καὶ ἐνταῦθα ἦν Κλέαρχον καταμα-
θεῖν ὡς ἐπεστάτει, ἐν μὲν τῇ ἀριστερᾷ χειρὶ τὸ δόρυ
ἔχων, ἐν δὲ τῇ δεξιᾷ βακτηρίαν· καὶ εἴ τις αὐτῷ δοκοίη
τῶν πρὸς τοῦτο τεταγμένων βλακεύειν, ἐκλεγόμενος
τὸν ἐπιτήδειον ἔπαισεν ἄν, καὶ ἅμα αὐτὸς προσ-
ελάμβανεν εἰς τὸν πηλὸν ἐμβαίνων· ὥστε πᾶσιν
12 αἰσχύνην εἶναι μὴ οὐ συσπουδάζειν. καὶ ἐτάχθησαν
πρὸς αὐτὸ οἱ εἰς τριάκοντα ἔτη γεγονότες· ἐπεὶ δὲ
Κλέαρχον ἑώρων σπουδάζοντα, προσελάμβανον καὶ
13 οἱ πρεσβύτεροι. πολὺ δὲ μᾶλλον ὁ Κλέαρχος ἔσπευδεν, ὑποπτεύων μὴ ἀεὶ οὕτω πλήρεις εἶναι τὰς τάφρους
ὕδατος· οὐ γὰρ ἦν ὥρα οἵα τὸ πεδίον ἄρδειν· ἀλλ᾽ ἵνα
πολλὰ τὰ ἄπορα φαίνοιτο τοῖς Ἕλλησι εἶναι εἰς τὴν
πορείαν, τούτου ἕνεκα βασιλέα ὑπώπτευεν ἐπὶ τὸ
πεδίον τὸ ὕδωρ ἀφεικέναι.

14   Πορευόμενοι δὲ ἀφίκοντο εἰς κώμας ὅθεν ἀπέδειξαν
οἱ ἡγεμόνες λαμβάνειν τὰ ἐπιτήδεια. ἐνῆν δὲ σῖτος
πολὺς καὶ οἶνος φοινίκων καὶ ὄξος ἑψητὸν ἀπὸ τῶν

deciding not to conclude the truce; to be sure," he said, "I suppose that our own soldiers will also feel the same fear." When, accordingly, it seemed that the proper time had come, he reported that he accepted the truce, and directed them to lead the way immediately to the provisions.

They proceeded, then, to lead the way, but Clearchus, although he had made the truce, kept his army in line of battle on the march, and commanded the rearguard himself. And they kept coming upon trenches and canals, full of water, which could not be crossed without bridges. They made bridges of a kind, however, out of the palm trees which had fallen and others which they cut down themselves. And here one could well observe how Clearchus commanded; he had his spear in his left hand and in his right a stick, and whenever he thought that anyone of the men assigned to this task was shirking, he would pick out the right man and deal him a blow, while at the same time he would get into the mud and lend a hand himself; the result was that everyone was ashamed not to match him in energy.[10] The men detailed to the work were all those up to thirty years of age, but the older men also took hold when they saw Clearchus in such energetic haste. Now Clearchus was in a far greater hurry because he suspected that the trenches were not always full of water in this way, for it was not a proper time to be irrigating the plain; his suspicion was, then, that the King had let the water into the plain in order that several obstacles in the way of their journey appear to exist for the Greeks.

The march at length brought them to villages where the guides directed them to get provisions. In these villages was grain in abundance and palm wine and a sour drink

[10] Cf. I. v. 7ff.

15 αὐτῶν. αὗται δὲ αἱ βάλανοι τῶν φοινίκων οἵας μὲν ἐν
τοῖς Ἕλλησιν ἔστιν ἰδεῖν τοῖς οἰκέταις ἀπέκειντο, αἱ
δὲ τοῖς δεσπόταις ἀποκείμεναι ἦσαν ἀπόλεκτοι, θαυ-
μάσιαι τὸ κάλλος καὶ τὸ μέγεθος, ἡ δὲ ὄψις ἠλέκτρου
οὐδὲν διέφερε· τὰς δέ τινας ξηραίνοντες τραγήματα
ἀπετίθεσαν. καὶ ἦν καὶ παρὰ πότον ἡδὺ μέν, κεφαλαλ-
16 γὲς δέ. ἐνταῦθα καὶ τὸν ἐγκέφαλον τοῦ φοίνικος πρῶτον ἔφαγον οἱ στρατιῶται, καὶ οἱ πολλοὶ ἐθαύμαζον τό
τε εἶδος καὶ τὴν ἰδιότητα τῆς ἡδονῆς. ἦν δὲ σφόδρα
καὶ τοῦτο κεφαλαλγές. ὁ δὲ φοῖνιξ ὅθεν ἐξαιρεθείη ὁ
ἐγκέφαλος ὅλος ἐξηραίνετο.

17 Ἐνταῦθα ἔμειναν ἡμέρας τρεῖς· καὶ παρὰ μεγάλου
βασιλέως ἦκε Τισσαφέρνης καὶ ὁ τῆς βασιλέως γυναικὸς ἀδελφὸς καὶ ἄλλοι Πέρσαι τρεῖς· δοῦλοι δὲ
πολλοὶ εἵποντο. ἐπεὶ δὲ ἀπήντησαν αὐτοῖς οἱ τῶν
Ἑλλήνων στρατηγοί, ἔλεγε πρῶτος Τισσαφέρνης δι᾽
18 ἑρμηνέως τοιάδε. Ἐγώ, ὦ ἄνδρες Ἕλληνες, γείτων
οἰκῶ τῇ Ἑλλάδι, καὶ ἐπεὶ ὑμᾶς εἶδον εἰς πολλὰ κἀμή-
χανα πεπτωκότας, εὕρημα ἐποιησάμην εἴ πως δυναίμην παρὰ βασιλέως αἰτήσασθαι δοῦναι ἐμοὶ ἀπο-
σῶσαι ὑμᾶς εἰς τὴν Ἑλλάδα. οἶμαι γὰρ ἂν οὐκ
ἀχαρίστως μοι ἔχειν οὔτε πρὸς ὑμῶν οὔτε πρὸς τῆς
19 πάσης Ἑλλάδος. ταῦτα δὲ γνοὺς ᾐτούμην βασιλέα,
λέγων αὐτῷ ὅτι δικαίως ἄν μοι χαρίζοιτο, ὅτι αὐτῷ
Κῦρόν τε ἐπιστρατεύοντα πρῶτος ἤγγειλα καὶ βοή-
θειαν ἔχων ἅμα τῇ ἀγγελίᾳ ἀφικόμην, καὶ μόνος τῶν
κατὰ τοὺς Ἕλληνας τεταγμένων οὐκ ἔφυγον, ἀλλὰ
διήλασα καὶ συνέμειξα βασιλεῖ ἐν τῷ ὑμετέρῳ στρα-

made from the same by boiling. As for the dates themselves of the palm, the sort that one can see in Greece were set apart for the servants, while those laid away for the masters were selected ones, remarkable for their beauty and size and with a colour altogether resembling that of amber; others, again, they would dry and store away for sweet-meats. These made a pleasant morsel also at a symposium, but were apt to cause headache. Here also the soldiers ate for the first time the crown of the palm, and most of them were surprised not alone at its appearance, but at the peculiar nature of its flavour. This, too, however, was exceedingly apt to cause headache. And when the crown was removed from a palm, the whole tree would wither.

In these villages they remained three days; and there came to them, as messengers from the Great King, Tissaphernes and the brother of the King's wife and three other Persians; and many slaves followed in their train. When the Greek generals met them, Tissaphernes, through an interpreter, began the speaking with the following words: "Men of Greece, in my own home I am a neighbour of yours, and when I saw you plunged into many difficulties, I thought it would be a piece of good fortune if I could in any way gain permission from the King to take you back safe to Greece. For I fancy I should not go without thanks, both from you and from all Greece. After reaching this conclusion I presented my request to the King, saying to him that it would be fair for him to do me a favour, because I was the first to report to him that Cyrus was marching against him, because along with my report I brought him aid also, and because I was the only man among those posted opposite the Greeks who did not take to flight, but, on the contrary, I charged through and joined forces with the

171

τοπέδῳ ἔνθα βασιλεὺς ἀφίκετο, ἐπεὶ Κῦρον ἀπέκτεινε
καὶ τοὺς σὺν Κύρῳ βαρβάρους ἐδίωξα σὺν τοῖσδε
τοῖς παροῦσι νῦν μετ᾽ ἐμοῦ, οἵπερ αὐτῷ εἰσι πιστότα-
20 τοι. καὶ περὶ μὲν τούτων ὑπέσχετό μοι βουλεύσεσθαι·
ἐρέσθαι δέ με ὑμᾶς ἐκέλευεν ἐλθόντα τίνος ἕνεκεν
ἐστρατεύσατε ἐπ᾽ αὐτόν. καὶ συμβουλεύω ὑμῖν με-
τρίως ἀποκρίνασθαι, ἵνα μοι εὐπρακτότερον ᾖ ἐάν τι
δύνωμαι ἀγαθὸν ὑμῖν παρ᾽ αὐτοῦ διαπράξασθαι.

21   Πρὸς ταῦτα μεταστάντες οἱ Ἕλληνες ἐβουλεύοντο·
καὶ ἀπεκρίναντο, Κλέαρχος δ᾽ ἔλεγεν· Ἡμεῖς οὔτε
συνήλθομεν ὡς βασιλεῖ πολεμήσοντες οὔτε ἐπορευόμεθα ἐπὶ βασιλέα, ἀλλὰ πολλὰς προφάσεις Κῦρος
ηὕρισκεν, ὡς καὶ σὺ εὖ οἶσθα, ἵνα ὑμᾶς τε ἀπαρα-
22 σκεύους λάβοι καὶ ἡμᾶς ἐνθάδε ἀναγάγοι. ἐπεὶ μέντοι
ἤδη αὐτὸν ἑωρῶμεν ἐν δεινῷ ὄντα, ᾐσχύνθημεν καὶ
θεοὺς καὶ ἀνθρώπους προδοῦναι αὐτόν, ἐν τῷ πρόσθεν
23 χρόνῳ παρέχοντες ἡμᾶς αὐτοὺς εὖ ποιεῖν. ἐπεὶ δὲ
Κῦρος τέθνηκεν, οὔτε βασιλεῖ ἀντιποιούμεθα τῆς ἀρχῆς οὔτ᾽ ἔστιν ὅτου ἕνεκα βουλοίμεθ᾽ ἂν τὴν βασιλέως
χώραν κακῶς ποιεῖν οὐδ᾽ αὐτὸν ἀποκτεῖναι ἂν ἐθέλοιμεν, πορευοίμεθα δ᾽ ἂν οἴκαδε, εἴ τις ἡμᾶς μὴ λυποίη·
ἀδικοῦντα μέντοι πειρασόμεθα σὺν τοῖς θεοῖς ἀμύνα-
σθαι· ἐὰν μέντοι τις ἡμᾶς καὶ εὖ ποιῶν ὑπάρχῃ, καὶ
τούτου εἴς γε δύναμιν οὐχ ἡττησόμεθα εὖ ποιοῦντες.
24 ὁ μὲν οὕτως εἶπεν· ἀκούσας δὲ ὁ Τισσαφέρνης Ταῦτα,
ἔφη, ἐγὼ ἀπαγγελῶ βασιλεῖ καὶ ὑμῖν πάλιν τὰ παρ᾽
ἐκείνου· μέχρι δ᾽ ἂν ἐγὼ ἥκω αἱ σπονδαὶ μενόντων·

King in your camp, where the King had arrived after slaying Cyrus, and I pursued the barbarians of Cyrus' army with the help of these men now present with me, men who are most faithful to the King. And, he promised me that he would consider this request of mine, but, meanwhile, he bade me come and ask you for what reason you took the field against him. Now I advise you to answer with moderation, that so it may be easier for me to obtain for you at his hands whatever good thing I may be able to obtain."

Hereupon the Greeks withdrew and proceeded to take counsel; then they gave their answer, Clearchus acting as spokesman: "We neither gathered together with the intention of making war upon the King nor were we marching against the King, but Cyrus kept finding many pretexts, as you also are well aware, in order that he might take you unprepared and bring us hither. When, however, the time came when we saw that he was in danger, we felt ashamed in the sight of gods and men to desert him, seeing that in former days we had been putting ourselves in the way of being benefited by him. But since Cyrus is dead, we are neither contending with the King for his realm nor is there any reason why we should desire to do harm to the King's territory or wish to slay the King himself, but rather we should return to our homes, if no one should molest us. If, however, anyone seeks to injure us, we shall try with the help of the gods to retaliate. On the other hand, if anyone is kind enough to do us a service, we shall not, so far as we have the power, be outdone in doing a service to him." So he spoke, and upon hearing his words Tissaphernes said: "This message I shall carry to the King, and bring back his to you; and until I return, let the truce continue, and we

ἀγορὰν δὲ ἡμεῖς παρέξομεν.

25 Καὶ εἰς μὲν τὴν ὑστεραίαν οὐχ ἧκεν· ὥσθ᾽ οἱ Ἕλληνες ἐφρόντιζον· τῇ δὲ τρίτῃ ἥκων ἔλεγεν ὅτι διαπε-
πραγμένος ἥκοι παρὰ βασιλέως δοθῆναι αὐτῷ σῴζειν
τοὺς Ἕλληνας, καίπερ πολλῶν ἀντιλεγόντων ὡς οὐκ
ἄξιον εἴη βασιλεῖ ἀφεῖναι τοὺς ἐφ᾽ ἑαυτὸν στρατευ-
26 σαμένους. τέλος δὲ εἶπε· Καὶ νῦν ἔξεστιν ὑμῖν πιστὰ
λαβεῖν παρ᾽ ἡμῶν ἦ μὴν φιλίαν παρέξειν ὑμῖν τὴν
χώραν καὶ ἀδόλως ἀπάξειν εἰς τὴν Ἑλλάδα ἀγορὰν
παρέχοντας· ὅπου δ᾽ ἂν μὴ παρέχωμεν ἀγοράν, λαμ-
27 βάνειν ὑμᾶς ἐκ τῆς χώρας ἐάσομεν τὰ ἐπιτήδεια. ὑμᾶς
δὲ αὖ ἡμῖν δεήσει ὀμόσαι ἦ μὴν πορεύσεσθαι ὡς διὰ
φιλίας ἀσινῶς σῖτα καὶ ποτὰ λαμβάνοντας ὁπόταν
μὴ ἀγορὰν παρέχωμεν· ἢν δὲ παρέχωμεν ἀγοράν,
28 ὠνουμένους ἕξειν τὰ ἐπιτήδεια. ταῦτα ἔδοξε, καὶ
ὤμοσαν καὶ δεξιὰς ἔδοσαν Τισσαφέρνης καὶ ὁ τῆς
βασιλέως γυναικὸς ἀδελφὸς τοῖς τῶν Ἑλλήνων στρατηγοῖς καὶ λοχαγοῖς καὶ ἔλαβον παρὰ τῶν Ἑλλήνων.
29 μετὰ δὲ ταῦτα Τισσαφέρνης εἶπε· Νῦν μὲν δὴ ἄπειμι
ὡς βασιλέα· ἐπειδὰν δὲ διαπράξωμαι ἃ δέομαι, ἥξω
συσκευασάμενος ὡς ἀπάξων ὑμᾶς εἰς τὴν Ἑλλάδα καὶ
αὐτὸς ἀπιὼν ἐπὶ τὴν ἐμαυτοῦ ἀρχήν.

IV. Μετὰ ταῦτα περιέμενον Τισσαφέρνην οἵ τε
Ἕλληνες καὶ ὁ Ἀριαῖος ἐγγὺς ἀλλήλων ἐστρατο-
πεδευμένοι ἡμέρας πλείους ἢ εἴκοσιν. ἐν δὲ ταύταις
ἀφικνοῦνται πρὸς Ἀριαῖον καὶ οἱ ἀδελφοὶ καὶ οἱ ἄλλοι
ἀναγκαῖοι καὶ πρὸς τοὺς σὺν ἐκείνῳ Περσῶν τινες,

will provide a market."[11]

The next day he did not return, and the Greeks, consequently, were anxious; but on the third day he came and said that he had secured permission from the King to save the Greeks, although many opposed the plan, urging that it was not fitting for the King to allow those who had undertaken a campaign against him to escape. In conclusion he said: "And now you may receive pledges from us that in very truth the territory you pass through shall be friendly and that we will lead you back to Greece without treachery, providing you with a market; and wherever we do not furnish a market we will allow you to take provisions from the country. And you, on your side, will have to swear to us that in very truth you will proceed as you would through a friendly country, doing no damage and taking food and drink from the country only when we do not provide a market, but that, if we do provide a market, you will obtain provisions by purchase." This was resolved upon, and Tissaphernes and the brother of the King's wife made oath and gave their right hands in pledge to the generals and captains of the Greeks, receiving the same also from the Greeks. After this Tissaphernes said: "Now I am going back to the King; but when I have accomplished what I desire, I shall return, fully equipped to conduct you back to Greece and to go home myself to my own province."

IV. After this the Greeks and Ariaeus, encamped close by one another, waited for Tissaphernes, more than twenty days. During this time Ariaeus' brothers and other relatives came to him and certain Persians came to his follow-

11 See note on I. ii. 18.

παραθαρρύνοντές[7] τε καὶ δεξιὰς ἔνιοι παρὰ βασιλέως
φέροντες μὴ μνησικακήσειν βασιλέα αὐτοῖς τῆς σὺν
Κύρῳ ἐπιστρατείας μηδὲ ἄλλου μηδενὸς τῶν παροι-
2 χομένων. τούτων δὲ γιγνομένων ἔνδηλοι ἦσαν οἱ περὶ
Ἀριαῖον ἧττον προσέχοντες τοῖς Ἕλλησι τὸν νοῦν·
ὥστε καὶ διὰ τοῦτο τοῖς μὲν πολλοῖς τῶν Ἑλλήνων
οὐκ ἤρεσκον, ἀλλὰ προσιόντες τῷ Κλεάρχῳ ἔλε-
3 γον καὶ τοῖς ἄλλοις στρατηγοῖς· Τί μένομεν ἢ οὐκ
ἐπιστάμεθα ὅτι βασιλεὺς ἡμᾶς ἀπολέσαι ἂν περὶ
παντὸς ποιήσαιτο, ἵνα καὶ τοῖς ἄλλοις Ἕλλησι φόβος
ᾖ ἐπὶ βασιλέα μέγαν στρατεύειν; καὶ νῦν μὲν ἡμᾶς
ὑπάγεται μένειν διὰ τὸ διεσπάρθαι αὐτῷ τὸ στρά-
τευμα· ἐπὴν δὲ πάλιν ἁλισθῇ αὐτῷ ἡ στρατιά, οὐκ
4 ἔστιν ὅπως οὐκ ἐπιθήσεται ἡμῖν. ἴσως δέ που ἢ
ἀποσκάπτει τι ἢ ἀποτειχίζει, ὡς ἄπορος ᾖ ἡ ὁδός. οὐ
γάρ ποτε ἑκών γε βουλήσεται ἡμᾶς ἐλθόντας εἰς τὴν
Ἑλλάδα ἀπαγγεῖλαι ὡς ἡμεῖς τοσοίδε ὄντες ἐνικῶμεν
τὴν βασιλέως δύναμιν ἐπὶ ταῖς θύραις αὐτοῦ καὶ
5 καταγελάσαντες ἀπήλθομεν. Κλέαρχος δὲ ἀπεκρίνατο
τοῖς ταῦτα λέγουσιν· Ἐγὼ ἐνθυμοῦμαι μὲν καὶ ταῦτα
πάντα· ἐννοῶ δ' ὅτι εἰ νῦν ἄπιμεν, δόξομεν ἐπὶ πολέμῳ ἀπιέναι καὶ παρὰ τὰς σπονδὰς ποιεῖν. ἔπειτα
πρῶτον μὲν ἀγορὰν οὐδεὶς παρέξει ἡμῖν οὐδὲ ὅθεν
ἐπισιτιούμεθα· αὖθις δὲ ὁ ἡγησόμενος οὐδεὶς ἔσται·
καὶ ἅμα ταῦτα ποιούντων ἡμῶν εὐθὺς Ἀριαῖος ἀφ-

---

[7] παραθαρρύνοντές some MSS.: others παρεθάρρυνον.

ers, offering encouragement, and some bringing pledges from the King that the King would bear them no ill-will because of their campaign with Cyrus against him or because of anything else in the past. While these things were going on, it was evident that Ariaeus and his followers paid less regard to the Greeks; this, accordingly, was another reason why the greater part of the Greeks were not pleased with them, and they would go to Clearchus and the other generals and say: "Why are we lingering? Do we not understand that the King would like above everything else to destroy us, in order that the rest of the Greeks also may be afraid to march against the Great King? For the moment he is scheming to keep us here because his army is scattered, but when he has collected his forces again, there is no question but that he will attack us. Or perhaps he is digging a trench or building a wall somewhere to cut us off and make our road impassable. For never, if he can help it, will he choose to let us go back to Greece and report that we, few as we are, were victorious over the King's forces at his very gates, and then laughed in his face and came home again." To those who talked in this way Clearchus replied: "I too have in mind all these things; but I reflect that if we go away now, it will seem that we are going away with hostile intent and are acting in violation of the truce. And then, in the first place, no one will provide us a market or a place from which we can get provisions; secondly, we shall have no one to guide us; again, the moment we take this course Ariaeus will instantly desert us; conse-

εστήξει·[8] ὥστε φίλος ἡμῖν οὐδεὶς λελείψεται, ἀλλὰ καὶ
6 οἱ πρόσθεν ὄντες πολέμιοι ἡμῖν ἔσονται. ποταμὸς δ᾽
εἰ μέν τις καὶ ἄλλος ἄρα ἡμῖν ἐστι διαβατέος οὐκ
οἶδα· τὸν δ᾽ οὖν Εὐφράτην οἴδαμεν ὅτι ἀδύνατον διαβῆναι κωλυόντων πολεμίων. οὐ μὲν δὴ ἂν μάχεσθαί
γε δέῃ, ἱππεῖς εἰσιν ἡμῖν σύμμαχοι, τῶν δὲ πολεμίων
ἱππεῖς εἰσι πλεῖστοι καὶ πλείστου ἄξιοι· ὥστε νικῶντες μὲν τίνα ἂν ἀποκτείναιμεν ἡττωμένων δὲ οὐδένα
7 οἷόν τε σωθῆναι. ἐγὼ μὲν οὖν βασιλέα, ᾧ οὕτω πολλά
ἐστι τὰ σύμμαχα, εἴπερ προθυμεῖται ἡμᾶς ἀπολέσαι,
οὐκ οἶδα ὅ τι δεῖ αὐτὸν ὀμόσαι καὶ δεξιὰν δοῦναι καὶ
θεοὺς ἐπιορκῆσαι καὶ τὰ ἑαυτοῦ πιστὰ ἄπιστα ποιῆσαι Ἕλλησί τε καὶ βαρβάροις. τοιαῦτα πολλὰ ἔλεγεν.
8   Ἐν δὲ τούτῳ ἧκε Τισσαφέρνης ἔχων τὴν ἑαυτοῦ
δύναμιν ὡς εἰς οἶκον ἀπιὼν καὶ Ὀρόντας τὴν ἑαυτοῦ
δύναμιν· ἦγε δὲ καὶ τὴν θυγατέρα τὴν βασιλέως ἐπὶ
9 γάμῳ. ἐντεῦθεν δὲ ἤδη Τισσαφέρνους ἡγουμένου καὶ
ἀγορὰν παρέχοντος ἐπορεύοντο· ἐπορεύετο δὲ καὶ Ἀριαῖος τὸ Κύρου βαρβαρικὸν ἔχων στράτευμα ἅμα
Τισσαφέρνει καὶ Ὀρόντᾳ καὶ συνεστρατοπεδεύετο
10 σὺν ἐκείνοις. οἱ δὲ Ἕλληνες ὑφορῶντες τούτους αὐτοὶ
ἐφ᾽ ἑαυτῶν ἐχώρουν ἡγεμόνας ἔχοντες. ἐστρατοπε-

[8] ἀφεστήξει some MSS., Hude/Peters, Mar.: other MSS. have
ἀποσταίη, which Gem. adopts, inserting ἂν after ἅμα, with
Rehdantz.

quently we shall have not a friend left, for even those who were friends before will be our enemies. Then remember the rivers—there may be others, for aught I know, that we must cross, but we know about the Euphrates at any rate, that it cannot possibly be crossed in the face of an enemy. Furthermore, in case fighting becomes necessary, we have no cavalry to help us, whereas the enemy's cavalry are exceedingly numerous and exceedingly efficient; hence if we are victorious, whom could we kill?[12] And if we are defeated, not one of us can be saved. For my part, therefore, I cannot see why the King, who has so many advantages on his side, should need, in case he is really eager to destroy us, to make oath and give pledge and forswear himself by the gods and make his good faith unfaithful in the eyes of Greeks and barbarians." Such arguments Clearchus was making in abundance.

Meanwhile Tissaphernes returned with his own forces as if intending to go back home, and likewise Orontas[13] with his forces; the latter was also taking home the King's daughter as his wife. Then they finally began the march, Tissaphernes taking the lead and providing a market; and Ariaeus with Cyrus' barbarian army kept with Tissaphernes and Orontas on the march and encamped with them. The Greeks, however, viewing them all with suspicion, proceeded by themselves, with their own guides. And the two

---

[12] Horsemen, of course, were at their best in following up a routed enemy.   [13] Satrap of Armenia; cf. III. iv. 13. He later led (362) the "satraps' revolt" against Artaxerxes, Diodorus XV. xci. 1 ff. He was half Bactrian (*OGIS* 264); he was honoured at Athens in c. 361 (*IG* II² 207a). He married the princess Rhodogune, Plutarch *Arta*. XXVII.7, *OGIS* 391–392.

δεύοντο δὲ ἑκάστοτε ἀπέχοντες ἀλλήλων παρασάγγην
καὶ πλέον· ἐφυλάττοντο δὲ ἀμφότεροι ὥσπερ πολεμίους ἀλλήλους, καὶ εὐθὺς τοῦτο ὑποψίαν παρεῖχεν·
11 ἐνίοτε δὲ καὶ ξυλιζόμενοι ἐκ τοῦ αὐτοῦ καὶ χόρτον καὶ
ἄλλα τοιαῦτα συλλέγοντες πληγὰς ἐνέτεινον ἀλλή-
12 λοις· ὥστε καὶ τοῦτο ἔχθραν παρεῖχε.

Διελθόντες δὲ τρεῖς σταθμοὺς ἀφίκοντο πρὸς τὸ
Μηδίας καλούμενον τεῖχος, καὶ παρῆλθον εἴσω αὐτοῦ.
ἦν δὲ ᾠκοδομημένον πλίνθοις ὀπταῖς ἐν ἀσφάλτῳ
κειμέναις, εὖρος εἴκοσι ποδῶν, ὕψος δὲ ἑκατόν· μῆκος
13 δ᾽ ἐλέγετο εἶναι εἴκοσι παρασάγγαι· ἀπέχει δὲ Βαβυλῶνος οὐ πολύ. ἐντεῦθεν δ᾽ ἐπορεύθησαν σταθμοὺς
δύο παρασάγγας ὀκτώ· καὶ διέβησαν διώρυχας δύο,
τὴν μὲν ἐπὶ γεφύρας, τὴν δ᾽ ἐζευγμένην πλοίοις ἑπτά·
αὗται δ᾽ ἦσαν ἀπὸ τοῦ Τίγρητος ποταμοῦ· κατετέτ-
μηντο δὲ ἐξ αὐτῶν καὶ τάφροι ἐπὶ τὴν χώραν, αἱ μὲν
πρῶται μεγάλαι, ἔπειτα δὲ ἐλάττους· τέλος δὲ καὶ
μικροὶ ὀχετοί, ὥσπερ ἐν τῇ Ἑλλάδι ἐπὶ τὰς μελίνας.

Καὶ ἀφικνοῦνται ἐπὶ τὸν Τίγρητα ποταμόν· πρὸς
ᾧ πόλις ἦν μεγάλη καὶ πολυάνθρωπος ᾗ ὄνομα
Σιττάκη, ἀπέχουσα τοῦ ποταμοῦ σταδίους πεντεκαί-
14 δεκα. οἱ μὲν οὖν Ἕλληνες παρ᾽ αὐτὴν ἐσκήνωσαν
ἐγγὺς παραδείσου μεγάλου καὶ καλοῦ καὶ δασέος
παντοίων δένδρων, οἱ δὲ βάρβαροι διαβεβηκότες τὸν
15 Τίγρητα· οὐ μέντοι καταφανεῖς ἦσαν. μετὰ δὲ τὸ
δεῖπνον ἔτυχον ἐν περιπάτῳ ὄντες πρὸ τῶν ὅπλων
Πρόξενος καὶ Ξενοφῶν· καὶ προσελθὼν ἄνθρωπός τις
ἠρώτησε τοὺς προφύλακας ποῦ ἂν ἴδοι Πρόξενον ἢ

parties encamped in every case a parasang or more from one another, and kept guard each against the other, as though against enemies—a fact which at once occasioned suspicion. Sometimes, moreover, when Greeks and barbarians were getting firewood from the same place or collecting fodder or other such things, they would come to blows with one another, and this also occasioned ill-will.

After travelling three stages they reached the so-called wall of Media,[14] and passed within it. It was built of baked bricks, laid in asphalt, and was twenty feet wide and a hundred feet high; its length was said to be twenty parasangs, and it is not far distant from Babylon. From there they proceeded two stages, eight parasangs, crossing on their way two canals, one by a stationary bridge and the other by a bridge made of seven boats. These canals issued from the Tigris river, and from them, again, ditches had been cut that ran into the country at first large, then smaller, and finally little channels, such as run to the millet fields in Greece.

Then they reached the Tigris river, near which was a large and populous city named Sittace, fifteen stadia from the river. The Greeks accordingly encamped beside this city, near a large and beautiful park, thickly covered with all sorts of trees, while the barbarians had crossed the Tigris before encamping, and were not within sight of the Greeks. After the evening meal Proxenus and Xenophon chanced to be walking in front of the place where the arms were stacked, when a man came up and asked the pickets where he could see Proxenus or Clearchus—he did not ask

14 See note on I. vii. 15.

Κλέαρχον· Μένωνα δὲ οὐκ ἐζήτει, καὶ ταῦτα παρ'
16 Ἀριαίου ὢν τοῦ Μένωνος ξένου. ἐπεὶ δὲ Πρόξενος
εἶπεν ὅτι αὐτός εἰμι ὃν ζητεῖς, εἶπεν ὁ ἄνθρωπος τάδε.
Ἔπεμψέ με Ἀριαῖος καὶ Ἀρτάοζος, πιστοὶ ὄντες Κύρῳ
καὶ ὑμῖν εὖνοι, καὶ κελεύουσι φυλάττεσθαι μὴ ὑμῖν
ἐπιθῶνται τῆς νυκτὸς οἱ βάρβαροι· ἔστι δὲ στράτευμα
17 πολὺ ἐν τῷ πλησίον παραδείσῳ. καὶ παρὰ τὴν
γέφυραν τοῦ Τίγρητος ποταμοῦ πέμψαι κελεύουσι
φυλακήν, ὡς διανοεῖται αὐτὴν λῦσαι Τισσαφέρνης
τῆς νυκτός, ἐὰν δύνηται, ὡς μὴ διαβῆτε ἀλλ' ἐν μέσῳ
18 ἀποληφθῆτε τοῦ ποταμοῦ καὶ τῆς διώρυχος. ἀκούσαντες ταῦτα ἄγουσιν αὐτὸν παρὰ τὸν Κλέαρχον καὶ
φράζουσιν ἃ λέγει. ὁ δὲ Κλέαρχος ἀκούσας ἐταράχθη
σφόδρα καὶ ἐφοβεῖτο.

19   Νεανίσκος δέ τις τῶν παρόντων ἐννοήσας εἶπεν ὡς
οὐκ ἀκόλουθα εἴη τό τε ἐπιθήσεσθαι καὶ τὸ λύσειν
τὴν γέφυραν. δῆλον γὰρ ὅτι ἐπιτιθεμένους ἢ νικᾶν
δεήσει ἢ ἡττᾶσθαι. ἐὰν μὲν οὖν νικῶσι, τί δεῖ λύειν
αὐτοὺς τὴν γέφυραν; οὐδὲ γὰρ ἂν πολλαὶ γέφυραι
20 ὦσιν ἔχοιμεν ἂν ὅποι φυγόντες ἡμεῖς σωθῶμεν. ἐὰν
δ' αὖ ἡμεῖς νικῶμεν, λελυμένης τῆς γεφύρας οὐχ
ἕξουσιν ἐκεῖνοι ὅποι φύγωσιν· οὐδὲ μὴν βοηθῆσαι
πολλῶν ὄντων πέραν οὐδεὶς αὐτοῖς δυνήσεται λελυμένης τῆς γεφύρας.

21   Ἀκούσας δὲ ὁ Κλέαρχος ταῦτα ἤρετο τὸν ἄγγελον
πόση τις εἴη χώρα ἡ ἐν μέσῳ τοῦ Τίγρητος καὶ τῆς
διώρυχος. ὁ δὲ εἶπεν ὅτι πολλὴ καὶ κῶμαι ἔνεισι καὶ
22 πόλεις πολλαὶ καὶ μεγάλαι. τότε δὴ καὶ ἐγνώσθη ὅτι

for Menon, despite the fact that he came from Ariaeus, Menon's friend. And when Proxenus said "I am the one you are looking for," the man made this statement: "I was sent here by Ariaeus and Artaozus, who were faithful to Cyrus and are friendly to you; they bid you be on your guard lest the barbarians attack you during the night, for there is a large army in the neighbouring park. They also bid you send a guard to the bridge over the Tigris river, because Tissaphernes intends to destroy it during the night, if he can, so that you may not cross, but may be cut off between the river and the canal." Upon hearing these words they took him to Clearchus and repeated his message. And when Clearchus heard it, he was exceedingly agitated and full of fear.

A young man who was present, however, fell to thinking, and then said that the two stories, that they intended to attack and intended to destroy the bridge, were not consistent. "For it is clear," he went on, "that by attacking, they must either be victorious or be defeated. Now if they are victorious, why should they need to destroy the bridge? For even if there were many bridges, we should have no place to which we could flee and save ourselves. But if it is we who are victorious, with the bridge destroyed they will have no place to which they can flee. And, furthermore, though there are troops in abundance on the other side, no one will be able to come to their aid with the bridge destroyed."

After hearing these words Clearchus asked the messenger about how extensive the territory between the Tigris and the canal was. He replied that it was a large tract, and that there were villages and many large towns in it. Then

οἱ βάρβαροι τὸν ἄνθρωπον ὑποπέμψαιεν, ὀκνοῦντες
μὴ οἱ Ἕλληνες διελόντες τὴν γέφυραν μείναιεν ἐν τῇ
νήσῳ ἐρύματα ἔχοντες ἔνθεν μὲν τὸν Τίγρητα, ἔνθεν
δὲ τὴν διώρυχα· τὰ δ᾽ ἐπιτήδεια ἔχοιεν ἐκ τῆς ἐν μέσῳ
χώρας πολλῆς καὶ ἀγαθῆς οὔσης καὶ τῶν ἐργασομέ-
νων ἐνόντων· εἶτα δὲ καὶ ἀποστροφὴ γένοιτο εἴ τις
βούλοιτο βασιλέα κακῶς ποιεῖν.

23   Μετὰ δὲ ταῦτα ἀνεπαύοντο· ἐπὶ μέντοι τὴν γέφυραν
ὅμως φυλακὴν ἔπεμψαν· καὶ οὔτε ἐπέθετο οὐδεὶς οὐδαμόθεν οὔτε πρὸς τὴν γέφυραν οὐδεὶς ἦλθε τῶν πολε-
24 μίων, ὡς οἱ φυλάττοντες ἀπήγγελλον. ἐπειδὴ δὲ ἕως
ἐγένετο, διέβαινον τὴν γέφυραν ἐζευγμένην πλοίοις
τριάκοντα καὶ ἑπτὰ ὡς οἷόν τε μάλιστα πεφυλαγ-
μένως· ἐξήγγελλον γάρ τινες τῶν παρὰ Τισσαφέρνους
Ἑλλήνων ὡς διαβαινόντων μέλλοιεν ἐπιθήσεσθαι.
ἀλλὰ ταῦτα μὲν ψευδῆ ἦν· διαβαινόντων μέντοι ὁ
Γλοῦς ἐπεφάνη μετ᾽ ἄλλων σκοπῶν εἰ διαβαίνοιεν τὸν
ποταμόν· ἐπειδὴ δὲ εἶδεν, ᾤχετο ἀπελαύνων.

25   Ἀπὸ δὲ τοῦ Τίγρητος ἐπορεύθησαν σταθμοὺς τέτταρας παρασάγγας εἴκοσιν ἐπὶ τὸν Φύσκον ποταμόν,
τὸ εὖρος πλέθρου· ἐπῆν δὲ γέφυρα. καὶ ἐνταῦθα ᾤκεῖτο
πόλις μεγάλη ὄνομα Ὦπις· πρὸς ἣν ἀπήντησε τοῖς
Ἕλλησιν ὁ Κύρου καὶ Ἀρταξέρξου νόθος ἀδελφὸς
ἀπὸ Σούσων καὶ Ἐκβατάνων στρατιὰν πολλὴν ἄγων
ὡς βοηθήσων βασιλεῖ· καὶ ἐπιστήσας τὸ ἑαυτοῦ
26 στράτευμα παρερχομένους τοὺς Ἕλληνας ἐθεώρει. ὁ

it was perceived that the barbarians had sent the man with
a false message out of fear that the Greeks might destroy
the bridge and establish themselves permanently on the
island, with the Tigris for a defence on one side and the
canal on the other; in that case, they thought, the Greeks
might get provisions from the territory between the river
and the canal, since it was extensive and fertile and there
were men in it to cultivate it; and furthermore, the spot
might also become a place of refuge for anyone who might
desire to do harm to the King.

After this the Greeks went to rest, yet they did, nevertheless, send a guard to the bridge; and no one attacked
the army from any quarter, nor did anyone of the enemy,
so the men on guard reported, come to the bridge. When
dawn came, they proceeded to cross the bridge, which was
made of thirty-seven boats, as guardedly as possible; for
they had reports from some of the Greeks who were with
Tissaphernes that the enemy would attack them while they
were crossing. But these reports were false. To be sure, in
the course of their passage Glus did appear, with some
others, watching to see if they were crossing the river, but
once he had seen, he went riding off.

From the Tigris they marched four stages, twenty parasangs, to the Physcus river, which was a plethrum in width
and had a bridge over it. There was situated a large city
named Opis, near which the Greeks met the bastard
brother of Cyrus and Artaxerxes, who was leading a large
army from Susa and Ecbatana[15] to the support, as he said,
of the King; and he halted his own army and watched the

[15] The capitals, respectively, of Elam and Media, and strategic
centers of the Achaemenid realm.

δὲ Κλέαρχος ἡγεῖτο μὲν εἰς δύο, ἐπορεύετο δὲ ἄλλοτε
καὶ ἄλλοτε ἐφιστάμενος· ὅσον δ' ἂν χρόνον τὸ ἡγούμενον τοῦ στρατεύματος ἐπιστῇ, τοσοῦτον ἦν ἀνάγκη
χρόνον δι' ὅλου τοῦ στρατεύματος γίγνεσθαι τὴν
ἐπίστασιν· ὥστε τὸ στράτευμα καὶ αὐτοῖς τοῖς Ἕλλησι δόξαι πάμπολυ εἶναι, καὶ τὸν Πέρσην ἐκπε-
27 πλῆχθαι θεωροῦντα. ἐντεῦθεν δ' ἐπορεύθησαν διὰ τῆς
Μηδίας σταθμοὺς ἐρήμους ἓξ παρασάγγας τριάκοντα
εἰς τὰς Παρυσάτιδος κώμας τῆς Κύρου καὶ βασιλέως
μητρός. ταύτας Τισσαφέρνης Κύρῳ ἐπεγγελῶν διαρπάσαι τοῖς Ἕλλησιν ἐπέτρεψε πλὴν ἀνδραπόδων.
ἐνῆν δὲ σῖτος πολὺς καὶ πρόβατα καὶ ἄλλα χρήματα.
28 ἐντεῦθεν δ' ἐπορεύθησαν σταθμοὺς ἐρήμους τέτταρας
παρασάγγας εἴκοσι τὸν Τίγρητα ποταμὸν ἐν ἀριστερᾷ ἔχοντες. ἐν δὲ τῷ πρώτῳ σταθμῷ πέραν τοῦ
ποταμοῦ πόλις ᾠκεῖτο μεγάλη καὶ εὐδαίμων ὄνομα
Καιναί, ἐξ ἧς οἱ βάρβαροι διῆγον ἐπὶ σχεδίαις διφθε-
ρίναις ἄρτους, τυρούς, οἶνον.

V. Μετὰ ταῦτα ἀφικνοῦνται ἐπὶ τὸν Ζαπάταν ποταμόν, τὸ εὖρος τεττάρων πλέθρων. καὶ ἐνταῦθα ἔμειναν ἡμέρας τρεῖς· ἐν δὲ ταύταις ὑποψίαι μὲν ἦσαν,
2 φανερὰ δὲ οὐδεμία ἐφαίνετο ἐπιβουλή. ἔδοξεν οὖν τῷ
Κλεάρχῳ συγγενέσθαι τῷ Τισσαφέρνει καὶ εἴ πως
δύναιτο παῦσαι τὰς ὑποψίας πρὶν ἐξ αὐτῶν πόλεμον
γενέσθαι· καὶ ἔπεμψέ τινα ἐροῦντα ὅτι συγγενέσθαι
αὐτῷ χρῄζοι. ὁ δὲ ἑτοίμως ἐκέλευεν ἥκειν.
3 Ἐπειδὴ δὲ ξυνῆλθον, λέγει ὁ Κλέαρχος τάδε. Ἐγώ,
ὦ Τισσαφέρνη, οἶδα μὲν ἡμῖν ὅρκους γεγενημένους

Greeks as they passed by. Clearchus led them two abreast, and halted now and then in his march; and whatever the length of time for which he halted the van of the army, just so long a time the halt would necessarily last through the entire army; the result was that even to the Greeks themselves their army seemed to be very large, and the Persian was astounded as he watched them. From there they marched through Media, six desert stages, thirty parasangs, to the villages of Parysatis,[16] the mother of Cyrus and the King. And Tissaphernes, by way of insulting Cyrus,[17] gave over these villages—save only the slaves they contained—to the Greeks to plunder. In them there was grain in abundance and cattle and other property. From there they marched four desert stages, twenty parasangs, keeping the Tigris river on the left. Across the river on the first stage was situated a large and prosperous city named Caenae, from which the barbarians brought over loaves, cheeses and wine, crossing upon rafts made of skins.

V. After this they reached the Zapatas river,[18] which was four plethra in width. There they remained three days. During this time suspicions were rife, it is true, but no plot came openly to light. Clearchus resolved, therefore, to have a meeting with Tissaphernes and put a stop to these suspicions, if he possibly could, before hostilities resulted from them; so he sent a messenger to say that he desired to meet him. And Tissaphernes readily bade him come.

When they had met, Clearchus spoke as follows: "I know, to be sure, Tissaphernes, that both of us have taken

[16] Cf. I. iv. 9.   [17] *i.e.* through the mother who "loved him better than her reigning son Artaxerxes" (I. i. 4).

[18] The Greater Zab, a tributary of the Tigris.

καὶ δεξιὰς δεδομένας μὴ ἀδικήσειν ἀλλήλους· φυλατ-
τόμενον δὲ σέ τε ὁρῶ ὡς πολεμίους ἡμᾶς καὶ ἡμεῖς
4 ὁρῶντες ταῦτα ἀντιφυλαττόμεθα. ἐπεὶ δὲ σκοπῶν
οὐδὲν δύναμαι οὔτε σὲ αἰσθέσθαι πειρώμενον ἡμᾶς
κακῶς ποιεῖν ἐγώ τε σαφῶς οἶδα ὅτι ἡμεῖς γε οὐδὲ
ἐπινοοῦμεν τοιοῦτον οὐδέν, ἔδοξέ μοι εἰς λόγους σοι
ἐλθεῖν, ὅπως εἰ δυναίμεθα ἐξέλοιμεν ἀλλήλων τὴν
5 ἀπιστίαν. καὶ γὰρ οἶδα ἀνθρώπους ἤδη τοὺς μὲν ἐκ
διαβολῆς τοὺς δὲ καὶ ἐξ ὑποψίας οἳ φοβηθέντες
ἀλλήλους φθάσαι βουλόμενοι πρὶν παθεῖν ἐποίησαν
ἀνήκεστα κακὰ τοὺς οὔτε μέλλοντας οὔτ' αὖ βου-
6 λομένους τοιοῦτον οὐδέν. τὰς οὖν τοιαύτας ἀγνωμοσύ-
νας νομίζων συνουσίαις μάλιστα ἂν παύεσθαι ἥκω
καὶ διδάσκειν σε βούλομαι ὡς σὺ ἡμῖν οὐκ ὀρθῶς
7 ἀπιστεῖς. πρῶτον μὲν γὰρ καὶ μέγιστον οἱ θεῶν ἡμᾶς
ὅρκοι κωλύουσι πολεμίους εἶναι ἀλλήλοις· ὅστις δὲ
τούτων σύνοιδεν αὑτῷ παρημεληκώς, τοῦτον ἐγὼ
οὔποτ' ἂν εὐδαιμονίσαιμι. τὸν γὰρ θεῶν πόλεμον οὐκ
οἶδα οὔτ'[9] ἀπὸ ποίου ἂν τάχους φεύγων τις ἀποφύγοι
οὔτ' εἰς ποῖον ἂν σκότος ἀποδραίη οὔθ' ὅπως ἂν εἰς
ἐχυρὸν χωρίον ἀποσταίη. πάντῃ γὰρ πάντα τοῖς θεοῖς
ὕποχα καὶ πανταχῇ πάντων ἴσον οἱ θεοὶ κρατοῦσι.

8   Περὶ μὲν δὴ τῶν θεῶν τε καὶ τῶν ὅρκων οὕτω
γιγνώσκω, παρ' οὓς ἡμεῖς τὴν φιλίαν συνθέμενοι
κατεθέμεθα· τῶν δ' ἀνθρωπίνων σὲ ἔγωγε ἐν τῷ

[9] οὐκ οἶδα οὔτ' some MSS., Mar.: οὐκ οἶδα other MSS.: οὔτ'
οἶδα Gem.

oaths and given pledges not to injure one another; yet I see
that you are on your guard against us as though we were
enemies, and we, observing this, are keeping guard on
our side. But since, upon inquiry, I am unable to ascertain
that you are trying to do us harm, and am perfectly sure
that we, for our part, are not even thinking of any such
thing against you, I resolved to have an interview with
you, so that, if possible, we might dispel this mutual distrust. For I know that there have been cases before now—
some of them the result of slander, others of mere suspicion—where men who have become fearful of one another
and wished to strike before they were struck, have done
irreparable harm to people who were neither intending
nor, for that matter, desiring to do anything of the sort to
them. In the belief, then, that such misunderstandings
would best be settled by conference, I have come here, and
I wish to point out to you that you are mistaken in distrusting us. For, first and chiefly, our oaths, sworn by the gods,
stand in the way of our being enemies of one another; and
the man who is conscious that he has disregarded such
oaths, I for my part should never account happy. For in war
with the gods I know not either by what swiftness of foot,
in trying to flee, one could make his escape, or into what
darkness he could steal away, or how he could withdraw
himself to a secure fortress. For all things in all places are
subject to the gods, and all alike the gods hold in their
control.[19]

"Touching the gods, then, and our oaths I am thus
minded, and to the keeping of the gods we consigned the
friendship which we covenanted; but as for things human,

[19] Cf. III. ii. 10, *Hell.* III. iv. 11. For gods' powers, *Mem.* I. i.
19.

9 παρόντι νομίζω μέγιστον εἶναι ἡμῖν ἀγαθόν. σὺν μὲν
γὰρ σοὶ πᾶσα μὲν ὁδὸς εὔπορος, πᾶς δὲ ποταμὸς
διαβατός, τῶν τε ἐπιτηδείων οὐκ ἀπορία· ἄνευ δὲ σοῦ
πᾶσα μὲν διὰ σκότους ἡ ὁδός· οὐδὲν γὰρ αὐτῆς ἐπι-
στάμεθα· πᾶς δὲ ποταμὸς δύσπορος, πᾶς δὲ ὄχλος
φοβερός, φοβερώτατον δ' ἐρημία· μεστὴ γὰρ πολλῆς
10 ἀπορίας ἐστίν. εἰ δὲ δὴ καὶ μανέντες σε κατακτεί-
ναιμεν, ἄλλο τι ἂν ἢ τὸν εὐεργέτην κατακτείναντες
πρὸς βασιλέα τὸν μέγιστον ἔφεδρον ἀγωνιζοίμεθα;[10]
ὅσων δὲ δὴ καὶ οἵων ἂν ἐλπίδων ἐμαυτὸν στερήσαιμι,
εἰ σέ τι κακὸν ἐπιχειρήσαιμι ποιεῖν, ταῦτα λέξω. ἐγὼ
11 γὰρ Κῦρον ἐπεθύμησά μοι φίλον γενέσθαι, νομίζων
τῶν τότε ἱκανώτατον εἶναι εὖ ποιεῖν ὃν βούλοιτο· σὲ
δὲ νῦν ὁρῶ τήν τε Κύρου δύναμιν καὶ χώραν ἔχοντα
καὶ τὴν σαυτοῦ ἀρχὴν σῴζοντα, τὴν δὲ βασιλέως
δύναμιν, ᾗ Κῦρος πολεμίᾳ ἐχρῆτο, σοὶ ταύτην σύμ-
12 μαχον οὖσαν. τούτων δὲ τοιούτων ὄντων τίς οὕτω
μαίνεται ὅστις οὐ βούλεται σοὶ φίλος εἶναι;

Ἀλλὰ μὴν ἐρῶ γὰρ καὶ ταῦτα ἐξ ὧν ἔχω ἐλπίδας
13 καὶ σὲ βουλήσεσθαι φίλον ἡμῖν εἶναι. οἶδα μὲν γὰρ
ὑμῖν Μυσοὺς λυπηροὺς ὄντας, οὓς νομίζω ἂν σὺν τῇ
παρούσῃ δυνάμει ταπεινοὺς ὑμῖν παρασχεῖν· οἶδα δὲ
καὶ Πισίδας· ἀκούω δὲ καὶ ἄλλα ἔθνη πολλὰ τοιαῦτα
εἶναι, ἃ οἶμαι ἂν παῦσαι ἐνοχλοῦντα ἀεὶ τῇ ὑμετέρᾳ
εὐδαιμονίᾳ. Αἰγυπτίους δέ, οἷς μάλιστα ὑμᾶς γιγνώ-

---

[10] ἀγωνιζοίμεθα some MSS., Hude/Peters, Mar.: πολεμήσομεν other MSS., which Gem. follows, bracketing ἂν above.

I believe that at this time you are to us the greatest good we possess. For, with you, every road is easy for us to traverse, every river is passable, supplies are not lacking; without you, all our road is through darkness—for none of it do we know—every river is hard to pass, every crowd excites our fears and most fearful of all is solitude—for it is crowded full of want. And if we should, in fact, be seized with madness and slay you, should we not certainly, after slaying our benefactor, be engaged in contest with the King, a fresh and most powerful opponent?[20] Again, how great and bright are the hopes of which I should rob myself if I attempted to do you any harm, I will relate to you. I set my heart upon having Cyrus for my friend because I thought that he was the best able of all the men of his time to benefit whom he pleased; but now I see that it is you who possess Cyrus' power and territory, while retaining your own besides, and that the power of the King, which Cyrus found hostile, is for you a support. Since this is so, who is so mad as not to desire to be your friend?

"And now for the other side—for I will go on to tell you the grounds upon which I base the hope that you will likewise desire to be our friend. I know that the Mysians are troublesome to you, and I believe that with the force I have I could make them your submissive servants; I know that the Pisidians also trouble you, and I hear that there are likewise many other tribes of the same sort; I could put a stop, I think, to their being a continual annoyance to your prosperity. As for the Egyptians, with whom I learn that

---

[20] The ἔφεδρος, in the language of Greek athletics, was the man who had "drawn a bye," and so waited for the result of a contest in order to engage the victor: see LSJ sv II 4.

σκω τεθυμωμένους, οὐχ ὁρῶ ποίᾳ δυνάμει συμμάχῳ
χρησάμενοι μᾶλλον ἂν κολάσαισθε τῆς νῦν σὺν ἐμοὶ
14 οὔσης. ἀλλὰ μὴν ἔν γε τοῖς πέριξ οἰκοῦσι σὺ εἰ μὲν
βούλοιό τῳ φίλος εἶναι ὡς μέγιστος ἂν εἴης, εἰ δέ τίς
σε λυποίη, ὡς δεσπότης ἂν ἀναστρέφοιο ἔχων ἡμᾶς
ὑπηρέτας, οἵ σοι οὐκ ἂν τοῦ μισθοῦ ἕνεκα μόνον
ὑπηρετοῖμεν ἀλλὰ καὶ τῆς χάριτος ἣν σωθέντες ὑπὸ
15 σοῦ σοὶ ἂν ἔχοιμεν δικαίως. ἐμοὶ μὲν ταῦτα πάντα
ἐνθυμουμένῳ οὕτω δοκεῖ θαυμαστὸν εἶναι τὸ σὲ ἡμῖν
ἀπιστεῖν ὥστε καὶ ἥδιστ᾽ ἂν ἀκούσαιμι τοὔνομα τίς
οὕτως ἐστὶ δεινὸς λέγειν ὥστε σε πεῖσαι λέγων ὡς
ἡμεῖς σοι ἐπιβουλεύομεν. Κλέαρχος μὲν οὖν τοσαῦτα
εἶπε· Τισσαφέρνης δὲ ὧδε ἀπημείφθη.
16 Ἀλλ᾽ ἥδομαι μέν, ὦ Κλέαρχε, ἀκούων σου φρο-
νίμους λόγους· ταῦτα γὰρ γιγνώσκων εἴ τι ἐμοὶ κακὸν
βουλεύοις, ἅμα ἄν μοι δοκεῖς καὶ σαυτῷ κακόνους
εἶναι. ὡς δ᾽ ἂν μάθῃς ὅτι οὐδ᾽ ἂν ὑμεῖς δικαίως οὔτε
17 βασιλεῖ οὔτ᾽ ἐμοὶ ἀπιστοίητε, ἀντάκουσον. εἰ γὰρ
ὑμᾶς ἐβουλόμεθα ἀπολέσαι, πότερά σοι δοκοῦμεν ἱππέων πλήθους ἀπορεῖν ἢ πεζῶν ἢ ὁπλίσεως ἐν ᾗ ὑμᾶς
μὲν βλάπτειν ἱκανοὶ εἴημεν ἄν, ἀντιπάσχειν δὲ οὐδεὶς
18 κίνδυνος; ἀλλὰ χωρίων ἐπιτηδείων ὑμῖν ἐπιτίθεσθαι
ἀπορεῖν ἄν σοι δοκοῦμεν; οὐ τοσαῦτα μὲν πεδία ἃ
ὑμεῖς φίλια ὄντα σὺν πολλῷ πόνῳ διαπορεύεσθε,
τοσαῦτα δὲ ὄρη ὁρᾶτε ὑμῖν ὄντα πορευτέα, ἃ ἡμῖν
ἔξεστι προκαταλαβοῦσιν ἄπορα ὑμῖν παρέχειν, τοσοῦτοι δ᾽ εἰσὶ ποταμοὶ ἐφ᾽ ὧν ἔξεστιν ἡμῖν ταμιεύεσθαι

you are especially angry, I do not see what force you could better employ to aid you in chastising them than the force which I now have. Again, take those who dwell around you: if you chose to be a friend to any, you could be the greatest possible friend, while if any were to annoy you, you could play the part of master over them in case you had us for supporters, for we should serve you, not only for the sake of pay, but also out of the gratitude that we should feel, and rightly feel, toward you, the man who had saved us. For my part, as I consider all these things the idea of your distrusting us seems to me so astonishing that I should be very glad indeed to hear the name of the man who is so clever a talker that his talk could persuade you that we were cherishing designs against you." Thus much Clearchus said, and Tissaphernes replied as follows:

"It is a pleasure to me, Clearchus, to hear your sensible words; for if, holding these views, you should devise any ill against me, you would at the same time, I think, be showing ill-will toward yourself also. And now, in order that you may learn that you likewise are mistaken in distrusting either the King or myself, take your turn in listening. If we were, in fact, desirous of destroying you, does it seem to you that we have not cavalry in abundance and infantry and military equipment, whereby we should be able to harm you without being in any danger of suffering harm ourselves? Or do you think that we should not have places suitable for attacking you? Do you not behold these vast plains, which even now, although they are friendly, it is costing you a deal of labour to traverse? and these great mountains you have to pass, which we can occupy in advance and render impassable for you? and have we not these great rivers, at which we can parcel out whatever

ὁπόσοις ἂν ὑμῶν βουλοίμεθα μάχεσθαι; εἰσὶ δ᾽ αὐτῶν
οὓς οὐδ᾽ ἂν παντάπασι διαβαίητε, εἰ μὴ ἡμεῖς ὑμᾶς
19 διαπορεύοιμεν. εἰ δ᾽ ἐν πᾶσι τούτοις ἡττώμεθα, ἀλλὰ
τό γέ τοι πῦρ κρεῖττον τοῦ καρποῦ ἐστιν· ὃν ἡμεῖς
δυναίμεθ᾽ ἂν κατακαύσαντες λιμὸν ὑμῖν ἀντιτάξαι, ᾧ
ὑμεῖς οὐδ᾽ εἰ πάνυ ἀγαθοὶ εἴητε μάχεσθαι ἂν
20 δύναισθε. πῶς ἂν οὖν ἔχοντες τοσούτους πόρους πρὸς
τὸ ὑμῖν πολεμεῖν, καὶ τούτων μηδένα ἡμῖν ἐπικίν-
δυνον, ἔπειτα ἐκ τούτων πάντων τοῦτον ἂν τὸν τρόπον
ἐξελοίμεθα ὃς μόνος μὲν πρὸς θεῶν ἀσεβής, μόνος δὲ
21 πρὸς ἀνθρώπων αἰσχρός; παντάπασι δὲ ἀπόρων ἐστὶ
καὶ ἀμηχάνων καὶ ἐν ἀνάγκῃ ἐχομένων, καὶ τούτων
πονηρῶν, οἵτινες ἐθέλουσι δι᾽ ἐπιορκίας τε πρὸς θεοὺς
καὶ ἀπιστίας πρὸς ἀνθρώπους πράττειν τι. οὐχ οὕτως
ἡμεῖς, ὦ Κλέαρχε, οὔτε ἀλόγιστοι οὔτε ἠλίθιοί ἐσμεν.
22 Ἀλλὰ τί δὴ ὑμᾶς ἐξὸν ἀπολέσαι οὐκ ἐπὶ τοῦτο
ἤλθομεν; εὖ ἴσθι ὅτι ὁ ἐμὸς ἔρως τούτου αἴτιος τοῦ
τοῖς Ἕλλησιν ἐμὲ πιστὸν γενέσθαι, καὶ ᾧ Κῦρος
ἀνέβη ξενικῷ διὰ μισθοδοσίαν πιστεύων τούτῳ ἐμὲ
23 καταβῆναι δι᾽ εὐεργεσίαν ἰσχυρόν. ὅσα δ᾽ ἐμοὶ χρήσιμοι ὑμεῖς ἐστε τὰ μὲν καὶ σὺ εἶπας, τὸ δὲ μέγιστον
ἐγὼ οἶδα· τὴν μὲν γὰρ ἐπὶ τῇ κεφαλῇ τιάραν βασιλεῖ
μόνῳ ἔξεστιν ὀρθὴν ἔχειν, τὴν δ᾽ ἐπὶ τῇ καρδίᾳ ἴσως
ἂν ὑμῶν παρόντων καὶ ἕτερος εὐπετῶς ἔχοι.

---

21 The first clause states a fact of Persian court etiquette; the
second is apparently intended to give Clearchus the impression

number of you we would choose to fight with—some, in fact, which you could not cross at all unless we carried you over? And if we were worsted at all these points, nevertheless it is certain that fire can worst crops; by burning them up we could bring famine into the field against you, and you could not fight against that, however brave you might be. Since, then, we have so many ways of making war upon you, no one of them dangerous to us, why, in such a case, should we choose out of them all that one way which alone is impious in the sight of the gods and shameful in the sight of men? For it is those who are utterly without ways and means, who are bound by necessity, and who are rascals in any case, that are willing to accomplish an object by perjury to the gods and unfaithfulness to men. As for us, Clearchus, we are not so unreasoning or foolish.

"But why, one might ask, when it was possible for us to destroy you, did we not proceed to do so? The reason for this, be well assured, was my eager desire to prove myself trustworthy to the Greeks, so that with the same mercenary force which Cyrus led up from the coast in the faith of wages paid, I might go back to the coast in the security of benefits conferred. And as for all the ways in which you are of use to me, you also have mentioned some of them, but it is I who know the most important: the King alone may wear upright the tiara that is upon the head, but another, too, with your help, might easily so wear the one that is upon the heart."[21]

that Tissaphernes aspires to the Persian throne, and for that reason really desires the friendship and help of the Greeks. Cf. Briant, *Histoire* I, 653.

XENOPHON

24 Ταῦτα εἰπὼν ἔδοξε τῷ Κλεάρχῳ ἀληθῆ λέγειν· καὶ
εἶπεν· Οὐκοῦν, ἔφη, οἵτινες τοιούτων ἡμῖν εἰς φιλίαν
ὑπαρχόντων πειρῶνται διαβάλλοντες ποιῆσαι πολεμί-
25 ους ἡμᾶς ἄξιοί εἰσι τὰ ἔσχατα παθεῖν; Καὶ ἐγὼ μέν
γε, ἔφη ὁ Τισσαφέρνης, εἰ βούλεσθέ μοι οἵ τε στρατηγοὶ καὶ οἱ λοχαγοὶ ἐλθεῖν, ἐν τῷ ἐμφανεῖ λέξω τοὺς
πρὸς ἐμὲ λέγοντας ὡς σὺ ἐμοὶ ἐπιβουλεύεις καὶ τῇ
26 σὺν ἐμοὶ στρατιᾷ. Ἐγὼ δέ, ἔφη ὁ Κλέαρχος, ἄξω
πάντας, καὶ σοὶ αὖ δηλώσω ὅθεν ἐγὼ περὶ σοῦ ἀκούω.
27 Ἐκ τούτων δὴ τῶν λόγων ὁ Τισσαφέρνης φιλοφρονούμενος τότε μὲν μένειν τε αὐτὸν ἐκέλευε καὶ σύνδειπνον ἐποιήσατο. τῇ δὲ ὑστεραίᾳ ὁ Κλέαρχος ἐλθὼν
ἐπὶ τὸ στρατόπεδον δῆλός τ᾽ ἦν πάνυ φιλικῶς οἰόμενος
διακεῖσθαι τῷ Τισσαφέρνει καὶ ἃ ἔλεγεν ἐκεῖνος
ἀπήγγελλεν, ἔφη τε χρῆναι ἰέναι παρὰ Τισσαφέρνην
οὓς ἐκέλευεν, καὶ οἳ ἂν ἐξελεγχθῶσι διαβάλλοντες
τῶν Ἑλλήνων, ὡς προδότας αὐτοὺς καὶ κακόνους τοῖς
28 Ἕλλησιν ὄντας τιμωρηθῆναι. ὑπώπτευε δὲ εἶναι τὸν
διαβάλλοντα Μένωνα, εἰδὼς αὐτὸν καὶ συγγεγενη-
μένον Τισσαφέρνει μετ᾽ Ἀριαίου καὶ στασιάζοντα
αὐτῷ καὶ ἐπιβουλεύοντα, ὅπως τὸ στράτευμα ἅπαν
29 πρὸς αὐτὸν λαβὼν φίλος ᾖ Τισσαφέρνει. ἐβούλετο δὲ
καὶ ὁ Κλέαρχος ἅπαν τὸ στράτευμα πρὸς ἑαυτὸν ἔχειν
τὴν γνώμην καὶ τοὺς παραλυποῦντας ἐκποδὼν εἶναι.
τῶν δὲ στρατιωτῶν ἀντέλεγόν τινες αὐτῷ μὴ ἰέναι
πάντας τοὺς λοχαγοὺς καὶ στρατηγοὺς μηδὲ πιστεύειν

196

In these things that he said Tissaphernes seemed to Clearchus to be speaking the truth; and Clearchus said: "Then do not those who are endeavouring by false charges to make us enemies, when we have such grounds for friendship, deserve to suffer the uttermost penalty?" "Yes," said Tissaphernes, "and for my part, if you generals and captains care to come to me, I will give you, publicly, the names of those who tell me that you are plotting against me and the army under my command." "And I," said Clearchus, "will bring them all, and in my turn will make known to you whence come the reports that I hear about you."

After this conversation Tissaphernes showed all kindness, inviting Clearchus at that time to stay with him and making him his guest at dinner. On the following day, when Clearchus returned to the Greek camp, he not only made it clear that he imagined he was on very friendly terms with Tissaphernes and reported the words which he had used, but he said that those whom Tissaphernes had invited must go to him, and that whoever among the Greeks should be convicted of making false charges ought to be punished, as traitors and foes to the Greeks. Now Clearchus suspected that the author of these slanders was Menon, for he was aware that Menon had not only had meetings with Tissaphernes, in company with Ariaeus, but was also organizing opposition to his own leadership and plotting against him, with the intention of winning over to himself the entire army and thereby securing the friendship of Tissaphernes. Clearchus desired, however, to have the entire army devoted to him and to put the troublesome members out of the way. As for the soldiers, some of them made objections to Clearchus' proposal, urging that the captains and generals should not all go and that they should not

30 Τισσαφέρνει. ὁ δὲ Κλέαρχος ἰσχυρῶς κατέτεινεν, ἔστε
διεπράξατο πέντε μὲν στρατηγοὺς ἰέναι, εἴκοσι δὲ
λοχαγούς· συνηκολούθησαν δὲ ὡς εἰς ἀγορὰν καὶ τῶν
ἄλλων στρατιωτῶν ὡς διακόσιοι.

31 Ἐπεὶ δὲ ἦσαν ἐπὶ θύραις ταῖς Τισσαφέρνους, οἱ
μὲν στρατηγοὶ παρεκλήθησαν εἴσω, Πρόξενος Βοιώτιος, Μένων Θετταλός, Ἀγίας Ἀρκάς, Κλέαρχος
Λάκων, Σωκράτης Ἀχαιός· οἱ δὲ λοχαγοὶ ἐπὶ ταῖς

32 θύραις ἔμενον. οὐ πολλῷ δὲ ὕστερον ἀπὸ τοῦ αὐτοῦ
σημείου οἵ τ' ἔνδον συνελαμβάνοντο καὶ οἱ ἔξω
κατεκόπησαν. μετὰ δὲ ταῦτα τῶν βαρβάρων τινὲς
ἱππέων διὰ τοῦ πεδίου ἐλαύνοντες ᾧτινι ἐντυγχάνοιεν

33 Ἕλληνι ἢ δούλῳ ἢ ἐλευθέρῳ πάντας ἔκτεινον. οἱ δὲ
Ἕλληνες τήν τε ἱππασίαν ἐθαύμαζον ἐκ τοῦ στρατοπέδου ὁρῶντες καὶ ὅ τι ἐποίουν ἠμφεγνόουν, πρὶν
Νίκαρχος Ἀρκὰς ἧκε φεύγων τετρωμένος εἰς τὴν
γαστέρα καὶ τὰ ἔντερα ἐν ταῖς χερσὶν ἔχων, καὶ εἶπε

34 πάντα τὰ γεγενημένα. ἐκ τούτου δὴ οἱ Ἕλληνες ἔθεον
ἐπὶ τὰ ὅπλα πάντες ἐκπεπληγμένοι καὶ νομίζοντες
αὐτίκα ἥξειν αὐτοὺς ἐπὶ τὸ στρατόπεδον.

35 Οἱ δὲ πάντες μὲν οὐκ ἦλθον, Ἀριαῖος δὲ καὶ Ἀρτάοζος καὶ Μιθραδάτης, οἳ ἦσαν Κύρῳ πιστότατοι· ὁ
δὲ τῶν Ἑλλήνων ἑρμηνεὺς ἔφη καὶ τὸν Τισσαφέρνους
ἀδελφὸν σὺν αὐτοῖς ὁρᾶν καὶ γιγνώσκειν· συνηκολού-
θουν δὲ καὶ ἄλλοι Περσῶν τεθωρακισμένοι εἰς τρια-

36 κοσίους. οὗτοι ἐπεὶ ἐγγὺς ἦσαν, προσελθεῖν ἐκέλευον
εἴ τις εἴη τῶν Ἑλλήνων στρατηγὸς ἢ λοχαγός, ἵνα

37 ἀπαγγείλωσι τὰ παρὰ βασιλέως. μετὰ ταῦτα ἐξῆλθον

trust Tissaphernes. But Clearchus vehemently insisted,[22] until he secured an agreement that five generals should go and twenty captains; and about two hundred of the soldiers also followed along, with the intention of going to market.

When they reached Tissaphernes' doors, the generals were invited in—Proxenus the Boeotian, Menon the Thessalian, Agias the Arcadian, Clearchus the Laconian, and Socrates the Achaean—while the captains waited at the doors. Not long afterward, at the same signal, those within were seized and those outside were cut down. After this some of the barbarian horsemen rode about over the plain and killed every Greek they met, whether slave or freeman. And the Greeks wondered at this riding about, as they saw it from their camp, and were puzzled to know what the horsemen were doing, until Nicarchus the Arcadian reached the camp in flight, wounded in his belly and holding his bowels in his hands, and told all that had happened. Thereupon the Greeks, one and all, ran to their arms, panic-stricken and believing that the enemy would come at once against the camp.

Not all of them came, however, but Ariaeus, Artaozus, and Mithradates, who had been most faithful friends of Cyrus, did come; and the interpreter of the Greeks said that with them he also saw and recognized Tissaphernes' brother; furthermore, they were followed by other Persians, armed with breastplates, to the number of three hundred. As soon as this party had come near, they directed whatever Greek general or captain there might be to come forward, in order that they might deliver a mes-

---

[22] Ctesias, *FGH* 688 F 27 reports that Clearchus went to Tissaphernes "against his will."

φυλαττόμενοι τῶν Ἑλλήνων στρατηγοὶ μὲν Κλεάνωρ
Ὀρχομένιος καὶ Σοφαίνετος Στυμφάλιος, σὺν αὐτοῖς
δὲ Ξενοφῶν Ἀθηναῖος, ὅπως μάθοι τὰ περὶ Προξένου·
Χειρίσοφος δὲ ἐτύγχανεν ἀπὼν ἐν κώμῃ τινὶ σὺν
38 ἄλλοις ἐπισιτιζομένοις. ἐπειδὴ δὲ ἔστησαν εἰς ἐπήκοον, εἶπεν Ἀριαῖος τάδε. Κλέαρχος μέν, ὦ ἄνδρες
Ἕλληνες, ἐπεὶ ἐπιορκῶν τε ἐφάνη καὶ τὰς σπονδὰς
λύων, ἔχει τὴν δίκην καὶ τέθνηκε, Πρόξενος δὲ καὶ
Μένων, ὅτι κατήγγειλαν αὐτοῦ τὴν ἐπιβουλήν, ἐν
μεγάλῃ τιμῇ εἰσιν. ὑμᾶς δὲ βασιλεὺς τὰ ὅπλα ἀπαιτεῖ·
αὑτοῦ γὰρ εἶναί φησιν, ἐπείπερ Κύρου ἦσαν τοῦ
39 ἐκείνου δούλου. πρὸς ταῦτα ἀπεκρίναντο οἱ Ἕλληνες,
ἔλεγε δὲ Κλεάνωρ ὁ Ὀρχομένιος· Ὦ κάκιστε ἀνθρώπων Ἀριαῖε καὶ οἱ ἄλλοι ὅσοι ἦτε Κύρου φίλοι, οὐκ
αἰσχύνεσθε οὔτε θεοὺς οὔτ᾽ ἀνθρώπους, οἵτινες ὀμό-
σαντες ἡμῖν τοὺς αὐτοὺς φίλους καὶ ἐχθροὺς νομιεῖν,
προδόντες ἡμᾶς σὺν Τισσαφέρνει τῷ ἀθεωτάτῳ τε καὶ
πανουργοτάτῳ τούς τε ἄνδρας αὐτοὺς οἷς ὤμνυτε ἀπο-
λωλέκατε καὶ τοὺς ἄλλους ἡμᾶς προδεδωκότες σὺν
40 τοῖς πολεμίοις ἐφ᾽ ἡμᾶς ἔρχεσθε; ὁ δὲ Ἀριαῖος εἶπε·
Κλέαρχος γὰρ πρόσθεν ἐπιβουλεύων φανερὸς ἐγένετο
Τισσαφέρνει τε καὶ Ὀρόντᾳ, καὶ πᾶσιν ἡμῖν τοῖς σὺν
41 τούτοις. ἐπὶ τούτοις Ξενοφῶν τάδε εἶπε. Κλέαρχος μὲν
τοίνυν εἰ παρὰ τοὺς ὅρκους ἔλυε τὰς σπονδάς, τὴν
δίκην ἔχει· δίκαιον γὰρ ἀπόλλυσθαι τοὺς ἐπιορκοῦν-
τας· Πρόξενος δὲ καὶ Μένων ἐπείπερ εἰσὶν ὑμέτεροι

sage from the King. After this two generals went forth from the Greek lines under guard, Cleanor the Orchomenian and Sophaenetus the Stymphalian, and with them Xenophon the Athenian, who wished to learn the fate of Proxenus; Cheirisophus, however, chanced to be away in a village in company with others who were getting provisions. And when the Greeks got within hearing distance, Ariaeus said: "Clearchus, men of Greece, inasmuch as he was shown to be perjuring himself and violating the truce, has received his deserts and is dead, but Proxenus and Menon, because they gave information about his plotting, are held in high honour. For yourselves, the King demands your arms; for he says that they belong to him, since they belonged to Cyrus, his slave."[23] To this the Greeks replied as follows, Cleanor the Orchomenian acting as spokesman: "Ariaeus, you basest of men, and all you others who were friends of Cyrus, are you not ashamed, either before gods or men, that, after giving us your oaths to count the same people friends and foes as we did, you have betrayed us, joining hands with Tissaphernes, that most godless and villainous man, and that you have not only destroyed the very men to whom you were then making oath, but have betrayed the rest of us and are come with our enemies against us?" And Ariaeus said: "But it was shown that long ago Clearchus was plotting against Tissaphernes and Orontas and all of us who are with them." Upon this Xenophon spoke as follows: "Well, then, if Clearchus was really transgressing the truce in violation of his oaths, he has his deserts, for it is right that perjurers should perish; but as for Proxenus and Menon, since they are your benefactors and

[23] Cf. n. to I. ix. 29.

μὲν εὐεργέται, ἡμέτεροι δὲ στρατηγοί, πέμψατε αὐτοὺς
δεῦρο· δῆλον γὰρ ὅτι φίλοι γε ὄντες ἀμφοτέροις
πειράσονται καὶ ὑμῖν καὶ ἡμῖν τὰ βέλτιστα συμ-
42 βουλεύειν. πρὸς ταῦτα οἱ βάρβαροι πολὺν χρόνον
διαλεχθέντες ἀλλήλοις ἀπῆλθον οὐδὲν ἀποκρινάμενοι.

VI. Οἱ μὲν δὴ στρατηγοὶ οὕτω ληφθέντες ἀνήχθη-
σαν ὡς βασιλέα καὶ ἀποτμηθέντες τὰς κεφαλὰς ἐτε-
λεύτησαν, εἷς μὲν αὐτῶν Κλέαρχος ὁμολογουμένως ἐκ
πάντων τῶν ἐμπείρως αὐτοῦ ἐχόντων δόξας γενέσθαι
2 ἀνὴρ καὶ πολεμικὸς καὶ φιλοπόλεμος ἐσχάτως. καὶ
γὰρ δὴ ἕως μὲν πόλεμος ἦν τοῖς Λακεδαιμονίοις πρὸς
τοὺς Ἀθηναίους παρέμενεν, ἐπειδὴ δὲ εἰρήνη ἐγένετο,
πείσας τὴν αὐτοῦ πόλιν ὡς οἱ Θρᾷκες ἀδικοῦσι τοὺς
Ἕλληνας καὶ διαπραξάμενος ὡς ἐδύνατο παρὰ τῶν
ἐφόρων ἐξέπλει ὡς πολεμήσων τοῖς ὑπὲρ Χερρονήσου
3 καὶ Περίνθου Θρᾳξίν. ἐπεὶ δὲ μεταγνόντες πως οἱ
ἔφοροι ἤδη ἔξω ὄντος ἀποστρέφειν αὐτὸν ἐπειρῶντο
ἐξ Ἰσθμοῦ, ἐνταῦθα οὐκέτι πείθεται, ἀλλ᾽ ᾤχετο πλέων
4 εἰς Ἑλλήσποντον. ἐκ τούτου καὶ ἐθανατώθη ὑπὸ τῶν
ἐν Σπάρτῃ τελῶν ὡς ἀπειθῶν. ἤδη δὲ φυγὰς ὢν ἔρχεται πρὸς Κῦρον, καὶ ὁποίοις μὲν λόγοις ἔπεισε Κῦρον
ἀλλαχοῦ γέγραπται, δίδωσι δὲ αὐτῷ Κῦρος μυρίους
5 δαρεικούς· ὁ δὲ λαβὼν οὐκ ἐπὶ ῥᾳθυμίαν ἐτράπετο,

---

24 *i.e.* the Greek colonists in the Thracian Chersonese.
25 The ephors, five in number, were the ruling officials at
Sparta.   26 Clearchus seems to have been one of an increasing
number of Spartan commanders who preferred foreign assign-

our generals, send them hither, for it is clear that, being friends of both parties, they will endeavour to give both you and ourselves the best advice." To this the barbarians made no answer, but, after talking for a long time with one another, they departed.

VI. The generals, then, after being thus seized, were taken to the King and put to death by being beheaded. One of them, Clearchus, by common consent of all who were personally acquainted with him, seemed to have shown himself a man who was both fitted for war and fond of war to the last degree. For, in the first place, as long as the Lacedaemonians were at war with the Athenians, he bore his part with them; then, as soon as peace had come, he persuaded his state that the Thracians were injuring the Greeks,[24] and, after gaining his point as best he could from the ephors,[25] set sail with the intention of making war upon the Thracians who dwelt beyond the Chersonese and Perinthus. When, however, the ephors changed their minds for some reason or other and, after he had already gone, tried to turn him back from the Isthmus of Corinth, at that point he declined to render further obedience, but went sailing off to the Hellespont.[26] As a result he was condemned to death by the authorities at Sparta on the ground of disobedience to orders. Being now an exile he came to Cyrus, and the arguments whereby he persuaded Cyrus are recorded elsewhere;[27] at any rate, Cyrus gave him ten thousand darics, and he, upon receiving this money, did

ments with broadly defined powers: cf. Dercylidas, *Hell.* III. i. 8 ff., and Xenophon's general comments, *Lac*. XIV. 4.

[27] Not in the *Anabasis* or his other works. He may think he had stated these arguments in I. i. 9.

ἀλλ' ἀπὸ τούτων τῶν χρημάτων συλλέξας στράτευμα
ἐπολέμει τοῖς Θραξί, καὶ μάχῃ τε ἐνίκησε καὶ ἀπὸ
τούτου δὴ ἔφερε καὶ ἦγε τούτους καὶ πολεμῶν διεγέ-
νετο μέχρι Κῦρος ἐδεήθη τοῦ στρατεύματος· τότε δὲ
ἀπῆλθεν ὡς σὺν ἐκείνῳ αὖ πολεμήσων.

6   Ταῦτα οὖν φιλοπολέμου μοι δοκεῖ ἀνδρὸς ἔργα
εἶναι, ὅστις ἐξὸν μὲν εἰρήνην ἄγειν ἄνευ αἰσχύνης καὶ
βλάβης αἱρεῖται πολεμεῖν, ἐξὸν δὲ ῥᾳθυμεῖν βούλεται
πονεῖν ὥστε πολεμεῖν, ἐξὸν δὲ χρήματα ἔχειν ἀκιν-
δύνως αἱρεῖται πολεμῶν μείονα ταῦτα ποιεῖν· ἐκεῖνος
δὲ ὥσπερ εἰς παιδικὰ ἢ εἰς ἄλλην τινὰ ἡδονὴν ἤθελε
7 δαπανᾶν εἰς πόλεμον. οὕτω μὲν φιλοπόλεμος ἦν· πολεμικὸς δὲ αὖ ταύτῃ ἐδόκει εἶναι ὅτι φιλοκίνδυνός τε ἦν
καὶ ἡμέρας καὶ νυκτὸς ἄγων ἐπὶ τοὺς πολεμίους καὶ
ἐν τοῖς δεινοῖς φρόνιμος, ὡς οἱ παρόντες πανταχοῦ
8 πάντες ὡμολόγουν. καὶ ἀρχικὸς δ' ἐλέγετο εἶναι ὡς
δυνατὸν ἐκ τοῦ τοιούτου τρόπου οἷον κἀκεῖνος εἶχεν.
ἱκανὸς μὲν γὰρ ὥς τις καὶ ἄλλος φροντίζειν ἦν ὅπως
ἔχοι ἡ στρατιὰ αὐτῷ τὰ ἐπιτήδεια καὶ παρασκευάζειν
ταῦτα, ἱκανὸς δὲ καὶ ἐμποιῆσαι τοῖς παροῦσιν ὡς
9 πειστέον εἴη Κλεάρχῳ. τοῦτο δ' ἐποίει ἐκ τοῦ χαλεπὸς
εἶναι· καὶ γὰρ ὁρᾶν στυγνὸς ἦν καὶ τῇ φωνῇ τραχύς,
ἐκόλαζέ τε ἰσχυρῶς, καὶ ὀργῇ ἐνίοτε, ὡς καὶ αὐτῷ
10 μεταμέλειν ἔσθ' ὅτε. καὶ γνώμῃ δ' ἐκόλαζεν· ἀκολά-
στου γὰρ στρατεύματος οὐδὲν ἡγεῖτο ὄφελος εἶναι,
ἀλλὰ καὶ λέγειν αὐτὸν ἔφασαν ὡς δέοι τὸν στρα-

not turn his thoughts to comfortable idleness, but used it
to collect an army and proceeded to make war upon the
Thracians. He defeated them in battle and from that time
on plundered them in every way, and he kept up the war
until Cyrus wanted his army; then he returned, still for the
purpose of making war, this time in company with Cyrus.

Now such conduct as this, in my opinion, reveals a man
fond of war. When he may enjoy peace without dishonour
or harm, he chooses war; when he may live in idleness, he
prefers toil, provided it be the toil of war; when he may
keep his money without risk, he elects to diminish it by
carrying on war. As for Clearchus, just as one spends upon
a loved one or upon any other pleasure, so he wanted to
spend upon war—such a lover he was of war. On the other
hand, he seemed to be fitted for war in that he was fond of
danger, ready by day or night to lead his troops against the
enemy, and self-possessed amid terrors, as all who were
with him on all occasions agreed. He was likewise said to
be fitted for command, so far as that was possible for a man
of such a disposition as his was. For example, he was competent, if ever a man was, in devising ways by which his
army might get provisions and in procuring them, and he
was competent also to impress it upon those who were with
him that Clearchus must be obeyed. This result he accomplished by being severe; for he was gloomy in appearance
and harsh in voice, and he used to punish severely, sometimes in anger, so that on occasion he would be sorry afterwards.[28] Yet he also punished on principle, for he believed
there was no good in an army that went without punishment; in fact, he used to say, it was reported, that a soldier

[28] Cf. *Hell.* V. iii. 7.

τιώτην φοβεῖσθαι μᾶλλον τὸν ἄρχοντα ἢ τοὺς πολεμίους, εἰ μέλλοι ἢ φυλακὰς φυλάξειν ἢ φίλων ἀφέξ-
11 εσθαι ἢ ἀπροφασίστως ἰέναι πρὸς τοὺς πολεμίους. ἐν
μὲν οὖν τοῖς δεινοῖς ἤθελον αὐτοῦ ἀκούειν σφόδρα καὶ
οὐκ ἄλλον ἡροῦντο οἱ στρατιῶται· καὶ γὰρ τὸ στυγνὸν
αὐτοῦ τότε φαιδρὸν[11] ἐν τοῖς ἄλλοις προσώποις ἔφασαν φαίνεσθαι καὶ τὸ χαλεπὸν ἐρρωμένον πρὸς τοὺς
πολεμίους ἐδόκει εἶναι, ὥστε σωτήριον, οὐκέτι χαλε-
12 πὸν ἐφαίνετο· ὅτε δ' ἔξω τοῦ δεινοῦ γένοιντο καὶ ἐξείη
πρὸς ἄλλους ἀρξομένους ἀπιέναι, πολλοὶ αὐτὸν ἀπ-
έλειπον· τὸ γὰρ ἐπίχαρι οὐκ εἶχεν, ἀλλ' ἀεὶ χαλεπὸς
ἦν καὶ ὠμός· ὥστε διέκειντο πρὸς αὐτὸν οἱ στρατιῶται
13 ὥσπερ παῖδες πρὸς διδάσκαλον. καὶ γὰρ οὖν φιλίᾳ
μὲν καὶ εὐνοίᾳ ἑπομένους οὐδέποτε εἶχεν· οἵτινες δὲ ἢ
ὑπὸ πόλεως τεταγμένοι ἢ ὑπὸ τοῦ δεῖσθαι ἢ ἄλλῃ τινὶ
ἀνάγκῃ κατεχόμενοι παρείησαν αὐτῷ, σφόδρα πει-
14 θομένοις ἐχρῆτο. ἐπεὶ δὲ ἄρξαιντο νικᾶν ξὺν αὐτῷ τοὺς
πολεμίους, ἤδη μεγάλα ἦν τὰ χρησίμους ποιοῦντα
εἶναι τοὺς σὺν αὐτῷ στρατιώτας· τό τε γὰρ πρὸς τοὺς
πολεμίους θαρραλέως ἔχειν παρῆν καὶ τὸ τὴν παρ'
ἐκείνου τιμωρίαν φοβεῖσθαι εὐτάκτους ἐποίει. τοιοῦτος
15 μὲν δὴ ἄρχων ἦν· ἄρχεσθαι δὲ ὑπὸ ἄλλων οὐ μάλα
ἐθέλειν ἐλέγετο. ἦν δὲ ὅτε ἐτελεύτα ἀμφὶ τὰ πεντήκοντα ἔτη.

16   Πρόξενος δὲ ὁ Βοιώτιος εὐθὺς μὲν μειράκιον ὢν

___

[11] After φαιδρὸν the MSS. have αὐτοῦ ἐν τοῖς ἄλλοις
προσώποις: Cobet places αὐτοῦ after στυγνὸν, which Peters ac-

must fear his commander more than the enemy if he were to perform guard duty or keep his hands from friends or without making excuses advance against the enemy. In the midst of dangers, therefore, the troops were ready to obey him implicitly and would choose no other to command them; for they said that at such times his gloominess appeared to be brightness in the faces of others, and his severity seemed to be resolution against the enemy, so that it appeared to betoken safety and to be no longer severity. But when they had got past the danger and could go off to serve under other commanders, many would desert him; for there was no attractiveness about him, but he was always severe and rough, so that the soldiers had the same feeling toward him that boys have toward a schoolmaster. For this reason, also, he never had men following him out of friendship and good-will, but such as were under him because they had been put in his hands by a government or by their own need or were under the compulsion of any other necessity, yielded him implicit obedience. And as soon as they began in his service to overcome the enemy, from that moment there were weighty reasons which made his soldiers efficient; for they had the feeling of confidence in the face of the enemy, and their fear of punishment at his hands kept them in a fine state of discipline. Such he was as a commander, but being commanded by others was not especially to his liking, so people said. He was about fifty years old at the time of his death.

Proxenus the Boeotian cherished from his earliest

---

cepts; Hude/Peters accept ἐν … προσώποις, which are widely rejected.

ἐπεθύμει γενέσθαι ἀνὴρ τὰ μεγάλα πράττειν ἱκανός·
καὶ διὰ ταύτην τὴν ἐπιθυμίαν ἔδωκε Γοργίᾳ ἀργύριον
17 τῷ Λεοντίνῳ. ἐπεὶ δὲ συνεγένετο ἐκείνῳ, ἱκανὸς νομίσας ἤδη εἶναι καὶ ἄρχειν καὶ φίλος ὢν τοῖς πρώτοις
μὴ ἡττᾶσθαι εὐεργετῶν, ἦλθεν εἰς ταύτας τὰς σὺν
Κύρῳ πράξεις· καὶ ᾤετο κτήσεσθαι ἐκ τούτων ὄνομα
18 μέγα καὶ δύναμιν μεγάλην καὶ χρήματα πολλά· τούτων δ' ἐπιθυμῶν σφόδρα ἔνδηλον αὖ καὶ τοῦτο εἶχεν,
ὅτι τούτων οὐδὲν ἂν ἐθέλοι κτᾶσθαι μετὰ ἀδικίας,
ἀλλὰ σὺν τῷ δικαίῳ καὶ καλῷ ᾤετο δεῖν τούτων
19 τυγχάνειν, ἄνευ δὲ τούτων μή. ἄρχειν δὲ καλῶν κἀγα-
θῶν ἱκανὸς ἦν· οὐ μέντοι οὔτ' αἰδῶ τοῖς στρατιώταις
αὑτοῦ οὔτε φόβον ἱκανὸς ἐμποιῆσαι, ἀλλὰ καὶ ᾐσχύ-
νετο μᾶλλον τοὺς στρατιώτας ἢ οἱ ἀρχόμενοι ἐκεῖνον·
καὶ φοβούμενος μᾶλλον ἦν φανερὸς τὸ ἀπεχθάνεσθαι
τοῖς στρατιώταις ἢ οἱ στρατιῶται τὸ ἀπιστεῖν ἐκείνῳ.
20 ᾤετο δὲ ἀρκεῖν πρὸς τὸ ἀρχικὸν εἶναι καὶ δοκεῖν τὸν
μὲν καλῶς ποιοῦντα ἐπαινεῖν, τὸν δὲ ἀδικοῦντα μὴ
ἐπαινεῖν. τοιγαροῦν αὐτῷ οἱ μὲν καλοί τε κἀγαθοὶ τῶν
συνόντων εὖνοι ἦσαν, οἱ δὲ ἄδικοι ἐπεβούλευον ὡς
εὐμεταχειρίστῳ ὄντι. ὅτε δὲ ἀπέθνησκεν ἦν ἐτῶν ὡς
τριάκοντα.

21 Μένων δὲ ὁ Θετταλὸς δῆλος ἦν ἐπιθυμῶν μὲν
πλούτου ἰσχυρῶς, ἐπιθυμῶν δὲ ἄρχειν, ὅπως πλείω
λαμβάνοι, ἐπιθυμῶν δὲ τιμᾶσθαι, ἵνα πλείω κερδαίνοι·
φίλος τε ἐβούλετο εἶναι τοῖς μέγιστον δυναμένοις, ἵνα

youth an eager desire to become a man capable of dealing
with great affairs, and because of this desire he paid money
to Gorgias of Leontini.[29] After having studied under him
and reaching the conclusion that he had now become competent to rule and, through friendship with the foremost
men of his day, to hold his own in conferring benefits, he
embarked upon this enterprise with Cyrus, expecting to
gain therefrom a famous name, great power, and abundant
wealth; but while vehemently desiring these great ends, he
nevertheless made it evident also that he would not care
to gain any one of them unjustly; rather, he thought that
he must secure them justly and honourably, or not at all.
As a leader, he was fit to command gentlemen, but he was
not capable of inspiring his soldiers with either respect for
himself or fear; on the contrary, he really stood in greater
awe of his men than they, whom he commanded, did of
him, and it was manifest that he was more afraid of incurring the hatred of his soldiers than they were of disobeying
him. His idea was that, for a man to be and to be thought
fit to command, it was enough that he should praise the
one who did right and withhold praise from the one who
did wrong. Consequently all among his associates who
were gentlemen were attached to him, but the unprinci-
pled would plot against him in the thought that he was easy
to deal with. At the time of his death he was about thirty
years old.

Menon the Thessalian was manifestly eager for enormous wealth—eager for command in order to get more
wealth and eager for honour in order to increase his gains;
and he desired to be a friend to the men who possessed

---

[29] The celebrated rhetorician and orator; see DK 82 A 5.

22 ἀδικῶν μὴ διδοίη δίκην. ἐπὶ δὲ τὸ κατεργάζεσθαι ὧν
ἐπιθυμοίη συντομωτάτην ᾤετο ὁδὸν εἶναι διὰ τοῦ
ἐπιορκεῖν τε καὶ ψεύδεσθαι καὶ ἐξαπατᾶν, τὸ δ' ἁπλοῦν
23 καὶ ἀληθὲς ἐνόμιζε τὸ αὐτὸ τῷ ἠλιθίῳ εἶναι. στέργων
δὲ φανερὸς μὲν ἦν οὐδένα, ὅτῳ δὲ φαίη φίλος εἶναι,
τούτῳ ἔνδηλος ἐγίγνετο ἐπιβουλεύων. καὶ πολεμίου
μὲν οὐδενὸς κατεγέλα, τῶν δὲ συνόντων πάντων ὡς
24 καταγελῶν ἀεὶ διελέγετο. καὶ τοῖς μὲν τῶν πολεμίων
κτήμασιν οὐκ ἐπεβούλευε· χαλεπὸν γὰρ ᾤετο εἶναι τὰ
τῶν φυλαττομένων λαμβάνειν· τὰ δὲ τῶν φίλων μόνος
25 ᾤετο εἰδέναι ὅτι ῥᾷστον ἀφύλακτα λαμβάνειν. καὶ
ὅσους μὲν αἰσθάνοιτο ἐπιόρκους καὶ ἀδίκους ὡς εὖ
ὡπλισμένους ἐφοβεῖτο, τοῖς δ' ὁσίοις καὶ ἀληθειαν
26 ἀσκοῦσιν ὡς ἀνάνδροις ἐπειρᾶτο χρῆσθαι. ὥσπερ δέ
τις ἀγάλλεται ἐπὶ θεοσεβείᾳ καὶ ἀληθείᾳ καὶ δι-
καιότητι, οὕτω Μένων ἠγάλλετο τῷ ἐξαπατᾶν δύνασθαι, τῷ πλάσασθαι ψεύδη, τῷ φίλους διαγελᾶν· τὸν
δὲ μὴ πανοῦργον τῶν ἀπαιδεύτων ἀεὶ ἐνόμιζεν εἶναι.
καὶ παρ' οἷς μὲν ἐπεχείρει πρωτεύειν φιλίᾳ, διαβάλ-
27 λων τοὺς πρώτους τούτῳ ᾤετο δεῖν κτήσασθαι. τὸ δὲ
πειθομένους τοὺς στρατιώτας παρέχεσθαι ἐκ τοῦ συν-
αδικεῖν αὐτοῖς ἐμηχανᾶτο. τιμᾶσθαι δὲ καὶ θερα-
πεύεσθαι ἠξίου ἐπιδεικνύμενος ὅτι πλεῖστα δύναιτο
καὶ ἐθέλοι ἂν ἀδικεῖν· εὐεργεσίαν δὲ κατέλεγεν, ὁπότε

greatest power in order that he might commit unjust deeds without suffering the penalty. Again, for the accomplishment of the objects upon which his heart was set, he imagined that the shortest route was by way of perjury and falsehood and deception, while he counted straightforwardness and truth the same thing as folly. Affection he clearly felt for nobody, and if he said that he was a friend to anyone, it would become plain that this man was the one he was plotting against. He would never ridicule an enemy, but he always gave the impression in conversation of ridiculing all his associates. Neither would he devise schemes against his enemies' property, for he saw difficulty in getting hold of the possessions of people who were on their guard; but he thought he was the only one who knew that it was easiest to get hold of the property of friends—just because it was unguarded. Again, all whom he found to be perjurers and wrongdoers he would fear, regarding them as well armed, while those who were pious and practised truth he would try to make use of, regarding them as weaklings. And just as a man prides himself upon piety, truthfulness, and justice, so Menon prided himself upon ability to deceive, the fabrication of lies, and the mocking of friends; but the man who was not a rascal he always thought of as belonging to the uneducated. Again, if he were attempting to be first in the friendship of anybody, he thought that slandering those who were already first was the necessary way of gaining this end. As for making his soldiers obedient, he managed that by bearing a share in their wrongdoing. He expected, indeed, to gain honour and attention by showing that he had the ability and would have the readiness to do the most wrongs; and he set it down as a kindness, whenever anyone broke off

τις αὐτοῦ ἀφίσταιτο, ὅτι χρώμενος αὐτῷ οὐκ ἀπώλεσεν αὐτόν.

28 Καὶ τὰ μὲν δὴ ἀφανῆ ἔξεστι περὶ αὐτοῦ ψεύδεσθαι, ἃ δὲ πάντες ἴσασι τάδ᾽ ἐστί. παρὰ Ἀριστίππου μὲν ἔτι ὡραῖος ὢν στρατηγεῖν διεπράξατο τῶν ξένων, Ἀριαίῳ δὲ βαρβάρῳ ὄντι, ὅτι μειρακίοις καλοῖς ἥδετο, οἰκειότατος ἔτι ὡραῖος ὢν ἐγένετο, αὐτὸς δὲ παιδικὰ
29 εἶχε Θαρύπαν ἀγένειος ὢν γενειῶντα. ἀποθνησκόντων δὲ τῶν συστρατήγων ὅτι ἐστράτευσαν ἐπὶ βασιλέα σὺν Κύρῳ, ταὐτὰ πεποιηκὼς οὐκ ἀπέθανε, μετὰ δὲ τὸν τῶν ἄλλων θάνατον τιμωρηθεὶς ὑπὸ βασιλέως ἀπέθανεν, οὐχ ὥσπερ Κλέαρχος καὶ οἱ ἄλλοι στρατηγοὶ ἀποτμηθέντες τὰς κεφαλάς, ὅσπερ τάχιστος θάνατος δοκεῖ εἶναι, ἀλλὰ ζῶν αἰκισθεὶς ἐνιαυτὸν ὡς πονηρὸς λέγεται τῆς τελευτῆς τυχεῖν.

30 Ἀγίας δὲ ὁ Ἀρκὰς καὶ Σωκράτης ὁ Ἀχαιὸς καὶ τούτω ἀπεθανέτην. τούτων δὲ οὔθ᾽ ὡς ἐν πολέμῳ κακῶν οὐδεὶς κατεγέλα οὔτ᾽ εἰς φιλίαν αὐτοὺς ἐμέμφετο. ἤστην δὲ ἄμφω ἀμφὶ τὰ πέντε καὶ τριάκοντα ἔτη ἀπὸ γενεᾶς.

with him, that he had not, while still on terms with such a one, destroyed him.

To be sure, in matters that are doubtful one may be mistaken about him, but the facts which everybody knows are the following. From Aristippus[30] he secured, while still in the bloom of youth, an appointment as general of his mercenaries; with Ariaeus, who was a barbarian, he became extremely intimate while still young for the reason that Ariaeus was fond of beautiful youths; and, lastly, he himself, while still beardless, had a bearded favorite named Tharypas.[31] Now when his fellow generals were put to death for joining Cyrus in his expedition against the King, he, who had done the same thing, was not so treated, but it was after the execution of the others that the King visited the punishment of death upon him; and he was not, like Clearchus and the rest of the generals, beheaded—a manner of death which is counted speediest—but, report says, was tortured alive for a year and so met the death of a scoundrel.

Agias the Arcadian and Socrates the Achaean were the two others who were put to death. No one ever laughed at these men as weaklings in war or found fault with them in the matter of friendship. They were both about thirty-five years of age.

[30] See I. i. 10, ii. l, and note on I. ii. 6.

[31] The reverse of what was expected, and hence shocking: see K. Dover, *Greek Homosexuality* (London and Cambridge Mass., 1978) 87.

Γ

2   I.[1] Ἐπεὶ δὲ οἵ τε στρατηγοὶ συνειλημμένοι ἦσαν
καὶ τῶν λοχαγῶν καὶ τῶν στρατιωτῶν οἱ συνεπόμενοι
ἀπωλώλεσαν, ἐν πολλῇ δὴ ἀπορίᾳ ἦσαν οἱ Ἕλληνες,
ἐννοούμενοι ὅτι ἐπὶ ταῖς βασιλέως θύραις ἦσαν,
κύκλῳ δὲ αὐτοῖς πάντῃ πολλὰ καὶ ἔθνη καὶ πόλεις
πολέμιαι ἦσαν, ἀγορὰν δὲ οὐδεὶς ἔτι παρέξειν ἔμελλεν, ἀπεῖχον δὲ τῆς Ἑλλάδος οὐ μεῖον ἢ μύρια στάδια,
ἡγεμὼν δ' οὐδεὶς τῆς ὁδοῦ ἦν, ποταμοὶ δὲ διεῖργον
ἀδιάβατοι ἐν μέσῳ τῆς οἴκαδε ὁδοῦ, προυδεδώκεσαν
δὲ αὐτοὺς καὶ οἱ σὺν Κύρῳ ἀναβάντες βάρβαροι,
μόνοι δὲ καταλελειμμένοι ἦσαν οὐδὲ ἱππέα οὐδένα
σύμμαχον ἔχοντες, ὥστε εὔδηλον ἦν ὅτι νικῶντες μὲν
οὐδ' ἂν ἕνα κατακάνοιεν, ἡττηθέντων δὲ αὐτῶν οὐδεὶς
3   ἂν λειφθείη· ταῦτα ἐννοούμενοι καὶ ἀθύμως ἔχοντες
ὀλίγοι μὲν αὐτῶν εἰς τὴν ἑσπέραν σίτου ἐγεύσαντο,
ὀλίγοι δὲ πῦρ ἀνέκαυσαν, ἐπὶ δὲ τὰ ὅπλα πολλοὶ οὐκ

---

[1] The summary prefixed to Book III (see note on II. i. 1) is as
follows: Ὅσα μὲν δὴ ἐν τῇ ἀναβάσει τῇ μετὰ Κύρου οἱ
Ἕλληνες ἔπραξαν μέχρι τῆς μάχης, καὶ ὅσα ἐπεὶ Κῦρος
ἐτελεύτησεν ἐγένετο ἀπιόντων τῶν Ἑλλήνων σὺν Τισσαφέρνει ἐν ταῖς σπονδαῖς, ἐν τῷ πρόσθεν λόγῳ δεδήλωται.

BOOK III

I.[1] After the generals had been seized and such of the captains and soldiers as accompanied them had been killed, the Greeks were naturally in great perplexity, reflecting that they were at the King's gates, that round about them on every side were many hostile tribes and cities, that no one would provide them a market any longer, that they were distant from Greece not less than ten thousand stadia, that they had no guide to show them the way, that they were cut off by impassable rivers which flowed across the homeward route, that the barbarians who had made the upward march with Cyrus had also betrayed them, and that they were left alone, without even a single horseman to support them, so that it was quite clear that if they should be victorious, they could not kill anyone,[2] while if they should be defeated, not one of them would be left alive. Full of these reflections and despondent as they were, but few of them tasted food at evening, few kindled a fire, and many did not come that night to their

---

[1] Summary (see note to text): The preceding narrative has described all that the Greeks did in the course of the upward march with Cyrus until the time of the battle, and all that took place after the death of Cyrus while the Greeks were on the way back with Tissaphernes during the period of the truce.

[2] See II. iv. 6 and the note.

ἦλθον ταύτην τὴν νύκτα, ἀνεπαύοντο δὲ ὅπου ἐτύγχανεν ἕκαστος, οὐ δυνάμενοι καθεύδειν ὑπὸ λύπης καὶ
πόθου πατρίδων, γονέων, γυναικῶν, παίδων, οὓς οὔποτ' ἐνόμιζον ἔτι ὄψεσθαι. οὕτω μὲν δὴ διακείμενοι
πάντες ἀνεπαύοντο.

4   Ἦν δέ τις ἐν τῇ στρατιᾷ Ξενοφῶν Ἀθηναῖος, ὃς
οὔτε στρατηγὸς οὔτε λοχαγὸς οὔτε στρατιώτης ὢν
συνηκολούθει, ἀλλὰ Πρόξενος αὐτὸν μετεπέμψατο οἴκοθεν ξένος ὢν ἀρχαῖος· ὑπισχνεῖτο δὲ αὐτῷ, εἰ ἔλθοι,
φίλον αὐτὸν Κύρῳ ποιήσειν, ὃν αὐτὸς ἔφη κρείττω
5 ἑαυτῷ νομίζειν τῆς πατρίδος. ὁ μέντοι Ξενοφῶν ἀναγνοὺς τὴν ἐπιστολὴν ἀνακοινοῦται Σωκράτει τῷ Ἀθη-
ναίῳ περὶ τῆς πορείας. καὶ ὁ Σωκράτης ὑποπτεύσας
μή τι πρὸς τῆς πόλεως ὑπαίτιον εἴη Κύρῳ φίλον
γενέσθαι, ὅτι ἐδόκει ὁ Κῦρος προθύμως τοῖς Λακεδαιμονίοις ἐπὶ τὰς Ἀθήνας συμπολεμῆσαι, συμβουλεύει
τῷ Ξενοφῶντι ἐλθόντα εἰς Δελφοὺς ἀνακοινῶσαι τῷ
6 θεῷ περὶ τῆς πορείας. ἐλθὼν δ' ὁ Ξενοφῶν ἐπήρετο
τὸν Ἀπόλλω τίνι ἂν θεῶν θύων καὶ εὐχόμενος κάλλιστα καὶ ἄριστα ἔλθοι τὴν ὁδὸν ἣν ἐπινοεῖ καὶ καλῶς
πράξας σωθείη. καὶ ἀνεῖλεν αὐτῷ ὁ Ἀπόλλων θεοῖς
7 οἷς ἔδει θύειν. ἐπεὶ δὲ πάλιν ἦλθε, λέγει τὴν μαντείαν
τῷ Σωκράτει. ὁ δ' ἀκούσας ᾐτιᾶτο αὐτὸν ὅτι οὐ τοῦτο
πρῶτον ἠρώτα πότερον λῷον εἴη αὐτῷ πορεύεσθαι ἢ
μένειν, ἀλλ' αὐτὸς κρίνας ἰτέον εἶναι τοῦτ' ἐπυνθάνετο

---

3 For this passage, see Intro.

quarters, but lay down wherever they each chanced to be, unable to sleep for grief and longing for their native states and parents, their wives and children, whom they thought they should never see again. Such was the state of mind in which they all lay down to rest.

There was a man in the army named Xenophon,[3] an Athenian, who was neither general nor captain nor common soldier, but had accompanied the expedition because Proxenus, an old friend of his, had sent him at his home an invitation to go with him; Proxenus had also promised him that, if he would go, he would make him a friend of Cyrus, whom he himself regarded, so he said, as worth more to him than was his native state. After reading Proxenus' letter Xenophon conferred with Socrates, the Athenian, about the proposed journey; and Socrates, suspecting that his becoming a friend of Cyrus might be a cause for accusation against Xenophon on the part of the Athenian government, for the reason that Cyrus was thought to have given the Lacedaemonians zealous aid in their war against Athens, advised Xenophon to go to Delphi and consult the god in regard to this journey. So Xenophon went and asked Apollo to what one of the gods he should sacrifice and pray in order best and most successfully to perform the journey which he had in mind and, after meeting with good fortune, to return home in safety; and Apollo in his response told him to what gods he must sacrifice. When Xenophon came back from Delphi, he reported the oracle to Socrates; and upon hearing about it Socrates found fault with him because he did not first put the question whether it were better for him to go or stay, but decided for himself that he was to go and then asked the god as to the best way of

ὅπως ἂν κάλλιστα πορευθείη. ἐπεὶ μέντοι οὕτως ἤρου,
ταῦτ᾽, ἔφη, χρὴ ποιεῖν ὅσα ὁ θεὸς ἐκέλευσεν.

8   Ὁ μὲν δὴ Ξενοφῶν οὕτω θυσάμενος οἷς ἀνεῖλεν ὁ
θεὸς ἐξέπλει, καὶ καταλαμβάνει ἐν Σάρδεσι Πρόξενον
καὶ Κῦρον μέλλοντας ἤδη ὁρμᾶν τὴν ἄνω ὁδόν, καὶ
9 συνεστάθη Κύρῳ. προθυμουμένου δὲ τοῦ Προξένου
καὶ ὁ Κῦρος συμπρουθυμεῖτο μεῖναι αὐτόν, εἶπε δὲ ὅτι
ἐπειδὰν τάχιστα ἡ στρατεία λήξῃ, εὐθὺς ἀποπέμψει
10 αὐτόν. ἐλέγετο δὲ ὁ στόλος εἶναι εἰς Πισίδας. ἐστρατεύετο μὲν δὴ οὕτως ἐξαπατηθείς—οὐχ ὑπὸ Προξένου·
οὐ γὰρ ᾔδει τὴν ἐπὶ βασιλέα ὁρμὴν οὐδὲ ἄλλος οὐδεὶς
τῶν Ἑλλήνων πλὴν Κλεάρχου· ἐπεὶ μέντοι εἰς Κιλικίαν ἦλθον, σαφὲς πᾶσιν ἤδη ἐδόκει εἶναι ὅτι ὁ στόλος εἴη ἐπὶ βασιλέα. φοβούμενοι δὲ τὴν ὁδὸν καὶ
ἄκοντες ὅμως οἱ πολλοὶ δι᾽ αἰσχύνην καὶ ἀλλήλων καὶ
Κύρου συνηκολούθησαν· ὧν εἷς καὶ Ξενοφῶν ἦν.

11   Ἐπεὶ δὲ ἀπορία ἦν, ἐλυπεῖτο μὲν σὺν τοῖς ἄλλοις
καὶ οὐκ ἐδύνατο καθεύδειν· μικρὸν δ᾽ ὕπνου λαχὼν
εἶδεν ὄναρ. ἔδοξεν αὐτῷ βροντῆς γενομένης σκηπτὸς
πεσεῖν εἰς τὴν πατρῴαν οἰκίαν, καὶ ἐκ τούτου λάμπε-
12 σθαι πᾶσα. περίφοβος δ᾽ εὐθὺς ἀνηγέρθη, καὶ τὸ ὄναρ
τῇ μὲν ἔκρινεν ἀγαθόν, ὅτι ἐν πόνοις ὢν καὶ κινδύνοις
φῶς μέγα ἐκ Διὸς ἰδεῖν ἔδοξε· τῇ δὲ καὶ ἐφοβεῖτο, ὅτι
ἀπὸ Διὸς μὲν βασιλέως τὸ ὄναρ ἐδόκει αὐτῷ εἶναι,
κύκλῳ δὲ ἐδόκει λάμπεσθαι τὸ πῦρ, μὴ οὐ δύναιτο ἐκ

going. "However," he added, "since you did put the question in that way, you must do all that the god directed."

Xenophon, accordingly, after offering the sacrifices to the gods that Apollo's oracle prescribed, set sail, overtook Proxenus and Cyrus at Sardis as they were on the point of beginning the upward march, and was introduced to Cyrus. And not only did Proxenus urge him to stay with them, but Cyrus also joined in this request, adding that as soon as the campaign came to an end, he would send Xenophon home at once; and the report was that the campaign was against the Pisidians. It was in this way, then, that Xenophon came to go on the expedition, quite deceived about its purpose—not, however, by Proxenus, for he did not know that the attack was directed against the King, nor did anyone else among the Greeks with the exception of Clearchus; but by the time they reached Cilicia, it seemed clear to everybody that the expedition was really against the King. Then, although the Greeks were fearful of the journey and unwilling to go on, most of them did, nevertheless, out of shame before one another and before Cyrus, continue the march. And Xenophon was one of this number.

Now when despair had set in, he was distressed as well as everybody else and was unable to sleep; but, getting at length a little sleep, he had a dream. It seemed to him that there was a clap of thunder and a bolt fell on his father's house, setting the whole house ablaze. He awoke at once in great fear, and judged the dream in one way an auspicious one, because in the midst of hardships and perils he had seemed to behold a great light from Zeus; but looking at it in another way he was fearful, since the dream came, as he thought, from Zeus the King and the fire appeared

τῆς χώρας ἐξελθεῖν τῆς βασιλέως, ἀλλ᾿ εἴργοιτο πάν-
13 τοθεν ὑπό τινων ἀποριῶν. ὁποῖόν τι μὲν δή ἐστι τὸ
τοιοῦτον ὄναρ ἰδεῖν ἔξεστι σκοπεῖν ἐκ τῶν συμβάντων
μετὰ τὸ ὄναρ. γίγνεται γὰρ τάδε. εὐθὺς ἐπειδὴ ἀνηγέρθη πρῶτον μὲν ἔννοια αὐτῷ ἐμπίπτει· τί κατάκειμαι;
ἡ δὲ νὺξ προβαίνει· ἅμα δὲ τῇ ἡμέρᾳ εἰκὸς τοὺς
πολεμίους ἥξειν. εἰ δὲ γενησόμεθα ἐπὶ βασιλεῖ, τί
ἐμποδὼν μὴ οὐχὶ πάντα μὲν τὰ χαλεπώτατα ἐπιδόν-
τας, πάντα δὲ τὰ δεινότατα παθόντας ὑβριζομένους
14 ἀποθανεῖν; ὅπως δ᾿ ἀμυνούμεθα οὐδεὶς παρασκευάζε-
ται οὐδὲ ἐπιμελεῖται, ἀλλὰ κατακείμεθα ὥσπερ ἐξὸν
ἡσυχίαν ἄγειν. ἐγὼ οὖν τὸν ἐκ ποίας πόλεως στρατηγὸν προσδοκῶ ταῦτα πράξειν; ποίαν δ᾿ ἡλικίαν ἐμαυτῷ ἐλθεῖν ἀναμείνω; οὐ γὰρ ἔγωγ᾿ ἔτι πρεσβύτερος
ἔσομαι, ἐὰν τήμερον προδῶ ἐμαυτὸν τοῖς πολεμίοις.
15 Ἐκ τούτου ἀνίσταται καὶ συγκαλεῖ τοὺς Προξένου
πρῶτον λοχαγούς. ἐπεὶ δὲ συνῆλθον, ἔλεξεν· Ἐγώ, ὦ
ἄνδρες λοχαγοί, οὔτε καθεύδειν δύναμαι, ὥσπερ οἶμαι
οὐδ᾿ ὑμεῖς, οὔτε κατακεῖσθαι ἔτι, ὁρῶν ἐν οἷς ἐσμέν.
16 οἱ μὲν γὰρ πολέμιοι δῆλον ὅτι οὐ πρότερον πρὸς ἡμᾶς
τὸν πόλεμον ἐξέφηναν πρὶν ἐνόμισαν καλῶς τὰ ἑαυτῶν
παρεσκευάσθαι, ἡμῶν δ᾿ οὐδεὶς οὐδὲν ἀντεπιμελεῖται
17 ὅπως ὡς κάλλιστα ἀγωνιούμεθα. καὶ μὴν εἰ ὑφησό-
μεθα καὶ ἐπὶ βασιλεῖ γενησόμεθα, τί οἰόμεθα πείσεσθαι; ὃς καὶ τοῦ ὁμομητρίου ἀδελφοῦ καὶ τεθνηκότος

---

4 This remark, and Xenophon's subsequent words to himself,

to blaze all about, lest he might not be able to escape out of the King's country, but might be shut in on all sides by various difficulties. Now what it really means to have such a dream one may learn from the events which followed the dream—and they were these: Firstly, on the moment of his awakening the thought occurred to him: "Why do I lie here?[4] The night is wearing on, and at daybreak it is likely that the enemy will be upon us. And if we fall into the King's hands, what is there to prevent our living to behold all the most grievous sights and to experience all the most dreadful sufferings, and then being put to death with insult? As for defending ourselves, however, no one is making preparations or taking thought for that, but we lie here just as if it were possible for us to enjoy our ease. What about myself, then? From what state am I expecting the general to come who is to perform these duties? And what age must I myself wait to attain? For surely I shall never be any older, if this day I give myself up to the enemy."

Then he arose and, as a first step, called together the captains of Proxenus. When they had gathered, he said: "Gentlemen, I am unable either to sleep, as I presume you are also, or to lie still any longer, when I see in what straits we now are. For the enemy manifestly did not begin open war upon us until the moment when they believed that their own preparations had been adequately made; but on our side no one is planning any counter-measures at all to ensure our making the best possible fight. And yet if we submit and fall into the King's hands, what do we imagine our fate is to be? Even in the case of his own brother, and,

are written in the tradition of military exhortation: note esp. Callinus 1.1 (West).

ἤδη ἀποτεμὼν τὴν κεφαλὴν καὶ τὴν χεῖρα ἀνεσταύρω-
σεν· ἡμᾶς δέ, οἷς κηδεμὼν μὲν οὐδεὶς πάρεστιν, ἐστρα-
τεύσαμεν δὲ ἐπ᾽ αὐτὸν ὡς δοῦλον ἀντὶ βασιλέως ποιήσοντες καὶ ἀποκτενοῦντες εἰ δυναίμεθα, τί ἂν οἰόμεθα
18 παθεῖν; ἆρ᾽ οὐκ ἂν ἐπὶ πᾶν ἔλθοι ὡς ἡμᾶς τὰ ἔσχατα
αἰκισάμενος πᾶσιν ἀνθρώποις φόβον παράσχοι τοῦ
στρατεῦσαί ποτε ἐπ᾽ αὐτόν; ἀλλ᾽ ὅπως τοι μὴ ἐπ᾽
ἐκείνῳ γενησόμεθα πάντα ποιητέον.

19   Ἐγὼ μὲν οὖν ἔστε μὲν αἱ σπονδαὶ ἦσαν οὔποτε
ἐπαυόμην ἡμᾶς μὲν οἰκτίρων, βασιλέα δὲ καὶ τοὺς σὺν
αὐτῷ μακαρίζων, διαθεώμενος αὐτῶν ὅσην μὲν χώραν
καὶ οἵαν ἔχοιεν, ὡς δὲ ἄφθονα τὰ ἐπιτήδεια, ὅσους δὲ
20 θεράποντας, ὅσα δὲ κτήνη, χρυσὸν δέ, ἐσθῆτα δέ· τὰ
δ᾽ αὖ τῶν στρατιωτῶν ὁπότε ἐνθυμοίμην, ὅτι τῶν μὲν
ἀγαθῶν τούτων οὐδενὸς ἡμῖν μετείη, εἰ μὴ πριαίμεθα,
ὅτου δ᾽ ὠνησόμεθα ᾔδειν ἔτι ὀλίγους ἔχοντας, ἄλλως
δέ πως πορίζεσθαι τὰ ἐπιτήδεια ἢ ὠνουμένους ⟨τοὺς⟩
ὅρκους ἤδη[2] κατέχοντας ἡμᾶς· ταῦτ᾽ οὖν λογιζόμενος
ἐνίοτε τὰς σπονδὰς μᾶλλον ἐφοβούμην ἢ νῦν τὸν
21 πόλεμον. ἐπεὶ μέντοι ἐκεῖνοι ἔλυσαν τὰς σπονδάς,
λελύσθαι μοι δοκεῖ καὶ ἡ ἐκείνων ὕβρις καὶ ἡ ἡμετέρα
ἀπορία. ἐν μέσῳ γὰρ ἤδη κεῖται ταῦτα τὰ ἀγαθὰ ἆθλα
ὁπότεροι ἂν ἡμῶν ἄνδρες ἀμείνονες ὦσιν, ἀγωνοθέται
δ᾽ οἱ θεοί εἰσιν, οἳ σὺν ἡμῖν, ὡς τὸ εἰκός, ἔσονται.
22 οὗτοι μὲν γὰρ αὐτοὺς ἐπιωρκήκασιν· ἡμεῖς δὲ πολλὰ

---

[2] ⟨τοὺς⟩ Hude; ἤδη Gem., Hude/Peters following Rehdantz:
ἤδη MSS.

yet more, when he was already dead, this man cut off his head and his hand and impaled them; as for ourselves, then, who have no one to intercede for us,[5] and who took the field against him with the intention of making him a slave rather than a king and of killing him if we could, what fate may we expect to suffer? Will he not do his utmost to inflict upon us the most outrageous tortures, and thus make all mankind afraid ever to undertake an expedition against him? We, then, must make every effort not to fall into his power.

"For my part, so long as the truce lasted I never ceased commiserating ourselves and congratulating the King and his followers; for I saw plainly what a great amount of fine land they possessed, what an abundance of provisions, what quantities of servants, cattle, gold, and apparel; but whenever I took thought of the situation of our own soldiers, I saw that we had no share in these good things, unless we bought them; I knew there were but few of us who still had money wherewith to buy; and I knew that our oaths restrained us from getting provisions in any other way than by purchase. Hence, with these considerations in mind, there were times I feared the truce more than I now fear war. But seeing that their own act has put an end to the truce, the end has likewise come, in my opinion, both of their arrogance and of our predicament. For now all these good things are offered as prizes for whichever of the two parties shall prove to be the braver men; and the judges of the contest are the gods, who, in all likelihood, will be on our side. For our enemies have sworn falsely by them, while we, with abundant possessions before our

5 Cf. i. 3 f.

ὁρῶντες ἀγαθὰ στερρῶς αὐτῶν ἀπειχόμεθα διὰ τοὺς
τῶν θεῶν ὅρκους· ὥστε ἐξεῖναί μοι δοκεῖ ἰέναι ἐπὶ τὸν
23 ἀγῶνα πολὺ σὺν φρονήματι μείζονι ἢ τούτοις. ἔτι δ᾽
ἔχομεν σώματα ἱκανώτερα τούτων καὶ ψύχη καὶ θάλ-
πη καὶ πόνους φέρειν· ἔχομεν δὲ καὶ ψυχὰς σὺν τοῖς
θεοῖς ἀμείνονας· οἱ δὲ ἄνδρες καὶ τρωτοὶ καὶ θνητοὶ
μᾶλλον ἡμῶν, ἢν οἱ θεοὶ ὥσπερ τὸ πρόσθεν νίκην
ἡμῖν διδῶσιν.

24 Ἀλλ᾽ ἴσως γὰρ καὶ ἄλλοι ταῦτ᾽ ἐνθυμοῦνται, πρὸς
τῶν θεῶν μὴ ἀναμένωμεν ἄλλους ἐφ᾽ ἡμᾶς ἐλθεῖν
παρακαλοῦντας ἐπὶ τὰ κάλλιστα ἔργα, ἀλλ᾽ ἡμεῖς
ἄρξωμεν τοῦ ἐξορμῆσαι καὶ τοὺς ἄλλους ἐπὶ τὴν
ἀρετήν· φάνητε τῶν λοχαγῶν ἄριστοι καὶ τῶν στρατη-
25 γῶν ἀξιοστρατηγότεροι. κἀγὼ δέ, εἰ μὲν ὑμεῖς ἐθέλετε
ἐξορμᾶν ἐπὶ ταῦτα, ἕπεσθαι ὑμῖν βούλομαι, εἰ δ᾽ ὑμεῖς
τάττετ᾽ ἐμὲ ἡγεῖσθαι, οὐδὲν προφασίζομαι τὴν ἡλικίαν, ἀλλὰ καὶ ἀκμάζειν ἡγοῦμαι ἐρύκειν ἀπ᾽ ἐμαυτοῦ
τὰ κακά.

26 Ὁ μὲν ταῦτ᾽ ἔλεξεν, οἱ δὲ λοχαγοὶ ἀκούσαντες
ἡγεῖσθαι ἐκέλευον πάντες, πλὴν Ἀπολλωνίδης τις ἦν
βοιωτιάζων τῇ φωνῇ· οὗτος δ᾽ εἶπεν ὅτι φλυαροίη
ὅστις λέγοι ἄλλως πως σωτηρίας ἂν τυχεῖν ἢ βασιλέα
πείσαντας, εἰ δύναιντο, καὶ ἅμα ἤρχετο λέγειν τὰς
27 ἀπορίας. ὁ μέντοι Ξενοφῶν μεταξὺ ὑπολαβὼν ἔλεξεν
ὧδε. Ὦ θαυμασιώτατε ἄνθρωπε, σύγε οὐδὲ ὁρῶν

eyes, have steadfastly kept our hands therefrom because of our oaths by the gods; hence we, I think, can go into the contest with far greater confidence than can our enemies. Besides, we have bodies more capable than theirs of bearing cold and heat and toil, and we likewise, by the blessing of the gods, have better souls; and these men are more liable than we to be wounded and killed, if the gods again, as on that former day, grant us victory.

"And now, since it may be that others also have these same thoughts in mind, let us not, in the name of the gods, wait for others to come to us and summon us to the noblest deeds, but let us take the lead ourselves and arouse the rest to valour. Show yourselves the best of the captains, and more worthy to be generals than the generals themselves. As for me, if you choose to set out upon this course, I am ready to follow you; but if you assign me the leadership, I do not plead my youth as an excuse;[6] rather, I believe I am in the very prime of my power to ward off dangers from my own head."

Such were Xenophon's words; and upon hearing what he said the officers bade him take the lead, all of them except a man named Apollonides, who spoke in the Boeotian dialect. This man maintained that anyone who said they could gain safety in any other way than by winning the King's consent through persuasion, if possible, was talking nonsense; and at the same time he began to recite the difficulties of their situation. But Xenophon interrupted him in the midst of his talk, and said: "You amazing fellow, you have eyes but still do not perceive, and you have

---

[6] On Xenophon's age, see Intro. Cf. VII. ii. 38.

γιγνώσκεις οὐδὲ ἀκούων μέμνησαι. ἐν ταὐτῷ γε μέντοι
ἦσθα τούτοις ὅτε βασιλεύς, ἐπεὶ Κῦρος ἀπέθανε, μέγα
φρονήσας ἐπὶ τούτῳ πέμπων ἐκέλευε παραδιδόναι τὰ
28 ὅπλα. ἐπεὶ δὲ ἡμεῖς οὐ παραδόντες, ἀλλ' ἐξωπλισμένοι
ἐλθόντες παρεσκηνήσαμεν αὐτῷ, τί οὐκ ἐποίησε
πρέσβεις πέμπων καὶ σπονδὰς αἰτῶν καὶ παρέχων τὰ
29 ἐπιτήδεια, ἔστε σπονδῶν ἔτυχεν; ἐπεὶ δ' αὖ οἱ στρατηγοὶ καὶ λοχαγοί, ὥσπερ δὴ σὺ κελεύεις, εἰς λόγους
αὐτοῖς ἄνευ ὅπλων ἦλθον πιστεύσαντες ταῖς σπονδαῖς, οὐ νῦν ἐκεῖνοι παιόμενοι, κεντούμενοι, ὑβριζόμε-
νοι οὐδὲ ἀποθανεῖν οἱ τλήμονες δύνανται, καὶ μάλ'
οἶμαι ἐρῶντες τούτου; ἃ σὺ πάντα εἰδὼς τοὺς μὲν
ἀμύνεσθαι κελεύοντας φλυαρεῖν φής, πείθειν δὲ πάλιν
30 κελεύεις ἰόντας; ἐμοὶ δέ, ὦ ἄνδρες, δοκεῖ τὸν ἄνθρωπον
τοῦτον μήτε προσίεσθαι εἰς ταὐτὸν ἡμῖν αὐτοῖς ἀφελο-
μένους τε τὴν λοχαγίαν σκεύη ἀναθέντας ὡς τοιούτῳ
χρῆσθαι. οὗτος γὰρ καὶ τὴν πατρίδα καταισχύνει καὶ
πᾶσαν τὴν Ἑλλάδα, ὅτι Ἕλλην ὢν τοιοῦτός ἐστιν.
31 Ἐντεῦθεν ὑπολαβὼν Ἀγασίας Στυμφάλιος εἶπεν·
Ἀλλὰ τούτῳ γε οὔτε τῆς Βοιωτίας προσήκει οὐδὲν
οὔτε τῆς Ἑλλάδος παντάπασιν, ἐπεὶ ἐγὼ αὐτὸν εἶδον
ὥσπερ Λυδὸν ἀμφότερα τὰ ὦτα τετρυπημένον. καὶ

---

7 A proverbial expression: Demosthenes XXV.89; cf. Aeschy-
lus, *Pr.* 447–8, *Ag.* 1623, and NT Matthew 13:13ff. Cf. Plato, *Phd.*
65b.

8 The Greeks considered it effeminate for a man to wear ear-
rings. His pierced ears, therefore, marked Apollonides as a bar-

ears but still do not remember.[7] You were present, surely, with the rest of these officers at the time when the King, after the death of Cyrus and in his elation over that event, sent and ordered us to give up our arms. But when, instead of giving them up, we equipped ourselves with them, and went and encamped beside him, what means did he leave untried—sending ambassadors, begging for a truce, offering us provisions—until in the end he obtained a truce? When, however, our generals and captains, following precisely the plan that you are now urging, went unarmed to a conference with them, relying upon the truce, what happened in that case? Are they not at this moment being beaten, tortured, insulted, unable even to die, hapless men that they are, even though they earnestly long, I imagine, for death? And do you, knowing all these things, say that they are talking nonsense who urge self-defence, and do you propose that we should again go and try persuasion? In my opinion, gentlemen, we should not simply refuse to admit this fellow to companionship with us, but should deprive him of his captaincy, lay packs on his back, and treat him as that sort of a creature. For the fellow is a disgrace both to his native state and to the whole of Greece, since, being a Greek, he is still a man of this kind."

Then Agasias, a Stymphalian, broke in and said: "For that matter, this fellow has nothing to do either with Boeotia or with any part of Greece at all, for I have noticed that he has both his ears pierced,[8] like a Lydian's."[9] In fact,

barian. See Anacreon *PMG* 388 = Athen. XII. 533, and cf. Aristotle, *Pr.* 961a.

[9] The Lydians were proverbially effeminate: Hdt. I. clv. 4.

32 εἶχεν οὕτως. τοῦτον μὲν οὖν ἀπήλασαν· οἱ δὲ ἄλλοι
παρὰ τὰς τάξεις ἰόντες ὅπου μὲν στρατηγὸς σῶς εἴη
τὸν στρατηγὸν παρεκάλουν, ὁπόθεν δὲ οἴχοιτο τὸν
ὑποστράτηγον, ὅπου δ' αὖ λοχαγὸς σῶς εἴη τὸν λοχα-
33 γόν. ἐπεὶ δὲ πάντες συνῆλθον, εἰς τὸ πρόσθεν τῶν
ὅπλων ἐκαθέζοντο· καὶ ἐγένοντο οἱ συνελθόντες στρατηγοὶ καὶ λοχαγοὶ ἀμφὶ τοὺς ἑκατόν. ὅτε δὲ ταῦτα ἦν
34 σχεδὸν μέσαι ἦσαν νύκτες. ἐνταῦθα Ἱερώνυμος Ἠλεῖος πρεσβύτατος ὢν τῶν Προξένου λοχαγῶν ἤρχετο
λέγειν ὧδε. Ἡμῖν, ὦ ἄνδρες στρατηγοὶ καὶ λοχαγοί,
ὁρῶσι τὰ παρόντα ἔδοξε καὶ αὐτοῖς συνελθεῖν καὶ
ὑμᾶς παρακαλέσαι, ὅπως βουλευσαίμεθα εἴ τι δυναίμεθα ἀγαθόν. λέξον δ', ἔφη, καὶ σύ, ὦ Ξενοφῶν, ἅπερ
καὶ πρὸς ἡμᾶς.

35 Ἐκ τούτου λέγει τάδε Ξενοφῶν· Ἀλλὰ ταῦτα μὲν
δὴ πάντες ἐπιστάμεθα, ὅτι βασιλεὺς καὶ Τισσαφέρνης οὓς μὲν ἐδυνήθησαν συνειλήφασιν ἡμῶν, τοῖς δ'
ἄλλοις δῆλον ὅτι ἐπιβουλεύουσιν, ὡς ἢν δύνωνται
ἀπολέσωσιν. ἡμῖν δέ γε οἶμαι πάντα ποιητέα ὡς
μήποτε ἐπὶ τοῖς βαρβάροις γενώμεθα, ἀλλὰ μᾶλλον
36 ἢν δυνώμεθα ἐκεῖνοι ἐφ' ἡμῖν. εὖ τοίνυν ἐπίστασθε ὅτι
ὑμεῖς τοσοῦτοι ὄντες ὅσοι νῦν συνεληλύθατε μέγιστον
ἔχετε καιρόν. οἱ γὰρ στρατιῶται οὗτοι πάντες πρὸς
ὑμᾶς ἀποβλέπουσι, κἂν μὲν ὑμᾶς ὁρῶσιν ἀθυμοῦντας,
πάντες κακοὶ ἔσονται, ἢν δὲ ὑμεῖς αὐτοί τε παρα-
σκευαζόμενοι φανεροὶ ἦτε ἐπὶ τοὺς πολεμίους καὶ

it was so. He, therefore, was driven away,[10] but the others proceeded to visit the various divisions of the army. Wherever a general was left alive, they would invite him to join them; where the general was gone, they invited the lieutenant-general; or, again, where only a captain was left, the captain. When all had come together, they seated themselves at the front of the encampment, and the generals and captains thus assembled amounted in number to about one hundred. By this time it was nearly midnight. Then Hieronymus the Elean, who was the eldest of Proxenus' captains, began to speak as follows: "Generals and captains, we have deemed it best, in view of the present situation, both to come together ourselves and to invite you to join us, in order that we may devise whatever good counsel we can. Repeat then, Xenophon," he added, "just what you said to us."

Thereupon Xenophon spoke as follows: " We all understand thus much, that the King and Tissaphernes have seized as many as they could of our number, and that they are manifestly plotting against the rest of us, to destroy us if they can. It is for us, then, in my opinion, to make every effort that we may never fall into the power of the barbarians, but that, if we can accomplish it, they may rather fall into our power. Be sure, therefore, that you, who have now come together in such numbers, have the grandest of opportunities. For all our soldiers here are looking to you; if they see that you are fainthearted, all of them will be cowards; but if you not only show that you are making preparations yourselves against the enemy, but call upon

---

[10] A textbook case of a scapegoat or φαρμακός: see W. Burkert, *Greek Religion* (Oxford and Cambridge Mass., 1985) 82–4.

τοὺς ἄλλους παρακαλῆτε, εὖ ἴστε ὅτι ἕψονται ὑμῖν καὶ
37 πειράσονται μιμεῖσθαι. ἴσως δέ τοι καὶ δίκαιόν ἐστιν
ὑμᾶς διαφέρειν τι τούτων. ὑμεῖς γάρ ἐστε στρατηγοί,
ὑμεῖς ταξίαρχοι καὶ λοχαγοί· καὶ ὅτε εἰρήνη ἦν, ὑμεῖς
καὶ χρήμασι καὶ τιμαῖς τούτων ἐπλεονεκτεῖτε· καὶ νῦν
τοίνυν ἐπεὶ πόλεμός ἐστιν, ἀξιοῦν δεῖ ὑμᾶς αὐτοὺς
ἀμείνους τε τοῦ πλήθους εἶναι καὶ προβουλεύειν τού-
38 των καὶ προπονεῖν, ἤν που δέῃ.

Καὶ νῦν πρῶτον μὲν οἶμαι ἂν ὑμᾶς μέγα ὀνῆσαι τὸ
στράτευμα, εἰ ἐπιμεληθείητε ὅπως ἀντὶ τῶν ἀπο-
λωλότων ὡς τάχιστα στρατηγοὶ καὶ λοχαγοὶ ἀντι-
κατασταθῶσιν. ἄνευ γὰρ ἀρχόντων οὐδὲν ἂν οὔτε
καλὸν οὔτε ἀγαθὸν γένοιτο ὡς μὲν συνελόντι εἰπεῖν
οὐδαμοῦ, ἐν δὲ δὴ τοῖς πολεμικοῖς παντάπασιν. ἡ μὲν
γὰρ εὐταξία σῴζειν δοκεῖ, ἡ δὲ ἀταξία πολλοὺς ἤδη
39 ἀπολώλεκεν. ἐπειδὰν δὲ καταστήσησθε τοὺς ἄρχοντας
ὅσους δεῖ, ἢν καὶ τοὺς ἄλλους στρατιώτας συλλέγητε
καὶ παραθαρρύνητε, οἶμαι ἂν ὑμᾶς πάνυ ἐν καιρῷ
40 ποιῆσαι. νῦν γὰρ ἴσως καὶ ὑμεῖς αἰσθάνεσθε ὡς
ἀθύμως μὲν ἦλθον ἐπὶ τὰ ὅπλα, ἀθύμως δὲ πρὸς τὰς
φυλακάς· ὥστε οὕτω γ᾽ ἐχόντων οὐκ οἶδα ὅ τι ἄν τις
χρήσαιτο αὐτοῖς, εἴτε νυκτὸς δέοι τι εἴτε καὶ ἡμέρας.
41 ἢν δέ τις αὐτῶν τρέψῃ τὰς γνώμας, ὡς μὴ τοῦτο μόνον
ἐννοῶνται τί πείσονται ἀλλὰ καὶ τί ποιήσουσι, πολὺ
42 εὐθυμότεροι ἔσονται. ἐπίστασθε γὰρ δὴ ὅτι οὔτε πλῆ-

---

11 Cf. *Iliad* XII. 310 ff.

the rest to do likewise, be well assured that they will follow
you and will try to imitate you. But perhaps it is really
proper that you should somewhat excel them. For you are
generals, you are lieutenant-generals and captains; while
peace lasted, you had the advantage of them alike in pay
and in standing; now, therefore, when a state of war exists,
it is right to expect that you should be superior to the
common soldiers, and that you should plan for them and
toil for them whenever there be need.[11]

"And now, firstly, I think you would do the army a great
service if you should see to it that generals and captains are
appointed as speedily as possible to take the places of those
who are lost. For without leaders nothing fine or useful can
be accomplished in any field, to put it broadly, and certainly not in warfare. For discipline, it seems, keeps men
in safety, while the lack of it has brought many before now
to destruction.[12] Secondly, when you have appointed all
the leaders that are necessary, I think you would perform
a very opportune act if you should gather together the rest
of the soldiers also and try to encourage them. For, as
matters stand now, perhaps you have observed for yourselves in what dejection they came to their quarters and in
what dejection they proceeded to their guard duty; and so
long as they are in this state, I know not what use one could
make of them, if there should be need of them either by
night or by day. If, however, we can turn the current of their
minds, so that they shall be thinking, not merely of what
they are to suffer, but likewise of what they are going to do,
they will be far more cheerful. For you understand, I am

---

[12] Order and discipline are central to Xenophon's thinking: cf.,
e.g. *Oec.* VIII, *Mem.* III. i. 7, *Cyr.* II. i. 27.

θός ἐστιν οὔτε ἰσχὺς ἡ ἐν τῷ πολέμῳ τὰς νίκας
ποιοῦσα, ἀλλ' ὁπότεροι ἂν σὺν τοῖς θεοῖς ταῖς ψυχαῖς
ἐρρωμενέστεροι ἴωσιν ἐπὶ τοὺς πολεμίους, τούτους ὡς
43 ἐπὶ τὸ πολὺ οἱ ἀντίοι οὐ δέχονται. ἐντεθύμημαι δ'
ἔγωγε, ὦ ἄνδρες, καὶ τοῦτο, ὅτι ὁπόσοι μὲν μαστεύ-
ουσι ζῆν ἐκ παντὸς τρόπου ἐν τοῖς πολέμοις, οὗτοι
μὲν κακῶς τε καὶ αἰσχρῶς ὡς ἐπὶ τὸ πολὺ ἀποθνήσκουσιν, ὁπόσοι δὲ τὸν μὲν θάνατον ἐγνώκασι πᾶσι
κοινὸν εἶναι καὶ ἀναγκαῖον ἀνθρώποις, περὶ δὲ τοῦ
καλῶς ἀποθνήσκειν ἀγωνίζονται, τούτους ὁρῶ μᾶλλόν
πως εἰς τὸ γῆρας ἀφικνουμένους καὶ ἕως ἂν ζῶσιν
44 εὐδαιμονέστερον διάγοντας. ἃ καὶ ἡμᾶς[3] δεῖ νῦν κατα-
μαθόντας, ἐν τοιούτῳ γὰρ καιρῷ ἐσμεν, αὐτούς τε
45 ἄνδρας ἀγαθοὺς εἶναι καὶ τοὺς ἄλλους παρακαλεῖν. ὁ
μὲν ταῦτ' εἰπὼν ἐπαύσατο.

Μετὰ τοῦτον δ' εἶπε Χειρίσοφος· Ἀλλὰ πρόσθεν
μέν, ὦ Ξενοφῶν, τοσοῦτον μόνον σε ἐγίγνωσκον ὅσον
ἤκουον Ἀθηναῖον εἶναι, νῦν δὲ καὶ ἐπαινῶ σε ἐφ' οἷς
λέγεις τε καὶ πράττεις καὶ βουλοίμην ἂν ὅτι πλείστους
46 εἶναι τοιούτους· κοινὸν γὰρ ἂν εἴη τὸ ἀγαθόν. καὶ νῦν,
ἔφη, μὴ μέλλωμεν, ὦ ἄνδρες, ἀλλ' ἀπελθόντες ἤδη
αἱρεῖσθε οἱ δεόμενοι ἄρχοντας, καὶ ἑλόμενοι ἥκετε εἰς
τὸ μέσον τοῦ στρατοπέδου καὶ τοὺς αἱρεθέντας ἄγετε·
ἔπειτ' ἐκεῖ συγκαλοῦμεν τοὺς ἄλλους στρατιώτας.
47 παρέστω δ' ἡμῖν, ἔφη, καὶ Τολμίδης ὁ κῆρυξ. καὶ ἅμα

---

[3] ἡμᾶς some MSS., Gem., Hude/Peters: ὑμᾶς other MSS.,
Mar.

sure, that it is neither numbers nor strength which wins victories in war; but whichever of the two sides it be whose troops, by the blessing of the gods, advance to the attack with stouter hearts, against those troops their adversaries generally refuse to stand. And in my own experience, gentlemen, I have observed this other fact, that those who are anxious in war to save their lives in any way they can, are the very men who usually meet with a base and shameful death; while those who have recognized that death is the common and inevitable portion of all mankind and therefore strive to meet death nobly, are precisely those who are somehow more likely to reach old age and who enjoy a happier existence while they do live. We, then, taking to heart this lesson, so suited to the crisis which now confronts us, must be brave men ourselves and call forth bravery in our fellows." With these words Xenophon ceased speaking.

After him Cheirisophus said: "Hitherto, Xenophon, I have known you only to the extent of having heard that you were an Athenian, but now I commend you both for your words and your deeds, and I should be glad if we had very many of your sort; for it would be a blessing to the entire army. And now, gentlemen," he went on, "let us not delay; withdraw and choose your commanders at once, you who need them, and after making your choices come to the middle of the camp and bring with you the men you have selected; then we will call a meeting there of all the troops. And let us make sure," he added, "'that Tolmides, the herald, is present." With these words he got up at once,

XENOPHON

ταῦτ᾽ εἰπὼν ἀνέστη, ὡς μὴ μέλλοιτο ἀλλὰ περαίνοιτο
τὰ δέοντα. ἐκ τούτου ᾑρέθησαν ἄρχοντες ἀντὶ μὲν
Κλεάρχου Τιμασίων Δαρδανεύς, ἀντὶ δὲ Σωκράτους
Ξανθικλῆς Ἀχαιός, ἀντὶ δὲ Ἀγίου Κλεάνωρ Ἀρκάς,[4]
ἀντὶ δὲ Μένωνος Φιλήσιος Ἀχαιός, ἀντὶ δὲ Προξένου
Ξενοφῶν Ἀθηναῖος.

II. Ἐπεὶ δὲ ᾕρηντο, ἡμέρα τε σχεδὸν ὑπέφαινε καὶ
εἰς τὸ μέσον ἧκον οἱ ἄρχοντες, καὶ ἔδοξεν αὐτοῖς
προφυλακὰς καταστήσαντας συγκαλεῖν τοὺς στρατιώτας. ἐπεὶ δὲ καὶ οἱ ἄλλοι στρατιῶται συνῆλθον,
ἀνέστη πρῶτον μὲν Χειρίσοφος ὁ Λακεδαιμόνιος καὶ
2 ἔλεξεν ὧδε. Ὦ ἄνδρες στρατιῶται, χαλεπὰ μὲν τὰ
παρόντα, ὁπότε ἀνδρῶν στρατηγῶν τοιούτων στερό-
μεθα καὶ λοχαγῶν καὶ στρατιωτῶν, πρὸς δ᾽ ἔτι καὶ οἱ
ἀμφὶ Ἀριαῖον οἱ πρόσθεν σύμμαχοι ὄντες προδεδώ-
3 κασιν ἡμᾶς· ὅμως δὲ δεῖ ἐκ τῶν παρόντων ἄνδρας
ἀγαθοὺς τελέθειν καὶ μὴ ὑφίεσθαι, ἀλλὰ πειρᾶσθαι
ὅπως ἢν μὲν δυνώμεθα καλῶς νικῶντες σῳζώμεθα· εἰ
δὲ μή, ἀλλὰ καλῶς γε ἀποθνῄσκωμεν, ὑποχείριοι δὲ
μηδέποτε γενώμεθα ζῶντες τοῖς πολεμίοις. οἶμαι γὰρ
ἂν ἡμᾶς τοιαῦτα παθεῖν οἷα τοὺς ἐχθροὺς οἱ θεοὶ
ποιήσειαν.

4 Ἐπὶ τούτῳ Κλεάνωρ ὁ Ὀρχομένιος ἀνέστη καὶ
ἔλεξεν ὧδε. Ἀλλ᾽ ὁρᾶτε μέν, ὦ ἄνδρες, τὴν βασιλέως
ἐπιορκίαν καὶ ἀσέβειαν, ὁρᾶτε δὲ τὴν Τισσαφέρνους
ἀπιστίαν, ὅστις λέγων ὡς γείτων τε εἴη τῆς Ἑλλάδος

---

[4] Κλεάνωρ Ἀρκάς some MSS., Hude/Peters, Mar.: Ἀρκάδος

234

that there might be no delay in carrying out the needful measures. Thereupon the commanders were chosen, Timasion the Dardanian in place of Clearchus, Xanthicles the Achaean in place of Socrates, Cleanor the Arcadian in place of Agias, Philesius the Achaean in place of Menon, and Xenophon the Athenian in place of Proxenus.

II. When these elections had been completed, and as day was just about beginning to break, the commanders met in the middle of the camp; and they resolved to station outposts and then call an assembly of the soldiers. As soon as they had come together, Cheirisophus the Lacedaemonian arose first and spoke as follows: "Fellow soldiers, painful indeed is our present situation, seeing that we are robbed of such generals and captains and soldiers, and, besides, that Ariaeus and his men, who were formerly our allies, have betrayed us; nevertheless, we must show ourselves brave men in such circumstances, and must not yield, but rather try to save ourselves by glorious victory if we can; otherwise, let us at least die a glorious death, and never fall into the hands of our enemies alive. For in that case I think we should meet the sort of sufferings that I pray the gods may visit upon our foes."

Then Cleanor the Orchomenian arose and spoke as follows: "Come, fellow soldiers, you see the perjury and impiety of the King; you see likewise the faithlessness of Tissaphernes. It was Tissaphernes who said[13] that he was a neighbour of Greece and that he would do his utmost to

---

[13] II. iii. 18.

Κλεάνωρ ὁ Ὀρχομένιος other MSS., which Gem. follows, bracketing Ἀρκάδος.

καὶ περὶ πλείστου ἂν ποιήσαιτο σῶσαι ἡμᾶς, καὶ ἐπὶ
τούτοις αὐτὸς ὀμόσας ἡμῖν, αὐτὸς δεξιὰς δούς, αὐτὸς
ἐξαπατήσας συνέλαβε τοὺς στρατηγούς, καὶ οὐδὲ Δία
ξένιον ᾐδέσθη, ἀλλὰ Κλεάρχῳ καὶ ὁμοτράπεζος γενόμενος αὐτοῖς τούτοις ἐξαπατήσας τοὺς ἄνδρας ἀπο-
5 λώλεκεν. Ἀριαῖος δέ, ὃν ἡμεῖς ἠθέλομεν βασιλέα
καθιστάναι, καὶ ἐδώκαμεν καὶ ἐλάβομεν πιστὰ μὴ
προδώσειν ἀλλήλους, καὶ οὗτος οὔτε τοὺς θεοὺς
δείσας οὔτε Κῦρον τεθνηκότα αἰδεσθείς, τιμώμενος
μάλιστα ὑπὸ Κύρου ζῶντος, νῦν πρὸς τοὺς ἐκείνου
ἐχθίστους ἀποστὰς ἡμᾶς τοὺς Κύρου φίλους κακῶς
6 ποιεῖν πειρᾶται. ἀλλὰ τούτους μὲν οἱ θεοὶ ἀποτεί-
σαιντο· ἡμᾶς δὲ δεῖ ταῦτα ὁρῶντας μήποτε ἐξαπατηθῆναι ἔτι ὑπὸ τούτων, ἀλλὰ μαχομένους ὡς ἂν δυνώμεθα κράτιστα τοῦτο ὅ τι ἂν δοκῇ τοῖς θεοῖς πάσχειν.
7   Ἐκ τούτου Ξενοφῶν ἀνίσταται ἐσταλμένος ἐπὶ
πόλεμον ὡς ἐδύνατο κάλλιστα, νομίζων, εἴτε νίκην
διδοῖεν οἱ θεοί, τὸν κάλλιστον κόσμον τῷ νικᾶν πρέ-
πειν, εἴτε τελευτᾶν δέοι, ὀρθῶς ἔχειν τῶν καλλίστων
ἑαυτὸν ἀξιώσαντα ἐν τούτοις τῆς τελευτῆς τυγχάνειν·
8 τοῦ λόγου δὲ ἤρχετο ὧδε. Τὴν μὲν τῶν βαρβάρων
ἐπιορκίαν τε καὶ ἀπιστίαν λέγει μὲν Κλεάνωρ, ἐπίστασθε δὲ καὶ ὑμεῖς οἶμαι. εἰ μὲν οὖν βουλόμεθα
πάλιν αὐτοῖς διὰ φιλίας ἰέναι, ἀνάγκη ἡμᾶς πολλὴν
ἀθυμίαν ἔχειν, ὁρῶντας καὶ τοὺς στρατηγούς, οἳ διὰ
πίστεως αὐτοῖς ἑαυτοὺς ἐνεχείρισαν, οἷα πεπόνθασιν·

save us; it was none other than he who gave us his oaths to confirm these words; and then he, Tissaphernes, the very man who had given such pledges, was the very man who deceived and seized our generals. More than that, he did not even reverence Zeus, the god of hospitality; instead, he entertained Clearchus at his own table[14] and then made that very act the means of deceiving and destroying the generals. Ariaeus, too, whom we were ready to make king,[15] with whom we exchanged pledges[16] not to betray one another, even he, showing neither fear of the gods nor honour for the memory of Cyrus dead, although he was most highly honoured by Cyrus living, has now gone over to the bitterest foes of that same Cyrus, and is trying to work harm to us, the friends of Cyrus. Well, may these men be duly punished by the gods; we, however, seeing their deeds, must never again be deceived by them, but must fight as stoutly as we can and meet whatever fortune the gods may please to send."

Hereupon Xenophon arose, arrayed for war in his finest dress. For he thought that if the gods should grant victory, the finest raiment was suited to victory; and if it should be his fate to die, it was proper, he thought, that inasmuch as he had accounted his office worthy of the most beautiful attire, in this attire he should meet his death. He began his speech as follows: "The perjury and faithlessness of the barbarians has been spoken of by Cleanor and is understood, I imagine, by the rest of you. If, then, it is our desire to be again on terms of friendship with them, we must needs feel great despondency when we see the fate of our generals, who trustingly put themselves in their hands; but

[14] II. v. 27.   [15] II. i. 4.   [16] II. ii. 8.

εἰ μέντοι διανοούμεθα σὺν τοῖς ὅπλοις ὧν τε πε-
ποιήκασι δίκην ἐπιθεῖναι αὐτοῖς καὶ τὸ λοιπὸν διὰ
παντὸς πολέμου αὐτοῖς ἰέναι, σὺν τοῖς θεοῖς πολλαὶ
ἡμῖν καὶ καλαὶ ἐλπίδες εἰσὶ σωτηρίας.

9   Τοῦτο δὲ λέγοντος αὐτοῦ πτάρνυταί τις· ἀκούσαντες δ᾽ οἱ στρατιῶται πάντες μιᾷ ὁρμῇ προσεκύνησαν
τὸν θεόν, καὶ ὁ Ξενοφῶν εἶπε· Δοκεῖ μοι, ὦ ἄνδρες,
ἐπεὶ περὶ σωτηρίας ἡμῶν λεγόντων οἰωνὸς τοῦ Διὸς
τοῦ σωτῆρος ἐφάνη, εὔξασθαι τῷ θεῷ τούτῳ θύσειν
σωτήρια ὅπου ἂν πρῶτον εἰς φιλίαν χώραν ἀφικώ-
μεθα, συνεπεύξασθαι δὲ καὶ τοῖς ἄλλοις θεοῖς θύσειν
κατὰ δύναμιν. καὶ ὅτῳ δοκεῖ ταῦτ᾽, ἔφη, ἀνατεινάτω
τὴν χεῖρα. καὶ ἀνέτειναν ἅπαντες. ἐκ τούτου ηὔξαντο
καὶ ἐπαιάνισαν. ἐπεὶ δὲ τὰ τῶν θεῶν καλῶς εἶχεν,
ἤρχετο πάλιν ὧδε.

10   Ἐτύγχανον λέγων ὅτι πολλαὶ καὶ καλαὶ ἐλπίδες
ἡμῖν εἶεν σωτηρίας. πρῶτον μὲν γὰρ ἡμεῖς μὲν ἐμπε-
δοῦμεν τοὺς τῶν θεῶν ὅρκους, οἱ δὲ πολέμιοι ἐπι-
ωρκήκασί τε καὶ τὰς σπονδὰς παρὰ τοὺς ὅρκους
λελύκασιν. οὕτω δ᾽ ἐχόντων εἰκὸς τοῖς μὲν πολεμίοις
ἐναντίους εἶναι τοὺς θεούς, ἡμῖν δὲ συμμάχους, οἵπερ
ἱκανοί εἰσι καὶ τοὺς μεγάλους ταχὺ μικροὺς ποιεῖν καὶ
τοὺς μικροὺς κἂν ἐν δεινοῖς ὦσι σῴζειν εὐπετῶς, ὅταν
11   βούλωνται. ἔπειτα δὲ ἀναμνήσω γὰρ ὑμᾶς καὶ τοὺς
τῶν προγόνων τῶν ἡμετέρων κινδύνους, ἵνα εἰδῆτε ὡς

---

17 The sneeze was a lucky sign, and particularly lucky because
it came at just the time when Xenophon was uttering the word

if our intention is to rely upon our arms, and not only to inflict punishment upon them for their past deeds, but henceforth to wage implacable war with them, we have—the gods willing—many fair hopes of deliverance."

As he was saying this a man sneezed,[17] and when the soldiers heard it, they all with one impulse made obeisance to the god;[18] and Xenophon said, "I move, gentlemen, since at the moment when we were talking about deliverance an omen from Zeus the Saviour was revealed to us, that we make a vow to sacrifice to that god thank-offerings for deliverance as soon as we reach a friendly land; and that we add a further vow to make sacrifices, to the extent of our ability, to the other gods also. All who are in favour of this motion," he said, "will raise their hands." And every man in the assembly raised his hand. Thereupon they made their vows and struck up the paean. These ceremonies duly performed, Xenophon began again with these words:

"I was saying that we have many fair hopes of deliverance. For, in the first place, we are standing true to the oaths we took in the name of the gods, while our enemies have perjured themselves and, in violation of their oaths, have broken the truce. This being so, it is fair to assume that the gods are their foes and our allies—and the gods are able speedily to make the strong weak and, when they so will, easily to deliver the weak, even though they be in dire perils. Secondly, I would remind you of the perils of our own forefathers, to show you not only that it is your

σωτηρίας, "deliverance." Cf. *Odyssey* XVII. 541.
[18] Zeus Soter, who was presumed to have sent the omen.

ἀγαθοῖς τε ὑμῖν προσήκει εἶναι σῴζονταί τε σὺν τοῖς
θεοῖς καὶ ἐκ πάνυ δεινῶν οἱ ἀγαθοί. ἐλθόντων μὲν γὰρ
Περσῶν καὶ τῶν σὺν αὐτοῖς παμπληθεῖ στόλῳ ὡς
ἀφανιούντων τὰς Ἀθήνας, ὑποστῆναι αὐτοὶ Ἀθηναῖοι
12 τολμήσαντες ἐνίκησαν αὐτούς. καὶ εὐξάμενοι τῇ Ἀρτέμιδι ὁπόσους κατακάνοιεν τῶν πολεμίων τοσαύτας
χιμαίρας καταθύσειν τῇ θεῷ, ἐπεὶ οὐκ εἶχον ἱκανὰς
εὑρεῖν, ἔδοξεν αὐτοῖς κατ' ἐνιαυτὸν πεντακοσίας θύειν,
13 καὶ ἔτι νῦν ἀποθύουσιν. ἔπειτα ὅτε Ξέρξης ὕστερον
ἀγείρας τὴν ἀναρίθμητον στρατιὰν ἦλθεν ἐπὶ τὴν
Ἑλλάδα, καὶ τότε ἐνίκων οἱ ἡμέτεροι πρόγονοι τοὺς
τούτων προγόνους καὶ κατὰ γῆν καὶ κατὰ θάλατταν.
ὧν ἔστι μὲν τεκμήρια ὁρᾶν τὰ τρόπαια, μέγιστον δὲ
μαρτύριον ἡ ἐλευθερία τῶν πόλεων ἐν αἷς ὑμεῖς ἐγένεσθε καὶ ἐτράφητε· οὐδένα γὰρ ἄνθρωπον δεσπότην
ἀλλὰ τοὺς θεοὺς προσκυνεῖτε. τοιούτων μέν ἐστε προγόνων.

14   Οὐ μὲν δὴ τοῦτό γε ἐρῶ ὡς ὑμεῖς καταισχύνετε
αὐτούς· ἀλλ' οὔπω πολλαὶ ἡμέραι ἀφ' οὗ ἀντιταξά-
μενοι τούτοις τοῖς ἐκείνων ἐκγόνοις πολλαπλασίους
15 ὑμῶν αὐτῶν ἐνικᾶτε σὺν τοῖς θεοῖς. καὶ τότε μὲν δὴ
περὶ τῆς Κύρου βασιλείας ἄνδρες ἦτε ἀγαθοί· νῦν δ'

---

[19] In the battle of Marathon, 490.   [20] According to
Herodotus (VI. cxvii) the Persian dead numbered 6,400.

[21] Herodotus (VII. clxxxv) puts the whole number of fighting
men in Xerxes' armament at 2,641,610.   [22] By sea at Salamis
(480) and by land at Plataea (479).

right to be brave men, but that brave men are delivered, with the help of the gods, even out of most dreadful dangers. For when the Persians and their followers came with a vast array to blot Athens out of existence, the Athenians dared, unaided, to withstand them, and won the victory.[19] And while they had vowed to Artemis that for every man they might slay of the enemy they would sacrifice a goat to the goddess, they were unable to find goats enough;[20] so they resolved to offer five hundred every year, and this sacrifice they are paying even to this day. Again, when Xerxes at a later time gathered together that countless[21] host and came against Greece, then too our forefathers were victorious, both by land and by sea,[22] over the forefathers of our enemies. As tokens of these victories we may, indeed, still behold the trophies,[23] but the strongest witness to them is the freedom of the states in which you were born and bred; for to no human creature do you pay homage as master,[24] but to the gods alone. It is from such ancestors, then, that you are sprung.

"Now I am far from intending to say that you disgrace them; in fact, not many days ago you set yourselves in array against these descendants of those ancient Persians and were victorious, with the aid of the gods, over many times your own numbers. And then, mark you, it was in Cyrus' contest for the throne that you proved yourselves brave

23 See, e.g., ML nos. 24–27.

24 Προσκύνησις involved an individual doing obeisance by bowing slightly and holding his hand before his mouth: see R.N. Frye, *Iranica Antiqua* 9 (1972) 106. It came to symbolize for the Greeks the servility and consequent weakness of easterners: cf. Isocrates *Pan.* 151, and see Brunt, Arrian, I, 538–539.

ὁπότε περὶ τῆς ὑμετέρας σωτηρίας ὁ ἀγών ἐστι πολὺ
δήπου ὑμᾶς προσήκει καὶ ἀμείνονας καὶ προθυμοτέ-
16 ρους εἶναι. ἀλλὰ μὴν καὶ θαρραλεωτέρους νῦν πρέπει
εἶναι πρὸς τοὺς πολεμίους. τότε μὲν γὰρ ἄπειροι ὄντες
αὐτῶν, τό τε πλῆθος ἄμετρον ὁρῶντες, ὅμως ἐτολμή-
σατε σὺν τῷ πατρίῳ φρονήματι ἰέναι εἰς αὐτούς· νῦν
δὲ ὁπότε καὶ πεῖραν ἤδη ἔχετε αὐτῶν ὅτι οὐ θέλουσι
καὶ πολλαπλάσιοι ὄντες δέχεσθαι ὑμᾶς, τί ἔτι ὑμῖν
προσήκει τούτους φοβεῖσθαι;

17   Μηδὲ μέντοι τοῦτο μεῖον δόξητε ἔχειν ὅτι οἱ Ἀρι-
αίου⁵ πρόσθεν σὺν ἡμῖν ταττόμενοι νῦν ἀφεστήκασιν.
ἔτι γὰρ οὗτοι κακίονές εἰσι τῶν ὑφ᾽ ἡμῶν ἡττημένων·
ἔφευγον γοῦν ἐκείνους καταλιπόντες ἡμᾶς. τοὺς δὲ
ἐθέλοντας φυγῆς ἄρχειν πολὺ κρεῖττον σὺν τοῖς πολεμίοις ταττομένους ἢ ἐν τῇ ἡμετέρᾳ τάξει ὁρᾶν.

18   Εἰ δέ τις ὑμῶν ἀθυμεῖ ὅτι ἡμῖν μὲν οὐκ εἰσὶν ἱππεῖς,
τοῖς δὲ πολεμίοις πολλοὶ πάρεισιν, ἐνθυμήθητε ὅτι οἱ
μύριοι ἱππεῖς οὐδὲν ἄλλο ἢ μύριοί εἰσιν ἄνθρωποι·
ὑπὸ μὲν γὰρ ἵππου ἐν μάχῃ οὐδεὶς πώποτε οὔτε
δηχθεὶς οὔτε λακτισθεὶς ἀπέθανεν, οἱ δὲ ἄνδρες εἰσὶν
19 οἱ ποιοῦντες ὅ τι ἂν ἐν ταῖς μάχαις γίγνηται. οὐκοῦν
τῶν γε ἱππέων πολὺ ἡμεῖς ἐπ᾽ ἀσφαλεστέρου ὀχήμα-
τός ἐσμεν· οἱ μὲν γὰρ ἐφ᾽ ἵππων κρέμανται φοβούμενοι οὐχ ἡμᾶς μόνον ἀλλὰ καὶ τὸ καταπεσεῖν· ἡμεῖς
δ᾽ ἐπὶ γῆς βεβηκότες πολὺ μὲν ἰσχυρότερον παίσομεν,
ἤν τις προσίῃ, πολὺ δὲ μᾶλλον ὅτου ἂν βουλώμεθα

---

⁵ Ἀριαίου Gem., Hude/Peters following Hug: Κύρειοι MSS.

men; but now, when the struggle is for your own safety, it is surely fitting that you should be far braver and more zealous. Furthermore, you ought now to be more confident in facing the enemy. For then you were unacquainted with them, and you saw that their numbers were beyond counting; nevertheless you dared, with all the spirit of your fathers, to charge upon them. But now, when you have already made actual trial of them and find that they have no desire, even though they are many times your number, to await your attack, what reason can remain for your being afraid of them?

"Again, do not suppose that you are the worse off because the followers of Ariaeus, who were formerly marshalled with us, have now deserted us. For they are even greater cowards than the men we defeated; at any rate they were taking to flight before them,[25] leaving us to shift for ourselves. And when we find men who are ready to set the example of flight, it is far better to see them drawn up with the enemy than on our own side.

"But if anyone of you is despondent because we are without horsemen while the enemy have plenty at hand, let him reflect that your ten thousand horsemen are nothing more than ten thousand men; for nobody ever lost his life in battle from the bite or kick of a horse, but it is the men who do whatever is done in battles. Moreover, we are on a far surer foundation than your horsemen: they are hanging on their horses' backs, afraid not only of us, but also of falling off; while we, standing upon the ground, shall strike with far greater force if anyone comes upon us and shall be far more likely to hit whomsoever we

[25] Cf. I. ix. 31–x. 1.

τευξόμεθα. ἑνὶ δὲ μόνῳ προέχουσιν οἱ ἱππεῖς· φεύγειν
20 αὐτοῖς ἀσφαλέστερόν ἐστιν ἢ ἡμῖν. εἰ δὲ δὴ τὰς μὲν
μάχας θαρρεῖτε, ὅτι δὲ οὐκέτι ὑμῖν Τισσαφέρνης ἡγή-
σεται οὐδὲ βασιλεὺς ἀγορὰν παρέξει, τοῦτο ἄχθεσθε,
σκέψασθε πότερον κρεῖττον Τισσαφέρνη ἡγεμόνα
ἔχειν, ὃς ἐπιβουλεύων ἡμῖν φανερός ἐστιν, ἢ οὓς ἂν
ἡμεῖς ἄνδρας λαβόντες ἡγεῖσθαι κελεύωμεν, οἳ εἴσον-
ται ὅτι ἤν τι περὶ ἡμᾶς ἁμαρτάνωσι, περὶ τὰς ἑαυτῶν
21 ψυχὰς καὶ σώματα ἁμαρτήσονται. τὰ δὲ ἐπιτήδεια
πότερον ὠνεῖσθαι κρεῖττον ἐκ τῆς ἀγορᾶς ἧς οὗτοι
παρεῖχον μικρὰ μέτρα πολλοῦ ἀργυρίου, μηδὲ τοῦτο
ἔτι ἔχοντας, ἢ αὐτοὺς λαμβάνειν, ἤνπερ κρατῶμεν,
μέτρῳ χρωμένους ὁπόσῳ ἂν ἕκαστος βούληται;
22 Εἰ δὲ ταῦτα μὲν γιγνώσκετε ὅτι κρείττονα, τοὺς δὲ
ποταμοὺς ἄπορον νομίζετε εἶναι καὶ μεγάλως ἡγεῖσθε
ἐξαπατηθῆναι διαβάντες, σκέψασθε εἰ ἄρα τοῦτο καὶ
μωρότατον πεποιήκασιν οἱ βάρβαροι. πάντες γὰρ οἱ
ποταμοί, ἢν καὶ πρόσω τῶν πηγῶν ἄποροι ὦσι, προσ-
ϊοῦσι πρὸς τὰς πηγὰς διαβατοὶ γίγνονται οὐδὲ τὸ
γόνυ βρέχοντες·
23 Εἰ δὲ μήθ᾽ οἱ ποταμοὶ διήσουσιν ἡγεμών τε μηδεὶς
ἡμῖν φανεῖται, οὐδ᾽ ὡς ἡμῖν γε ἀθυμητέον. ἐπιστάμεθα

---

26 *e.g.* the Tigris (II. iv. 13–24).

27 *viz.* In leading the Greeks across (*i.e.* to the eastern bank of)
the Tigris. For, Xenophon argues (see below), the Greeks will now
be compelled to march to the source of the river in order to cross,
and hence will be living on the country so much the longer a time.

aim at. In one point alone your horsemen have the advantage—flight is safer for them than it is for us. Suppose, however, that you do not lack confidence about the fighting, but are troubled because you are no longer to have Tissaphernes to guide you or the King to provide a market. If this be the case, I ask you to consider whether it is better to have Tissaphernes for a guide, the man who is manifestly plotting against us, or such people as we may ourselves capture and may order to serve as guides, men who will know that if they make any mistake in anything that concerns us, they will be making a mistake in that which concerns their own lives and limbs. And as for provisions, is it the better plan to buy from the market which these barbarians have provided—small measures for large prices, when we have no money left, either—or to appropriate for ourselves, in case we are victorious, and to use as large a measure as each one of us pleases?

"But in these points, let us say, you realize that our present situation is better; you believe, however, that the rivers are a difficulty, and you think you were immensely deceived when you crossed them;[26] then consider whether this is not really a surpassingly foolish thing that the barbarians have done.[27] For all rivers, even though they be impassable at a distance from their sources, become passable, without even wetting your knees, as you approach toward the sources.

"But assume that the rivers will not afford us a crossing and that we shall find no one to guide us; even in that case we ought not to be despondent. For we know that the

γὰρ Μυσούς, οὓς οὐκ ἂν ἡμῶν φαίημεν βελτίους
εἶναι, οἳ ἐν βασιλέως χώρᾳ πολλάς τε καὶ εὐδαίμονας
καὶ μεγάλας πόλεις οἰκοῦσιν, ἐπιστάμεθα δὲ Πισίδας
ὡσαύτως, Λυκάονας δὲ καὶ αὐτοὶ εἴδομεν ὅτι ἐν τοῖς
πεδίοις τὰ ἐρυμνὰ καταλαβόντες τὴν τούτων χώραν
24 καρποῦνται· καὶ ἡμᾶς δ᾽ ἂν ἔφην ἔγωγε χρῆναι μήπω
φανεροὺς εἶναι οἴκαδε ὡρμημένους, ἀλλὰ κατασκευ-
άζεσθαι ὡς αὐτοῦ οἰκήσοντας. οἶδα γὰρ ὅτι καὶ
Μυσοῖς βασιλεὺς πολλοὺς μὲν ἡγεμόνας ἂν δοίη,
πολλοὺς δ᾽ ἂν ὁμήρους τοῦ ἀδόλως ἐκπέμψειν, καὶ
ὁδοποιήσειέ γ᾽ ἂν αὐτοῖς καὶ εἰ σὺν τεθρίπποις βούλοιντο ἀπιέναι. καὶ ἡμῖν γ᾽ ἂν οἶδ᾽ ὅτι τρισάσμενος
ταῦτ᾽ ἐποίει, εἰ ἑώρα ἡμᾶς μένειν κατασκευαζομένους.
25 ἀλλὰ γὰρ δέδοικα μὴ ἂν ἅπαξ μάθωμεν ἀργοὶ ζῆν
καὶ ἐν ἀφθόνοις βιοτεύειν, καὶ Μήδων δὲ καὶ Περσῶν
καλαῖς καὶ μεγάλαις γυναιξὶ καὶ παρθένοις ὁμιλεῖν,
μὴ ὥσπερ οἱ λωτοφάγοι ἐπιλαθώμεθα τῆς οἴκαδε
26 ὁδοῦ. δοκεῖ οὖν μοι εἰκὸς καὶ δίκαιον εἶναι πρῶτον εἰς
τὴν Ἑλλάδα καὶ πρὸς τοὺς οἰκείους πειρᾶσθαι ἀφι-
κνεῖσθαι καὶ ἐπιδεῖξαι τοῖς Ἕλλησιν ὅτι ἑκόντες
πένονται, ἐξὸν αὐτοῖς τοὺς νῦν σκληρῶς ἐκεῖ πολιτεύ-
οντας ἐνθάδε κομισαμένους πλουσίους ὁρᾶν.

Ἀλλὰ γάρ, ὦ ἄνδρες, πάντα ταῦτα τἀγαθὰ δῆλον
27 ὅτι τῶν κρατούντων ἐστί· τοῦτο δὴ δεῖ λέγειν, πῶς ἂν

---

28 Peoples of Asia Minor who were in essence autonomous; cf.
esp. I. ii. 19, II. v. 13, *Mem.* III. v. 26. See also Intro.

Mysians whom we should not admit to be better men than ourselves, inhabit many large and prosperous cities in the King's territory, we know that the same is true of the Pisidians, and as for the Lycaonians[28] we even saw with our own eyes that they had seized the strongholds in the plains and were reaping for themselves the lands of these Persians; so, in our case, my own view would be that we ought not yet to let it be seen that we have set out for home; we ought, rather, to be making our arrangements as if we intended to settle here. For I know that to the Mysians the King would not only give plenty of guides, but plenty of hostages, to guarantee a safe conduct for them out of his country; in fact, he would build a road for them, even if they wanted, to take their departure in four-horse chariots. And I know that he would be thrice glad to do the same for us, if he saw that we were preparing to stay here. I really fear, however, that if we once learn to live in idleness and luxury, and to consort with the tall and beautiful women and maidens of these Medes and Persians, we may, like the Lotus Eaters,[29] forget our homeward way. Therefore, I think it is right and proper that our first endeavour should be to return to our kindred and friends in Greece, and to point out to the Greeks that it is by their own choice that they are poor; for they could bring here the people who are now living a hard life at home, and could see them in the enjoyment of riches.

"It is really a plain fact, gentlemen, that all these good things belong to those who have the strength to possess them; but I must go on to another point, how we can march

[29] An allusion to *Odyssey*, IX. 94 ff. This entire section is full of panhellenic "big talk."

πορευοίμεθά τε ὡς ἀσφαλέστατα καὶ εἰ μάχεσθαι δέοι
ὡς κράτιστα μαχοίμεθα. πρῶτον μὲν τοίνυν, ἔφη,
δοκεῖ μοι κατακαῦσαι τὰς ἁμάξας ἃς ἔχομεν, ἵνα μὴ
τὰ ζεύγη ἡμῶν στρατηγῇ, ἀλλὰ πορευώμεθα ὅπῃ ἂν
τῇ στρατιᾷ συμφέρῃ· ἔπειτα καὶ τὰς σκηνὰς συγκατα-
καῦσαι. αὗται γὰρ αὖ ὄχλον μὲν παρέχουσιν ἄγειν,
συνωφελοῦσι δ᾽ οὐδὲν οὔτε εἰς τὸ μάχεσθαι οὔτ᾽ εἰς
28 τὸ τὰ ἐπιτήδεια ἔχειν. ἔτι δὲ καὶ τῶν ἄλλων σκευῶν τὰ
περιττὰ ἀπαλλάξωμεν πλὴν ὅσα πολέμου ἕνεκεν ἢ
σίτων ἢ ποτῶν ἔχομεν, ἵνα ὡς πλεῖστοι μὲν ἡμῶν ἐν
τοῖς ὅπλοις ὦσιν, ὡς ἐλάχιστοι δὲ σκευοφορῶσι. κρα-
τουμένων μὲν γὰρ ἐπίστασθε ὅτι πάντα ἀλλότρια· ἢν
δὲ κρατῶμεν, καὶ τοὺς πολεμίους δεῖ σκευοφόρους
ἡμετέρους νομίζειν.

29 Λοιπόν μοι εἰπεῖν ὅπερ καὶ μέγιστον νομίζω εἶναι.
ὁρᾶτε γὰρ καὶ τοὺς πολεμίους ὅτι οὐ πρόσθεν ἐξ-
ενεγκεῖν ἐτόλμησαν πρὸς ἡμᾶς πόλεμον πρὶν τοὺς
στρατηγοὺς ἡμῶν συνέλαβον, νομίζοντες ὄντων μὲν
τῶν ἀρχόντων καὶ ἡμῶν πειθομένων ἱκανοὺς εἶναι
ἡμᾶς περιγενέσθαι τῷ πολέμῳ, λαβόντες δὲ τοὺς
ἄρχοντας ἀναρχίᾳ ἂν καὶ ἀταξίᾳ ἐνόμιζον ἡμᾶς ἀπο-
30 λέσθαι. δεῖ οὖν πολὺ μὲν τοὺς ἄρχοντας ἐπιμε-
λεστέρους γενέσθαι τοὺς νῦν τῶν πρόσθεν, πολὺ δὲ
τοὺς ἀρχομένους εὐτακτοτέρους καὶ πειθομένους μᾶλ-
31 λον τοῖς ἄρχουσι νῦν ἢ πρόσθεν· ἢν δέ τις ἀπειθῇ,
ψηφίσασθαι τὸν ἀεὶ ὑμῶν ἐντυγχάνοντα σὺν τῷ
ἄρχοντι κολάζειν· οὕτως οἱ πολέμιοι πλεῖστον ἐψευσμένοι ἔσονται· τῇδε γὰρ τῇ ἡμέρᾳ μυρίους ὄψονται

most safely and, if we have to fight, can fight to the best advantage. In the first place, then," Xenophon proceeded, "I think we should burn up the wagons which we have, so that our cattle may not be our captains, but we can take whatever route may be best for the army. Secondly, we should burn up our tents also; for these, again, are a bother to carry, and no help at all either for fighting or for obtaining provisions. Furthermore, let us abandon all our other superfluous baggage, keeping only such articles as we use for war, or in eating and drinking, in order that we may have the largest possible number of men under arms and the least number carrying baggage. For when men are conquered, you are aware that all their possessions become the property of others; but if we are victorious, we may regard the enemy as our packbearers.

"It remains for me to mention the one matter which I believe is really of the greatest importance. You observe that our enemies did not muster up courage to begin hostilities against us until they had seized our generals; for they believed that so long as we had our commanders and were obedient to them, we were able to worst them in war, but when they had got possession of our commanders, they believed that the want of leadership and of discipline would be the ruin of us. Therefore our present commanders must show themselves far more vigilant than their predecessors, and the men in the ranks must be far more orderly and more obedient to their commanders now than they used to be. We must pass a vote that, in case anyone is disobedient, whoever of you may be at hand at the time shall join with the officer in punishing him; in this way the enemy will find themselves mightily deceived; for to-day

ἀνθ᾿ ἑνὸς Κλεάρχους τοὺς οὐδενὶ ἐπιτρέψοντας κακῷ
32 εἶναι. ἀλλὰ γὰρ καὶ περαίνειν ἤδη ὥρα· ἴσως γὰρ οἱ
πολέμιοι αὐτίκα παρέσονται. ὅτῳ οὖν ταῦτα δοκεῖ
καλῶς ἔχειν, ἐπικυρωσάτω ὡς τάχιστα, ἵνα ἔργῳ
περαίνηται. εἰ δέ τι ἄλλο βέλτιον ἢ ταύτῃ, τολμάτω
καὶ ὁ ἰδιώτης διδάσκειν· πάντες γὰρ κοινῆς σωτηρίας
δεόμεθα.

33 Μετὰ ταῦτα Χειρίσοφος εἶπεν· Ἀλλ᾿ εἰ μέν τινος
ἄλλου δεῖ πρὸς τούτοις οἷς λέγει Ξενοφῶν, καὶ αὐτίκα
ἐξέσται ποιεῖν· ἃ δὲ νῦν εἴρηκε δοκεῖ μοι ὡς τάχιστα
ψηφίσασθαι ἄριστον εἶναι· καὶ ὅτῳ δοκεῖ ταῦτα, ἀνατεινάτω τὴν χεῖρα. ἀνέτειναν πάντες.

34 Ἀναστὰς δὲ πάλιν εἶπε Ξενοφῶν· Ὦ ἄνδρες, ἀκούσατε ὧν προσδεῖν δοκεῖ μοι. δῆλον ὅτι πορεύεσθαι
ἡμᾶς δεῖ ὅπου ἕξομεν τὰ ἐπιτήδεια· ἀκούω δὲ κώμας
35 εἶναι καλὰς οὐ πλέον εἴκοσι σταδίων ἀπεχούσας· οὐκ
ἂν οὖν θαυμάζοιμι εἰ οἱ πολέμιοι, ὥσπερ οἱ δειλοὶ
κύνες τοὺς μὲν παριόντας διώκουσί τε καὶ δάκνουσιν,
ἢν δύνωνται, τοὺς δὲ διώκοντας φεύγουσιν, εἰ καὶ
36 αὐτοὶ ἡμῖν ἀπιοῦσιν ἐπακολουθοῖεν. ἴσως οὖν ἀσφαλέστερον ἡμῖν πορεύεσθαι πλαίσιον ποιησαμένους
τῶν ὅπλων, ἵνα τὰ σκευοφόρα καὶ ὁ πολὺς ὄχλος ἐν
ἀσφαλεστέρῳ ᾖ. εἰ οὖν νῦν ἀποδειχθείη τίνα χρὴ
ἡγεῖσθαι τοῦ πλαισίου καὶ τὰ πρόσθεν κοσμεῖν καὶ
τίνας ἐπὶ τῶν πλευρῶν ἑκατέρων εἶναι, τίνας δ᾿

---

[30] Clearchus was notoriously a stern disciplinarian; cf. II. vi.
8 ff.

they will behold, not one Clearchus[30] but ten thousand, who will not suffer anybody to be a bad soldier. But it is time now to be acting instead of talking; for perhaps the enemy will soon be at hand. Whoever, then, thinks that these proposals are good should ratify them with all speed, that they may be carried out in action. But if any other plan is thought better than mine, let anyone, even though he be a private soldier, feel free to present it; for the safety of all is the need of all."

After this Cheirisophus said: "Whether we need to do anything else besides what Xenophon proposes it will be possible immediately to do it; but on the proposals which he has already made I think it is best for us to vote as speedily as possible. Whoever is in favour of these measures, let him raise his hand." They all raised their hands.

Then Xenophon arose once more and said: 'Hear, gentlemen, what I believe is also required. It is clear that we must make our way to a place where we can get provisions; and I hear that there are fine villages at a distance of not more than twenty stadia. I would not be surprised, then, if the enemy—after the fashion of cowardly dogs that chase passers-by and bite them, if they can, but run away from anyone who chases them—if the enemy in the same way should follow at our heels as we retire. Hence it will be safer, perhaps, for us to march with the hoplites formed into a hollow square,[31] so that the baggage train and the great crowd of camp followers may be in a safer place. If, then, it should be settled at once who are to lead the square and marshal the van, who are to be on either flank, and who

---

31 Cf. III. iv. 19; see also *Hell*. VI. v. 18–19 and *Hell. Oxy*. XI. 3.

ὀπισθοφυλακεῖν, οὐκ ἂν ὁπότε οἱ πολέμιοι ἔλθοιεν
βουλεύεσθαι ἡμᾶς δέοι, ἀλλὰ χρῴμεθ' ἂν εὐθὺς τοῖς
37 τεταγμένοις. εἰ μὲν οὖν ἄλλο τις βέλτιον ὁρᾷ, ἄλλως
ἐχέτω· εἰ δὲ μή, Χειρίσοφος μὲν ἡγοῖτο, ἐπειδὴ καὶ
Λακεδαιμόνιός ἐστι· τῶν δὲ πλευρῶν ἑκατέρων δύο τὼ
πρεσβυτάτω στρατηγὼ ἐπιμελοίσθην· ὀπισθοφυλα-
κοῖμεν δ' ἡμεῖς οἱ νεώτατοι ἐγὼ καὶ Τιμασίων τὸ νῦν
38 εἶναι. τὸ δὲ λοιπὸν πειρώμενοι ταύτης τῆς τάξεως
βουλευσόμεθα ὅ τι ἂν ἀεὶ κράτιστον δοκῇ εἶναι. εἰ δέ
τις ἄλλο ὁρᾷ βέλτιον, λεξάτω. ἐπεὶ δ' οὐδεὶς ἀντέλεγεν, εἶπεν· Ὅτῳ δοκεῖ ταῦτα, ἀνατεινάτω τὴν χεῖρα.
39 ἔδοξε ταῦτα. Νῦν τοίνυν, ἔφη, ἀπιόντας ποιεῖν δεῖ τὰ
δεδογμένα. καὶ ὅστις τε ὑμῶν τοὺς οἰκείους ἐπιθυμεῖ
ἰδεῖν, μεμνήσθω ἀνὴρ ἀγαθὸς εἶναι· οὐ γὰρ ἔστιν
ἄλλως τούτου τυχεῖν· ὅστις τε ζῆν ἐπιθυμεῖ, πειράσθω
νικᾶν· τῶν μὲν γὰρ νικώντων τὸ κατακαίνειν, τῶν δὲ
ἡττωμένων τὸ ἀποθνήσκειν ἐστί· καὶ εἴ τις δὲ χρημάτων ἐπιθυμεῖ, κρατεῖν πειράσθω· τῶν γὰρ νικώντων
ἐστὶ καὶ τὰ ἑαυτῶν σῴζειν καὶ τὰ τῶν ἡττωμένων
λαμβάνειν.

III. Τούτων λεχθέντων ἀνέστησαν καὶ ἀπελθόντες
κατέκαιον τὰς ἁμάξας καὶ τὰς σκηνάς, τῶν δὲ περιτ-
τῶν ὅτου μὲν δέοιτό τις μετεδίδοσαν ἀλλήλοις, τὰ δὲ
ἄλλα εἰς τὸ πῦρ ἐρρίπτουν. ταῦτα ποιήσαντες ἠριστο-
ποιοῦντο. ἀριστοποιουμένων δὲ αὐτῶν ἔρχεται Μιθρα-

---

[32] Cf. II. v. 35.

to guard the rear, we should not need to be taking counsel at the time when the enemy comes upon us, but we should find our men at once in their places ready for action. Now if anyone sees another plan which is better, let us follow that plan; but if not, I propose that Cheirisophus take the lead, especially since he is a Lacedaemonian, that the two oldest generals have charge of the two flanks, and that, for the present, we who are the youngest, Timasion and I, command the rear. And for the future, as we make trial of this formation we can adopt whatever course may seem from time to time to be best. If anyone sees a better plan, let him present it." No one having any opposing view to express, Xenophon said: "Whoever is in favour of these measures, let him raise his hand." The motion was carried. "And now," he continued, "we must go back and put into execution what has been resolved upon. And whoever among you desires to see his friends again, let him remember to show himself a brave man; for in no other way can he accomplish this desire. Again, whoever is desirous of saving his life, let him strive for victory; for it is the victors that slay and the defeated that are slain. Or if anyone longs for wealth, let him also strive to conquer; for conquerors not only keep their own possessions, but gain the possessions of the conquered."

III. After these words of Xenophon's the assembly arose, and all went back to camp and proceeded to burn the wagons and the tents. As for the superfluous articles of baggage, whatever anybody needed they shared with one another, but the rest they threw into the fire. When they had done all this, they set about preparing breakfast; and while they were so engaged, Mithradates[32] approached

δάτης σὺν ἱππεῦσιν ὡς τριάκοντα, καὶ καλεσάμενος
2 τοὺς στρατηγοὺς εἰς ἐπήκοον λέγει ὧδε. Ἐγώ, ὦ
ἄνδρες Ἕλληνες, καὶ Κύρῳ πιστὸς ἦν, ὡς ὑμεῖς ἐπίστασθε, καὶ νῦν ὑμῖν εὔνους· καὶ ἐνθάδε δ᾽ εἰμὶ σὺν
πολλῷ φόβῳ διάγων. εἰ οὖν ὁρῴην ὑμᾶς σωτήριόν τι
βουλευομένους, ἔλθοιμι ἂν πρὸς ὑμᾶς καὶ τοὺς θεράποντας πάντας ἔχων. λέξατε οὖν πρός με τί ἐν νῷ
ἔχετε ὡς φίλον τε καὶ εὔνουν καὶ βουλόμενον κοινῇ
3 σὺν ὑμῖν τὸν στόλον ποιεῖσθαι. βουλευομένοις τοῖς
στρατηγοῖς ἔδοξεν ἀποκρίνασθαι τάδε· καὶ ἔλεγε Χει-
ρίσοφος· Ἡμῖν δοκεῖ, εἰ μέν τις ἐᾷ ἡμᾶς ἀπιέναι
οἴκαδε, διαπορεύεσθαι τὴν χώραν ὡς ἂν δυνώμεθα
ἀσινέστατα· ἢν δέ τις ἡμᾶς τῆς ὁδοῦ ἐπικωλύῃ,[6] δια-
4 πολεμεῖν τούτῳ ὡς ἂν δυνώμεθα κράτιστα. ἐκ τούτου
ἐπειρᾶτο Μιθραδάτης διδάσκειν ὡς ἄπορον εἴη βασιλέως ἄκοντος σωθῆναι. ἔνθα δὴ ἐγιγνώσκετο ὅτι
ὑπόπεμπτος εἴη· καὶ γὰρ τῶν Τισσαφέρνους τις
5 οἰκείων παρηκολουθήκει πίστεως ἕνεκα. καὶ ἐκ τούτου
ἐδόκει τοῖς στρατηγοῖς βέλτιον εἶναι δόγμα ποιήσασθαι τὸν πόλεμον ἀκήρυκτον εἶναι ἔστ᾽ ἐν τῇ πολεμίᾳ
εἶεν· διέφθειρον γὰρ προσιόντες τοὺς στρατιώτας, καὶ
ἕνα γε λοχαγὸν διέφθειραν Νίκαρχον Ἀρκάδα, καὶ
ᾤχετο ἀπιὼν νυκτὸς σὺν ἀνθρώποις ὡς εἴκοσι.
6   Μετὰ ταῦτα ἀριστήσαντες καὶ διαβάντες τὸν
Ζαπάταν ποταμὸν ἐπορεύοντο τεταγμένοι τὰ ὑποζύγια

---

[6] ἐπικωλύῃ corrector of one MS., Gem., Hude/Peters: ἀπο-
κωλύῃ other MSS., Mar.

with about thirty horsemen, summoned the Greek generals within earshot, and spoke as follows: "Men of Greece, I was faithful to Cyrus, as you know for yourselves, and I am now friendly to you; indeed, I am tarrying here in great fear. Therefore if I should see that you were taking salutary measures, I should join you and bring all my retainers with me. Tell me, then, what you have in mind, in the assurance that I am your friend and well-wisher, and am desirous of making the journey in company with you." The generals held council and voted to return the following answer, Cheirisophus acting as spokesman: "It is our resolve, in case no one hinders our homeward march, to proceed through the country doing the least possible damage, but if anyone tries to prevent us from making the journey, to fight it out with him to the best of our power." Thereupon Mithradates undertook to show that there was no possibility of their effecting a safe return unless the King so pleased. Then it became clear to the Greeks that his mission was a treacherous one; indeed, one of Tissaphernes' relatives had followed along, to see that he kept faith. The generals consequently decided that it was best to pass a decree that there should be no negotiations with the enemy in this war so long as they should be in the enemy's country. For the barbarians kept coming and trying to corrupt the soldiers; in the case of one captain, Nicarchus the Arcadian, they actually succeeded, and he decamped during the night, taking with him about twenty men.

After this they took breakfast, crossed the Zapatas[33] river, and set out on the march in the formation decided

33 Cf. II v. I.

καὶ τὸν ὄχλον ἐν μέσῳ ἔχοντες. οὐ πολὺ δὲ προεληλυ-
θότων αὐτῶν ἐπιφαίνεται πάλιν ὁ Μιθραδάτης, ἱππέας
ἔχων ὡς διακοσίους καὶ τοξότας καὶ σφενδονήτας εἰς

7 τετρακοσίους μάλα ἐλαφροὺς καὶ εὐζώνους. καὶ προσ-
ήει μὲν ὡς φίλος ὢν πρὸς τοὺς Ἕλληνας· ἐπεὶ δ᾽ ἐγγὺς
ἐγένοντο, ἐξαπίνης οἱ μὲν αὐτῶν ἐτόξευον καὶ ἱππεῖς
καὶ πεζοί, οἱ δ᾽ ἐσφενδόνων, καὶ ἐτίτρωσκον. οἱ δὲ
ὀπισθοφύλακες τῶν Ἑλλήνων ἔπασχον μὲν κακῶς,
ἀντεποίουν δ᾽ οὐδέν· οἵ τε γὰρ Κρῆτες βραχύτερα τῶν
Περσῶν ἐτόξευον καὶ ἅμα ψιλοὶ ὄντες εἴσω τῶν ὅπλων
κατεκέκλειντο, οἱ δὲ ἀκοντισταὶ βραχύτερα ἠκόντιζον

8 ἢ ὡς ἐξικνεῖσθαι τῶν σφενδονητῶν. ἐκ τούτου Ξενοφῶντι ἐδόκει διωκτέον εἶναι· καὶ ἐδίωκον τῶν τε ὁπλιτῶν καὶ τῶν πελταστῶν οἳ ἔτυχον σὺν αὐτῷ ὀπισθοφυ-
λακοῦντες· διώκοντες δὲ οὐδένα κατελάμβανον τῶν

9 πολεμίων. οὔτε γὰρ ἱππεῖς ἦσαν τοῖς Ἕλλησιν οὔτε οἱ
πεζοὶ τοὺς πεζοὺς ἐκ πολλοῦ φεύγοντας ἐδύναντο
καταλαμβάνειν ἐν ὀλίγῳ χωρίῳ· πολὺ γὰρ οὐχ οἷόν

10 τε ἦν ἀπὸ τοῦ ἄλλου στρατεύματος διώκειν· οἱ δὲ
βάρβαροι ἱππεῖς καὶ φεύγοντες ἅμα ἐτίτρωσκον εἰς
τοὔπισθεν τοξεύοντες ἀπὸ τῶν ἵππων, ὁπόσον δὲ προ-
διώξειαν οἱ Ἕλληνες, τοσοῦτον πάλιν ἐπαναχωρεῖν

11 μαχομένους ἔδει. ὥστε τῆς ἡμέρας ὅλης διῆλθον οὐ

---

[34] See ii. 36.

upon,[34] with the baggage animals and the camp followers in the middle of the square. They had not proceeded far when Mithradates appeared again, accompanied by about two hundred horsemen and by bowmen and slingers—exceedingly active and nimble troops—to the number of four hundred. He approached the Greeks as if he were a friend, but when his party had got close at hand, on a sudden some of them, horse and foot alike, began shooting with their bows and others with slings, and they inflicted wounds. And the Greek rearguard, while suffering severely, could not retaliate at all; for the Cretan[35] bowmen not only had a shorter range than the Persians, but besides, since they had no armour, they were shut in within the lines of the hoplites; and the Greek javelin-men could not throw far enough to reach the enemy's slingers. Xenophon consequently decided that they must pursue the Persians, and this they did, with such of the hoplites and peltasts as were guarding the rear with him; but in their pursuit they failed to catch a single man of the enemy. For the Greeks had no horsemen, and their foot soldiers were not able to overtake the enemy's foot soldiers—since the latter had a long start in their flight—within a short distance; and a long pursuit, far away from the main Greek army, was not possible. Again, the barbarian horsemen even while they were in flight would inflict wounds by shooting behind them from their horses; and whatever distance the Greeks might at any time gain in advance in their pursuit, all that distance they were obliged to fall back fighting. The result was that

[35] See I. ii. 9. The Cretans were the most famous archers of antiquity: see, e.g., Thuc. VI. xxv. 2; Caesar, *BG* II. 7; Plutarch, *Gracch.* XXXVII. 4; Arrian, *An.* II. ix. 3.

πλέον πέντε καὶ εἴκοσι σταδίων, ἀλλὰ δείλης ἀφίκοντο εἰς τὰς κώμας.

Ἔνθα δὴ πάλιν ἀθυμία ἦν. καὶ Χειρίσοφος καὶ οἱ πρεσβύτατοι τῶν στρατηγῶν Ξενοφῶντα ᾐτιῶντο ὅτι ἐδίωκεν ἀπὸ τῆς φάλαγγος καὶ αὐτός τε ἐκινδύνευε καὶ τοὺς πολεμίους οὐδὲν μᾶλλον ἐδύνατο βλάπτειν.
12 ἀκούσας δὲ Ξενοφῶν ἔλεγεν ὅτι ὀρθῶς αἰτιῷντο καὶ αὐτὸ τὸ ἔργον αὐτοῖς μαρτυροίη. ἀλλ' ἐγώ, ἔφη, ἠναγκάσθην διώκειν, ἐπειδὴ ἑώρων ἡμᾶς ἐν τῷ μένειν κακῶς μὲν πάσχοντας, ἀντιποιεῖν δὲ οὐδὲν δυνα-
13 μένους. ἐπειδὴ δὲ ἐδιώκομεν, ἀληθῆ, ἔφη, ὑμεῖς λέγετε· κακῶς μὲν γὰρ ποιεῖν οὐδὲν μᾶλλον ἐδυνάμεθα τοὺς
14 πολεμίους, ἀνεχωροῦμεν δὲ παγχαλέπως. τοῖς οὖν θεοῖς χάρις ὅτι οὐ σὺν πολλῇ ῥώμῃ ἀλλὰ σὺν ὀλίγοις ἦλθον, ὥστε βλάψαι μὲν μὴ μεγάλα, δηλῶσαι δὲ ὧν
15 δεόμεθα. νῦν γὰρ οἱ πολέμιοι τοξεύουσι καὶ σφενδονῶσιν ὅσον οὔτε οἱ Κρῆτες ἀντιτοξεύειν δύνανται οὔτε οἱ ἐκ χειρὸς βάλλοντες ἐξικνεῖσθαι· ὅταν δὲ αὐτοὺς διώκωμεν, πολὺ μὲν οὐχ οἷόν τε χωρίον ἀπὸ τοῦ στρατεύματος διώκειν, ἐν ὀλίγῳ δὲ οὐδ' εἰ ταχὺς εἴη πεζὸς πεζὸν ἂν διώκων καταλάβοι ἐκ τόξου ῥύμα-
16 τος. ἡμεῖς οὖν εἰ μέλλομεν τούτους εἴργειν ὥστε μὴ δύνασθαι βλάπτειν ἡμᾶς πορευομένους, σφενδονητῶν τὴν ταχίστην δεῖ καὶ ἱππέων. ἀκούω δ' εἶναι ἐν τῷ

during the whole day they travelled not more than twenty-five stadia. They did arrive, however, towards evening at the villages.[36]

Here again there was despondency. And Cheirisophus and the eldest of the generals found fault with Xenophon for leaving the main body of the army to undertake a pursuit, and thus endangering himself without being able, for all that, to do the enemy any harm. When Xenophon heard their words, he replied that they were right in finding fault with him, and that the outcome bore witness of itself for their view. "But," he continued, "I was compelled to pursue when I saw that by keeping our places we were suffering severely and were still unable to strike a blow ourselves. As to what happened, however, when we did pursue, you are quite right: we were no better able to inflict harm upon the enemy, and it was only with the utmost difficulty that we effected our own withdrawal. Let us thank the gods, therefore, that they came, not with a large force, but with a handful, so that without doing us any great damage they have revealed our needs. For at present the enemy can shoot arrows and sling stones so far that neither our Cretan bowmen nor our javelin-men can reach them in reply; and when we pursue them, a long chase, away from our main body, is out of the question, and in a short chase no foot soldier, even if he is swift, can overtake another foot soldier who has a bow-shot the start of him. Hence, if we intend to put an end to the possibility of their harming us on our march, we need slingers ourselves at once, and horsemen

---

[36] *i.e.* those mentioned in ii. 34.

στρατεύματι ἡμῶν Ῥοδίους, ὧν τοὺς πολλούς φασιν
ἐπίστασθαι σφενδονᾶν, καὶ τὸ βέλος αὐτῶν καὶ δι-
17 πλάσιον φέρεσθαι τῶν Περσικῶν σφενδονῶν. ἐκεῖναι
γὰρ διὰ τὸ χειροπληθέσι τοῖς λίθοις σφενδονᾶν ἐπὶ
βραχὺ ἐξικνοῦνται, οἱ δὲ Ῥόδιοι καὶ ταῖς μολυβδίσιν
18 ἐπίστανται χρῆσθαι. ἢν οὖν αὐτῶν ἐπισκεψώμεθα
τίνες πέπανται σφενδόνας, καὶ τούτων τῷ⁷ μὲν δῶμεν
αὐτῶν ἀργύριον, τῷ δὲ ἄλλας πλέκειν ἐθέλοντι ἄλλο
ἀργύριον τελῶμεν, καὶ τῷ σφενδονᾶν ἐντεταλμένῳ
ἐθέλοντι ἄλλην τινὰ ἀτέλειαν εὑρίσκωμεν, ἴσως τινὲς
19 φανοῦνται ἱκανοὶ ἡμᾶς ὠφελεῖν. ὁρῶ δὲ ἵππους ὄντας
ἐν τῷ στρατεύματι, τοὺς μέν τινας παρ᾽ ἐμοί, τοὺς δὲ
τῶν Κλεάρχου καταλελειμμένους, πολλοὺς δὲ καὶ
ἄλλους αἰχμαλώτους σκευοφοροῦντας. ἂν οὖν τούτους
πάντας ἐκλέξαντες σκευοφόρα μὲν ἀντιδῶμεν, τοὺς δὲ
ἵππους εἰς ἱππέας κατασκευάσωμεν, ἴσως καὶ οὗτοί
20 τι τοὺς φεύγοντας ἀνιάσουσιν. ἔδοξε καὶ ταῦτα. καὶ
ταύτης τῆς νυκτὸς σφενδονῆται μὲν εἰς διακοσίους
ἐγένοντο, ἵπποι δὲ καὶ ἱππεῖς ἐδοκιμάσθησαν τῇ ὑστεραίᾳ εἰς πεντήκοντα, καὶ σπολάδες καὶ θώρακες αὐτοῖς ἐπορίσθησαν, καὶ ἵππαρχος ἐπεστάθη Λύκιος ὁ
Πολυστράτου Ἀθηναῖος.

IV. Μείναντες δὲ ταύτην τὴν ἡμέραν τῇ ἄλλῃ ἐπο-

---

⁷ Τούτων τῷ some MSS.; τούτῳ others.

---

37 Rhodian slingers were hardly less famous than Cretan bowmen. Arrian remembered the Cyreans' predicament, *An.* II. vii. 8.

also. Now I am told that there are Rhodians[37] in our army, that most of them understand the use of the sling, and that their missile carries no less than twice as far as those from the Persian slings. For the latter have only a short range because the stones that are used in them are as large as the hand can hold; the Rhodians, however, are versed also in the art of slinging leaden bullets. If, therefore, we should ascertain who among them possess slings, and if to one of them we should give their wage; to another who is willing, payment to construct yet more slings; and if for the one assigned to be a slinger, we should devise some sort of exemption, it may be that men will come forward who will be capable of helping us. Again, I observe that there are horses in the army—a few at my own quarters, others that made part of Clearchus' troop and were left behind,[38] and many others that have been taken from the enemy and are used as pack-animals. If, then, we should pick out all these horses, replacing them with mules, and should equip them for cavalry, it may be that this cavalry also will cause some annoyance to the enemy when they are in flight." These proposals also were adopted, and in the course of that night a company of two hundred slingers was organized, while on the following day horses and horsemen to the number of fifty were examined and accepted, and leather tunics and breastplates were provided for them; and Lycius, the son of Polystratus, an Athenian, was put in command of the troop.

IV. That day they remained quiet, but the next morning

For the Ten Thousand's difficulties in "combined arms," see J.K. Anderson, *Military Theory and Practice* (Berkeley, 1970) 115 ff.

[38] *i.e.* when Clearchus' cavalry deserted to the King (II. ii. 7).

ρεύοντο πρῶτερον ἀναστάντες· χαράδραν γὰρ ἔδει
αὐτοὺς διαβῆναι ἐφ' ᾗ ἐφοβοῦντο μὴ ἐπιθοῖντο αὐτοῖς
2 διαβαίνουσιν οἱ πολέμιοι. διαβεβηκόσι δὲ αὐτοῖς
πάλιν ἐπιφαίνεται ὁ Μιθραδάτης, ἔχων ἱππέας
χιλίους, τοξότας δὲ καὶ σφενδονήτας εἰς τετρακισχι-
λίους· τοσούτους γὰρ ᾔτησε Τισσαφέρνη, καὶ ἔλαβεν
ὑποσχόμενος, ἂν τούτους λάβῃ, παραδώσειν αὐτῷ
τοὺς Ἕλληνας, καταφρονήσας, ὅτι ἐν τῇ πρόσθεν
προσβολῇ ὀλίγους ἔχων ἔπαθε μὲν οὐδέν, πολλὰ δὲ
3 κακὰ ἐνόμιζε ποιῆσαι. ἐπεὶ δὲ οἱ Ἕλληνες διαβεβηκότες ἀπεῖχον τῆς χαράδρας ὅσον ὀκτὼ
σταδίους, διέβαινε καὶ ὁ Μιθραδάτης ἔχων τὴν
δύναμιν. παρήγγελτο δὲ τῶν τε πελταστῶν οὓς ἔδει
διώκειν καὶ τῶν ὁπλιτῶν, καὶ τοῖς ἱππεῦσιν εἴρητο
θαρροῦσι διώκειν ὡς ἐφεψομένης ἱκανῆς δυνάμεως.
4 ἐπεὶ δὲ ὁ Μιθραδάτης κατειλήφει, καὶ ἤδη σφενδόναι
καὶ τοξεύματα ἐξικνοῦντο, ἐσήμηνε τοῖς Ἕλλησι τῇ
σάλπιγγι, καὶ εὐθὺς ἔθεον ὁμόσε οἷς εἴρητο καὶ οἱ
ἱππεῖς ἤλαυνον· οἱ δὲ οὐκ ἐδέξαντο, ἀλλ' ἔφευγον ἐπὶ
5 τὴν χαράδραν. ἐν ταύτῃ τῇ διώξει τοῖς βαρβάροις τῶν
τε πεζῶν ἀπέθανον πολλοὶ καὶ τῶν ἱππέων ἐν τῇ
χαράδρᾳ ζωοὶ ἐλήφθησαν εἰς ὀκτωκαίδεκα. τοὺς δὲ
ἀποθανόντας αὐτοκέλευστοι οἱ Ἕλληνες ᾐκίσαντο, ὡς
ὅτι φοβερώτατον τοῖς πολεμίοις εἴη ὁρᾶν.
6   Καὶ οἱ μὲν πολέμιοι οὕτω πράξαντες ἀπῆλθον, οἱ

they set forth, after rising earlier than usual; for there was a gorge they had to cross, and they were afraid that the enemy might attack them as they were crossing. It was only after they had crossed it, however, that Mithradates appeared again, accompanied by a thousand horsemen and about four thousand bowmen and slingers. For these were the numbers he had requested from Tissaphernes, and these numbers he had obtained upon his promise that, if such a force were given him, he would deliver the Greeks into Tissaphernes' hands; for he had come to despise them, seeing that in his earlier attack with a small force he had done a great deal of harm, as he thought, without suffering any loss himself. When, accordingly, the Greeks were across the gorge and about eight stadia beyond it, Mithradates also proceeded to make the crossing with his troops. Now orders had already been given to such of the Greek peltasts and hoplites as were to pursue the enemy, and the horsemen had been directed to be bold in urging the pursuit, in the assurance that an adequate force would follow at their heels. As soon, then, as Mithradates had caught up, so that his sling-stones and arrows were just beginning to reach their marks, the trumpet gave its signal to the Greeks, and on the instant the foot soldiers who were under orders rushed upon the enemy and the horsemen charged; and the enemy did not await their attack, but fled towards the gorge. In this pursuit the barbarians had many of their infantry killed, while of their cavalry no less than eighteen were taken alive in the gorge. And the Greek troops, unbidden save by their own impulse, disfigured the bodies of the dead, in order that the sight of them might inspire the utmost terror in the enemy.

After faring thus badly the enemy departed, while the

δὲ Ἕλληνες ἀσφαλῶς πορευόμενοι τὸ λοιπὸν τῆς
7 ἡμέρας ἀφίκοντο ἐπὶ τὸν Τίγρητα ποταμόν. ἐνταῦθα
πόλις ἦν ἐρήμη μεγάλη, ὄνομα δ' αὐτῇ ἦν Λάρισα·
ᾤκουν δ' αὐτὴν τὸ παλαιὸν Μῆδοι. τοῦ δὲ τείχους
αὐτῆς ἦν τὸ εὖρος πέντε καὶ εἴκοσι πόδες, ὕψος δ'
ἑκατόν· τοῦ δὲ κύκλου ἡ περίοδος δύο παρασάγγαι·
ᾠκοδόμητο δὲ πλίνθοις κεραμεαῖς· κρηπὶς δ' ὑπῆν
8 λιθίνη τὸ ὕψος εἴκοσι ποδῶν. ταύτην βασιλεὺς ὁ
Περσῶν ὅτε παρὰ Μήδων τὴν ἀρχὴν ἐλάμβανον Πέρσαι πολιορκῶν οὐδενὶ τρόπῳ ἐδύνατο ἑλεῖν· ἥλιον δὲ
νεφέλη προκαλύψασα⁸ ἠφάνισε μέχρι ἐξέλιπον οἱ
9 ἄνθρωποι, καὶ οὕτως ἑάλω. παρὰ ταύτην τὴν πόλιν ἦν
πυραμὶς λιθίνη, τὸ μὲν εὖρος ἑνὸς πλέθρου, τὸ δὲ ὕψος
δύο πλέθρων. ἐπὶ ταύτης πολλοὶ τῶν βαρβάρων ἦσαν
ἐκ τῶν πλησίον κωμῶν ἀποπεφευγότες.

10 Ἐντεῦθεν δ' ἐπορεύθησαν σταθμὸν ἕνα παρασάγγας ἓξ πρὸς τεῖχος ἔρημον μέγα πρὸς πόλει κείμενον·
ὄνομα δὲ ἦν τῇ πόλει Μέσπιλα· Μῆδοι δ' αὐτήν ποτε
ᾤκουν. ἦν δὲ ἡ μὲν κρηπὶς λίθου ξεστοῦ κογχυλιάτου,
τὸ εὖρος πεντήκοντα ποδῶν καὶ τὸ ὕψος πεντήκοντα.
11 ἐπὶ δὲ ταύτῃ ἐπῳκοδόμητο πλίνθινον τεῖχος, τὸ μὲν

---

⁸ ἥλιον δὲ νεφέλη προκαλύψασα Hude/Peters, Mar., following Brodaeus: ἥλιος δὲ νεφέλην προκαλύψας MSS., Gem.

---

³⁹ This city, called by Xenophon "Larisa," was the great
Assyrian city of Nimrud or Kalhu (Genesis 10:11, 12).
⁴⁰ Cyrus the Great (558–529).

Greeks continued their march unmolested through the remainder of the day and arrived at the Tigris river. Here was a large deserted city;[39] its name was Larisa, and it was inhabited in ancient times by the Medes. Its wall was twenty-five feet in breadth and a hundred in height, and the whole circuit of the wall was two parasangs. It was built of clay bricks, and rested upon a stone foundation twenty feet high. This city was besieged by the king[40] of the Persians at the time when the Persians were seeking to wrest from the Medes their empire, but he could in no way capture it. A cloud, however, overspread the sun and hid it from sight until the inhabitants abandoned their city; and thus it was taken. Near by this city was a pyramid of stone,[41] a plethrum in breadth and two plethra in height; and upon this pyramid were many barbarians who had fled away from the neighbouring villages.

From this place they marched one stage, six parasangs, to a great stronghold, deserted and lying beside a city. The name of this city was Mespila,[42] and it was once inhabited by the Medes. The foundation of its wall was made of polished stone full of shells, and was fifty feet in breadth and fifty in height. Upon this foundation was built a wall

[41] A ziggurat is probably what was seen.

[42] The ruins which Xenophon saw here were those of Nineveh, the famous capital of the Assyrian Empire. It is revealing that he can characterize this great Assyrian city (as well as Kalhu above) with the casual and misleading statement that "it was once inhabited by the Medes." In fact, the capture of Nineveh by the Medes (c. 600) was the precise event which *closed* the important period of its history, and it remained under the control of the Medes only during the succeeding half-century, *i.e.* until the Median Empire was in its turn overthrown by the Persians (549).

εὖρος πεντήκοντα ποδῶν, τὸ δὲ ὕψος ἑκατόν· τοῦ δὲ
τείχους ἡ περίοδος ἓξ παρασάγγαι. ἐνταῦθα λέγεται
Μήδεια γυνὴ βασιλέως καταφυγεῖν ὅτε ἀπώλλυσαν

12 τὴν ἀρχὴν ὑπὸ Περσῶν Μῆδοι. ταύτην δὲ τὴν πόλιν
πολιορκῶν ὁ Περσῶν βασιλεὺς οὐκ ἐδύνατο οὔτε
χρόνῳ ἑλεῖν οὔτε βίᾳ· Ζεὺς δ' ἐμβροντήτους ποιεῖ τοὺς
ἐνοικοῦντας, καὶ οὕτως ἑάλω.

13 Ἐντεῦθεν δ' ἐπορεύθησαν σταθμὸν ἕνα παρασάγγας τέτταρας. εἰς τοῦτον δὲ τὸν σταθμὸν Τισσαφέρνης ἐπεφάνη, οὕς τε αὐτὸς ἱππέας ἦλθεν ἔχων καὶ τὴν
Ὀρόντα δύναμιν τοῦ τὴν βασιλέως θυγατέρα ἔχοντος
καὶ οὓς Κῦρος ἔχων ἀνέβη βαρβάρους καὶ οὓς ὁ
βασιλέως ἀδελφὸς ἔχων βασιλεῖ ἐβοήθει, καὶ πρὸς
τούτοις ὅσους βασιλεὺς ἔδωκεν αὐτῷ, ὥστε τὸ στρά-

14 τευμα πάμπολυ ἐφάνη. ἐπεὶ δ' ἐγγὺς ἐγένετο, τὰς μὲν
τῶν τάξεων ὄπισθεν καταστήσας, τὰς δὲ εἰς τὰ πλάγια
παραγαγὼν ἐμβαλεῖν μὲν οὐκ ἐτόλμησεν οὐδ' ἐβούλετο διακινδυνεύειν, σφενδονᾶν δὲ παρήγγειλε καὶ

15 τοξεύειν. ἐπεὶ δὲ διαταχθέντες οἱ Ῥόδιοι ἐσφεν-
δόνησαν καὶ οἱ Σκύθαι τοξόται ἐτόξευσαν καὶ οὐδεὶς
ἡμάρτανεν ἀνδρός (οὐδὲ γὰρ εἰ πάνυ προυθυμεῖτο
ῥᾴδιον ἦν), καὶ ὁ Τισσαφέρνης μάλα ταχέως ἔξω
βελῶν ἀπεχώρει καὶ αἱ ἄλλαι τάξεις ἀπεχώρησαν.

---

43 Astyages, the last king of Media.
44 *i.e.* from his province in Asia Minor, when he came to inform Artaxerxes of Cyrus' designs against him. See I. ii. 4.
45 Cf. II. iv. 8.   46 Cf. II. iv. 25.

of brick, fifty feet in breadth and a hundred in height; and the circuit of the wall was six parasangs. Here, as the story goes, Medea, the king's[43] wife, took refuge at the time when the Medes were deprived of their empire by the Persians. To this city also the king of the Persians laid siege, but he was unable to capture it either by length of siege or by storm; Zeus, however, rendered the inhabitants thunderstruck, and thus the city was taken.

From this place they marched one stage, four parasangs. In the course of this stage Tissaphernes made his appearance, having under his command the cavalry which he had himself brought with him,[44] the troops of Orontas,[45] who was married to the King's daughter, the barbarians whom Cyrus had brought with him on his upward march, and those with whom the King's brother had come to the aid of the King;[46] besides these contingents Tissaphernes had all the troops that the King had given him; the result was that his army appeared exceedingly large. When he got near the Greeks, he stationed some of his battalions in their rear and moved others into position on their flanks; then, although he could not muster up the courage to close with them and had no desire to risk a decisive battle, he ordered his men to discharge their slings and let fly their arrows. But when the Rhodian slingers and the Scythian bowmen, posted at intervals here and there, sent back an answering volley, and not a man among them missed his mark (for even if he had been very eager to do so, it would not have been easy),[47] then Tissaphernes withdrew out of range with all speed, and the other battalions followed his example.

[47] *i.e.* on account of the dense throng of the enemy.

16 Καὶ τὸ λοιπὸν τῆς ἡμέρας οἱ μὲν ἐπορεύοντο, οἱ δ'
εἵποντο· καὶ οὐκέτι ἐσίνοντο οἱ βάρβαροι τῇ τότε
ἀκροβολίσει· μακρότερον γὰρ οἵ γε Ῥόδιοι τῶν Περ-
17 σῶν ἐσφενδόνων, καὶ τῶν τοξοτῶν.⁹ μεγάλα δὲ καὶ τὰ
τόξα τὰ Περσικά ἐστιν· ὥστε χρήσιμα ἦν ὁπόσα
ἁλίσκοιτο τῶν τοξευμάτων τοῖς Κρησί, καὶ διετέλουν
χρώμενοι τοῖς τῶν πολεμίων τοξεύμασι, καὶ ἐμελέτων
τοξεύειν ἄνω ἱέντες μακράν. ηὑρίσκετο δὲ καὶ νεῦρα
πολλὰ ἐν ταῖς κώμαις καὶ μόλυβδος, ὥστε χρῆσθαι
18 εἰς τὰς σφενδόνας. καὶ ταύτῃ μὲν τῇ ἡμέρᾳ, ἐπεὶ
κατεστρατοπεδεύοντο οἱ Ἕλληνες κώμαις ἐπιτυχόντες,
ἀπῆλθον οἱ βάρβαροι μεῖον ἔχοντες τῇ ἀκροβολίσει·
τὴν δ' ἐπιοῦσαν ἡμέραν ἔμειναν οἱ Ἕλληνες καὶ ἐπε-
σιτίσαντο· ἦν γὰρ πολὺς σῖτος ἐν ταῖς κώμαις. τῇ δ'
ὑστεραίᾳ ἐπορεύοντο διὰ τοῦ πεδίου, καὶ Τισσαφέρνης
εἵπετο ἀκροβολιζόμενος.

19 Ἔνθα δὲ οἱ Ἕλληνες ἔγνωσαν πλαίσιον ἰσόπλευ-
ρον ὅτι πονηρὰ τάξις εἴη πολεμίων ἑπομένων. ἀνάγκη
γάρ ἐστιν, ἢν συγκύπτῃ τὰ κέρατα τοῦ πλαισίου ἢ
ὁδοῦ στενοτέρας οὔσης ἢ ὀρέων ἀναγκαζόντων ἢ γεφύρας, ἐκθλίβεσθαι τοὺς ὁπλίτας καὶ πορεύεσθαι
πονήρως, ἅμα μὲν πιεζομένους, ἅμα δὲ ταραττομένους,
ὥστε δυσχρήστους εἶναι ἀνάγκη ἀτάκτους ὄντας·
20 ὅταν δ' αὖ διάσχῃ τὰ κέρατα, ἀνάγκη διασπᾶσθαι
τοὺς τότε ἐκθλιβομένους καὶ κενὸν γίγνεσθαι τὸ

⁹ Mar. follows Madvig in regarding the text here as corrupt.

For the rest of the day the one army continued its march and the other its pursuit. And the barbarians were no longer[48] able to do any harm by their skirmishing at long range; for the Rhodian slingers carried farther with their missiles than the Persians, farther even than the Persian bowmen. Now, the Persian bows are large, and consequently the Cretans could make good use of all the arrows that fell into their hands; in fact, they were continually using the enemy's arrows, and practised themselves in longrange work by shooting them into the air.[49] In the villages, furthermore, the Greeks found gut in abundance and lead for the use of their slingers. As for that day's doings, when the Greeks came upon some villages and proceeded to encamp, the barbarians withdrew, having had the worst of it in the skirmishing. The following day the Greeks remained quiet and collected supplies, for there was an abundance of corn in the villages. On the day thereafter they continued their march through the plain, and Tissaphernes hung upon their rear and kept up the skirmishing.

Then it was that the Greeks found out that a square is a poor formation when an enemy is following. For if the wings draw together, either because a road is unusually narrow or because mountains or a bridge make it necessary, it is inevitable that the hoplites should be squeezed out of line and should march with difficulty, inasmuch as they are crowded together and are likewise in confusion; the result is that, being in disorder, they are by necessity of little service. Furthermore, when the wings draw apart again, those who had just been squeezed out are inevitably

[48] Cf. iii. 7–10.
[49] So that the arrows could be easily recovered.

μέσον τῶν κεράτων, καὶ ἀθυμεῖν τοὺς ταῦτα πάσχοντας πολεμίων ἑπομένων. καὶ ὁπότε δέοι γέφυραν διαβαίνειν ἢ ἄλλην τινὰ διάβασιν, ἔσπευδεν ἕκαστος
βουλόμενος φθάσαι πρῶτος· καὶ εὐεπίθετον ἦν ἐν-
21 ταῦθα τοῖς πολεμίοις. ἐπεὶ δὲ ταῦτ᾽ ἔγνωσαν οἱ στρατηγοί, ἐποίησαν ἓξ λόχους ἀνὰ ἑκατὸν ἄνδρας, καὶ
λοχαγοὺς ἐπέστησαν καὶ ἄλλους πεντηκοντῆρας καὶ
ἄλλους ἐνωμοτάρχους. οὕτω δὲ πορευόμενοι, ὁπότε μὲν
συγκύπτοι τὰ κέρατα, ὑπέμενον ὕστεροι οἱ λοχαγοί,
ὥστε μὴ ἐνοχλεῖν τοῖς κέρασι, τότε[10] δὲ παρῆγον
22 ἔξωθεν τῶν κεράτων. ὁπότε δὲ διάσχοιεν αἱ πλευραὶ
τοῦ πλαισίου, τὸ μέσον ἀνεξεπίμπλασαν, εἰ μὲν στε-
νότερον εἴη τὸ διέχον, κατὰ λόχους, εἰ δὲ πλατύτερον,
κατὰ πεντηκοστῦς, εἰ δὲ πάνυ πλατύ, κατ᾽ ἐνωμοτίας·
23 ὥστε ἀεὶ ἔκπλεων εἶναι τὸ μέσον. εἰ δὲ καὶ διαβαίνειν
τινὰ δέοι διάβασιν ἢ γέφυραν, οὐκ ἐταράττοντο, ἀλλ᾽

[10] Τότε some MSS., Mar.: τοὺς others. Gem., reading τοὺς,
inserts οἱ μὲν before ὕστεροι, following Mangelsdorf. After
ὕστεροι the MSS. have οἱ λοχαγοί which Mar. and Gem.
bracket.

[50] *i.e.* commanders of fifties and twenty-fives, or of half and
quarter companies.

[51] The formation is a hollow square. Xenophon means by
"wings" (κέρατα, here and above) the right and left ends of the
division which formed the front of the square, and by "flanks"
(πλευραί) the divisions which formed the sides of the square.
Apparently three of the special companies were stationed at the
middle of the front side of the square (cf. §43 below) and the other
three in the corresponding position at the rear.

scattered, the space between the wings is left unoccupied, and the men affected are out of spirits when an enemy is close behind them. Again, as often as the army had to pass over a bridge or make any other crossing, every man would hurry, in the desire to be the first one across, and that gave the enemy a fine chance to make an attack. When the generals came to realize these difficulties, they formed six companies of a hundred men each and put a captain at the head of each company, adding also platoon and squad commanders.[50] Proceeding in this fashion, when the wings drew together on the march,[51] the rearmost captains would drop back, so as not to interfere with the wings, and for the time being would move along behind the wings; and when the flanks of the square drew apart again, they would fill up the space between the wings, by companies in case this space was rather narrow, by platoons in case it was broader, or, if it was very broad, by squads,[52] the idea being, to have the gap filled up in any event. Again, if the army had to make some crossing or to pass over a bridge, there was no

[52] The squad, or quarter company, consisting of 25 men (i.e. 24 + the leader), normally marched three abreast, *i.e.* with a front of three and a depth of eight. The company might be formed in any one of three ways: (*a*) one squad front and four deep, (*b*) two squads front and two deep, or (*c*) four squads front and one deep. Three companies ranged alongside one another information (*a*) would thus have a front of three squads or nine men, in formation (*b*) a front of eighteen men, and in formation (*c*) a front of thirty-six men. It is these three dispositions of the three special companies at the front of the square which Xenophon terms, respectively, "by companies," "by platoons," and "by squads."

ἐν τῷ μέρει οἱ λόχοι[11] διέβαινον· καὶ εἴ που δέοι τι τῆς
φάλαγγος, ἐπιπαρῆσαν οὗτοι. τούτῳ τῷ τρόπῳ
ἐπορεύθησαν σταθμοὺς τέτταρας.

24   Ἡνίκα δὲ τὸν πέμπτον ἐπορεύοντο, εἶδον βασίλειόν
τι καὶ περὶ αὐτὸ κώμας πολλάς, τὴν δὲ ὁδὸν πρὸς τὸ
χωρίον τοῦτο διὰ γηλόφων ὑψηλῶν γιγνομένην, οἳ
καθῆκον ἀπὸ τοῦ ὄρους ὑφ᾽ ᾧ ἦσαν αἱ κῶμαι.[12] καὶ
εἶδον μὲν τοὺς λόφους ἄσμενοι οἱ Ἕλληνες, ὡς εἰκὸς
25   τῶν πολεμίων ὄντων ἱππέων· ἐπεὶ δὲ πορευόμενοι ἐκ
τοῦ πεδίου ἀνέβησαν ἐπὶ τὸν πρῶτον γήλοφον καὶ
κατέβαινον, ὡς ἐπὶ τὸν ἕτερον ἀναβαῖεν, ἐνταῦθα
ἐπιγίγνονται οἱ βάρβαροι καὶ ἀπὸ τοῦ ὑψηλοῦ εἰς τὸ
26   πρανὲς ἔβαλλον, ἐσφενδόνων, ἐτόξευον ὑπὸ μαστίγων,
καὶ πολλοὺς κατετίτρωσκον καὶ ἐκράτησαν τῶν
Ἑλλήνων γυμνήτων καὶ κατέκλεισαν αὐτοὺς εἴσω τῶν
ὅπλων· ὥστε παντάπασι ταύτην τὴν ἡμέραν ἄχρηστοι
ἦσαν ἐν τῷ ὄχλῳ ὄντες καὶ οἱ σφενδονῆται καὶ οἱ
27   τοξόται. ἐπεὶ δὲ πιεζόμενοι οἱ Ἕλληνες ἐπεχείρησαν
διώκειν, σχολῇ μὲν ἐπὶ τὸ ἄκρον ἀφικνοῦνται ὁπλῖται
28   ὄντες, οἱ δὲ πολέμιοι ταχὺ ἀπεπήδων. πάλιν δὲ ὁπότε
ἀπίοιεν πρὸς τὸ ἄλλο στράτευμα ταὐτὰ ἔπασχον, καὶ
ἐπὶ τοῦ δευτέρου γηλόφου ταὐτὰ ἐγίγνετο, ὥστε ἀπὸ

---

[11] Οἱ λόχοι Hude/Peters, Gem., following Valckenaer: οἱ
λοχαγοὶ MSS.

[12] ἦσαν αἱ κῶμαι Hude/Peters, Gem., following Schenkl: ἦν
ἡ κώμη MSS.

confusion, but each company crossed over in its turn; and
if any help was needed in any part of the army, these troops
would make their way to the spot. In this fashion the
Greeks proceeded four stages.

In the course of the fifth stage they caught sight of a
palace of some sort, with many villages round about it, and
they observed that the road to this place passed over high
hills, which stretched down from the mountain at whose
foot the villages were situated. And the Greeks were well
pleased to see the hills, as was natural considering that
the enemy's force was cavalry;[53] when, however, in their
march out of the plain they had mounted to the top of the
first hill, and were descending it, so as to ascend the next,
at this moment the barbarians came upon them and down
from the hilltop discharged their missiles and sling-stones
and arrows, fighting under the lash.[54] They were wounding
many, and they got the better of the Greek light troops
and shut them up within the lines of the hoplites, so that
these troops, being mingled with the non-combatants,
were entirely useless throughout that day, slingers and
bowmen alike. And when the Greeks, hard-pressed as
they were, undertook to pursue the attacking force, they
reached the hilltop but slowly, being heavy troops, while
the enemy sprang quickly out of reach; and every time
they returned from a pursuit to join the main army, they
suffered again in the same way.[55] On the second hill
the same experiences were repeated, and hence after

[53] Which is most effective in a level country.

[54] Like Xerxes' troops at Thermopylae (Hdt. VII. ccxxiii). Driving troops under the lash was an important element in Greek
conceptions of the Persians.   [55] *i.e.* as described in §§25–26.

273

τοῦ τρίτου γηλόφου ἔδοξεν αὐτοῖς μὴ κινεῖν τοὺς
στρατιώτας πρὶν ἀπὸ τῆς δεξιᾶς πλευρᾶς τοῦ πλαι-
29 σίου ἀνήγαγον πελταστὰς πρὸς τὸ ὄρος. ἐπεὶ δ' οὗτοι
ἐγένοντο ὑπὲρ τῶν ἑπομένων πολεμίων, οὐκέτι ἐπετίθεντο οἱ πολέμιοι τοῖς καταβαίνουσι, δεδοικότες μὴ
ἀποτμηθείησαν καὶ ἀμφοτέρωθεν αὐτῶν γένοιντο οἱ
30 πολέμιοι. οὕτω τὸ λοιπὸν τῆς ἡμέρας πορευόμενοι, οἱ
μὲν ἐν τῇ ὁδῷ κατὰ τοὺς γηλόφους, οἱ δὲ κατὰ τὸ ὄρος
ἐπιπαριόντες, ἀφίκοντο εἰς τὰς κώμας· καὶ ἰατροὺς
κατέστησαν ὀκτώ· πολλοὶ γὰρ ἦσαν οἱ τετρωμένοι.
31   Ἐνταῦθα ἔμειναν ἡμέρας τρεῖς καὶ τῶν τετρωμένων
ἕνεκα καὶ ἅμα ἐπιτήδεια πολλὰ εἶχον, ἄλευρα, οἶνον,
κριθὰς ἵπποις συμβεβλημένας πολλάς. ταῦτα δὲ συν-
ενηνεγμένα ἦν τῷ σατραπεύοντι τῆς χώρας. τετάρτῃ
32 δ' ἡμέρᾳ καταβαίνουσιν εἰς τὸ πεδίον. ἐπεὶ δὲ κατέλα-
βεν αὐτοὺς Τισσαφέρνης σὺν τῇ δυνάμει, ἐδίδαξεν
αὐτοὺς ἡ ἀνάγκη κατασκηνῆσαι οὗ πρῶτον εἶδον
κώμην καὶ μὴ πορεύεσθαι ἔτι μαχομένους· πολλοὶ γὰρ
ἦσαν οἱ ἀπόμαχοι, οἵ τε τετρωμένοι καὶ οἱ ἐκείνους
33 φέροντες καὶ οἱ τῶν φερόντων τὰ ὅπλα δεξάμενοι. ἐπεὶ
δὲ κατεσκήνησαν καὶ ἐπεχείρησαν αὐτοῖς ἀκροβολίζεσθαι οἱ βάρβαροι πρὸς τὴν κώμην προσιόντες, πολὺ
περιῆσαν οἱ Ἕλληνες· πολὺ γὰρ διέφερεν ἐκ χώρας
ὁρμῶντας ἀλέξασθαι ἢ πορευομένους ἐπιοῦσι τοῖς
πολεμίοις μάχεσθαι.

---

[56] Cf. §24.

ascending the third hill they decided not to stir the troops from its crest until they had led up a force of peltasts from the right flank of the square to a position on the mountain.[56] As soon as this force had got above the hostile troops that were hanging upon the Greek rear, the latter desisted from attacking the Greek army in its descent, for fear that they might be cut off and find themselves enclosed on both sides by their foes. In this way the Greeks continued their march for the remainder of the day, the one division by the road leading over the hills while the other followed a parallel course along the mountain slope, and so arrived at the villages. There they appointed eight surgeons, for the wounded were many.

In these villages they remained for three days, not only for the sake of the wounded, but likewise because they had provisions in abundance—flour, wine, and great stores of barley that had been collected for horses, all these supplies having been gathered together by the acting satrap of the district. On the fourth day they proceeded to descend into the plain. But when Tissaphernes and his command overtook them, necessity taught them to encamp in the first village they caught sight of, and not to continue the plan of marching and fighting at the same time; for a large number of the Greeks were unfit for combat, not only the wounded, but also those who were carrying them and the men who took in charge the arms of these carriers. When they had encamped, and the barbarians, approaching toward the village, attempted to attack them at long range, the Greeks had much the better of it; for to occupy a position and therefrom ward off an attack was a very different thing from being on the march and fighting with the enemy as they followed after.

34 Ἡνίκα δ᾽ ἦν ἤδη δείλη, ὥρα ἦν ἀπιέναι τοῖς πολε-
μίοις· οὔποτε γὰρ μεῖον ἀπεστρατοπεδεύοντο οἱ βάρβαροι τοῦ Ἑλληνικοῦ ἑξήκοντα σταδίων, φοβούμενοι
35 μὴ τῆς νυκτὸς οἱ Ἕλληνες ἐπιθῶνται αὐτοῖς. πονηρὸν
γὰρ νυκτός ἐστι στράτευμα Περσικόν. οἵ τε γὰρ ἵπποι
αὐτοῖς δέδενται καὶ ὡς ἐπὶ τὸ πολὺ πεποδισμένοι εἰσὶ
τοῦ μὴ φεύγειν ἕνεκα εἰ λυθείησαν, ἐάν τέ τις θόρυβος
γίγνηται, δεῖ ἐπισάξαι τὸν ἵππον Πέρσῃ ἀνδρὶ καὶ
χαλινῶσαι δεῖ καὶ θωρακισθέντα ἀναβῆναι ἐπὶ τὸν
ἵππον. ταῦτα δὲ πάντα χαλεπὰ νύκτωρ καὶ θορύβου
ὄντος ποιεῖν. τούτου ἕνεκα πόρρω ἀπεσκήνουν τῶν
Ἑλλήνων.

36 Ἐπεὶ δὲ ἐγίγνωσκον αὐτοὺς οἱ Ἕλληνες βουλομένους ἀπιέναι καὶ διαγγελλομένους, ἐκήρυξε τοῖς Ἕλλησι συσκευάζεσθαι ἀκουόντων τῶν πολεμίων. καὶ
χρόνον μέν τινα ἐπέσχον τῆς πορείας οἱ βάρβαροι,
ἐπειδὴ δὲ ὀψὲ ἐγίγνετο, ἀπῇσαν· οὐ γὰρ ἐδόκει λύειν
αὐτοὺς νυκτὸς πορεύεσθαι καὶ κατάγεσθαι ἐπὶ τὸ
37 στρατόπεδον. ἐπειδὴ δὲ σαφῶς ἀπιόντας ἤδη ἑώρων
οἱ Ἕλληνες, ἐπορεύοντο καὶ αὐτοὶ ἀναζεύξαντες καὶ
διῆλθον ὅσον ἑξήκοντα σταδίους. καὶ γίγνεται τοσοῦτον μεταξὺ τῶν στρατευμάτων ὥστε τῇ ὑστεραίᾳ οὐκ
ἐφάνησαν οἱ πολέμιοι οὐδὲ τῇ τρίτῃ, τῇ δὲ τετάρτῃ
νυκτὸς προελθόντες καταλαμβάνουσι χωρίον ὑπερ-
δέξιον οἱ βάρβαροι, ᾗ ἔμελλον οἱ Ἕλληνες παριέναι,
ἀκρωνυχίαν ὄρους, ὑφ᾽ ἣν ἡ κατάβασις ἦν εἰς τὸ
πεδίον.

38 Ἐπειδὴ δὲ ἑώρα Χειρίσοφος προκατειλημμένην

As soon as it came to be late in the afternoon, it was time for the enemy to withdraw. For in no instance did the barbarians encamp at a distance of less than sixty stadia from the Greek camp, out of fear that the Greeks might attack them during the night. For a Persian army at night is a sorry thing. Their horses are tethered, and usually hobbled also to prevent their running away if they get loose from the tether, and hence in case of any alarm a Persian has to put saddle-cloth and bridle on his horse, and then has also to put on his own breastplate and mount his horse—and all these things are difficult to do at night and in the midst of confusion. It was for this reason that the Persians encamped at a considerable distance from the Greeks.

When the Greeks became aware that they were desirous of withdrawing and were passing the word along, the order to pack up luggage was proclaimed to the Greek troops within hearing of the enemy. For a time the barbarians delayed their setting out, but when it began to grow late, they went off; for they thought it did not pay to be on the march and arriving at their camp in the night. When the Greeks saw at length that they were clearly departing, they broke camp and took the road themselves, and accomplished a march of no less than sixty stadia. Thus the two armies got so far apart that on the next day the enemy did not appear, nor yet on the third; on the fourth day, however, after pushing forward by night the barbarians occupied a high position on the right side of the road by which the Greeks were to pass, a spur of the mountain, namely, along the base of which ran the route leading down into the plain.

As soon as Cheirisophus observed that the spur was

τὴν ἀκρωνυχίαν, καλεῖ Ξενοφῶντα ἀπὸ τῆς οὐρᾶς καὶ
κελεύει λαβόντα τοὺς πελταστὰς παραγενέσθαι εἰς τὸ
39 πρόσθεν· ὁ δὲ Ξενοφῶν τοὺς μὲν πελταστὰς οὐκ ἦγεν·
ἐπιφαινόμενον γὰρ ἑώρα Τισσαφέρνη καὶ τὸ στράτευμα πᾶν· αὐτὸς δὲ προσελάσας ἠρώτα Τί καλεῖς; ὁ
δὲ λέγει αὐτῷ· Ἔξεστιν ὁρᾶν· προκατείληπται γὰρ
ἡμῖν ὁ ὑπὲρ τῆς καταβάσεως λόφος, καὶ οὐκ ἔστι
40 παρελθεῖν, εἰ μὴ τούτους ἀποκόψομεν. ἀλλὰ τί οὐκ
ἦγες τοὺς πελταστάς; ὁ δὲ λέγει ὅτι οὐκ ἐδόκει αὐτῷ
ἔρημα καταλιπεῖν τὰ ὄπισθεν πολεμίων ἐπιφαινο-
μένων. Ἀλλὰ μὴν ὥρα γ᾽, ἔφη, βουλεύεσθαι πῶς τις
41 τοὺς ἄνδρας ἀπελᾷ ἀπὸ τοῦ λόφου. ἐνταῦθα Ξενοφῶν
ὁρᾷ τοῦ ὄρους τὴν κορυφὴν ὑπὲρ αὐτοῦ τοῦ ἑαυτῶν
στρατεύματος οὖσαν, καὶ ἀπὸ ταύτης ἔφοδον ἐπὶ τὸν
λόφον ἔνθα ἦσαν οἱ πολέμιοι, καὶ λέγει· Κράτιστον,
ὦ Χειρίσοφε, ἡμῖν ἵεσθαι ὡς τάχιστα ἐπὶ τὸ ἄκρον·
ἢν γὰρ τοῦτο λάβωμεν, οὐ δυνήσονται μένειν οἱ ὑπὲρ
τῆς ὁδοῦ. ἀλλά, εἰ βούλει, μένε ἐπὶ τῷ στρατεύματι,
ἐγὼ δ᾽ ἐθέλω πορεύεσθαι· εἰ δὲ χρῄζεις, πορεύου ἐπὶ
42 τὸ ὄρος, ἐγὼ δὲ μενῶ αὐτοῦ. Ἀλλὰ δίδωμί σοι, ἔφη ὁ
Χειρίσοφος, ὁπότερον βούλει ἑλέσθαι. εἰπὼν ὁ Ξενοφῶν ὅτι νεώτερός ἐστιν αἱρεῖται πορεύεσθαι, κελεύει
δέ οἱ συμπέμψαι ἀπὸ τοῦ στόματος ἄνδρας· μακρὸν
43 γὰρ ἦν ἀπὸ τῆς οὐρᾶς λαβεῖν. καὶ ὁ Χειρίσοφος
συμπέμπει τοὺς ἀπὸ τοῦ στόματος πελταστάς, ἔλαβε

already occupied, he summoned Xenophon from the rear, directing him to come to the front and bring the peltasts with him. Xenophon, however, would not bring the peltasts, for he could see Tissaphernes and his whole army coming into view;[57] but he rode forward himself and asked, "Why are you summoning me?" Cheirisophus replied, "It is perfectly evident; the hill overhanging our downward road has been occupied ahead of us, and there is no getting by unless we dislodge these people. Why did you not bring the peltasts?" Xenophon answered that he had not thought it best to leave the rear unprotected when hostile troops were coming into sight. "Well, at any rate," said Cheirisophus, "it is high time to be thinking how we are to drive these fellows from the height." Then Xenophon observed that the summit of the mountain was close above their own army and that from this summit there was a way of approach to the hill where the enemy were; and he said, "Our best plan, Cheirisophus, is to drive with all speed for the mountain top; for if we once get possession of that, those men above our road will not be able to hold their position. If you choose, then, stay in command of the army, and I will go; or, if you prefer, you make for the mountain top, and I will stay here." "Well," said Cheirisophus, "I leave it to you to choose which part you wish." Then Xenophon, remarking that he was younger, elected to go, but he urged Cheirisophus to send with him some troops from the front; for it would have been too long a journey to bring up men from the rear. Cheirisophus accordingly sent with him the peltasts at the front, replacing them with those

[57] *i.e.* from the rear.

δὲ τοὺς κατὰ μέσον πλαισίου. συνέπεσθαι δ' ἐκέλευσεν αὐτῷ[13] καὶ τοὺς τριακοσίους οὓς αὐτὸς εἶχε τῶν
ἐπιλέκτων ἐπὶ τῷ στόματι τοῦ πλαισίου.

44 Ἐντεῦθεν ἐπορεύοντο ὡς ἐδύναντο τάχιστα. οἱ δ'
ἐπὶ τοῦ λόφου πολέμιοι ὡς ἐνόησαν αὐτῶν τὴν πορείαν
ἐπὶ τὸ ἄκρον, εὐθὺς καὶ αὐτοὶ ὥρμησαν ἁμιλλᾶσθαι
45 ἐπὶ τὸ ἄκρον. καὶ ἐνταῦθα πολλὴ μὲν κραυγὴ ἦν τοῦ
Ἑλληνικοῦ στρατεύματος διακελευομένων τοῖς ἑαυτῶν, πολλὴ δὲ κραυγὴ τῶν ἀμφὶ Τισσαφέρνη τοῖς
46 ἑαυτῶν διακελευομένων. Ξενοφῶν δὲ παρελαύνων ἐπὶ
τοῦ ἵππου παρεκελεύετο· Ἄνδρες, νῦν ἐπὶ τὴν Ἑλλάδα
νομίζετε ἁμιλλᾶσθαι, νῦν πρὸς [τοὺς] παῖδας καὶ [τὰς]
γυναῖκας, νῦν ὀλίγον πονήσαντες ἀμαχεὶ τὴν λοιπὴν
47 πορευσόμεθα. Σωτηρίδας δὲ ὁ Σικυώνιος εἶπεν· Οὐκ
ἐξ ἴσου, ὦ Ξενοφῶν, ἐσμέν· σὺ μὲν γὰρ ἐφ' ἵππου
48 ὀχεῖ, ἐγὼ δὲ χαλεπῶς κάμνω τὴν ἀσπίδα φέρων. καὶ
ὃς ἀκούσας ταῦτα καταπηδήσας ἀπὸ τοῦ ἵππου ὠθεῖ-
ται αὐτὸν ἐκ τῆς τάξεως καὶ τὴν ἀσπίδα ἀφελόμενος
ὡς ἐδύνατο τάχιστα ἔχων ἐπορεύετο· ἐτύγχανε δὲ καὶ
θώρακα ἔχων τὸν ἱππικόν· ὥστ' ἐπιέζετο. καὶ τοῖς μὲν
ἔμπροσθεν ὑπάγειν παρεκελεύετο, τοῖς δὲ ὄπισθεν
49 παριέναι μόλις ἑπόμενος. οἱ δ' ἄλλοι στρατιῶται παί-
ουσι καὶ βάλλουσι καὶ λοιδοροῦσι τὸν Σωτηρίδαν,
ἔστε ἠνάγκασαν λαβόντα τὴν ἀσπίδα πορεύεσθαι. ὁ
δ' ἀναβάς, ἕως μὲν βάσιμα ἦν, ἐπὶ τοῦ ἵππου ἦγεν,

13 αὐτῷ some MSS., Mar.: αὐτοὺς others. Gem. brackets
αὐτοὺς, following Rehdantz.

that were inside the square; he also ordered the three hundred picked men[58] under his own command at the front of the square to join Xenophon's force.

Then they set out with all possible speed. But no sooner had the enemy upon the hill observed their dash for the summit of the mountain than they also set off, to race with the Greeks for this summit. Then there was a deal of shouting from the Greek army as they urged on their friends, and just as much shouting from Tissaphernes' troops to urge on their men. And Xenophon, riding along the lines upon his horse, cheered his troops forward: "Men," he said, "believe that now you are struggling for Greece, for children and wives; now a little toil and no more fighting for the rest of our journey." But Soteridas the Sicyonian said: "We are not on an equality, Xenophon; you are riding on horseback, while I am desperately tired with carrying my shield." When Xenophon heard that, he leaped down from his horse and pushed Soteridas out of his place in the line, then took his shield away from him and marched on with it as fast as he could; he had on also, as it happened, his cavalry breastplate, and the result was that he was heavily burdened. And he urged the men in front of him to keep going, while he told those who were behind to pass along by him, for he found it hard to keep up. The rest of the soldiers, however, struck and pelted and abused Soteridas until they forced him to take his shield and march on. Then Xenophon remounted, and as long as riding was possible, led the way on horseback, but when the ground became

---

[58] See §21 above and note thereon. Three hundred was a conventional size for a medium to small detachment, both at Sparta and elsewhere: thus Hdt. I. lxxxii, VII. ccii, IX. lxiv; Thuc. V. lxxii. 4 (Spartans); Plutarch *Pel*. XVIII (Theban Sacred Band).

ἐπεὶ δὲ ἄβατα ἦν, καταλιπὼν τὸν ἵππον ἔσπευδε πεζῇ.
καὶ φθάνουσιν ἐπὶ τῷ ἄκρῳ γενόμενοι τοὺς πολεμίους.

V. Ἔνθα δὴ οἱ μὲν βάρβαροι στραφέντες ἔφευγον
ᾗ ἕκαστος ἐδύνατο, οἱ δὲ Ἕλληνες εἶχον τὸ ἄκρον. οἱ
δὲ ἀμφὶ Τισσαφέρνη καὶ Ἀριαῖον ἀποτραπόμενοι
ἄλλην ὁδὸν ᾤχοντο. οἱ δὲ ἀμφὶ Χειρίσοφον καταβάντες εἰς τὸ πεδίον[14] ἐστρατοπεδεύοντο ἐν κώμῃ
μεστῇ πολλῶν ἀγαθῶν. ἦσαν δὲ καὶ ἄλλαι κῶμαι
πολλαὶ πλήρεις πολλῶν ἀγαθῶν ἐν τούτῳ τῷ πεδίῳ
2 παρὰ τὸν Τίγρητα ποταμόν. ἡνίκα δ᾽ ἦν δείλη ἐξαπίνης οἱ πολέμιοι ἐπιφαίνονται ἐν τῷ πεδίῳ, καὶ τῶν
Ἑλλήνων κατέκοψάν τινας τῶν ἐσκεδασμένων ἐν τῷ
πεδίῳ καθ᾽ ἁρπαγήν· καὶ γὰρ νομαὶ πολλαὶ βοσκη-
μάτων διαβιβαζόμεναι εἰς τὸ πέραν τοῦ ποταμοῦ κατ-
3 ελήφθησαν. ἐνταῦθα Τισσαφέρνης καὶ οἱ σὺν αὐτῷ
καίειν ἐπεχείρησαν τὰς κώμας. καὶ τῶν Ἑλλήνων
μάλα ἠθύμησάν τινες, ἐννοούμενοι μὴ τὰ ἐπιτήδεια,
4 εἰ καύσοιεν, οὐκ ἔχοιεν ὁπόθεν λαμβάνοιεν. καὶ οἱ μὲν
ἀμφὶ Χειρίσοφον ἀπῇσαν ἐκ τῆς βοηθείας· ὁ δὲ Ξενοφῶν ἐπεὶ κατέβη, παρελαύνων τὰς τάξεις ἡνίκα ⟨οἱ⟩[15]
ἀπὸ τῆς βοηθείας ἀπήντησαν οἱ Ἕλληνες ἔλεγεν·
5 Ὁρᾶτε, ὦ ἄνδρες Ἕλληνες, ὑφιέντας τὴν χώραν ἤδη
ὑμετέραν εἶναι; ἃ γὰρ ὅτε ἐσπένδοντο διεπράττοντο,
μὴ κάειν τὴν βασιλέως χώραν, νῦν αὐτοὶ καίουσιν ὡς
ἀλλοτρίαν. ἀλλ᾽ ἐάν που καταλίπωσί γε αὐτοῖς

[14] εἰς τὸ πεδίον omitted by one MS.
[15] οἱ added by Schenkl.

too difficult, he left his horse behind and hurried forward on foot. And they reached the summit before the enemy.

V. Then it was that the barbarians turned about and fled, every man for himself, while the Greeks held possession of the summit. As for the troops under Tissaphernes and Ariaeus, they turned off by another road and were gone; and the army under Cheirisophus descended into the plain[59] and encamped in a village stored with abundant supplies. There were likewise many other villages richly stored with supplies in this plain on the banks of the Tigris. When it came to be late in the day, all of a sudden the enemy appeared in the plain and cut to pieces some of the Greeks who were scattered about there in quest of plunder; in fact, many herds of cattle had been captured while they were being taken across to the other side of the river. Then Tissaphernes and his followers attempted to burn the villages; and some of the Greeks got exceedingly despondent, out of apprehension that they would not have a place from which to get provisions in case the enemy should succeed in this attempt. Meanwhile Cheirisophus and his men, who had gone to the rescue of the plunderers, were returning; and when Xenophon had come down from the mountain, he rode along the lines upon falling in with the Greeks of the rescuing party and said: "Do you observe, men of Greece, that they admit the country is now ours? For while they stipulated when they made the treaty that there should be no burning of the King's territory, now they are doing that very thing themselves, as though the land were another's. At any rate, if they leave supplies anywhere

[59] See iv. 37 *fin.*

ἐπιτήδεια, ὄψονται καὶ ἡμᾶς ἐνταῦθα πορευομένους.

6 ἀλλ᾽, ὦ Χειρίσοφε, ἔφη, δοκεῖ μοι βοηθεῖν ἐπὶ τοὺς
κάοντας ὡς ὑπὲρ τῆς ἡμετέρας. ὁ δὲ Χειρίσοφος εἶπεν·
Οὔκουν ἔμοιγε δοκεῖ· ἀλλὰ καὶ ἡμεῖς, ἔφη, κάωμεν,
καὶ οὕτω θᾶττον παύσονται.

7 Ἐπεὶ δὲ ἐπὶ τὰς σκηνὰς ἀπῆλθον, οἱ μὲν ἄλλοι περὶ
τὰ ἐπιτήδεια ἦσαν, στρατηγοὶ δὲ καὶ λοχαγοὶ συνῆλθον. καὶ ἐνταῦθα πολλὴ ἀπορία ἦν. ἔνθεν μὲν γὰρ
ὄρη ἦν ὑπερύψηλα, ἔνθεν δὲ ὁ ποταμὸς τοσοῦτος τὸ
βάθος ὡς μηδὲ τὰ δόρατα ὑπερέχειν πειρωμένοις τοῦ
8 βάθους. ἀπορουμένοις δ᾽ αὐτοῖς προσελθών τις ἀνὴρ
Ῥόδιος εἶπεν· Ἐγὼ θέλω, ὦ ἄνδρες, διαβιβάσαι ὑμᾶς
κατὰ τετρακισχιλίους ὁπλίτας, ἂν ἐμοὶ ὧν δέομαι
9 ὑπηρετήσητε καὶ τάλαντον μισθὸν πορίσητε. ἐρωτώμενος δὲ ὅτου δέοιτο, Ἀσκῶν, ἔφη, δισχιλίων δεήσο-
μαι· πολλὰ δ᾽ ὁρῶ ταῦτα πρόβατα καὶ αἶγας καὶ βοῦς
καὶ ὄνους, ἃ ἀποδαρέντα καὶ φυσηθέντα ῥᾳδίως ἂν
10 παρέχοι τὴν διάβασιν. δεήσομαι δὲ καὶ τῶν δεσμῶν
οἷς χρῆσθε περὶ τὰ ὑποζύγια· τούτοις ζεύξας τοὺς
ἀσκοὺς πρὸς ἀλλήλους, ὁρμίσας ἕκαστον ἀσκὸν
λίθους ἀρτήσας καὶ ἀφεὶς ὥσπερ ἀγκύρας εἰς τὸ ὕδωρ,
διαγαγὼν καὶ ἀμφοτέρωθεν δήσας ἐπιβαλῶ ὕλην καὶ
11 γῆν ἐπιφορήσω· ὅτι μὲν οὖν οὐ καταδύσεσθε αὐτίκα
μάλα εἴσεσθε· πᾶς γὰρ ἀσκὸς δύο ἄνδρας ἕξει τοῦ μὴ
καταδῦναι. ὥστε δὲ μὴ ὀλισθάνειν ἡ ὕλη καὶ ἡ γῆ
12 σχήσει. ἀκούσασι ταῦτα τοῖς στρατηγοῖς τὸ μὲν

---

[60] Cf. I. v. 10, II. iv. 28.

for their own use, they shall behold us also proceeding to that spot. But, Cheirisophus," he went on, "it seems to me that we ought to attack the enemy setting the fires, like men defending their own country." "Well, it doesn't seem so to me," said Cheirisophus; "rather, let us set about burning ourselves, and then they will stop the sooner."

When they had come back to their quarters, the troops were busy about provisions, but the generals and captains gathered in council. And here there was great despondency. For on one side of them were exceedingly high mountains and on the other side a river so deep that not even their spears reached above water when they tried its depth. In the midst of their perplexity a Rhodian came to them and said: "I stand ready, gentlemen, to set you across the river, four thousand hoplites at a time, if you will provide me with the means that I require and give me a talent for pay." Upon being asked what his requirements were, he replied: "I shall need two thousand skins. Many are these sheep and goats and cattle and asses I see; take off their skins and blow them up, and they would easily provide the means of crossing.[60] I shall want also the girths which you use on the beasts of burden; with these I shall tie the skins to one another and also moor each skin by fastening stones to the girths and letting them down into the water like anchors; then I shall carry the line of skins across the river, make it fast at both ends, and pile on brushwood and earth. As for your not sinking, then, you may be sure in an instant on that point, for every skin will keep two men from sinking; and as regards slipping, the brushwood and the earth will prevent that." After hearing these words the generals thought that while the idea was a

ἐνθύμημα χαρίεν ἐδόκει εἶναι, τὸ δ' ἔργον ἀδύνατον.
ἦσαν γὰρ οἱ κωλύσοντες πέραν πολλοὶ ἱππεῖς, οἳ
εὐθὺς τοῖς πρώτοις οὐδὲν ἂν ἐπέτρεπον τούτων ποιεῖν.

13   Ἐνταῦθα τὴν μὲν ὑστεραίαν ἐπανεχώρουν[16] εἰς
τοὔμπαλιν εἰς τὰς ἀκαύστους κώμας, κατακαύσαντες
ἔνθεν ἐξῇσαν· ὥστε οἱ πολέμιοι οὐ προσήλαυνον,
ἀλλὰ ἐθεῶντο καὶ ὅμοιοι ἦσαν θαυμάζοντες ὅποι ποτὲ
14   τρέψονται οἱ Ἕλληνες καὶ τί ἐν νῷ ἔχοιεν. ἐνταῦθα οἱ
μὲν ἄλλοι στρατιῶται ἀμφὶ τὰ ἐπιτήδεια ἦσαν· οἱ δὲ
στρατηγοὶ πάλιν συνῆλθον, καὶ συναγαγόντες τοὺς
αἰχμαλώτους ἤλεγχον τὴν κύκλῳ πᾶσαν χώραν τίς
15   ἑκάστη εἴη. οἱ δὲ ἔλεγον ὅτι τὰ πρὸς μεσημβρίαν τῆς
ἐπὶ Βαβυλῶνα εἴη καὶ Μηδίαν, δι' ἧσπερ ἥκοιεν, ἡ δὲ
πρὸς ἕω ἐπὶ Σοῦσά τε καὶ Ἐκβάτανα φέροι, ἔνθα
θερίζειν καὶ ἐαρίζειν λέγεται βασιλεύς, ἡ δὲ διαβάντι
τὸν ποταμὸν πρὸς ἑσπέραν ἐπὶ Λυδίαν καὶ Ἰωνίαν
φέροι, ἡ δὲ διὰ τῶν ὀρέων καὶ πρὸς ἄρκτον τετραμ-
16   μένη ὅτι εἰς Καρδούχους ἄγοι. τούτους δὲ ἔφασαν
οἰκεῖν ἀνὰ τὰ ὄρη καὶ πολεμικοὺς εἶναι, καὶ βασιλέως
οὐκ ἀκούειν, ἀλλὰ καὶ ἐμβαλεῖν ποτε εἰς αὐτοὺς
βασιλικὴν στρατιὰν δώδεκα μυριάδας· τούτων δ'
οὐδένα ἀπονοστῆσαι διὰ τὴν δυσχωρίαν. ὁπότε μέντοι
πρὸς τὸν σατράπην ἐν τῷ πεδίῳ σπείσαιντο, καὶ

---

[16] ἐπανεχώρουν some MSS., Hude/Peters, Gem.: ὑπαν-
εχώρουν other MSS., Mar.

clever one, the execution of it was impossible. For there were people on the other side of the river to thwart it, a large force of horsemen, namely, who at the very outset would prevent the first comers from carrying out any part of the plan.

Under these circumstances they marched all the next day in the reverse direction, going back to the unburned villages,[61] after burning the one from which they withdrew. The result was that, instead of making an attack, the enemy merely gazed at the Greeks, and appeared to be wondering where in the world they would turn and what they had in mind. At the close of the day, while the rest of the army went after provisions, the generals held another meeting, at which they brought together the prisoners that had been taken and enquired of them about each district of all the surrounding country. The prisoners said that the region to the south lay on the road towards Babylon and Media, the identical province they had just passed through; that the road to the eastward led to Susa and Ecbatana, where the King is said to spend his summers and springs; across the river and on to the west was the way to Lydia and Ionia; while the route through the mountains and northward led to the country of the Carduchians. These Carduchians, they said, dwelt up among the mountains, were a warlike people, and were not subjects of the King;[62] in fact, a royal army of one hundred and twenty thousand men had once invaded them, and, by reason of the ruggedness of the country, not a man of all that number came back. Still, whenever they made a treaty with the satrap in the plain,

[61] See §§1 and 3 above.   [62] Obviously, another autonomous region such as those mentioned at III. ii. 23.

ἐπιμειγνύναι σφῶν τε πρὸς ἐκείνους καὶ ἐκείνων πρὸς
ἑαυτούς.

17 Ἀκούσαντες ταῦτα οἱ στρατηγοὶ ἐκάθισαν χωρὶς
τοὺς ἑκασταχόσε φάσκοντας εἰδέναι, οὐδὲν δῆλον
ποιήσαντες ὅποι πορεύεσθαι ἔμελλον. ἐδόκει δὲ τοῖς
στρατηγοῖς ἀναγκαῖον εἶναι διὰ τῶν ὀρέων εἰς Καρδούχους ἐμβάλλειν· τούτους γὰρ διελθόντας ἔφασαν
εἰς Ἀρμενίαν ἥξειν, ἧς Ὀρόντας ἦρχε πολλῆς καὶ
εὐδαίμονος. ἐντεῦθεν δ᾽ εὔπορον ἔφασαν εἶναι ὅποι τις
18 ἐθέλοι πορεύεσθαι. ἐπὶ τούτοις ἐθύσαντο, ὅπως ὁπη-
νίκα καὶ δοκοίη τῆς ὥρας τὴν πορείαν ποιοῖντο· τὴν
γὰρ ὑπερβολὴν τῶν ὀρέων ἐδεδοίκεσαν μὴ προκατα-
ληφθείη· καὶ παρήγγειλαν, ἐπειδὴ δειπνήσειαν, συσκευασαμένους πάντας ἀναπαύεσθαι, καὶ ἕπεσθαι
ἡνίκ᾽ ἄν τις παραγγέλλῃ.

some of the people of the plain did have dealings with the Carduchians and some of the Carduchians with them.

After listening to these statements the generals set aside those who claimed to know the way in every direction, without giving the least clue as to the direction in which they proposed to march. The opinion of the generals however, was that they must make their way through the mountains into the country of the Carduchians; for the prisoners said that after passing through this country they would come to Armenia, the large and prosperous province of which Orontas was ruler; and from there, they said, it was easy to go in any direction one chose. Thereupon the generals offered sacrifice, so that they could begin the march at the moment they thought best[63]—for they feared that the pass over the mountains might be occupied in advance; and they issued orders that when the troops had dined, every man should pack up his belongings and go to rest, and then fall into line as soon as the word of command was given.

[63] As a rule it was immediately before an army set out that sacrifice was offered. See, in general, Burkert, *Greek Religion*, 267.

5 I.[1] Ἡνίκα δ᾽ ἦν ἀμφὶ τὴν τελευταίαν φυλακὴν καὶ
ἐλείπετο τῆς νυκτὸς ὅσον σκοταίους διελθεῖν τὸ πεδίον, τηνικαῦτα ἀναστάντες ἀπὸ παραγγέλσεως πορευ-

---

[1] The summary prefixed to Book IV (see note on II. i. 1) is as
follows: Ὅσα μὲν δὴ ἐν τῇ ἀναβάσει ἐγένετο μέχρι τῆς
μάχης, καὶ ὅσα μετὰ τὴν μάχην ἐν ταῖς σπονδαῖς ἃς
βασιλεὺς καὶ οἱ σὺν Κύρῳ ἀναβάντες Ἕλληνες ἐποιήσαντο,
καὶ ὅσα παραβάντος τὰς σπονδὰς βασιλέως καὶ Τισσαφέρνους ἐπολεμήθη πρὸς τοὺς Ἕλληνας ἐπακολουθοῦντος τοῦ
Περσῶν στρατεύματος, ἐν τῷ πρόσθεν λόγῳ δεδήλωται. ἐπεὶ
δὲ ἀφίκοντο ἔνθα ὁ μὲν Τίγρης ποταμὸς παντάπασιν ἄπορος
ἦν διὰ τὸ βάθος καὶ μέγεθος, πάροδος δὲ οὐκ ἦν, ἀλλὰ τὰ
Καρδούχεια ὄρη ἀπότομα ὑπὲρ αὐτοῦ τοῦ ποταμοῦ ἐ-
κρέματο, ἐδόκει δὴ τοῖς στρατηγοῖς διὰ τῶν ὀρέων πορευτέον
εἶναι. ἤκουον γὰρ τῶν ἁλισκομένων ὅτι εἰ διέλθοιεν τὰ Καρδούχεια ὄρη, ἐν τῇ Ἀρμενίᾳ τὰς πηγὰς τοῦ Τίγρητος ποταμοῦ, ἣν μὲν βούλωνται, διαβήσονται, ἢν δὲ μὴ βούλωνται,
περιίασι. καὶ τοῦ Εὐφράτου δὲ τὰς πηγὰς ἐλέγετο οὐ πρόσω
τοῦ Τίγρητος εἶναι, καὶ ἔστιν οὕτως ἔχον. τὴν δ᾽ εἰς τοὺς
Καρδούχους ἐμβολὴν ὧδε ποιοῦνται, ἅμα μὲν λαθεῖν
πειρώμενοι, ἅμα δὲ φθάσαι πρὶν τοὺς πολεμίους καταλαβεῖν
τὰ ἄκρα.

---

[1] Summary (see note to text): The preceding narrative has
described all that took place on the upward march until the time

BOOK IV

I.[1] When it was about the last watch, and enough of the night remained to allow them to cross the plain in the dark, at that time they arose upon the word of command

of the battle, all that happened after the battle during the truce concluded by the King and the Greeks who had made the upward march in company with Cyrus, and likewise the whole course of the warfare carried on against the Greeks after the King and Tissaphernes had broken the truce, when the Persian army was hanging upon the Greek rear. When the Greeks finally reached a point where the Tigris river was quite impassable by reason of its depth and width, and where there was no passage along side the river, since the Carduchian mountains hung sheer and close above it, the generals were forced to the conclusion that they must make their way through the mountains. For they heard from the prisoners who were taken that once they had passed through the Carduchian mountains and reached Armenia, they could there cross the headwaters of the Tigris river, if they so desired, or, if they preferred, could go round them. They were also informed that the headwaters of the Euphrates were not far from those of the Tigris—and such is indeed the case. Now they conducted their invasion of the country of the Carduchians in the following way, since they were seeking not only to escape observation, but at the same time to reach the heights before the enemy could take possession of them.

6 ὅμενοι ἀφικνοῦνται ἅμα τῇ ἡμέρᾳ πρὸς τὸ ὄρος. ἔνθα
δὴ Χειρίσοφος μὲν ἡγεῖτο τοῦ στρατεύματος λαβὼν
τὸ ἀμφ᾽ αὑτὸν καὶ τοὺς γυμνῆτας πάντας, Ξενοφῶν
δὲ σὺν τοῖς ὀπισθοφύλαξιν ὁπλίταις εἵπετο οὐδένα
ἔχων γυμνῆτα· οὐδεὶς γὰρ κίνδυνος ἐδόκει εἶναι μή
7 τις ἄνω πορευομένων ἐκ τοῦ ὄπισθεν ἐπίσποιτο. καὶ
ἐπὶ μὲν τὸ ἄκρον ἀναβαίνει Χειρίσοφος πρίν τινα
αἰσθέσθαι τῶν πολεμίων· ἔπειτα δ᾽ ὑφηγεῖτο· ἐφείπετο
δὲ ἀεὶ τὸ ὑπερβάλλον τοῦ στρατεύματος εἰς τὰς κώμας
8 τὰς ἐν τοῖς ἄγκεσί τε καὶ μυχοῖς τῶν ὀρέων. ἔνθα δὴ
οἱ μὲν Καρδοῦχοι ἐκλιπόντες τὰς οἰκίας ἔχοντες καὶ
γυναῖκας καὶ παῖδας ἔφευγον ἐπὶ τὰ ὄρη. τὰ δὲ ἐπιτήδεια πολλὰ ἦν λαμβάνειν, ἦσαν δὲ καὶ χαλκώμασι
παμπόλλοις κατεσκευασμέναι αἱ οἰκίαι, ὧν οὐδὲν ἔφερον οἱ Ἕλληνες, οὐδὲ τοὺς ἀνθρώπους ἐδίωκον, ὑπο-
φειδόμενοι, εἴ πως ἐθελήσειαν οἱ Καρδοῦχοι διέναι
αὐτοὺς ὡς διὰ φιλίας τῆς χώρας, ἐπείπερ βασιλεῖ
9 πολέμιοι ἦσαν· τὰ μέντοι ἐπιτήδεια ὅτῳ τις ἐπιτυγχά-
νοι ἐλάμβανον· ἀνάγκη γὰρ ἦν. οἱ δὲ Καρδοῦχοι οὔτε
καλούντων ὑπήκουον οὔτε ἄλλο φιλικὸν οὐδὲν ἐποίουν.
10 ἐπεὶ δὲ οἱ τελευταῖοι τῶν Ἑλλήνων κατέβαινον εἰς τὰς
κώμας ἀπὸ τοῦ ἄκρου ἤδη σκοταῖοι—διὰ γὰρ τὸ
στενὴν εἶναι τὴν ὁδὸν ὅλην τὴν ἡμέραν ἡ ἀνάβασις
αὐτοῖς ἐγένετο καὶ κατάβασις εἰς τὰς κώμας—τότε δὴ
συλλεγέντες τινὲς τῶν Καρδούχων τοῖς τελευταίοις

---

2 It will be remembered that light troops had proved more ser-

and set out on their march; and they reached the mountain at daybreak. Here Cheirisophus, with his own division and all the light-armed troops, led the van, while Xenophon followed behind with the hoplites of the rearguard, but without any light troops at all; for there seemed to be no danger of any pursuit from behind while they were proceeding uphill.[2] And Cheirisophus reached the summit of the pass before any one of the enemy perceived him; then he led on slowly, and each division of the army as it passed over the summit followed along to the villages which lay in the hollows and nooks of the mountains. Then it was that the Carduchians abandoned their houses and fled to the mountains with their wives and children. As for provisions, there was an abundance for the Greeks to take, and the houses were also supplied with bronze vessels in great numbers; the Greeks, however, did not carry off any of these, and did not pursue the people themselves, refraining from harshness on the chance that the Carduchians might perhaps be willing to let them pass through their country in friendship, seeing that they also were enemies of the King; but they did take whatever they chanced upon in the way of provisions, for that was necessary. The Carduchians, however, would neither listen when they called to them nor give any other sign of friendliness. And when the rearguard of the Greeks was descending from the summit of the pass to the villages—and by this time it was dark, for on account of the road being narrow their ascent and descent into the villages lasted through the entire day—at this moment some of the Carduchians gathered together

viceable than hoplites in the recent skirmishes with the Persians. Cf. III. iv. 15–17, 24–30, 38–43.

ἐπετίθεντο, καὶ ἀπέκτεινάν τινας καὶ λίθοις καὶ τοξεύμασι κατέτρωσαν, ὀλίγοι ὄντες· ἐξ ἀπροσδοκήτου γὰρ
11 αὐτοῖς ἐπέπεσε τὸ Ἑλληνικόν. εἰ μέντοι τότε πλείους
συνελέγησαν, ἐκινδύνευσεν ἂν διαφθαρῆναι πολὺ τοῦ
στρατεύματος. καὶ ταύτην μὲν τὴν νύκτα οὕτως ἐν ταῖς
κώμαις ηὐλίσθησαν· οἱ δὲ Καρδοῦχοι πυρὰ πολλὰ
ἔκαιον κύκλῳ ἐπὶ τῶν ὀρέων καὶ συνεώρων ἀλλήλους.
12 Ἅμα δὲ τῇ ἡμέρᾳ συνελθοῦσι τοῖς στρατηγοῖς καὶ
λοχαγοῖς τῶν Ἑλλήνων ἔδοξε τῶν τε ὑποζυγίων τὰ
ἀναγκαῖα καὶ δυνατώτατα ἔχοντας πορεύεσθαι, κατα-
λιπόντας τἆλλα, καὶ ὅσα ἦν νεωστὶ αἰχμάλωτα
13 ἀνδράποδα ἐν τῇ στρατιᾷ πάντα ἀφεῖναι. σχολαίαν
γὰρ ἐποίουν τὴν πορείαν πολλὰ ὄντα τὰ ὑποζύγια καὶ
τὰ αἰχμάλωτα, πολλοὶ δὲ οἱ ἐπὶ τούτοις ὄντες ἀπόμαχοι ἦσαν, διπλάσιά τε τὰ ἐπιτήδεια ἔδει πορίζεσθαι
καὶ φέρεσθαι πολλῶν τῶν ἀνθρώπων ὄντων. δόξαν δὲ
ταῦτα ἐκήρυξαν οὕτω ποιεῖν.
14 Ἐπειδὴ δὲ ἀριστήσαντες ἐπορεύοντο, ὑποστάντες
ἐν στενῷ οἱ στρατηγοί, εἴ τι εὑρίσκοιεν τῶν εἰρημένων
μὴ ἀφειμένον, ἀφῃροῦντο, οἱ δ' ἐπείθοντο, πλὴν εἴ τίς
τι ἔκλεψεν, οἷον ἢ παιδὸς ἐπιθυμήσας ἢ γυναικὸς τῶν
εὐπρεπῶν. καὶ ταύτην μὲν τὴν ἡμέραν οὕτως ἐπορεύθησαν, τὰ μέν τι μαχόμενοι τὰ δέ τι ἀναπαυόμενοι.
15 εἰς δὲ τὴν ὑστεραίαν γίγνεται χειμὼν πολύς, ἀναγκαῖον δ' ἦν πορεύεσθαι· οὐ γὰρ ἦν ἱκανὰ τἀπιτήδεια.

and attacked the hindmost Greeks; and they killed some and wounded others severely with stones and arrows, though they were themselves but few in number; for the Greek army had come upon them unexpectedly. If, however, a larger number of them had gathered together at that time, a great part of the army would have been in danger of being destroyed. Thus the Greeks bivouacked for that night in the villages, while the Carduchians kindled many fires round about upon the mountains and kept themselves in sight of one another.

At daybreak the generals and captains of the Greeks came together and resolved to keep with them on the march only the indispensable and most powerful baggage animals and to leave the rest behind; likewise, to let go all the newly-taken captives that were in the army, to the last man. For the baggage animals and the captives, numerous as they were, made the march slow, and the large number of men who had charge of them were thus taken out of the fighting line; besides, with so many people to feed it was necessary to procure and to carry twice the amount of provisions. This decision once reached, they published the order to carry it into effect

When they had breakfasted and were setting out upon the march, the generals, quietly stationed in the defile, proceeded to take away from the troops such of the things specified as had not been given up if they found any; and the soldiers submitted, except in cases where a man had smuggled something in, either a handsome boy or woman, for example, that he had set his heart upon. So they went on for that day, now fighting a little and now resting. On the next day there was a heavy storm, but they had to continue their march, for they had not an adequate supply

XENOPHON

καὶ ἡγεῖτο μὲν Χειρίσοφος, ὠπισθοφυλάκει δὲ Ξενο-
16 φῶν. καὶ οἱ πολέμιοι ἰσχυρῶς ἐπετίθεντο, καὶ στενῶν
ὄντων τῶν χωρίων ἐγγὺς προσιόντες ἐτόξευον καὶ
ἐσφενδόνων· ὥστε ἠναγκάζοντο οἱ Ἕλληνες ἐπιδιώ-
κοντες καὶ πάλιν ἀναχάζοντες σχολῇ πορεύεσθαι· καὶ
θαμινὰ παρήγγελλεν ὁ Ξενοφῶν ὑπομένειν, ὅτε οἱ
17 πολέμιοι ἰσχυρῶς ἐπικέοιντο. ἔνθα ὁ Χειρίσοφος
ἄλλοτε μὲν ὅτε παρεγγυῷτο ὑπέμενε, τότε δὲ οὐχ
ὑπέμενεν, ἀλλ᾿ ἦγε ταχέως καὶ παρηγγύα ἕπεσθαι,
ὥστε δῆλον ἦν ὅτι πρᾶγμά τι εἴη· σχολὴ δ᾿ οὐκ ἦν
ἰδεῖν παρελθόντι τὸ αἴτιον τῆς σπουδῆς· ὥστε ἡ πο-
18 ρεία ὁμοία φυγῇ ἐγίγνετο τοῖς ὀπισθοφύλαξι. καὶ
ἐνταῦθα ἀποθνήσκει ἀνὴρ ἀγαθὸς Λακωνικὸς Κλεώνυ-
μος τοξευθεὶς διὰ τῆς ἀσπίδος καὶ τῆς σπολάδος εἰς
τὰς πλευράς, καὶ Βασίας Ἀρκὰς διαμπερὲς τὴν κε-
φαλήν.

19   Ἐπεὶ δὲ ἀφίκοντο ἐπὶ σταθμόν, εὐθὺς ὥσπερ εἶχεν
ὁ Ξενοφῶν ἐλθὼν πρὸς τὸν Χειρίσοφον ᾐτιᾶτο αὐτὸν
ὅτι οὐχ ὑπέμεινεν, ἀλλ᾿ ἠναγκάζοντο φεύγοντες ἅμα
μάχεσθαι. καὶ νῦν δύο καλώ τε καὶ ἀγαθὼ ἄνδρε
τέθνατον καὶ οὔτε ἀνελέσθαι οὔτε θάψαι ἐδυνάμεθα.
20 ἀποκρίνεται ὁ Χειρίσοφος· Βλέψον, ἔφη, πρὸς τὰ ὄρη
καὶ ἰδὲ ὡς ἄβατα πάντα ἐστί· μία δ᾿ αὕτη ὁδὸς ἦν
ὁρᾷς ὀρθία, καὶ ἐπὶ ταύτῃ ἀνθρώπων ὁρᾶν ἔξεστί σοι

of provisions; and Cheirisophus led the way while Xenophon commanded the rearguard. Here the enemy began a vigorous attack, and in the narrow places on the road came close up to discharge their bows and slings. The result was that the Greeks were forced to give chase and then fall back, and hence made but slow progress; and time after time, when the enemy pressed them hard, Xenophon would send word to Cheirisophus to wait a little. Now while Cheirisophus was accustomed to wait whenever such word was given, on this occasion he did not do so, but led on rapidly and passed back the order to keep up with him. It was evident, therefore, that something was the matter, but there was no time to go forward and find out the reason for his haste; consequently the progress of the rearguard became more like a flight than a march. Then it was that a brave man was killed, Cleonymus the Laconian, who was pierced in the side by an arrow that went through his shield and cuirass; also Basias the Arcadian, who was shot clean through the head.[3]

As soon as they reached a halting place, Xenophon went straight to Cheirisophus, just as he was, and proceeded to reproach him for not waiting, but compelling them to flee and fight at the same time; "and now," he went on, "two fine, brave fellows have lost their lives, and we were not able to pick up their bodies or bury them." Cheirisophus' reply was, "Take a look," said he, "at the mountains, and observe how impassable all of them are. The only road is the one there, which you see, a steep one, too, and on that you can see the great crowd of people who have taken

[3] Death notices of individuals are rare in the *Anabasis*: perhaps these are meant as Homeric touches.

ὄχλον τοσοῦτον, οἳ κατειληφότες φυλάττουσι τὴν ἔκ-
21 βασιν. ταῦτ' ἐγὼ ἔσπευδον καὶ διὰ τοῦτό σε οὐχ
ὑπέμενον, εἴ πως δυναίμην φθάσαι πρὶν κατειλῆφθαι
τὴν ὑπερβολήν· οἱ δ' ἡγεμόνες οὓς ἔχομεν οὔ φασιν
22 εἶναι ἄλλην ὁδόν. ὁ δὲ Ξενοφῶν λέγει· Ἀλλ' ἐγὼ ἔχω
δύο ἄνδρας. ἐπεὶ γὰρ ἡμῖν πράγματα παρεῖχον, ἐν-
ηδρεύσαμεν, ὅπερ ἡμᾶς καὶ ἀναπνεῦσαι ἐποίησε, καὶ
ἀπεκτείναμέν τινας αὐτῶν, καὶ ζῶντας προυθυμήθημεν
λαβεῖν αὐτοῦ τούτου ἕνεκα ὅπως ἡγεμόσιν εἰδόσι τὴν
χώραν χρησαίμεθα.

23   Καὶ εὐθὺς ἀγαγόντες τοὺς ἀνθρώπους ἤλεγχον δια-
λαβόντες εἴ τινα εἰδεῖεν ἄλλην ὁδὸν ἢ τὴν φανεράν.
ὁ μὲν οὖν ἕτερος οὐκ ἔφη καὶ μάλα πολλῶν φόβων
προσαγομένων· ἐπεὶ δὲ οὐδὲν ὠφέλιμον ἔλεγεν, ὁρῶν-
24 τος τοῦ ἑτέρου κατεσφάγη. ὁ δὲ λοιπὸς ἔλεξεν ὅτι
οὗτος μὲν διὰ ταῦτα οὐ φαίη εἰδέναι, ὅτι αὐτῷ τυγχά-
νοι θυγάτηρ ἐκεῖ παρ' ἀνδρὶ ἐκδεδομένη· αὐτὸς δ' ἔφη
ἡγήσεσθαι δυνατὴν καὶ ὑποζυγίοις πορεύεσθαι ὁδόν.
25 ἐρωτώμενος δ' εἰ εἴη τι ἐν αὐτῇ δυσπάριτον χωρίον,
ἔφη εἶναι ἄκρον ὃ εἰ μή τις προκαταλήψοιτο, ἀδύνατον
ἔσεσθαι παρελθεῖν.

26   Ἐνταῦθα ἐδόκει συγκαλέσαντας λοχαγοὺς καὶ
πελταστὰς καὶ τῶν ὁπλιτῶν λέγειν τε τὰ παρόντα καὶ
ἐρωτᾶν εἴ τις αὐτῶν ἔστιν ὅστις ἀνὴρ ἀγαθὸς ἐθέλοι
27 ἂν γενέσθαι καὶ ὑποστὰς ἐθελοντὴς πορεύεσθαι. ὑφ-

possession of it and are guarding our way out. That's the reason why I was hurrying and why I would not wait for you, for I hoped to reach the pass and occupy it before they did. The guides that we have say there is no other road." And Xenophon answered, "Well, I also have two men. For at the time when the enemy were giving us trouble, we set an ambush. It allowed us, for one thing, to catch our breath; but, besides, we killed a number of them, and we took especial pains to get some prisoners for this very purpose, of being able to employ as guides men who know the country."

They brought up the two men at once and questioned them separately as to whether they knew any other road besides the one that was in plain sight. The first man said he did not, despite all the numerous threats that were made to him; and since he would give no information, he was slaughtered before the eyes of the second one. The latter now said that the reason why this first man had maintained that he did not know any other road, was because he chanced to have a daughter living in that neighbourhood with a husband to whom he had given her; but as for himself, he said that he would lead the Greeks by a road that could be traversed even by baggage animals. Upon being asked whether there was any point on it which was difficult to pass, he replied that there was a height which they could not possibly pass unless they should seize it beforehand.

Thereupon it was decided to call together the captains, both of peltasts and hoplites, to set forth to them the existing situation, and to ask if there was any one among them who would like to prove himself a brave man and to undertake this expedition as a volunteer. Volunteers came for-

ἵσταται τῶν μὲν ὁπλιτῶν Ἀριστώνυμος Μεθυδριεὺς
Ἀρκὰς καὶ Ἀγασίας Στυμφάλιος Ἀρκάς, ἀντιστα-
σιάζων δὲ αὐτοῖς Καλλίμαχος Παρράσιος Ἀρκὰς καὶ
οὗτος ἔφη ἐθέλειν πορεύεσθαι προσλαβὼν ἐθελοντὰς
ἐκ παντὸς τοῦ στρατεύματος· Ἐγὼ γάρ, ἔφη, οἶδα ὅτι
28 ἔψονται πολλοὶ τῶν νέων ἐμοῦ ἡγουμένου. ἐκ τούτου
ἐρωτῶσιν εἴ τις καὶ τῶν γυμνήτων ταξιάρχων ἐθέλοι
συμπορεύεσθαι. ὑφίσταται Ἀριστέας Χῖος, ὃς πολλα-
χοῦ πολλοῦ ἄξιος τῇ στρατιᾷ εἰς τὰ τοιαῦτα ἐγένετο.

II. Καὶ ἦν μὲν δείλη ἤδη, οἱ δ' ἐκέλευον αὐτοὺς
ἐμφαγόντας πορεύεσθαι. καὶ τὸν ἡγεμόνα δήσαντες
παραδιδόασιν αὐτοῖς, καὶ συντίθενται τὴν μὲν νύκτα,
ἢν λάβωσι τὸ ἄκρον, τὸ χωρίον φυλάττειν, ἅμα δὲ τῇ
ἡμέρᾳ τῇ σάλπιγγι σημαίνειν· καὶ τοὺς μὲν ἄνω ὄντας
ἰέναι ἐπὶ τοὺς κατέχοντας τὴν φανερὰν ἔκβασιν, αὐτοὶ
δὲ συμβοηθήσειν ἐκβαίνοντες ὡς ἂν δύνωνται τάχι-
2 στα. ταῦτα συνθέμενοι οἱ μὲν οὖν ἐπορεύοντο πλῆθος
ὡς δισχίλιοι· καὶ ὕδωρ πολὺ ἦν ἐξ οὐρανοῦ· Ξενοφῶν
δὲ ἔχων τοὺς ὀπισθοφύλακας ἡγεῖτο πρὸς τὴν φανερὰν ἔκβασιν, ὅπως ταύτῃ τῇ ὁδῷ οἱ πολέμιοι προσ-
έχοιεν τὸν νοῦν καὶ ὡς μάλιστα λάθοιεν οἱ περιόντες.
3 ἐπεὶ δὲ ἦσαν ἐπὶ χαράδρᾳ οἱ ὀπισθυφύλακες ἣν ἔδει
διαβάντας πρὸς τὸ ὄρθιον ἐκβαίνειν, τηνικαῦτα
ἐκύλινδον οἱ βάρβαροι ὀλοιτρόχους ἁμαξιαίους καὶ
μείζους καὶ ἐλάττους, οἳ φερόμενοι πρὸς τὰς πέτρας

---

4 See i. 20.   5 *i.e.* the volunteers.

ward, from the hoplites Aristonymus of Methydrium an Arcadian and Agasias of Stymphalus an Arcadian, and in rivalry with them Callimachus of Parrhasia an Arcadian; this man said that he was ready to make the expedition and take with him volunteers from the entire army; "for I know," he continued, "that many of the young men will follow if I am in the lead." Then they asked whether any one among the captains of light troops wanted to join in the march. The volunteer was Aristeas of Chios, who on many occasions proved himself valuable to the army for such services.

II. It was already late afternoon, and they ordered the volunteers to eat quickly and set out. They also bound the guide and turned him over to the volunteers, and made an agreement with them that in case they should capture the height, they were to guard it through the night and give a signal at daybreak with the trumpet; then those on the height were to proceed against the Carduchians who were holding the visible way out,[4] while the main army was to come to their support, pushing forward as fast as it could. This agreement concluded, the volunteers, about two thousand in number, then set out on their march; and there was a heavy downpour of rain; at the same time Xenophon with the rearguard began advancing toward the visible way out, in order that the enemy might be giving their attention to that road and that the party[5] taking the roundabout route might, so far as possible, escape observation. But as soon as the troops of the rearguard were at a gorge which they had to cross before marching up the steep hill, at that moment the barbarians began to roll down round stones large enough for a wagon-load, with larger and smaller ones also; they came down with a crash upon the rocks

301

πταίοντες διεσφενδονῶντο. καὶ παντάπασιν οὐδὲ πελά-
4 σαι οἷόν τ᾽ ἦν τῇ εἰσόδῳ. ἔνιοι δὲ τῶν λοχαγῶν, εἰ μὴ
ταύτῃ δύναιντο, ἄλλῃ ἐπειρῶντο· καὶ ταῦτα ἐποίουν
μέχρι σκότος ἐγένετο· ἐπεὶ δὲ ᾤοντο ἀφανεῖς εἶναι
ἀπιόντες, τότε ἀπῆλθον ἐπὶ τὸ δεῖπνον· ἐτύγχανον δὲ
καὶ ἀνάριστοι ὄντες αὐτῶν οἱ ὀπισθοφυλακήσαντες.
οἱ μέντοι πολέμιοι οὐδὲν ἐπαύσαντο δι᾽ ὅλης τῆς
νυκτὸς κυλίνδοντες τοὺς λίθους· τεκμαίρεσθαι δ᾽ ἦν
τῷ ψόφῳ.

5 Οἱ δ᾽ ἔχοντες τὸν ἡγεμόνα κύκλῳ περιιόντες καταλαμβάνουσι τοὺς φύλακας ἀμφὶ πῦρ καθημένους· καὶ
τοὺς μὲν κατακανόντες τοὺς δὲ καταδιώξαντες αὐτοὶ
6 ἐνταῦθ᾽ ἔμενον ὡς τὸ ἄκρον κατέχοντες. οἱ δ᾽ οὐ
κατεῖχον, ἀλλὰ μαστὸς ἦν ὑπὲρ αὐτῶν παρ᾽ ὃν ἦν ἡ
στενὴ αὕτη ὁδὸς ἐφ᾽ ᾗ ἐκάθηντο οἱ φύλακες. ἔφοδος
μέντοι αὐτόθεν ἐπὶ τοὺς πολεμίους ἦν οἳ ἐπὶ τῇ φανερᾷ
ὁδῷ ἐκάθηντο. καὶ τὴν μὲν νύκτα ἐνταῦθα διήγαγον·
7 ἐπεὶ δ᾽ ἡμέρα ὑπέφαινεν, ἐπορεύοντο σιγῇ συντεταγ-
μένοι ἐπὶ τοὺς πολεμίους· καὶ γὰρ ὁμίχλη ἐγένετο,
ὥστ᾽ ἔλαθον ἐγγὺς προσελθόντες. ἐπεὶ δὲ εἶδον
ἀλλήλους, ἥ τε σάλπιγξ ἐφθέγξατο καὶ ἀλαλάξαντες
ἵεντο ἐπὶ τοὺς ἀνθρώπους. οἱ δὲ οὐκ ἐδέξαντο, ἀλλὰ
λιπόντες τὴν ὁδὸν φεύγοντες ὀλίγοι ἀπέθνησκον·
8 εὔζωνοι γὰρ ἦσαν. οἱ δὲ ἀμφὶ Χειρίσοφον ἀκούσαντες

---

⁶ *i.e.* "the guards" whom they expected to find upon the height
mentioned (i. 25, ii. 1). See below.

below and the fragments of them flew in all directions, so that it was quite impossible even to approach the ascending road. Then some of the captains, unable to proceed by this route, would try another, and they kept this up until darkness came on. It was not until they imagined that their withdrawal would be unobserved that they went back to dinner—and it chanced that their rearguard had had no breakfast either. The enemy, however, never stopped rolling down their stones all through the night, as one could judge from the noise.

Meanwhile the party with the guide, proceeding by a roundabout route, found the guards[6] sitting around a fire, and after killing some of them and chasing away the others they remained at the post themselves, supposing that they held the height. In fact, they were not holding it, for there was a round hill above them and past it ran this narrow road upon which the guards had been sitting. Nevertheless, from the place they did hold there was a way of approach to the spot, upon the visible road,[7] where the main body of the enemy were stationed. At this place, then, they passed the night, and when day was beginning to break, they took up their march silently in battle array against the enemy; for there was a mist, and consequently they got close up to them without being observed. When they did catch sight of one another, the trumpet sounded and the Greeks raised the battle cry and rushed upon the enemy. And the Carduchians did not meet their attack, but abandoned the road and took to flight; only a few of them, however, were killed, for they were agile fellows. Meanwhile Cheirisophus and his command, hearing the trum-

[7] i.e. the one mentioned in i. 20, 23, ii. 1.

τῆς σάλπιγγος εὐθὺς ἵεντο ἄνω κατὰ τὴν φανερὰν
ὁδόν· ἄλλοι δὲ τῶν στρατηγῶν κατὰ ἀτριβεῖς ὁδοὺς
ἐπορεύοντο ᾗ ἔτυχον ἕκαστοι ὄντες, καὶ ἀναβάντες ὡς
9 ἐδύναντο ἀνίμων ἀλλήλους τοῖς δόρασι. καὶ οὗτοι
πρῶτοι συνέμειξαν τοῖς προκαταλαβοῦσι τὸ χωρίον.

Ξενοφῶν δὲ ἔχων τῶν ὀπισθοφυλάκων τοὺς ἡμίσεις
ἐπορεύετο ᾗπερ οἱ τὸν ἡγεμόνα ἔχοντες· εὐοδωτάτη
γὰρ ἦν τοῖς ὑποζυγίοις· τοὺς δὲ ἡμίσεις ὄπισθεν τῶν
10 ὑποζυγίων ἔταξε. πορευόμενοι δ᾽ ἐντυγχάνουσι λόφῳ
ὑπὲρ τῆς ὁδοῦ κατειλημμένῳ ὑπὸ τῶν πολεμίων, οὓς
ἢ ἀποκόψαι ἦν ἀνάγκη ἢ διεζεῦχθαι ἀπὸ τῶν ἄλλων
Ἑλλήνων. καὶ αὐτοὶ μὲν ἂν ἐπορεύθησαν ᾗπερ οἱ
ἄλλοι, τὰ δὲ ὑποζύγια οὐκ ἦν ἄλλῃ ἢ ταύτῃ ἐκβῆναι.
11 ἔνθα δὴ παρακελευσάμενοι ἀλλήλοις προσβάλλουσι
πρὸς τὸν λόφον ὀρθίοις τοῖς λόχοις, οὐ κύκλῳ ἀλλὰ
καταλιπόντες ἄφοδον τοῖς πολεμίοις, εἰ βούλοιντο
12 φεύγειν. καὶ τέως μὲν αὐτοὺς ἀναβαίνοντας ὅπῃ ἐδύναντο ἕκαστος οἱ βάρβαροι ἐτόξευον καὶ ἔβαλλον,
ἐγγὺς δ᾽ οὐ προσίεντο, ἀλλὰ φυγῇ λείπουσι τὸ χωρίον. καὶ τοῦτόν τε παρεληλύθεσαν οἱ Ἕλληνες καὶ
ἕτερον ὁρῶντες ἔμπροσθεν λόφον κατεχόμενον ἐπὶ
13 τοῦτον αὖθις ἐδόκει πορεύεσθαι. ἐννοήσας δ᾽ ὁ Ξενοφῶν μή, εἰ ἔρημον καταλίποι τὸν ἑαλωκότα λόφον,
πάλιν λαβόντες οἱ πολέμιοι ἐπιθοῖντο τοῖς ὑποζυγίοις

---

8 Cheirisophus and his command.
9 Which "could be traversed even by baggage animals," i. 24.

pet, charged immediately up the visible road; and some of
the other generals made their way without following any
road from the points where they severally chanced to be
and, clambering up as best they could, pulled one another
up with their spears; and it was they who were first to join
the troops that had already gained possession of the place.

But Xenophon with half the rearguard set out by the
same route which the party with the guide had followed,
because this was the easiest route for the baggage animals;
and behind the baggage animals he posted the other half
of the rearguard. As they proceeded they came upon a hill
above the road which had been seized by the enemy, and
found themselves compelled either to dislodge them or be
completely separated from the rest of the Greeks; and
while, so far as the troops themselves were concerned, they
might have taken the same route that the rest[8] followed,
the baggage animals could not get through by any other
road than this one[9] by which Xenophon was proceeding.
Then and there, accordingly, with words of cheer to one
another, they charged upon the hill with their companies
in column, not surrounding it, but leaving the enemy a way
of retreat in case they chose to use it. For a while, as the
Greeks were climbing up by whatever way they severally
could, the barbarians discharged arrows and other missiles
upon them; they did not let them get near, however, but
took to flight and abandoned the place. No sooner had the
Greeks passed by this hill, than they saw a second one
ahead similarly occupied by the enemy, and decided to
proceed against this one in its turn. Xenophon, however,
becoming apprehensive lest, if he should leave unoccupied
the hill he had just captured, the enemy might take possession of it again and attack the baggage train as it passed

παριοῦσιν—ἐπὶ πολὺ δ᾽ ἦν τὰ ὑποζύγια ἅτε διὰ στενῆς
τῆς ὁδοῦ πορευόμενα—καταλείπει ἐπὶ τοῦ λόφου
λοχαγοὺς Κηφισόδωρον Κηφισοφῶντος Ἀθηναῖον καὶ
Ἀμφικράτην Ἀμφιδήμου Ἀθηναῖον καὶ Ἀρχαγόραν
Ἀργεῖον φυγάδα, αὐτὸς δὲ σὺν τοῖς λοιποῖς ἐπορεύετο
ἐπὶ τὸν δεύτερον λόφον, καὶ τῷ αὐτῷ τρόπῳ καὶ τοῦτον
αἱροῦσιν.

14   Ἔτι δὲ αὐτοῖς τρίτος μαστὸς λοιπὸς ἦν πολὺ ὀρθι-
ώτατος ὁ ὑπὲρ τῆς ἐπὶ τῷ πυρὶ καταληφθείσης φυ-
15 λακῆς τῆς νυκτὸς ὑπὸ τῶν ἐθελοντῶν. ἐπεὶ δ᾽ ἐγγὺς
ἐγένοντο οἱ Ἕλληνες, λείπουσιν οἱ βάρβαροι ἀμαχητὶ
τὸν μαστόν, ὥστε θαυμαστὸν πᾶσι γενέσθαι καὶ
ὑπώπτευον δείσαντας αὐτοὺς μὴ κυκλωθέντες πολι-
ορκοῖντο ἀπολιπεῖν. οἱ δ᾽ ἄρα ἀπὸ τοῦ ἄκρου καθορῶν-
τες τὰ ὄπισθεν γιγνόμενα πάντες ἐπὶ τοὺς ὀπισθοφύ-
16 λακας ἐχώρουν. καὶ Ξενοφῶν μὲν σὺν τοῖς νεωτάτοις
ἀνέβαινεν ἐπὶ τὸ ἄκρον, τοὺς δὲ ἄλλους ἐκέλευσεν
ὑπάγειν, ὅπως οἱ τελευταῖοι λόχοι προσμείξειαν, καὶ
προελθόντας κατὰ τὴν ὁδὸν ἐν τῷ ὁμαλῷ θέσθαι τὰ
ὅπλα εἶπε.

17   Καὶ ἐν τούτῳ τῷ χρόνῳ ἦλθεν Ἀρχαγόρας ὁ Ἀρ-
γεῖος πεφευγὼς καὶ λέγει ὡς ἀπεκόπησαν ἀπὸ τοῦ
πρώτου λόφου καὶ ὅτι τεθνᾶσι Κηφισόδωρος καὶ
Ἀμφικράτης καὶ οἱ ἄλλοι ὅσοι μὴ ἁλόμενοι κατὰ τῆς

---

[10] The one originally mentioned by the Carduchian guide. See
i. 25, ii. 6.

(and the train stretched out a long way because of the narrowness of the road it was following), left three captains upon the hill, Cephisodorus, son of Cephisophon, an Athenian, Amphicrates, son of Amphidemus, also an Athenian, and Archagoras, an Argive exile; while he himself with the rest of the troops proceeded against the second hill, which they captured in the same fashion as the first.

There still remained a third round hill,[10] far the steepest of them all, the one that rose above the guard post, by the fire, which had been captured during the night by the volunteers. But when the Greeks got near this hill, the barbarians abandoned it without striking a blow, so that everybody was filled with surprise and imagined that they had quit the place out of fear that they might be surrounded and blockaded. As it proved, however, they had seen, looking down from their height, what was going on farther back, and were all setting out to attack the Greek rearguard.[11] Meanwhile Xenophon proceeded to climb the abandoned height with his youngest troops, ordering the rest to move on slowly in order that the hindmost companies might catch up; then they were to advance along the road and halt under arms on the plateau[12] at the top of the pass.

At this time Archagoras the Argive came up in flight and reported that the Greeks had been dislodged from the first hill, that Cephisodorus and Amphicrates had been killed, and likewise all the rest except such as had leaped down

[11] *i.e.* the three companies left upon the first hill, which the main body of Xenophon's troops had now passed by. See below.

[12] Into which the ἔκβασις, or "way out," ultimately led.

18 πέτρας πρὸς τοὺς ὀπισθοφύλακας ἀφίκοντο. ταῦτα δὲ
διαπραξάμενοι οἱ βάρβαροι ἧκον ἐπ' ἀντίπορον λόφον
τῷ μαστῷ· καὶ ὁ Ξενοφῶν διελέγετο αὐτοῖς δι'
19 ἑρμηνέως περὶ σπονδῶν καὶ τοὺς νεκροὺς ἀπῄτει. οἱ δὲ
ἔφασαν ἀποδώσειν ἐφ' ᾧ μὴ καίειν τὰς οἰκίας. συν-
ωμολόγει ταῦτα ὁ Ξενοφῶν. ἐν ᾧ δὲ τὸ μὲν ἄλλο
στράτευμα παρῄει, οἱ δὲ ταῦτα διελέγοντο, πάντες οἱ
ἐκ τούτου τοῦ τόπου συνερρύησαν. ἐνταῦθα ἵσταντο οἱ
20 πολέμιοι. καὶ ἐπεὶ ἤρξαντο καταβαίνειν ἀπὸ τοῦ
μαστοῦ πρὸς τοὺς ἄλλους ἔνθα τὰ ὅπλα ἔκειτο, ἵεντο
δὴ οἱ πολέμιοι πολλῷ πλήθει καὶ θορύβῳ· καὶ ἐπεὶ
ἐγένοντο ἐπὶ τῆς κορυφῆς τοῦ μαστοῦ ἀφ' οὗ Ξενοφῶν
κατέβαινεν, ἐκυλίνδον πέτρας· καὶ ἑνὸς μὲν κατέαξαν
τὸ σκέλος, Ξενοφῶντα δὲ ὁ ὑπασπιστὴς ἔχων τὴν
21 ἀσπίδα ἀπέλιπεν· Εὐρύλοχος δὲ Λουσιεὺς Ἀρκὰς
προσέδραμεν αὐτῷ ὁπλίτης, καὶ πρὸ ἀμφοῖν προβε-
βλημένος ἀπεχώρει, καὶ οἱ ἄλλοι πρὸς τοὺς συντεταγ-
μένους ἀπῆλθον.

22 Ἐκ δὲ τούτου πᾶν ὁμοῦ ἐγένετο τὸ Ἑλληνικόν, καὶ
ἐσκήνησαν αὐτοῦ ἐν πολλαῖς καὶ καλαῖς οἰκίαις καὶ
ἐπιτηδείοις δαψιλέσι· καὶ γὰρ οἶνος πολὺς ἦν, ὃν ἐν
23 λάκκοις κονιατοῖς εἶχον. Ξενοφῶν δὲ καὶ Χειρίσοφος
διεπράξαντο ὥστε λαβόντες τοὺς νεκροὺς ἀποδοῦναι
τὸν ἡγεμόνα· καὶ πάντα ἐποίησαν τοῖς ἀποθανοῦσιν
ἐκ τῶν δυνατῶν ὥσπερ νομίζεται ἀνδράσιν ἀγαθοῖς.

---

[13] In this case the reference is manifestly to the division behind the baggage train (§9).   [14] See §14 above.

the rocks and reached the rearguard.[13] After accomplishing this achievement the barbarians came to a hill opposite the round hill,[14] and Xenophon, through an interpreter, spoke with them regarding a truce and asked them to give back the bodies of the Greek dead. They replied that they would give them back on condition that the Greeks should not burn their houses. To this Xenophon agreed. But while the rest of the army was passing by and they were engaged in this conference, all the people from that neighbourhood had streamed together. There the enemy were coming to a halt. As soon as Xenophon and his men began to descend from the round hill, towards the rest of the Greeks at the place where their march had been halted, the enemy took this opportunity to rush upon them in great force and with a great deal of uproar. When they had reached the crest of the hill from which Xenophon was descending, they proceeded to roll down stones. They broke one man's leg, and Xenophon found himself deserted by the servant who was carrying his shield; but Eurylochus of Lusi an Arcadian, a hoplite, ran up to him and, keeping his shield held out in front of them both, fell back with him; and the rest also made good their retreat to the main array.

Then the entire Greek army united, and the troops took up quarters there in many fine houses and in the midst of abundant supplies; for the inhabitants had quantities of wine which they kept in cement-lined cisterns. Meanwhile Xenophon and Cheirisophus effected an arrangement whereby to recover the bodies of their dead and then give back the guide; and they rendered to the dead, so far as their means permitted, all the usual honours that are paid to brave men.

24   Τῇ δὲ ὑστεραίᾳ ἄνευ ἡγεμόνος ἐπορεύοντο· μαχόμενοι δ' οἱ πολέμιοι καὶ ὅπῃ εἴη στενὸν χωρίον προ-
25 καταλαμβάνοντες ἐκώλυον τὰς παρόδους. ὁπότε μὲν
οὖν τοὺς πρώτους κωλύοιεν, Ξενοφῶν ὄπισθεν ἐκβαίνων πρὸς τὰ ὄρη ἔλυε τὴν ἀπόφραξιν τῆς παρόδου
τοῖς πρώτοις ἀνωτέρω πειρώμενος γίγνεσθαι τῶν
26 κωλυόντων, ὁπότε δὲ τοῖς ὄπισθεν ἐπιθοῖντο, Χειρίσοφος ἐκβαίνων καὶ πειρώμενος ἀνωτέρω γίγνεσθαι τῶν
κωλυόντων ἔλυε τὴν ἀπόφραξιν τῆς παρόδου τοῖς
ὄπισθεν· καὶ ἀεὶ οὕτως ἐβοήθουν ἀλλήλοις καὶ ἰσχυ-
27 ρῶς ἀλλήλων ἐπεμέλοντο. ἦν δὲ καὶ ὁπότε αὐτοῖς τοῖς
ἀναβᾶσι πολλὰ πράγματα παρεῖχον οἱ βάρβαροι
πάλιν καταβαίνουσιν· ἐλαφροὶ γὰρ ἦσαν ὥστε καὶ
ἐγγύθεν φεύγοντες ἀποφεύγειν· οὐδὲν γὰρ εἶχον ἄλλο
28 ἢ τόξα καὶ σφενδόνας. ἄριστοι δὲ καὶ τοξόται ἦσαν·
εἶχον δὲ τόξα ἐγγὺς τριπήχη, τὰ δὲ τοξεύματα πλέον
ἢ διπήχη· εἷλκον δὲ τὰς νευρὰς ὁπότε τοξεύοιεν πρὸς
τὸ κάτω τοῦ τόξου τῷ ἀριστερῷ ποδὶ προσβαίνοντες.
τὰ δὲ τοξεύματα ἐχώρει διὰ τῶν ἀσπίδων καὶ διὰ τῶν
θωράκων. ἐχρῶντο δὲ αὐτοῖς οἱ Ἕλληνες, ἐπεὶ λάβοιεν, ἀκοντίοις ἐναγκυλῶντες. ἐν τούτοις τοῖς χωρίοις
οἱ Κρῆτες χρησιμώτατοι ἐγένοντο. ἦρχε δὲ αὐτῶν
Στρατοκλῆς Κρής.

III. Ταύτην δ' αὖ τὴν ἡμέραν ηὐλίσθησαν ἐν ταῖς
κώμαις ταῖς ὑπὲρ τοῦ πεδίου τοῦ παρὰ τὸν Κεντρίτην

---

15 See i. 18.

On the next day they continued their march without a guide, while the enemy, by fighting and by seizing positions in advance wherever the road was narrow, tried to prevent their passage. Accordingly, whenever they blocked the march of the van, Xenophon would push forward from the rear to the mountains and break the blockade of the passage for the van by trying to get higher than those who were halting it, and whenever they attacked the rear, Cheirisophus would sally forth and, by trying to get higher than the obstructing force, would break the blockade of the passage-way for the rear; in this way they continually aided one another and took zealous care for one another. There were times, indeed, when the barbarians caused a great deal of trouble even to the troops who had climbed to a higher position, when they were coming down again; for their men were so agile that even if they took to flight from close at hand, they could escape; for they had nothing to carry except bows and slings. As bowmen they were most excellent; they had bows nearly three cubits long and their arrows were more than two cubits, and when they shot, they would draw their strings by pressing with the left foot against the lower end of the bow; and their arrows would go straight through shields and breastplates.[15] Whenever they got hold of them, the Greeks would use these arrows as javelins, fitting them with thongs. In these regions the Cretans made themselves exceedingly useful. They were commanded by a Cretan named Stratocles.

III. For that day again[16] they found quarters in the villages that lie above the plain bordering the Centrites

---

[16] On the preceding night also they had been quartered in villages (ii. 22).

ποταμόν, εὖρος ὡς δίπλεθρον, ὃς ὁρίζει τὴν Ἀρμενίαν
καὶ τὴν τῶν Καρδούχων χώραν. καὶ οἱ Ἕλληνες
ἐνταῦθα ἀνέπνευσαν ἄσμενοι ἰδόντες πεδίον· ἀπεῖχε
δὲ τῶν ὀρέων ὁ ποταμὸς ἓξ ἢ ἑπτὰ στάδια τῶν Καρ-
2 δούχων. τότε μὲν οὖν ηὐλίσθησαν μάλα ἡδέως καὶ
τἀπιτήδεια ἔχοντες καὶ πολλὰ τῶν παρεληλυθότων
πόνων μνημονεύοντες. ἑπτὰ γὰρ ἡμέρας ὅσασπερ
ἐπορεύθησαν διὰ τῶν Καρδούχων πάσας μαχόμενοι
διετέλεσαν, καὶ ἔπαθον κακὰ ὅσα οὐδὲ τὰ σύμπαντα
ὑπὸ βασιλέως καὶ Τισσαφέρνους. ὡς οὖν ἀπηλλαγ-
μένοι τούτων ἡδέως ἐκοιμήθησαν.

3   Ἅμα δὲ τῇ ἡμέρᾳ ὁρῶσιν ἱππέας που πέραν τοῦ
ποταμοῦ ἐξωπλισμένους ὡς κωλύσοντας διαβαίνειν,
πεζοὺς δ' ἐπὶ ταῖς ὄχθαις παρατεταγμένους ἄνω τῶν
ἱππέων ὡς κωλύσοντας εἰς τὴν Ἀρμενίαν ἐκβαίνειν.
4 ἦσαν δ' οὗτοι Ὀρόντα καὶ Ἀρτούχα Ἀρμένιοι καὶ
Μάρδοι καὶ Χαλδαῖοι μισθοφόροι. ἐλέγοντο δὲ οἱ
Χαλδαῖοι ἐλεύθεροί τε καὶ ἄλκιμοι εἶναι· ὅπλα δ' εἶχον
5 γέρρα μακρὰ καὶ λόγχας. αἱ δὲ ὄχθαι αὗται ἐφ' ὧν
παρατεταγμένοι οὗτοι ἦσαν τρία ἢ τέτταρα πλέθρα
ἀπὸ τοῦ ποταμοῦ ἀπεῖχον· ὁδὸς δὲ μία ὁρωμένη ἦν
ἄγουσα ἄνω ὥσπερ χειροποίητος· ταύτῃ ἐπειρῶντο
6 διαβαίνειν οἱ Ἕλληνες. ἐπεὶ δὲ πειρωμένοις τό τε ὕδωρ

---

17 Satrap of Armenia; cf. II. iv. 8, 9; III. iv. 13, V. 17.
18 A Persian general.
19 Cf. V. v. 17. More autonomous peoples. "Chaldaean" is normally reserved for Babylonians, esp. the priestly class. See, e.g.,

river, which is about two plethra in width and separates
Armenia and the country of the Carduchians. There the
Greeks took breath, glad to behold a plain; for the river
was distant six or seven stadia from the mountains of the
Carduchians. At the time, then, they went into their quarters very happily, for they had provisions and likewise many
recollections of the hardships that were now past. For during all the seven days of their march through the land of
the Carduchians they were continually fighting, and they
suffered more evils than all which they had suffered taken
together at the hands of the King and Tissaphernes. In the
feeling, therefore, that they were rid of these troubles they
lay down happily to rest.

At daybreak, however, they caught sight of horsemen
at a place across the river, fully armed and ready to prevent
their passage, and likewise foot soldiers drawn up in line
of battle upon the bluffs above the horsemen, to prevent
their pushing up into Armenia. All these were the troops
of Orontas[17] and Artuchas,[18] and consisted of Armenians,
Mardians, and Chaldaean mercenaries. The Chaldaeans
were said to be an independent and valiant people; they
had as weapons long wicker shields and lances.[19] Now the
bluffs just mentioned, upon which these troops were
drawn up, were distant three or four plethra from the river,
and there was only one road to be seen that led up them,
apparently an artificial road; so at this point[20] the Greeks
undertook to cross the river. When they made the attempt,

D. Asheri, *Erodoto* I (Milan, 1988) 372. These people would have
to be different; cf. VII.24, addition.

[20] *i.e.* opposite this road, where they naturally expected to find
a practicable ford.

ὑπὲρ τῶν μαστῶν ἐφαίνετο, καὶ τραχὺς ἦν ὁ ποταμὸς
μεγάλοις λίθοις καὶ ὀλισθηροῖς, καὶ οὔτ᾽ ἐν τῷ ὕδατι
τὰ ὅπλα ἦν ἔχειν· εἰ δὲ μή, ἥρπαζεν ὁ ποταμός· ἐπί
τε τῆς κεφαλῆς τὰ ὅπλα εἴ τις φέροι, γυμνοὶ ἐγίγνοντο
πρὸς τὰ τοξεύματα καὶ τἆλλα βέλη· ἀνεχώρησαν οὖν
καὶ αὐτοῦ ἐστρατοπεδεύσαντο παρὰ τὸν ποταμόν.
7   ἔνθα δὲ αὐτοὶ τὴν πρόσθεν νύκτα ἦσαν ἐπὶ τοῦ ὄρους
ἑώρων τοὺς Καρδούχους πολλοὺς συνειλεγμένους ἐν
τοῖς ὅπλοις. ἐνταῦθα δὴ πολλὴ ἀθυμία ἦν τοῖς Ἕλλησιν, ὁρῶσι μὲν τοῦ ποταμοῦ τὴν δυσπορίαν, ὁρῶσι δὲ
τοὺς διαβαίνειν κωλύσοντας, ὁρῶσι δὲ τοῖς διαβαίνουσιν ἐπικεισομένους τοὺς Καρδούχους ὄπισθεν.
8   Ταύτην μὲν οὖν τὴν ἡμέραν καὶ νύκτα ἔμειναν ἐν
πολλῇ ἀπορίᾳ ὄντες. Ξενοφῶν δὲ ὄναρ εἶδεν· ἔδοξεν ἐν
πέδαις δεδέσθαι, αὗται δὲ αὐτῷ αὐτόμαται περιρ-
ρυῆναι, ὥστε λυθῆναι καὶ διαβαίνειν ὁπόσον ἐβούλετο. ἐπεὶ δὲ ὄρθρος ἦν, ἔρχεται πρὸς τὸν Χειρίσοφον
καὶ λέγει ὅτι ἐλπίδας ἔχει καλῶς ἔσεσθαι, καὶ διηγεῖ-
9   ται αὐτῷ τὸ ὄναρ. ὁ δὲ ἥδετό τε καὶ ὡς τάχιστα ἕως
ὑπέφαινεν ἐθύοντο πάντες παρόντες οἱ στρατηγοί. καὶ
τὰ ἱερὰ καλὰ ἦν εὐθὺς ἐπὶ τοῦ πρώτου, καὶ ἀπιόντες
ἀπὸ τῶν ἱερῶν οἱ στρατηγοὶ καὶ λοχαγοὶ παρήγγελλον τῇ στρατιᾷ ἀριστοποιεῖσθαι.
10   Ἀριστῶντι δὲ τῷ Ξενοφῶντι προστρέχετον δύο
νεανίσκω· ᾔδεσαν γὰρ πάντες ὅτι ἐξείη αὐτῷ καὶ

however, the water proved to be more than breast deep and the river bed was rough with large, slippery stones; furthermore, they could not carry their shields in the water, for if they tried that, the current would snatch them away, while if a man carried them on his head, his body was left unprotected against arrows and other missiles; so they turned back and went into camp there by the side of the river. Meanwhile, at the point where they had themselves spent the previous night, on the mountain side, they could see the Carduchians gathered together under arms in great numbers. Then it was that deep despondency fell upon the Greeks, as they saw before them a river difficult to cross, beyond it troops that would obstruct their crossing, and behind them the Carduchians, ready to fall upon their rear when they tried to cross.

That day and night, accordingly, they remained there, in great perplexity. But Xenophon had a dream; he thought that he was bound in fetters, but that the fetters fell off from him of their own accord, so that he was released and could take as long steps[21] as he pleased. When dawn came, he went to Cheirisophus, told him he had hopes that all would be well, and related to him his dream. Cheirisophus was pleased, and as soon as day began to break, all the generals were at hand and proceeded to offer sacrifices. And with the very first victim the omens were favourable. Then the generals and captains withdrew from the sacrifice and gave orders to the troops to get their breakfasts.

While Xenophon was breakfasting, two young men came running up to him; for all knew that they might go

21 διαβαίνειν, which also means "to cross" a river (see above). Here lay the good omen of the dream.

ἀριστῶντι καὶ δειπνοῦντι προσελθεῖν καὶ εἰ καθεύδοι
ἐπεγείραντα εἰπεῖν, εἴ τίς τι ἔχοι τῶν πρὸς τὸν πόλε-

11 μον. καὶ τότε ἔλεγον ὅτι τυγχάνοιεν φρύγανα συλλέγοντες ὡς ἐπὶ πῦρ, κἄπειτα κατίδοιεν ἐν τῷ πέραν ἐν
πέτραις καθηκούσαις ἐπ᾽ αὐτὸν τὸν ποταμὸν γέροντά
τε καὶ γυναῖκα καὶ παιδίσκας ὥσπερ μαρσίπους

12 ἱματίων κατατιθεμένους ἐν πέτρᾳ ἀντρώδει. ἰδοῦσι δὲ
σφίσι δόξαι ἀσφαλὲς εἶναι διαβῆναι· οὐδὲ γὰρ τοῖς
πολεμίοις ἱππεῦσι προσβατὸν εἶναι κατὰ τοῦτο. ἐκ-
δύντες δ᾽ ἔφασαν ἔχοντες τὰ ἐγχειρίδια γυμνοὶ ὡς
νευσόμενοι διαβαίνειν· πορευόμενοι δὲ πρόσθεν διαβῆναι πρὶν βρέξαι τὰ αἰδοῖα· καὶ διαβάντες,
λαβόντες τὰ ἱμάτια πάλιν ἥκειν.

13   Εὐθὺς οὖν Ξενοφῶν αὐτός τε ἔσπενδε καὶ τοῖς
νεανίσκοις ἐγχεῖν ἐκέλευε καὶ εὔχεσθαι τοῖς φήνασι
θεοῖς τά τε ὀνείρατα καὶ τὸν πόρον καὶ τὰ λοιπὰ
ἀγαθὰ ἐπιτελέσαι. σπείσας δ᾽ εὐθὺς ἦγε τοὺς νεανί-
σκους παρὰ τὸν Χειρίσοφον, καὶ διηγοῦνται ταῦτα.

14 ἀκούσας δὲ καὶ ὁ Χειρίσοφος σπονδὰς ἐποίει. σπεί-
σαντες δὲ τοῖς μὲν ἄλλοις παρήγγελλον συσκευάζεσθαι, αὐτοὶ δὲ συγκαλέσαντες τοὺς στρατηγοὺς ἐβουλεύοντο ὅπως ἂν κάλλιστα διαβαῖεν καὶ τούς τε
ἔμπροσθεν νικῷεν καὶ ὑπὸ τῶν ὄπισθεν μηδὲν πά-

15 σχοιεν κακόν. καὶ ἔδοξεν αὐτοῖς Χειρίσοφον μὲν
ἡγεῖσθαι καὶ διαβαίνειν ἔχοντα τὸ ἥμισυ τοῦ

---

[22] The practice of a good leader: cf. Teleutias, *Hell.* V. i. 14.

to him whether he was breakfasting or dining, and that if he were asleep, they might awaken him and tell him whatever they might have to tell that concerned the war.[22] In the present case the young men reported that they had happened to be gathering dry sticks for the purpose of making a fire, and that while so occupied they had descried across the river, among some rocks that reached down to the very edge of the river, an old man and a woman and some little girls putting away what looked like bags of clothes in a cavernous rock. When they saw this proceeding, they said, they made up their minds that it was safe for them to cross, for this was a place that was not accessible to the enemy's cavalry. They accordingly stripped, keeping only their daggers, and started across naked, supposing that they would have to swim; but they went on and got across without wetting themselves up to the middle; once on the other side, they took the clothes and came back again.

Upon hearing this report Xenophon immediately proceeded to pour a libation himself, and directed his attendants to fill a cup for the young men and to pray to the gods who had revealed the dream and the ford, to bring to fulfilment the other blessings also. The libation accomplished, he at once led the young men to Cheirisophus, and they repeated their story to him. And upon hearing it Cheirisophus also made libation. Thereafter they gave orders to the troops to pack up their baggage, while they themselves called together the generals and took counsel as to how they might best effect a crossing so as to defeat the enemy in front without suffering any harm from those in their rear. The decision was, that Cheirisophus should take the lead with half the army and attempt a crossing,

στρατεύματος, τὸ δ' ἥμισυ ἔτι ὑπομένειν σὺν Ξενοφῶντι, τὰ δὲ ὑποζύγια καὶ τὸν ὄχλον ἐν μέσῳ τούτων
διαβαίνειν.

16 Ἐπεὶ δὲ καλῶς ταῦτα εἶχεν ἐπορεύοντο· ἡγοῦντο δ'
οἱ νεανίσκοι ἐν ἀριστερᾷ ἔχοντες τὸν ποταμόν· ὁδὸς
17 δὲ ἦν ἐπὶ τὴν διάβασιν ὡς τέτταρες στάδιοι. πορευομένων δ' αὐτῶν ἀντιπαρῇσαν αἱ τάξεις τῶν ἱππέων.
ἐπειδὴ δὲ ἦσαν κατὰ τὴν διάβασιν καὶ τὰς ὄχθας τοῦ
ποταμοῦ, ἔθεντο τὰ ὅπλα, καὶ αὐτὸς πρῶτος Χειρίσοφος στεφανωσάμενος καὶ ἀποδὺς ἐλάμβανε τὰ ὅπλα
καὶ τοῖς ἄλλοις πᾶσι παρήγγελλε, καὶ τοὺς λοχαγοὺς
ἐκέλευεν ἄγειν τοὺς λόχους ὀρθίους, τοὺς μὲν ἐν ἀριστερᾷ τοὺς δ' ἐν δεξιᾷ ἑαυτοῦ. καὶ οἱ μὲν μάντεις
18 ἐσφαγιάζοντο εἰς τὸν ποταμόν· οἱ δὲ πολέμιοι ἐτόξευόν
19 τε καὶ ἐσφενδόνων· ἀλλ' οὔπω ἐξικνοῦντο· ἐπεὶ δὲ καλὰ
ἦν τὰ σφάγια, ἐπαιάνιζον πάντες οἱ στρατιῶται καὶ
ἀνηλάλαζον, συνωλόλυζον δὲ καὶ αἱ γυναῖκες ἅπασαι.
πολλαὶ γὰρ ἦσαν ἑταῖραι ἐν τῷ στρατεύματι.

20 Καὶ Χειρίσοφος μὲν ἐνέβαινε καὶ οἱ σὺν ἐκείνῳ· ὁ
δὲ Ξενοφῶν τῶν ὀπισθοφυλάκων λαβὼν τοὺς εὐζωνο-
τάτους ἔθει ἀνὰ κράτος πάλιν ἐπὶ τὸν πόρον τὸν κατὰ
τὴν ἔκβασιν τὴν εἰς τὰ τῶν Ἀρμενίων ὄρη, προσποι-
ούμενος ταύτῃ διαβὰς ἀποκλείσειν τοὺς παρὰ τὸν
21 ποταμὸν ἱππέας. οἱ δὲ πολέμιοι ὁρῶντες μὲν τοὺς ἀμφὶ

---

[23] As the Spartans were accustomed to do when going into
battle; cf. I. iv. 2–3.

that the other half with Xenophon should stay behind for a while, and that the baggage animals and camp followers should cross between the two divisions.

When these arrangements had been satisfactorily made, they set out, the young men leading the way and keeping the river on the left; and the distance to the ford was about four stadia. As they proceeded, the squadrons of the enemy's cavalry kept along opposite to them. When they reached the ford and the river bank, they halted under arms, and Cheirisophus put a wreath upon his head,[23] threw off his cloak, and took up his arms, giving orders to all the others to do the same; he also directed the captains to lead their companies in column, part of them upon his left and the rest upon his right. Meanwhile the soothsayers were offering sacrifice to the river, and the enemy were shooting arrows and discharging slings, but not yet reaching their mark; and when the sacrifices proved favourable, all the soldiers struck up the paean and raised the war shout, while the women, everyone of them, joined their cries with the shouting of the men—for there were a large number of prostitutes in the camp.

Then Cheirisophus and his division proceeded into the river; but Xenophon took the nimblest troops of the rearguard and began running back at full speed to the ford[24] that was opposite the road which led out into the Armenian mountains, pretending that he meant to cross at that point and thus cut off[25] the horsemen who were by the side of the river. The enemy thereupon, when they saw Cheiriso-

[24] *i.e.* the original ford, which had proved impracticable (§§ 5–6).

[25] *i.e.* by attacking them on the flank.

Χειρίσοφον εὐπετῶς τὸ ὕδωρ διαπερῶντας, ὁρῶντες δὲ
τοὺς ἀμφὶ Ξενοφῶντα θέοντας εἰς τοὔμπαλιν, δείσαντες μὴ ἀποληφθείησαν φεύγουσιν ἀνὰ κράτος ὡς πρὸς
τὴν τοῦ ποταμοῦ ἄνω ἔκβασιν. ἐπεὶ δὲ κατὰ τὴν ὁδὸν
22 ἐγένοντο, ἔτεινον ἄνω πρὸς τὸ ὄρος. Λύκιος δ' ὁ τὴν
τάξιν ἔχων τῶν ἱππέων καὶ Αἰσχίνης ὁ τὴν τάξιν τῶν
πελταστῶν τῶν ἀμφὶ Χειρίσοφον ἐπεὶ ἑώρων ἀνὰ
κράτος φεύγοντας, εἵποντο· οἱ δὲ στρατιῶται ἐβόων
μὴ ἀπολείπεσθαι, ἀλλὰ συνεκβαίνειν ἐπὶ τὸ ὄρος.
23 Χειρίσοφος δ' αὖ ἐπεὶ διέβη, τοὺς ἱππέας οὐκ ἐδίωκεν,
εὐθὺς δὲ κατὰ τὰς προσηκούσας ὄχθας ἐπὶ τὸν ποταμὸν ἐξέβαινεν ἐπὶ τοὺς ἄνω πολεμίους. οἱ δὲ ἄνω,
ὁρῶντες μὲν τοὺς ἑαυτῶν ἱππέας φεύγοντας, ὁρῶντες
δ' ὁπλίτας σφίσιν ἐπιόντας, ἐκλείπουσι τὰ ὑπὲρ τοῦ
ποταμοῦ ἄκρα.

24 Ξενοφῶν δ' ἐπεὶ τὰ πέραν ἑώρα καλῶς γιγνόμενα,
ἀπεχώρει τὴν ταχίστην πρὸς τὸ διαβαῖνον στρά-
τευμα· καὶ γὰρ οἱ Καρδοῦχοι φανεροὶ ἤδη ἦσαν εἰς
τὸ πεδίον καταβαίνοντες ὡς ἐπιθησόμενοι τοῖς τελευ-
25 ταίοις. καὶ Χειρίσοφος μὲν τὰ ἄνω κατεῖχε, Λύκιος δὲ
σὺν ὀλίγοις ἐπιχειρήσας ἐπιδιῶξαι ἔλαβε τῶν σκευο-
φόρων τὰ ὑπολειπόμενα καὶ μετὰ τούτων ἐσθῆτά τε
26 καλὴν καὶ ἐκπώματα. καὶ τὰ μὲν σκευοφόρα τῶν
Ἑλλήνων καὶ ὁ ὄχλος ἀκμὴν διέβαινε, Ξενοφῶν δὲ
στρέψας πρὸς τοὺς Καρδούχους ἀντία τὰ ὅπλα ἔθετο,

phus and his division crossing the river without difficulty and likewise saw Xenophon and his men running back, were seized with fear that they might be cut off, and they fled at full speed to reach the road which led up from the river. This road once gained, they hastened on upward in the direction of the mountain. Then Lycius, who commanded the squadron of Greek cavalry; and Aeschines, commander of the battalion of peltasts that was with Cheirisophus, upon seeing the enemy in full flight set off in pursuit, while the rest of the Greek troops shouted to them not to fall behind, but to follow those fleeing right up to the mountain. As for Cheirisophus, after getting across he chose not to pursue the hostile cavalry, but immediately pushed up over the bluffs that reached down to the river against the infantry on top of them.[26] And these troops, seeing their own cavalry in flight and hoplites advancing upon them, abandoned the heights above the river.

Xenophon no sooner saw that all was going well on the other side than he started back with all speed to join the troops that were crossing, for by this time the Carduchians could be seen descending into the plain with the manifest intention of attacking the hindmost. Meanwhile Cheirisophus was in possession of the bluffs, and Lycius, venturing a pursuit with his small squadron,[27] had captured the straggling portion of the enemy's baggage train, and with it fine apparel and drinking cups. And now, with the Greek baggage train and the camp followers in the very act of crossing, Xenophon wheeled his troops so that they took a position facing the Carduchians, and gave orders to the

[26] See §3 above.
[27] Which numbered only fifty men (III. iii. 20).

καὶ παρήγγειλε τοῖς λοχαγοῖς κατ᾽ ἐνωμοτίας ποιήσασθαι ἕκαστον τὸν ἑαυτοῦ λόχον, παρ᾽ ἀσπίδα παρα-
γαγόντας τὴν ἐνωμοτίαν ἐπὶ φάλαγγος· καὶ τοὺς μὲν
λοχαγοὺς καὶ τοὺς ἐνωμοτάρχους πρὸς τῶν Καρδούχων ἰέναι, οὐραγοὺς δὲ καταστήσασθαι πρὸς τοῦ
27 ποταμοῦ. οἱ δὲ Καρδοῦχοι ὡς ἑώρων τοὺς ὀπισθοφύλακας τοῦ ὄχλου ψιλουμένους καὶ ὀλίγους ἤδη φαι-
νομένους, θᾶττον δὴ ἐπῇσαν ᾠδάς τινας ᾄδοντες. ὁ δὲ
Χειρίσοφος, ἐπεὶ τὰ παρ᾽ αὐτῷ ἀσφαλῶς εἶχε, πέμπει
παρὰ Ξενοφῶντα τοὺς πελταστὰς καὶ σφενδονήτας
καὶ τοξότας καὶ κελεύει ποιεῖν ὅ τι ἂν παραγγέλλῃ.
28 ἰδὼν δὲ αὐτοὺς διαβαίνοντας ὁ Ξενοφῶν πέμψας ἄγγελον κελεύει αὐτοῦ μεῖναι ἐπὶ τοῦ ποταμοῦ μὴ διαβάν-
τας· ὅταν δ᾽ ἄρξωνται αὐτοὶ διαβαίνειν, ἐναντίους
ἔνθεν καὶ ἔνθεν σφῶν ἐμβαίνειν ὡς διαβησομένους,
διηγκυλωμένους τοὺς ἀκοντιστὰς καὶ ἐπιβεβλημένους
τοὺς τοξότας· μὴ πρόσω δὲ τοῦ ποταμοῦ προβαίνειν.
29 τοῖς δὲ παρ᾽ ἑαυτῷ παρήγγειλεν, ἐπειδὰν σφενδόνη
ἐξικνῆται καὶ ἀσπὶς ψοφῇ, παιανίσαντας θεῖν εἰς τοὺς
πολεμίους, ἐπειδὰν δ᾽ ἀναστρέψωσιν οἱ πολέμιοι καὶ
ἐκ τοῦ ποταμοῦ ὁ σαλπικτὴς σημήνῃ τὸ πολεμικόν,
ἀναστρέψαντας ἐπὶ δόρυ ἡγεῖσθαι μὲν τοὺς οὐραγούς,
θεῖν δὲ πάντας καὶ διαβαίνειν ὅτι τάχιστα ᾗ ἕκαστος
τὴν τάξιν εἶχεν, ὡς μὴ ἐμποδίζειν ἀλλήλους· ὅτι οὗτος
ἄριστος ἔσοιτο ὃς ἂν πρῶτος ἐν τῷ πέραν γένηται.

captains that each man of them should form his own company by squads,[28] moving each squad by the left into line of battle; then the captains and squad leaders were to face toward the Carduchians and station file closers on the side next to the river. But as soon as the Carduchians saw the rearguard stripped of the crowd of camp followers and looking now like a small body, they advanced to the attack all the more rapidly, singing certain songs. As for Cheirisophus, since everything was safe on his side, he sent back to Xenophon the peltasts, slingers, and bowmen, and directed them to do whatever Xenophon might order. But when he saw them beginning to cross, Xenophon sent a messenger and directed them to stay where they were, on the bank of the river, without crossing; at the moment, however, when his own men should begin to cross, they were to enter the river opposite them, on this side and that, as though they were going to cross it, the javelin men with hand on the thong and the bowmen with arrow on the string; but they were not to proceed far into the river. The orders he gave to his own men were, that when slingstones reached them and shields rang, they were to strike up the paean and charge upon the enemy, and when the enemy turned to flight and the trumpeter on the river-bank sounded the charge,[29] they were to face about to the right, the file closers were to take the lead, and all of them were to run and cross as fast as they could with every man keeping his proper place in the line, so that they should not interfere with one another; and he that got to the other side first would be the best man.

[28] See III. iv. 21–22, and note thereon.
[29] In order to deceive the enemy.

30   Οἱ δὲ Καρδοῦχοι ὁρῶντες ὀλίγους ἤδη τοὺς λοι-
πούς—πολλοὶ γὰρ καὶ τῶν μένειν τεταγμένων ᾤχοντο
ἐπιμελόμενοι οἱ μὲν ὑποζυγίων, οἱ δὲ σκευῶν, οἱ δ᾽
ἑταιρῶν—ἐνταῦθα δὴ ἐπέκειντο θρασέως καὶ ἤρξαντο
31   σφενδονᾶν καὶ τοξεύειν. οἱ δὲ Ἕλληνες παιανίσαντες
ὥρμησαν δρόμῳ ἐπ᾽ αὐτούς· οἱ δὲ οὐκ ἐδέξαντο· καὶ
γὰρ ἦσαν ὡπλισμένοι ὡς μὲν ἐν τοῖς ὄρεσιν ἱκανῶς
πρὸς τὸ ἐπιδραμεῖν καὶ φεύγειν, πρὸς δὲ τὸ εἰς χεῖρας
32   δέχεσθαι οὐχ ἱκανῶς. ἐν τούτῳ σημαίνει ὁ σαλπικτής·
καὶ οἱ μὲν πολέμιοι ἔφευγον πολὺ ἔτι θᾶττον, οἱ δὲ
Ἕλληνες τἀναντία στρέψαντες ἔσπευδον διὰ τοῦ πο-
33   ταμοῦ ὅτι τάχιστα. τῶν δὲ πολεμίων οἱ μέν τινες
αἰσθόμενοι πάλιν ἔδραμον ἐπὶ τὸν ποταμὸν καὶ τοξεύοντες ὀλίγους ἔτρωσαν, οἱ δὲ πολλοὶ καὶ πέραν
34   ὄντων τῶν Ἑλλήνων ἔτι φανεροὶ ἦσαν φεύγοντες. οἱ
δὲ ὑπαντήσαντες ἀνδριζόμενοι καὶ προσωτέρω τοῦ
καιροῦ προϊόντες ὕστερον τῶν μετὰ Ξενοφῶντος διέβησαν πάλιν· καὶ ἐτρώθησάν τινες καὶ τούτων.

IV. Ἐπεὶ δὲ διέβησαν, συνταξάμενοι ἀμφὶ μέσον
ἡμέρας ἐπορεύθησαν διὰ τῆς Ἀρμενίας πεδίον ἅπαν
καὶ λείους γηλόφους οὐ μεῖον ἢ πέντε παρασάγγας·
οὐ γὰρ ἦσαν ἐγγὺς τοῦ ποταμοῦ κῶμαι διὰ τοὺς
2   πολέμους τοὺς πρὸς τοὺς Καρδούχους. εἰς δὲ ἣν ἀφίκοντο κώμην μεγάλη τε ἦν καὶ βασίλειον εἶχε τῷ
σατράπῃ καὶ ἐπὶ ταῖς πλείσταις οἰκίαις τύρσεις ἐπῆ-
3   σαν· ἐπιτήδεια δ᾽ ἦν δαψιλῆ. ἐντεῦθεν δ᾽ ἐπορεύθησαν
σταθμοὺς δύο παρασάγγας δέκα μέχρι ὑπερῆλθον
τὰς πηγὰς τοῦ Τίγρητος ποταμοῦ. ἐντεῦθεν δ᾽ ἐπορεύ-

Now the Carduchians, seeing that those who were left were by this time few in number (for many even of those detailed to stay had gone off to look after pack animals or baggage or women, as the case might be), at that moment proceeded to press upon them boldly and began to sling stones and shoot arrows. Then the Greeks struck up the paean and charged at them on the run, and they did not meet the attack; for while they were equipped well enough for attack and retreat in the mountains, their equipment was not adequate for hand-to-hand fighting. At that instant the Greek trumpeter sounded his signal; and while the enemy began to flee much faster than before, the Greeks turned about and were hastening through the river at top speed. Some of the enemy, perceiving this movement, ran back to the river and wounded a few Greeks with arrows, but most of them, even when the Greeks were on the other side, could still be seen continuing their flight. But the troops that came to meet Xenophon, behaving like men and advancing farther than they should have gone, crossed back again in the rear of Xenophon's command; and some of them also were wounded.

IV. When they had accomplished the crossing, they formed in line of battle about midday and marched through Armenia, over entirely level country and gently sloping hills, not less than five parasangs; for there were no villages near the river because of the wars between the Armenians and Carduchians. The village which they finally reached was a large one and had a palace for the satrap, while most of the houses were surmounted by turrets; and provisions were plentiful. From there they marched two stages, ten parasangs, until they passed the headwaters of the Tigris river. From there they marched three stages,

θησαν σταθμοὺς τρεῖς παρασάγγας πεντεκαίδεκα ἐπὶ
τὸν Τηλεβόαν ποταμόν. οὗτος δ' ἦν καλὸς μέν, μέγας
4 δ' οὔ· κῶμαι δὲ πολλαὶ περὶ τὸν ποταμὸν ἦσαν. ὁ δὲ
τόπος οὗτος Ἀρμενία ἐκαλεῖτο ἡ πρὸς ἑσπέραν. ὕπαρχος δ' ἦν αὐτῆς Τιρίβαζος, ὁ καὶ βασιλεῖ φίλος
γενόμενος, καὶ ὁπότε παρείη, οὐδεὶς ἄλλος βασιλέα
5 ἐπὶ τὸν ἵππον ἀνέβαλλεν. οὗτος προσήλασεν ἱππέας
ἔχων, καὶ προπέμψας ἑρμηνέα εἶπεν ὅτι βούλοιτο
διαλεχθῆναι τοῖς ἄρχουσι. τοῖς δὲ στρατηγοῖς ἔδοξεν
ἀκοῦσαι· καὶ προσελθόντες εἰς ἐπήκοον ἠρώτων τί
6 θέλοι. ὁ δὲ εἶπεν ὅτι σπείσασθαι βούλοιτο ἐφ' ᾧ μήτε
αὐτὸς τοὺς Ἕλληνας ἀδικεῖν μήτε ἐκείνους καίειν τὰς
οἰκίας, λαμβάνειν τε τἀπιτήδεια ὅσων δέοιντο. ἔδοξε
ταῦτα τοῖς στρατηγοῖς καὶ ἐσπείσαντο ἐπὶ τούτοις.

7 Ἐντεῦθεν δ' ἐπορεύθησαν σταθμοὺς τρεῖς διὰ πεδίου παρασάγγας πεντεκαίδεκα· καὶ Τιρίβαζος παρ-
ηκολούθει ἔχων τὴν ἑαυτοῦ δύναμιν ἀπέχων ὡς δέκα
σταδίους· καὶ ἀφίκοντο εἰς βασίλεια καὶ κώμας πέριξ
8 πολλὰς πολλῶν τῶν ἐπιτηδείων μεστάς. στρατοπε-
δευομένων δ' αὐτῶν γίγνεται τῆς νυκτὸς χιὼν πολλή·
καὶ ἕωθεν ἔδοξε διασκηνῆσαι τὰς τάξεις καὶ τοὺς
στρατηγοὺς κατὰ τὰς κώμας· οὐ γὰρ ἑώρων πολέμιον
οὐδένα καὶ ἀσφαλὲς ἐδόκει εἶναι διὰ τὸ πλῆθος τῆς
9 χιόνος. ἐνταῦθα εἶχον τὰ ἐπιτήδεια ὅσα ἐστὶν ἀγαθά,
ἱερεῖα, σῖτον, οἴνους παλαιοὺς εὐώδεις, ἀσταφίδας,

---

[30] Subordinate to the satrap of all Armenia, Orontas. On the
subordinate governor see *Hell.* III. i. 10 ff.

fifteen parasangs, to the Teleboas river. This was a beautiful
river, though not a large one, and there were many villages
about it. This region was called Western Armenia. Its lieu-
tenant-governor[30] was Tiribazus,[31] who had proved himself
a friend to the King and, so often as he was present, was
the only man permitted to help the King mount his horse.
He rode up to the Greeks with a body of horsemen, and
sending forward an interpreter, said that he wished to confer with their commanders. The generals decided to hear
what he had to say, and, after approaching within hearing
distance, they asked him what he wanted. He replied that
he wished to conclude a treaty with these conditions, that
he on his side would not harm the Greeks, and that they
should not burn the houses, but might take all the provisions they needed. This proposition was accepted by the
generals, and they concluded a treaty on these terms.

From there they marched three stages, fifteen parasangs, through level country, Tiribazus and his command
following along at a distance of about ten stadia from them;
and they reached a palace with many villages round about
it full of provisions in abundance. While they were in camp
there, there was a heavy fall of snow[32] during the night, and
in the morning they decided to quarter the several divisions of the army, with their commanders, in the different
villages; for there was no enemy within sight, and the plan
seemed to be a safe one by reason of the great quantity of
snow. There they had all possible good things in the way of
supplies—animals for sacrifice, grain, old wines with a fine

[31] On the role of this important figure in the 380s see *Hell*. IV.
viii. 16, V. i. 28 ff.

[32] It was now late in November.

ὄσπρια παντοδαπά. τῶν δὲ ἀποσκεδαννυμένων τινὲς
ἀπὸ τοῦ στρατοπέδου ἔλεγον ὅτι κατίδοιεν νύκτωρ
10 πολλὰ πυρὰ φαίνοντα. ἐδόκει δὴ τοῖς στρατηγοῖς οὐκ
ἀσφαλὲς εἶναι διασκηνοῦν, ἀλλὰ συναγαγεῖν τὸ
στράτευμα πάλιν. ἐντεῦθεν συνῆλθον· καὶ γὰρ ἐδόκει
11 διαιθριάζειν. νυκτερευόντων δ᾽ αὐτῶν ἐνταῦθ᾽ ἐπιπίπτει
χιὼν ἄπλατος, ὥστε ἀπέκρυψε καὶ τὰ ὅπλα καὶ τοὺς
ἀνθρώπους κατακειμένους· καὶ τὰ ὑποζύγια συνεπό-
δισεν ἡ χιών· καὶ πολὺς ὄκνος ἦν ἀνίστασθαι· κατα-
κειμένων γὰρ ἀλεεινὸν ἦν ἡ χιὼν ἐπιπεπτωκυῖα ὅτῳ
12 μὴ παραρρυείη. ἐπεὶ δὲ Ξενοφῶν ἐτόλμησε γυμνὸς
ἀναστὰς σχίζειν ξύλα, τάχα ἀναστάς τις καὶ ἄλλος
ἐκείνου ἀφελόμενος ἔσχιζεν. ἐκ δὲ τούτου καὶ οἱ ἄλλοι
13 ἀναστάντες πῦρ ἔκαιον καὶ ἐχρίοντο· πολὺ γὰρ ἐνταῦθα ηὑρίσκετο χρῖμα, ᾧ ἐχρῶντο ἀντ᾽ ἐλαίου, σύειον
καὶ σησάμινον καὶ ἀμυγδάλινον ἐκ τῶν πικρῶν καὶ
τερμίνθινον. ἐκ δὲ τῶν αὐτῶν τούτων καὶ μύρον
ηὑρίσκετο.

14 Μετὰ ταῦτα ἐδόκει πάλιν διασκηνητέον εἶναι κατὰ[2]
τὰς κώμας εἰς στέγας. ἔνθα δὴ οἱ στρατιῶται σὺν
πολλῇ κραυγῇ καὶ ἡδονῇ ἦσαν ἐπὶ τὰς στέγας καὶ τὰ
ἐπιτήδεια· ὅσοι δὲ ὅτε τὸ[3] πρότερον ἀπῇσαν τὰς οἰκίας
ἐνέπρησαν ὑπὸ ἀτασθαλίας, δίκην ἐδίδοσαν κακῶς
15 σκηνοῦντες. ἐντεῦθεν ἔπεμψαν νυκτὸς Δημοκράτην
Τημνίτην ἄνδρας δόντες ἐπὶ τὰ ὄρη ἔνθα ἔφασαν οἱ

---

[2] κατά Pithoeus, followed by Peters: most MSS. have εἰς.
[3] ὅτε τὸ Hude/Peters, Mar., following one MS.: other MSS.
and Gem. omit.

bouquet, dried grapes, and beans of all sorts. But some men who straggled away from their quarters reported that they saw in the night the gleam of a great many fires. The generals accordingly decided that it was unsafe to have their divisions in separate quarters, and that they must bring all the troops together again; so they came together, especially as the storm seemed to be clearing up. But there came such a terrible fall of snow while they were bivouacked there that it completely covered both the arms and the men as they slept, besides hampering the baggage animals; and everybody was very reluctant to get up, for as the men lay there the snow that had fallen upon them—in case it did not slip off—was a source of warmth. But once Xenophon had mustered the courage to get up without his cloak and set about splitting wood, another man also speedily got up, took the axe away from him, and went on with the splitting. Thereupon the rest got up and proceeded to build fires and anoint themselves; for they found ointment there in abundance which they used in place of olive oil—made of pork fat, sesame, bitter almonds, or turpentine. They found also a fragrant oil made out of these same ingredients.

After this it was deemed necessary to distribute the troops again to quarters in the houses throughout the several villages. Then followed plenty of joyful shouting as the men went back to their houses and provisions, and all those who just before had wantonly burned the houses they were leaving, paid the penalty by getting poor quarters. After this they sent Democrates of Temnus with a body of troops during the night to the mountains where the stragglers said

ἀποσκεδαννύμενοι καθορᾶν τὰ πυρά· οὗτος γὰρ ἐδόκει
καὶ πρότερον πολλὰ ἤδη ἀληθεῦσαι τοιαῦτα, τὰ ὄντα

16 τε ὡς ὄντα καὶ τὰ μὴ ὄντα ὡς οὐκ ὄντα. πορευθεὶς δὲ
τὰ μὲν πυρὰ οὐκ ἔφη ἰδεῖν, ἄνδρα δὲ συλλαβὼν ἧκεν
ἄγων ἔχοντα τόξον Περσικὸν καὶ φαρέτραν καὶ σάγα-

17 ριν οἷανπερ καὶ Ἀμαζόνες ἔχουσιν. ἐρωτώμενος δὲ
ποδαπὸς εἴη Πέρσης μὲν ἔφη εἶναι, πορεύεσθαι δ᾽ ἀπὸ
τοῦ Τιριβάζου στρατοπέδου, ὅπως ἐπιτήδεια λάβοι. οἱ
δ᾽ ἠρώτων αὐτὸν τὸ στράτευμα ὁπόσον τε εἴη καὶ ἐπὶ

18 τίνι συνειλεγμένον. ὁ δὲ εἶπεν ὅτι Τιρίβαζος εἴη ἔχων
τήν τε αὐτοῦ δύναμιν καὶ μισθοφόρους Χάλυβας καὶ
Τάοχους· παρεσκευάσθαι δὲ αὐτὸν ἔφη ὡς ἐπὶ τῇ
ὑπερβολῇ τοῦ ὄρους ἐν τοῖς στενοῖς ᾗπερ μοναχῇ εἴη
πορεία, ἐνταῦθα ἐπιθησόμενον τοῖς Ἕλλησιν.

19 Ἀκούσασι τοῖς στρατηγοῖς ταῦτα ἔδοξε τὸ στράτευμα συναγαγεῖν· καὶ εὐθὺς φύλακας καταλιπόντες
καὶ στρατηγὸν ἐπὶ τοῖς μένουσι Σοφαίνετον Στυμφάλιον ἐπορεύοντο ἔχοντες ἡγεμόνα τὸν ἁλόντα ἄνθρω-

20 πον. ἐπειδὴ δὲ ὑπερέβαλλον τὰ ὄρη, οἱ πελτασταὶ
προϊόντες καὶ κατιδόντες τὸ στρατόπεδον οὐκ ἔμειναν
τοὺς ὁπλίτας, ἀλλ᾽ ἀνακραγόντες ἔθεον ἐπὶ τὸ στρατό-

21 πεδον. οἱ δὲ βάρβαροι ἀκούσαντες τὸν θόρυβον οὐχ
ὑπέμειναν, ἀλλ᾽ ἔφευγον· ὅμως δὲ καὶ ἀπέθανόν τινες
τῶν βαρβάρων καὶ ἵπποι ἑάλωσαν εἰς εἴκοσι καὶ ἡ
σκηνὴ ἡ Τιριβάζου ἑάλω καὶ ἐν αὐτῇ κλῖναι ἀργυρό-
ποδες καὶ ἐκπώματα καὶ οἱ ἀρτοκόποι καὶ οἱ οἰνοχόοι

they had seen the fires; for this Democrates enjoyed the reputation of having made accurate reports in many previous cases of the same sort, describing what were facts as facts and what were fictions as fictions. Upon his return he stated that he had not seen the fires; he had captured, however, and brought back with him a man with a Persian bow and quiver and a battleaxe of the same sort that Amazons carry.[33] When this man was asked from what country he came, he said he was a Persian and was on his way from the camp of Tiribazus to get provisions. They asked him how large Tiribazus' army was and for what purpose it had been gathered. He replied that it was Tiribazus with his own forces and Chalybian and Taochian mercenaries, and that he had made his preparations with the idea of taking a position upon the mountain pass, in the defile through which ran the only road, and there attacking the Greeks.

When the generals heard these statements, they resolved to bring the troops together into a camp; then, after leaving a garrison and Sophaenetus the Stymphalian as general in command of those who stayed behind, they set out at once, with the captured man as guide. As soon as they had begun to cross the mountains, the peltasts, pushing on ahead and having caught sight of the enemy's camp, did not wait for the hoplites, but raised a shout and charged upon the camp. When the barbarians heard the uproar, they did not wait to offer resistance, but took to flight; nevertheless, some of them were killed, about twenty horses were captured, and likewise Tiribazus' tent, with silver-footed couches in it, and drinking cups, and people

[33] For depictions of Amazons wielding a *sagaris* see *LIMC* I.2 470 no. 233a, 476 no. 285, 510 no. 647, 512 no. 644.

22 φάσκοντες εἶναι. ἐπειδὴ δὲ ἐπύθοντο ταῦτα οἱ τῶν
ὁπλιτῶν στρατηγοί, ἐδόκει αὐτοῖς ἀπιέναι τὴν ταχίστην ἐπὶ τὸ στρατόπεδον, μή τις ἐπίθεσις γένοιτο τοῖς
καταλελειμμένοις. καὶ εὐθὺς ἀνακαλεσάμενοι τῇ σάλπιγγι ἀπῆσαν, καὶ ἀφικνοῦνται αὐθημερὸν ἐπὶ τὸ
στρατόπεδον.

V. Τῇ δ' ὑστεραίᾳ ἐδόκει πορευτέον εἶναι ὅπῃ δύναιντο τάχιστα πρὶν ἢ συλλεγῆναι τὸ στράτευμα
πάλιν καὶ καταλαβεῖν τὰ στενά. συσκευασάμενοι δ'
εὐθὺς ἐπορεύοντο διὰ χιόνος πολλῆς ἡγεμόνας ἔχοντες
πολλούς· καὶ αὐθημερὸν ὑπερβαλόντες τὸ ἄκρον ἐφ'
ᾧ ἔμελλεν ἐπιτίθεσθαι Τιρίβαζος κατεστρατοπεδεύ-
2 σαντο. ἐντεῦθεν δ' ἐπορεύθησαν σταθμοὺς ἐρήμους
τρεῖς παρασάγγας πεντεκαίδεκα ἐπὶ τὸν Εὐφράτην
ποταμόν, καὶ διέβαινον αὐτὸν βρεχόμενοι πρὸς τὸν
ὀμφαλόν. ἐλέγοντο δ' οὐδ' αἱ πηγαὶ πρόσω εἶναι.

3   Ἐντεῦθεν ἐπορεύοντο διὰ χιόνος πολλῆς καὶ πεδίου
σταθμοὺς τρεῖς παρασάγγας[4] τρεῖς καὶ δέκα. ὁ δὲ
τρίτος ἐγένετο χαλεπὸς καὶ ἄνεμος βορρᾶς ἐναντίος
ἔπνει παντάπασιν ἀποκαίων πάντα καὶ πηγνὺς τοὺς
4 ἀνθρώπους. ἔνθα δὴ τῶν μάντεών τις εἶπε σφαγι-
άσασθαι τῷ ἀνέμῳ, καὶ σφαγιάζεται· καὶ πᾶσι δὴ
περιφανῶς ἔδοξεν λῆξαι τὸ χαλεπὸν τοῦ πνεύματος.
ἦν δὲ τῆς χιόνος τὸ βάθος ὄργυα· ὥστε καὶ τῶν
ὑποζυγίων καὶ τῶν ἀνδραπόδων πολλὰ ἀπώλετο καὶ

---

[4] τρεῖς παρασάγγας added by Gem.

who said they were his bakers and his cup-bearers.[34] As soon as the generals of the hoplites learned of these results, they deemed it best to go back as speedily as possible to their own camp, lest some attack might be made upon those they had left behind. So they immediately sounded the recall with the trumpet and set out on the return journey, arriving at their camp on the same day.

V. On the next day it seemed that they must continue their march with all speed, before the hostile army could be gathered together again and take possession of the narrow passes. They accordingly packed up and set out at once, marching through deep snow with a large number of guides; and before the day ended they crossed over the summit at which Tiribazus was intending to attack them and went into camp. From there they marched three stages through barren country, fifteen parasangs, to the Euphrates river, and crossed it, wetting themselves up to the navel;[35] and report was that the sources of the river were not far distant.

From there they marched over a plain and through deep snow three stages, thirteen parasangs. The third stage proved a hard one, with the north wind, which blew full in their faces, absolutely blasting everything and freezing the men. Then it was that one of the soothsayers bade them offer sacrifice to the wind, and sacrifice was offered; and it seemed quite clear to everybody that the violence of the wind abated. But the depth of the snow was a fathom, so that many of the baggage animals and slaves perished, and

[34] Cf. a similar capture of a Persian grandee's tent: Mardonius' tent after Plataea, Hdt. IX. lxxxii.

[35] Cf. Xenophon's own remarks, III. ii. 22.

5 τῶν στρατιωτῶν ὡς τριάκοντα. διεγένοντο δὲ τὴν
νύκτα πῦρ καίοντες· ξύλα δ᾽ ἦν ἐν τῷ σταθμῷ πολλά.
οἱ δὲ ὀψὲ προσιόντες ξύλα οὐκ εἶχον· οἱ οὖν πάλαι
ἥκοντες καὶ πῦρ καίοντες οὐ προσίεσαν πρὸς τὸ πῦρ
τοὺς ὀψίζοντας, εἰ μὴ μεταδοῖεν αὐτοῖς πυροὺς ἢ ἄλλο
εἴ τι ἔχοιεν βρωτόν. ἔνθα δὴ μετεδίδοσαν ἀλλήλοις

6 ὧν εἶχον ἕκαστοι. ἔνθα δὲ τὸ πῦρ ἐκαίετο, διατηκο-
μένης τῆς χιόνος βόθροι ἐγίγνοντο μεγάλοι ἔστε ἐπὶ
τὸ δάπεδον· οὗ δὴ παρῆν μετρεῖν τὸ βάθος τῆς χιόνος.

7 Ἐντεῦθεν δὲ τὴν ἐπιοῦσαν ἡμέραν ὅλην ἐπορεύοντο
διὰ χιόνος, καὶ πολλοὶ τῶν ἀνθρώπων ἐβουλιμίασαν.
Ξενοφῶν δ᾽ ὀπισθοφυλακῶν καὶ καταλαμβάνων τοὺς
πίπτοντας τῶν ἀνθρώπων ἠγνόει ὅ τι τὸ πάθος εἴη.

8 ἐπειδὴ δὲ εἶπέ τις αὐτῷ τῶν ἐμπείρων ὅτι σαφῶς
βουλιμιῶσι κἄν τι φάγωσιν ἀναστήσονται, περιὼν
περὶ τὰ ὑποζύγια, εἴ πού τι ὁρῴη βρωτόν, διεδίδου
καὶ διέπεμπε διδόντας τοὺς δυναμένους παρατρέχειν

9 τοῖς βουλιμιῶσιν. ἐπειδὴ δέ τι ἐμφάγοιεν, ἀνίσταντο
καὶ ἐπορεύοντο.

Πορευομένων δὲ Χειρίσοφος μὲν ἀμφὶ κνέφας πρὸς
κώμην ἀφικνεῖται, καὶ ὑδροφορούσας ἐκ τῆς κώμης
πρὸς τῇ κρήνῃ γυναῖκας καὶ κόρας καταλαμβάνει

10 ἔμπροσθεν τοῦ ἐρύματος. αὗται ἠρώτων αὐτοὺς τίνες
εἶεν. ὁ δ᾽ ἑρμηνεὺς εἶπε περσιστὶ ὅτι παρὰ βασιλέως
πορεύονται πρὸς τὸν σατράπην. αἱ δὲ ἀπεκρίναντο ὅτι

---

36 Penalty for tardiness; cf. *Hell*. VI. ii. 28.

about thirty of the soldiers. They got through that night by keeping up fires, for there was wood in abundance at the haltingplace; those who came up late, however, had none, and consequently the men who had arrived early and were keeping a fire would not allow the late comers to get near it unless they gave them a share of their wheat or anything else they had that was edible.[36] So then they shared with one another what they severally possessed. Now where the fire was kindled the snow melted, and the result was great holes clear down to the ground; and there, of course, one could measure the depth of the snow.

From there they marched all the following day through snow, and many of the men fell ill with hunger-sickness. And Xenophon, with the rearguard, as he came upon the men who were falling by the way, did not know what the trouble was. But as soon as a person who was acquainted with the disease had told him that they manifestly had hunger-sickness, and if they were given something to eat would be able to get up, he went around among the baggage animals, and wherever he saw anything that was edible, he would distribute it among the sick men, or send off in different directions people who had the strength to run along the lines, to give it to them. And when they had eaten something, they would get up and continue the march.

As the army went on, Cheirisophus reached a village about dusk, and found at the spring outside the wall women and girls who had come from the village to fetch water. They asked the Greeks who they were, and the interpreter replied in Persian that they were on their way from the King to the satrap. The women answered that he

οὐκ ἐνταῦθα εἴη, ἀλλ᾽ ἀπέχοι ὅσον παρασάγγην. οἱ
δ᾽, ἐπεὶ ὀψὲ ἦν, πρὸς τὸν κώμαρχον συνεισέρχονται
11 εἰς τὸ ἔρυμα σὺν ταῖς ὑδροφόροις. Χειρίσοφος μὲν
οὖν καὶ ὅσοι ἐδυνήθησαν τοῦ στρατεύματος ἐνταῦθα
ἐστρατοπεδεύσαντο, τῶν δ᾽ ἄλλων στρατιωτῶν οἱ μὴ
δυνάμενοι διατελέσαι τὴν ὁδὸν ἐνυκτέρευσαν ἄσιτοι
καὶ ἄνευ πυρός· καὶ ἐνταῦθά τινες ἀπώλοντο τῶν
στρατιωτῶν.

12 Ἐφείποντο δὲ τῶν πολεμίων συνειλεγμένοι τινὲς
καὶ τὰ μὴ δυνάμενα τῶν ὑποζυγίων ἥρπαζον καὶ
ἀλλήλοις ἐμάχοντο περὶ αὐτῶν. ἐλείποντο δὲ τῶν
στρατιωτῶν οἵ τε διεφθαρμένοι ὑπὸ τῆς χιόνος τοὺς
ὀφθαλμοὺς οἵ τε ὑπὸ τοῦ ψύχους τοὺς δακτύλους τῶν
13 ποδῶν ἀποσεσηπότες. ἦν δὲ τοῖς μὲν ὀφθαλμοῖς ἐπι-
κούρημα τῆς χιόνος εἴ τις μέλαν τι ἔχων πρὸ τῶν
ὀφθαλμῶν ἐπορεύετο, τῶν δὲ ποδῶν εἴ τις κινοῖτο καὶ
μηδέποτε ἡσυχίαν ἔχοι καὶ εἰς τὴν νύκτα ὑπολύοιτο·
14 ὅσοι δὲ ὑποδεδεμένοι ἐκοιμῶντο, εἰσεδύοντο εἰς τοὺς
πόδας οἱ ἱμάντες καὶ τὰ ὑποδήματα περιεπήγνυντο·
καὶ γὰρ ἦσαν, ἐπειδὴ ἐπέλιπε τὰ ἀρχαῖα ὑποδήματα,
καρβάτιναι πεποιημέναι ἐκ τῶν νεοδάρτων βοῶν.

15 Διὰ τὰς τοιαύτας οὖν ἀνάγκας ὑπελείποντό τινες
τῶν στρατιωτῶν· καὶ ἰδόντες μέλαν τι χωρίον διὰ τὸ
ἐκλελοιπέναι αὐτόθεν τὴν χιόνα ἥκαζον τετηκέναι· καὶ
ἐτετήκει διὰ κρήνην τινὰ ἣ πλησίον ἦν ἀτμίζουσα ἐν
νάπῃ· ἐνταῦθ᾽ ἐκτραπόμενοι ἐκάθηντο καὶ οὐκ ἔφασαν
16 πορεύεσθαι. ὁ δὲ Ξενοφῶν ἔχων <τοὺς>⁵ ὀπισθοφύ-

was not there, but about a parasang away. Then, inasmuch as it was late, the Greeks accompanied the water-carriers within the wall to visit the village chief. So it was that Cheirisophus and all the troops who could muster strength enough to reach the village, went into quarters there, but such of the others as were unable to complete the journey spent the night in the open without food or fire; and in this way some of the soldiers perished.

Meanwhile they were being followed by the enemy, some of whom had banded together and were seizing such of the pack animals as lacked the strength to go on, and fighting over them with one another. Some of the soldiers likewise were falling behind—those whose eyes had been blinded by the snow, or whose toes had rotted off by reason of the cold. It was a protection to the eyes against the snow if a man marched with something black in front of them, and a protection to the feet if one kept moving and never rested, and if he took off his shoes for the night; but in all cases where men slept with their shoes on, the straps sank into their flesh and the shoes froze on their feet; for what they were wearing, since their old footwear had given out, were rough shoes made of freshly flayed ox-hides.

It was under compulsion of such difficulties that some of the soldiers were falling behind; and seeing a spot that was dark because the snow just there had disappeared, they surmised that it had melted; and in fact it had melted, on account of a spring which was near by, steaming in a dell; here they turned aside and sat down, refusing to go any farther. But when Xenophon with the rearguard ob-

---

5 τοὺς added by Krüger.

XENOPHON

λακας ὡς ἤσθετο, ἐδεῖτο αὐτῶν πάσῃ τέχνῃ καὶ μηχανῇ μὴ ἀπολείπεσθαι, λέγων ὅτι ἕπονται πολλοὶ πολέμιοι συνειλεγμένοι, καὶ τελευτῶν ἐχαλέπαινεν. οἱ δὲ σφάττειν ἐκέλευον· οὐ γὰρ ἂν δύνασθαι πορευθῆναι.

17 ἐνταῦθα ἔδοξε κράτιστον εἶναι τοὺς ἑπομένους πολεμίους φοβῆσαι, εἴ τις δύναιτο, μὴ ἐπιπέσοιεν τοῖς κάμνουσι. καὶ ἦν μὲν σκότος ἤδη, οἱ δὲ προσῆσαν

18 πολλῷ θορύβῳ ἀμφὶ ὧν εἶχον διαφερόμενοι. ἔνθα δὴ οἱ ὀπισθοφύλακες ἅτε ὑγιαίνοντες ἐξαναστάντες ἔδραμον εἰς τοὺς πολεμίους· οἱ δὲ κάμνοντες ἀνακραγόντες ὅσον ἐδύναντο μέγιστον τὰς ἀσπίδας πρὸς τὰ δόρατα ἔκρουσαν. οἱ δὲ πολέμιοι δείσαντες ἧκαν αὑτοὺς κατὰ τῆς χιόνος εἰς τὴν νάπην, καὶ οὐδεὶς ἔτι οὐδαμοῦ ἐφθέγξατο.

19 Καὶ Ξενοφῶν μὲν καὶ οἱ σὺν αὐτῷ εἰπόντες τοῖς ἀσθενοῦσιν ὅτι τῇ ὑστεραίᾳ ἥξουσί τινες ἐπ᾽ αὐτούς, πορευόμενοι πρὶν τέτταρα στάδια διελθεῖν ἐντυγχάνουσιν ἐν τῇ ὁδῷ ἀναπαυομένοις ἐπὶ τῆς χιόνος τοῖς στρατιώταις ἐγκεκαλυμμένοις, καὶ οὐδὲ φυλακὴ οὐδεμία καθειστήκει· καὶ ἀνίστασαν αὐτούς. οἱ δ᾽ ἔλεγον

20 ὅτι οἱ ἔμπροσθεν οὐχ ὑποχωροῖεν. ὁ δὲ παριὼν καὶ παραπέμπων τῶν πελταστῶν τοὺς ἰσχυροτάτους ἐκέλευε σκέψασθαι τί εἴη τὸ κωλῦον. οἱ δὲ ἀπήγγελλον

21 ὅτι ὅλον οὕτως ἀναπαύοιτο τὸ στράτευμα. ἐνταῦθα καὶ οἱ περὶ Ξενοφῶντα ηὐλίσθησαν αὐτοῦ ἄνευ πυρὸς καὶ ἄδειπνοι, φυλακὰς οἵας ἐδύναντο καταστησάμενοι. ἐπεὶ δὲ πρὸς ἡμέραν ἦν, ὁ μὲν Ξενοφῶν πέμψας πρὸς τοὺς ἀσθενοῦντας τοὺς νεωτάτους ἀναστήσαντας ἐκέ-

served them, he begged them by all manner of means not to be left behind, telling them that a large body of the enemy had gathered and were pursuing, and finally he became angry. They told him, however, to kill them, for they could not go on. In this situation it seemed to be best to frighten the pursuing enemy, if they could, in order to prevent their falling upon the sick men. It was dark by this time, and the enemy were coming on with a great uproar, quarrelling over the booty they had. Then the men of the rearguard, since they were sound and well, started up and charged upon the enemy, while the invalids raised as big a shout as they could and clashed their shields against their spears. And the enemy, seized with fear, threw themselves down over the snow into the dell, and not a sound was heard from them afterwards.

Thereupon Xenophon and his men, after telling the invalids that on the next day people would come back after them, continued their march, but before they had gone four stadia they came upon their comrades lying down in the road upon the snow, wrapped up in their cloaks, and without so much as a single guard posted. They tried to get them up, but the men said that the troops in front would not make way for them. Xenophon accordingly passed along and, sending forward the strongest of the peltasts, directed them to see what the hindrance was. They reported back that the whole army was resting in this way. Thereupon Xenophon also and his party bivouacked where they were, without a fire and without dinner, after stationing such guards as they could. When it came toward morning, Xenophon sent the youngest of his troops to the sick

λευεν ἀναγκάζειν προϊέναι.

22   Ἐν δὲ τούτῳ Χειρίσοφος πέμπει τῶν ἐκ τῆς κώμης
σκεψομένους πῶς ἔχοιεν οἱ τελευταῖοι. οἱ δὲ ἅσμενοι
ἰδόντες τοὺς μὲν ἀσθενοῦντας τούτοις παρέδοσαν κο-
μίζειν ἐπὶ τὸ στρατόπεδον, αὐτοὶ δὲ ἐπορεύοντο, καὶ
πρὶν εἴκοσι στάδια διεληλυθέναι ἦσαν πρὸς τῇ κώμῃ
23   ἔνθα Χειρίσοφος ηὐλίζετο. ἐπεὶ δὲ συνεγένοντο ἀλλήλοις, ἔδοξε κατὰ τὰς κώμας ἀσφαλὲς εἶναι τὰς τάξεις
σκηνοῦν. καὶ Χειρίσοφος μὲν αὐτοῦ ὑπέμεινεν, οἱ δὲ
ἄλλοι διαλαχόντες ἃς ἑώρων κώμας ἐπορεύοντο ἕκα-
24   στοι τοὺς ἑαυτῶν ἔχοντες. ἔνθα δὴ Πολυκράτης Ἀθηναῖος λοχαγὸς ἐκέλευσεν ἀφιέναι ἑαυτόν· καὶ λαβὼν
τοὺς εὐζώνους, θέων ἐπὶ τὴν κώμην ἣν εἰλήχει Ξενοφῶν καταλαμβάνει πάντας ἔνδον τοὺς κωμήτας καὶ
τὸν κώμαρχην, καὶ πώλους εἰς δασμὸν βασιλεῖ τρε-
φομένους ἑπτακαίδεκα, καὶ τὴν θυγατέρα τοῦ κωμάρ-
χου ἐνάτην ἡμέραν γεγαμημένην· ὁ δ' ἀνὴρ αὐτῆς
λαγὼς ᾤχετο θηράσων καὶ οὐχ ἑάλω ἐν τῇ κώμῃ.

25   Αἱ δ' οἰκίαι ἦσαν κατάγειοι, τὸ μὲν στόμα ὥσπερ
φρέατος, κάτω δ' εὐρεῖαι· αἱ δὲ εἴσοδοι τοῖς μὲν
ὑποζυγίοις ὀρυκταί, οἱ δὲ ἄνθρωποι κατέβαινον κατὰ
κλίμακος. ἐν δὲ ταῖς οἰκίαις ἦσαν αἶγες, οἶες, βόες,
ὄρνιθες, καὶ τὰ ἔκγονα τούτων· τὰ δὲ κτήνη πάντα

---

37 Cf. §§34–35. This later passage makes clear that the horses
were to be sacrificed to the sun-god = Mithra: see Briant, *Histoire*
I, 262. Cf. the sacred Nisaean horses, Hdt. VII. xl, III. cvi, Arrian,
An. VII. xiii. 1.   38 Robert Curzon, in the mid-nineteenth cen-

men with orders to make them get up and force them to
proceed.

Meanwhile Cheirisophus sent some of the troops quartered in the village to find out how the people at the rear
were faring. Xenophon's party were glad enough to see
them, and turned over the invalids to them to carry on to
the camp, while they themselves continued their journey,
and before completing twenty stadia reached the village
where Cheirisophus was quartered. When all had come
together, the generals decided that it was safe for the different divisions of the army to take up quarters in the
several villages. Cheirisophus accordingly remained where
he was, while the other generals distributed by lot the
villages within sight, and all set off with their respective
commands. Then it was that Polycrates, an Athenian captain, asked to be detached from his division; and with an
active group of men he ran to the village which had fallen
to Xenophon's lot and there took possession of all the villagers, the village chief included, seventeen colts which
were being reared for tribute to the King,[37] and the village
chief's daughter, who had been married eight days before;
her husband, however, was off hunting hares, and was not
taken in the village.

The houses here were underground, with a mouth like
that of a well, but spacious below; and while entrances
were tunnelled down for the beasts of burden, the human
inhabitants descended by a ladder.[38] In the houses were
goats, sheep, cattle, fowls, and their young; and all the ani-

tury, described precisely these structures near Erzerum: *Armenia*
(New York, 1854) 55–58. Cf. Vitruvius II. i. 5. See also D. Lang,
Armenia (London, 1970) 119.

26 χιλῷ ἔνδον ἐτρέφοντο. ἦσαν δὲ καὶ πυροὶ καὶ κριθαὶ
καὶ ὄσπρια καὶ οἶνος κρίθινος ἐν κρατῆρσιν. ἐνῆσαν
δὲ καὶ αὐταὶ αἱ κριθαὶ ἰσοχειλεῖς, καὶ κάλαμοι ἐνέκε-
ιντο, οἱ μὲν μείζους οἱ δὲ ἐλάττους, γόνατα οὐκ ἔχον-
27 τες· τούτους ἔδει ὁπότε τις διψῴη λαβόντα εἰς τὸ
στόμα μύζειν. καὶ πάνυ ἄκρατος ἦν, εἰ μή τις ὕδωρ
ἐπιχέοι· καὶ πάνυ ἡδὺ συμμαθόντι τὸ πόμα ἦν.

28 Ὁ δὲ Ξενοφῶν τὸν ἄρχοντα τῆς κώμης ταύτης
σύνδειπνον ἐποιήσατο καὶ θαρρεῖν αὐτὸν ἐκέλευε
λέγων ὅτι οὔτε τῶν τέκνων στερήσοιτο τήν τε οἰκίαν
αὐτοῦ ἀντεμπλήσαντες τῶν ἐπιτηδείων ἀπίασιν, ἢν
ἀγαθόν τι τῷ στρατεύματι ἐξηγησάμενος φαίνηται
29 ἔστ' ἂν ἐν ἄλλῳ ἔθνει γένωνται. ὁ δὲ ταῦτα ὑπισχνεῖτο, καὶ φιλοφρονούμενος οἶνον ἔφρασεν ἔνθα
ἦν κατορωρυγμένος. ταύτην μὲν οὖν τὴν νύκτα δι-
ασκηνήσαντες οὕτως ἐκοιμήθησαν ἐν πᾶσιν ἀφθόνοις
πάντες οἱ στρατιῶται, ἐν φυλακῇ ἔχοντες τὸν κωμάρχην καὶ τὰ τέκνα αὐτοῦ ὁμοῦ ἐν ὀφθαλμοῖς.

30 Τῇ δ' ἐπιούσῃ ἡμέρᾳ Ξενοφῶν λαβὼν τὸν κωμάρχην πρὸς Χειρίσοφον ἐπορεύετο· ὅπου δὲ παρίοι
κώμην, ἐτρέπετο πρὸς τοὺς ἐν ταῖς κώμαις καὶ κατελάμβανε πανταχοῦ εὐωχουμένους καὶ εὐθυμουμένους,
καὶ οὐδαμόθεν ἀφίεσαν πρὶν παραθεῖεν αὐτοῖς ἄρι-
31 στον· οὐκ ἦν δ' ὅπου οὐ παρετίθεσαν ἐπὶ τὴν αὐτὴν
τράπεζαν κρέα ἄρνεια, ἐρίφεια, χοίρεια, μόσχεια,
ὀρνίθεια, σὺν πολλοῖς ἄρτοις τοῖς μὲν πυρίνοις τοῖς
32 δὲ κριθίνοις. ὁπότε δέ τις φιλοφρονούμενός τῳ βού-

mals were reared and took their fodder there in the houses. Here were also wheat, barley, and beans, and barleywine in large bowls. Floating on the top of this drink were the barley-grains and in it were straws, some larger and others smaller, without joints; and when one was thirsty, he had to take these straws into his mouth and suck. It was an extremely strong drink unless one diluted it with water, and extremely good when one was used to it.

Xenophon made the chief man of this village his guest at dinner and bade him be of good cheer, telling him that he should not be deprived of his children, and that before they went away they would fill his house with provisions by way of reward in case he should prove to have given the army good guidance until they should reach another tribe. He promised to do this, and in a spirit of kindliness told them where there was wine buried. For that night, then, all Xenophon's soldiers, in this village where they were thus separately quartered, went to bed amid an abundance of everything, keeping the village chief under guard and his children all together within sight.[39]

On the next day Xenophon took the village chief and set out to visit Cheirisophus; whenever he passed a village, he would turn aside to visit the troops quartered there, and everywhere he found them faring sumptuously and in fine spirits; there was no place from which the men would let them go until they had served them breakfast, and no place where they did not serve on the same table lamb, kid, pork, veal, and poultry, together with many loaves of bread, some of wheat and some of barley. And whenever a

[39] This section suggests the komarch held broad powers. See S. Hornblower CAH[2], VI, 51.

λοιτο προπιεῖν, εἷλκεν ἐπὶ τὸν κρατῆρα, ἔνθεν ἐπι-
κύψαντα ἔδει ῥοφοῦντα πίνειν ὥσπερ βοῦν. καὶ τῷ
κωμάρχῃ ἐδίδοσαν λαμβάνειν ὅ τι βούλοιτο. ὁ δὲ
ἄλλο μὲν οὐδὲν ἐδέχετο, ὅπου δέ τινα τῶν συγγενῶν
33 ἴδοι, πρὸς ἑαυτὸν ἀεὶ ἐλάμβανεν. ἐπεὶ δ᾽ ἦλθον πρὸς
Χειρίσοφον, κατελάμβανε κἀκείνους σκηνοῦντας
ἐστεφανωμένους τοῦ ξηροῦ χιλοῦ στεφάνοις, καὶ δια-
κονοῦντας Ἀρμενίους παῖδας σὺν ταῖς βαρβαρικαῖς
στολαῖς· τοῖς δὲ παισὶν ἐδείκνυσαν ὥσπερ ἐνεοῖς ὅ τι
δέοι ποιεῖν.

34   Ἐπεὶ δ᾽ ἀλλήλους ἐφιλοφρονήσαντο Χειρίσοφος
καὶ Ξενοφῶν, κοινῇ δὴ ἀνηρώτων τὸν κωμάρχην διὰ
τοῦ περσίζοντος ἑρμηνέως τίς εἴη ἡ χώρα. ὁ δ᾽ ἔλεγεν
ὅτι Ἀρμενία. καὶ πάλιν ἠρώτων τίνι οἱ ἵπποι τρέφοιντο. ὁ δ᾽ ἔλεγεν ὅτι βασιλεῖ δασμός· τὴν δὲ
πλησίον χώραν ἔφη εἶναι Χάλυβας, καὶ τὴν ὁδὸν
35 ἔφραζεν ᾗ εἴη. καὶ αὐτὸν τότε μὲν ᾤχετο ἄγων ὁ
Ξενοφῶν πρὸς τοὺς ἑαυτοῦ οἰκέτας, καὶ ἵππον ὃν
εἰλήφει παλαίτερον δίδωσι τῷ κωμάρχῃ ἀναθρέψαντι
καταθῦσαι, ὅτι ἤκουεν αὐτὸν ἱερὸν εἶναι τοῦ Ἡλίου,
δεδιὼς μὴ ἀποθάνῃ· ἐκεκάκωτο γὰρ ὑπὸ τῆς πορείας·
αὐτὸς δὲ τῶν πώλων λαμβάνει, καὶ τῶν ἄλλων στρα-
36 τηγῶν καὶ λοχαγῶν ἔδωκεν ἑκάστῳ πῶλον. ἦσαν δ᾽ οἱ
ταύτῃ ἵπποι μείονες μὲν τῶν Περσικῶν, θυμοει-
δέστεροι δὲ πολύ. ἐνταῦθα δὴ καὶ διδάσκει ὁ
κωμάρχης περὶ τοὺς πόδας τῶν ἵππων καὶ τῶν ὑπο-

man wanted out of good fellowship to drink another's health, he would draw him to the bowl, and then one had to stoop over and drink from it, sucking like an ox. To the village chief they offered the privilege of taking whatever he wanted. He declined for the most part to accept anything, but whenever he caught sight of one of his kinsmen, he would always take the man to his side. Again, when they reached Cheirisophus, Xenophon found his troops also feasting in their quarters, crowned with wreaths of hay and served by Armenian boys in their strange, foreign dress; and they were showing the boys what to do by signs, as if they were deaf and dumb.

As soon as Cheirisophus and Xenophon had exchanged warm greetings, they together asked the village chief, through their Persian-speaking interpreter, what this land was. He replied that it was Armenia. They asked him again for whom the horses were being reared. He answered, as tribute for the King; and he said that the neighbouring country was that of the Chalybians, and told them where the road was. Then Xenophon took the village chief back for the time to his own household, and gave him a horse that he had got when it was rather old, to fatten up and sacrifice, for he understood that it was sacred to the Sun-god. He did this out of fear that the horse might die, for it had been injured by the journey; and he took for himself one of the colts[40] and gave his generals and captains also a colt apiece. The horses of this region were smaller than the Persian horses, but very much more spirited. It was here also that the village chief instructed them about wrapping small bags round the feet of their horses and beasts of

40 See §24 above.

ζυγίων σακία περιειλεῖν, ὅταν διὰ τῆς χιόνος ἄγωσιν·
ἄνευ γὰρ τῶν σακίων κατεδύοντο μέχρι τῆς γαστρός.

VI. Ἐπεὶ δ᾽ ἡμέρα ἦν ὀγδόη, τὸν μὲν ἡγεμόνα
παραδίδωσι Χειρισόφῳ, τοὺς δὲ οἰκέτας καταλείπει[6]
πλὴν τοῦ υἱοῦ τοῦ ἄρτι ἡβάσκοντος. τοῦτον δὲ Ἐπι-
σθένει Ἀμφιπολίτῃ παραδίδωσι φυλάττειν, ὅπως εἰ
καλῶς ἡγήσοιτο, ἔχων καὶ τοῦτον ἀπίοι. καὶ εἰς τὴν
οἰκίαν αὐτοῦ εἰσεφόρησαν ὡς ἐδύναντο πλεῖστα, καὶ
2 ἀναζεύξαντες ἐπορεύοντο. ἡγεῖτο δ᾽ αὐτοῖς ὁ κωμάρχης λελυμένος διὰ χιόνος· καὶ ἤδη τε ἦν ἐν τῷ τρίτῳ
σταθμῷ, καὶ Χειρίσοφος αὐτῷ ἐχαλεπάνθη ὅτι οὐκ εἰς
κώμας ἤγαγεν. ὁ δ᾽ ἔλεγεν ὅτι οὐκ εἶεν ἐν τῷ τόπῳ
3 τούτῳ. ὁ δὲ Χειρίσοφος αὐτὸν ἔπαισεν μέν, ἔδησε δ᾽
οὔ. ἐκ δὲ τούτου ἐκεῖνος τῆς νυκτὸς ἀποδρὰς ᾤχετο
καταλιπὼν τὸν υἱόν. τοῦτό γε δὴ Χειρισόφῳ καὶ Ξενοφῶντι μόνον διάφορον ἐν τῇ πορείᾳ ἐγένετο, ἡ τοῦ
ἡγεμόνος κάκωσις καὶ ἀμέλεια. Ἐπισθένης δὲ ἠράσθη
τοῦ παιδὸς καὶ οἴκαδε κομίσας πιστοτάτῳ ἐχρῆτο.

4 Μετὰ τοῦτο ἐπορεύθησαν ἑπτὰ σταθμοὺς ἀνὰ πέντε
παρασάγγας τῆς ἡμέρας παρὰ τὸν Φᾶσιν ποταμόν,
5 εὖρος πλεθριαῖον. ἐντεῦθεν ἐπορεύθησαν σταθμοὺς
δύο παρασάγγας δέκα· ἐπὶ δὲ τῇ εἰς τὸ πεδίον ὑπερβολῇ ἀπήντησαν αὐτοῖς Χάλυβες καὶ Τάοχοι καὶ
6 Φασιανοί. Χειρίσοφος δ᾽ ἐπεὶ κατεῖδε τοὺς πολεμίους
ἐπὶ τῇ ὑπερβολῇ, ἐπαύσατο πορευόμενος, ἀπέχων εἰς

---

[6] After καταλείπει the MSS. have τῷ κωμάρχῃ: Gem. brackets, following Rehdantz: Hude/Peters omit.

burden when they were going through the snow; for without these bags the animals would sink in up to their bellies.

VI. When seven days had passed, Xenophon gave over the village chief to Cheirisophus to act as guide, leaving his family behind with the exception of his son, who was just coming into the prime of youth; this son he gave into the keeping of Episthenes of Amphipolis, in order that the father, if he should serve them well as guide, might take him also back with him. Then, after putting into his house as large a quantity of supplies as they could,[41] they broke camp and set out upon the march. The village chief, who was not bound,[42] guided their way through the snow; but by the time they were on the third stage Cheirisophus got angry with him for not leading them to villages. He replied that there were none in this region. Then Cheirisophus struck him, but neglected to bind him. The result was that he stole away during the night, leaving his son behind. And this was the only cause of difference between Cheirisophus and Xenophon during the course of the march, this ill-treatment of the guide and carelessness in not guarding him. Episthenes, however, fell in love with the boy, took him home with him, and found him absolutely faithful.

After this they marched seven stages at the rate of five parasangs a day to the Phasis river, which was a plethrum in width. From there they marched two stages, ten parasangs; and on the pass leading over to the plain they encountered a body of Chalybians, Taochians, and Phasians. As soon as Cheirisophus caught sight of the enemy on the pass, he halted, while still at a distance of about thirty

[41] See §28 above.
[42] Cf. ii. 1.

τριάκοντα σταδίους, ἵνα μὴ κατὰ κέρας ἄγων πλησιάσῃ τοῖς πολεμίοις· παρήγγειλε δὲ καὶ τοῖς ἄλλοις παράγειν τοὺς λόχους, ὅπως ἐπὶ φάλαγγος γένοιτο τὸ
7 στράτευμα. ἐπεὶ δὲ ἦλθον οἱ ὀπισθοφύλακες, συνεκάλεσε τοὺς στρατηγοὺς καὶ λοχαγούς, καὶ ἔλεξεν ὧδε. Οἱ μὲν πολέμιοι, ὡς ὁρᾶτε, κατέχουσι τὰς ὑπερβολὰς τοῦ ὄρους· ὥρα δὲ βουλεύεσθαι ὅπως ὡς
8 κάλλιστα ἀγωνιούμεθα. ἐμοὶ μὲν οὖν δοκεῖ παραγγεῖλαι μὲν ἀριστοποιεῖσθαι τοῖς στρατιώταις, ἡμᾶς δὲ βουλεύεσθαι εἴτε τήμερον εἴτε αὔριον δοκεῖ
9 ὑπερβάλλειν τὸ ὄρος. Ἐμοὶ δέ γε, ἔφη ὁ Κλεάνωρ, δοκεῖ, ἐπὰν τάχιστα ἀριστήσωμεν, ἐξοπλισαμένους ὡς τάχιστα ἰέναι ἐπὶ τοὺς ἄνδρας. εἰ γὰρ διατρίψομεν τὴν τήμερον ἡμέραν, οἵ τε νῦν ἡμᾶς ὁρῶντες πολέμιοι θαρραλεώτεροι ἔσονται καὶ ἄλλους εἰκὸς τούτων θαρρούντων πλείους προσγενέσθαι.

10 Μετὰ τοῦτον Ξενοφῶν εἶπεν· Ἐγὼ δ᾽ οὕτω γιγνώσκω. εἰ μὲν ἀνάγκη ἐστὶ μάχεσθαι, τοῦτο δεῖ παρασκευάσασθαι ὅπως ὡς κράτιστα μαχούμεθα· εἰ δὲ βουλόμεθα ὡς ῥᾷστα ὑπερβάλλειν, τοῦτό μοι δοκεῖ σκεπτέον εἶναι ὅπως ὡς ἐλάχιστα μὲν τραύματα λάβωμεν, ὡς ἐλάχιστα δὲ σώματα ἀνδρῶν ἀποβάλω-
11 μεν. τὸ μὲν οὖν ὄρος ἐστὶ τὸ ὁρώμενον πλέον ἢ ἐφ᾽ ἑξήκοντα στάδια, ἄνδρες δ᾽ οὐδαμοῦ φυλάττοντες ἡμᾶς φανεροί εἰσιν ἀλλ᾽ ἢ κατ᾽ αὐτὴν τὴν ὁδόν· πολὺ οὖν κρεῖττον τοῦ ἐρήμου ὄρους καὶ κλέψαι τι πειρᾶσθαι λαθόντας καὶ ἁρπάσαι φθάσαντας, εἰ δυναί-

stadia, in order not to get near the enemy while his troops were marching in column; and he gave orders to the other officers also to move along their companies so as to bring the army into line of battle.[43] When the rearguard had come up, he called the generals and captains together and spoke as follows: "The enemy, as you see, are in possession of the pass over the mountain, and it is time for us to take counsel as to how we can best make our fight. My own view is, that we should give orders to the soldiers to get their breakfast while we ourselves consider whether it is best to attempt to cross over the mountain today or tomorrow." "My opinion is," said Cleanor, "that as soon as we have breakfasted, we should arm ourselves and attack these men as quickly as possible. For if we waste this day, not only will the enemy who are now looking at us become bolder, but others, in greater numbers, when these are once embold-ened, are likely to join them."

After Cleanor had spoken, Xenophon said: "And I think this way: if it is necessary for us to fight, our preparation should have this end in view, to make the strongest possible fight; but if we wish to effect a passage in the easiest way we can, then, in my opinion, our consideration should be on this point, how we may sustain the fewest wounds and sacrifice the fewest lives. Now this mountain—or the part of it that we see—extends over more than sixty stadia, but as for men to guard it against us, none are to be seen anywhere except on the road above; it is far better, there-fore, to turn to the unoccupied part of the mountain and try to steal a position by eluding the enemy's observation

---

[43] *i.e.* to bring companies which had been marching in column, *viz.* one behind another, into line abreast of one another.

μεθα, μᾶλλον ἢ πρὸς ἰσχυρὰ χωρία καὶ ἄνδρας
12 παρεσκευασμένους μάχεσθαι. πολὺ γὰρ ῥᾷον ὄρθιον
ἀμαχεὶ ἰέναι ἢ ὁμαλὲς ἔνθεν καὶ ἔνθεν πολεμίων
ὄντων, καὶ νύκτωρ ἀμαχεὶ μᾶλλον ἂν τὰ πρὸ ποδῶν
ὁρῴη τις ἢ μεθ' ἡμέραν μαχόμενος, καὶ ἡ τραχεῖα τοῖς
ποσὶν ἀμαχεὶ ἰοῦσιν εὐμενεστέρα ἢ ἡ ὁμαλὴ τὰς
13 κεφαλὰς βαλλομένοις. καὶ κλέψαι δ' οὐκ ἀδύνατόν μοι
δοκεῖ εἶναι, ἐξὸν μὲν νυκτὸς ἰέναι, ὡς μὴ ὁρᾶσθαι,
ἐξὸν δ' ἀπελθεῖν τοσοῦτον ὡς μὴ αἴσθησιν παρέχειν.
δοκοῦμεν δ' ἄν μοι ταύτῃ προσποιούμενοι προσβαλεῖν
ἐρημοτέρῳ ἂν τῷ ἄλλῳ ὄρει χρῆσθαι· μένοιεν γὰρ ἂν
αὐτοῦ μᾶλλον ἀθρόοι οἱ πολέμιοι. ἀτὰρ τί ἐγὼ περὶ
14 κλοπῆς συμβάλλομαι; ὑμᾶς γὰρ ἔγωγε, ὦ Χειρίσοφε,
ἀκούω τοὺς Λακεδαιμονίους ὅσοι ἐστὲ τῶν ὁμοίων
εὐθὺς καὶ ἐκ παίδων κλέπτειν μελετᾶν, καὶ οὐκ
αἰσχρὸν εἶναι ἀλλὰ καλὸν κλέπτειν ὅσα μὴ κωλύει
15 νόμος. ὅπως δὲ ὡς κράτιστα κλέπτητε[7] καὶ πειρᾶσθε
λανθάνειν, νόμιμον ἄρα[8] ὑμῖν ἐστιν, ἐὰν ληφθῆτε
κλέπτοντες, μαστιγοῦσθαι. νῦν οὖν μάλα σοι καιρός
ἐστιν ἐπιδείξασθαι τὴν παιδείαν, καὶ φυλάξασθαι
μέντοι μὴ ληφθῶμεν κλέπτοντες τοῦ ὄρους, ὡς μὴ
πληγὰς λάβωμεν.

16 Ἀλλὰ μέντοι, ἔφη ὁ Χειρίσοφος, κἀγὼ ὑμᾶς τοὺς
Ἀθηναίους ἀκούω δεινοὺς εἶναι κλέπτειν τὰ δημόσια,

---

[7] κράτιστα κλέπτητε some MSS., Hude/Peters, Mar.:
τάχιστα κλέπτειν τε (καὶ πειρᾶσθαι) other MSS.: τάχιστα
κλέπτοντες Gem.   [8] ἄρα some MSS., Hude/Peters, Mar.:
μὲν γὰρ other MSS.: παρ' Gem., following Rehdantz.

and to seize it by getting ahead of them, if we can, rather than to fight against strong places and men prepared. For it is far easier to march uphill without fighting than over level ground with enemies on this side and that; one can see what is in front of him more easily by night if he is not fighting than by day if he is fighting; and the rough road is more comfortable to men who are going over it on foot without fighting than the smooth road to men who are being pelted on the head. And as for stealing a position, that does not seem to me impossible, for we can go during the night so as not to be seen, and we can get far enough away from the enemy so as not to be heard. I do think, however, that if we should make a feint of attacking here, we should find the rest of the mountain all the more deserted, for the enemy would be more likely to remain in a body where they are. But why should I be the man to make suggestions about stealing? For, as I hear, Cheirisophus, you Lacedaemonians, at least those among you who belong to the peers,[44] practise stealing even from childhood, and count it not disgraceful but honourable to steal anything that the law does not prevent you from taking. And in order that you may steal with all possible skill and may try not to be caught at it, it is the law of your land that, if you are caught stealing, you are flogged.[45] Now, therefore, is just the time for you to display your training, and to take care that we do not get caught stealing any of the mountain, so that we shall not get a beating."

"Well, for all that," said Cheirisophus, "I hear on my side that you Athenians are terribly clever at stealing the

---

[44] For the ὅμοιοι of Sparta, see *Hell*. III. iii. 5, *Lac*. X. 7.
[45] Cf. *Lac*. II. 6–9.

καὶ μάλα ὄντος δεινοῦ τοῦ κινδύνου τῷ κλέπτοντι, καὶ
τοὺς κρατίστους μέντοι μάλιστα, εἴπερ ὑμῖν οἱ κράτιστοι ἄρχειν ἀξιοῦνται· ὥστε ὥρα καὶ σοὶ ἐπιδείκνυ-
17 σθαι τὴν παιδείαν. Ἐγὼ μὲν τοίνυν, ἔφη ὁ Ξενοφῶν,
ἕτοιμός εἰμι τοὺς ὀπισθοφύλακας ἔχων, ἐπειδὰν δει-
πνήσωμεν, ἰέναι καταληψόμενος τὸ ὄρος. ἔχω δὲ καὶ
ἡγεμόνας· οἱ γὰρ γυμνῆτες τῶν ἑπομένων ἡμῖν κλω-
πῶν ἔλαβόν τινας ἐνεδρεύσαντες· τούτων καὶ πυνθάνομαι ὅτι οὐκ ἄβατόν ἐστι τὸ ὄρος, ἀλλὰ νέμεται αἰξὶ
καὶ βουσίν· ὥστε ἐάνπερ ἅπαξ λάβωμέν τι τοῦ ὄρους,
18 βατὰ καὶ τοῖς ὑποζυγίοις ἔσται. ἐλπίζω δὲ οὐδὲ τοὺς
πολεμίους μενεῖν ἔτι, ἐπειδὰν ἴδωσιν ἡμᾶς ἐν τῷ ὁμοίῳ
ἐπὶ τῶν ἄκρων· οὐδὲ γὰρ νῦν ἐθέλουσι καταβαίνειν εἰς
19 τὸ ἴσον ἡμῖν. ὁ δὲ Χειρίσοφος εἶπε· Καὶ τί δεῖ σὲ
ἰέναι καὶ καταλιπεῖν τὴν ὀπισθοφυλακίαν; ἀλλὰ
20 ἄλλους πέμψον, ἂν μή τινες ἐθελούσιοι[9] φαίνωνται. ἐκ
τούτου Ἀριστώνυμος Μεθυδριεὺς ἔρχεται ὁπλίτας
ἔχων καὶ Ἀριστέας Χῖος γυμνῆτας καὶ Νικόμαχος
Οἰταῖος γυμνῆτας· καὶ σύνθημα ἐποιήσαντο, ὁπότε
21 ἔχοιεν τὰ ἄκρα, πυρὰ καίειν πολλά. ταῦτα συνθέμενοι
ἠρίστων· ἐκ δὲ τοῦ ἀρίστου προήγαγεν ὁ Χειρίσοφος
τὸ στράτευμα πᾶν ὡς δέκα σταδίους πρὸς τοὺς
πολεμίους, ὅπως ὡς μάλιστα δοκοίη ταύτῃ προσάξειν.
22 Ἐπειδὴ δὲ ἐδείπνησαν καὶ νὺξ ἐγένετο, οἱ μὲν
ταχθέντες ᾤχοντο[10] καὶ καταλαμβάνουσι τὸ ὄρος, οἱ

---

[9] ἐθελούσιοι most MSS., Hude/Peters, Gem.: ἐθέλοντες
ἀγαθοὶ one MS., Mar.   [10] ἀπήρχοντο some MSS., Gem.,
Hude/Peters: ᾤχοντο other MSS., Mar.

public funds, even though the danger is terribly great for the stealer, and, in fact, that your best people do it most, at least if they really are your best who are deemed worthy to rule; hence it is time for you also to be displaying your training." "Well," said Xenophon, "I am ready to set out with the rearguard, as soon as we have dined, to seize possession of the mountain. And I have guides, too; for the light troops set an ambush and captured some of the thieves who are following us. From these men I also learn that the mountain is not impassable, but is pastured with goats and cattle; therefore if we once get possession of any part of the mountain, our pack animals will find it passable. And I hope that the enemy will remove themselves from our way as soon as they see us on a level with them upon the heights; for they are not willing now to come down and meet us on our level." Then Cheirisophus said: "But why should you be the one to go, and leave your post with the rearguard? Send others rather, unless some offer themselves as volunteers." At that, Aristonymus of Methydrium, commanding hoplites, came forward, and Aristeas the Chian with light troops, and Nicomachus the Oetaean with light troops; and they made an agreement that as soon as they were in possession of the heights, they would kindle a number of fires. This agreement concluded, they proceeded to take breakfast; and immediately after breakfast Cheirisophus led the whole army forward about ten stadia toward the enemy, in order to make them quite certain that he was going to advance upon them by this road.

After they had had dinner and night had come on, the men appointed to the task set forward and gained possession of the mountain, while the remainder of the troops

δὲ ἄλλοι αὐτοῦ ἀνεπαύοντο. οἱ δὲ πολέμιοι ἐπεὶ
ᾔσθοντο τὸ ὄρος ἐχόμενον, ἐγρηγόρεσαν καὶ ἔκαιον
23 πυρὰ πολλὰ διὰ νυκτός. ἐπειδὴ δὲ ἡμέρα ἐγένετο
Χειρίσοφος μὲν θυσάμενος ἦγε κατὰ τὴν ὁδόν, οἱ δὲ
24 τὸ ὄρος καταλαβόντες κατὰ τὰ ἄκρα ἐπῇσαν. τῶν δὲ
πολεμίων τὸ μὲν πολὺ ἔμενεν ἐπὶ τῇ ὑπερβολῇ τοῦ
ὄρους, μέρος δ' αὐτῶν ἀπήντα τοῖς κατὰ τὰ ἄκρα. πρὶν
δὲ ὁμοῦ εἶναι τοὺς πολλοὺς ἀλλήλοις συμμειγνύασιν
οἱ κατὰ τὰ ἄκρα, καὶ νικῶσιν οἱ Ἕλληνες καὶ διώκου-
25 σιν. ἐν τούτῳ δὲ καὶ οἱ ἐκ τοῦ πεδίου οἱ μὲν πελτασταὶ
τῶν Ἑλλήνων δρόμῳ ἔθεον πρὸς τοὺς παρατεταγμένους, Χειρίσοφος δὲ βάδην ταχὺ ἐφείπετο σὺν τοῖς
26 ὁπλίταις. οἱ δὲ πολέμιοι οἱ ἐπὶ τῇ ὁδῷ ἐπειδὴ τὸ ἄνω
ἑώρων ἡττώμενον, φεύγουσι· καὶ ἀπέθανον μὲν οὐ
πολλοὶ αὐτῶν, γέρρα δὲ πάμπολλα ἐλήφθη· ἃ οἱ
Ἕλληνες ταῖς μαχαίραις κόπτοντες ἀχρεῖα ἐποίουν.
27 ὡς δ' ἀνέβησαν, θύσαντες καὶ τρόπαιον στησάμενοι
κατέβησαν εἰς τὸ πεδίον, καὶ εἰς κώμας πολλῶν καὶ
ἀγαθῶν γεμούσας ἦλθον.

VII. Ἐκ δὲ τούτων ἐπορεύθησαν εἰς Ταόχους σταθμοὺς πέντε παρασάγγας τριάκοντα· καὶ τὰ ἐπιτήδεια
ἐπέλιπε· χωρία γὰρ ᾤκουν ἰσχυρὰ οἱ Τάοχοι, ἐν οἷς
2 καὶ τὰ ἐπιτήδεια ἅπαντα εἶχον ἀνακεκομισμένοι. ἐπεὶ
δ' ἀφίκοντο πρὸς χωρίον ὃ πόλιν μὲν οὐκ εἶχεν οὐδ'
οἰκίας—συνεληλυθότες δ' ἦσαν αὐτόσε καὶ ἄνδρες καὶ
γυναῖκες καὶ κτήνη πολλά—Χειρίσοφος μὲν οὖν πρὸς
τοῦτο προσέβαλλεν εὐθὺς ἥκων· ἐπειδὴ δὲ ἡ πρώτη

rested where they were. And when the enemy perceived that the mountain was occupied, they stayed awake and kept many fires burning through the night. As soon as day came Cheirisophus offered sacrifice and led the army forward along the road, while the party that had seized the mountain advanced along the heights. As for the enemy, the majority remained at the pass over the mountain, but a part of them went to meet the detachment on the heights. Now before the two main bodies got near one another, those upon the heights came to close combat with each other, and the Greeks were victorious and began their pursuit. Meanwhile the main body of the Greeks was moving upward from the plain, the peltasts charging at a run upon the enemy's battleline and Cheirisophus following at a quick-step with the hoplites. But the enemy on the road no sooner saw their detachment on the heights being defeated than they took to flight; and while not many of them were killed, a great number of wicker shields were captured, which the Greeks rendered useless by slashing them with their sabres. When they had climbed to the top of the pass, after offering sacrifice and setting up a trophy they descended into the plain on the farther side, and reached villages full of many good things.

VII. After this they marched into the country of the Taochians five stages, thirty parasangs; and their provisions had run low, for the Taochians dwelt in strongholds, and in these strongholds they kept all their provisions stored away. Now when the Greeks arrived at one of them which contained no town nor houses, but was only a place where men and women and a great number of cattle were gathered, Cheirisophus proceeded to attack this stronghold as soon as he reached it; and when his first battalion grew

355

τάξις ἀπέκαμνεν, ἄλλη προσῄει καὶ αὖθις ἄλλη· οὐ
γὰρ ἦν ἀθρόοις περιστῆναι, ἀλλ' ἀπότομον ἦν κύκλῳ.

3   Ἐπειδὴ δὲ Ξενοφῶν ἦλθε σὺν τοῖς ὀπισθοφύλαξι
καὶ πελτασταῖς καὶ ὁπλίταις, ἐνταῦθα δὴ λέγει Χειρί-
σοφος· Εἰς καλὸν ἥκετε· τὸ γὰρ χωρίον αἱρετέον· τῇ
γὰρ στρατιᾷ οὐκ ἔστι τὰ ἐπιτήδεια, εἰ μὴ ληψόμεθα
4   τὸ χωρίον. ἐνταῦθα δὴ κοινῇ ἐβουλεύοντο· καὶ τοῦ
Ξενοφῶντος ἐρωτῶντος τί τὸ κωλῦον εἴη εἰσελθεῖν,
εἶπεν ὁ Χειρίσοφος· Μία αὕτη πάροδός ἐστιν ἣν ὁρᾷς·
ὅταν δέ τις ταύτῃ πειρᾶται παριέναι, κυλινδοῦσι λίθους ὑπὲρ ταύτης τῆς ὑπερεχούσης πέτρας· ὃς δ' ἂν
καταληφθῇ, οὕτω διατίθεται. ἅμα δ' ἔδειξε συντετριμ-
5   μένους ἀνθρώπους καὶ σκέλη καὶ πλευράς. Ἢν δὲ τοὺς
λίθους ἀναλώσωσιν, ἔφη ὁ Ξενοφῶν, ἄλλο τι ἢ οὐδὲν
κωλύει παριέναι; οὐ γὰρ δὴ ἐκ τοῦ ἐναντίου ὁρῶμεν εἰ
μὴ ὀλίγους τούτους ἀνθρώπους, καὶ τούτων δύο ἢ
6   τρεῖς ὡπλισμένους. τὸ δὲ χωρίον, ὡς καὶ σὺ ὁρᾷς,
σχεδὸν τρία ἡμίπλεθρά ἐστιν ὃ δεῖ βαλλομένους διελ-
θεῖν· τούτου δὲ ὅσον πλέθρον δασὺ πίτυσι διαλειπού-
σαις μεγάλαις, ἀνθ' ὧν ἑστηκότες ἄνδρες τί ἂν
πάσχοιεν ἢ ὑπὸ τῶν φερομένων λίθων ἢ ὑπὸ τῶν
κυλινδομένων; τὸ λοιπὸν οὖν γίγνεται ὡς ἡμίπλεθρον,
7   ὃ δεῖ ὅταν λωφήσωσιν οἱ λίθοι παραδραμεῖν. Ἀλλὰ
εὐθύς, ἔφη ὁ Χειρίσοφος, ἐπειδὰν ἀρξώμεθα εἰς τὸ
δασὺ προσιέναι, φέρονται οἱ λίθοι πολλοί. Αὐτὸ ἄν,
ἔφη, τὸ δέον εἴη· θᾶττον γὰρ ἀναλώσουσι τοὺς λίθους.
ἀλλὰ πορευώμεθα ἔνθεν ἡμῖν μικρόν τι παραδραμεῖν

weary, another advanced to the attack, and yet another; for it was not possible for them to surround the place in continuous line, because its sides were precipitous.

The moment Xenophon came up with the rearguard, consisting of both peltasts and hoplites, Cheirisophus said to him: "You have come in the nick of time; for the place must be captured; for the army has no provisions unless we capture this place." Then they took counsel together, and when Xenophon asked what it was that prevented their effecting an entrance, Cheirisophus replied: "There is this one way of approach which you see, but when one tries to go along by this way, they roll down stones from this overhanging rock; and whoever gets caught, is served in this fashion"—and with the words he pointed out men with their legs and ribs crushed. "But suppose they use up their stones," said Xenophon, "there is nothing then, is there, to hinder one's passing? For surely there is nothing we can see on the other side except a few men yonder, and only two or three of them are armed. Furthermore, as you can see for yourself, the distance we must traverse under attack is about a plethrum and a half. Now as much as a plethrum of that distance is covered with tall, scattered pine trees, and if men should stand behind them, what harm could they suffer either from the flying stones or the rolling ones? The remaining space, then, amounts to about half a plethrum, and that we must cross on the run at a moment when the stones stop coming." "But," said Cheirisophus, "the very moment we begin to push out toward the trees, the stones fly in quantities." "Precisely the thing we want," said Xenophon, "for they will use up their stones the sooner. But let us make our way to a spot from which we shall have only a short distance to run

ἔσται, ἢν δυνώμεθα, καὶ ἀπελθεῖν ῥᾴδιον, ἢν βουλώμεθα.

8 Ἐντεῦθεν ἐπορεύοντο Χειρίσοφος καὶ Ξενοφῶν καὶ
Καλλίμαχος Παρράσιος λοχαγός· τούτου γὰρ ἡ
ἡγεμονία ἦν τῶν ὀπισθοφυλάκων λοχαγῶν ἐκείνῃ τῇ
ἡ ἡμέρᾳ· οἱ δὲ ἄλλοι λοχαγοὶ ἔμενον ἐν τῷ ἀσφαλεῖ.
μετὰ τοῦτο οὖν ἀπῆλθον ὑπὸ τὰ δένδρα ἄνθρωποι ὡς
ἑβδομήκοντα, οὐχ ἁθρόοι ἀλλὰ καθ' ἕνα, ἕκαστος
9 φυλαττόμενος ὡς ἐδύνατο. Ἀγασίας δὲ ὁ Στυμφάλιος
καὶ Ἀριστώνυμος Μεθυδριεύς, καὶ οὗτοι τῶν ὀπισθοφυλάκων λοχαγοὶ ὄντες, καὶ ἄλλοι δέ, ἐφέστασαν ἔξω
τῶν δένδρων· οὐ γὰρ ἦν ἀσφαλῶς ἐν τοῖς δένδροις
10 ἑστάναι πλέον ἢ τὸν ἕνα λόχον. ἔνθα δὴ Καλλίμαχος
μηχανᾶταί τι· προέτρεχεν ἀπὸ τοῦ δένδρου ὑφ' ᾧ ἦν
αὐτὸς δύο ἢ τρία βήματα· ἐπεὶ δὲ οἱ λίθοι φέροιντο,
ἀνεχάζετο εὐπετῶς· ἐφ' ἑκάστης δὲ προδρομῆς πλέον
11 ἢ δέκα ἅμαξαι πετρῶν ἀνηλίσκοντο. ὁ δὲ Ἀγασίας ὡς
ὁρᾷ τὸν Καλλίμαχον ἃ ἐποίει, καὶ τὸ στράτευμα πᾶν
θεώμενον, δείσας μὴ οὐ πρῶτος παραδράμῃ εἰς τὸ
χωρίον, οὔτε[11] τὸν Ἀριστώνυμον πλησίον ὄντα παρακαλέσας οὐδὲ Εὐρύλοχον τὸν Λουσιέα ἑταίρους ὄντας
οὐδὲ ἄλλον οὐδένα χωρεῖ αὐτός, καὶ παρέρχεται
12 πάντας. ὁ δὲ Καλλίμαχος ὡς ὁρᾷ αὐτὸν παριόντα,
ἐπιλαμβάνεται αὐτοῦ τῆς ἴτυος· ἐν δὲ τούτῳ παραθεῖ
αὐτοὺς Ἀριστώνυμος Μεθυδριεύς, καὶ μετὰ τοῦτον

---

[11] οὔτε Hude/Peters: οὐ Gem., following Rehdantz: οὐδὲ
MSS., Mar.

across, in case we can do that, and an easy retreat, in case we choose to come back."

Thereupon Cheirisophus and Xenophon set forth, and with them Callimachus of Parrhasia, a captain; for he was the officer of the day in command of the captains of the rearguard; and the other captains remained in a place of safety. Following this lead about seventy men got out under shelter of the trees, not all together, but one by one, each protecting himself as best he could. But Agasias of Stymphalus and Aristonymus of Methydrium, who were likewise captains of the rearguard, and others also, took places outside the cover of the trees, for not more than the one company[46] could stand among them with safety. At that moment Callimachus hit upon a scheme: he would run forward two or three steps from the particular tree he was under and, when the stones began to fly, would draw back without any trouble; and at every one of his dashes more than ten cart-loads of stones would be used up. But when Agasias saw what Callimachus was doing, and with the whole army for spectators, he became fearful that he would not be the first to make the run across to the stronghold; so without asking Aristonymus or Eurylochus of Lusi (though the former was close by and both were his friends) or any one else to join him, he dashed forward himself and proceeded to go past everybody. Callimachus, however, when he saw him going by, seized the rim of his shield; and at that moment Aristonymus of Methydrium ran past both

---

[46] *viz.* Callimachus' company.

Εὐρύλοχος Λουσιεύς· πάντες γὰρ οὗτοι ἀντεποιοῦντο
ἀρετῆς καὶ διηγωνίζοντο πρὸς ἀλλήλους· καὶ οὕτως
ἐρίζοντες αἱροῦσι τὸ χωρίον. ὡς γὰρ ἅπαξ εἰσέδρα-
μον, οὐδεὶς ἔτι πέτρος ἄνωθεν ἠνέχθη.

13   Ἐνταῦθα δὴ δεινὸν ἦν θέαμα. αἱ γὰρ γυναῖκες
ῥίπτουσαι τὰ παιδία εἶτα καὶ ἑαυτὰς ἐπικατερρίπτουν,
καὶ οἱ ἄνδρες ὡσαύτως. ἔνθα δὴ καὶ Αἰνείας ὁ Στυμφάλιος λοχαγὸς ἰδών τινα θέοντα ὡς ῥίψοντα ἑαυτὸν
14   στολὴν ἔχοντα καλὴν ἐπιλαμβάνεται ὡς κωλύσων· ὁ
δὲ αὐτὸν ἐπισπᾶται, καὶ ἀμφότεροι ᾤχοντο κατὰ τῶν
πετρῶν φερόμενοι καὶ ἀπέθανον. ἐντεῦθεν ἄνθρωποι
μὲν πάνυ ὀλίγοι ἐλήφθησαν, βόες δὲ καὶ ὄνοι πολλοὶ
καὶ πρόβατα.

15   Ἐντεῦθεν ἐπορεύθησαν διὰ Χαλύβων σταθμοὺς
ἑπτὰ παρασάγγας πεντήκοντα. οὗτοι ἦσαν ὧν διῆλθον
ἀλκιμώτατοι, καὶ εἰς χεῖρας ᾖσαν. εἶχον δὲ θώρακας
λινοῦς μέχρι τοῦ ἤτρου, ἀντὶ δὲ τῶν πτερύγων σπάρτα
16   πυκνὰ ἐστραμμένα. εἶχον δὲ καὶ κνημῖδας καὶ κράνη
καὶ παρὰ τὴν ζώνην μαχαίριον ὅσον ξυήλην Λακω-
νικήν, ᾧ ἔσφαττον ὧν κρατεῖν δύναιντο, καὶ ἀποτέμ-
νοντες ἂν τὰς κεφαλὰς ἔχοντες ἐπορεύοντο, καὶ ᾖδον
καὶ ἐχόρευον ὁπότε οἱ πολέμιοι αὐτοὺς ὄψεσθαι ἔμελλον. εἶχον δὲ καὶ δόρυ ὡς πεντεκαίδεκα πήχεων μίαν
17   λόγχην ἔχον. οὗτοι ἐνέμενον ἐν τοῖς πολίσμασιν· ἐπεὶ
δὲ παρέλθοιεν οἱ Ἕλληνες, εἵποντο ἀεὶ μαχόμενοι.

---

[47] This spear is impossibly long. Note that the detail comes in
a section of ethnography, where exaggeration is not uncommon.

of them, and upon his heels Eurylochus of Lusi. For all these four were rivals in valour and continually striving with one another; and in thus contending they captured the stronghold, for once they had rushed in not a stone came down any more from above.

Then came a dreadful spectacle: the women threw their little children down from the rocks and then threw themselves down after them, and the men did likewise. In the midst of this scene Aeneas of Stymphalus, a captain, catching sight of a man, who was wearing a fine robe, running to cast himself down, seized hold of him in order to stop him; but the man dragged Aeneas along after him, and both went flying down the cliffs and were killed. In this stronghold only a very few human beings were captured, but they secured cattle and asses in large numbers and sheep.

From there they marched through the land of the Chalybians seven stages, fifty parasangs. These were the most valiant of all the peoples they passed through, and would come to hand-to-hand encounter. They had corselets of linen reaching down to the groin, with a thick fringe of plaited cords instead of flaps. They had greaves also and helmets, and at the girdle a knife about as long as a Laconian dagger, with which they would slaughter whomever they might be able to vanquish; then they would cut off their heads and carry them along on their march, and they would sing and dance whenever they were likely to be seen by the enemy. They carried also a spear about fifteen cubits long, with a point at only one end.[47] These people would stay within their towns, and when the Greeks had passed by, they would follow them, always skirmishing with

361

ᾤκουν δὲ ἐν τοῖς ὀχυροῖς, καὶ τὰ ἐπιτήδεια ἐν τούτοις
ἀνακεκομισμένοι ἦσαν· ὥστε μηδὲν λαμβάνειν αὐτόθεν τοὺς Ἕλληνας, ἀλλὰ διετράφησαν τοῖς κτήνεσιν
18 ἃ ἐκ τῶν Ταόχων ἔλαβον. ἐκ τούτου οἱ Ἕλληνες
ἀφίκοντο ἐπὶ τὸν Ἅρπασον ποταμόν, εὗρος τεττάρων
πλέθρων. ἐντεῦθεν ἐπορεύθησαν διὰ Σκυθηνῶν σταθμοὺς τέτταρας παρασάγγας εἴκοσι διὰ πεδίου εἰς
κώμας· ἐν αἷς ἔμειναν ἡμέρας τρεῖς καὶ ἐπεσιτίσαντο.
19   Ἐντεῦθεν διῆλθον σταθμοὺς τέτταρας παρασάγγας εἴκοσι πρὸς πόλιν μεγάλην καὶ εὐδαίμονα καὶ
οἰκουμένην ἣ ἐκαλεῖτο Γυμνιάς. ἐκ ταύτης ὁ τῆς
χώρας ἄρχων[12] τοῖς Ἕλλησιν ἡγεμόνα πέμπει, ὅπως
20 διὰ τῆς ἑαυτῶν πολεμίας χώρας ἄγοι αὐτούς. ἐλθὼν
δ᾽ ἐκεῖνος λέγει ὅτι ἄξει αὐτοὺς πέντε ἡμερῶν εἰς
χωρίον ὅθεν ὄψονται θάλατταν· εἰ δὲ μή, τεθνάναι
ἐπηγγείλατο. καὶ ἡγούμενος ἐπειδὴ ἐνέβαλεν εἰς τὴν
πολεμίαν, παρεκελεύετο αἴθειν καὶ φθείρειν τὴν χώ-
ραν· ᾧ καὶ δῆλον ἐγένετο ὅτι τούτου ἔνεκα ἔλθοι, οὐ
21 τῆς τῶν Ἑλλήνων εὐνοίας. καὶ ἀφικνοῦνται ἐπὶ τὸ
ὄρος τῇ πέμπτῃ ἡμέρᾳ· ὄνομα δὲ τῷ ὄρει ἦν Θήχης.
ἐπεὶ δὲ οἱ πρῶτοι ἐγένοντο ἐπὶ τοῦ ὄρους καὶ κατεῖδον
22 τὴν θάλατταν, κραυγὴ πολλὴ ἐγένετο. ἀκούσας δὲ ὁ
Ξενοφῶν καὶ οἱ ὀπισθοφύλακες ᾠήθησαν καὶ ἔμπροσθεν ἄλλους ἐπιτίθεσθαι πολεμίους· εἵποντο γὰρ
καὶ ὄπισθεν ἐκ τῆς καιομένης χώρας, καὶ αὐτῶν οἱ

___

[12] ὁ τῆς χώρας ἄρχων Gem., Hude/Peters, following
Schneider: τῆς χώρας ὁ ἄρχων MSS., which Mar. follows,
though marking the passage as corrupt.

them. Their dwellings were in strongholds, and therein they had stored away all their provisions; hence the Greeks could get nothing in this country, but they subsisted on the cattle they had taken from the Taochians. Leaving this land, the Greeks arrived at the Harpasus river, which was four plethra in width. From there they marched through the territory of the Scytheni four stages, twenty parasangs, over a level plain, and they arrived at some villages, and there remained for three days and collected provisions.

From there they journeyed four stages, twenty parasangs, to a large and prosperous inhabited city which was called Gymnias. From this city the ruler of the land sent the Greeks a guide, in order to lead them through territory that was hostile to his own. When the guide came, he said that he would lead them within five days to a place from which they could see the sea;[48] if he failed to do so, he was ready to accept death. Thus taking the lead, when he had brought them into the hostile territory, he kept urging them to spread abroad fire and ruin, thereby making it clear that it was with this end in view that he had come, and not out of good-will toward the Greeks. On the fifth day they did in fact reach the mountain; its name was Theches. Now as soon as the vanguard got to the top of the mountain and caught sight of the sea, a great shout went up. And when Xenophon and the rearguard heard it, they imagined that other enemies were attacking also in front; for enemies were also following behind them from the district that was in flames, and the rearguard had killed

[48] The Euxine, or modern Black Sea.

ὀπισθοφύλακες ἀπέκτεινάν τέ τινας καὶ ἐζώγρησαν
ἐνέδραν ποιησάμενοι, καὶ γέρρα ἔλαβον δασειῶν
23 βοῶν ὠμοβόϊνα ἀμφὶ τὰ εἴκοσιν. ἐπειδὴ δὲ ⟨ἡ⟩[13] βοὴ
πλείων τε ἐγίγνετο καὶ ἐγγύτερον καὶ οἱ ἀεὶ ἐπιόντες
ἔθεον δρόμῳ ἐπὶ τοὺς ἀεὶ βοῶντας καὶ πολλῷ μεῖζων
ἐγίγνετο ἡ βοὴ ὅσῳ δὴ πλείους ἐγίγνοντο, ἐδόκει δὴ
24 μεῖζόν τι εἶναι τῷ Ξενοφῶντι, καὶ ἀναβὰς ἐφ᾽ ἵππον
καὶ Λύκιον καὶ τοὺς ἱππέας ἀναλαβὼν παρεβοήθει·
καὶ τάχα δὴ ἀκούουσι βοώντων τῶν στρατιωτῶν
Θάλαττα θάλαττα καὶ παρεγγυώντων. ἔνθα δὴ ἔθεον
ἅπαντες καὶ οἱ ὀπισθοφύλακες, καὶ τὰ ὑποζύγια
25 ἠλαύνετο καὶ οἱ ἵπποι. ἐπεὶ δὲ ἀφίκοντο πάντες ἐπὶ τὸ
ἄκρον, ἐνταῦθα δὴ περιέβαλλον ἀλλήλους καὶ στρατηγοὺς καὶ λοχαγοὺς δακρύοντες. καὶ ἐξαπίνης ὅτου
δὴ παρεγγυήσαντος οἱ στρατιῶται φέρουσι λίθους καὶ
26 ποιοῦσι κολωνὸν μέγαν. ἐνταῦθα ἀνετίθεσαν δερμά-
των πλῆθος ὠμοβοΐνων καὶ βακτηρίας καὶ τὰ αἰχμάλωτα γέρρα, καὶ ὁ ἡγεμὼν αὐτός τε κατέτεμνε τὰ
27 γέρρα καὶ τοῖς ἄλλοις διεκελεύετο. μετὰ ταῦτα τὸν
ἡγεμόνα οἱ Ἕλληνες ἀποπέμπουσι δῶρα δόντες ἀπὸ
κοινοῦ ἵππον καὶ φιάλην ἀργυρᾶν καὶ σκευὴν Περ-
σικὴν καὶ δαρεικοὺς δέκα· ᾔτει δὲ μάλιστα τοὺς
δακτυλίους, καὶ ἔλαβε πολλοὺς παρὰ τῶν στρατιωτῶν.
κώμην δὲ δείξας αὐτοῖς οὗ σκηνήσουσι καὶ τὴν ὁδὸν
ἣν πορεύσονται εἰς Μάκρωνας, ἐπεὶ ἑσπέρα ἐγένετο,

[13] ἡ added by Krüger.

some of them and captured others by setting an ambush, and had also taken about twenty wicker shields covered with raw, shaggy ox-hides. But as the shout kept getting louder and nearer, as the successive ranks that came up all began to run at full speed toward the ranks ahead that were one after another joining in the shout, and as the shout kept growing far louder as the number of men grew steadily greater, it became quite clear to Xenophon that here was something of unusual importance; so he mounted a horse, took with him Lycius and the cavalry, and pushed ahead to lend aid; and in a moment they heard the soldiers shouting, "The Sea! The Sea!" and passing the word along. Then all the troops of the rearguard likewise broke into a run, and the pack animals began racing ahead and the horses. And when all had reached the summit, then indeed they fell to embracing one another, and generals and captains as well, with tears in their eyes. And on a sudden, at the bidding of some one or other, the soldiers began to bring stones and to build a great cairn. Thereon they placed as offerings a quantity of raw ox-hides and walking-sticks and the cap-tured wicker shields; and the guide not only cut these shields to pieces himself, but urged the others to do so.[49] After this the Greeks dismissed the guide with gifts from the common stock—a horse, a silver cup, a Persian dress, and ten darics; but what he particularly asked the men for was their rings, and he got a considerable number of them. Then he showed them a village to encamp in and the road they were to follow to the country of the Macronians, and,

[49] Still trying to fulfil his real mission of harming his people's enemies. Cf. §§19–20 above.

ᾤχετο τῆς νυκτὸς ἀπιών.

VIII. Ἐντεῦθεν δ᾽ ἐπορεύθησαν οἱ Ἕλληνες διὰ
Μακρώνων σταθμοὺς τρεῖς παρασάγγας δέκα. τῇ
πρώτῃ δὲ ἡμέρᾳ ἀφίκοντο ἐπὶ τὸν ποταμὸν ὃς ὥριζε
2 τήν τε τῶν Μακρώνων καὶ τὴν τῶν Σκυθηνῶν. εἶχον
δ᾽ ὑπὲρ δεξιῶν χωρίον οἷον χαλεπώτατον καὶ ἐξ ἀρι-
στερᾶς ἄλλον ποταμόν, εἰς ὃν ἐνέβαλλεν ὁ ὁρίζων, δι᾽
οὗ ἔδει διαβῆναι. ἦν δὲ οὗτος δασὺς δένδρεσι παχέσι
μὲν οὔ, πυκνοῖς δέ. ταῦτα ἐπεὶ προσῆλθον οἱ Ἕλληνες
ἔκοπτον, σπεύδοντες ἐκ τοῦ χωρίου ὡς τάχιστα ἐξελ-
3 θεῖν. οἱ δὲ Μάκρωνες ἔχοντες γέρρα καὶ λόγχας καὶ
τριχίνους χιτῶνας κατ᾽ ἀντιπέρας τῆς διαβάσεως
παρατεταγμένοι ἦσαν καὶ ἀλλήλοις διεκελεύοντο καὶ
λίθους εἰς τὸν ποταμὸν ἔρριπτον· ἐξικνοῦντο δὲ οὒ οὐδ᾽
ἔβλαπτον οὐδέν.

4 Ἔνθα δὴ προσέρχεται Ξενοφῶντι τῶν πελταστῶν
ἀνὴρ Ἀθήνησι φάσκων δεδουλευκέναι, λέγων ὅτι
γιγνώσκοι τὴν φωνὴν τῶν ἀνθρώπων. καὶ οἶμαι, ἔφη,
ἐμὴν ταύτην πατρίδα εἶναι· καὶ εἰ μή τι κωλύει, ἐθέλω
5 αὐτοῖς διαλεχθῆναι. Ἀλλ᾽ οὐδὲν κωλύει, ἔφη, ἀλλὰ
διαλέγου καὶ μάθε πρῶτον τίνες εἰσίν. οἱ δ᾽ εἶπον
ἐρωτήσαντος ὅτι Μάκρωνες. Ἐρώτα τοίνυν, ἔφη, αὐτοὺς τί ἀντιτέτακται καὶ χρῄζουσιν ἡμῖν πολέμιοι
6 εἶναι. οἱ δ᾽ ἀπεκρίναντο Ὅτι καὶ ὑμεῖς[14] ἐπὶ τὴν
ἡμετέραν χώραν ἔρχεσθε. λέγειν ἐκέλευον οἱ στρατη-

---

[14] καὶ ὑμεῖς some MSS., Hude/Peters, Mar.: ὑμεῖς corrector
of one MS., Gem.

as soon as evening came, took his departure during the night.

VIII. From there the Greeks marched through the country of the Macronians three stages, ten parasangs. On the first of these days they reached the river which separated the territory of the Macronians from that of the Scytheni. There they had on the right, above them, an exceedingly difficult bit of ground, and on the left another river, into which the boundary stream that they had to cross emptied. Now this stream was fringed with trees, not large ones, but of thick growth, and when the Greeks came up, they began felling them in their haste to get out of the place as speedily as possible. But the Macronians, armed with wicker shields and lances and hair tunics, were drawn up in line of battle opposite the place where the Greeks must cross, and they were cheering one another on and throwing stones into the stream; but they never reached the Greeks or did them any harm.

At this moment one of the peltasts came up to Xenophon, a man who said that he had been a slave at Athens, saying that he knew the language of these people; "I think," he went on, "that this is my native country, and if there is nothing to hinder, I should like to have a talk with them." "Well, there is nothing to hinder," said Xenophon; "so talk with them, and learn, to begin with, who they are." In reply to his inquiry they said, "Macronians." "Well, then," said Xenophon, "ask them why they are arrayed against us and want to be our enemies." They replied, "Because you are coming against our land." The generals

γοὶ ὅτι οὐ κακῶς γε ποιήσοντες, ἀλλὰ βασιλεῖ πολε-
μήσαντες ἀπερχόμεθα εἰς τὴν Ἑλλάδα, καὶ ἐπὶ θάλατ-
7 ταν βουλόμεθα ἀφικέσθαι. ἠρώτων ἐκεῖνοι εἰ δοῖεν ἂν
τούτων τὰ πιστά. οἱ δ' ἔφασαν καὶ δοῦναι καὶ λαβεῖν
ἐθέλειν. ἐντεῦθεν διδόασιν οἱ Μάκρωνες βαρβαρικὴν
λόγχην τοῖς Ἕλλησιν, οἱ δὲ Ἕλληνες ἐκείνοις Ἑλλη-
νικήν· ταῦτα γὰρ ἔφασαν πιστὰ εἶναι· θεοὺς δ' ἐπε-
μαρτύραντο ἀμφότεροι.

8 Μετὰ δὲ τὰ πιστὰ εὐθὺς οἱ Μάκρωνες τὰ δένδρα
συνεξέκοπτον τήν τε ὁδὸν ὡδοποίουν ὡς διαβιβάσον-
τες ἐν μέσοις ἀναμεμειγμένοι τοῖς Ἕλλησι, καὶ ἀγορὰν οἵαν ἐδύναντο παρεῖχον, καὶ παρήγαγον ἐν τρισὶν
ἡμέραις ἕως ἐπὶ τὰ Κόλχων ὅρια κατέστησαν τοὺς
9 Ἕλληνας. ἐνταῦθα ἦν ὄρος μέγα, προσβατὸν δέ·[15] καὶ
ἐπὶ τούτου οἱ Κόλχοι παρατεταγμένοι ἦσαν. καὶ τὸ
μὲν πρῶτον οἱ Ἕλληνες ἀντιπαρετάξαντο φάλαγγα,
ὡς οὕτως ἄξοντες πρὸς τὸ ὄρος· ἔπειτα δὲ ἔδοξε τοῖς
στρατηγοῖς βουλεύσασθαι συλλεγεῖσιν ὅπως ὡς κάλλιστα ἀγωνιοῦνται.

10 Ἔλεξεν οὖν Ξενοφῶν ὅτι δοκεῖ παύσαντας τὴν
φάλαγγα λόχους ὀρθίους ποιῆσαι· ἡ μὲν γὰρ φάλαγξ
διασπασθήσεται εὐθύς· τῇ μὲν γὰρ ἄνοδον τῇ δὲ
εὔοδον εὑρήσομεν τὸ ὄρος· καὶ εὐθὺς τοῦτο ἀθυμίαν
ποιήσει ὅταν τεταγμένοι εἰς φάλαγγα ταύτην δι-

---

[15] μέγα, προσβατὸν δέ some MSS., Hude/Peters, Mar.:
μέγα corrector of one MS., Gem.

directed the man to say, "We have not come to do you any harm whatever, but we have been at war with the King and are on our way back to Greece, and we want to reach the sea." The Macronians asked whether they would give pledges to this effect. They replied that they were ready both to give and to receive pledges. Thereupon the Macronians gave the Greeks a barbarian lance and the Greeks gave them a Greek lance, for the Macronians declared that these were pledges; and both sides called the gods to witness.

After this exchange of pledges the Macronians at once began to help the Greeks cut down the trees and to build the road in order to get them across, mingling freely with the Greeks; and they supplied as good a market as they could, and conducted the Greeks on their way for three days, until they brought them to the boundaries of the Colchians. At this place was a great mountain, but accessible; and upon this mountain the Colchians were drawn up in line of battle. At first the Greeks formed an opposing line of battle, with the intention of advancing in this way upon the mountain, but afterwards the generals decided to gather together and take counsel as to how they could best make the contest.

Xenophon accordingly said that in his opinion they should give up the line of battle and form the companies in column.[50] "For the line," he continued, "will be broken up at once; for we shall find the mountain hard to traverse at some points and easy at others; and the immediate result will be discouragement, when men who are formed in line

[50] See vi. 6, and note. Of course it is the opposite movement that is now in contemplation.

11 εσπασμένην ὁρῶσιν. ἔπειτα ἢν μὲν ἐπὶ πολλοὺς
τεταγμένοι προσάγωμεν, περιττεύσουσιν ἡμῶν οἱ
πολέμιοι καὶ τοῖς περιττοῖς χρήσονται ὅ τι ἂν βού-
λωνται· ἐὰν δὲ ἐπ᾽ ὀλίγων τεταγμένοι ἴωμεν, οὐδὲν ἂν
εἴη θαυμαστὸν εἰ διακοπείη ἡμῶν ἡ φάλαγξ ὑπὸ
ἀθρόων καὶ βελῶν καὶ ἀνθρώπων πολλῶν ἐμπεσόν-
των· εἰ δέ πη τοῦτο ἔσται, τῇ ὅλῃ φάλαγγι κακὸν
12 ἔσται. ἀλλά μοι δοκεῖ ὀρθίους τοὺς λόχους ποιησαμένους τοσοῦτον χωρίον κατασχεῖν διαλιπόντας τοῖς
λόχοις ὅσον ἔξω τοὺς ἐσχάτους λόχους γενέσθαι τῶν
πολεμίων κεράτων· καὶ οὕτως ἐσόμεθα τῆς τε τῶν
πολεμίων φάλαγγος ἔξω οἱ ἔσχατοι λόχοι, καὶ ὀρθίους ἄγοντες οἱ κράτιστοι ἡμῶν πρῶτοι προσίασιν,
ᾗ τε ἂν εὔοδον ᾖ, ταύτῃ ἕκαστος ἄξει ὁ λοχαγός.[16]
13 καὶ εἴς τε τὸ διαλεῖπον οὐ ῥᾴδιον ἔσται τοῖς πολεμίοις
εἰσελθεῖν ἔνθεν καὶ ἔνθεν λόχων ὄντων, διακόψαι τε
οὐ ῥᾴδιον ἔσται λόχον ὄρθιον προσιόντα· ἐάν τέ τις
πιέζηται τῶν λόχων, ὁ πλησίον βοηθήσει. ἤν τε εἷς
πη δυνηθῇ τῶν λόχων ἐπὶ τὸ ἄκρον ἀναβῆναι, οὐδεὶς
μηκέτι μείνῃ τῶν πολεμίων.
14 Ταῦτα ἔδοξε, καὶ ἐποίουν ὀρθίους τοὺς λόχους.
Ξενοφῶν δὲ ἀπιὼν ἐπὶ τὸ εὐώνυμον ἀπὸ τοῦ δεξιοῦ
ἔλεγε τοῖς στρατιώταις· Ἄνδρες, οὗτοί εἰσιν οὓς ὁρᾶτε

---

[16] ὁ λοχαγός Gem., Hude/Peters following Krüger: the MSS.
have ὁ λόχος, which Mar. retains but brackets.

of battle see the line broken up. Furthermore, if we advance upon them formed in a line many ranks deep, the enemy will outflank us, and will use their outflanking wing for whatever purpose they please; on the other hand, if we advance in a line a few ranks deep, it would be nothing surprising if our line should be cut through by a multitude both of missiles and men falling upon us in a mass; and if this happens at any point, it will be bad for the whole line. But it seems to me we should form the companies in column and, by leaving spaces between them, cover enough ground so that the outermost companies should get beyond the enemy's wings; in this way not only shall we, the outermost units, outflank the enemy's line, but advancing in column our best men will be in the van of the attack, and wherever it is good going, there each captain will lead forward his men. And it will not be easy for the enemy to push into the space between the columns when there are companies on this side and that, and not any easier for him to cut through a company that is advancing in column. Again, if any one of the companies is hard pressed, its neighbour will come to its aid; and if one single company can somehow climb to the summit, not a man of the enemy will stand any longer."

This plan was decided upon, and they proceeded to form the companies in column. And as Xenophon was going back from the right wing to the left,[51] he said to the troops: "Soldiers, these men yonder whom you see are the

---

[51] Cheirisophus was commander of the van, Xenophon of the rear. The van of an army on the march became the right wing of the line of battle and the rear the left wing. It was at Cheirisophus' post, on the right, that the council was held.

μόνοι ἔτι ἡμῖν ἐμποδὼν τὸ μὴ ἤδη εἶναι ἔνθα πάλαι
σπεύδομεν· τούτους, ἤν πως δυνώμεθα, καὶ ὠμοὺς δεῖ
καταφαγεῖν.

15 Ἐπεὶ δ' ἐν ταῖς χώραις ἕκαστοι ἐγένοντο καὶ τοὺς
λόχους ὀρθίους ἐποιήσαντο, ἐγένοντο μὲν λόχοι τῶν
ὁπλιτῶν ἀμφὶ τοὺς ὀγδοήκοντα, ὁ δὲ λόχος ἕκαστος
σχεδὸν εἰς τοὺς ἑκατόν· τοὺς δὲ πελταστὰς καὶ τοὺς
τοξότας τριχῇ ἐποιήσαντο, τοὺς μὲν τοῦ εὐωνύμου
ἔξω, τοὺς δὲ τοῦ δεξιοῦ, τοὺς δὲ κατὰ μέσον, σχεδὸν

16 ἑξακοσίους ἑκάστους. ἐκ τούτου παρηγγύησαν οἱ
στρατηγοὶ εὔχεσθαι· εὐξάμενοι δὲ καὶ παιανίσαντες
ἐπορεύοντο. καὶ Χειρίσοφος μὲν καὶ Ξενοφῶν καὶ οἱ
σὺν αὐτοῖς πελτασταὶ τῆς τῶν πολεμίων φάλαγγος

17 ἔξω γενόμενοι ἐπορεύοντο· οἱ δὲ πολέμιοι ὡς εἶδον
αὐτούς, ἀντιπαραθέοντες οἱ μὲν ἐπὶ τὸ δεξιὸν οἱ δὲ ἐπὶ
τὸ εὐώνυμον διεσπάσθησαν, καὶ πολὺ τῆς αὐτῶν

18 φάλαγγος ἐν τῷ μέσῳ κενὸν ἐποίησαν. ἰδόντες δὲ
αὐτοὺς διχάζοντας[17] οἱ κατὰ τὸ Ἀρκαδικὸν πελτασταί,
ὧν ἦρχεν Αἰσχίνης ὁ Ἀκαρνάν, νομίσαντες φεύγειν
ἀνακραγόντες ἔθεον· καὶ οὗτοι πρῶτοι ἐπὶ τὸ ὄρος
ἀναβαίνουσι· συνεφείπετο δὲ αὐτοῖς καὶ τὸ Ἀρκαδικὸν

19 ὁπλιτικόν, ὧν ἦρχε Κλεάνωρ ὁ Ὀρχομένιος. οἱ δὲ

---

[17] ἰδόντες ... διχάζοντας omitted by corrector of one MS.

---

[52] A phrase as old as Homer, *Iliad* IV. 35–36, XXII. 346–7, XXIV
212–13. Cf. *Hell*. III. iii. 6.

only ones who still stand in the way of our being forthwith at the place we have long been striving to reach; if we possibly can, we must simply eat these fellows raw."[52]

When the officers had got to their several positions and had formed their companies in column, the result was about eighty companies of hoplites with each company numbering close upon one hundred;[53] the peltasts and the bowmen, on the other hand, they formed in three divisions, one beyond the left wing of the hoplites, the second beyond the right, and the third in the centre, each division numbering about six hundred men.[54] After this the generals passed along the order to offer prayer, and when they had prayed and sung the paean they set forth. Now Cheirisophus and Xenophon[55] and the peltasts with them got beyond the wings of the enemy's line in their advance; and when the enemy saw this, they ran out, some to the right and others to the left, to confront them, with the result that their line was pulled apart and a large portion of it in the centre was left deserted. Then, having noticed the enemy dividing, the peltasts of the Arcadian division, who were commanded by Aeschines the Acarnanian, got the idea that they were in flight, set up a shout and began to run; and they were the first to reach the summit of the mountain, while following close after them came the Arcadian division of hoplites, under the command of Cleanor of Orchomenus. As for the enemy, once the peltasts began

[53] A total of 8000 as compared with an original strength of 11,700.   [54] One thousand eight hundred as compared with an original 2300.

[55] On the right and left wings respectively. See note on §14 above.

πολέμιοι, ὡς ἤρξαντο θεῖν, οὐκέτι ἔστησαν, ἀλλὰ
φυγῇ ἄλλος ἄλλῃ ἐτράπετο.

Οἱ δὲ Ἕλληνες ἀναβάντες ἐστρατοπεδεύοντο ἐν
20 πολλαῖς κώμαις καὶ τἀπιτήδεια πολλὰ ἐχούσαις. καὶ
τὰ μὲν ἄλλα οὐδὲν ὅ τι καὶ ἐθαύμασαν· τὰ δὲ σμήνη
πολλὰ ἦν αὐτόθι, καὶ τῶν κηρίων ὅσοι ἔφαγον τῶν
στρατιωτῶν πάντες ἄφρονές τε ἐγίγνοντο καὶ ἤμουν
καὶ κάτω διεχώρει αὐτοῖς καὶ ὀρθὸς οὐδεὶς ἐδύνατο
ἵστασθαι, ἀλλ' οἱ μὲν ὀλίγον ἐδηδοκότες σφόδρα
μεθύουσιν ἐῴκεσαν, οἱ δὲ πολὺ μαινομένοις, οἱ δὲ καὶ
21 ἀποθνήσκουσιν. ἔκειντο δὲ οὕτω πολλοὶ ὥσπερ τρο-
πῆς γεγενημένης, καὶ πολλὴ ἦν ἀθυμία. τῇ δ' ὑστεραίᾳ ἀπέθανε μὲν οὐδείς, ἀμφὶ δὲ τὴν αὐτήν που ὥραν
ἀνεφρόνουν· τρίτῃ δὲ καὶ τετάρτῃ ἀνίσταντο ὥσπερ
ἐκ φαρμακοποσίας.

22 Ἐντεῦθεν δ' ἐπορεύθησαν δύο σταθμοὺς παρασάγγας ἑπτά, καὶ ἦλθον ἐπὶ θάλατταν εἰς Τραπεζοῦντα
πόλιν Ἑλληνίδα οἰκουμένην ἐν τῷ Εὐξείνῳ Πόντῳ,
Σινωπέων ἀποικίαν ἐν τῇ Κόλχων χώρᾳ. ἐνταῦθα
ἔμειναν ἡμέρας ἀμφὶ τὰς τριάκοντα ἐν ταῖς τῶν Κόλ-
23 χων κώμαις· κἀντεῦθεν ὁρμώμενοι ἐλῄζοντο τὴν Κολ-
χίδα. ἀγορὰν δὲ παρεῖχον τῷ στρατοπέδῳ Τραπεζούντιοι, καὶ ἐδέξαντό τε τοὺς Ἕλληνας καὶ ξένια ἔδοσαν
24 βοῦς καὶ ἄλφιτα καὶ οἶνον. συνδιεπράττοντο δὲ καὶ
ὑπὲρ τῶν πλησίον Κόλχων τῶν ἐν τῷ πεδίῳ μάλιστα
οἰκούντων, καὶ ξένια καὶ παρ' ἐκείνων ἦλθον βόες.

to run they no longer stood their ground, but betook themselves here and there in flight.

After accomplishing the ascent the Greeks took up quarters in numerous villages, which contained provisions in abundance. Now for the most part there was nothing here which they really found strange; but the swarms of bees in the neighbourhood were numerous, and the soldiers who ate of the honey all went off their heads, and suffered from vomiting and diarrhoea, and not one of them could stand up, but those who had eaten a little were like people exceedingly drunk, while those who had eaten a great deal seemed like crazy, or even, in some cases, dying men.[56] So they lay there in great numbers as though the army had suffered a defeat, and great despondency prevailed. On the next day, however, no one had died, and at approximately the same hour as they had eaten the honey they began to come to their senses; and on the third or fourth day they got up, as if from a drugging.

From there they marched two stages, seven parasangs, and reached the sea at Trapezus, an inhabited Greek city on the Euxine Sea, a colony of the Sinopeans in the territory of Colchis. There they remained about thirty days in the villages of the Colchians, and from these as a base plundered Colchis. And the Trapezuntians supplied a market for the army, received the Greeks kindly, and gave them oxen, barley-meal, and wine as gifts of hospitality. They likewise took part in negotiations with the Greeks in behalf of the near-by Colchians, who dwelt for the most part on the plain, and from these people also the Greeks received hospitable gifts of oxen.

[56] Cf. Dioscorides, *Materia Medica* II. 82.

25 Μετὰ δὲ τοῦτο τὴν θυσίαν ἣν ηὔξαντο παρεσκευ-
άζοντο· ἦλθον δ' αὐτοῖς ἱκανοὶ βόες ἀποθῦσαι τῷ Διὶ
τῷ σωτῆρι καὶ τῷ Ἡρακλεῖ ἡγεμόσυνα καὶ τοῖς
ἄλλοις δὲ θεοῖς ἃ ηὔξαντο. ἐποίησαν δὲ καὶ ἀγῶνα
γυμνικὸν ἐν τῷ ὄρει ἔνθαπερ ἐσκήνουν. εἵλοντο δὲ
Δρακόντιον Σπαρτιάτην, ὃς ἔφυγε παῖς ἔτι ὢν οἴκοθεν,
παῖδα ἄκων κατακανὼν ξυήλῃ πατάξας, δρόμου τ'
26 ἐπιμεληθῆναι καὶ τοῦ ἀγῶνος προστατῆσαι. ἐπειδὴ δὲ
ἡ θυσία ἐγένετο, τὰ δέρματα παρέδοσαν τῷ Δρακον-
τίῳ, καὶ ἡγεῖσθαι ἐκέλευον ὅπου τὸν δρόμον πεποιηκὼς εἴη. ὁ δὲ δείξας οὗπερ ἑστηκότες ἐτύγχανον·
Οὗτος ὁ λόφος, ἔφη, κάλλιστος τρέχειν ὅπου ἄν τις
βούληται. Πῶς οὖν, ἔφασαν, δυνήσονται παλαίειν ἐν
σκληρῷ καὶ δασεῖ οὕτως; ὁ δ' εἶπε· Μᾶλλόν τι
27 ἀνιάσεται ὁ καταπεσών. ἠγωνίζοντο δὲ παῖδες μὲν
στάδιον τῶν αἰχμαλώτων οἱ πλεῖστοι, δόλιχον δὲ
Κρῆτες πλείους ἢ ἑξήκοντα ἔθεον πάλην δὲ καὶ πυγ-
μὴν καὶ παγκράτιον,[18] καὶ καλὴ θέα ἐγένετο. πολλοὶ
γὰρ κατέβησαν καὶ ἄτε θεωμένων τῶν ἑταίρων πολλὴ
28 φιλονικία ἐγίγνετο. ἔθεον δὲ καὶ ἵπποι καὶ ἔδει αὐτοὺς
κατὰ τοῦ πρανοῦς ἐλάσαντας ἐν τῇ θαλάττῃ ἀνα-

[18] After παγκράτιον Peters accepts Schenkl's supplement
καί: one MS. has ἕτεροι, which Mar. prints, but regards as corrupt:
Gem. reads Ἀρκάδες, following Matthias.

---

[57] See III. ii. 9.   [58] The hides of sacrificial victims, which
were to be offered as prizes in the games. Cf. *Iliad*, XXII. 159.
[59] The regular short race in the Greek games.

After this they made ready the sacrifice which they had vowed;[57] and a sufficient number of oxen had come to them so that they could pay their thank-offerings to Zeus the Deliverer, to Heracles for guidance, and to the other gods according as they had vowed. They instituted also athletic games on the mountain side, just where they were encamped; and they chose Dracontius, a Spartan, who had been exiled from home as a boy because he had accidentally killed another boy with the stroke of a dagger, to look out for a race-course and to act as manager of the games. When, accordingly, the sacrifice had been completed, they turned over the hides[58] to Dracontius and bade him lead the way to the place he had fixed upon for his race-course. He pointed out the precise spot where they chanced to be standing, and said, "This hill is superb for running, wherever you please." "How, then," they said, "can men wrestle on ground so hard and overgrown as this is?" And he replied, "The one that is thrown will get hurt a bit more." The events were, a stadium race[59] for boys, most of them belonging to the captives, a long race,[60] in which more than sixty Cretans took part, wrestling, boxing, and the pancratium;[61] and it made a fine spectacle;[62] for there were a great many entries and, inasmuch as the comrades of the contestants were looking on, there was a great deal of rivalry. There were horseraces also, and the riders had to drive their horses down the steep slope, turn them around on

60 The δόλιχος seems to have varied from six to twenty-four stadia.

61 A combination of boxing and wrestling.

62 This is the main point: the ordered, successful army holding athletic games is a thing of beauty. Cf. *Hell*. III. iv. 16 ff.

στρέψαντας πάλιν ἄνω πρὸς τὸν βωμὸν ἄγειν. καὶ
κάτω μὲν οἱ πολλοὶ ἐκυλινδοῦντο· ἄνω δὲ πρὸς τὸ
ἰσχυρῶς ὄρθιον μόγις βάδην ἐπορεύοντο οἱ ἵπποι·
ἔνθα πολλὴ κραυγὴ καὶ γέλως καὶ παρακέλευσις
ἐγίγνετο.

the shore, and bring them back up again to the altar.[63] And on the way down most of the horses rolled over and over, while on the way up, against the exceedingly steep incline, they found it hard to keep on at a walk; so there was much shouting and laughter and cheering.

[63] The altar on which the sacrifices had been offered served as a starting-point for the races.

E

2   I.[1] Ἐκ δὲ τούτου συνελθόντες ἐβουλεύοντο περὶ τῆς
λοιπῆς πορείας· ἀνέστη δὲ πρῶτος Λέων Θούριος καὶ
ἔλεξεν ὧδε. Ἐγὼ μὲν τοίνυν, ἔφη, ὦ ἄνδρες, ἀπείρηκα
ἤδη συσκευαζόμενος καὶ βαδίζων καὶ τρέχων καὶ τὰ
ὅπλα φέρων καὶ ἐν τάξει ἰὼν καὶ φυλακὰς φυλάττων
καὶ μαχόμενος, ἐπιθυμῶ δὲ ἤδη παυσάμενος τούτων
τῶν πόνων, ἐπεὶ θάλατταν ἔχομεν, πλεῖν τὸ λοιπὸν καὶ
ἐκταθεὶς ὥσπερ Ὀδυσσεὺς ἀφικέσθαι εἰς τὴν Ἑλλά-
3 δα. ταῦτα ἀκούσαντες οἱ στρατιῶται ἀνεθορύβησαν
ὡς εὖ λέγοι· καὶ ἄλλος ταὐτὰ ἔλεγε, καὶ πάντες οἱ
παριόντες. ἔπειτα δὲ Χειρίσοφος ἀνέστη καὶ εἶπεν
4   ὧδε. Φίλος μοί ἐστιν, ὦ ἄνδρες, Ἀναξίβιος, ναυαρχῶν
δὲ καὶ τυγχάνει. ἢν οὖν πέμψητέ με, οἴομαι ἂν ἐλθεῖν

---

[1] The summary prefixed to Book V (see note on II. i. 1) reads:
Ὅσα μὲν δὴ ἐν τῇ ἀναβάσει τῇ μετὰ Κύρου ἔπραξαν οἱ
Ἕλληνες, καὶ ἐν τῇ πορείᾳ τῇ μέχρι ἐπὶ θάλατταν τὴν ἐν τῷ
Εὐξείνῳ Πόντῳ, καὶ ὡς εἰς Τραπεζοῦντα πόλιν Ἑλληνίδα
ἀφίκοντο, καὶ ὡς ἀπέθυσαν ἃ ηὔξαντο σωτήρια θύσειν ἔνθα
πρῶτον εἰς φιλίαν γῆν ἀφίκοιντο, ἐν τῷ πρόσθεν λόγῳ δεδήλωται.

---

[1] Summary (see note to text): The preceding narrative has

BOOK V

I.[1] After this they gathered together and proceeded to take counsel in regard to the remainder of their journey; and the first man to get up was Leon of Thurii, who spoke as follows: "Well, I, for my part, gentlemen," he said, "am tired by this time of packing up and walking and running and carrying my arms and marching in line and standing guard and fighting, and what I long for now is to be rid of these toils, since we have the sea, and to sail the rest of the way, and so reach Greece stretched out on my back, like Odysseus."[2] Upon hearing these words the soldiers shouted out that he was quite right; and another man said the same thing, and in fact all who rose to speak. Then Cheirisophus got up and spoke as follows: "I have a friend Anaxibius, gentlemen, and he happens also to be Admiral.[3] So if you will send me to him, I presume I can bring back

---

described all that the Greeks did on their upward march with Cyrus and on their journey to the shore of the Euxine Sea, how they arrived at the Greek city of Trapezus, and how they paid the thank offerings for deliverance which they had vowed to sacrifice at the place where they should first reach a friendly land.

[2] See *Odyssey*, XIII. 75–118.

[3] Not "an" admiral, for ναύαρχος was the distinctive title of the commanding officer of the Lacedaemonian fleet. See, e.g., *Hell*. I. v. 1 ff.

καὶ τριήρεις ἔχων καὶ πλοῖα τὰ ἡμᾶς ἄξοντα· ὑμεῖς δὲ
εἴπερ πλεῖν βούλεσθε, περιμένετε ἔστ᾽ ἂν ἐγὼ ἔλθω·
ἥξω δὲ ταχέως. ἀκούσαντες ταῦτα οἱ στρατιῶται
ἤσθησάν τε καὶ ἐψηφίσαντο πλεῖν αὐτὸν ὡς τάχιστα.

5   Μετὰ τοῦτον Ξενοφῶν ἀνέστη καὶ ἔλεξεν ὧδε. Χειρίσοφος μὲν δὴ ἐπὶ πλοῖα στέλλεται, ἡμεῖς δὲ ἀνα-
μενοῦμεν. ὅσα μοι οὖν δοκεῖ καιρὸς εἶναι ποιεῖν ἐν τῇ
6 μονῇ, ταῦτα ἐρῶ. πρῶτον μὲν τὰ ἐπιτήδεια δεῖ πορίζεσθαι ἐκ τῆς πολεμίας· οὔτε γὰρ ἀγορὰ ἔστιν ἱκανὴ
οὔτε ὅτου ὠνησόμεθα εὐπορία εἰ μὴ ὀλίγοις τισίν· ἡ
δὲ χώρα πολεμία· κίνδυνος οὖν πολλοὺς ἀπόλλυσθαι,
ἢν ἀμελῶς τε καὶ ἀφυλάκτως πορεύησθε ἐπὶ τὰ ἐπιτή-
7 δεια. ἀλλά μοι δοκεῖ σὺν προνομαῖς λαμβάνειν τὰ
ἐπιτήδεια, ἄλλως δὲ μὴ πλανᾶσθαι, ὡς σῴζησθε, ἡμᾶς
δὲ τούτων ἐπιμελεῖσθαι. ἔδοξε ταῦτα.

8   Ἔτι τοίνυν ἀκούσατε καὶ τάδε. ἐπὶ λείαν γὰρ ὑμῶν
ἐκπορεύσονταί τινες. οἴομαι οὖν βέλτιστον εἶναι ἡμῖν
εἰπεῖν τὸν μέλλοντα ἐξιέναι, φράζειν δὲ καὶ ὅποι, ἵνα
καὶ τὸ πλῆθος εἰδῶμεν τῶν ἐξιόντων καὶ τῶν μενόντων
καὶ συμπαρασκευάζωμεν, ἐάν τι δέῃ, κἂν βοηθῆσαί
τισι καιρὸς ᾖ, εἰδῶμεν ὅποι δεήσει βοηθεῖν, καὶ ἐάν
τις τῶν ἀπειροτέρων ἐγχειρῇ ποι, συμβουλεύωμεν πειρώμενοι εἰδέναι τὴν δύναμιν ἐφ᾽ οὓς ἂν ἴωσιν. ἔδοξε
καὶ ταῦτα.

9   Ἐννοεῖτε δὲ καὶ τόδε, ἔφη. σχολὴ τοῖς πολεμίοις

with me ships of war and merchant vessels to carry us; for yourselves, if you really wish to go by sea, wait until I return; and I shall return speedily." When they heard this, the soldiers were delighted, and voted that Cheirisophus should set sail with all speed.

After him Xenophon rose and spoke as follows: "Cheirisophus, then, is setting off after ships, and we are to stay here; I am going to speak, therefore, of all the things that it seems to me proper for us to be doing while we wait. In the first place, we must obtain provisions from hostile territory, for we neither have an adequate market, nor have we, with some few exceptions, the means wherewith to buy; but the territory is hostile, and hence there is danger that many of you will perish if you set out after provisions carelessly and unguardedly. Rather, it seems to me that you ought to get your provisions in foraging parties and not roam about at random, in order that you may be kept safe, and that we generals ought to have charge of this matter." This proposal was adopted.

"Listen, then, to this further point. Some of you are to journey forth after plunder. Now I think it is best for the man who is going out to inform us of the fact and to tell us also where he is going, in order that we may know the number of men who are going out and the number who are staying behind; then we can help, if need be, in making preparations, and if there be occasion to go to any one's assistance, we shall know where we are to go with such assistance, and if a man who is without experience is making an attempt in any quarter, we can advise him by trying to ascertain the strength of those against whom he may be going." This proposal also was adopted.

"Then," he said, "consider this matter also. Our ene-

λήζεσθαι, καὶ δικαίως ἡμῖν ἐπιβουλεύουσιν· ἔχομεν
γὰρ τὰ ἐκείνων· ὑπερκάθηνται δὲ ἡμῶν. φυλακὰς δή
μοι δοκεῖ δεῖν περὶ τὸ στρατόπεδον εἶναι· ἐὰν οὖν κατὰ
μέρος φυλάττωμεν καὶ σκοπῶμεν, ἧττον ἂν δύναιντο
ἡμᾶς θηρᾶν οἱ πολέμιοι.

10 Ἔτι τοίνυν τάδε ὁρᾶτε. εἰ μὲν ἠπιστάμεθα σαφῶς
ὅτι ἥξει πλοῖα Χειρίσοφος ἄγων ἱκανά, οὐδὲν ἂν ἔδει
ὧν μέλλω λέγειν· νῦν δ᾽ ἐπεὶ τοῦτο ἄδηλον, δοκεῖ μοι
πειρᾶσθαι πλοῖα συμπαρασκευάζειν καὶ αὐτόθεν. ἢν
μὲν γὰρ ἔλθῃ, ὑπαρχόντων ἐνθάδε ἐν ἀφθονωτέροις
πλευσούμεθα· ἢν δὲ μὴ ἄγῃ, τοῖς ἐνθάδε χρησόμεθα.

11 ὁρῶ δὲ ἐγὼ πλοῖα πολλάκις παραπλέοντα· εἰ οὖν
αἰτησάμενοι παρὰ Τραπεζουντίων μακρὰ πλοῖα κατά-
γοιμεν καὶ φυλάττοιμεν αὐτά, τὰ² πηδάλια παραλυό-
μενοι, ἕως ἂν ἱκανὰ τὰ ἄξοντα γένηται, ἴσως ἂν οὐκ
ἀπορήσαιμεν κομιδῆς οἵας δεόμεθα. ἔδοξε καὶ ταῦτα.

12 Ἐννοήσατε δ᾽, ἔφη, εἰ εἰκὸς καὶ τρέφειν ἀπὸ κοινοῦ
οὓς ἂν καταγάγωμεν ὅσον ἂν χρόνον ἡμῶν ἕνεκεν
μένωσι, καὶ ναῦλον συνθέσθαι, ὅπως ὠφελοῦντες καὶ
ὠφελῶνται. ἔδοξε καὶ ταῦτα.

13 Δοκεῖ τοίνυν μοι, ἔφη, ἢν ἄρα καὶ ταῦτα ἡμῖν μὴ
ἐκπεραίνηται ὥστε ἀρκεῖν πλοῖα, τὰς ὁδοὺς ἃς δυσπό-
ρους ἀκούομεν εἶναι ταῖς παρὰ θάλατταν οἰκούσαις
πόλεσιν ἐντείλασθαι ὁδοποιεῖν· πείσονται γὰρ καὶ διὰ

---

² αὐτὰ τὰ some MSS., Mar.: αὐτὰ other MSS.: τὰ Gem.,
following Hartman.

mies have leisure for plundering and they are plotting against us—quite properly, seeing that we have appropriated what was theirs; and they are posted up above us. So it seems to me that we ought to have guards around our camp; supposing, then, that we take turns in standing guard and keeping watch, the enemy would be less able to harry us.

"Here is still another point to note. If we knew beyond doubt that Cheirisophus would bring back with him an adequate number of ships, there would be no need of what I am about to say; but since in fact that is uncertain, I think we should try to do our part by procuring ships here also. For if he does come, then with those at hand here we shall have a more abundant supply to sail in; while if he does not, we shall use those which we have here. Now I see ships sailing past frequently, and if we can get the people of Trapezus to give us men-of-war and so bring these ships into port and keep them under guard, taking off their rudders meanwhile, until we get enough to carry us, perhaps we should not lack such means of transport as we need." This proposal also was adopted.

"Again," he said, "do you not think it reasonable that we should maintain from our common fund whichever sailors we are bringing into port for as long a time as they may be waiting for our sakes, and that we should agree upon a price for our passage, so that in conferring a benefit upon us they may also benefit themselves?" This proposal also was adopted.

"Now it seems to me," he continued, "that if perchance this plan also shall fail to provide us with enough ships, we must turn to the roads, which we hear are difficult to travel, and direct the cities that are situated along the sea to repair

τὸ φοβεῖσθαι καὶ διὰ τὸ βούλεσθαι ἡμῶν ἀπαλλαγῆναι.

14 Ἐνταῦθα δὴ ἀνέκραγον ὡς οὐ δέοι ὁδοιπορεῖν. ὁ δὲ ὡς ἔγνω τὴν ἀφροσύνην αὐτῶν, ἐπεψήφισε μὲν οὐδέν, τὰς δὲ πόλεις ἑκούσας ἔπεισεν ὁδοποιεῖν, λέγων ὅτι θᾶττον ἀπαλλάξονται, ἢν εὔποροι γένωνται αἱ 15 ὁδοί. ἔλαβον δὲ καὶ πεντηκόντορον παρὰ τῶν Τραπεζουντίων, ᾗ ἐπέστησαν Δέξιππον Λάκωνα περίοικον. οὗτος ἀμελήσας τοῦ συλλέγειν πλοῖα ἀποδρὰς ᾤχετο ἔξω τοῦ Πόντου, ἔχων τὴν ναῦν. οὗτος μὲν οὖν δίκαια ἔπαθεν ὕστερον· ἐν Θρᾴκῃ γὰρ παρὰ Σεύθῃ πολυπραγμονῶν τι ἀπέθανεν ὑπὸ Νικάνδρου τοῦ Λάκωνος. 16 ἔλαβον δὲ καὶ τριακόντορον, ᾗ ἐπεστάθη Πολυκράτης Ἀθηναῖος, ὃς ὁπόσα λαμβάνοι πλοῖα κατῆγεν ἐπὶ τὸ στρατόπεδον. καὶ τὰ μὲν ἀγώγιμα εἴ τι ἦγον ἐξαιρούμενοι φύλακας καθίστασαν, ὅπως σῶα εἴη, τοῖς δὲ 17 πλοίοις ἐχρήσαντο[3] εἰς παραγωγήν. ἐν ᾧ δὲ ταῦτα ἦν ἐπὶ λείαν ἐξῇσαν οἱ Ἕλληνες, καὶ οἱ μὲν ἐλάμβανον, οἱ δὲ καὶ οὔ. Κλεαίνετος δὲ ἐξαγαγὼν καὶ τὸν ἑαυτοῦ καὶ ἄλλον λόχον πρὸς χωρίον χαλεπὸν αὐτός τε ἀπέθανε καὶ ἄλλοι πολλοὶ τῶν σὺν αὐτῷ.

II. Ἐπεὶ δὲ τὰ ἐπιτήδεια οὐκέτι ἦν λαμβάνειν ὥστε ἀπαυθημερίζειν ἐπὶ τὸ στρατόπεδον, ἐκ τούτου λαβὼν

---

[3] ἐχρήσαντο some MSS., Hude/Peters, Mar.: χρήσαιντο other MSS., Gem.

[4] The perioeci were the inhabitants of the outlying Laconian towns; they were free, but not Spartan citizens. They formed part

them; for they will obey, not only from fear, but also from the desire to be rid of us."

At this the soldiers set up a shout, saying that they did not want to go by land. And Xenophon, realizing their foolishness, did not put any proposal regarding this matter to vote, but persuaded the cities to repair the roads voluntarily, urging that they would be rid of the army the more quickly if the roads should be made easy to travel. Furthermore, they got a fifty-oared warship from the people of Trapezus, and put it under the command of Dexippus, a Laconian perioecus.[4] This fellow, however, paying no heed to the duty of collecting vessels, slipped away with his man-of-war and left the Euxine. He did indeed get his deserts afterwards; for while engaged in some intrigue at the court of Seuthes[5] in Thrace he was killed by Nicander the Laconian. They also got a thirty-oared galley, and put it under the command of Polycrates the Athenian, who brought in to the camp all the merchant vessels that he captured. And they would unload the cargoes, in case the ships had any, and put them under guard, in order to keep these safe, and they used the vessels themselves for transport service. While these things were going on, the Greeks were making forays in quest of booty, and while some parties were securing it, others did not. And in one case, when Cleaenetus led forth his own company and another against a difficult stronghold, the commander himself was killed and many of his men besides.

II. The time came when it was no longer possible to obtain provisions and return to the camp on the same day.

of the highly differentiated underclass at Sparta: cf. *Hell.* III. iii. 6, V. iii. 9. [5] See VII. ii. 31–34.

Ξενοφῶν ἡγεμόνας τῶν Τραπεζουντίων ἐξάγει εἰς
Δρίλας τὸ ἥμισυ τοῦ στρατεύματος, τὸ δὲ ἥμισυ
κατέλιπε φυλάττειν τὸ στρατόπεδον· οἱ γὰρ Κόλχοι,
ἅτε ἐκπεπτωκότες τῶν οἰκιῶν, πολλοὶ ἦσαν ἀθρόοι καὶ
2 ὑπερεκάθηντο ἐπὶ τῶν ἄκρων. οἱ δὲ Τραπεζούντιοι
ὁπόθεν μὲν τὰ ἐπιτήδεια ῥᾴδιον ἦν λαβεῖν οὐκ ἦγον·
φίλοι γὰρ αὐτοῖς ἦσαν· εἰς δὲ τοὺς Δρίλας προθύμως
ἦγον, ὑφ᾽ ὧν κακῶς ἔπασχον, εἰς χωρία τε ὀρεινὰ καὶ
δύσβατα καὶ ἀνθρώπους πολεμικωτάτους τῶν ἐν τῷ
Πόντῳ.

3 Ἐπεὶ δὲ ἦσαν ἐν τῇ ἄνω χώρᾳ οἱ Ἕλληνες, ὁποῖα
τῶν χωρίων τοῖς Δρίλαις ἁλώσιμα εἶναι ἐδόκει ἐμ-
πιμπράντες ἀπῇσαν· καὶ οὐδὲν ἦν λαμβάνειν εἰ μὴ ὗς
ἢ βοῦς ἢ ἄλλο τι κτῆνος τὸ πῦρ διαπεφευγός. ἐν δὲ
ἦν χωρίον μητρόπολις αὐτῶν· εἰς τοῦτο πάντες συνερ-
ρυήκεσαν. περὶ δὲ τοῦτο ἦν χαράδρα ἰσχυρῶς βαθεῖα,
4 καὶ πρόσοδοι χαλεπαὶ πρὸς τὸ χωρίον. οἱ δὲ πελτασταὶ προδραμόντες στάδια πέντε ἢ ἓξ τῶν ὁπλιτῶν,
διαβάντες τὴν χαράδραν, ὁρῶντες πρόβατα πολλὰ καὶ
ἄλλα χρήματα προσέβαλλον πρὸς τὸ χωρίον· συν-
είποντο δὲ καὶ δορυφόροι πολλοὶ οἱ ἐπὶ τὰ ἐπιτήδεια
ἐξωρμημένοι· ὥστε ἐγένοντο οἱ διαβάντες πλείους ἢ
5 δισχίλιοι ἄνθρωποι.[4] ἐπεὶ δὲ μαχόμενοι οὐκ ἐδύναντο
λαβεῖν τὸ χωρίον, καὶ γὰρ τάφρος ἦν περὶ αὐτὸ εὐρεῖα
ἀναβεβλημένη καὶ σκόλοπες ἐπὶ τῆς ἀναβολῆς καὶ

---

[4] διχίλιοι ἄνθρωποι Matthias, followed by Hude/Peters,
Mar.: εἰς χιλίλους ἀνθρώπους one MS., others omit εἰς.

Then Xenophon took some men from Trapezus for guides and led forth half the army to the country of the Drilae, leaving the other half behind to guard the camp—because the Colchians, since they had been driven out of their houses, were now gathered together in one great body and had taken a position on the heights above the camp. For the Trapezuntians would not lead the Greeks to districts from which provisions could be secured easily, because they were friendly to the people of those districts; but they were eager to lead them into the territory of the Drilae, at whose hands they were continually suffering losses, though their country was mountainous and difficult to traverse and its inhabitants the most warlike of all that dwell upon the Euxine.

When the Greeks had reached the highlands, the Drilae set fire to such of their strongholds as seemed to them easy to capture, and fell back; and the Greeks could secure nothing except an occasional pig or ox or other animal that had escaped the fire. There was one stronghold, however, which was their metropolis, and into this they had all streamed. Around it was an exceedingly deep ravine, and the approaches to the place were difficult. Now the peltasts, who had run five or six stadia ahead of the hoplites, crossed this ravine and, seeing quantities of sheep and other property, essayed an attack upon the stronghold; in their train there followed a considerable number of spearmen who had set out after provisions, so that the party that crossed the ravine amounted to more than two thousand men. But when they found themselves unable with all their fighting to capture the place (for there was a wide trench around it, backed by a rampart, and upon the

τύρσεις πυκναὶ ξύλιναι πεποιημέναι, ἀπιέναι δὴ ἐπ-
6 εχείρουν· οἱ δὲ ἐπέκειντο αὐτοῖς. ὡς δὲ οὐκ ἐδύναντο
ἀποτρέχειν, ἦν γὰρ ἐφ᾽ ἑνὸς ἡ κατάβασις ἐκ τοῦ
χωρίου εἰς τὴν χαράδραν, πέμπουσι πρὸς Ξενοφῶντα·
7 ὁ δὲ ἡγεῖτο τοῖς ὁπλίταις. ὁ δὲ ἐλθὼν λέγει ὅτι ἔστι
χωρίον χρημάτων πολλῶν μεστόν· τοῦτο οὔτε λαβεῖν
δυνάμεθα· ἰσχυρὸν γάρ ἐστιν· οὔτε ἀπελθεῖν ῥᾴδιον·
μάχονται γὰρ ἐπεξεληλυθότες καὶ ἡ ἄφοδος χαλεπή.
8   Ἀκούσας ταῦτα ὁ Ξενοφῶν προσαγαγὼν πρὸς τὴν
χαράδραν τοὺς μὲν ὁπλίτας θέσθαι ἐκέλευσε τὰ ὅπλα,
αὐτὸς δὲ διαβὰς σὺν τοῖς λοχαγοῖς ἐσκοπεῖτο πότερον
εἴη κρεῖττον ἀπαγαγεῖν καὶ τοὺς διαβεβηκότας ἢ καὶ
τοὺς ὁπλίτας διαβιβάζειν, ὡς ἁλόντος ἂν τοῦ χωρίου.
9 ἐδόκει γὰρ τὸ μὲν ἀπαγαγεῖν οὐκ εἶναι ἄνευ πολλῶν
νεκρῶν, ἑλεῖν δ᾽ ἂν ᾤοντο καὶ οἱ λοχαγοὶ τὸ χωρίον,
καὶ ὁ Ξενοφῶν συνεχώρησε τοῖς ἱεροῖς πιστεύσας· οἱ
γὰρ μάντεις ἀποδεδειγμένοι ἦσαν ὅτι μάχη μὲν ἔσται,
10 τὸ δὲ τέλος καλὸν τῆς ἐξόδου. καὶ τοὺς μὲν λοχαγοὺς
πέμπει διαβιβάσοντας τοὺς ὁπλίτας, αὐτὸς δ᾽ ἔμενεν
ἀναχωρίσας ἅπαντας τοὺς πελταστάς, καὶ οὐδένα εἴα
11 ἀκροβολίζεσθαι. ἐπεὶ δ᾽ ἧκον οἱ ὁπλῖται, ἐκέλευσε τὸν
λόχον ἕκαστον ποιῆσαι τῶν λοχαγῶν ὡς ἂν κράτιστα
οἴηται ἀγωνιεῖσθαι· ἦσαν γὰρ οἱ λοχαγοὶ πλησίον
ἀλλήλων οἳ πάντα τὸν χρόνον ἀλλήλοις περὶ ἀνδρα-

rampart palisades had been set and wooden towers constructed at frequent intervals), their next move was to try to withdraw; and then the enemy pressed hard upon them. To get away by running proved impossible, inasmuch as the descent from the stronghold to the ravine only allowed them to go in single file, and they accordingly sent a messenger to Xenophon, who was at the head of the hoplites. The messenger came and reported: "There is a stronghold full of all kinds of stores. We cannot capture it, for it is strong; and we cannot easily get away, for the defenders rush out and attack us, and the road that leads back is a difficult one."

Upon hearing this message Xenophon led on to the ravine, ordered the hoplites to halt there under arms, and himself crossed over with the captains and looked about to see whether it was better to withdraw the troops that had already crossed, or to lead over the hoplites also, on the presumption that the stronghold could be captured. The withdrawal, it seemed clear, could not be accomplished without the loss of many lives, while the capture of the place, in the opinion of the captains, was feasible, and Xenophon fell in with their opinion, in reliance upon his sacrifices; for the seers had declared that while there would be fighting to do, the issue of the expedition would be fortunate. Accordingly he sent the captains to bring over the hoplites, while he himself remained on the further side, having drawn back the entire body of peltasts and forbidding any one to shoot at long range. Upon the arrival of the hoplites he ordered each of the captains to form his company in the way he thought it would fight most effectively; for near one another were the captains who had all the time been vying with one another in valour. This order

12 γαθίας ἀντεποιοῦντο. καὶ οἱ μὲν ταῦτ' ἐποίουν· ὁ δὲ
τοῖς πελτασταῖς πᾶσι παρήγγειλε διηγκυλωμένους
ἰέναι, ὡς ὁπόταν σημήνῃ ἀκοντίζειν δεῆσον, καὶ τοὺς
τοξότας ἐπιβεβλῆσθαι ἐπὶ ταῖς νευραῖς, ὡς ὁπόταν
σημήνῃ τοξεύειν δεῆσον, καὶ τοὺς γυμνῆτας λίθων
ἔχειν μεστὰς τὰς διφθέρας· καὶ τοὺς ἐπιτηδείους ἔπεμψε τούτων ἐπιμεληθῆναι.

13 Ἐπεὶ δὲ πάντα παρεσκεύαστο καὶ οἱ λοχαγοὶ καὶ
οἱ ὑπολόχαγοι καὶ οἱ ἀξιοῦντες τούτων μὴ χείρους
εἶναι πάντες παρατεταγμένοι ἦσαν, καὶ ἀλλήλους μὲν
δὴ συνεώρων· μηνοειδὴς γὰρ διὰ τὸ χωρίον ἡ τάξις
14 ἦν· ἐπεὶ δ' ἐπαιάνισαν καὶ ἡ σάλπιγξ ἐφθέγξατο, ἅμα
τε τῷ Ἐνυαλίῳ ἠλέλιξαν καὶ ἔθεον δρόμῳ οἱ ὁπλῖται,
καὶ τὰ βέλη ὁμοῦ ἐφέρετο, λόγχαι, τοξεύματα, σφενδόναι, πλεῖστοι δ' ἐκ τῶν χειρῶν λίθοι, ἦσαν δὲ οἳ καὶ
15 πῦρ προσέφερον. ὑπὸ δὲ τοῦ πλήθους τῶν βελῶν
ἔλιπον οἱ πολέμιοι τά τε σταυρώματα καὶ τὰς τύρσεις·
ὥστε Ἀγασίας Στυμφάλιος καὶ Φιλόξενος Πελληνεὺς[5]
καταθέμενοι τὰ ὅπλα ἐν χιτῶνι μόνον ἀνέβησαν, καὶ
ἄλλος ἄλλον[6] εἷλκε, καὶ ἄλλος ἀνεβεβήκει, καὶ ἑ-
αλώκει τὸ χωρίον, ὡς ἐδόκει.

16 Καὶ οἱ μὲν πελτασταὶ καὶ οἱ ψιλοὶ ἐσδραμόντες
ἥρπαζον ὅ τι ἕκαστος ἐδύνατο· ὁ δὲ Ξενοφῶν στὰς
κατὰ τὰς πύλας ὁπόσους ἐδύνατο κατεκώλυσε τῶν

---

[5] One MS. omits καὶ Φιλόξενος Πελληνεύς.
[6] ἄλλος ἄλλον some MSS., Hude/Peters, Mar.: ἄλλος other
MSS., Gem.

they proceeded to carry out, and meanwhile Xenophon passed word to all the peltasts to advance with hand on the thong, so that they could discharge their javelins when the signal indicated it was needed, to the bowmen to have their arrows upon the string, ready to shoot upon the signal, and to the slingers to have their bags full of stones; and he despatched the proper persons to look after all these things.

When all preparations had been made and the captains, lieutenants, and those among the men who claimed to be not inferior to them in bravery were all grouped together in the line[6] and, moreover, watching one another (for the line was crescent-shaped, to conform with the position they were attacking), then they struck up the paean and the trumpet sounded, and then, at the same moment, they raised the war cry to Enyalius, the hoplites charged forward on the run, and the missiles began to fly all together—spears, arrows, sling-stones, and very many stones thrown by hand, while some of the men employed fire-brands also. By reason of the quantity of the missiles the enemy abandoned both their ramparts and their towers, so that Agasias the Stymphalian and Philoxenus the Pellenean, putting aside their arms and clad only in tunic, climbed up, the one pulled up the other, and meanwhile another had made the climb, so that the capture of the stronghold was accomplished, as it seemed.

Thereupon the peltasts and the light troops rushed in and proceeded to snatch whatever plunder they severally could; but Xenophon, taking his stand at the gates, kept out

[6] A formation which the captain judged to be the "most effective" (§11 above).

ὁπλιτῶν ἔξω· πολέμιοι γὰρ ἄλλοι ἐφαίνοντο ἐπ᾽ ἄκροις

17 τισὶν ἰσχυροῖς. οὐ πολλοῦ δὲ χρόνου μεταξὺ γενομέ-
νου κραυγή τε ἐγένετο ἔνδον καὶ ἔφευγον οἱ μὲν καὶ
ἔχοντες ἃ ἔλαβον, τάχα δέ τις καὶ τετρωμένος· καὶ
πολὺς ἦν ὠθισμὸς ἀμφὶ τὰ θύρετρα. καὶ ἐρωτώμενοι
οἱ ἐκπίπτοντες ἔλεγον ὅτι ἄκρα τέ ἐστιν ἔνδον καὶ οἱ
πολέμιοι πολλοί, οἳ παίουσιν ἐκδεδραμηκότες τοὺς

18 ἔνδον ἀνθρώπους. ἐνταῦθα ἀνειπεῖν ἐκέλευσε Τολμίδην τὸν κήρυκα ἰέναι εἴσω τὸν βουλόμενόν τι λαμβάνειν. καὶ ἵενται πολλοὶ εἴσω, καὶ νικῶσι τοὺς ἐκπίπτοντας οἱ εἰσωθούμενοι καὶ κατακλείουσι τοὺς

19 πολεμίους πάλιν εἰς τὴν ἄκραν. καὶ τὰ μὲν ἔξω τῆς
ἄκρας πάντα διηρπάσθη, καὶ ἐξεκομίσαντο οἱ Ἕλλη-
νες· οἱ δὲ ὁπλῖται ἔθεντο τὰ ὅπλα, οἱ μὲν περὶ τὰ
σταυρώματα, οἱ δὲ κατὰ τὴν ὁδὸν τὴν ἐπὶ τὴν ἄκραν

20 φέρουσαν. ὁ δὲ Ξενοφῶν καὶ οἱ λοχαγοὶ ἐσκόπουν εἰ
οἷόν τε εἴη τὴν ἄκραν λαβεῖν· ἦν γὰρ οὕτω σωτηρία
ἀσφαλής, ἄλλως δὲ παγχάλεπον ἐδόκει εἶναι ἀπελ-
θεῖν· σκοπουμένοις δὲ αὐτοῖς ἔδοξε παντάπασιν ἀνά-
λωτον εἶναι τὸ χωρίον.

21 Ἐνταῦθα παρεσκευάζοντο τὴν ἄφοδον, καὶ τοὺς μὲν
σταυροὺς ἕκαστοι τοὺς καθ᾽ αὑτοὺς διήρουν, καὶ τοὺς
ἀχρείους καὶ φορτία ἔχοντας ἐξεπέμποντο καὶ τῶν
ὁπλιτῶν τὸ πλῆθος καταλιπόντες οἱ λοχαγοὶ οἷς ἕκα-

22 στος ἐπίστευεν. ἐπεὶ δὲ ἤρξαντο ἀποχωρεῖν, ἐπεξέθεον
ἔνδοθεν πολλοὶ γέρρα καὶ λόγχας ἔχοντες καὶ κνημῖ-

as many as he could of the hoplites, for the reason that other enemies were coming into view upon certain strong heights. After no long interval a shout arose within and men came pouring forth in flight, some carrying with them what they had seized, then soon a number of men that were wounded; and there was a great deal of pushing about the gates. When those who were tumbling out were questioned, they said that there was a citadel within, that the enemy were numerous, and that they had sallied forth and were dealing blows upon the men inside. Then Xenophon ordered Tolmides the herald to proclaim that whoever wanted to get any plunder should go in. At that many proceeded to rush into the gates, and the crowd that was pushing in overcame the crowd that was tumbling out and shut up the enemy again in their citadel. So everything outside the citadel was seized and carried off by the Greeks, and the hoplites took up their position, some about the ramparts, others along the road leading up to the citadel. Meanwhile Xenophon and the captains were looking to see whether it was possible to capture the citadel; for in that case their safety was secured, while otherwise they thought it would be very difficult to effect their withdrawal; but the upshot of their consideration was, that the place was quite impregnable.

Then they made preparations for the withdrawal: they tore down the palisades, each division taking those on its own front, and sent off the men who were unfit for service or were carrying burdens, and likewise the greater part of the hoplites, the captains keeping behind only those troops that they each relied upon. But the moment they began to retire, there rushed out upon them from within a great crowd of men armed with wicker shields, spears, greaves,

δας καὶ κράνη Παφλαγονικά, καὶ ἄλλοι ἐπὶ τὰς οἰκίας
ἀνέβαινον τὰς ἔνθεν καὶ ἔνθεν τῆς εἰς τὴν ἄκραν
23 φερούσης ὁδοῦ· ὥστε οὐδὲ διώκειν ἀσφαλὲς ἦν κατὰ
τὰς πύλας τὰς εἰς τὴν ἄκραν φερούσας. καὶ γὰρ ξύλα
μεγάλα ἐπερρίπτουν ἄνωθεν, ὥστε χαλεπὸν ἦν καὶ
μένειν καὶ ἀπιέναι· καὶ ἡ νὺξ φοβερὰ ἦν ἐπιοῦσα.
24   Μαχομένων δὲ αὐτῶν καὶ ἀπορουμένων θεῶν τις
αὐτοῖς μηχανὴν σωτηρίας δίδωσιν. ἐξαπίνης γὰρ ἀν-
έλαμψεν οἰκία τῶν ἐν δεξιᾷ ὅτου δὴ ἐνάψαντος. ὡς δ᾽
αὕτη συνέπιπτεν, ἔφευγον οἱ ἀπὸ τῶν ἐν δεξιᾷ οἰκιῶν.
25 ὡς δὲ ἔμαθεν ὁ Ξενοφῶν τοῦτο παρὰ τῆς τύχης,
ἐνάπτειν ἐκέλευε καὶ τὰς ἐν ἀριστερᾷ οἰκίας, αἳ ξύλιναι ἦσαν, ὥστε καὶ ταχὺ ἐκαίοντο. ἔφευγον οὖν καὶ
26 οἱ ἀπὸ τούτων τῶν οἰκιῶν. οἱ δὲ κατὰ στόμα δὴ ἔτι
μόνοι ἐλύπουν καὶ δῆλοι ἦσαν ὅτι ἐπικείσονται ἐν τῇ
ἐξόδῳ τε καὶ καταβάσει. ἐνταῦθα παραγγέλλει φορεῖν
ξύλα ὅσοι ἐτύγχανον ἔξω ὄντες τῶν βελῶν εἰς τὸ
μέσον ἑαυτῶν καὶ τῶν πολεμίων. ἐπεὶ δὲ ἱκανὰ ἤδη
ἦν, ἐνῆψαν· ἐνῆπτον δὲ καὶ τὰς παρ᾽ αὐτὸ τὸ χαρά-
κωμα οἰκίας, ὅπως οἱ πολέμιοι ἀμφὶ ταῦτα ἔχοιεν.
27 οὕτω μόλις ἀπῆλθον ἀπὸ τοῦ χωρίου, πῦρ ἐν μέσῳ
ἑαυτῶν καὶ τῶν πολεμίων ποιησάμενοι. καὶ κατεκαύθη
πᾶσα ἡ πόλις καὶ αἱ οἰκίαι καὶ αἱ τύρσεις καὶ τὰ
σταυρώματα καὶ τἆλλα πάντα πλὴν τῆς ἄκρας.
28   Τῇ δὲ ὑστεραίᾳ ἀπῆσαν οἱ Ἕλληνες ἔχοντες τὰ

and Paphlagonian helmets, while others set about climbing to the tops of the houses that were on either side of the road leading up to the citadel. The result was that even a pursuit in the direction of the gates that led into the citadel was unsafe; for they would hurl down great logs from above, so that it was difficult either to remain or to retire. And the approach of night was also a cause for fear.

In the midst of their fighting and perplexity some god gave to the Greeks a means of salvation. For of a sudden one of the houses on the right, set on fire by somebody or other, broke into a blaze; and as it began to fall in, there began a general flight from the other houses on the right side of the road. The moment Xenophon grasped this opportunity which chance had given him, he gave orders to set fire to the houses on the left also, which were of wood and so fell to burning very quickly. The result was that the people in these houses likewise took to flight. It was only the enemy in their front who were now left to trouble the Greeks and manifestly intended to attack them as they passed out and down the hill. At this stage Xenophon sent out orders that all who chanced to be out of range of the missiles should set about bringing up logs and put them in the open space between their own forces and the enemy. As soon as enough logs had been collected, they set fire to them; and meanwhile they set fire also to the houses which were close along the palisade, so that the enemy's attention might be occupied with these. It was in this way that they effected, with difficulty, their withdrawal from the stronghold, by putting fire between themselves and the enemy. And the whole city was burned down, houses, towers, palisades, and everything else except the citadel.

On the next day the Greeks were for returning to camp

ἐπιτήδεια. ἐπεὶ δὲ τὴν κατάβασιν ἐφοβοῦντο τὴν εἰς
Τραπεζοῦντα, πρανὴς γὰρ ἦν καὶ στενή, ψευδενέδραν
29 ἐποιήσαντο· καὶ ἀνὴρ Μυσὸς τὸ γένος[7] καὶ τοὔνομα
τοῦτο ἔχων τῶν Κρητῶν λαβὼν δέκα ἔμενεν ἐν λασίῳ
χωρίῳ καὶ προσεποιεῖτο τοὺς πολεμίους πειρᾶσθαι
λανθάνειν· αἱ δὲ πέλται αὐτῶν ἄλλοτε καὶ ἄλλοτε
30 διεφαίνοντο χαλκαῖ οὖσαι. οἱ μὲν οὖν πολέμιοι ταῦτα
διορῶντες ἐφοβοῦντο ὡς ἐνέδραν οὖσαν· ἡ δὲ στρατιὰ
ἐν τούτῳ κατέβαινεν. ἐπεὶ δὲ ἐδόκει ἤδη ἱκανὸν ὑπ-
εληλυθέναι, τῷ Μυσῷ ἐσήμηνε φεύγειν ἀνὰ κράτος·
31 καὶ ὃς ἐξαναστὰς φεύγει καὶ οἱ σὺν αὐτῷ. καὶ οἱ μὲν
ἄλλοι Κρῆτες, ἁλίσκεσθαι γὰρ ἔφασαν τῷ δρόμῳ,
ἐκπεσόντες ἐκ τῆς ὁδοῦ εἰς ὕλην κατὰ τὰς νάπας
καλινδούμενοι ἐσώθησαν, ὁ Μυσὸς δὲ κατὰ τὴν ὁδὸν
32 φεύγων ἐβόα βοηθεῖν· καὶ ἐβοήθησαν αὐτῷ, καὶ ἀν-
έλαβον τετρωμένον. καὶ αὐτοὶ ἐπὶ πόδα ἀνεχώρουν
βαλλόμενοι οἱ βοηθήσαντες καὶ ἀντιτοξεύοντές τινες
τῶν Κρητῶν. οὕτως ἀφίκοντο ἐπὶ τὸ στρατόπεδον
πάντες σῶοι ὄντες.

III. Ἐπεὶ δὲ οὔτε Χειρίσοφος ἧκεν οὔτε πλοῖα ἱκανὰ
ἦν οὔτε τὰ ἐπιτήδεια ἦν λαμβάνειν ἔτι, ἐδόκει ἀπιτέον
εἶναι. καὶ εἰς μὲν τὰ πλοῖα τούς τε ἀσθενοῦντας
ἐνεβίβασαν καὶ τοὺς ὑπὲρ τετταράκοντα ἔτη καὶ παῖδας καὶ γυναῖκας καὶ τῶν σκευῶν ὅσα μὴ ἀνάγκη ἦν

---

[7] τὸ γένος omitted by some MSS.

with their provisions. But inasmuch as they feared the descent to Trapezus (for the way was steep and narrow), they laid a false ambuscade: a Mysian by race, who likewise bore the name of Mysus,[7] took ten of the Cretans, stayed behind in a bit of undergrowth, and pretended to be trying to keep out of sight of the enemy; but their shields, which were of bronze, would now and then gleam through the bushes. So the enemy, catching glimpses of these proceedings, were fearful that it was an ambuscade; and meanwhile the Greek army was making its descent. When it seemed that they had got down far enough, a signal was given to the Mysian to flee at the top of his speed, and he and his companions arose and took to flight. The Cretans of the party (for they said that they were as good as captured if they ran) plunged out of the road into the woods, and by tumbling down through the ravines made their escape, but the Mysian held to the road in his flight and kept shouting for help; and they did go to his aid, and picked him up wounded. Then the rescuers in their turn proceeded to retreat, faces to the front, while the enemy kept throwing missiles at them and some of the Cretans replied with their arrows. In this way they all reached the camp safe and sound.

III. And now, seeing that Cheirisophus was not returned,[8] that they had not an adequate number of ships,[9] and that it was no longer possible to get provisions, they resolved to depart by land. On board the ships they embarked the sick, those who were more than forty years of age, the women and children, and all the baggage which

[7] Which itself means "Mysian." The name, if authentic, would be rare: cf. Theopompus, *FGH* 115 F 344: Magnes from Magnesia.　　[8] See i. 4.　　[9] i. 10–16.

ἔχειν. καὶ Φιλήσιον καὶ Σοφαίνετον τοὺς πρεσβυτά-
τους τῶν στρατηγῶν εἰσβιβάσαντες τούτων ἐκέλευον
2 ἐπιμελεῖσθαι· οἱ δὲ ἄλλοι ἐπορεύοντο· ἡ δὲ ὁδὸς ὡδο-
ποιημένη ἦν. καὶ ἀφικνοῦνται πορευόμενοι εἰς Κερασοῦντα τριταῖοι πόλιν Ἑλληνίδα ἐπὶ θαλάττῃ Σινωπέων ἄποικον ἐν τῇ Κολχίδι χώρᾳ. ἐνταῦθα ἔμειναν
3 ἡμέρας δέκα· καὶ ἐξέτασις σὺν τοῖς ὅπλοις ἐγίγνετο
καὶ ἀριθμός, καὶ ἐγένοντο ὀκτακισχίλιοι καὶ ἑξακόσιοι. οὗτοι ἐσώθησαν. οἱ δὲ ἄλλοι ἀπώλοντο ὑπό τε
τῶν πολεμίων καὶ χιόνος καὶ εἴ τις νόσῳ.

4   Ἐνταῦθα καὶ διαλαμβάνουσι τὸ ἀπὸ τῶν αἰχμαλώτων ἀργύριον γενόμενον. καὶ τὴν δεκάτην, ἣν τῷ
Ἀπόλλωνι ἐξεῖλον καὶ τῇ Ἐφεσίᾳ Ἀρτέμιδι, διέλαβον
οἱ στρατηγοὶ τὸ μέρος ἕκαστος φυλάττειν τοῖς θεοῖς·
5 ἀντὶ δὲ Χειρισόφου Νέων ὁ Ἀσιναῖος ἔλαβε. Ξενοφῶν
οὖν τὸ μὲν τοῦ Ἀπόλλωνος ἀνάθημα ποιησάμενος
ἀνατίθησιν εἰς τὸν ἐν Δελφοῖς τῶν Ἀθηναίων θησαυ-
ρὸν καὶ ἐπέγραψε τό τε αὑτοῦ ὄνομα καὶ τὸ Προξένου,
6 ὃς σὺν Κλεάρχῳ ἀπέθανεν· ξένος γὰρ ἦν αὐτοῦ. τὸ δὲ
τῆς Ἀρτέμιδος τῆς Ἐφεσίας, ὅτ᾽ ἀπῄει σὺν Ἀγησιλάῳ
ἐκ τῆς Ἀσίας τὴν εἰς Βοιωτοὺς ὁδόν, καταλείπει παρὰ
Μεγαβύζῳ τῷ τῆς Ἀρτέμιδος νεωκόρῳ, ὅτι αὐτὸς κιν-
δυνεύσων ἐδόκει ἰέναι, καὶ ἐπέστειλεν, ἣν μὲν αὐτὸς

---

[10] i. 13–14.   [11] Cf. IV. viii. 15 and notes thereon.
[12] II. v.   [13] III. i. 4–10.
[14] In 394, ending in the hard-fought battle of Coronea, at
which Xenophon was probably present. Cf. *Hell.* IV. ii. 1–8, iii.
1–21.

they did not need to keep with them. They put aboard also Philesius and Sophaenetus, the eldest of the generals, and bade them take charge of the enterprise; then the rest took up the march, the road having been already constructed.[10] And on the third day of their journey they reached Cerasus, a Greek city on the sea, being a colony planted by the Sinopeans in the territory of Colchis. There they remained ten days; and the troops were reviewed under arms and numbered, and there proved to be eight thousand six hundred men.[11] So many were left alive. The rest had perished at the hands of the enemy or in the snow, a few also by disease.

There, also, they divided the money received from the sale of the captives. And the tithe, which they set apart for Apollo and for Artemis of the Ephesians, was distributed among the generals, each taking his portion to keep safely for the gods; and the portion that fell to Cheirisophus was given to Neon the Asinaean. As for Xenophon, he caused a votive offering to be made out of Apollo's share of his portion and dedicated it in the treasury of the Athenians at Delphi, inscribing upon it his own name and that of Proxenus, who was killed with Clearchus;[12] for Proxenus was his friend.[13] The share which belonged to Artemis of the Ephesians he left behind, at the time when he was returning from Asia with Agesilaus to take part in the campaign against Boeotia,[14] in charge of Megabyzus, the sacristan of Artemis,[15] for the reason that his own journey seemed likely to be a dangerous one; and his instructions were that in case he should escape with his life, the money

[15] The temple of Artemis at Ephesus was held in great honor by the Persians: see Briant, *Histoire* I, 722.

σωθῇ, αὐτῷ ἀποδοῦναι· εἰ δέ τι πάθοι[8] ἀναθεῖναι
ποιησάμενον τῇ Ἀρτέμιδι ὅ τι οἴοιτο χαριεῖσθαι τῇ
θεῷ.

7   Ἐπεὶ δ᾽ ἔφευγεν ὁ Ξενοφῶν, κατοικοῦντος ἤδη
αὐτοῦ ἐν Σκιλλοῦντι ὑπὸ τῶν Λακεδαιμονίων οἰκισθέν-
τος παρὰ τὴν Ὀλυμπίαν ἀφικνεῖται Μεγάβυζος εἰς
Ὀλυμπίαν θεωρήσων καὶ ἀποδίδωσι τὴν παρακατα-
θήκην αὐτῷ. Ξενοφῶν δὲ λαβὼν χωρίον ὠνεῖται τῇ
8   θεῷ ὅπου ἀνεῖλεν ὁ θεός. ἔτυχε δὲ διαρρέων διὰ τοῦ
χωρίου ποταμὸς Σελινοῦς. καὶ ἐν Ἐφέσῳ δὲ παρὰ τὸν
τῆς Ἀρτέμιδος νεὼν Σελινοῦς ποταμὸς παραρρεῖ. καὶ
ἰχθύες τε ἐν ἀμφοτέροις ἔνεισι καὶ κόγχαι· ἐν δὲ τῷ
ἐν Σκιλλοῦντι χωρίῳ καὶ θῆραι πάντων ὁπόσα ἐστὶν
9   ἀγρευόμενα θηρία. ἐποίησε δὲ καὶ βωμὸν καὶ ναὸν
ἀπὸ τοῦ ἱεροῦ ἀργυρίου, καὶ τὸ λοιπὸν δὲ ἀεὶ δεκα-
τεύων τὰ ἐκ τοῦ ἀγροῦ ὡραῖα θυσίαν ἐποίει τῇ θεῷ,
καὶ πάντες οἱ πολῖται καὶ οἱ πρόσχωροι ἄνδρες καὶ
γυναῖκες μετεῖχον τῆς ἑορτῆς. παρεῖχε δὲ ἡ θεὸς τοῖς
σκηνοῦσιν ἄλφιτα, ἄρτους, οἶνον, τραγήματα, καὶ τῶν
θυομένων ἀπὸ τῆς ἱερᾶς νομῆς λάχος, καὶ τῶν θηρευο-
10   μένων δέ. καὶ γὰρ θήραν ἐποιοῦντο εἰς τὴν ἑορτὴν οἵ
τε Ξενοφῶντος παῖδες καὶ οἱ τῶν ἄλλων πολιτῶν, οἱ
δὲ βουλόμενοι καὶ ἄνδρες συνεθήρων· καὶ ἡλίσκετο
τὰ μὲν ἐξ αὐτοῦ τοῦ ἱεροῦ χώρου, τὰ δὲ καὶ ἐκ τῆς
Φολόης, σύες καὶ δορκάδες καὶ ἔλαφοι.

---

[8] εἰ δέ τι πάθοι some MSS.: ἤν δέ τι πάθῃ other MSS.

was to be returned to him, but in case any ill should befall him, Megabyzus was to cause to be made and dedicated to Artemis whatever offering he thought would please the goddess.

In the time of Xenophon's exile[16] and while he was living at Scillus,[17] near Olympia, where he had been established as a colonist by the Lacedaemonians, Megabyzus came to Olympia to attend the games and returned to him his deposit. Upon receiving it Xenophon bought a plot of ground for the goddess in a place which Apollo's oracle appointed. As it chanced, there flowed through the plot a river named Selinus; and at Ephesus likewise a Selinus river flows past the temple of Artemis. In both streams, moreover, there are fish and mussels, while in the plot at Scillus there is hunting of all manner of beasts of the chase. Here Xenophon built an altar and a temple with the sacred money, and from that time forth he would every year take the tithe of the products of the land in their season and offer sacrifice to the goddess, all the citizens and the men and women of the neighborhood taking part in the festival. And the goddess would provide for the banqueters barley meal and loaves of bread, wine and sweetmeats, and a portion of the sacrificial victims from the sacred herd as well as of the victims taken in the chase. For Xenophon's sons and the sons of the other citizens used to have a hunting expedition at the time of the festival, and any grown men who so wished would join them; and they captured their game partly from the sacred precinct itself and partly from Mount Pholöe—boars and gazelles and stags.[18]

[16] See Intro.　　[17] Cf. Paus. V. vi. 5.　　[18] An idealized scene of Greek piety and *xenia*: cf. Burkert, *Greek Religion*, 67, 259; R. Parker, *Athenian Religion* (Oxford, 1996) 78 n.41.

11 Ἔστι δὲ ὁ τόπος ᾗ ἐκ Λακεδαίμονος εἰς Ὀλυμπίαν
πορεύονται ὡς εἴκοσι στάδιοι ἀπὸ τοῦ ἐν Ὀλυμπίᾳ
Διὸς ἱεροῦ. ἔνι δ᾽ ἐν τῷ ἱερῷ χώρῳ καὶ λειμὼν καὶ ὄρη
δένδρων μεστά, ἱκανὰ σῦς καὶ αἶγας καὶ βοῦς τρέφειν
καὶ ἵππους, ὥστε καὶ τὰ τῶν εἰς τὴν ἑορτὴν ἰόντων
12 ὑποζύγια εὐωχεῖσθαι. περὶ δὲ αὐτὸν τὸν ναὸν ἄλσος
ἡμέρων δένδρων ἐφυτεύθη ὅσα ἐστὶ τρωκτὰ ὡραῖα. ὁ
δὲ ναὸς ὡς μικρὸς μεγάλῳ τῷ ἐν Ἐφέσῳ ᾔκασται, καὶ
τὸ ξόανον ἔοικεν ὡς κυπαρίττινον χρυσῷ ὄντι τῷ ἐν
13 Ἐφέσῳ. καὶ στήλη ἔστηκε παρὰ τὸν ναὸν γράμματα
ἔχουσα· ΙΕΡΟΣ Ο ΧΩΡΟΣ ΤΗΣ ΑΡΤΕΜΙΔΟΣ. ΤΟΝ ΕΧΟΝΤΑ
ΚΑΙ ΚΑΡΠΟΥΜΕΝΟΝ ΤΗΝ ΜΕΝ ΔΕΚΑΤΗΝ ΚΑΤΑΘΥΕΙΝ
ΕΚΑΣΤΟΥ ΕΤΟΥΣ, ΕΚ ΔΕ ΤΟΥ ΠΕΡΙΤΤΟΥ ΤΟΝ ΝΑΟΝ ΕΠΙ-
ΣΚΕΤΑΖΕΙΝ. ΑΝ ΔΕ ΤΙΣ ΜΗ ΠΟΙΗΙ ΤΑΥΤΑ ΤΗΙ ΘΕΩΙ ΜΕΛΗΣΕΙ.

IV. Ἐκ Κερασοῦντος δὲ κατὰ θάλατταν μὲν
ἐκομίζοντο οἵπερ καὶ πρόσθεν, οἱ δὲ ἄλλοι κατὰ γῆν
2 ἐπορεύοντο. ἐπεὶ δὲ ἦσαν ἐπὶ τοῖς Μοσσυνοίκων ὁρί-
οις, πέμπουσιν εἰς αὐτοὺς Τιμησίθεον τὸν Τραπεζούν-
τιον πρόξενον ὄντα τῶν Μοσσυνοίκων, ἐρωτῶντες πότερον ὡς διὰ φιλίας ἢ διὰ πολεμίας πορεύσονται τῆς
χώρας. οἱ δὲ εἶπον ὅτι οὐ διήσοιεν· ἐπίστευον γὰρ τοῖς
3 χωρίοις. ἐντεῦθεν λέγει ὁ Τιμησίθεος ὅτι πολέμιοι
εἰσὶν αὐτοῖς οἱ ἐκ τοῦ ἐπέκεινα. καὶ ἐδόκει καλέσαι
ἐκείνους, εἰ βούλοιντο συμμαχίαν ποιήσασθαι· καὶ

---

19 That is, with multiple breasts and animal figures: see *LIMC*
2.1, 755–57, and 2.2, 564–73. Artemis Ephesia is otherwise never
found in mainland Greece.   20 See iii. 1.

The place is situated on the road which leads from Lacedaemon to Olympia, and is about twenty stadia from the temple of Zeus at Olympia. Within the sacred precinct there is meadowland and tree-covered hills, suited for the rearing of swine, goats, cattle and horses, so that even the draught animals which bring people to the festival have their feast also. Immediately surrounding the temple is a grove of cultivated trees, producing all sorts of dessert fruits in their season. The temple itself is like the one at Ephesus, although small as compared with great, and the image of the goddess, although cypress wood as compared with gold, is like the Ephesian image.[19] Beside the temple stands a tablet with this inscription: THE PLACE IS SACRED TO ARTEMIS. HE WHO HOLDS IT AND ENJOYS ITS FRUITS MUST OFFER THE TITHE EVERY YEAR IN SACRIFICE, AND FROM THE REMAINDER MUST KEEP THE TEMPLE IN REPAIR. IF ANY ONE LEAVE THESE THINGS UNDONE, THE GODDESS WILL LOOK TO IT.

IV. Leaving Cerasus, the people who had thus far been conveyed by sea[20] went on as before, while the rest continued their journey by land. When they reached the boundary of the Mossynoecians,[21] they sent to them Timesitheus the Trapezuntian, who was official representative of the Mossynoecians at Trapezus, and asked whether in marching through their country they were to regard it as friendly or hostile. The Mossynoecians replied that they would not permit them to pass through; for they trusted in their strongholds. Then Timesitheus told the Greeks that the Mossynoecians who dwelt farther on were hostile to them, and it was decided to summon them and see whether they

---

[21] Lit. *dwellers in Mossyns,* or wooden towers. See §26 below.

4 πεμφθεὶς ὁ Τιμησίθεος ἧκεν ἄγων τοὺς ἄρχοντας. ἐπεὶ
δὲ ἀφίκοντο, συνῆλθον οἵ τε τῶν Μοσσυνοίκων ἄρχον-
5 τες καὶ οἱ στρατηγοὶ τῶν Ἑλλήνων· καὶ ἔλεξε Ξενοφῶν, ἡρμήνευε δὲ Τιμησίθεος· ᾿Ω ἄνδρες Μοσσύνοικοι, ἡμεῖς βουλόμεθα διασωθῆναι πρὸς τὴν Ἑλλάδα
πεζῇ· πλοῖα γὰρ οὐκ ἔχομεν. κωλύουσι δὲ οὗτοι ἡμᾶς
6 οὓς ἀκούομεν ὑμῖν πολεμίους εἶναι. εἰ οὖν βούλεσθε,
ἔξεστιν ὑμῖν ἡμᾶς λαβεῖν συμμάχους καὶ τιμωρήσασθαι εἴ τί πώποτε ὑμᾶς οὗτοι ἠδίκησαν, καὶ τὸ λοιπὸν
7 ὑμῖν ὑπηκόους εἶναι τούτους. εἰ δὲ ἡμᾶς ἀφήσετε,
σκέψασθε πόθεν αὖθις ἂν τοσαύτην δύναμιν λάβοιτε
8 σύμμαχον. πρὸς ταῦτα ἀπεκρίνατο ὁ ἄρχων τῶν Μοσσυνοίκων ὅτι καὶ βούλοιντο ταῦτα καὶ δέχοιντο τὴν
9 ξυμμαχίαν. ῎Αγετε δή, ἔφη ὁ Ξενοφῶν, τί ἡμῶν δεή-
σεσθε χρήσασθαι, ἂν σύμμαχοι ὑμῶν γενώμεθα, καὶ
ὑμεῖς τί οἷοί τε ἔσεσθε ἡμῖν συμπρᾶξαι περὶ τῆς
10 διόδου; οἱ δὲ εἶπον ὅτι ἱκανοί ἐσμεν εἰς τὴν χώραν
εἰσβάλλειν ἐκ τοῦ ἐπὶ θάτερα τὴν τῶν ὑμῖν τε καὶ
ἡμῖν πολεμίων, καὶ δεῦρο ὑμῖν πέμψαι ναῦς τε καὶ
ἄνδρας οἵτινες ὑμῖν συμμαχοῦνταί τε καὶ τὴν ὁδὸν
ἡγήσονται.

11 Ἐπὶ τούτοις πιστὰ δόντες καὶ λαβόντες ᾤχοντο.
καὶ ἧκον τῇ ὑστεραίᾳ ἄγοντες τριακόσια πλοῖα μονό-
ξυλα καὶ ἐν ἑκάστῳ τρεῖς ἄνδρας, ὧν οἱ μὲν δύο
12 ἐκβάντες εἰς τάξιν ἔθεντο τὰ ὅπλα, ὁ δὲ εἷς ἔμενε. καὶ
οἱ μὲν λαβόντες τὰ πλοῖα ἀπέπλευσαν, οἱ δὲ μένοντες
ἐξετάξαντο ὧδε. ἔστησαν ἀνὰ ἑκατὸν μάλιστα οἷον

wanted to conclude an alliance; so Timesitheus was sent to them, and brought back with him their chiefs. When they arrived, these chiefs of the Mossynoecians and the generals of the Greeks met together; and Xenophon spoke as follows, Timesitheus acting as interpreter: "Mossynoecians, we desire to make our way to Greece in safety by land, for we have no ships; but these people, who, as we hear, are your enemies, are blocking our passage. If you wish, therefore, it is within your power to secure us as allies, to exact vengeance for any wrong these people have ever done you, and to make them henceforth your subjects. But if you dismiss us with a refusal, where, bethink you, could you ever again secure so large a force to help fight your battles?" To these words the chief of the Mossynoecians replied that they desired this arrangement and accepted the alliance. "Well, then," said Xenophon, "what use will you want to make of us if we become your allies, and what assistance will you, in your turn, be able to render us in the matter of our passage through this territory?" They replied: "We are able to invade this land of your enemies and ours from the opposite side, and to send to you here not only ships, but men who will aid you in the fighting and will guide you on your way."

After confirming this agreement by giving and receiving pledges they departed. Then next day they returned, bringing with them three hundred canoes, each made out of a single log and each containing three men, two of whom disembarked and fell into line under arms, while the third remained in the canoe. Then the second group took their canoes and sailed back again, and those who stayed behind marshalled themselves in the following way. They took position in lines of about a hundred each, like choral danc-

χοροὶ ἀντιστοιχοῦντες ἀλλήλοις, ἔχοντες γέρρα πάντες λευκῶν βοῶν δασέα, ἠκασμένα κιττοῦ πετάλῳ, ἐν
δὲ τῇ δεξιᾷ παλτὸν ὡς ἐξάπηχυ, ἔμπροσθεν μὲν
λόγχην ἔχον, ὄπισθεν δὲ αὐτοῦ τοῦ ξύλου σφαι-
13 ροειδές. χιτωνίσκους δὲ ἐνεδεδύκεσαν ὑπὲρ γονάτων,
πάχος ὡς λινοῦ στρωματοδέσμου, ἐπὶ τῇ κεφαλῇ δὲ
κράνη σκύτινα οἷάπερ τὰ Παφλαγονικά, κρωβύλον
ἔχοντα κατὰ μέσον, ἐγγύτατα τιαροειδῆ· εἶχον δὲ καὶ
14 σαγάρεις σιδηρᾶς. ἐντεῦθεν ἐξῆρχε μὲν αὐτῶν εἷς, οἱ
δὲ ἄλλοι πάντες ἐπορεύοντο ᾄδοντες ἐν ῥυθμῷ, καὶ
διελθόντες διὰ τῶν τάξεων καὶ διὰ τῶν ὅπλων τῶν
Ἑλλήνων ἐπορεύοντο εὐθὺς πρὸς τοὺς πολεμίους ἐπὶ
15 χωρίον ὃ ἐδόκει ἐπιμαχώτατον εἶναι. ᾠκεῖτο δὲ τοῦτο
πρὸ τῆς πόλεως τῆς μητροπόλεως καλουμένης αὐτοῖς
καὶ ἐχούσης τὸ ἀκρότατον τῶν Μοσσυνοίκων. καὶ περὶ
τούτου ὁ πόλεμος ἦν· οἱ γὰρ ἀεὶ τοῦτ' ἔχοντες ἐδόκουν
ἐγκρατεῖς εἶναι καὶ πάντων Μοσσυνοίκων, καὶ ἔφασαν τούτους οὐ δικαίως ἔχειν τοῦτο, ἀλλὰ κοινὸν ὂν
καταλαβόντας πλεονεκτεῖν.

16   Εἵποντο δ' αὐτοῖς καὶ τῶν Ἑλλήνων τινές, οὐ
ταχθέντες ὑπὸ τῶν στρατηγῶν, ἀλλὰ ἁρπαγῆς ἕνεκεν.
οἱ δὲ πολέμιοι προσιόντων τέως μὲν ἡσύχαζον· ἐπεὶ
δ' ἐγγὺς ἐγένοντο τοῦ χωρίου, ἐκδραμόντες τρέπονται
αὐτούς, καὶ ἀπέκτειναν συχνοὺς τῶν βαρβάρων καὶ
τῶν συναναβάντων Ἑλλήνων τινάς, καὶ ἐδίωκον μέχρι
17 οὗ εἶδον τοὺς Ἕλληνας βοηθοῦντας· εἶτα δὲ ἀποτρα-

---

[22] Cf. IV. vii. 16 and note thereon.

ers ranged opposite one another, all of them with wicker shields covered with white, shaggy ox-hide and like an ivy leaf in shape, and each man holding in his right hand a lance about six cubits long, with a spearhead at one end[22] and a round ball at the butt end of the shaft. They wore short tunics which did not reach their knees and were as thick as a linen bag for bedclothes, and upon their heads leather helmets just such as the Paphlagonian helmets, with a tuft in the middle very like a tiara in shape; and they had also iron battle-axes. After they had formed their lines one of them led off, and the rest after him, every man of them, fell into a rhythmic march and song, and passing through the battalions and through the quarters of the Greeks they went straight on against the enemy, toward a stronghold which seemed to be especially assailable. It was situated in front of the city which is called by them their metropolis and contains the chief citadel of the Mossynoecians. In fact, it was for the possession of this citadel that the war was going on; for those who at any time held it were deemed to be masters of all the other Mossynoecians, and they said that the present occupants did not hold it by right, but that it was common property and they had seized it in order to gain a selfish advantage.

The attacking party was followed by some of the Greeks, not under orders from their generals, but seeking plunder. As they approached, the enemy for a time kept quiet; but when they had got near the stronghold, they sallied forth and put them to flight, killing a considerable number of the barbarians and some of the Greeks who had gone up the hill with them, and pursuing the rest until they saw the Greeks coming to the rescue; then they turned and

πόμενοι ᾤχοντο, καὶ ἀποτεμόντες τὰς κεφαλὰς τῶν
νεκρῶν ἐπεδείκνυσαν τοῖς τε Ἕλλησι καὶ τοῖς ἑαυτῶν
18 πολεμίοις, καὶ ἅμα ἐχόρευον νόμῳ τινὶ ᾄδοντες. οἱ δὲ
Ἕλληνες μάλα ἤχθοντο ὅτι τούς τε πολεμίους ἐπεποιήκεσαν θρασυτέρους καὶ ὅτι οἱ ἐξελθόντες Ἕλληνες σὺν αὐτοῖς ἐπεφεύγεσαν μάλα ὄντες συχνοί· ὃ
οὔπω πρόσθεν ἐπεποιήκεσαν ἐν τῇ στρατείᾳ.

19 Ξενοφῶν δὲ συγκαλέσας τοὺς Ἕλληνας εἶπεν· Ἄνδρες στρατιῶται, μηδὲν ἀθυμήσητε ἕνεκα τῶν γεγενη-
μένων· ἴστε γὰρ ὅτι καὶ ἀγαθὸν οὐ μεῖον τοῦ κακοῦ
20 γεγένηται. πρῶτον μὲν γὰρ ἐπίστασθε ὅτι οἱ μέλλον-
τες ἡμῖν ἡγεῖσθαι τῷ ὄντι πολέμιοί εἰσιν οἷσπερ καὶ
ἡμᾶς ἀνάγκη· ἔπειτα δὲ καὶ τῶν Ἑλλήνων οἱ ἀφρον-
τιστήσαντες τῆς σὺν ἡμῖν τάξεως καὶ ἱκανοὶ ἡγησά-
μενοι εἶναι ξὺν τοῖς βαρβάροις ταὐτὰ πράττειν ἅπερ
σὺν ἡμῖν δίκην δεδώκασιν· ὥστε αὖθις ἧττον τῆς
21 ἡμετέρας τάξεως ἀπολείψονται. ἀλλ᾽ ὑμᾶς δεῖ παρασκευάζεσθαι ὅπως καὶ τοῖς φίλοις οὖσι τῶν βαρβάρων δόξετε κρείττους αὐτῶν εἶναι καὶ τοῖς πολεμίοις
δηλώσετε ὅτι οὐχ ὁμοίοις ἀνδράσι μαχοῦνται νῦν τε
καὶ ὅτε τοῖς ἀτάκτοις ἐμάχοντο.

22   Ταύτην μὲν οὖν τὴν ἡμέραν οὕτως ἔμειναν· τῇ δὲ
ὑστεραίᾳ θύσαντες ἐπεὶ ἐκαλλιερήσαντο, ἀριστήσαντες, ὀρθίους τοὺς λόχους ποιησάμενοι, καὶ τοὺς
βαρβάρους ἐπὶ τὸ εὐώνυμον κατὰ ταὐτὰ ταξάμενοι
ἐπορεύοντο τοὺς τοξότας μεταξὺ τῶν λόχων ὀρθίων

fell back, and after cutting off the heads of the dead men displayed them to the Greeks and to their own enemies, at the same time dancing to a kind of strain which they sang. And the Greeks were exceedingly angry, not only because the enemy had been made bolder, but because the Greeks who went to the attack with the barbarians had taken to flight, though in very considerable numbers—a thing which they had never done before in the course of the expedition.

Then Xenophon called the Greeks together and said: "Fellow soldiers, do not by any means lose heart on account of what has happened; for be sure that a good thing also has happened, no less important than the evil thing. In the first place, you know that those who are to guide us are really enemies to the people whose enemies we also are compelled to be; secondly, and touching our own men, those among them who paid no attention to the battle formation we use and got the idea that they could accomplish the same results in company with the barbarians as they could with us, have paid the penalty—another time they will be less likely to leave our ordered lines. But you must make ready to prove to our friends among the barbarians that you are better men than they, and to show the enemy that they are not going to fight against the same sort of men now as the disorderly mass they met before."[23]

It was thus that the Greeks spent that day; but on the next, after obtaining favourable omens from their sacrifices, they took breakfast, formed the companies in column, and began the march, with the barbarians in the same formation posted on the left, the bowmen distributed in

[23] Cf. *Oec*. VIII. 4 ff.

ἔχοντες, ὑπολειπομένους δὲ μικρὸν τοῦ στόματος τῶν
23 ὁπλιτῶν. ἦσαν γὰρ τῶν πολεμίων οἱ εὔζωνοι κατα-
τρέχοντες τοῖς λίθοις ἔβαλλον. τούτους οὖν ἀνέστελ-
λον οἱ τοξόται καὶ πελτασταί. οἱ δ᾽ ἄλλοι βάδην
ἐπορεύοντο πρῶτον μὲν ἐπὶ τὸ χωρίον ἀφ᾽ οὗ τῇ
προτεραίᾳ οἱ βάρβαροι ἐτρέφθησαν καὶ οἱ σὺν αὐτοῖς·
24 ἐνταῦθα γὰρ οἱ πολέμιοι ἦσαν ἀντιτεταγμένοι. τοὺς
μὲν οὖν πελταστὰς ἐδέξαντο οἱ βάρβαροι καὶ ἐμάχοντο, ἐπειδὴ δὲ ἐγγὺς ἦσαν οἱ ὁπλῖται, ἐτράποντο. καὶ
οἱ μὲν πελτασταὶ εὐθὺς εἵποντο διώκοντες ἄνω πρὸς
25 τὴν πόλιν, οἱ δὲ ὁπλῖται ἐν τάξει εἵποντο. ἐπεὶ δὲ ἄνω
ἦσαν πρὸς ταῖς τῆς μητροπόλεως οἰκίαις, ἐνταῦθα δὴ
οἱ πολέμιοι ὁμοῦ δὴ πάντες γενόμενοι ἐμάχοντο καὶ
ἐξηκόντιζον τοῖς παλτοῖς, καὶ ἄλλα δόρατα ἔχοντες
παχέα μακρά, ὅσα ἀνὴρ ἂν φέροι μόλις, τούτοις
26 ἐπειρῶντο ἀμύνεσθαι ἐκ χειρός. ἐπεὶ δὲ οὐχ ὑφίεντο
οἱ Ἕλληνες, ἀλλὰ ὁμόσε ἐχώρουν, ἔφευγον οἱ βάρβαροι καὶ ἐντεῦθεν, ἅπαντες λιπόντες[9] τὸ χωρίον. ὁ δὲ
βασιλεὺς αὐτῶν ὁ ἐν τῷ μόσσυνι τῷ ἐπ᾽ ἄκρου ᾠκο-
δομημένῳ, ὃν τρέφουσι πάντες κοινῇ αὐτοῦ μένοντα
καὶ φυλάττοντα, οὐκ ἤθελεν ἐξελθεῖν, οὐδὲ ὁ ἐν τῷ
πρότερον αἱρεθέντι χωρίῳ, ἀλλ᾽ αὐτοῦ σὺν τοῖς μοσ-
σύνοις κατεκαύθησαν.
27   Οἱ δὲ Ἕλληνες διαρπάζοντες τὰ χωρία ηὕρισκον

9 ἅπαντες λιπόντες Hude/Peters: ἔλειπον (ἔλιπον) ἅπαντες
MSS.

412

the spaces between the companies, which were in column, a small distance from the van of the hoplites. For the enemy had some nimble troops who kept running down the hill and pelting the Greeks with stones; these fellows, then, were held back by the bowmen and peltasts. The rest of the Greek army, proceeding at a walk, advanced first against the stronghold from which the barbarians and those with them had been put to flight on the preceding day; for it was there that the enemy were now drawn up to oppose them. The barbarians did, indeed, meet the attack of the peltasts and engaged them in battle, but when the hoplites got near them, they fled. The peltasts at once made after them and pursued them up the hill to the city, while the hoplites followed along, still keeping their lines. When they were at the top and near the houses of the metropolis, at that moment all the troops of the enemy massed together and did battle; they hurled their lances, and with other spears which they had, so thick and long that a man could only carry them with difficulty, tried to defend themselves in hand to hand fighting. As the Greeks, however, refused to give way, but kept pushing on to close quarters, the barbarians took to flight from that point also, every man of them having abandoned the fortress. Their king in his wooden tower built upon the citadel, whom all the people jointly maintain while he remains there on guard, refused to come forth, as did also the commander of the stronghold[24] which had been captured earlier, so they were burned up where they were, along with their towers.

In plundering the strongholds the Greeks found in the

---

[24] *i.e.* the one mentioned above, §§14, 23

θησαυροὺς ἐν ταῖς οἰκίαις ἄρτων νενημένων περυσινῶν[10] ὡς ἔφασαν οἱ Μοσσύνοικοι, τὸν δὲ νέον σῖτον
σὺν τῇ καλάμῃ ἀποκείμενον· ἦσαν δὲ ζειαὶ αἱ πλεῖ-
28 σται. καὶ δελφίνων τεμάχη ἐν ἀμφορεῦσιν ηὑρίσκετο
τεταριχευμένα καὶ στέαρ ἐν τεύχεσι τῶν δελφίνων, ᾧ
ἐχρῶντο οἱ Μοσσύνοικοι καθάπερ οἱ Ἕλληνες τῷ
29 ἐλαίῳ· κάρυα δὲ ἐπὶ τῶν ἀνώγεων ἦν πολλὰ τὰ πλατέα
οὐκ ἔχοντα διαφυὴν οὐδεμίαν. τούτων καὶ πλείστῳ
σίτῳ ἐχρῶντο ἕψοντες καὶ ἄρτους ὀπτῶντες. οἶνος δὲ
ηὑρίσκετο ὃς ἄκρατος μὲν ὀξὺς ἐφαίνετο εἶναι ὑπὸ τῆς
αὐστηρότητος, κερασθεὶς δὲ εὐώδης τε καὶ ἡδύς.

30 Οἱ μὲν δὴ Ἕλληνες ἀριστήσαντες ἐνταῦθα ἐπορεύοντο τοῦ πρόσω, παραδόντες τὸ χωρίον τοῖς συμ-
μαχήσασι τῶν Μοσσυνοίκων. ὁπόσα δὲ καὶ ἄλλα
παρῆσαν χωρία τῶν σὺν τοῖς πολεμίοις ὄντων, τὰ
εὐπροσοδώτατα οἱ μὲν ἔλειπον, οἱ δὲ ἑκόντες προσ-
31 εχώρουν. τὰ δὲ πλεῖστα τοιάδε ἦν τῶν χωρίων. ἀπεῖχον αἱ πόλεις ἀπ᾽ ἀλλήλων στάδια ὀγδοήκοντα, αἱ δὲ
πλέον αἱ δὲ μεῖον· ἀναβοώντων δὲ ἀλλήλων συνή-
κουον εἰς τὴν ἑτέραν ἐκ τῆς ἑτέρας πόλεως· οὕτως
32 ὑψηλή τε καὶ κοίλη ἡ χώρα ἦν. ἐπεὶ δὲ πορευόμενοι
ἐν τοῖς φίλοις ἦσαν, ἐπεδείκνυσαν αὐτοῖς παῖδας τῶν
εὐδαιμόνων σιτευτούς, τεθραμμένους καρύοις ἐφθοῖς,
ἁπαλοὺς καὶ λευκοὺς σφόδρα καὶ οὐ πολλοῦ δέοντας

---

[10] περυσινῶν Suda, followed by Hude/Peters, Mar.: πατρίους
MSS., Gem.

houses stores, as the Mossynoecians described them, of heaped up loaves from last year's grain, while the new grain was laid away with the straw, the most of it being spelt. They also found slices of dolphin salted away in jars, and in other vessels dolphin blubber, which the Mossynoecians used in the same way as the Greeks use olive oil; and on the upper floors of the houses there were large quantities of flat nuts, without any divisions.[25] Out of these nuts, by boiling them and baking them into loaves, they made the bread which they used most. The Greeks also found wine, which by reason of its harshness appeared to be sharp when taken unmixed, but mixed with water was fragrant and delicious.

When they had breakfasted there, the Greeks took up their onward march, after handing over the fortress to the Mossynoecians who had helped them in the fighting. As for the other strongholds which they passed by, belonging to those who sided with the enemy, the most accessible were in some cases abandoned by their occupants, in other cases surrendered voluntarily. The greater part of these places were of the following description: The towns were eighty stadia distant from one another, some more, and some less; but the inhabitants could hear one another shouting from one town to the next, such heights and valleys there were in the country. And when the Greeks, as they proceeded, were among the friendly Mossynoecians, they would exhibit to them fattened children of the wealthy inhabitants, who had been nourished on boiled nuts and were soft and white to an extraordinary degree,

[25] *i.e.* such as walnuts have. Xenophon probably means hazelnuts or filberts (LSJ *sv* κάρυον).

ἴσους τὸ μῆκος καὶ τὸ πλάτος εἶναι, ποικίλους δὲ τὰ
νῶτα καὶ τὰ ἔμπροσθεν πάντα ἐστιγμένους ἀνθέμια.

33 ἐζήτουν δὲ καὶ ταῖς ἑταίραις ἃς ἦγον οἱ Ἕλληνες,
ἐμφανῶς συγγίγνεσθαι· νόμος γὰρ ἦν οὗτός σφισι.

34 λευκοὶ δὲ πάντες οἱ ἄνδρες καὶ αἱ γυναῖκες. τούτους
ἔλεγον οἱ στρατευσάμενοι βαρβαρωτάτους διελθεῖν
καὶ πλεῖστον τῶν Ἑλληνικῶν νόμων κεχωρισμένους.
ἔν τε γὰρ ὄχλῳ ὄντες ἐποίουν ἅπερ ἂν ἄλλοι ἐν ἐρημίᾳ
ποιήσειαν, μόνοι τε ὄντες ὅμοια ἔπραττον ἅπερ ἂν μετ᾽
ἄλλων ὄντες, διελέγοντό τε αὑτοῖς καὶ ἐγέλων ἐφ᾽
ἑαυτοῖς καὶ ὠρχοῦντο ἐφιστάμενοι ὅπου τύχοιεν
ὥσπερ ἄλλοις ἐπιδεικνύμενοι.

V. Διὰ ταύτης τῆς χώρας οἱ Ἕλληνες, διά τε τῆς
πολεμίας καὶ τῆς φιλίας, ἐπορεύθησαν ὀκτὼ στα-
θμούς, καὶ ἀφικνοῦνται εἰς Χάλυβας. οὗτοι ὀλίγοι τε
ἦσαν καὶ ὑπήκοοι τῶν Μοσσυνοίκων, καὶ ὁ βίος ἦν
τοῖς πλείστοις αὐτῶν ἀπὸ σιδηρείας. ἐντεῦθεν ἀφι-

2 κνοῦνται εἰς Τιβαρηνούς. ἡ δὲ τῶν Τιβαρηνῶν χώρα
πολὺ ἦν πεδινωτέρα καὶ χωρία εἶχεν ἐπὶ θαλάττῃ
ἧττον ἐρυμνά. καὶ οἱ στρατηγοὶ ἔχρῃζον πρὸς τὰ
χωρία προσβάλλειν καὶ τὴν στρατιὰν ὀνηθῆναί τι,
καὶ τὰ ξένια ἃ ἧκε παρὰ Τιβαρηνῶν οὐκ ἐδέχοντο,
ἀλλ᾽ ἐπιμεῖναι κελεύσαντες ἔστε βουλεύσαιντο ἐθύ-

3 οντο. καὶ πολλὰ καταθυσάντων τέλος ἀπεδείξαντο οἱ
μάντεις πάντες γνώμην ὅτι οὐδαμῇ προσίοιντο οἱ θεοὶ

---

[26] Apparently an outlying tribe of the people whose territory
the Greeks had previously passed through. Cf. IV. vii. 15 ff.

and pretty nearly equal in length and breadth, with their backs adorned with many colours and their fore parts all tattooed with flower patterns. These Mossynoecians wanted also to have intercourse openly with the women who accompanied the Greeks, for that was their own fashion. And all of them were white, the men and the women alike. They were said by the Greeks who served on the expedition as the most uncivilized people whose country they traversed, the furthest removed from Greek customs. For they habitually did in public the things that other people would do only in private, and when they were alone they would behave just as if they were in the company of others, talking to themselves, laughing at themselves, and dancing in whatever spot they chanced to be, as though they were giving an exhibition to others.

V. Through this country, both the hostile and the friendly portions of it, the Greeks marched eight stages, reaching then the land of the Chalybians.[26] These people were few in number and subject to the Mossynoecians, and most of them gained their livelihood from working in iron. Next they reached the country of the Tibarenians,[27] which was much more level and had fortresses upon the seacoast that were less strong. The generals were desirous of attacking these fortresses, so as to get a little something for the army, and accordingly they would not accept the gifts of hospitality which came from the Tibarenians, but, directing them to wait until they should take counsel, proceeded to offer sacrifices. After many victims had been sacrificed all the seers finally declared the opinion that the gods in

[27] Cf. Ephorus, *FGH* 70 F 43.

τὸν πόλεμον. ἐντεῦθεν δὴ τὰ ξένια ἐδέξαντο, καὶ ὡς
διὰ φιλίας πορευόμενοι δύο ἡμέρας ἀφίκοντο εἰς Κοτύωρα πόλιν Ἑλληνίδα, Σινωπέων ἄποικον, ὄντας δ᾽
ἐν τῇ Τιβαρηνῶν χώρᾳ.[11]

5   Ἐνταῦθα ἔμειναν ἡμέρας τετταράκοντα πέντε. ἐν
δὲ ταύταις πρῶτον μὲν τοῖς θεοῖς ἔθυσαν, καὶ πομπὰς
ἐποίησαν κατὰ ἔθνος ἕκαστοι τῶν Ἑλλήνων καὶ ἀγῶ-
6   νας γυμνικούς. τὰ δ᾽ ἐπιτήδεια ἐλάμβανον τὰ μὲν ἐκ
τῆς Παφλαγονίας, τὰ δ᾽ ἐκ τῶν χωρίων τῶν Κοτυ-
ωριτῶν· οὐ γὰρ παρεῖχον ἀγοράν, οὐδὲ εἰς τὸ τεῖχος
τοὺς ἀσθενοῦντας ἐδέχοντο.

7   Ἐν τούτῳ ἔρχονται ἐκ Σινώπης πρέσβεις, φοβούμενοι περὶ τῶν Κοτυωριτῶν τῆς τε πόλεως, ἦν γὰρ
ἐκείνων καὶ φόρον ἐκείνοις ἔφερον, καὶ περὶ τῆς χώρας, ὅτι ἤκουον δῃουμένην. καὶ ἐλθόντες εἰς τὸ στρατόπεδον ἔλεγον· προηγόρει δὲ Ἑκατώνυμος δεινὸς
8   νομιζόμενος εἶναι λέγειν· Ἔπεμψεν ἡμᾶς, ὦ ἄνδρες
στρατιῶται, ἡ τῶν Σινωπέων πόλις ἐπαινέσοντάς τε
ὑμᾶς ὅτι νικᾶτε Ἕλληνες ὄντες βαρβάρους, ἔπειτα δὲ
καὶ συνησθησομένους ὅτι διὰ πολλῶν τε καὶ δεινῶν,
ὡς ἡμεῖς ἀκούομεν, πραγμάτων σεσωσμένοι πάρεστε·
9   ἀξιοῦμεν δὲ Ἕλληνες ὄντες καὶ αὐτοὶ ὑφ᾽ ὑμῶν ὄντων

---

11 §4 in the MSS. reads: Μέχρι ἐνταῦθα ἐπέζευσεν ἡ
στρατιά. πλῆθος τῆς καταβάσεως τῆς ὁδοῦ ἀπὸ τῆς ἐν Βα-
βυλῶνι μάχης ἄχρι εἰς Κοτύωρα σταθμοὶ ἑκατὸν εἴκοσι δύο,
παρασάγγαι ἑξακόσιοι καὶ εἴκοσι, στάδιοι μύριοι καὶ ὀκτακισχίλιοι καὶ ἑξακόσιοι, χρόνου πλῆθος ὀκτὼ μῆνες. This passage is regarded by edd. generally as an interpolation. Cf. II. ii. 6.

no wise permitted war. So then the generals accepted the gifts of hospitality, and proceeding as through a friendly country for two days, they arrived at Cotyora, a Greek city and a colony of the Sinopeans, dwelling as they were in the territory of the Tibarenians.[28]

There they remained forty-five days. During this time they first of all sacrificed to the gods, and all the several groups of the Greeks, nation by nation, instituted festal processions and athletic contests. As for provisions, they got them partly from Paphlagonia and partly from the estates of the Cotyorites; for the latter would not provide them with a market, nor would they receive their sick within the walls of the city.

Meanwhile ambassadors came from Sinope, full of fears not only for the city of the Cotyorites (for it belonged to them and its inhabitants paid them tribute), but also for its territory, because they heard it was being laid waste. And coming to the Greek camp they spoke as follows, Hecatonymus, who was regarded as a clever orator, being their spokesman: "Soldiers," he said, "the city of the Sinopeans has sent us, first, to applaud you as Greeks who stand victors over barbarians, and, secondly, to congratulate you that you have made your way through many dreadful troubles, as we hear, in safety to this place. Now we claim, being ourselves Greeks, to receive from you, who are Greeks also, good treatment and no ill; for we, on our

[28] §4 (see note to text): As far as this point the army travelled by land. The length in distance of the downward journey, from the battlefield near Babylon to Cotyora, was one hundred and twenty-two stages, six hundred and twenty parasangs, or eighteen thousand, six hundred stadia; and in time, eight months. [18,600 stadia = c. 2050 English miles.]

Ἑλλήνων ἀγαθὸν μέν τι πάσχειν, κακὸν δὲ μηδέν·
οὐδὲ γὰρ ἡμεῖς ὑμᾶς οὐδὲν πώποτε ὑπήρξαμεν κακῶς
10 ποιοῦντες. Κοτυωρῖται δὲ οὗτοί εἰσι μὲν ἡμέτεροι
ἄποικοι, καὶ τὴν χώραν ἡμεῖς αὐτοῖς ταύτην παρα-
δεδώκαμεν βαρβάρους ἀφελόμενοι· διὸ καὶ δασμὸν
ἡμῖν φέρουσιν οὗτοι τεταγμένον καὶ Κερασούντιοι καὶ
Τραπεζούντιοι· ὥστε ὅ τι ἂν τούτους κακὸν ποιήσητε
11 ἡ Σινωπέων πόλις νομίζει πάσχειν. νῦν δὲ ἀκούομεν
ὑμᾶς εἴς τε τὴν πόλιν βίᾳ παρεληλυθότας ἐνίους
σκηνοῦν ἐν ταῖς οἰκίαις καὶ ἐκ τῶν χωρίων βίᾳ λαμ-
12 βάνειν ὧν ἂν δέησθε οὐ πείθοντας. ταῦτ᾽ οὖν οὐκ
ἀξιοῦμεν· εἰ δὲ ταῦτα ποιήσετε, ἀνάγκη ἡμῖν καὶ
Κορύλαν καὶ Παφλαγόνας καὶ ἄλλον ὅντινα ἂν δυνώμεθα φίλον ποιεῖσθαι.

13   Πρὸς ταῦτα ἀναστὰς Ξενοφῶν ὑπὲρ τῶν στρατιωτῶν εἶπεν· Ἡμεῖς δέ, ὦ ἄνδρες Σινωπεῖς, ἥκομεν
ἀγαπῶντες ὅτι τὰ σώματα διεσωσάμεθα καὶ τὰ ὅπλα·
οὐ γὰρ ἦν δυνατὸν ἅμα τε χρήματα ἄγειν καὶ φέρειν
14 καὶ τοῖς πολεμίοις μάχεσθαι. καὶ νῦν ἐπεὶ εἰς τὰς
Ἑλληνίδας πόλεις ἤλθομεν, ἐν Τραπεζοῦντι μέν, παρεῖχον γὰρ ἡμῖν ἀγοράν, ὠνούμενοι εἴχομεν τὰ ἐπιτήδεια, καὶ ἀνθ᾽ ὧν ἐτίμησαν ἡμᾶς καὶ ξένια ἔδωκαν τῇ
στρατιᾷ, ἀντετιμῶμεν αὐτούς, καὶ εἴ τις αὐτοῖς φίλος
ἦν τῶν βαρβάρων, τούτων ἀπειχόμεθα· τοὺς δὲ πολεμίους αὐτῶν ἐφ᾽ οὓς αὐτοὶ ἡγοῖντο κακῶς ἐποιοῦμεν
15 ὅσον ἐδυνάμεθα. ἐρωτᾶτε δὲ αὐτοὺς ὁποίων τινῶν
ἡμῶν ἔτυχον· πάρεισι γὰρ ἐνθάδε οὓς ἡμῖν ἡγεμόνας

side, have never set the example by doing you any manner of harm. These Cotyorites are our colonists, and it was we who gave over to them this land, after we had taken it away from barbarians; therefore they pay us a stated tribute, as do the people of Cerasus and Trapezus; hence whatever harm you may do to these Cotyorites, the city of the Sinopeans regards as done to itself. At present we hear, firstly, that you have made your way into the city by force, some of you, and are quartered in the houses, and, secondly, that you are taking from the estates by force whatever you may need without asking leave. Now these things we do not deem proper; and if you continue to do them, you force us to make friends with Corylas[29] and the Paphlagonians and whomever else we can."

In reply to these words Xenophon, on behalf of the soldiers, rose and said: "For ourselves, men of Sinope, we have come back well content to have saved our bodies and our arms; for it was not possible at one and the same time to gather plunder and to fight with the enemy. As to our doings now, since we have reached Greek cities, we got our provisions in Trapezus by purchase, for the Trapezuntians provided us a market, and in return for the honours they bestowed upon us and the gifts of hospitality they gave the army, we paid them like honours; if any of the barbarians were their friends, we kept our hands off them, while upon their enemies, against whom they would themselves lead us, we wrought all the harm we could. Ask them what sort of people they found us to be; for the men are here pre-

---

[29] Ruler of Paphlagonia, apparently an autonomous region. Xenophon in *Hell*. IV. i. 3 ff. mentions one Otys as king of the Paphlagonians.

16 διὰ φιλίαν ἡ πόλις συνέπεμψεν. ὅποι δ' ἂν ἐλθόντες
ἀγορὰν μὴ ἔχωμεν, ἄν τε εἰς βάρβαρον γῆν ἄν τε εἰς
Ἑλληνίδα, οὐχ ὕβρει ἀλλὰ ἀνάγκῃ λαμβάνομεν τὰ
17 ἐπιτήδεια. καὶ Καρδούχους μὲν καὶ Ταόχους καὶ Χαλ-
δαίους καίπερ βασιλέως οὐχ ὑπηκόους ὄντας, ὅμως,
καὶ μάλα φοβεροὺς ὄντας, πολεμίους ἐκτησάμεθα διὰ
τὸ ἀνάγκην εἶναι λαμβάνειν τὰ ἐπιτήδεια, ἐπεὶ ἀγορὰν
18 οὐ παρεῖχον. Μάκρωνας δέ γε καὶ βαρβάρους ὄντας,
ἐπεὶ ἀγορὰν οἵαν ἐδύναντο παρεῖχον, φίλους τε ἐνομί-
ζομεν εἶναι καὶ βίᾳ οὐδὲν ἐλαμβάνομεν τῶν ἐκείνων.
19 Κοτυωρίτας δέ, οὓς ὑμετέρους φατὲ εἶναι, εἴ τι
αὐτῶν εἰλήφαμεν, αὐτοὶ αἴτιοί εἰσιν· οὐ γὰρ ὡς φίλοι
προσεφέροντο ἡμῖν, ἀλλὰ κλείσαντες τὰς πύλας οὔτε
εἴσω ἐδέχοντο οὔτε ἔξω ἀγορὰν ἔπεμπον· ᾐτιῶντο δὲ
20 τὸν παρ' ὑμῶν ἁρμοστὴν τούτων αἴτιον εἶναι. ὃ δὲ
λέγεις βίᾳ παρελθόντας σκηνοῦν, ἡμεῖς ἠξιοῦμεν τοὺς
κάμνοντας εἰς τὰς στέγας δέξασθαι· ἐπεὶ δὲ οὐκ
ἀνέῳγον τὰς πύλας, ᾗ ἡμᾶς ἐδέχετο αὐτὸ τὸ χωρίον
ταύτῃ εἰσελθόντες ἄλλο μὲν οὐδὲν βίαιον ἐποιήσαμεν,
σκηνοῦσι δ' ἐν ταῖς στέγαις οἱ κάμνοντες τὰ αὑτῶν
δαπανῶντες, καὶ τὰς πύλας φρουροῦμεν, ὅπως μὴ ἐπὶ
τῷ ὑμετέρῳ ἁρμοστῇ ὦσιν οἱ κάμνοντες ἡμῶν, ἀλλ'
21 ἐφ' ἡμῖν ᾖ κομίσασθαι ὅταν βουλώμεθα. οἱ δὲ ἄλλοι,
ὡς ὁρᾶτε, σκηνοῦμεν ὑπαίθριοι ἐν τῇ τάξει, παρεσκευασμένοι, ἂν μέν τις εὖ ποιῇ, ἀντευποιεῖν, ἂν δὲ κακῶς,
ἀλέξασθαι.

sent whom the city of Trapezus, out of friendship, sent with us as guides. On the other hand, wherever we come, whether it be to a barbarian or to a Greek land, and have no market at which to buy, we take provisions, not out of arrogance, but from necessity. The Carduchians, for example, and the Taochians and Chaldaeans were not subjects of the King and were exceedingly formidable, yet, even so, we made enemies of them because of this necessity of taking provisions, inasmuch as they would not provide a market. The Macronians, for their part, provided us as good a market as they could, and we therefore regarded them as friends, barbarians though they were, and took by force not a thing that belonged to them.

"As for the Cotyorites, whom you claim as yours, if we have taken anything that belonged to them, they are themselves to blame; for they did not behave toward us as friends, but shut their gates and would neither admit us within nor send a market without; and they alleged that the governor set over them by you was responsible for this conduct. In regard to your statement about people making their way into the city by force and being quartered there, we asked them to receive our sick into their houses; but when they refused to open their gates, we went in at a point where the place of itself received us; and we have done no deed of force save only that our sick are quartered in the houses, paying their own expenses, and that we are guarding the gates, in order that our sick may not be in the power of your governor, but that it may be in our power to get them back when we so wish. The rest of us, as you see, are quartered in the open in our regular formation, all ready, in case one does us a kindness, to return the like, or if it is an injury, to return that.

423

22 Ἃ δὲ ἠπείλησας ὡς ἢν ὑμῖν δοκῇ Κορύλαν καὶ
Παφλαγόνας συμμάχους ποιήσεσθε ἐφ᾽ ἡμᾶς, ἡμεῖς
δὲ ἢν μὲν ἀνάγκῃ ᾖ πολεμήσομεν καὶ ἀμφοτέροις· ἤδη
γὰρ καὶ ἄλλοις πολλαπλασίοις ὑμῶν ἐπολεμήσαμεν.
ἂν δὲ δοκῇ ἡμῖν καὶ φίλον ποιεῖσθαι τὸν Παφλα-
23 γόνα—ἀκούομεν δὲ αὐτὸν καὶ ἐπιθυμεῖν τῆς ὑμετέρας
πόλεως καὶ χωρίων τῶν ἐπιθαλαττίων—πειρασόμεθα
συμπράττοντες αὐτῷ ὧν ἐπιθυμεῖ φίλοι γίγνεσθαι.

24 Ἐκ τούτου μάλα μὲν δῆλοι ἦσαν οἱ συμπρέσβεις
τῷ Ἑκατωνύμῳ χαλεπαίνοντες τοῖς εἰρημένοις, παρελθὼν δ᾽ αὐτῶν ἄλλος εἶπεν ὅτι οὐ πόλεμον ποιησόμενοι
ἥκοιεν ἀλλὰ ἐπιδείξοντες ὅτι φίλοι εἰσί. καὶ ξενίοις,
ἢν μὲν ἔλθητε πρὸς τὴν Σινωπέων πόλιν, ἐκεῖ δεξόμεθα, νῦν δὲ τοὺς ἐνθάδε κελεύσομεν διδόναι ἃ δύναν-
25 ται· ὁρῶμεν γὰρ πάντα ἀληθῆ ὄντα ἃ λέγετε. ἐκ τούτου
ξένιά τε ἔπεμπον οἱ Κοτυωρῖται καὶ οἱ στρατηγοὶ τῶν
Ἑλλήνων ἐξένιζον τοὺς τῶν Σινωπέων πρέσβεις, καὶ
πρὸς ἀλλήλους πολλά τε καὶ φιλικὰ διελέγοντο· τά τε
ἄλλα καὶ περὶ τῆς λοιπῆς πορείας ἀνεπυνθάνοντο ὧν
ἑκάτεροι ἐδέοντο.

VI. Ταύτῃ μὲν τῇ ἡμέρᾳ τοῦτο τὸ τέλος ἐγένετο. τῇ
δὲ ὑστεραίᾳ συνέλεξαν οἱ στρατηγοὶ τοὺς στρατιώτας,
καὶ ἐδόκει αὐτοῖς περὶ τῆς λοιπῆς πορείας παρακαλέ-
σαντας τοὺς Σινωπέας βουλεύεσθαι. εἴτε γὰρ πεζῇ
δέοι πορεύεσθαι, χρήσιμοι ἂν ἐδόκουν εἶναι οἱ Σινω-
πεῖς· ἔμπειροι γὰρ ἦσαν τῆς Παφλαγονίας· εἴτε κατὰ
θάλατταν, προσδεῖν ἐδόκει Σινωπέων· μόνοι γὰρ ἂν
ἐδόκουν ἱκανοὶ εἶναι πλοῖα παρασχεῖν ἀρκοῦντα τῇ

"As to the threat you uttered, that if you thought best you would, enlist Corylas and the Paphlagonians as allies against us, we on our side are quite ready to make war with you both if it be necessary; for we have made war ere now with others who were many times your numbers. But if we think best to make a friend of the Paphlagonian—and we hear that he has a desire for your city and strongholds on the coast—we shall try to prove ourselves his friends by aiding him to accomplish his desires."

Hereupon Hecatonymus' fellow ambassadors made it very clear that they were angry with him for the words he had spoken, and one of them took the floor and said that they had not come to make war, but to show that they were friends. "And if you come," he continued, "to the city of the Sinopeans, we shall receive you there with gifts of hospitality, and now we shall direct the people of this city to give you what they can; for we see that all you say is true." After this the Cotyorites sent gifts of hospitality, and the generals of the Greeks entertained the ambassadors of the Sinopeans, and they had a great deal of friendly conversation with one another on general matters, while in particular they made such inquiries as each party wished in regard to the rest of the journey.

VI. Such was the end of that day. On the next the generals called an assembly of the soldiers, and they decided to invite the Sinopeans to join them in deliberating about the rest of their journey. For if they should have to proceed by land, it seemed that the Sinopeans would be useful to them, by virtue of their acquaintance with Paphlagonia; and if they were to go by sea, there was still need, they thought, of the Sinopeans, inasmuch as they were the only people who could provide ships enough for the army. They

XENOPHON

2 στρατιᾷ. καλέσαντες οὖν τοὺς πρέσβεις συνεβουλεύ-
οντο, καὶ ἠξίουν Ἕλληνας ὄντας Ἕλλησι τούτῳ πρῶτον καλῶς δέχεσθαι τῷ εὔνους τε εἶναι καὶ τὰ βέλτιστα συμβουλεύειν.

3 Ἀναστὰς δὲ Ἑκατώνυμος πρῶτον μὲν ἀπελογή-
σατο περὶ οὗ εἶπεν ὡς τὸν Παφλαγόνα φίλον ποιή-
σοιντο, ὅτι οὐχ ὡς τοῖς Ἕλλησι πολεμησόντων σφῶν
εἴποι, ἀλλ᾽ ὅτι ἐξὸν τοῖς βαρβάροις φίλους εἶναι τοὺς
Ἕλληνας αἱρήσονται. ἐπεὶ δὲ συμβουλεύειν ἐκέλευον,

4 ἐπευξάμενος εἶπεν ὧδε. Εἰ μὲν συμβουλεύοιμι ἃ βέλ-
τιστά μοι δοκεῖ εἶναι, πολλά μοι κἀγαθὰ γένοιτο· εἰ δὲ
μή, τἀναντία. αὕτη γὰρ ἡ ἱερὰ συμβουλὴ λεγομένη
δοκεῖ μοι παρεῖναι· νῦν γὰρ δὴ ἂν μὲν εὖ συμ-
βουλεύσας φανῶ, πολλοὶ ἔσονται οἱ ἐπαινοῦντές με,

5 ἂν δὲ κακῶς, πολλοὶ ἔσεσθε οἱ καταρώμενοι. πράγματα μὲν οὖν οἶδ᾽ ὅτι πολὺ πλείω ἕξομεν, ἐὰν κατὰ
θάλατταν κομίζησθε· ἡμᾶς γὰρ δεήσει τὰ πλοῖα
πορίζειν· ἢν δὲ κατὰ γῆν στέλλησθε, ὑμᾶς δεήσει τοὺς

6 μαχομένους εἶναι· ὅμως δὲ λεκτέα ἃ γιγνώσκω· ἔμπειρος γάρ εἰμι καὶ τῆς χώρας τῆς Παφλαγόνων καὶ
τῆς δυνάμεως. ἔχει γὰρ ἀμφότερα, καὶ πεδία κάλλι-

7 στα καὶ ὄρη ὑψηλότατα. καὶ πρῶτον μὲν οἶδα εὐθὺς
ᾗ τὴν εἰσβολὴν ἀνάγκη ποιεῖσθαι· οὐ γὰρ ἔστιν ἄλλη
ἢ ᾗ τὰ κέρατα τοῦ ὄρους τῆς ὁδοῦ καθ᾽ ἑκάτερά ἐστιν
ὑψηλά, ἃ κρατεῖν κατέχοντες καὶ πάνυ ὀλίγοι δύναιντ᾽

426

accordingly invited the ambassadors in and proceeded to take counsel with them, asking them, as Greeks dealing with Greeks, to make a beginning of their kindly reception by showing friendliness and offering the best advice.

Then Hecatonymus rose and, in the first place, defended himself in the matter of his remark that they would make a friend of the Paphlagonian, by saying that he did not mean that his own people would make war upon the Greeks, but rather that despite the opportunity they had to be friends of the barbarians they would choose the Greeks instead. But when they told him to proceed to give some advice, he began with a prayer to the gods as follows: "If I should give the advice which in my judgment is best, may many blessings come to me; otherwise, the opposite. For what men term 'sacred counsel'[30] seems verily to be my portion; since today if I be found to have given good counsel, there will be many to praise me, but if it be ill, there will be many among you to curse me. Now I know that we shall have far more trouble if you are conveyed by sea, for upon us will fall the duty of providing the ships; while if you journey by land, upon you will fall the task of doing the fighting. Nevertheless, I must say what I believe; for I am acquainted with both the country of the Paphlagonians and their power. Their country possesses these two things, the fairest plains and the loftiest mountains. And, in the first place, I know at once where you must make your entry: there is no place save where the peaks of the mountains rise high on either side of the road; holding these peaks a mere handful of men could command the pass, and

[30] Hecatonymus alludes to the proverb "Counsel is a sacred thing," *i.e.* it must be given honestly. Cf. Plato, *Theages* 122b.

ἄν· τούτων δὲ κατεχομένων οὐδ᾽ ἂν οἱ πάντες ἄνθρωποι
δύναιντ᾽ ἂν διελθεῖν. ταῦτα δὲ καὶ δείξαιμι ἄν, εἴ μοί
8 τινα βούλεσθε συμπέμψαι. ἔπειτα δὲ οἶδα καὶ πεδία
ὄντα καὶ ἱππείαν ἣν αὐτοὶ οἱ βάρβαροι νομίζουσι
κρείττω εἶναι ἁπάσης τῆς βασιλέως ἱππείας. καὶ νῦν
οὗτοι οὐ παρεγένοντο βασιλεῖ καλοῦντι, ἀλλὰ καὶ
μεῖζον φρονεῖ ὁ ἄρχων αὐτῶν.

9 Ἢν δὲ καὶ δυνηθῆτε τά τε ὄρη κλέψαι ἢ φθάσαι
λαβόντες καὶ ἐν τῷ πεδίῳ κρατῆσαι μαχόμενοι τούς τε
ἱππέας τούτων καὶ πεζῶν μυριάδας πλέον ἢ δώδεκα,
ἥξετε ἐπὶ τοὺς ποταμούς, πρῶτον μὲν τὸν Θερμώδοντα,
εὖρος τριῶν πλέθρων, ὃν χαλεπὸν οἶμαι διαβαίνειν
ἄλλως τε καὶ πολεμίων πολλῶν μὲν ἔμπροσθεν ὄντων,
πολλῶν δὲ ὄπισθεν ἑπομένων· δεύτερον δὲ Ἶριν, τρί-
πλεθρον ὡσαύτως· τρίτον δὲ Ἅλυν, οὐ μεῖον δυοῖν
σταδίοιν, ὃν οὐκ ἂν δύναισθε ἄνευ πλοίων διαβῆναι·
πλοῖα δὲ τίς ἔσται ὁ παρέχων; ὡς δ᾽ αὕτως καὶ ὁ
Παρθένιος ἄβατος· ἐφ᾽ ὃν ἔλθοιτε ἄν, εἰ τὸν Ἅλυν
διαβαίητε.

10 Ἐγὼ μὲν οὖν οὐ χαλεπὴν ὑμῖν εἶναι νομίζω τὴν
πορείαν ἀλλὰ παντάπασιν ἀδύνατον. ἂν δὲ πλέητε,
ἔστιν ἐνθένδε μὲν εἰς Σινώπην παραπλεῦσαι, ἐκ Σινώπης δὲ εἰς Ἡράκλειαν· ἐξ Ἡρακλείας δὲ οὔτε πεζῇ
οὔτε κατὰ θάλατταν ἀπορία· πολλὰ γὰρ πλοῖα ἔστι
καὶ ἐν Ἡρακλείᾳ.

11 Ἐπεὶ δὲ ταῦτ᾽ ἔλεξεν, οἱ μὲν ὑπώπτευον φιλίας
ἕνεκα τῆς Κορύλα λέγειν· καὶ γὰρ ἦν πρόξενος αὐτῷ·
οἱ δὲ καὶ ὡς δῶρα ληψόμενον διὰ τὴν συμβουλὴν

if they are so held, not all the men in the world could effect a passage. All this I could even point out if you wish to send some one to the spot with me. Secondly, I know that they have plains and a cavalry which the barbarians themselves regard as superior to the whole of the King's cavalry. Indeed, only now these Paphlagonians have failed to present themselves when the King summoned them, for their ruler is too proud to obey.

"If you should, after all, find yourselves able not only to seize the mountains, whether by stealth or by anticipating the enemy, but also on the plain to conquer in battle both their cavalry and their more than one hundred and twenty thousand infantry, you will come to the rivers. First is the Thermodon, three plethra in width, which I fancy would be difficult to cross, especially with great numbers of the enemy in front and great numbers following behind; second, the Iris, likewise three plethra wide; third, the Halys, not less than two stadia in width, which you could not cross without boats—and who will there be to supply you with boats?—and similarly impassable is the Parthenius also, to which you would come if you should get across the Halys.

"For my part, therefore, I believe that this journey is not merely difficult for you, but a thing of utter impossibility. If you go by sea, however, you can coast along from here to Sinope, and from Sinope to Heracleia; and from Heracleia on there is no difficulty either by land or by water, for there are ships in abundance also at Heracleia."

When he had thus spoken, some of his hearers were suspicious that he spoke as he did out of friendship for Corylas, for he was his official representative at Sinope; others imagined that he even had the idea of obtaining gifts

ταύτην· οἱ δὲ ὑπώπτευον καὶ τούτου ἕνεκα λέγειν ὡς
μὴ πεζῇ ἰόντες τὴν Σινωπέων τι χώραν κακὸν ἐργά-
ζοιντο. οἱ δ' οὖν Ἕλληνες ἐψηφίσαντο κατὰ θάλατταν
12 τὴν πορείαν ποιεῖσθαι. μετὰ ταῦτα Ξενοφῶν εἶπεν· Ὦ
Σινωπεῖς, οἱ μὲν ἄνδρες ᾕρηνται πορείαν ἣν ὑμεῖς
συμβουλεύετε· οὕτω δὲ ἔχει· εἰ μὲν μέλλει πλοῖα ἔσεσθαι ἱκανὰ ὡς ἀριθμῷ ἕνα μὴ καταλείπεσθαι ἐνθάδε,
ἡμεῖς ἂν πλέοιμεν· εἰ δὲ μέλλοιμεν οἱ μὲν καταλείψε-
σθαι οἱ δὲ πλεύσεσθαι, οὐκ ἂν ἐμβαίημεν εἰς τὰ
13 πλοῖα. γιγνώσκομεν γὰρ ὅτι ὅπου μὲν ἂν κρατῶμεν,
δυναίμεθ' ἂν καὶ σῴζεσθαι καὶ τὰ ἐπιτήδεια ἔχειν· εἰ
δέ που ἥττους τῶν πολεμίων ληφθησόμεθα, εὔδηλον
δὴ ὅτι ἐν ἀνδραπόδων χώρᾳ ἐσόμεθα. ἀκούσαντες
14 ταῦτα οἱ πρέσβεις ἐκέλευον πέμπειν πρέσβεις. καὶ
πέμπουσι Καλλίμαχον Ἀρκάδα καὶ Ἀρίστωνα Ἀθηναῖον καὶ Σαμόλαν Ἀχαιόν. καὶ οἱ μὲν ᾤχοντο.

15 Ἐν δὲ τούτῳ τῷ χρόνῳ Ξενοφῶντι, ὁρῶντι μὲν
ὁπλίτας πολλοὺς τῶν Ἑλλήνων, ὁρῶντι δὲ πελταστὰς
πολλοὺς καὶ τοξότας καὶ σφενδονήτας καὶ ἱππέας δὲ
καὶ μάλα ἤδη διὰ τὴν τριβὴν ἱκανούς, ὄντας δ' ἐν τῷ
Πόντῳ, ἔνθα οὐκ ἂν ἀπ' ὀλίγων χρημάτων τοσαύτη
δύναμις παρεσκευάσθη, καλὸν αὐτῷ ἐδόκει εἶναι
χώραν καὶ δύναμιν τῇ Ἑλλάδι προσκτήσασθαι πόλιν
16 κατοικίσαντας. καὶ γενέσθαι ἂν αὐτῷ ἐδόκει μεγάλη,
καταλογιζομένῳ τό τε αὐτῶν πλῆθος καὶ τοὺς περι-

on account of this advice; while still others suspected that the real purpose of his speech was to prevent the Greeks from going by land and so doing some harm to the territory of the Sinopeans. At any rate, however, the Greeks voted to make the journey by sea. After this Xenophon said: "Men of Sinope, my troops have chosen the route which you advise; but the matter stands in this way: if there are to be ships enough so that not so much as one man will be left behind here, we shall set sail; but if the plan should be to let some of us stay behind and others sail, we shall not set foot on the ships. For we know that wherever we hold the upper hand, we should be able both to keep ourselves safe and to obtain provisions; but let us once get caught where we are weaker than the enemy, and it is perfectly clear that we shall be in the position of slaves." Upon hearing these words the envoys told them to send ambassadors. And they sent Callimachus the Arcadian, Ariston the Athenian, and Samolas the Achaean. These men accordingly set out.

At this time, as Xenophon's eyes rested upon a great body of Greek hoplites, and likewise upon a great body of peltasts, bowmen, slingers, and horsemen also, all of them now exceedingly efficient through constant service and all there in Pontus[31] where so large a force could not have been gathered by any slight outlay of money, it seemed to him that it was a fine thing to gain additional territory and power for Greece by founding a city. It would become a great city, he thought, as he reckoned up their own numbers and the peoples who dwelt around the Euxine. And

---

[31] Xenophon uses the term Πόντος both of the Euxine Sea and of the region along its south-eastern coast. See below.

οἰκοῦντας τὸν Πόντον. καὶ ἐπὶ τούτοις ἐθύετο πρίν τινι
εἰπεῖν τῶν στρατιωτῶν Σιλανὸν παρακαλέσας τὸν

17 Κύρου μάντιν γενόμενον τὸν Ἀμπρακιώτην. ὁ δὲ Σιλανὸς δεδιὼς μὴ γένηται ταῦτα καὶ καταμείνῃ που ἡ
στρατιά, ἐκφέρει εἰς τὸ στράτευμα λόγον ὅτι Ξενοφῶν
βούλεται καταμεῖναι τὴν στρατιὰν καὶ πόλιν οἰκίσαι

18 καὶ ἑαυτῷ ὄνομα καὶ δύναμιν περιποιήσασθαι. αὐτὸς
δ᾽ ὁ Σιλανὸς ἐβούλετο ὅτι τάχιστα εἰς τὴν Ἑλλάδα
ἀφικέσθαι· οὓς γὰρ παρὰ Κύρου ἔλαβε τρισχιλίους
δαρεικοὺς ὅτε τὰς δέκα ἡμέρας ἠλήθευσε θυόμενος
Κύρῳ, διεσεσώκει.

19 Τῶν δὲ στρατιωτῶν, ἐπεὶ ἤκουσαν, τοῖς μὲν ἐδόκει
βέλτιστον εἶναι καταμεῖναι, τοῖς δὲ πολλοῖς οὔ. Τιμασίων δὲ ὁ Δαρδανεὺς καὶ Θώραξ ὁ Βοιώτιος πρὸς
ἐμπόρους τινὰς παρόντας τῶν Ἡρακλεωτῶν καὶ Σινωπέων λέγουσιν ὅτι εἰ μὴ ἐκποριοῦσι τῇ στρατιᾷ
μισθὸν ὥστε ἔχειν τὰ ἐπιτήδεια ἐκπλέοντας, ὅτι κιν-
δυνεύσει μεῖναι τοσαύτη δύναμις ἐν τῷ Πόντῳ· βούλεται γὰρ Ξενοφῶν καὶ ἡμᾶς παρακαλεῖ, ἐπειδὰν ἔλθῃ

20 τὰ πλοῖα, τότε εἰπεῖν ἐξαίφνης τῇ στρατιᾷ· Ἄνδρες,
νῦν μὲν ὁρῶμεν ὑμᾶς ἀπόρους ὄντας καὶ ἐν τῷ ἀπόπλῳ
ἔχειν τὰ ἐπιτήδεια καὶ ὡς οἴκαδε[12] ἀπελθόντας ὀνῆσαί
τι τοὺς οἴκοι· εἰ δὲ βούλεσθε τῆς κύκλῳ χώρας περὶ
τὸν Πόντον οἰκουμένης ἐκλεξάμενοι ὅποι ἂν βούλησθε

12 ὡς οἴκαδε some MSS., Gem., Hude/Peters, Mar.: οἴκαδε
other MSS., Cobet.

---

32 Xenophon as *oikistes*, or founder of a colony, offering sacri-

with a view to this project, before speaking about it to any of the soldiers, he offered sacrifices, summoning for that purpose Silanus the Ambraciot, who had been the soothsayer of Cyrus.[32] Silanus, however, fearing that this thing might come to pass and that the army might settle down somewhere, carried forth to the troops a report that Xenophon wanted them to settle down, so that he could found a city and win for himself a name and power. As for Silanus, his own desire was to reach Greece as quickly as possible; for the three thousand darics, which he had received from Cyrus at the time when he sacrificed for him and had told the truth about the ten days,[33] he had brought safely through.

When the soldiers heard this report, some of them thought it was best to settle down, but the majority thought otherwise. And Timasion the Dardanian and Thorax the Boeotian said to some Heracleot and Sinopean merchants who were there, that if they did not provide pay for the troops so that they would have provisions for the voyage from Cotyora, there would be danger of that great force remaining in Pontus. "For Xenophon," they went on, "wishes and is urging that as soon as the ships come, we should then say all of a sudden to the army: 'Soldiers, now we see that you are without means either to supply yourselves with provisions on the homeward voyage, or to do anything for your people at home assuming you get back there; but if you wish to pick out some spot in the country that lies round about the Euxine and put to shore wherever

fices on the site of a future city: cf. Arrian, *An*. III. i. 5, and see I. Malkin, *Religion and Colonization in Ancient Greece* (Leiden, 1987) 102–4.   [33] See I. vii. 18.

433

κατασχεῖν, καὶ τὸν μὲν ἐθέλοντα ἀπιέναι οἴκαδε, τὸν
δ᾽ ἐθέλοντα μένειν αὐτοῦ, πλοῖα δ᾽ ὑμῖν πάρεστιν,
ὥστε ὅπῃ ἂν βούλησθε ἐξαίφνης ἂν ἐπιπέσοιτε.

21 Ἀκούσαντες ταῦτα οἱ ἔμποροι ἀπήγγελλον ταῖς
πόλεσι· συνέπεμψε δ᾽ αὐτοῖς Τιμασίων Δαρδανεὺς
Εὐρύμαχόν τε τὸν Δαρδανέα καὶ Θώρακα τὸν Βοιώτιον
τὰ αὐτὰ ταῦτα ἐροῦντας. Σινωπεῖς δὲ καὶ Ἡρακλεῶται
ταῦτα ἀκούσαντες πέμπουσι πρὸς τὸν Τιμασίωνα καὶ
κελεύουσι προστατεῦσαι λαβόντα χρήματα ὅπως ἐκ-
22 πλεύσῃ ἡ στρατιά. ὁ δὲ ἄσμενος ἀκούσας ἐν συλλόγῳ
τῶν στρατιωτῶν ὄντων λέγει τάδε. Οὐ δεῖ προσέχειν
μονῇ, ὦ ἄνδρες, οὐδὲ τῆς Ἑλλάδος οὐδὲν περὶ πλείονος ποιεῖσθαι. ἀκούω δέ τινας θύεσθαι ἐπὶ τούτῳ οὐδ᾽
23 ὑμῖν λέγοντας. ὑπισχνοῦμαι δὲ ὑμῖν, ἂν ἐκπλέητε, ἀπὸ
νουμηνίας μισθοφορὰν παρέξειν κυζικηνὸν ἑκάστῳ
τοῦ μηνός· καὶ ἄξω ὑμᾶς εἰς τὴν Τρῳάδα, ἔνθεν καί
εἰμι φυγάς, καὶ ὑπάρξει ὑμῖν ἡ ἐμὴ πόλις· ἑκόντες γάρ
24 με δέξονται. ἡγήσομαι δὲ αὐτὸς ἐγὼ ἔνθεν πολλὰ
χρήματα λήψεσθε. ἔμπειρος δέ εἰμι τῆς Αἰολίδος καὶ
τῆς Φρυγίας καὶ τῆς Τρῳάδος καὶ τῆς Φαρναβάζου
ἀρχῆς πάσης, τὰ μὲν διὰ τὸ ἐκεῖθεν εἶναι, τὰ δὲ διὰ
τὸ συνεστρατεῦσθαι ἐν αὐτῇ σὺν Κλεάρχῳ τε καὶ
Δερκυλίδᾳ.

---

[34] An electrum coin of Cyzicus, an important Greek city on the
Propontis. The main unit of exchange in the Pontus region, it was
worth approx. 25 Attic drachmas.

[35] Persian satrap of Lesser Phrygia and Bithynia.

[36] A Spartan general, he worked closely with Pharnabazus in

you may wish—he who so desires to go back home and he who so desires to stay behind—here are your ships, so that you could make a sudden attack at whatever point you may wish.'"

Upon hearing this statement the merchants carried it back to their cities; and along with them Timasion the Dardanian sent Eurymachus the Dardanian and Thorax the Boeotian to report these same things. When the Sinopeans and Heracleots heard it, they sent to Timasion and urged him to take in charge, for a fee, the matter of getting the army to sail away. He received this proposal gladly, and when the soldiers were gathered in assembly addressed them as follows: "You ought not, soldiers, to set your thoughts on remaining here, nor to esteem anything more highly than Greece. But I hear that certain people are offering sacrifices over this matter, with not so much as a word to you. Now I promise, in case you set sail from here, to provide you with pay from the first of the month at the rate of a Cyzicene[34] per month to each man; and I will take you to Troas, the place from which I am an exile, and my city will be at your service; for they will receive me willingly. Then I myself will lead you to places from which you will get an abundance of wealth. I am acquainted with Aeolis, Phrygia, Troas, and the entire province of Pharnabazus,[35] partly because I come from that region, and partly because I have campaigned there with Clearchus and Dercylidas."[36]

the Peloponnesian War (Thuc. VIII. lxi–lxii); he evidently quarrelled with the Persian, and while commander of Spartan forces later in Asia Minor (which included Xenophon and the Cyreans), attacked his satrapy (*Hell.* III. i. 8–ii. 20).

25 Ἀναστὰς αὖθις Θώραξ ὁ Βοιώτιος, ὃς ἀεὶ περὶ
στρατηγίας Ξενοφῶντι ἐμάχετο, ἔφη, εἰ ἐξέλθοιεν ἐκ
τοῦ Πόντου, ἔσεσθαι αὐτοῖς Χερρόνησον χώραν καλὴν καὶ εὐδαίμονα ὥστε τῷ βουλομένῳ ἐνοικεῖν, τῷ δὲ
μὴ βουλομένῳ ἀπιέναι οἴκαδε. γελοῖον δὲ εἶναι ἐν τῇ
Ἑλλάδι οὔσης χώρας πολλῆς καὶ ἀφθόνου ἐν τῇ
26 βαρβάρων μαστεύειν. ἔστε δ᾽ ἄν, ἔφη, ἐκεῖ γένησθε,
κἀγὼ καθάπερ Τιμασίων ὑπισχνοῦμαι ὑμῖν τὴν
μισθοφοράν. ταῦτα δὲ ἔλεγεν εἰδὼς ἃ Τιμασίωνι οἱ
Ἡρακλεῶται καὶ οἱ Σινωπεῖς ἐπαγγέλλοιντο ὥστε ἐκπλεῖν. ὁ δὲ Ξενοφῶν ἐν τούτῳ ἐσίγα.

27 Ἀναστὰς δὲ Φιλήσιος καὶ Λύκων οἱ Ἀχαιοὶ ἔλεγον
ὡς δεινὸν εἴη ἰδίᾳ μὲν Ξενοφῶντα πείθειν τε κατα-
μένειν καὶ θύεσθαι ὑπὲρ τῆς μονῆς, εἰς δὲ τὸ κοινὸν
μηδὲν ἀγορεύειν περὶ τούτων. ὥστε ἠναγκάσθη ὁ
28 Ξενοφῶν ἀναστῆναι καὶ εἰπεῖν τάδε. Ἐγώ, ὦ ἄνδρες,
θύομαι μὲν ὡς ὁρᾶτε ὁπόσα δύναμαι καὶ ὑπὲρ ὑμῶν
καὶ ὑπὲρ ἐμαυτοῦ ὅπως ταῦτα τυγχάνω καὶ λέγων καὶ
νοῶν καὶ πράττων ὁποῖα μέλλει ὑμῖν τε κάλλιστα καὶ
ἄριστα ἔσεσθαι καὶ ἐμοί. καὶ νῦν ἐθυόμην περὶ αὐτοῦ
τούτου εἰ ἄμεινον εἴη ἄρχεσθαι λέγειν εἰς ὑμᾶς καὶ
πράττειν περὶ τούτων ἢ παντάπασι μηδὲ ἅπτεσθαι τοῦ
29 πράγματος. Σιλανὸς δέ μοι ὁ μάντις ἀπεκρίνατο τὸ
μὲν μέγιστον, τὰ ἱερὰ καλὰ εἶναι· ᾔδει γὰρ καὶ ἐμὲ
οὐκ ἄπειρον ὄντα διὰ τὸ ἀεὶ παρεῖναι τοῖς ἱεροῖς· ἔλεξε
δὲ ὅτι ἐν τοῖς ἱεροῖς φαίνοιτό τις δόλος καὶ ἐπιβουλὴ

Next rose Thorax the Boeotian, who was always at odds with Xenophon over the generalship of the army, and said that once they got out of the Euxine they would have the Chersonese, a fair and prosperous country, where any one who so desired might dwell, while any who did not desire to do this, might return home. It was ridiculous, he said, when there was plenty of fertile land in Greece, to be hunting for it in the domain of the barbarians. "And until you reach that spot," he continued, "I also, like Timasion, promise you regular pay." All this he said with full knowledge of what the Heracleots and the Sinopeans were promising Timasion for getting the army to sail away. Xenophon meanwhile was silent.

Then Philesius and Lycon the Achaeans rose and said that it was outrageous for Xenophon to be privately urging people to settle down and sacrificing with a view to that plan, while publicly saying not a word about the matter. Thus Xenophon was compelled to rise and speak as follows: "I offer, soldiers, as you see, all the sacrifices I can both on your behalf and my own in order that I may perchance say and think and do such things as will be fairest and best both for you and me.[37] And in the present case I was sacrificing for guidance on this point only, whether it was better to begin to speak before you and to act regarding this project, or not to touch the matter at all. Now Silanus, the soothsayer, answered me in respect to the main issue that the omens were favourable (for he knew well enough that I was not unacquainted with divination, being always present at the sacrifices); but he said that there appeared in the omens a kind of fraud and plot

[37] Cf. *Hipp.* I. 1.

437

ἐμοί, ὡς ἄρα γιγνώσκων ὅτι αὐτὸς ἐπεβούλευε διαβάλλειν με πρὸς ὑμᾶς. ἐξήνεγκε γὰρ τὸν λόγον ὡς
ἐγὼ πράττειν ταῦτα διανοοίμην ἤδη οὐ πείσας ὑμᾶς.

30 ἐγὼ δὲ εἰ μὲν ἑώρων ἀποροῦντας ὑμᾶς, τοῦτ᾽ ἂν ἐσκόπουν ἀφ᾽ οὗ ἂν γένοιτο ὥστε λαβόντας ὑμᾶς πόλιν
τὸν μὲν βουλόμενον ἀποπλεῖν ἤδη, τὸν δὲ μὴ βουλόμενον, ἐπεὶ κτήσαιτο ἱκανὰ ὥστε καὶ τοὺς ἑαυτοῦ

31 οἰκείους ὠφελῆσαί τι. ἐπεὶ δὲ ὁρῶ ὑμῖν καὶ τὰ πλοῖα
πέμποντας Ἡρακλεώτας καὶ Σινωπέας ὥστε ἐκπλεῖν,
καὶ μισθὸν ὑπισχνουμένους ὑμῖν ἄνδρας ἀπὸ νουμηνίας, καλόν μοι δοκεῖ εἶναι σῳζομένους ἔνθα βουλόμεθα μισθὸν τῆς σωτηρίας λαμβάνειν, καὶ αὐτός τε
παύομαι ἐκείνης τῆς διανοίας, καὶ ὁπόσοι πρὸς ἐμὲ
προσῇσαν λέγοντες ὡς χρὴ ταῦτα πράττειν, ἅμα
παύεσθαί φημι χρῆναι.

32 Οὕτω γὰρ γιγνώσκω· ὁμοῦ μὲν ὄντες πολλοὶ ὥσπερ
νυνὶ δοκεῖτε ἄν μοι καὶ ἔντιμοι εἶναι καὶ ἔχειν τὰ
ἐπιτήδεια· ἐν γὰρ τῷ κρατεῖν ἐστι καὶ τὸ λαμβάνειν
τὰ τῶν ἡττόνων· διασπασθέντες δ᾽ ἂν καὶ κατὰ μικρὰ
γενομένης τῆς δυνάμεως οὔτ᾽ ἂν τροφὴν δύναισθε

33 λαμβάνειν οὔτε χαίροντες ἂν ἀπαλλάξαιτε. δοκεῖ οὖν
μοι ἅπερ ὑμῖν, ἐκπορεύεσθαι εἰς τὴν Ἑλλάδα, καὶ ἐάν
τις μείνῃ ἢ ἀπολιπὼν ληφθῇ πρὶν ἐν ἀσφαλεῖ εἶναι
πᾶν τὸ στράτευμα, κρίνεσθαι αὐτὸν ὡς ἀδικοῦντα. καὶ
ὅτῳ δοκεῖ, ἔφη, ταῦτα, ἀράτω τὴν χεῖρα. ἀνέτειναν
ἅπαντες.

against me, manifestly because he knew that he was himself plotting to traduce me before you. For he spread abroad the report that I was intending to do these things at once, without getting your consent. Now if I saw that you were without resources, I should be looking about for a plan by which you might get possession of a city, with the provision that afterwards he who chose might sail back home at once, while he who did not wish to go at once might return after he had accumulated enough to bestow a little something upon his people at home. But since, in fact, I see that the Heracleots and Sinopeans are sending you the ships in which to sail away, and that men are promising you pay from the first of the month, it seems to me it is a fine thing to be carried safely where we want to go and at the same time to receive pay for our preservation; therefore I renounce that other project for myself, and I say, to all those who have come to me and expressed the view that it ought to be carried out, that they at the same time should renounce it too.

"For I hold this opinion: standing together and in force, as you are now, I think you will be held in honour and will have provisions, for in strength lies the opportunity to wrest away the possessions of the weaker; but let yourselves get separated and your force broken up into small parts, and you would neither be able to obtain food to live on nor would you come off unharmed. I think, therefore, just as you do, that we should set out for Greece, and that if it does come to pass that any man stays behind or is caught deserting before the entire army is in a place of safety, he should be brought to trial as a wrong-doer. And whoever is of this opinion," he continued, "let him raise his hand." Up went every hand.

34 Ὁ δὲ Σιλανὸς ἐβόα, καὶ ἐπεχείρει λέγειν ὡς δίκαιον
εἴη ἀπιέναι τὸν βουλόμενον. οἱ δὲ στρατιῶται οὐκ
ἠνείχοντο, ἀλλ᾽ ἠπείλουν αὐτῷ ὅτι εἰ λήψονται ἀπο-
35 διδράσκοντα, τὴν δίκην ἐπιθήσοιεν. ἐντεῦθεν ἐπεὶ
ἔγνωσαν οἱ Ἡρακλεῶται ὅτι ἐκπλεῖν δεδογμένον εἴη
καὶ Ξενοφῶν αὐτὸς ἐπεψηφικὼς εἴη, τὰ μὲν πλοῖα
πέμπουσι, τὰ δὲ χρήματα ἃ ὑπέσχοντο Τιμασίωνι καὶ
36 Θώρακι ἐψευσμένοι ἦσαν τῆς μισθοφορᾶς. ἐνταῦθα δὲ
ἐκπεπληγμένοι ἦσαν καὶ ἐδέδισαν τὴν στρατιὰν οἱ
τὴν μισθοφορὰν ὑπεσχημένοι. παραλαβόντες οὖν
οὗτοι καὶ τοὺς ἄλλους στρατηγοὺς οἷς ἀνεκεκοίνωντο
ἃ πρόσθεν ἔπραττον, πάντες δ᾽ ἦσαν πλὴν Νέωνος
τοῦ Ἀσιναίου, ὃς Χειρισόφῳ ὑπεστρατήγει, Χειρίσοφος δὲ οὔπω παρῆν, ἔρχονται πρὸς Ξενοφῶντα, καὶ
λέγουσιν ὅτι μεταμέλοι αὐτοῖς, καὶ δοκοίη κράτιστον
εἶναι πλεῖν εἰς Φᾶσιν, ἐπεὶ πλοῖα ἔστι, καὶ κατασχεῖν
37 τὴν Φασιανῶν χώραν. Αἰήτου δὲ υἱδοῦς ἐτύγχανε
βασιλεύων αὐτῶν. Ξενοφῶν δὲ ἀπεκρίνατο ὅτι οὐδὲν
ἂν τούτων εἴποι εἰς τὴν στρατιάν· ὑμεῖς δὲ συλλέξαντες, ἔφη, εἰ βούλεσθε, λέγετε. ἐνταῦθα ἀποδείκνυται
Τιμασίων ὁ Δαρδανεὺς γνώμην μὴ ἐκκλησιάζειν ἀλλὰ
τοὺς αὑτοῦ ἕκαστον λοχαγοὺς πρῶτον πειρᾶσθαι πείθειν. καὶ ἀπελθόντες ταῦτ᾽ ἐποίουν.

VII. Ταῦτα οὖν οἱ στρατιῶται ἀνεπύθοντο πρατ-
τόμενα. καὶ ὁ Νέων λέγει ὡς Ξενοφῶν ἀναπεπεικὼς
τοὺς ἄλλους στρατηγοὺς διανοεῖται ἄγειν τοὺς στρα-
2 τιώτας ἐξαπατήσας πάλιν εἰς Φᾶσιν. ἀκούσαντες δ᾽
οἱ στρατιῶται χαλεπῶς ἔφερον, καὶ σύλλογοι ἐγί-

Silanus, however, began shouting, and attempted to say that it was fair for any one who so chose to leave the army. But the soldiers would not allow him to speak, and they threatened him that as surely as they caught him running away, they would inflict due punishment upon him. After that, when the Heracleots learned that it had been voted to sail away, and that Xenophon himself had put the question to vote, they did send the ships, but in the matter of the money they had promised to Timasion and Thorax they turned out to be deceivers in the payment. Consequently the men who had promised the pay were panic-stricken, and stood in fear of the army. They therefore took with them the other generals to whom they had communicated their earlier doings—namely, all the generals except Neon the Asinaean, who was acting as lieutenant for Cheirisophus because Cheirisophus had not yet returned—and came to Xenophon, with the message that they had changed their minds and thought it was best to sail to the Phasis, inasmuch as there were ships at hand, and seize the land of the Phasians. Their king, as it chanced, was a grandson of Aeetes. Xenophon replied that he would not say a word to the army about this plan; "but," he went on, "gather the men together and speak to them yourselves, if you wish." Then Timasion the Dardanian declared it as his opinion that they should not hold an assembly, but that each general should first endeavour to persuade his own captains. So they went away and set about doing this.

VII. The soldiers, accordingly, learned by inquiry the matters being carried out. And Neon said that Xenophon had won over the other generals and was intending to deceive the soldiers and lead them back to the Phasis. Upon hearing these words the soldiers were exceedingly angry;

γνοντο καὶ κύκλοι συνίσταντο καὶ μάλα φοβεροὶ
ἦσαν μὴ ποιήσειαν οἷα καὶ τοὺς τῶν Κόλχων κήρυκας
ἐποίησαν καὶ τοὺς ἀγορανόμους. ὅσοι γὰρ μὴ εἰς τὴν

3 θάλατταν κατέφυγον κατελεύσθησαν.[13] ἐπεὶ δὲ ᾐσθάνετο Ξενοφῶν, ἔδοξεν αὐτῷ ὡς τάχιστα συναγαγεῖν
αὐτῶν ἀγοράν, καὶ μὴ ἐᾶσαι συλλεγῆναι αὐτομάτους·

4 καὶ ἐκέλευσε τὸν κήρυκα συλλέξαι ἀγοράν. οἱ δ' ἐπεὶ
τοῦ κήρυκος ἤκουσαν, συνέδραμον καὶ μάλα ἑτοίμως.
ἐνταῦθα Ξενοφῶν τῶν μὲν στρατηγῶν οὐ κατηγόρει,
ὅτι ἦλθον πρὸς αὐτόν, λέγει δὲ ὧδε.

5 Ἀκούω τινὰ διαβάλλειν, ὦ ἄνδρες, ἐμὲ ὡς ἐγὼ ἄρα
ἐξαπατήσας ὑμᾶς μέλλω ἄγειν εἰς Φᾶσιν. ἀκούσατε
οὖν μου πρὸς θεῶν, καὶ ἐὰν μὲν ἐγὼ φαίνωμαι ἀδικῶν,
οὐ χρή με ἐνθένδε ἀπελθεῖν πρὶν ἂν δῶ τὴν δίκην· ἂν
δ' ὑμῖν φαίνωνται ἀδικοῦντες οἱ ἐμὲ διαβάλλοντες,

6 οὕτως αὐτοῖς χρῆσθαι ὥσπερ ἄξιον. ὑμεῖς δ', ἔφη,
ἴστε δήπου ὅθεν ἥλιος ἀνίσχει καὶ ὅπου δύεται, καὶ
ὅτι ἐὰν μέν τις εἰς τὴν Ἑλλάδα μέλλῃ ἰέναι, πρὸς
ἑσπέραν δεῖ πορεύεσθαι· ἢν δέ τις βούληται εἰς τοὺς
βαρβάρους, τοὔμπαλιν πρὸς ἕω. ἔστιν οὖν ὅστις τοῦτο
ἂν δύναιτο ὑμᾶς ἐξαπατῆσαι ὡς ἥλιος ἔνθεν μὲν
ἀνίσχει, δύεται δὲ ἐνταῦθα, ἔνθα δὲ δύεται, ἀνίσχει δ'

7 ἐντεῦθεν; ἀλλὰ μὴν καὶ τοῦτό γε ἐπίστασθε ὅτι βορέας
μὲν ἔξω τοῦ Πόντου εἰς τὴν Ἑλλάδα φέρει, νότος δὲ
εἴσω εἰς Φᾶσιν, καὶ λέγεται, ὅταν βορρᾶς πνέῃ, ὡς

---

[13] ὅσοι … κατελεύσθησαν del. by Rehdantz.

meetings were held, groups of them collected, and it was greatly to be feared that they would do the sort of things they had done to the heralds of the Colchians and the market clerks; for whoever did not escape to the sea were stoned to death.[38] When Xenophon became aware of the situation, he decided to call an assembly of the men as speedily as possible and not to allow them to gather of their own accord; so he directed the herald to call an assembly. And as soon as the soldiers heard the herald, they rushed together with the utmost readiness. Then Xenophon, without mentioning against the generals the matter of their visit to him, spoke as follows:

"I hear, soldiers, that some one is bringing a charge against me, namely, that I am going to deceive you and lead you to the Phasis. In the name of the gods, then, give ear to my words, and if it appears that I am guilty of wrong, I ought not to leave this spot without paying the penalty; but if it appears to you that my accusers are guilty of wrong, they ought to be dealt with in such manner as they deserve. You doubtless know," he continued, "where the sun rises and where it sets; likewise, that if a man is to go to Greece, he must journey toward the west, while if he wishes to go to the lands of the barbarians, he must travel in the opposite direction, that is, toward the east. Now is there any one who could deceive you in this matter, by maintaining that the place where the sun rises is the one where it sets and the place where it sets is the one where it rises? Again, you surely know this also, that the north wind carries one out of the Euxine to Greece, while the south wind carries you within, to the Phasis—indeed, the saying is, 'When the

[38] As described by Xenophon in the following speech, §§13 ff.

καλοὶ πλοῖ εἰσιν εἰς τὴν Ἑλλάδα. τοῦτ᾽ οὖν ἔστιν ὅπως
τις ἂν ὑμᾶς ἐξαπατήσαι ὥστε ἐμβαίνειν ὁπόταν νότος
8 πνέῃ; ἀλλὰ γὰρ ὁπόταν γαλήνη ᾖ ἐμβιβῶ. οὐκοῦν ἐγὼ
μὲν ἐν ἑνὶ πλοίῳ πλευσοῦμαι, ὑμεῖς δὲ τοὐλάχιστον ἐν
ἑκατόν. πῶς ἂν οὖν ἐγὼ ἢ βιασαίμην ὑμᾶς σὺν ἐμοὶ
9 πλεῖν μὴ βουλομένους ἢ ἐξαπατήσας ἄγοιμι; ποιῶ δ᾽
ὑμᾶς ἐξαπατηθέντας καὶ καταγοητευθέντας ὑπ᾽ ἐμοῦ
ἥκειν εἰς Φᾶσιν· καὶ δὴ ἀποβαίνομεν εἰς τὴν χώραν·
γνώσεσθε δήπου ὅτι οὐκ ἐν τῇ Ἑλλάδι ἐστέ· καὶ ἐγὼ
μὲν ἔσομαι ὁ ἐξηπατηκὼς εἷς ὑμᾶς, ὑμεῖς δὲ οἱ ἐξ-
ηπατημένοι ἐγγὺς μυρίων ἔχοντες ὅπλα. πῶς ἂν οὖν
ἀνὴρ μᾶλλον δοίη δίκην ἢ οὕτω περὶ αὑτοῦ τε καὶ
ὑμῶν βουλευόμενος;

10 Ἀλλ᾽ οὗτοί εἰσιν οἱ λόγοι ἀνδρῶν καὶ ἠλιθίων
κἀμοὶ φθονούντων, ὅτι ἐγὼ ὑφ᾽ ὑμῶν τιμῶμαι. καίτοι
οὐ δικαίως γ᾽ ἄν μοι φθονοῖεν· τίνα γὰρ αὐτῶν ἐγὼ
κωλύω ἢ λέγειν εἴ τίς τι ἀγαθὸν δύναται ἐν ὑμῖν, ἢ
μάχεσθαι εἴ τις ἐθέλει ὑπὲρ ὑμῶν τε καὶ ἑαυτοῦ, ἢ
ἐγρηγορέναι περὶ τῆς ὑμετέρας ἀσφαλείας ἐπιμελό-
μενον; τί γάρ, ἄρχοντας αἱρουμένων ὑμῶν ἐγώ τινι
ἐμποδών εἰμι; παρίημι, ἀρχέτω· μόνον ἀγαθόν τι
11 ποιῶν ὑμᾶς φαινέσθω. ἀλλὰ γὰρ ἐμοὶ μὲν ἀρκεῖ περὶ
τούτων τὰ εἰρημένα· εἰ δέ τις ὑμῶν ἢ αὐτὸς ἐξαπατηθῆναι ἂν οἴεται ταῦτα ἢ ἄλλον ἐξαπατῆσαι ταῦτα,
12 λέγων διδασκέτω. ὅταν δὲ τούτων ἅλις ἔχητε, μὴ
ἀπέλθητε πρὶν ἂν ἀκούσητε οἷον ὁρῶ ἐν τῇ στρατιᾷ
ἀρχόμενον πρᾶγμα· ὃ εἰ ἔπεισι καὶ ἔσται οἷον ὑπο-

444

north wind doth blow, fair voyaging to Greece.' In this matter, again, is it possible that any one could deceive you into embarking when the south wind is blowing? But I am going to put you aboard, you may say, when it is calm. Well, I shall be sailing on one ship, you on a hundred at least. How, then, could I either force you to voyage along with me if you did not choose, or deceive you into following my lead? But suppose you have been deceived and bewitched by me and we have come to the Phasis; we accordingly disembark upon the shore; you will perceive, likely enough, that you are not in Greece; and I, who have done the deceiving, will be one lone man, while you, the deceived, will be close to ten thousand, with arms in your hands. Then how could a man bring down punishment upon himself more surely than by planning in that way for himself and for you?

"No, these are the stories of foolish men, jealous of me because I enjoy honour at your hands. And yet they should not in fairness feel such jealousy; for whom among them do I hinder either from saying any good word he can before you, or from fighting if he will in your behalf and his own, or from being watchful in his care for your safety? Well, then, do I stand in any one's way when you are choosing commanders? I yield, let him be commander; only let it be shown that he renders you good service. For my part, however, what I have said on these points seems to me sufficient; but if any one among you imagines either that he could be deceived himself by such tales, or could deceive another by these tales, let him speak and explain. And when you have had enough of this, do not go away until you have heard what manner of evil I see beginning to show itself in the army; for if it comes upon us and proves

δείκνυσιν, ὥρα ἡμῖν βουλεύεσθαι ὑπὲρ ἡμῶν αὐτῶν
μὴ κάκιστοί τε καὶ αἴσχιστοι ἄνδρες φανῶμεν καὶ
πρὸς θεῶν καὶ πρὸς ἀνθρώπων καὶ φίλων καὶ πολεμίων.

13 Ἀκούσαντες δὲ ταῦτα οἱ στρατιῶται ἐθαύμασάν τε
ὅ τι εἴη καὶ λέγειν ἐκέλευον. ἐκ τούτου ἄρχεται πάλιν·
Ἐπίστασθέ που ὅτι χωρία ἦν ἐν τοῖς ὄρεσι βαρβα-
ρικά, φίλια τοῖς Κερασουντίοις, ὅθεν κατιόντες τινὲς
καὶ ἱερεῖα ἐπώλουν ὑμῖν καὶ ἄλλα ὧν εἶχον, δοκοῦσι
δέ μοι καὶ ὑμῶν τινες εἰς τὸ ἐγγυτάτω χωρίον τούτων
14 ἐλθόντες ἀγοράσαντές τι πάλιν ἀπελθεῖν. τοῦτο καταμαθὼν Κλεάρετος ὁ λοχαγὸς ὅτι καὶ μικρὸν εἴη καὶ
ἀφύλακτον διὰ τὸ φίλιον νομίζειν εἶναι, ἔρχεται ἐπ'
αὐτοὺς τῆς νυκτὸς ὡς πορθήσων, οὐδενὶ ἡμῶν εἰπών.
15 διενενόητο δέ, εἰ λάβοι τόδε τὸ χωρίον, εἰς μὲν τὸ
στράτευμα μηκέτι ἐλθεῖν, εἰσβὰς δὲ εἰς πλοῖον ἐν ᾧ
ἐτύγχανον οἱ σύσκηνοι αὐτοῦ παραπλέοντες, καὶ ἐν-
θέμενος εἴ τι λάβοι, ἀποπλέων οἴχεσθαι ἔξω τοῦ
Πόντου. καὶ ταῦτα συνωμολόγησαν αὐτῷ οἱ ἐκ τοῦ
16 πλοίου σύσκηνοι, ὡς ἐγὼ νῦν αἰσθάνομαι. παρακαλέσας οὖν ὁπόσους ἔπεισεν ἦγεν ἐπὶ τὸ χωρίον. πορευό-
μενον δ' αὐτὸν φθάνει ἡμέρα γενομένη, καὶ συστάντες
οἱ ἄνθρωποι ἀπὸ ἰσχυρῶν τόπων βάλλοντες καὶ παί-
οντες τόν τε Κλεάρετον ἀποκτείνουσι καὶ τῶν ἄλλων
συχνούς, οἱ δέ τινες καὶ εἰς Κερασοῦντα αὐτῶν ἀπο-

---

39 Cf. above, i. 8; Clearetus does not follow the recommenda-
tions of Xenophon.

to be as serious as it now shows signs of being, it is time for us to be taking counsel for ourselves, in order that we may not appear as most wicked and base men, both in the sight of gods and mankind, of friends and enemies."

Upon hearing these words the soldiers fell to wondering what the thing was, and they bade Xenophon go on. So he began again: "You know, perhaps, that in the mountains there were barbarian strongholds, friendly to the Cerasuntians, from which people would come down and sell you cattle and other things which they had, and also, I believe, some of you went to the nearest of these strongholds and did some buying and came back again. Clearetus the captain, learning that this place was not only small, but also unguarded, for the reason that its inhabitants deemed themselves friendly, set forth against them by night with the idea of plundering the place, and without a word to any one of us.[39] It was his intention, in case he should capture this stronghold, not to come back again to the army, but to embark on a vessel upon which his messmates chanced to be sailing along the coast, to put aboard whatever plunder he might secure, and sailing out of the Euxine to go away. Indeed, as I now learn, his messmates on the vessel had concluded an agreement with him to this effect. He accordingly summoned all the men he could persuade, and set out at their head to march against the stronghold. While he was still on the march, however, the break of day surprised him, and the people of the place gathered together and, by throwing missiles and dealing blows from strong positions, killed Clearetus and a good many of his followers, although some of them did make their way back to

17 χωροῦσι. ταῦτα δ' ἦν ἐν τῇ ἡμέρᾳ ᾗ ἡμεῖς δεῦρο
ἐξωρμῶμεν πεζῇ· τῶν δὲ παραπλεόντων ἔτι τινὲς ἦσαν
ἐν Κερασοῦντι, οὔπω ἀνηγμένοι.

Μετὰ τοῦτο, ὡς οἱ Κερασούντιοι λέγουσιν, ἀφικνοῦνται τῶν ἐκ τοῦ χωρίου τρεῖς ἄνδρες τῶν γεραιτέ-
18 ρων πρὸς τὸ κοινὸν τὸ ἡμέτερον χρῄζοντες ἐλθεῖν. ἐπεὶ
δ' ἡμᾶς οὐ κατέλαβον, πρὸς τοὺς Κερασουντίους ἔλεγον ὅτι θαυμάζοιεν τί ἡμῖν δόξειεν ἐλθεῖν ἐπ' αὐτούς.
ἐπεὶ μέντοι σφεῖς λέγειν, ἔφασαν, ὅτι οὐκ ἀπὸ κοινοῦ
γένοιτο τὸ πρᾶγμα, ἥδεσθαί τε αὐτοὺς καὶ μέλλειν
ἐνθάδε πλεῖν, ὡς ἡμῖν λέξειαν τὰ γενόμενα, καὶ τοὺς
νεκροὺς κελεύειν [αὐτοὺς]¹⁴ θάπτειν λαβόντας τοὺς
19 τούτου δεομένους. τῶν δ' ἀποφυγόντων τινὰς Ἑλλήνων
τυχεῖν ἔτι ὄντας ἐν Κερασοῦντι· αἰσθόμενοι δὲ τοὺς
βαρβάρους ὅποι ἴοιεν αὐτοί τε ἐτόλμησαν βάλλειν
τοῖς λίθοις καὶ τοῖς ἄλλοις παρεκελεύοντο. καὶ οἱ
ἄνδρες ἀποθνήσκουσι τρεῖς ὄντες οἱ πρέσβεις κατα-
λευσθέντες.

20 Ἐπεὶ δὲ τοῦτο ἐγένετο, ἔρχονται πρὸς ἡμᾶς οἱ
Κερασούντιοι καὶ λέγουσι τὸ πρᾶγμα· καὶ ἡμεῖς οἱ
στρατηγοὶ ἀκούσαντες ἠχθόμεθά τε τοῖς γεγενημένοις
καὶ ἐβουλευόμεθα σὺν τοῖς Κερασουντίοις ὅπως ἂν
21 ταφείησαν οἱ τῶν Ἑλλήνων νεκροί. συγκαθήμενοι δ'
ἔξωθεν τῶν ὅπλων ἐξαίφνης ἀκούομεν θορύβου πολλοῦ Παῖε, παῖε, βάλλε, βάλλε, καὶ τάχα δὴ ὁρῶμεν
πολλοὺς προσθέοντας λίθους ἔχοντας ἐν ταῖς χερσί,

¹⁴ αὐτοὺς Hude brackets.

Cerasus. All this happened on the day when we were setting forth to come here by land; and some of those who were going by sea along the coast were still at Cerasus, not having as yet set sail.

"After this, as the Cerasuntians say, there arrived at Cerasus three of the inhabitants of the stronghold, all elderly men, desiring to come before our general assembly. But since they did not find us, they addressed themselves to the Cerasuntians, saying that they wondered why we had seen fit to make an attack upon them. When, however, the Cerasuntians replied, so their statement ran, that it was not by public authority that the affair took place, the envoys were pleased, and were intending to sail here in order to tell us what had happened, and to bid those concerned to retrieve and bury the corpses. Now it chanced that some of the Greeks who had escaped were still at Cerasus; and when they learned where the barbarians were going, they committed the shamelessness of not only attacking them with stones themselves, but urging others to do the same. And the men were killed, these three, who were ambassadors, stoned to death.

"When this had taken place, the Cerasuntians came to us and told us of the affair; and we generals, upon hearing the story, were distressed at what had happened, and we proceeded to take counsel with the Cerasuntians as to how the bodies of the Greek dead might be buried. While we were in session outside the camp, we suddenly heard a great uproar and shouts of 'Strike! strike! pelt! pelt!' and in a moment we saw a crowd of men rushing toward us with stones in their hands and others picking up stones. And the

22 τοὺς δὲ καὶ ἀναιρουμένους. καὶ οἱ μὲν Κερασούντιοι,
ὡς ἂν καὶ ἑορακότες τὸ παρ' αὑτοῖς πρᾶγμα, δείσαντες
ἀποχωροῦσι πρὸς τὰ πλοῖα. ἦσαν δὲ νὴ Δία καὶ ἡμῶν
23 οἳ ἔδεισαν. ἐγώ γε μὴν ἦλθον πρὸς αὐτοὺς καὶ ἠρώτων
ὅ τι ἐστὶ τὸ πρᾶγμα. τῶν δὲ ἦσαν μὲν οἳ οὐδὲν ᾔδεσαν,
ὅμως δὲ λίθους εἶχον ἐν ταῖς χερσίν. ἐπεὶ δὲ καὶ εἰδότι
τινὶ ἐπέτυχον, λέγει μοι ὅτι οἱ ἀγορανόμοι δεινότατα
24 ποιοῦσι τὸ στράτευμα. ἐν τούτῳ τις ὁρᾷ τὸν ἀγορα-
νόμον Ζήλαρχον πρὸς τὴν θάλατταν ἀποχωροῦντα,
καὶ ἀνέκραγεν· οἱ δὲ ὡς ἤκουσαν, ὥσπερ ἢ συὸς
25 ἀγρίου ἢ ἐλάφου φανέντος ἵενται ἐπ' αὐτόν. οἱ δ' αὖ
Κερασούντιοι ὡς εἶδον ὁρμῶντας καθ' αὑτούς, σαφῶς
νομίσαντες ἐπὶ σφᾶς ἵεσθαι, φεύγουσι δρόμῳ καὶ
ἐμπίπτουσιν εἰς τὴν θάλατταν. συνεισέπεσον δὲ καὶ
ἡμῶν αὐτῶν τινες, καὶ ἐπνίγετο ὅστις νεῖν μὴ ἐτύγχα-
26 νεν ἐπιστάμενος. καὶ τούτους τί δοκεῖτε; ἠδίκουν μὲν
οὐδέν, ἔδεισαν δὲ μὴ λύττα τις ὥσπερ κυσὶν ἡμῖν
ἐμπεπτώκοι.

Εἰ οὖν ταῦτα τοιαῦτα ἔσται, θεάσασθε οἷα ἡ κατά-
27 στασις ἡμῖν ἔσται τῆς στρατιᾶς. ὑμεῖς μὲν οἱ πάντες
οὐκ ἔσεσθε κύριοι οὔτε ἀνελέσθαι πόλεμον ᾧ ἂν
βούλησθε οὔτε καταλῦσαι, ἰδίᾳ δὲ ὁ βουλόμενος ἄξει
στράτευμα ἐφ' ὅ τι ἂν ἐθέλῃ. κἄν τινες πρὸς ὑμᾶς
ἴωσι πρέσβεις ἢ εἰρήνης δεόμενοι ἢ ἄλλου τινός,
κατακανόντες τούτους οἱ βουλόμενοι ποιήσουσιν ὑμᾶς

Cerasuntians, as they too would have witnessed the affair
in their own city, were naturally terrified, and hurried back
toward their ships. For that matter, by Zeus, there were
some of our own number who were terrified. I went up to
the men, however, and asked what the trouble was. Some
of them did not know at all, but nevertheless they had
stones in their hands. When I did come upon a man who
knew, he told me that the supervisors of the market were
treating the army most outrageously. At this moment some
one saw the supervisor, Zelarchus, retreating toward the
sea, and set up a shout; and when the rest heard it, they
rushed upon him as though a wild boar or a stag had been
sighted. And now the Cerasuntians, seeing this rush in
their neighbourhood and believing it was undoubtedly directed against themselves, took to running in their flight
and threw themselves into the sea. Some of our own men
also plunged in with them, and any who did not chance to
know how to swim were drowned. Now what think you
about these Cerasuntians? They had done no wrong, but
they were afraid that a kind of madness, such as attacks
dogs,[40] had seized upon us.

"Now if these doings are to go on in this way, observe
what the situation of your army will be. You, the general
body, will not have it in your power either to undertake war
upon whom you please or to bring war to an end, but any
individual who wishes will be leading an army to gain any
end he may desire. And if people come to you as ambassadors, either desiring peace or anything else, any who
choose will kill them and prevent you from hearing the

---

[40] i.e., rabies: Aristotle, *Hist. Animal.* 604a5. For comparison
to human frenzy, cf. Hippocrates, *VM* xix. See also below §32.

28 τῶν λόγων μὴ ἀκοῦσαι τῶν πρὸς ὑμᾶς ἰόντων. ἔπειτα
δὲ οὓς μὲν ἂν ὑμεῖς ἅπαντες ἕλησθε ἄρχοντας, ἐν
οὐδεμιᾷ χώρᾳ ἔσονται, ὅστις δ᾽ ἂν ἑαυτὸν ἕληται
στρατηγὸν καὶ ἐθέλῃ λέγειν Βάλλε, βάλλε, οὗτος
ἔσται ἱκανὸς καὶ ἄρχοντα κατακανεῖν καὶ ἰδιώτην ὃν
ἂν ὑμῶν ἐθέλῃ ἄκριτον, ἢν ὦσιν οἱ πεισόμενοι αὐτῷ,
29 ὥσπερ καὶ νῦν ἐγένετο. οἷα δὲ ὑμῖν καὶ διαπεπράχασιν
οἱ αὐθαίρετοι οὗτοι στρατηγοὶ σκέψασθε. Ζήλαρχος
μὲν ὁ ἀγορανόμος εἰ μὲν ἀδικεῖ ὑμᾶς, οἴχεται ἀποπλέων οὐ δοὺς ὑμῖν δίκην· εἰ δὲ μὴ ἀδικεῖ, φεύγει ἐκ
τοῦ στρατεύματος δείσας μὴ ἀδίκως ἄκριτος ἀποθάνῃ.
30 οἱ δὲ καταλεύσαντες τοὺς πρέσβεις διεπράξαντο ὑμῖν
μόνοις μὲν τῶν Ἑλλήνων εἰς Κερασοῦντα μὴ ἀσφαλὲς
εἶναι ἂν μὴ σὺν ἰσχύι ἀφικνεῖσθαι· τοὺς δὲ νεκροὺς
οὓς πρόσθεν αὐτοὶ οἱ κατακανόντες ἐκέλευον θάπτειν,
τούτους διεπράξαντο μηδὲ σὺν κηρυκείῳ ἔτι ἀσφαλὲς
εἶναι ἀνελέσθαι. τίς γὰρ ἐθελήσει κῆρυξ ἰέναι κήρυκας ἀπεκτονώς; ἀλλ᾽ ἡμεῖς Κερασουντίων θάψαι
αὐτοὺς ἐδεήθημεν.
31 Εἰ μὲν οὖν ταῦτα καλῶς ἔχει, δοξάτω ὑμῖν, ἵνα ὡς
τοιούτων ἐσομένων καὶ φυλακὴν ἰδίᾳ ποιήσῃ τις καὶ
32 τὰ ἐρυμνὰ ὑπερδέξια πειρᾶται ἔχων σκηνοῦν. εἰ μέντοι
ὑμῖν δοκεῖ θηρίων ἀλλὰ μὴ ἀνθρώπων εἶναι τὰ τοιαῦτα ἔργα, σκοπεῖτε παυλάν τινα αὐτῶν· εἰ δὲ μή,
πρὸς Διὸς πῶς ἢ θεοῖς θύσομεν ἡδέως ποιοῦντες ἔργα
ἀσεβῆ, ἢ τοῖς πολεμίοις πῶς μαχούμεθα, ἢν ἀλλήλους

words of those who come to confer with you. Furthermore, the men whom you as a body may choose for commanders will be of no account, but whoever may choose himself general and will raise the cry 'Pelt, pelt,' that man will have the power to slay either commander or private, any one of you he pleases, without a trial, provided—as indeed it came about in the present case—there are people who will obey him. Consider the sort of things these self-chosen generals have actually accomplished for you. Take Zelarchus, the supervisor: supposing he has done you wrong, he has sailed off without paying you the penalty; supposing he is not guilty, he has fled from the army out of fear that he might be slain unjustly and without a trial. Take those who stoned to death the ambassadors: they have accomplished this result, that for you alone of all the Greeks it is not safe to enter Cerasus unless with a strong force; and as for the dead whom previously the very men who killed them proposed burying, the result accomplished is that now it is not safe to pick up their bodies even for one who carries a herald's staff. For who will care to go as herald when he has the blood of heralds upon his hands? So we requested the Cerasuntians to bury them.

"Now if these things are right, do you so resolve, in order that, with the understanding that such deeds are to be done, a man may establish his own private guard and may endeavour to hold possession of the strong places overhanging him on the right when he encamps. If, however, you think that such deeds are those of wild beasts and not of human beings, look about for some means of stopping them; otherwise, how, in the name of Zeus, shall we offer glad sacrifices to the gods when we are doing impious deeds, or how shall we fight with our enemies if we are

33 κατακαίνωμεν; πόλις δὲ φιλία τίς ἡμᾶς δέξεται, ἥτις
ἂν ὁρᾷ τοσαύτην ἀνομίαν ἐν ἡμῖν; ἀγορὰν δὲ τίς ἄξει
θαρρῶν, ἢν περὶ τὰ μέγιστα τοιαῦτα ἐξαμαρτάνοντες
φαινώμεθα; οὗ δὲ δὴ πάντων ᾠόμεθα τεύξεσθαι ἐπαίνου, τίς ἂν ἡμᾶς τοιούτους ὄντας ἐπαινέσειεν;[15] ἡμεῖς
μὲν γὰρ οἶδ᾽ ὅτι πονηροὺς ἂν φαίημεν εἶναι τοὺς τὰ
τοιαῦτα ποιοῦντας.

34 Ἐκ τούτου ἀνιστάμενοι πάντες ἔλεγον τοὺς μὲν
τούτων ἀρξαντας δοῦναι δίκην, τοῦ δὲ λοιποῦ μηκέτι
ἐξεῖναι ἀνομίας ἄρξαι· ἐὰν δέ τις ἄρξῃ, ὑπάγεσθαι
αὐτοὺς θανάτου· τοὺς δὲ στρατηγοὺς εἰς δίκας πάντας
καταστῆσαι· εἶναι δὲ δίκας καὶ εἴ τι ἄλλο τις ἠδίκητο
ἐξ οὗ Κῦρος ἀπέθανε· δικαστὰς δὲ τοὺς λοχαγοὺς
35 ἐποιήσαντο. παραινοῦντος δὲ Ξενοφῶντος καὶ τῶν
μάντεων συμβουλευόντων ἔδοξε καθῆραι τὸ στράτευμα. καὶ ἐγένετο καθαρμός.

VIII. Ἔδοξε δὲ καὶ τοὺς στρατηγοὺς δίκην ὑπο-
σχεῖν τοῦ παρεληλυθότος χρόνου. καὶ διδόντων Φιλήσιος μὲν ὦφλε καὶ Ξανθικλῆς τῆς φυλακῆς τῶν γαυλι-
κῶν χρημάτων τὸ μείωμα εἴκοσι μνᾶς, Σοφαίνετος δέ,
ὅτι αἱρεθεὶς[16] κατημέλει, δέκα μνᾶς.

Ξενοφῶντος δὲ κατηγόρησάν τινες φάσκοντες παί-

---

[15] τίς ἂν ... ἐπαινέσειεν some MSS., Hude/Peters, Mar.: τίς
(ἂν omitted) ... ἐπαινέσει Gem. following Dindorf: τίς ...
ἐπαινέσειεν other MSS.

[16] After αἱρεθεὶς editors generally, following Leunclavius, assume a lacuna.

slaying one another? And what friendly city will receive us
when it sees so great lawlessness amongst us? Who will
dare to supply us a market if in matters of the greatest
import we show ourselves guilty of such offences? And in
that land[41] where we were fancying that we would obtain
praise from every one, who would praise us if we are men
of this sort? For we ourselves, I am quite sure, should say
that people who perform such deeds are scoundrels."

Hereupon all rose and proposed that the men who began this affair should be duly punished, and that henceforth no one should be again permitted to make a beginning of lawlessness; but if any should so begin, they were
to be put on trial for their lives; and the generals were to
bring all offenders to trial, and trials were likewise to be
held in the matter of any other offences which any one had
committed since the time when Cyrus was killed; and they
appointed the captains to serve as a jury.[42] Further, upon
the recommendation of Xenophon, and by the advice of
the soothsayers, it was resolved to purify the army. So the
rites of purification were performed.

VIII. It was likewise resolved that the generals should
undergo an inquiry with reference to their past conduct.
When they presented their statements, Philesius and Xanthicles were condemned, for their careless guarding of the
merchantmen's cargoes,[43] to pay the loss incurred, namely,
twenty minas, and Sophaenetus, for neglect of duty in the
office to which he had been chosen,[44] was fined ten minas.

Accusations were also made against Xenophon by certain men who claimed that he was beating them, and they

---

[41] Greece.   [42] For military courts, cf. Lysias XIV. 5, XV.
1–4; Plato, *Lg.* 943a-b.   [43] Cf. i. 16.   [44] Cf. iii. 1.

εσθαι ὑπ' αὐτοῦ καὶ ὡς ὑβρίζοντος τὴν κατηγορίαν

2 ἐποιοῦντο. καὶ ὁ Ξενοφῶν ἐκέλευσεν εἰπεῖν τὸν πρῶτον λέξαντα ποῦ καὶ ἐπλήγη. ὁ δὲ ἀπεκρίνατο· Ὅπου καὶ

3 τῷ ῥίγει ἀπωλλύμεθα καὶ χιὼν πλείστη ἦν. ὁ δὲ εἶπεν· Ἀλλὰ μὴν εἰ χειμῶνός γε ὄντος οἵου λέγεις, σίτου δὲ ἐπιλελοιπότος, οἴνου δὲ μηδ' ὀσφραίνεσθαι παρόν, ὑπὸ δὲ πόνων πολλῶν ἀπαγορευόντων, πολεμίων δὲ ἑπομένων, εἰ ἐν τοιούτῳ καιρῷ ὕβριζον, ὁμολογῶ καὶ τῶν ὄνων ὑβριστότερος εἶναι, οἷς φασιν ὑπὸ τῆς ὕβρεως κόπον οὐκ ἐγγίγνεσθαι. ὅμως δὲ καὶ λέξον,

4 ἔφη, ἐκ τίνος ἐπλήγης. πότερον ᾔτουν τί σε καὶ ἐπεί μοι οὐκ ἐδίδους ἔπαιον; ἀλλ' ἀπῄτουν, ἀλλὰ περὶ

5 παιδικῶν μαχόμενος, ἀλλὰ μεθύων παρῴνησα; ἐπεὶ δὲ τούτων οὐδὲν ἔφησεν, ἐπήρετο αὐτὸν εἰ ὁπλιτεύοι. οὐκ ἔφη· πάλιν εἰ πελτάζοι. οὐδὲ τοῦτ' ἔφη, ἀλλ' ἡμίονον ἤλαυνον ταχθεὶς ὑπὸ τῶν συσκήνων ἐλεύθερος ὤν.

6 ἐνταῦθα δὴ ἀναγιγνώσκει αὐτὸν καὶ ἤρετο· Ἦ σὺ εἶ ὁ τὸν κάμνοντα ἀπαγαγών; Ναὶ μὰ Δί', ἔφη· σὺ γὰρ ἠνάγκαζες· τὰ δὲ τῶν ἐμῶν συσκήνων σκεύη διέρρι-

7 ψας. Ἀλλ' ἡ μὲν διάρριψις, ἔφη ὁ Ξενοφῶν, τοιαύτη τις ἐγένετο. διέδωκα ⟨ἄλλα⟩[17] ἄλλοις ἄγειν καὶ ἐκέλευσα πρὸς ἐμὲ ἀπαγαγεῖν, καὶ ἀπολαβὼν ἅπαντα σῶα ἀπέδωκά σοι, ἐπεὶ καὶ σὺ ἐμοὶ ἀπέδειξας τὸν

---

17 ἄλλα added by Mehler.

---

45 A very serious charge; maintaining that an illegal act was committed out of *hybris* implied that the accused acted wilfully

were making the accusation on the grounds that he was acting out of arrogance.[45] Xenophon bade the first man who spoke to state where it was that he had struck him. He replied, "In the place where we were perishing with cold and there was an enormous amount of snow." And Xenophon said, "Well, really, with weather of the sort you describe and provisions used up and no chance even to get a smell of wine, when many of us were becoming exhausted with hardships and the enemy were at our heels, if at such a time as that I wantonly abused you, I admit that I am more wanton even than the ass, which, because of its wantonness, so the saying runs, is not subject to fatigue. Nevertheless, do tell us," he said, "for what reason you were struck. Did I ask you for something, and then strike you because you would not give it to me? Did I demand something back? Was it in a fight over a boy? Was it an act of drunken violence?" When the man replied that it was none of these things, Xenophon asked him if he was a hoplite. He said no. Was he a peltast, then? No, not that either, he said, but he was driving a mule, assigned to that post by his messmates, although he was a free man. At that Xenophon recognized him, and asked: "Are you the fellow who carried off the sick man?" "Yes, by Zeus," he replied, "for you forced me to do so; and you scattered my messmates' baggage all about." "Why, the scattering," said Xenophon, "was after this fashion: I distributed the baggage among others to carry and directed them to bring it back to me, and when I got it back, I returned the whole of it to you intact when

and with malice: cf. Demosthenes LIV and D. MacDowell, *Greece and Rome* 23 (1976) 14–31.

ἄνδρα. οἷον δὲ τὸ πρᾶγμα ἐγένετο ἀκούσατε, ἔφη· καὶ
γὰρ ἄξιον.

8   Ἀνὴρ κατελείπετο διὰ τὸ μηκέτι δύνασθαι πορεύεσθαι. καὶ ἐγὼ τὸν μὲν ἄνδρα τοσοῦτον ἐγίγνωσκον
ὅτι εἷς ἡμῶν εἴη· ἠνάγκασα δὲ σὲ τοῦτον ἄγειν, ὡς μὴ
ἀπόλοιτο· καὶ γάρ, ὡς ἐγὼ οἶμαι, πολέμιοι ἡμῖν
9 ἐφείποντο. συνέφη τοῦτο ὁ ἄνθρωπος. Οὐκοῦν, ἔφη ὁ
Ξενοφῶν, ἐπεὶ προύπεμψά σε, καταλαμβάνω αὖθις
σὺν τοῖς ὀπισθοφύλαξι προσιὼν βόθρον ὀρύττοντα
ὡς κατορύξοντα τὸν ἄνθρωπον, καὶ ἐπιστὰς ἐπήνουν
10 σε. ἐπεὶ δὲ παρεστηκότων ἡμῶν συνέκαμψε τὸ σκέλος
ἀνήρ, ἀνέκραγον οἱ παρόντες ὅτι ζῇ ὁ ἀνήρ, σὺ δ᾽
εἶπας· Ὁπόσα γε βούλεται· ὡς ἔγωγε αὐτὸν οὐκ ἄξω.
ἐνταῦθα ἔπαισά σε· ἀληθῆ λέγεις· ἔδοξας γάρ μοι
11 εἰδότι ἐοικέναι ὅτι ἔζη. Τί οὖν, ἔφη, ἧττόν τι ἀπέθανεν,
ἐπεὶ ἐγώ σοι ἀπέδειξα αὐτόν; Καὶ γὰρ ἡμεῖς, ἔφη ὁ
Ξενοφῶν, πάντες ἀποθανούμεθα· τούτου οὖν ἕνεκα
ζῶντας ἡμᾶς δεῖ κατορυχθῆναι;

12   Τοῦτον μὲν ἀνέκραγον ὡς ὀλίγας παίσειεν· ἄλλους
δ᾽ ἐκέλευε λέγειν διὰ τί ἕκαστος ἐπλήγη. ἐπεὶ δὲ οὐκ
13 ἀνίσταντο, αὐτὸς ἔλεγεν· Ἐγώ, ὦ ἄνδρες, ὁμολογῶ
παῖσαι δὴ ἄνδρας ἕνεκεν ἀταξίας ὅσοις σῴζεσθαι μὲν
ἦρκει δι᾽ ὑμᾶς ἐν τάξει τε ἰόντων καὶ μαχομένων ὅπου
δέοι, αὐτοὶ δὲ λιπόντες τὰς τάξεις προθέοντες ἁρπάζειν ἤθελον καὶ ὑμῶν πλεονεκτεῖν. εἰ δὲ τοῦτο πάντες
14 ἐποιοῦμεν, ἅπαντες ἂν ἀπωλόμεθα. ἤδη δὲ καὶ μαλακι-

you, for your part, had shown me the sick man. But listen, all of you;" he continued, "and hear how the affair happened; for the story is worth hearing.

"A man was being left behind because he was unable to keep going any longer. I was acquainted with the man only so far as to know that he was one of our number, and I forced you, sir, to carry him in order that he might not perish; for, as I remember, the enemy were following after us." To that the fellow agreed. "Well," Xenophon continued, "after I had sent you on ahead, I overtook you again, as I came along with the rearguard, and found you digging a hole to bury the man in, and I stopped and commended you. But when, as we were standing by, the man drew up his leg, all of us cried out, 'The man is alive'; and you said, 'Let him be alive just as much as he pleases; I, for my part, am not going to carry him.' Then I struck you; your story is true; for it looked to me as if you knew that he was alive." "Well, what of that," the fellow said; "didn't he die all the same after I had shown him to you?" "Why," said Xenophon, "all of us are likewise going to die; but should we on that account be buried alive?"

As for this fellow, everybody cried out that Xenophon had given him fewer blows than he deserved. Then he directed the rest to state the reason why each one of them had been struck. When they failed to rise, he went on himself: "I admit, soldiers, that I have indeed struck men for neglect of discipline, the men who were content to be kept safe thanks to you who marched in due order and fought wherever there was need, while they themselves would leave the ranks and run on ahead in the desire to secure plunder and to enjoy an advantage over you. For if all of us had behaved in this way, all of us alike would have

ζόμενόν τινα καὶ οὐκ ἐθέλοντα ἀνίστασθαι ἀλλὰ προϊ-
έμενον αὑτὸν τοῖς πολεμίοις καὶ ἔπαισα καὶ ἐβια-
σάμην πορεύεσθαι. ἐν γὰρ τῷ ἰσχυρῷ χειμῶνι καὶ
αὐτός ποτε ἀναμένων τινὰς συσκευαζομένους καθεζό-
μενος συχνὸν χρόνον κατέμαθον ἀναστὰς μόλις καὶ
15 τὰ σκέλη ἐκτείνας. ἐν ἐμαυτῷ οὖν πεῖραν λαβὼν ἐκ
τούτου καὶ ἄλλον, ὁπότε ἴδοιμι καθήμενον καὶ βλα-
κεύοντα, ἤλαυνον· τὸ γὰρ κινεῖσθαι καὶ ἀνδρίζεσθαι
παρεῖχε θερμασίαν τινὰ καὶ ὑγρότητα, τὸ δὲ καθῆσθαι καὶ ἡσυχίαν ἔχειν ἑώρων ὑπουργὸν ὂν τῷ τε
ἀποπήγνυσθαι τὸ αἷμα καὶ τῷ ἀποσήπεσθαι τοὺς τῶν
ποδῶν δακτύλους, ἅπερ πολλοὺς καὶ ὑμεῖς ἴστε πα-
16 θόντας. ἄλλον δέ γε ἴσως ἀπολειπόμενόν που διὰ
ῥᾳστώνην καὶ κωλύοντα καὶ ὑμᾶς τοὺς πρόσθεν καὶ
ἡμᾶς τοὺς ὄπισθεν πορεύεσθαι ἔπαισα πύξ, ὅπως μὴ
17 λόγχῃ ὑπὸ τῶν πολεμίων παίοιτο. καὶ γὰρ οὖν νῦν
ἔξεστιν αὐτοῖς σωθεῖσιν, εἴ τι ὑπ’ ἐμοῦ ἔπαθον παρὰ
τὸ δίκαιον, δίκην λαβεῖν. εἰ δ’ ἐπὶ τοῖς πολεμίοις
ἐγένοντο, τί μέγα ἂν οὕτως ἔπαθον ὅτου δίκην ἂν
ἠξίουν λαμβάνειν;

18 Ἁπλοῦς μοι, ἔφη, ὁ λόγος· ἐγὼ γὰρ εἰ μὲν ἐπ’
ἀγαθῷ ἐκόλασά τινα, ἀξιῶ ὑπέχειν δίκην οἵαν καὶ
γονεῖς υἱοῖς καὶ διδάσκαλοι παισί· καὶ γὰρ οἱ ἰατροὶ
19 καίουσι καὶ τέμνουσιν ἐπ’ ἀγαθῷ· εἰ δὲ ὕβρει νομίζετέ
με ταῦτα πράττειν, ἐνθυμήθητε ὅτι νῦν ἐγὼ θαρρῶ σὺν
τοῖς θεοῖς μᾶλλον ἢ τότε καὶ θρασύτερός εἰμι νῦν ἢ
τότε καὶ οἶνον πλείω πίνω, ἀλλ’ ὅμως οὐδένα παίω· ἐν

perished. Again, when a man behaved like a weakling and refused to get up, preferring to surrender himself to the enemy, I did indeed strike him and use violence to compel him to go on. For once during the severe weather I myself remained seated for quite a long time, waiting for some people who were packing up, and I discovered that it was hard work to get up and stretch my legs. Having tested the matter, then, in my own case, I used after that to drive on any other man whom I might see sitting down and shirking; for getting into motion and acting like a man produced a certain amount of warmth and suppleness, while sitting and keeping quiet tended, as I saw, to make the blood freeze and the toes rot off, just the misfortunes which many people suffered, as you know for yourselves. In still another case, the man, perhaps, who fell behind somewhere out of indolence and prevented both you in the van and us in the rear from going on, I struck such a one with the fist in order that the enemy might not strike him with the lance. Indeed, that is the reason why these people, having been saved, now have it in their power to obtain satisfaction for whatever they suffered unjustly at my hands. But if they had fallen into the hands of the enemy, what suffering would they have experienced so great that they would now be asking to obtain satisfaction for it?

"My defence," he continued, "is simple: if it was for his good that I punished any one, I think I should render the sort of account that parents render to sons and teachers to pupils; for that matter, surgeons also burn and cut patients for their good; but if you believe it was out of cruelty that I do these things, take note that now, by the blessing of the gods, I am more confident than I was then and that I am bolder now than then and drink more wine, but nev-

20 εὐδίᾳ γὰρ ὁρῶ ὑμᾶς. ὅταν δε χειμὼν ᾖ καὶ θάλαττα
μεγάλη ἐπιφέρηται, οὐχ ὁρᾶτε ὅτι καὶ νεύματος μόνου
ἕνεκα χαλεπαίνει μὲν πρῳρεὺς τοῖς ἐν πρῴρᾳ, χαλεπαίνει δὲ κυβερνήτης τοῖς ἐν πρύμνῃ; ἱκανὰ γὰρ ἐν
τῷ τοιούτῳ καὶ μικρὰ ἁμαρτηθέντα πάντα συνεπι-
21 τρῖψαι. ὅτι δὲ δικαίως ἔπαιον αὐτοὺς καὶ ὑμεῖς κατ-
εδικάσατε· ἔχοντες ξίφη, οὐ ψήφους, παρέστατε, καὶ
ἐξῆν ὑμῖν ἐπικουρεῖν αὐτοῖς, εἰ ἐβούλεσθε· ἀλλὰ μὰ
Δία οὔτε τούτοις ἐπεκουρεῖτε οὔτε σὺν ἐμοὶ τὸν ἀτα-
22 κτοῦντα ἐπαίετε. τοιγαροῦν ἐξουσίαν ἐποιήσατε τοῖς
κακοῖς αὐτῶν ὑβρίζειν ἐῶντες αὐτούς.

Οἶμαι γάρ, εἰ ἐθέλετε σκοπεῖν, τοὺς αὐτοὺς εὑρή-
σετε καὶ τότε κακίστους καὶ νῦν ὑβριστοτάτους.
23 Βοΐσκος γοῦν ὁ πύκτης ὁ Θετταλὸς τότε μὲν διεμάχετο
ὡς κάμνων ἀσπίδα μὴ φέρειν, νῦν δέ, ὡς ἀκούω,
24 Κοτυωριτῶν πολλοὺς ἤδη ἀποδέδυκεν. ἢν οὖν σωφρονῆτε, τοῦτον τἀναντία ποιήσετε ἢ τοὺς κύνας ποιοῦσι·
τοὺς μὲν γὰρ κύνας τοὺς χαλεποὺς τὰς μὲν ἡμέρας
διδέασι, τὰς δὲ νύκτας ἀφιᾶσι, τοῦτον δέ, ἢν σωφρονῆτε, τὴν νύκτα μὲν δήσετε, τὴν δὲ ἡμέραν ἀφήσετε.
25 Ἀλλὰ γάρ, ἔφη, θαυμάζω ὅτι εἰ μέν τινι ὑμῶν
ἀπηχθόμην, μέμνησθε καὶ οὐ σιωπᾶτε, εἰ δέ τῳ ἢ
χειμῶνα ἐπεκούφισα ἢ πολέμιον ἀπήρυξα ἢ ἀσθε-
νοῦντι ἢ ἀποροῦντι συνεξεπόρισά τι, τούτων δὲ οὐδεὶς
μέμνηται, οὐδ' εἴ τινα καλῶς τι ποιοῦντα ἐπήνεσα οὐδ'
εἴ τιν' ἄνδρα ὄντα ἀγαθὸν ἐτίμησα ὡς ἐδυνάμην, οὐδὲν

ertheless I strike no man—for the reason that I see you are in calm waters. But when it is stormy weather and a high sea is running, do you not observe that even for a mere nod the lookout gets angry with the people at the prow and the helmsman angry with the people at the stern? For in such a situation even small blunders are enough to ruin everything. But you rendered judgment yourselves that I was justified in striking those men; for you stood by, with swords, not ballots, in your hands, and it was within your power to come to their aid if you chose; but, by Zeus, you would neither give those people aid nor would you join with me in striking such as violated discipline. Consequently you gave the bad among them freedom to act wantonly by thus letting them alone.

"For I think, if you care to look into the matter, you will find it is the very same men who were then most cowardly that are now most wanton. At any rate, Boïscus the boxer, of Thessaly, then fought hard to escape carrying his shield, on the plea that he was tired; but now, as I hear, he has already stripped off the clothes of many Cotyorites. If you are wise, therefore, you will do to this fellow the opposite of what people do to dogs; for dogs that are savage are tied up by day and let loose by night, but this fellow, if you are wise, you will tie up by night and let loose by day.

"But really," he continued, "I am surprised that if ever I incurred the ill-will of any one among you, you remember that and are not silent about it, while if I gave relief to anyone in the cold, or warded off an enemy from him, or helped to provide something for him when he was sick or in want, these acts, on the other hand, are not remembered by anybody; nor, again, if I praised a man for a deed well done, or honoured according to my ability a man who was

26 τούτων μέμνησθε. ἀλλὰ μὴν καλόν γε καὶ δίκαιον καὶ
ὅσιον καὶ ἥδιον τῶν ἀγαθῶν μᾶλλον ἢ τῶν κακῶν
μεμνῆσθαι.

Ἐκ τούτου μὲν δὴ ἀνίσταντο καὶ ἀνεμίμνησκον.
καὶ περιεγένετο ὥστε καλῶς ἔχειν.

brave, do you remember any of these things. Yet surely it is more honourable and fair, more righteous and gracious to remember good deeds than evil."

Then people began getting up and recalling past incidents, and all turned out well in the end.

I. Ἐκ τούτου δὲ ἐν τῇ διατριβῇ οἱ μὲν ἀπὸ τῆς
ἀγορᾶς ἔζων, οἱ δὲ καὶ ληζόμενοι ἐκ τῆς Παφλαγονίας. ἐκλώπευον δὲ καὶ οἱ Παφλαγόνες εὖ μάλα τοὺς
ἀποσκεδαννυμένους, καὶ τῆς νυκτὸς τοὺς πρόσω σκηνοῦντας ἐπειρῶντο κακουργεῖν· καὶ πολεμικώτατα
2 πρὸς ἀλλήλους εἶχον ἐκ τούτων. ὁ δὲ Κορύλας, ὃς
ἐτύγχανε τότε Παφλαγονίας ἄρχων, πέμπει παρὰ τοὺς
Ἕλληνας πρέσβεις ἔχοντας ἵππους καὶ στολὰς κα-
λάς, λέγοντας ὅτι Κορύλας ἕτοιμος εἴη τοὺς Ἕλληνας
3 μήτε ἀδικεῖν μήτε ἀδικεῖσθαι. οἱ δὲ στρατηγοὶ ἀπεκρίναντο ὅτι περὶ μὲν τούτων σὺν τῇ στρατιᾷ βουλεύ-
σοιντο, ἐπὶ ξένια δὲ ἐδέχοντο αὐτούς· παρεκάλεσαν δὲ
καὶ τῶν ἄλλων ἀνδρῶν οὓς ἐδόκουν δικαιοτάτους εἶναι.
4 θύσαντες δὲ τῶν αἰχμαλώτων βοῶν καὶ ἄλλα ἱερεῖα
εὐωχίαν μὲν ἀρκοῦσαν παρεῖχον, κατακείμενοι δὲ ἐν
στιβάσιν ἐδείπνουν, καὶ ἔπινον ἐκ κερατίνων ποτη-
ρίων, οἷς ἐνετύγχανον ἐν τῇ χώρᾳ.
5 Ἐπεὶ δὲ σπονδαί τ᾽ ἐγένοντο καὶ ἐπαιάνισαν, ἀνέστησαν πρῶτοι μὲν Θρᾷκες καὶ πρὸς αὐλὸν ὠρχήσαν-

BOOK VI

I. After this, while they delayed at Cotyora, some of the men lived by purchasing from the market[1] and others by pillaging the territory of Paphlagonia. The Paphlagonians, however, were extremely clever in kidnapping the stragglers, and at night time they tried to inflict harm upon such of the Greeks as were quartered at some distance from the rest; consequently they and the Greeks were in a very hostile mood toward one another. Then Corylas,[2] who chanced at the time to be ruler of Paphlagonia, sent ambassadors to the Greeks, with horses and fine raiment, bearing word that Corylas was ready to do the Greeks no wrong and to suffer no wrong at their hands. The generals replied that they would take counsel with the army on this matter, but meanwhile they received the ambassadors as their guests at dinner, inviting in also such of the other men in the army as seemed to them best entitled to an invitation. By sacrificing some of the cattle they had captured and also other animals they provided an adequate feast, and they dined reclining upon straw mats and drank from cups made of horn which they found in the country.

After they had made libations and sung the paean, two Thracians rose up first and began a dance in full armour

---

[1] Cf. V. v. 24 ff.   [2] Cf. V. v. 12 and note.

το σὺν τοῖς ὅπλοις καὶ ἥλλοντο ὑψηλά τε καὶ κούφως
καὶ ταῖς μαχαίραις ἐχρῶντο· τέλος δὲ ὁ ἕτερος τὸν
ἕτερον παίει, ὡς πᾶσι δοκεῖν πεπληγέναι τὸν ἄνδρα·[1]

6 ὁ δ' ἔπεσε τεχνικῶς πως. καὶ ἀνέκραγον οἱ Παφλαγόνες. καὶ ὁ μὲν σκυλεύσας τὰ ὅπλα τοῦ ἑτέρου ἐξῄει
ᾄδων τὸν Σιτάλκαν· ἄλλοι δὲ τῶν Θρᾳκῶν τὸν ἕτερον

7 ἐξέφερον ὡς τεθνηκότα· ἦν δὲ οὐδὲν πεπονθώς. μετὰ
τοῦτο Αἰνιᾶνες καὶ Μάγνητες ἀνέστησαν, οἳ ὠρχοῦντο

8 τὴν καρπαίαν καλουμένην ἐν τοῖς ὅπλοις. ὁ δὲ τρόπος
τῆς ὀρχήσεως ἦν, ὁ μὲν παραθέμενος τὰ ὅπλα σπείρει
καὶ ζευγηλατεῖ πυκνὰ μεταστρεφόμενος ὡς φοβούμενος, λῃστὴς δὲ προσέρχεται· ὁ δ' ἐπὰν προΐδηται,
ἀπαντᾷ ἁρπάσας τὰ ὅπλα καὶ μάχεται πρὸ τοῦ
ζεύγους· καὶ οὗτοι ταῦτ' ἐποίουν ἐν ῥυθμῷ πρὸς τὸν
αὐλόν· καὶ τέλος ὁ λῃστὴς δήσας τὸν ἄνδρα καὶ τὸ
ζεῦγος ἀπάγει· ἐνίοτε δὲ καὶ ὁ ζευγηλάτης τὸν λῃστήν·
εἶτα παρὰ τοὺς βοῦς ζεύξας ὀπίσω τὼ χεῖρε δεδεμένον

9 ἐλαύνει. μετὰ τοῦτο Μυσὸς εἰσῆλθεν ἐν ἑκατέρᾳ τῇ
χειρὶ ἔχων πέλτην, καὶ τοτὲ μὲν ὡς δύο ἀντιτατ-
τομένων μιμούμενος ὠρχεῖτο, τοτὲ δὲ ὡς πρὸς ἕνα
ἐχρῆτο ταῖς πέλταις, τοτὲ δ' ἐδινεῖτο καὶ ἐξεκυβίστα
ἔχων τὰς πέλτας, ὥστε ὄψιν ἔχων καλὴν φαίνεσθαι.

10 τέλος δὲ τὸ Περσικὸν ὠρχεῖτο κρούων τὰς πέλτας καὶ
ὤκλαζε καὶ ἐξανίστατο· καὶ ταῦτα πάντα ἐν ῥυθμῷ

---

[1] The reading of Athenaeus: the MSS. offer a variety of other
readings.

to the music of a flute, leaping high and lightly and using their sabres; finally, one struck the other; it seemed to everyone that the man had been mortally wounded; and he fell artfully. And the Paphlagonians set up a cry. Then the first man despoiled the other of his arms and marched out singing the Sitalcas,[3] while other Thracians carried off the fallen dancer, as though he were dead; in fact, he had not been hurt at all. After this some Aenianians and Magnesians arose and danced under arms the so-called carpaea.[4] The manner of the dance was this: a man is sowing and driving a yoke of oxen, his arms laid at one side, and he turns about frequently as one in fear; a robber approaches; as soon as the sower sees him coming, he snatches up his arms, goes to meet him, and fights with him to save his oxen. The two men do all this in rhythm to the music of the flute. Finally, the robber binds the man and drives off the oxen; or sometimes the master of the oxen binds the robber, and then he yokes him alongside the oxen, his hands tied behind him, and drives off. After this a Mysian came in carrying a light shield in each hand, and at one moment in his dance he would go through a pantomime as though two men were arrayed against him; again he would use his shields as though against one antagonist, and again he would whirl and throw somersaults while holding the shields in his hands, so that he seemed to offer a fine spectacle. Lastly, he danced the Persian dance, clashing his shields together and crouching down and then rising up again; and all this he did, keeping time to the music

---

[3] A Thracian war-song, apparently composed in honour of an early king named Sitalcas. This passage is quoted by Athenaeus, I. 15E.   [4] A dance known to us from this passage only.

11 πρὸς τὸν αὐλὸν ἐποίει. ἐπὶ δὲ τούτῳ ἐπιόντες οἱ Μαν-
τινεῖς καὶ ἄλλοι τινὲς τῶν Ἀρκάδων ἀναστάντες ἐξωπλισμένοι ὡς ἐδύναντο κάλλιστα ᾖσάν τε ἐν ῥυθμῷ
πρὸς τὸν ἐνόπλιον ῥυθμὸν αὐλούμενον καὶ ἐπαιάνισαν
καὶ ὠρχήσαντο ὥσπερ ἐν ταῖς πρὸς τοὺς θεοὺς προσ-
όδοις. ὁρῶντες δὲ οἱ Παφλαγόνες δεινὰ ἐποιοῦντο
12 πάσας τὰς ὀρχήσεις ἐν ὅπλοις εἶναι. ἐπὶ τούτοις ὁρῶν
ὁ Μυσὸς ἐκπεπληγμένους αὐτούς, πείσας τῶν Ἀρκάδων τινὰ πεπαμένον ὀρχηστρίδα εἰσάγει σκευάσας ὡς
ἐδύνατο κάλλιστα καὶ ἀσπίδα δοὺς κούφην αὐτῇ. ἡ
13 δὲ ὠρχήσατο πυρρίχην ἐλαφρῶς. ἐνταῦθα κρότος ἦν
πολύς, καὶ οἱ Παφλαγόνες ἤροντο εἰ καὶ αἱ γυναῖκες
συνεμάχοντο αὐτοῖς. οἱ δ' ἔλεγον ὅτι αὗται καὶ αἱ
τρεψάμεναι εἶεν βασιλέα ἐκ τοῦ στρατοπέδου. τῇ μὲν
οὖν νυκτὶ ταύτῃ τοῦτο τὸ τέλος ἐγένετο.

14 Τῇ δὲ ὑστεραίᾳ προσῆγον αὐτοὺς εἰς τὸ στράτευ-
μα· καὶ ἔδοξε τοῖς στρατιώταις μήτε ἀδικεῖν Παφλαγόνας μήτε ἀδικεῖσθαι. μετὰ τοῦτο οἱ μὲν πρέσβεις
ᾤχοντο· οἱ δὲ Ἕλληνες, ἐπειδὴ πλοῖα ἱκανὰ ἐδόκει
παρεῖναι, ἀναβάντες ἔπλεον ἡμέραν καὶ νύκτα πνεύ-
15 ματι καλῷ ἐν ἀριστερᾷ ἔχοντες τὴν Παφλαγονίαν. τῇ
δ' ἄλλῃ ἀφικνοῦνται εἰς Σινώπην καὶ ὡρμίσαντο εἰς
Ἁρμήνην τῆς Σινώπης. Σινωπεῖς δὲ οἰκοῦσι μὲν ἐν τῇ
Παφλαγονικῇ, Μιλησίων δὲ ἄποικοί εἰσιν. οὗτοι δὲ
ξένια πέμπουσι τοῖς Ἕλλησιν ἀλφίτων μὲν μεδίμνους
τρισχιλίους, οἴνου δὲ κεράμια χίλια καὶ πεντακόσια.

---

5 A famous war-dance from Sparta: see Athenaeus XIV. 631A.

of the flute. After him the Mantineans came forward and some of the other Arcadians arose, arrayed in the finest arms and accoutrements they could command, and marched in time to the accompaniment of a martial rhythm played on the flute and sang the paean and danced, just as the Arcadians do in their festal processions in honour of the gods. And the Paphlagonians, as they looked on, thought it most strange that all the dances were under arms. Thereupon the Mysian, seeing how astounded they were, persuaded one of the Arcadians who had a dancing girl to let him bring her in, after dressing her up in the finest way he could and giving her a light shield. And she danced the Pyrrhic[5] with grace. Then there was great applause, and the Paphlagonians asked whether their women also fought by their side. And the Greeks replied that these women were precisely the ones who put the King to flight from his camp. Such was the end of that evening.

On the next day they introduced the ambassadors to the army, and the soldiers passed a resolution to do the Paphlagonians no wrong and to suffer no wrong at their hands. After this the ambassadors departed, and the Greeks, inasmuch as it seemed that vessels enough were at hand, embarked and sailed for a day and a night with a fair wind keeping Paphlagonia on the left. On the second day they reached Sinope, and came to anchor at Harmene, in the territory of Sinope. The Sinopeans dwell, indeed, in Paphlagonia, but are colonists of the Milesians. And they sent to the Greeks, as gifts of hospitality, three thousand *medimni*[6] of barley meal and fifteen hundred jars of wine.

[6] The *medimnus* = about a bushel and a half.

16　Καὶ Χειρίσοφος ἐνταῦθα ἦλθε τριήρη ἔχων. καὶ οἱ
μὲν στρατιῶται προσεδόκων ἄγοντά τι σφίσιν ἥκειν·
ὁ δ' ἦγε μὲν οὐδέν, ἀπήγγελλε δὲ ὅτι ἐπαινοίη αὐτοὺς
καὶ Ἀναξίβιος ὁ ναύαρχος καὶ οἱ ἄλλοι, καὶ ὅτι
ὑπισχνεῖτο Ἀναξίβιος, εἰ ἀφίκοιντο ἔξω τοῦ Πόντου,
17　μισθοφορὰν αὐτοῖς ἔσεσθαι. καὶ ἐν ταύτῃ τῇ Ἁρμήνῃ
ἔμειναν οἱ στρατιῶται ἡμέρας πέντε.

　　Ὡς δὲ τῆς Ἑλλάδος ἐδόκουν ἐγγὺς γίγνεσθαι, ἤδη
μᾶλλον ἢ πρόσθεν εἰσῄει αὐτοὺς ὅπως ἂν καὶ ἔχοντές
18　τι οἴκαδε ἀφίκοιντο. ἡγήσαντο οὖν, εἰ ἕνα ἕλοιντο
ἄρχοντα, μᾶλλον ἂν ἢ πολυαρχίας οὔσης δύνασθαι
τὸν ἕνα χρῆσθαι τῷ στρατεύματι καὶ νυκτὸς καὶ
ἡμέρας, καὶ εἴ τι δέοι λανθάνειν, μᾶλλον ἂν κρύπτε-
σθαι, καὶ εἴ τι αὖ δέοι φθάνειν, ἧττον ἂν ὑστερίζειν·
οὐ γὰρ ἂν λόγων δεῖν πρὸς ἀλλήλους, ἀλλὰ τὸ δόξαν
τῷ ἑνὶ περαίνεσθαι ἄν· τὸν δ' ἔμπροσθεν χρόνον ἐκ
τῆς νικώσης ἔπραττον πάντα οἱ στρατηγοί.

19　　Ὡς δὲ ταῦτα διενοοῦντο, ἐτράποντο ἐπὶ τὸν Ξενο-
φῶντα· καὶ οἱ λοχαγοὶ ἔλεγον προσιόντες αὐτῷ ὅτι ἡ
στρατιὰ οὕτω γιγνώσκει, καὶ εὔνοιαν ἐνδεικνύμενος
20　ἕκαστός τις ἔπειθεν αὐτὸν ὑποστῆναι τὴν ἀρχήν. ὁ δὲ
Ξενοφῶν τῇ μὲν ἐβούλετο ταῦτα, νομίζων καὶ τὴν
τιμὴν μείζω οὕτως ἑαυτῷ γίγνεσθαι πρὸς τοὺς φίλους
καὶ εἰς τὴν πόλιν τοὔνομα μεῖζον ἀφίξεσθαι αὐτοῦ,
τυχὸν δὲ καὶ ἀγαθοῦ τινος ἂν αἴτιος τῇ στρατιᾷ

---

7 Cf. V. i. 3–4.

Here Cheirisophus[7] also came, with a man-of-war. And the soldiers expected that he had brought them something; in fact, however, he brought nothing, save the report that the admiral Anaxibius and the others commended them, and that Anaxibius promised that if they got outside the Euxine, they should have regular pay. Here at Harmene the troops remained for five days.

By this time, since it seemed that they were getting near Greece, the question came into their minds more than before how they might reach home with a little something in hand. They came to the conclusion, therefore, that if they should choose one commander, that one man would be able to handle the army better, whether by night or day, than a number of commanders—that if there should be need of concealment, he would be better able to keep matters secret, or again, if there should be need of getting ahead of an adversary, he would be less likely to be too late; for, thought the soldiers, there would be no need of conferences of generals with one another, but the plan resolved upon by the one man would be carried through, whereas in the past the generals had acted in all matters in accordance with a majority vote.

As they thought over these things they turned to Xenophon; the captains came to him and said that this was the opinion of the army, and each one of them, with manifestations of good will, urged him to undertake the command. As for Xenophon, he was inclined on some accounts to accept the command, for he thought that if he did so the greater would be the honour he would enjoy among his friends and the greater his name when it should reach his city, while, furthermore, it might chance that he could be the means of accomplishing some good thing for the army.

473

21 γενέσθαι. τὰ μὲν δὴ τοιαῦτα ἐνθυμήματα ἐπῆρεν
αὐτὸν ἐπιθυμεῖν αὐτοκράτορα γενέσθαι ἄρχοντα.
ὁπότε δ᾽ αὖ ἐνθυμοῖτο ὅτι ἄδηλον μὲν παντὶ ἀνθρώπῳ
ὅπῃ τὸ μέλλον ἕξει, διὰ τοῦτο δὲ καὶ κίνδυνος εἴη καὶ
τὴν προειργασμένην δόξαν ἀποβαλεῖν, ἠπορεῖτο.

22 Ἀπορουμένῳ δὲ αὐτῷ διακρῖναι ἔδοξε κράτιστον
εἶναι τοῖς θεοῖς ἀνακοινῶσαι· καὶ παραστησάμενος
δύο ἱερεῖα ἐθύετο τῷ Διὶ τῷ βασιλεῖ, ὅσπερ αὐτῷ
μαντευτὸς ἦν ἐκ Δελφῶν· καὶ τὸ ὄναρ δὴ ἀπὸ τούτου
τοῦ θεοῦ ἐνόμιζεν ἑορακέναι ὃ εἶδεν ὅτε ἤρχετο ἐπὶ τὸ

23 συνεπιμελεῖσθαι τῆς στρατιᾶς καθίστασθαι. καὶ ὅτε
ἐξ Ἐφέσου δὲ ὡρμᾶτο Κύρῳ συσταθησόμενος, ἀετὸν
ἀνεμιμνῄσκετο αὐτῷ δεξιὸν φθεγγόμενον, καθήμενον
μέντοι, ὅνπερ ὁ μάντις ⟨ὁ⟩[2] προπέμπων αὐτὸν ἔλεγεν
ὅτι μέγας μὲν οἰωνὸς εἴη καὶ οὐκ ἰδιωτικός, καὶ ἔνδο-
ξος, ἐπίπονος μέντοι· τὰ γὰρ ὄρνεα μάλιστα ἐπιτίθεσθαι τῷ ἀετῷ καθημένῳ· οὐ μέντοι χρηματιστικὸν
εἶναι τὸν οἰωνόν· τὸν γὰρ ἀετὸν περιπετόμενον μᾶλλον

24 λαμβάνειν τὰ ἐπιτήδεια. οὕτω δὴ θυομένῳ αὐτῷ δια-
φανῶς ὁ θεὸς σημαίνει μήτε προσδεῖσθαι τῆς ἀρχῆς
μήτε εἰ αἱροῖντο ἀποδέχεσθαι. τοῦτο μὲν δὴ οὕτως
ἐγένετο.

25 Ἡ δὲ στρατιὰ συνῆλθε, καὶ πάντες ἔλεγον ἕνα
αἱρεῖσθαι· καὶ ἐπεὶ τοῦτο ἔδοξε, προυβάλλοντο αὐτόν.

[2] ὁ added by Poppo.

Such considerations, then, roused in him an earnest desire
to become sole commander. On the other hand, when he
reflected that no man can see clearly how the future will
turn out and that for this reason there was danger that he
might even lose the reputation he had already won, he was
doubtful.

Unable as he was to decide the question, it seemed best
to him to consult the gods; and he accordingly brought two
victims to the altar and proceeded to offer sacrifice to King
Zeus, the very god that the oracle at Delphi had prescribed
for him;[8] and it was likewise from this god, as he believed,
that the dream[9] came which he had at the time when he
took the first steps toward assuming a share in the charge
of the army. Moreover, he recalled that when he was setting out from Ephesus to be introduced to Cyrus[10] an eagle
screamed upon his right; it was sitting, however, and the
soothsayer who was conducting him said that while the
omen was one suited to the great rather than to an ordinary
person, and while it betokened glory, it nevertheless por-
tended suffering, for the reason that other birds are most
apt to attack the eagle when it is sitting; still, he said, the
omen did not betoken gain, for it is rather while the eagle
is on the wing that it gets its food. So it was, then, that
Xenophon made sacrifice, and the god signified to him
quite clearly that he should neither strive for the command
nor accept it in case he should be chosen. Such was the
issue of this matter.

Then the army came together, and all the speakers
urged that a single commander be chosen; when this had
been resolved upon, they proceeded to nominate Xeno-

[8] Cf. III. i. 5 ff.   [9] Cf. III. i. 11 f.   [10] Cf. III. i. 8.

ἐπεὶ δὲ ἐδόκει δῆλον εἶναι ὅτι αἱρήσονται αὐτόν, εἴ τις ἐπιψηφίζοι, ἀνέστη καὶ ἔλεξε τάδε.

26 Ἐγώ, ὦ ἄνδρες, ἥδομαι μὲν ὑπὸ ὑμῶν τιμώμενος, εἴπερ ἄνθρωπός εἰμι, καὶ χάριν ἔχω καὶ εὔχομαι δοῦναί μοι τοὺς θεοὺς αἴτιόν τινος ὑμῖν ἀγαθοῦ γενέσθαι· τὸ μέντοι ἐμὲ προκριθῆναι ὑπὸ ὑμῶν ἄρχοντα Λακεδαιμονίου ἀνδρὸς παρόντος οὔτε ὑμῖν μοι δοκεῖ συμφέρον εἶναι, ἀλλ᾽ ἧττον ἂν διὰ τοῦτο τυγχάνειν, εἴ τι δέοισθε παρ᾽ αὐτῶν· ἐμοί τε αὖ οὐ πάνυ τι νομίζω 27 ἀσφαλὲς εἶναι τοῦτο· ὁρῶ γὰρ ὅτι καὶ τῇ πατρίδι μου οὐ πρόσθεν ἐπαύσαντο πολεμοῦντες πρὶν ἐποίησαν πᾶσαν τὴν πόλιν ὁμολογεῖν Λακεδαιμονίους καὶ αὐ- 28 τῶν ἡγεμόνας εἶναι. ἐπεὶ δὲ τοῦτο ὡμολόγησαν, εὐθὺς ἐπαύσαντο πολεμοῦντες καὶ οὐκέτι πέρα ἐπολιόρ- κησαν τὴν πόλιν. εἰ οὖν ταῦτα ὁρῶν ἐγὼ δοκοίην ὅπου δυναίμην ἐνταῦθ᾽ ἄκυρον ποιεῖν τὸ ἐκείνων ἀξίωμα, 29 ἐκεῖνο ἐννοῶ μὴ λίαν ἂν ταχὺ σωφρονισθείην. ὃ δὲ ὑμεῖς ἐννοεῖτε, ὅτι ἧττον ἂν στάσις εἴη ἑνὸς ἄρχοντος ἢ πολλῶν, εὖ ἴστε ὅτι ἄλλον μὲν ἑλόμενοι οὐχ εὑρή- σετε ἐμὲ στασιάζοντα· νομίζω γὰρ ὅστις ἐν πολέμῳ ὢν στασιάζει πρὸς ἄρχοντα, τοῦτον πρὸς τὴν ἑαυτοῦ σωτηρίαν στασιάζειν· ἐὰν δὲ ἐμὲ ἕλησθε, οὐκ ἂν θαυμάσαιμι εἴ τινα εὕροιτε καὶ ὑμῖν καὶ ἐμοὶ ἀχθό- μενον.

30 Ἐπεὶ δὲ ταῦτα εἶπε, πολὺ μᾶλλον ἐξανίσταντο λέγοντες ὡς δέοι αὐτὸν ἄρχειν. Ἀγασίας δὲ Στυμ-

---

11 Cf. *Hell.* II. ii. 20.

476

phon. And when it seemed clear that they would elect him as soon as the question should be put to vote, he arose and spoke as follows:

"I am happy, soldiers, since I am a human being, to be honoured by you, and I am grateful also, and I pray that the gods may grant me opportunity to be the means of bringing you some benefit; still, I think that for me to be preferred by you as commander when a Lacedaemonian is at hand, is not expedient for you—for you would be less likely on this account to obtain any favour you might desire from the Lacedaemonians—and for myself, on the other hand, I believe it is not altogether safe. For I see that the Lacedaemonians did not cease waging war upon my native state until they had made all her citizens acknowledge that the Lacedaemonians were their leaders also.[11] But just as soon as this acknowledgment had been made, they straightway ceased waging war and no longer continued to besiege the city. Now if I, being aware of these things, should seem to be trying to make their authority null and void wherever I could, I suspect that I might very speedily be brought back to reason on that point. As to your own thought, that there would be less factiousness with one commander than with many, be well assured that if you choose another, you will not find me acting factiously—for I believe that when a man engaged in war factiously opposes a commander, that man is factiously opposing his own safety; but if you choose me, I should not be surprised if you should find some one else feeling angry both with you and with myself."

When he had thus spoken, an even greater number of people stood up, saying that he ought to be commander. And Agasias the Stymphalian said that it was ridiculous if

477

φάλιος εἶπεν ὅτι γελοῖον εἴη, εἰ οὕτως ἔχοι· ἢ ὀργιοῦν-
ται Λακεδαιμόνιοι καὶ ἐὰν σύνδειπνοι συνελθόντες μὴ
Λακεδαιμόνιον συμποσίαρχον αἱρῶνται· ἐπεὶ εἰ οὕτω
γε τοῦτο ἔχει, ἔφη, οὐδὲ λοχαγεῖν ἡμῖν ἔξεστιν, ὡς
ἔοικεν, ὅτι Ἀρκάδες ἐσμέν. ἐνταῦθα δὴ ὡς εὖ εἰπόντος
τοῦ Ἀγασίου ἀνεθορύβησαν.

31   Καὶ ὁ Ξενοφῶν ἐπεὶ ἑώρα πλείονος ἐνδέον, παρελθὼν εἶπεν· Ἀλλ᾽, ὦ ἄνδρες, ἔφη, ὡς πάνυ εἰδῆτε,
ὀμνύω ὑμῖν θεοὺς πάντας καὶ πάσας, ἦ μὴν ἐγώ, ἐπεὶ
τὴν ὑμετέραν γνώμην ᾐσθανόμην, ἐθυόμην εἰ βέλτιον
εἴη ὑμῖν τε ἐμοὶ ἐπιτρέψαι ταύτην τὴν ἀρχὴν καὶ ἐμοὶ
ὑποστῆναι· καί μοι οἱ θεοὶ οὕτως ἐν τοῖς ἱεροῖς ἐσήμη-
ναν ὡς καὶ ἰδιώτην ἂν γνῶναι ὅτι ταύτης μοναρχίας
ἀπέχεσθαί με δεῖ.

32   Οὕτω δὴ Χειρίσοφον αἱροῦνται. Χειρίσοφος δ᾽ ἐπεὶ
ᾑρέθη, παρελθὼν εἶπεν· Ἀλλ᾽, ὦ ἄνδρες, τοῦτο μὲν
ἴστε, ὅτι οὐδ᾽ ἂν ἔγωγε ἐστασίαζον, εἰ ἄλλον εἵλεσθε·
Ξενοφῶντα μέντοι, ἔφη, ὠνήσατε οὐχ ἑλόμενοι· ὡς καὶ
νῦν Δέξιππος ἤδη διέβαλλεν αὐτὸν πρὸς Ἀναξίβιον
ὅ τι ἐδύνατο καὶ μάλα ἐμοῦ αὐτὸν σιγάζοντος. ὁ δ᾽
ἔφη νομίζειν αὐτὸν Τιμασίωνι μᾶλλον συνάρχειν
ἐθελῆσαι[3] Δαρδανεῖ ὄντι τοῦ Κλεάρχου στρατεύματος
33   ἢ ἑαυτῷ Λάκωνι ὄντι. ἐπεὶ μέντοι ἐμὲ εἵλεσθε, ἔφη,
καὶ ἐγὼ πειράσομαι ὅ τι ἂν δύνωμαι ὑμᾶς ἀγαθὸν

----

[3] συνάρχειν ἐθελῆσαι some MSS., Hude/Peters: ἄρχειν
συνεθελῆσαι other MSS., Mar.: συνάρχειν ἂν ἐθελῆσαι Cobet,
Gem.

the situation was as Xenophon described it. "Will the Lacedaemonians also be angry," he said, "if guests at dinner come together and fail to choose a Lacedaemonian as master of the feast? For if the matter stands in that way, we are not free even to be captains, it would seem, because we are Arcadians." Thereupon the soldiers raised a shout, saying that Agasias was quite right.

Then Xenophon, seeing that something more was needed, came forward and spoke again: "Well, soldiers," he said, "that you may understand the matter fully I swear to you by all the gods and goddesses that in very truth, when I became aware of your intention, I offered sacrifices to learn whether it was best for you to entrust to me this command and for me to undertake it; and the gods gave me such signs in the sacrifices that even a layman could perceive that I must withhold myself from accepting this sole command."

Under these circumstances, then, they chose Cheirisophus. And after being chosen Cheirisophus came forward and spoke as follows: "Well, soldiers, be sure of this, that I also should not have acted factiously if you had chosen another; as for Xenophon, however," he continued, "you did him a kindness by not choosing him; for even now Dexippus[12] has already been falsely accusing him, as far as he could, to Anaxibius, even though I tried hard to silence him. He said he believed that Xenophon preferred to share the command of Clearchus' army with Timasion, a Dardanian, than with himself, a Laconian. However," Cheirisophus went on, "since you have chosen me, I shall endeavour to render you whatever service I can. And do

12 Cf. V. i. 15.

ποιεῖν. καὶ ὑμεῖς οὕτω παρασκευάζεσθε ὡς αὔριον, ἐὰν
πλοῦς ᾖ, ἀναξόμενοι· ὁ δὲ πλοῦς ἔσται εἰς Ἡράκλειαν·
ἅπαντας οὖν δεῖ ἐκεῖσε πειρᾶσθαι κατασχεῖν· τὰ δ᾽
ἄλλα, ἐπειδὰν ἐκεῖσε ἔλθωμεν, βουλευσόμεθα.

II. Ἐντεῦθεν τῇ ὑστεραίᾳ ἀναγαγόμενοι πνεύματι
ἔπλεον καλῷ ἡμέρας δύο παρὰ γῆν. καὶ παραπλέοντες
ἐθεώρουν τήν τε Ἰασονίαν ἀκτήν, ἔνθα ἡ Ἀργὼ λέγεται ὁρμίσασθαι, καὶ τῶν ποταμῶν τὰ στόματα, πρῶτον
μὲν τοῦ Θερμώδοντος, ἔπειτα δὲ τοῦ Ἴριος, ἔπειτα δὲ
τοῦ Ἅλυος, μετὰ δὲ τοῦτον τοῦ Παρθενίου· τοῦτον δὲ
παραπλεύσαντες[4] ἀφίκοντο εἰς Ἡράκλειαν πόλιν Ἑλληνίδα, Μεγαρέων ἄποικον, οὖσαν δ᾽ ἐν τῇ Μαριαν-
2 δυνῶν χώρᾳ. καὶ ὡρμίσαντο παρὰ τῇ Ἀχερουσιάδι
Χερρονήσῳ, ἔνθα λέγεται ὁ Ἡρακλῆς ἐπὶ τὸν Κέρ-
βερον κύνα καταβῆναι ᾗ νῦν τὰ σημεῖα δεικνύασι τῆς
3 καταβάσεως τὸ βάθος πλέον ἢ ἐπὶ δύο στάδια. ἐνταῦθα τοῖς Ἕλλησιν οἱ Ἡρακλεῶται ξένια πέμπουσιν
ἀλφίτων μεδίμνους τρισχιλίους καὶ οἴνου κεράμια
δισχίλια καὶ βοῦς εἴκοσι καὶ οἷς ἑκατόν. ἐνταῦθα διὰ
τοῦ πεδίου ῥεῖ ποταμὸς Λύκος ὄνομα, εὖρος ὡς δύο
πλέθρων.

4 Οἱ δὲ στρατιῶται συλλεγέντες ἐβουλεύοντο τὴν
λοιπὴν πορείαν πότερον κατὰ γῆν ἢ κατὰ θάλατταν
χρὴ πορευθῆναι ἐκ τοῦ Πόντου. ἀναστὰς δὲ Λύκων

4 These remarks are geographically impossible; consequently,
editors have generally rejected them. However, the errors may
simply be Xenophon's: cf. Cawkwell, *Persian Expedition*, 270 n. 3.

you make your preparations to put to sea tomorrow if it be sailing weather. The voyage will be to Heracleia; every one of us, therefore, must try to come to land there; and we shall take counsel about our further doings when we have arrived there."

II. On the next day they set sail from Sinope and voyaged for two days with a fair wind along the coast. And coursing along, they saw Jason's Cape, where the Argo is said to have come to anchor, and the mouths of the rivers, first the Thermodon, then the Iris, third the Halys, and after that the Parthenius; and after they had passed this river they arrived at Heracleia, a Greek city and a colony of the Megarians, situated in the territory of the Mariandynians.[13] And they came to anchor alongside the Acherusian Chersonese, where Heracles is said to have descended to Hades after the dog Cerberus, at a spot where they now show the marks of his descent, reaching to a depth of more than two stadia.[14] Here the Heracleots sent to the Greeks, as gifts of hospitality, three thousand *medimni* of barley meal, two thousand jars of wine, twenty cattle, and a hundred sheep. And in this place there flows through the plain a river named the Lycus, about two plethra in width.

Then the soldiers gathered together and proceeded to take counsel about the remainder of the journey, that is, whether they had better go on from the Euxine by land or by sea. And Lycon the Achaean rose and said: "I am

[13] For what follows, cf. S. Burstein, *Outpost of Hellenism: the Emergence of Heraclea on the Black Sea* (Berkeley, 1976) 39–41.

[14] Cf. the work of the Heracleot Herodorus, *FGH* 31 F 31: local pride and tourism.

Ἀχαιὸς εἶπε· Θαυμάζω μέν, ὦ ἄνδρες, τῶν στρατηγῶν
ὅτι οὐ πειρῶνται ἡμῖν ἐκπορίζειν σιτηρέσιον· τὰ μὲν
γὰρ ξένια οὐ μὴ γένηται τῇ στρατιᾷ τριῶν ἡμερῶν
σιτία· ὁπόθεν δ᾽ ἐπισιτισάμενοι πορευσόμεθα οὐκ
ἔστιν, ἔφη. ἐμοὶ οὖν δοκεῖ αἰτεῖν τοὺς Ἡρακλεώτας μὴ
5 ἔλαττον ἢ τρισχιλίους κυζικηνούς· ἄλλος δ᾽ εἶπε μὴ
ἔλαττον ἢ μυρίους· καὶ ἑλομένους πρέσβεις αὐτίκα
μάλα ἡμῶν καθημένων πέμπειν πρὸς τὴν πόλιν, καὶ
εἰδέναι ὅ τι ἂν ἀπαγγέλλωσι, καὶ πρὸς ταῦτα βου-
6 λεύεσθαι. ἐντεῦθεν προυβάλλοντο πρέσβεις πρῶτον
μὲν Χειρίσοφον, ὅτι ἄρχων ᾕρητο· ἔστι δ᾽ οἳ καὶ
Ξενοφῶντα. οἱ δὲ ἰσχυρῶς ἀπεμάχοντο· ἀμφοῖν γὰρ
ταῦτα ἐδόκει μὴ ἀναγκάζειν πόλιν Ἑλληνίδα καὶ
7 φιλίαν ὅ τι μὴ αὐτοὶ ἐθέλοντες διδοῖεν. ἐπεὶ δ᾽ οὗτοι
ἐδόκουν ἀπρόθυμοι εἶναι, πέμπουσι Λύκωνα Ἀχαιὸν
καὶ Καλλίμαχον Παρράσιον καὶ Ἀγασίαν Στυμφάλιον. οὗτοι ἐλθόντες ἔλεγον τὰ δεδογμένα· τὸν δὲ
Λύκωνα ἔφασαν καὶ ἐπαπειλεῖν, εἰ μὴ ποιήσοιεν
8 ταῦτα. ἀκούσαντες δ᾽ οἱ Ἡρακλεῶται βουλεύσεσθαι
ἔφασαν· καὶ εὐθὺς τά τε χρήματα ἐκ τῶν ἀγρῶν
συνῆγον καὶ τὴν ἀγορὰν εἴσω ἀνεσκεύασαν, καὶ αἱ
πύλαι ἐκέκλειντο καὶ ἐπὶ τῶν τειχῶν ὅπλα ἐφαίνοντο.
9   Ἐκ τούτου οἱ ταράξαντες ταῦτα τοὺς στρατηγοὺς
ᾐτιῶντο διαφθείρειν τὴν πρᾶξιν· καὶ συνίσταντο οἱ
Ἀρκάδες καὶ οἱ Ἀχαιοί· προειστήκει δὲ μάλιστα

astonished, soldiers that the generals do not endeavour to supply us with money to buy provisions; for our gifts of hospitality will not make three days' rations for the army; and there is no place," said he, "from which we can procure provisions before beginning our journey. I move, therefore, that we demand of the Heracleots not less than three thousand Cyzicenes"[15] —another man said, not less than ten thousand—"and that we choose ambassadors this very moment, while we are in session here, send them to the city, hear whatever report they may bring back, and take counsel in the light of that." Thereupon they went to nominating ambassadors, first Cheirisophus, because he had been chosen commander, and some nominated Xenophon also. Both men, however, offered vigorous resistance; for both held the same view—that they ought not to coerce a friendly city of Greeks into giving what they did not offer of their own accord. As these two seemed disinclined to act, they sent Lycon the Achaean, Callimachus the Parrhasian, and Agasias the Stymphalian. These men went and put before the Heracleots the resolutions adopted by the army; and Lycon, so the report ran, even added threats, in case they should refuse compliance. After hearing the ambassadors, the Heracleots said that they would consider the matter; and immediately they set about gathering their property from the country and moved the market within the walls; meanwhile the gates had been closed and arms were to be seen upon the walls.

Thereupon those who had brought about this agitation accused the generals of spoiling their undertaking; and the Arcadians and Achaeans proceeded to band themselves

15 Cf. note on V. vi. 23.

αὐτῶν Καλλίμαχός τε ὁ Παρράσιος καὶ Λύκων ὁ
10 Ἀχαιός. οἱ δὲ λόγοι ἦσαν αὐτοῖς ὡς αἰσχρὸν εἴη
ἄρχειν Ἀθηναῖον Πελοποννησίων καὶ Λακεδαιμονίων,
μηδεμίαν δύναμιν παρεχόμενον εἰς τὴν στρατιάν, καὶ
τοὺς μὲν πόνους σφᾶς ἔχειν, τὰ δὲ κέρδη ἄλλους, καὶ
ταῦτα τὴν σωτηρίαν σφῶν κατειργασμένων· εἶναι γὰρ
τοὺς κατειργασμένους Ἀρκάδας καὶ Ἀχαιούς, τὸ δ᾽
ἄλλο στράτευμα οὐδὲν εἶναι (καὶ ἦν δὲ τῇ ἀληθείᾳ
ὑπὲρ ἥμισυ τοῦ ἄλλου στρατεύματος Ἀρκάδες καὶ
11 Ἀχαιοί)· εἰ οὖν σωφρονοῖεν, αὐτοὶ συστάντες καὶ
στρατηγοὺς ἑλόμενοι ἑαυτῶν καθ᾽ ἑαυτούς τ᾽ ἂν τὴν
πορείαν ποιοῖντο καὶ πειρῷντο ἀγαθόν τι λαμβάνειν.
12 ταῦτ᾽ ἔδοξε· καὶ ἀπολιπόντες Χειρίσοφον εἴ τινες ἦσαν
παρ᾽ αὐτῷ Ἀρκάδες ἢ Ἀχαιοὶ καὶ Ξενοφῶντα συν-
έστησαν καὶ στρατηγοὺς αἱροῦνται ἑαυτῶν δέκα·
τούτους δὲ ἐψηφίσαντο ἐκ τῆς νικώσης ὅ τι δοκοίη
τοῦτο ποιεῖν. ἡ μὲν οὖν τοῦ παντὸς ἀρχὴ Χειρισόφῳ
ἐνταῦθα κατελύθη ἡμέρᾳ ἕκτῃ ἢ ἑβδόμῃ ἀφ᾽ ἧς ᾑρέθη.
13 Ξενοφῶν μέντοι ἐβούλετο κοινῇ μετ᾽ αὐτοῦ τὴν
πορείαν ποιεῖσθαι, νομίζων οὕτως ἀσφαλεστέραν εἶναι ἢ ἰδίᾳ ἕκαστον στέλλεσθαι· ἀλλὰ Νέων ἔπειθεν
αὐτὸν καθ᾽ αὑτὸν πορεύεσθαι, ἀκούσας τοῦ Χειρισόφου ὅτι Κλέανδρος ὁ ἐν Βυζαντίῳ ἁρμοστὴς φαίη

---

16 The independence of the Arcadians and Achaeans is note-
worthy: both came from regions in Greece popular for the recruit-

together, under the leadership particularly of Callimachus the Parrhasian and Lycon the Achaean. Their words were to this effect, that it was shameful that Peloponnesians and Lacedaemonians should be under the command of an Athenian who contributed no troops to the army, and that the hardships should fall to themselves and the gains to others, all despite the fact that the preservation of the army was their achievement; for it was, they said, the Arcadians and Achaeans who had achieved this result, and the rest of the army amounted to nothing (in truth the Arcadians and Achaeans constituted more than half of the entire army); if they were wise, therefore, they would band together by themselves, choose generals from their own number, make the journey by themselves, and try to get a little good out of it. This course was resolved upon, and whatever Arcadians or Achaeans there were with Cheirisophus and Xenophon left these commanders and joined forces, and they chose ten generals from their own number, decreeing that these ten were to do whatever might be decided upon by vote of the majority.[16] So it was that the supreme command of Cheirisophus came to an end then and there, on the sixth or seventh day from the day of his election.

Xenophon, however, was desirous of making the journey in company with Cheirisophus, believing that this was a safer plan than for each of them to proceed independently; but Neon[17] urged him to go by himself, for he had heard from Cheirisophus that Cleander, the Lacedae-

ment of mercenaries, and that would wield considerable power later as federal states.

[17] Cheirisophus' lieutenant (cf. V. vi. 36).

14 τριήρεις ἔχων ἥξειν εἰς Κάλπης λιμένα· ὅπως οὖν
μηδεὶς μετάσχοι, ἀλλ' αὐτοὶ καὶ οἱ αὐτῶν στρατιῶται
ἐκπλεύσειαν ἐπὶ τῶν τριήρων, διὰ ταῦτα συνεβούλευε.
καὶ Χειρίσοφος, ἅμα μὲν ἀθυμῶν τοῖς γεγενημένοις,
ἅμα δὲ μισῶν ἐκ τούτου τὸ στράτευμα, ἐπιτρέπει αὐτῷ
15 ποιεῖν ὅ τι βούλεται. Ξενοφῶν δὲ ἔτι μὲν ἐπεχείρησεν
ἀπαλλαγεὶς τῆς στρατιᾶς ἐκπλεῦσαι· θυομένῳ δὲ αὐτῷ
τῷ ἡγεμόνι Ἡρακλεῖ καὶ κοινουμένῳ, πότερα λῷον καὶ
ἄμεινον εἴη στρατεύεσθαι ἔχοντι τοὺς παραμείναντας
τῶν στρατιωτῶν ἢ ἀπαλλάττεσθαι, ἐσήμηνεν ὁ θεὸς
16 τοῖς ἱεροῖς συστρατεύεσθαι. οὕτω γίγνεται τὸ στράτευμα τρίχα, Ἀρκάδες μὲν καὶ Ἀχαιοὶ πλείους ἢ
τετρακισχίλιοι καὶ πεντακόσιοι, ὁπλῖται πάντες, Χειρισόφῳ δ' ὁπλῖται μὲν εἰς τετρακοσίους καὶ χιλίους,
πελτασταὶ δὲ εἰς ἑπτακοσίους, οἱ Κλεάρχου Θρᾷκες,
Ξενοφῶντι δὲ ὁπλῖται μὲν εἰς ἑπτακοσίους καὶ χιλίους,
πελτασταὶ δὲ εἰς τριακοσίους· ἱππικὸν δὲ μόνος οὗτος
εἶχεν, ἀμφὶ τετταράκοντα ἱππέας.

17 Καὶ οἱ μὲν Ἀρκάδες διαπραξάμενοι πλοῖα παρὰ
τῶν Ἡρακλεωτῶν πρῶτοι πλέουσιν, ὅπως ἐξαίφνης
ἐπιπεσόντες τοῖς Βιθυνοῖς λάβοιεν ὅτι πλεῖστα· καὶ
ἀποβαίνουσιν εἰς Κάλπης λιμένα κατὰ μέσον πως τῆς
18 Θρᾴκης. Χειρίσοφος δ' εὐθὺς ἀπὸ τῆς πόλεως τῶν
Ἡρακλεωτῶν ἀρξάμενος πεζῇ ἐπορεύετο διὰ τῆς
χώρας· ἐπεὶ δὲ εἰς τὴν Θρᾴκην ἐνέβαλε, παρὰ τὴν
19 θάλατταν ᾔει· καὶ γὰρ ἠσθένει. Ξενοφῶν δὲ πλοῖα

---

[18] Consulted because important locally.

monian governor at Byzantium, had said he was coming to
Calpe Harbour with triremes; it was Neon's purpose, then,
that no one else should get a share in this opportunity, but
that he himself and Cheirisophus and their soldiers should
sail away upon the triremes, and this was the reason for his
advice to Xenophon. As for Cheirisophus, he was so despondent over what had happened and, besides, felt such
hatred toward the army for its action, that he allowed Neon
to do whatever he chose. For a time, indeed, Xenophon
did try to get clear of the army and sail away home; but
when he sacrificed to Heracles the Leader,[18] consulting
him as to whether it was better and more proper for him
to continue the journey with such of the soldiers as had
remained with him, or to be rid of them, the god indicated
to him by the sacrifices that he should stay with them. Thus
the army was split into three parts: first, the Arcadians and
Achaeans, more than four thousand five hundred in
number, all hoplites; secondly, Cheirisophus' troops, to the
number of fourteen hundred hoplites and seven hundred
peltasts, the latter being Clearchus' Thracians; and thirdly,
Xenophon's force, numbering seventeen hundred hoplites
and three hundred peltasts; Xenophon alone, however, had
horsemen, to the number of about forty.

The Arcadians, managing to obtain ships from the Heracleots, set sail first, with the intention of making an unexpected descent upon the Bithynians and thus securing the
greatest possible amount of booty; and they disembarked
at Calpe Harbour, about halfway along the Thracian coast.
But Cheirisophus went by land from the very beginning
of his journey from the city of the Heracleots, travelling
across country; when, however, he had entered Thrace, he
proceeded along the coast, for the reason that he was ill.

λαβὼν ἀποβαίνει ἐπὶ τὰ ὅρια τῆς Θρᾴκης καὶ τῆς Ἡρακλεώτιδος καὶ διὰ μεσογείας ἐπορεύετο.

2 III. Ἔπραξαν δ' αὐτῶν ἕκαστοι τάδε. οἱ μὲν Ἀρκάδες ὡς ἀπέβησαν νυκτὸς εἰς Κάλπης λιμένα, πορεύονται εἰς τὰς πρώτας κώμας, στάδια ἀπὸ θαλάττης ὡς τριάκοντα. ἐπεὶ δὲ φῶς ἐγένετο, ἦγεν ἕκαστος ὁ στρατηγὸς τὸν αὑτοῦ λόχον ἐπὶ κώμην· ὁποία δὲ μείζων

3 ἐδόκει εἶναι, σύνδυο λόχους ἦγον οἱ στρατηγοί. συνεβάλοντο δὲ καὶ λόφον εἰς ὃν δέοι πάντας ἁλίζεσθαι· καὶ ἅτε ἐξαίφνης ἐπιπεσόντες ἀνδράποδά τε πολλὰ

4 ἔλαβον καὶ πρόβατα πολλὰ περιεβάλοντο. οἱ δὲ Θρᾷκες ἠθροίζοντο οἱ διαφυγόντες· πολλοὶ δὲ διέφυγον πελτασταὶ ὄντες ὁπλίτας ἐξ αὐτῶν τῶν χειρῶν. ἐπεὶ δὲ συνελέγησαν, πρῶτον μὲν τῷ Σμίκρητος λόχῳ ἑνὸς τῶν Ἀρκάδων στρατηγῶν ἀπιόντι ἤδη εἰς τὸ συγκεί-

5 μενον καὶ πολλὰ χρήματα ἄγοντι ἐπιτίθενται. καὶ τέως μὲν ἐμάχοντο ἅμα πορευόμενοι οἱ Ἕλληνες, ἐπὶ δὲ διαβάσει χαράδρας τρέπονται αὐτούς, καὶ αὐτόν τε τὸν Σμίκρητα ἀποκτιννύασι καὶ τοὺς ἄλλους πάντας· ἄλλου δὲ λόχου τῶν δέκα στρατηγῶν τοῦ Ἡγησάνδρου ὀκτὼ μόνους κατέλιπον· καὶ αὐτὸς Ἡγήσανδρος ἐσώθη.

6 Καὶ οἱ ἄλλοι δὲ λοχαγοὶ συνῆλθον οἱ μὲν σὺν πράγμασιν οἱ δὲ ἄνευ πραγμάτων· οἱ δὲ Θρᾷκες ἐπεὶ ηὐτύχησαν τοῦτο τὸ εὐτύχημα, συνεβόων τε ἀλλήλους καὶ συνελέγοντο ἐρρωμένως τῆς νυκτός. καὶ ἅμα ἡμέρᾳ κύκλῳ περὶ τὸν λόφον ἔνθα οἱ Ἕλληνες

Xenophon, finally, took ships, disembarked at the boundaries separating Thrace and the territory of Heracleia, and made his way through the back country.

III. The fortunes of the several divisions were as follows. The Arcadians after disembarking by night at Calpe Harbour proceeded to the first villages, about thirty stadia from the sea. When daylight came, each general led his own company against a village, except that where a village seemed unusually large, the generals combined two companies for the attack upon it. They also fixed upon a hill as the place where all the troops were afterwards to gather; and since their onset was unexpected, they took many captives and secured a large number of sheep. The Thracians who escaped them, however, began to gather—and many had escaped, inasmuch as they were light troops against hoplites, from the very hands of the Arcadians. When they had come together in a body, they first attacked the company under Smicres, one of the Arcadian generals, as it was already withdrawing to the appointed place with a great quantity of booty. For a while the Greeks fought as they marched, but at the crossing of a gorge the Thracians put them to rout, and they killed not only Smicres himself, but the rest of the company to a man; in another of the companies belonging to the ten generals, the one commanded by Hegesander, they left behind only eight men alive, Hegesander himself being one of them.

The other company commanders succeeded in getting together, some of them with difficulty, others without any difficulty; but the Thracians, having gained this success, kept shouting to one another and collecting their forces energetically during the night. At daybreak they proceeded to form their lines all round the hill where the

ἐστρατοπεδεύοντο ἐτάττοντο καὶ ἱππεῖς πολλοὶ καὶ
7 πελτασταί, καὶ ἀεὶ πλέονες συνέρρεον· καὶ προσέβαλλον πρὸς τοὺς ὁπλίτας ἀσφαλῶς· οἱ μὲν γὰρ Ἕλληνες
οὔτε τοξότην εἶχον οὔτε ἀκοντιστὴν οὔτε ἱππέα· οἱ δὲ
προσθέοντες καὶ προσελαύνοντες ἠκόντιζον· ὁπότε δὲ
8 αὐτοῖς ἐπίοιεν, ῥᾳδίως ἀπέφευγον· ἄλλοι δὲ ἄλλῃ
ἐπετίθεντο. καὶ τῶν μὲν πολλοὶ ἐτιτρώσκοντο, τῶν δὲ
οὐδείς· ὥστε κινηθῆναι οὐκ ἐδύναντο ἐκ τοῦ χωρίου,
ἀλλὰ τελευτῶντες καὶ ἀπὸ τοῦ ὕδατος εἶργον αὐτοὺς
9 οἱ Θρᾷκες. ἐπεὶ δὲ ἀπορία πολλὴ ἦν, διελέγοντο περὶ
σπονδῶν· καὶ τὰ μὲν ἄλλα ὡμολόγητο αὐτοῖς, ὁμήρους δὲ οὐκ ἐδίδοσαν οἱ Θρᾷκες αἰτούντων τῶν Ἑλλήνων, ἀλλ' ἐν τούτῳ ἴσχετο. τὰ μὲν δὴ τῶν Ἀρκάδων
οὕτως εἶχε.

10 Χειρίσοφος δὲ ἀσφαλῶς πορευόμενος παρὰ θάλατταν ἀφικνεῖται εἰς Κάλπης λιμένα.

Ξενοφῶντι δὲ διὰ τῆς μεσογείας πορευομένῳ οἱ
ἱππεῖς προκαταθέοντες[5] ἐντυγχάνουσι πρεσβύταις
πορευομένοις ποι. καὶ ἐπεὶ ἤχθησαν παρὰ Ξενοφῶντα,
ἐρωτᾷ αὐτοὺς εἴ που ᾔσθηνται ἄλλου στρατεύματος
11 ὄντος Ἑλληνικοῦ. οἱ δὲ ἔλεγον πάντα τὰ γεγενημένα,
καὶ νῦν ὅτι πολιορκοῦνται ἐπὶ λόφου, οἱ δὲ Θρᾷκες
πάντες περικεκυκλωμένοι εἶεν αὐτούς. ἐνταῦθα τοὺς
μὲν ἀνθρώπους τούτους ἐφύλαττεν ἰσχυρῶς, ὅπως

---

[5] προκαταθέοντες some MSS., Gem.: καταθέοντες other
MSS., Mar.

Greeks were encamping, their troops consisting of horsemen in large numbers and peltasts, while still more were
continually streaming together; and they made attacks
upon the hoplites without danger to themselves, inasmuch
as the Greeks had neither bowman nor javelin thrower nor
horseman; so they would come running or riding up and
throw their javelins, and when the Greeks charged upon
them, they would easily get away; and different parties
kept attacking at different points.[19] Hence on the one side
many were being wounded, on the other side not a man;
the result was, that the Greeks were not able to stir from
the spot, and at last the Thracians were even cutting them
off from their water supply. When their embarrassment
became serious, they opened negotiations for a truce; and
on every other point an agreement had been reached, but
the Thracians refused to give the hostages which the
Greeks demanded, and in this particular there was a hitch.
Such, then, was the situation of the Arcadians.

As to Cheirisophus, he pursued his march in safety
along the coast and arrived at Calpe Harbour.

Xenophon, lastly, was proceeding through the back
country when his horsemen, riding on in advance, chanced
upon some old men who were journeying somewhere or
other. When they were brought to Xenophon, he asked
them whether they had heard of another army anywhere,
a Greek army. And they told him all that had happened,
adding that at present the Greeks were being besieged
upon a hill, with the Thracians in full force completely
surrounding them. Then Xenophon kept these men under

[19] The fatal weakness of the hoplite exposed: cf. *Hell*. IV. v.
11 ff.

491

ἡγεμόνες εἶεν ὅποι δέοι· σκοποὺς δὲ καταστήσας
12 συνέλεξε τοὺς στρατιώτας καὶ ἔλεξεν· Ἄνδρες στρατιῶται, τῶν Ἀρκάδων οἱ μὲν τεθνᾶσιν, οἱ δὲ λοιποὶ ἐπὶ
λόφου τινὸς πολιορκοῦνται. νομίζω δ' ἔγωγε, εἰ ἐκεῖνοι
ἀπολοῦνται, οὐδ' ἡμῖν εἶναι οὐδεμίαν σωτηρίαν, οὕτω
μὲν πολλῶν ὄντων τῶν πολεμίων, οὕτω δὲ τεθαρ-
13 ρηκότων. κράτιστον οὖν ἡμῖν ὡς τάχιστα βοηθεῖν τοῖς
ἀνδράσιν, ὅπως εἰ ἔτι εἰσὶ σῶοι, σὺν ἐκείνοις μαχώ-
μεθα καὶ μὴ μόνοι λειφθέντες μόνοι καὶ κινδυνεύω-
16 μεν.[6] ἡμεῖς γὰρ ἀποδραίημεν ἂν οὐδαμοῖ ἐνθένδε·
(14) πολλὴ μὲν γάρ, ἔφη, εἰς Ἡράκλειαν πάλιν ἀπιέναι,
πολλὴ δὲ εἰς Χρυσόπολιν διελθεῖν· οἱ δὲ πολέμιοι
πλησίον· εἰς Κάλπης δὲ λιμένα, ἔνθα Χειρίσοφον
εἰκάζομεν εἶναι, εἰ σέσωσται, ἐλαχίστη ὁδός. ἀλλὰ δὴ
ἐκεῖ μὲν οὔτε πλοῖά ἐστιν οἷς ἀποπλευσούμεθα,
μένουσι δὲ αὐτοῦ οὐδὲ μιᾶς ἡμέρας ἔστι τὰ ἐπιτήδεια.
17 τῶν δὲ πολιορκουμένων ἀπολομένων σὺν τοῖς Χειρι-
(15) σόφου μόνοις κάκιόν ἐστι διακινδυνεύειν ἢ τῶνδε
σωθέντων πάντας εἰς ταὐτὸν ἐλθόντας κοινῇ τῆς
σωτηρίας ἔχεσθαι. ἀλλὰ χρὴ παρασκευασαμένους
τὴν γνώμην πορεύεσθαι ὡς νῦν ἢ εὐκλεῶς τελευτῆσαι
ἔστιν ἢ κάλλιστον ἔργον ἐργάσασθαι Ἕλληνας
18 τοσούτους σώσαντας. καὶ ὁ θεὸς ἴσως ἄγει οὕτως, ὃς
(16) τοὺς μεγαληγορήσαντας ὡς πλέον φρονοῦντας τα-
πεινῶσαι βούλεται, ἡμᾶς δὲ τοὺς ἀπὸ τῶν θεῶν ἀρχο-

---

[6] In the transposition indicated by the following section numbers Gem., Mar., and Hude/Peters follow Rehdantz.

492

strict guard, in order that they might serve as guides wherever he might need to go; and after stationing watchers he called the troops together and spoke as follows: "Fellow soldiers, some of the Arcadians have been killed and the remainder of them are being besieged upon a certain hill. Now it is my own belief that if they are to perish, there is no salvation for us either, the enemy being so numerous and made so confident by their success. Therefore it is best for us to go to the rescue of these men with all speed, so that if they are still alive, we may have their aid in the fighting, instead of being left alone and alone facing the danger. For there is no place to which we can ourselves steal away from here; for to go back to Heracleia," he said, "is a long journey, and it is a long journey through to Chrysopolis, and meanwhile the enemy are close at hand; to Calpe Harbour, where we presume Cheirisophus is, in case he has come through safely, is the shortest distance. But firstly, mark you, having arrived there we have neither ships wherein to sail away nor provisions for so much as a single day if we remain in the place; and secondly, it is worse to have the blockaded force destroyed and take our chances in company with Cheirisophus' troops only, than to have these men saved and then unite all our forces and together strive for deliverance. We must set forth, then, prepared in our minds for either meeting today a glorious death or accomplishing a most noble deed in saving so many Greeks. And it may be that the god is guiding events in this way, he who wills that those who talked boastfully, as though possessed of superior wisdom, should be brought low, and that we, who always begin with the

μένους ἐντιμοτέρους ἐκείνων καταστῆσαι. ἀλλ᾽ ἕπεσθαι χρὴ καὶ προσέχειν τὸν νοῦν, ὡς ἂν τὸ παραγ-
14 γελλόμενον δύνησθε ποιεῖν. νῦν μὲν οὖν στρατο-
(17) πεδευσώμεθα προελθόντες ὅσον ἂν δοκῇ καιρὸς εἶναι
εἰς τὸ δειπνοποιεῖσθαι· ἕως δ᾽ ἂν πορευώμεθα, Τιμασίων ἔχων τοὺς ἱππέας προελαυνέτω ἐφορῶν ἡμᾶς
καὶ σκοπείτω τὰ ἔμπροσθεν, ὡς μηδὲν ἡμᾶς λάθῃ.

15 Ταῦτ᾽ εἰπὼν ἡγεῖτο. παρέπεμψε δὲ καὶ τῶν γυμνή-
(18) των ἀνθρώπους εὐζώνους εἰς τὰ πλάγια καὶ εἰς τὰ
ἄκρα, ὅπως εἴ πού τί ποθεν καθορῷεν, σημαίνοιεν·
ἐκέλευε δὲ καίειν ἅπαντα ὅτῳ ἐντυγχάνοιεν καυσίμῳ.
19 οἱ δ᾽ ἱππεῖς διασπειρόμενοι ἐφ᾽ ὅσον καλῶς εἶχεν
ἔκαιον, καὶ οἱ πελτασταὶ ἐπιπαριόντες κατὰ τὰ ἄκρα
ἔκαιον πάντα ὅσα καύσιμα ἑώρων, καὶ ἡ στρατιὰ δέ,
εἴ τινι παραλειπομένῳ ἐντυγχάνοιεν· ὥστε πᾶσα ἡ
χώρα αἴθεσθαι ἐδόκει καὶ τὸ στράτευμα πολὺ εἶναι.
20 ἐπεὶ δὲ ὥρα ἦν, κατεστρατοπεδεύσαντο ἐπὶ λόφον
ἐκβάντες, καὶ τά τε τῶν πολεμίων πυρὰ ἑώρων, ἀπεῖχον δὲ ὡς τετταράκοντα σταδίους, καὶ αὐτοὶ ὡς
21 ἐδύναντο πλεῖστα πυρὰ ἔκαιον. ἐπεὶ δὲ ἐδείπνησαν
τάχιστα, παρηγγέλθη τὰ πυρὰ κατασβεννύναι πάντα.
καὶ τὴν μὲν νύκτα φυλακὰς ποιησάμενοι ἐκάθευδον·
ἅμα δὲ τῇ ἡμέρᾳ προσευξάμενοι τοῖς θεοῖς, συνταξάμενοι ὡς εἰς μάχην ἐπορεύοντο ᾗ ἐδύναντο
22 τάχιστα. Τιμασίων δὲ καὶ οἱ ἱππεῖς ἔχοντες τοὺς

---

[20] *i.e.* consult the gods before undertaking any enterprise. The
expresssion was proverbial.

gods,[20] should be set in a place of higher honour than those
boasters. And now you must keep in line and on the alert,
so that you can carry out the orders that are given. For the
present, then, let us go forward as far as may seem consistent with our time for dining, and then encamp; and so long
as we are on the march, let Timasion with the cavalry ride
on in advance, keeping us in sight, and spy out what is
ahead, in order that nothing may escape our attention."

With these words he proceeded to lead the way. Furthermore, he sent out on the flanks and to the neighbouring heights some of the more active of the light-armed
troops in order that they might signal to the army in case
they should sight anything anywhere from any point of
observation; and he directed them to burn everything they
found that could be burned. So the horsemen, scattering
as widely as was proper, went to burning, the peltasts, making their way along the heights abreast of the main army,
burned all they saw which was combustible, and the main
army likewise burned anything they found that had been
passed over; the result was, that the whole country seemed
to be ablaze and the army seemed to be a large one. When
the time had come, they ascended a hill and encamped;
from there they could see the campfires of the enemy,
distant about forty stadia, and they kindled as many fires
themselves as they could. Immediately after they had
dined, however, the order was given to extinguish every
one of the fires. Then, after stationing guards, they slept
the night through; and at daybreak they offered prayer to
the gods, formed their lines for battle, and set forth at the
fastest possible pace. And Timasion and the horsemen,

ἡγεμόνας καὶ προελαύνοντες ἔλαθον αὑτοὺς ἐπὶ τῷ
λόφῳ γενόμενοι ἔνθα ἐπολιορκοῦντο οἱ Ἕλληνες. καὶ
οὐχ ὁρῶσιν οὔτε φίλιον στράτευμα οὔτε πολέμιον (καὶ
ταῦτα ἀπαγγέλλουσι πρὸς τὸν Ξενοφῶντα καὶ τὸ
στράτευμα), γράδια δὲ καὶ γερόντια καὶ πρόβατα
23 ὀλίγα καὶ βοῦς καταλελειμμένους. καὶ τὸ μὲν πρῶτον
θαῦμα ἦν τί εἴη τὸ γεγενημένον, ἔπειτα δὲ καὶ τῶν
καταλελειμμένων ἐπυνθάνοντο ὅτι οἱ μὲν Θρᾷκες εὐθὺς
ἀφ' ἑσπέρας ᾤχοντο ἀπιόντες, ἕωθεν καὶ τοὺς Ἕλληνας δὲ ἔφασαν οἴχεσθαι· ὅποι δέ, οὐκ εἰδέναι.

24 Ταῦτα ἀκούσαντες οἱ ἀμφὶ Ξενοφῶντα, ἐπεὶ ἠρί-
στησαν, συσκευασάμενοι ἐπορεύοντο, βουλόμενοι ὡς
τάχιστα συμμεῖξαι τοῖς ἄλλοις εἰς Κάλπης λιμένα.
καὶ πορευόμενοι ἑώρων τὸν στίβον τῶν Ἀρκάδων καὶ
Ἀχαιῶν κατὰ τὴν ἐπὶ Κάλπης ὁδόν. ἐπεὶ δὲ ἀφίκοντο
εἰς τὸ αὐτό, ἄσμενοί τε εἶδον ἀλλήλους καὶ ἠσπάζοντο
25 ὥσπερ ἀδελφούς. καὶ ἐπυνθάνοντο οἱ Ἀρκάδες τῶν
περὶ Ξενοφῶντα τί τὰ πυρὰ κατασβέσειαν· ἡμεῖς μὲν
γάρ, ἔφασαν, ᾠόμεθα ὑμᾶς τὸ μὲν πρῶτον, ἐπειδὴ τὰ
πυρὰ οὐκέθ' ἑωρῶμεν, τῆς νυκτὸς ἥξειν ἐπὶ τοὺς πολε-
μίους· καὶ οἱ πολέμιοι δέ, ὥς γε ἡμῖν ἐδόκουν, τοῦτο
δείσαντες ἀπῆλθον· σχεδὸν γὰρ ἀμφὶ τοῦτον τὸν χρό-
26 νον ἀπῇσαν. ἐπεὶ δὲ οὐκ ἀφικνεῖσθε, ὁ δὲ χρόνος
ἐξῆκεν, ᾠόμεθα ὑμᾶς πυθομένους τὰ παρ' ἡμῖν φοβη-
θέντας οἴχεσθαι ἀποδράντας ἐπὶ θάλατταν· καὶ ἐδόκει

riding on ahead with the guides, found themselves without knowing it upon the hill where the Greeks had been besieged. They could see no army, however, either friendly or hostile (and this fact they reported back to Xenophon and the main body), but only some wretched old women and men and a few sheep and cattle that had been left behind. At first they could only wonder what the thing was that had happened, but afterwards they managed to find out from the people who had been left behind that the Thracians had disappeared immediately after nightfall, and the Greeks also, they said, had gone at dawn; but where, they did not know.

Upon hearing this report Xenophon and his men packed up, as soon as they had breakfasted, and set forth, wishing as speedily as possible to join their comrades at Calpe Harbour. As they proceeded, they could see the track of the Arcadians and Achaeans along the road leading towards Calpe. When the two detachments came together, the men were delighted to see one another, and greeted one another like brothers.[21] And the Arcadians inquired of Xenophon's troops why they had put out their fires; "for we imagined at first," they said, "when we could no longer see your fires, that you meant to come against the enemy during the night; and the enemy likewise, so at least it seemed to us, feared this, and on that account departed; for it was at about that time that they went away. But when you were not arriving, although the requisite time had passed, we supposed that you had learned of our situation and, seized with fear, had stealthily made off toward the sea; and we

21 Cf. IV. vii. 25.

ἡμῖν μὴ ἀπολείπεσθαι ὑμῶν. οὕτως οὖν καὶ ἡμεῖς
δεῦρο ἐπορεύθημεν.

IV. Ταύτην μὲν οὖν τὴν ἡμέραν αὐτοῦ ηὐλίζοντο ἐπὶ
τοῦ αἰγιαλοῦ πρὸς τῷ λιμένι. τὸ δὲ χωρίον τοῦτο ὃ
καλεῖται Κάλπης λιμὴν ἔστι μὲν ἐν τῇ Θρᾴκῃ τῇ ἐν τῇ
Ἀσίᾳ· ἀρξαμένη δὲ ἡ Θρᾴκη αὕτη ἐστὶν ἀπὸ τοῦ
στόματος τοῦ Πόντου μέχρι Ἡρακλείας ἐπὶ δεξιὰ εἰς
2 τὸν Πόντον εἰσπλέοντι. καὶ τριήρει μέν ἐστιν εἰς
Ἡράκλειαν ἐκ Βυζαντίου κώπαις ἡμέρας μάλα μακρᾶς
πλοῦς· ἐν δὲ τῷ μέσῳ ἄλλη μὲν πόλις οὐδεμία οὔτε
φιλία οὔτε Ἑλληνίς, ἀλλὰ Θρᾷκες Βιθυνοί· καὶ οὓς ἂν
λάβωσι τῶν Ἑλλήνων ἢ ἐκπίπτοντας ἢ ἄλλως πως
3 δεινὰ ὑβρίζειν λέγονται τοὺς Ἕλληνας. ὁ δὲ Κάλπης
λιμὴν ἐν μέσῳ μὲν κεῖται ἑκατέρωθεν πλεόντων ἐξ
Ἡρακλείας καὶ Βυζαντίου, ἔστι δ᾽ ἐν τῇ θαλάττῃ
προκείμενον χωρίον, τὸ μὲν εἰς τὴν θάλατταν καθῆκον
αὐτοῦ πέτρα ἀπορρώξ, ὕψος ὅπῃ ἐλάχιστον οὐ μεῖον
εἴκοσιν ὀργυῶν, ὁ δὲ αὐχὴν ὁ εἰς τὴν γῆν ἀνήκων τοῦ
χωρίου μάλιστα τεττάρων πλέθρων τὸ εὖρος· τὸ δ᾽
ἐντὸς τοῦ αὐχένος χωρίον ἱκανὸν μυρίοις ἀνθρώποις
4 οἰκῆσαι. λιμὴν δ᾽ ὑπ᾽ αὐτῇ τῇ πέτρᾳ τὸ πρὸς ἑσπέραν
αἰγιαλὸν ἔχων. κρήνη δὲ ἡδέος ὕδατος καὶ ἄφθονος
ῥέουσα ἐπ᾽ αὐτῇ τῇ θαλάττῃ ὑπὸ τῇ ἐπικρατείᾳ τοῦ
χωρίου. ξύλα δὲ πολλὰ μὲν καὶ ἄλλα, πάνυ δὲ πολλὰ
5 καὶ καλὰ ναυπηγήσιμα ἐπ᾽ αὐτῇ τῇ θαλάττῃ. τὸ δὲ
ὄρος εἰς μεσόγειαν μὲν ἀνήκει ὅσον ἐπὶ εἴκοσι
σταδίους, καὶ τοῦτο γεῶδες καὶ ἄλιθον· τὸ δὲ παρὰ

thought it best not to be left behind. That was the reason, then, why we also proceeded here."

IV. During that day they bivouacked where they were, upon the beach by the harbour. Now this place which is called Calpe Harbour is situated in Thrace-in-Asia; and this portion of Thrace begins at the mouth of the Euxine and extends as far as Heracleia, being on the right as one sails into the Euxine. It is an especially long day's journey for a trireme to row from Byzantium to Heracleia, and between the two places there is no other city, either friendly or Greek, only Bithynian Thracians; and they are said to abuse outrageously any Greeks they may find shipwrecked or may capture in any other way. As for Calpe Harbour, it lies midway on the voyage between Heracleia and Byzantium and is a bit of land jutting out into the sea, the part of it which extends seaward being a precipitous mass of rock, not less than twenty fathoms high at its lowest point, and the isthmus which connects this head with the mainland being about four plethra in width; and the space to the seaward of the isthmus is large enough for ten thousand people to dwell in.[22] At the very foot of the rock there is a harbour whose beach faces toward the west, and an abundantly flowing spring of fresh water close to the shore of the sea and commanded by the headland. There is also a great deal of timber of various sorts, but an especially large amount of fine ship-timber, on the very shore of the sea.[23] The ridge extends back into the interior for about twenty stadia, and this stretch has deep soil and is free from stones, while the land bordering the coast is thickly cov-

[22] Xenophon's point seems clear: another opportunity for colonization.   [23] Cf. Theopompus, *FGH* 115 F 15.

θάλατταν πλέον ἢ ἐπὶ εἴκοσι σταδίους δασὺ πολλοῖς
6 καὶ παντοδαποῖς καὶ μεγάλοις ξύλοις. ἡ δὲ ἄλλη
χώρα καλὴ καὶ πολλή, καὶ κῶμαι ἐν αὐτῇ εἰσι πολλαὶ
καὶ οἰκούμεναι· φέρει γὰρ ἡ γῆ καὶ κριθὰς καὶ πυροὺς
καὶ ὄσπρια πάντα καὶ μελίνας καὶ σήσαμα καὶ σῦκα
ἀρκοῦντα καὶ ἀμπέλους πολλὰς καὶ ἡδυοίνους καὶ
τἆλλα πάντα πλὴν ἐλαῶν.

7 Ἡ μὲν χώρα ἦν τοιαύτη. ἐσκήνουν δ' ἐν τῷ αἰγιαλῷ
πρὸς τῇ θαλάττῃ· εἰς δὲ τὸ πόλισμα ἂν γενόμενον οὐκ
ἐβούλοντο στρατοπεδεύεσθαι, ἀλλὰ ἐδόκει καὶ τὸ
ἐλθεῖν ἐνταῦθα ἐξ ἐπιβουλῆς εἶναι, βουλομένων τινῶν
8 κατοικίσαι πόλιν. τῶν γὰρ στρατιωτῶν οἱ πλεῖστοι
ἦσαν οὐ σπάνει βίου ἐκπεπλευκότες ἐπὶ ταύτην τὴν
μισθοφοράν, ἀλλὰ τὴν Κύρου ἀρετὴν ἀκούοντες, οἱ
μὲν καὶ ἄνδρας ἄγοντες, οἱ δὲ καὶ προσανηλωκότες
χρήματα, καὶ τούτων ἕτεροι ἀποδεδρακότες πατέρας
καὶ μητέρας, οἱ δὲ καὶ τέκνα καταλιπόντες ὡς χρήματ'
αὐτοῖς κτησάμενοι ἥξοντες πάλιν, ἀκούοντες καὶ τοὺς
ἄλλους τοὺς παρὰ Κύρῳ πολλὰ καὶ ἀγαθὰ πράττειν.
τοιοῦτοι ὄντες ἐπόθουν εἰς τὴν Ἑλλάδα σῴζεσθαι.

9 Ἐπειδὴ δὲ ὑστέρᾳ ἡμέρᾳ ἐγένετο τῆς εἰς ταὐτὸν
συνόδου, ἐπ' ἐξόδῳ ἐθύετο Ξενοφῶν· ἀνάγκη γὰρ ἦν
ἐπὶ τὰ ἐπιτήδεια ἐξάγειν· ἐπενόει δὲ καὶ τοὺς νεκροὺς
θάπτειν. ἐπεὶ δὲ τὰ ἱερὰ καλὰ ἐγένετο, εἵποντο καὶ οἱ

ered for a distance of more than twenty stadia with an abundance of heavy timber of all sorts. The rest of the region is fair and extensive, and contains many inhabited villages; for the land produces barley, wheat, beans of all kinds, millet and sesame, a sufficient quantity of figs, an abundance of grapes which yield a good sweet wine, and in fact everything except olives.

Such was the country thereabouts. The men took up quarters on the beach by the sea, refusing to encamp on the spot which might become a city; indeed, the fact of their coming to this place at all seemed to them the result of scheming on the part of some people who wished to found a city. For most of the soldiers had sailed away from Greece to undertake this service for pay, not because their means were scanty, but because they knew by report of the noble character of Cyrus; some brought other men with them, some had even spent money of their own on the enterprise, while still another class had abandoned fathers and mothers, or had left children behind with the idea of getting money to bring back to them, all because they heard that the other people who served with Cyrus enjoyed abundant good fortune. Being men of this sort, therefore, they longed to return in safety to Greece.[24]

On the day after the reunion of the three divisions Xenophon offered sacrifice with a view to an expedition; for it was necessary to go out after provisions and, besides, he intended to bury the Arcadian dead. When the sacrifices proved favourable, the Arcadians also followed

[24] An important characterization of the variety of the Cyreans' motives; perhaps a response to criticism of them by men such as Isocrates, *Pan.* CXLVI.

Ἀρκάδες, καὶ τοὺς μὲν νεκροὺς τοὺς πλείστους ἔνθαπερ ἔπεσον ἑκάστους ἔθαψαν· ἤδη γὰρ ἦσαν πεμ-
πταῖοι καὶ οὐχ οἷόν τε ἀναιρεῖν ἔτι ἦν· ἐνίους δὲ τοὺς
ἐκ τῶν ὁδῶν συνενεγκόντες ἔθαψαν ἐκ τῶν ὑπαρχόντων ὡς ἐδύναντο κάλλιστα· οὓς δὲ μὴ ηὕρισκον,
κενοτάφιον αὐτοῖς ἐποίησαν μέγα, καὶ στεφάνους
10 ἐπέθεσαν. ταῦτα δὲ ποιήσαντες ἀνεχώρησαν ἐπὶ τὸ
στρατόπεδον. καὶ τότε μὲν δειπνήσαντες ἐκοιμήθησαν.
τῇ δὲ ὑστεραίᾳ συνῆλθον οἱ στρατιῶται πάντες· συν-
ῆγε δὲ μάλιστα Ἀγασίας τε ὁ Στυμφάλιος λοχαγὸς
καὶ Ἱερώνυμος Ἠλεῖος λοχαγὸς καὶ ἄλλοι οἱ πρεσ-
11 βύτατοι τῶν Ἀρκάδων. καὶ δόγμα ἐποιήσαντο, ἐάν τις
τοῦ λοιποῦ μνησθῇ δίχα τὸ στράτευμα ποιεῖν, θανάτῳ
αὐτὸν ζημιοῦσθαι, καὶ κατὰ χώραν ἀπιέναι ᾗπερ
πρόσθεν εἶχε τὸ στράτευμα καὶ ἄρχειν τοὺς πρόσθεν
στρατηγούς. καὶ Χειρίσοφος μὲν ἤδη ἐτετελευτήκει
φάρμακον πιὼν πυρέττων· τὰ δ᾽ ἐκείνου Νέων Ἀσιναῖος παρέλαβε.

12 Μετὰ δὲ ταῦτα ἀναστὰς εἶπε Ξενοφῶν· Ὦ ἄνδρες
στρατιῶται, τὴν μὲν πορείαν, ὡς ἔοικε, δῆλον ὅτι πεζῇ
ποιητέον· οὐ γὰρ ἔστι πλοῖα· ἀνάγκη δὲ πορεύεσθαι
ἤδη· οὐ γὰρ ἔστι μένουσι τὰ ἐπιτήδεια. ἡμεῖς μὲν οὖν,
ἔφη, θυσόμεθα· ὑμᾶς δὲ δεῖ παρασκευάζεσθαι ὡς
μαχουμένους εἴ ποτε καὶ ἄλλοτε· οἱ γὰρ πολέμιοι
13 ἀνατεθαρρήκασιν. ἐκ τούτου ἐθύοντο οἱ στρατηγοί,
μάντις δὲ παρῆν Ἀρηξίων Ἀρκάς· ὁ δὲ Σιλανὸς ὁ

with the rest,[25] and they buried the greater part of the dead just where they each had fallen; for they had already lain unburied five days, and it was not now possible to carry away the bodies; some that lay upon the roads, however, they did gather together and honour with as fine a burial as their means allowed, while for those they could not find, they erected a great cenotaph, and placed wreaths upon it. After doing all this they returned to their camp, and then took dinner and went to bed. On the following day all the soldiers held a meeting, the chief movers in the matter being Agasias the Stymphalian, a captain, Hieronymus the Elean, also a captain, and some others from among the eldest of the Arcadians. They passed a resolution that if any man from this time forth should suggest dividing the army, he should be punished with death, and further, that the army should return to the same organization which formerly obtained, and that the former generals should resume command. Now by this time Cheirisophus had died, from the effects of a medicine which he took for a fever;[26] and his command passed to Neon the Asinaean.

After this Xenophon rose and said: "Fellow soldiers, it is clear that our journey, as it seems, must be made by land, for we have no ships; and we must set out at once, for we have no provisions if we remain here. We, then," he continued, "will sacrifice; you must prepare yourselves to fight if ever you did; for the enemy have renewed their courage." Thereupon the generals proceeded to sacrifice, the soothsayer who was present being Arexion the Arcadian; for

[25] *i.e.* no longer insisting upon their independent organization.
[26] Cf. ii. 18.

Ἀμπρακιώτης ἤδη ἀπεδεδράκει πλοῖον μισθωσάμενος
ἐξ Ἡρακλείας. θυομένοις δὲ ἐπὶ τῇ ἀφόδῳ οὐκ
14 ἐγίγνετο τὰ ἱερά. ταύτην μὲν οὖν τὴν ἡμέραν ἐπαύσαντο. καί τινες ἐτόλμων λέγειν ὡς ὁ Ξενοφῶν βουλόμενος τὸ χωρίον οἰκίσαι πέπεικε τὸν μάντιν λέγειν ὡς
15 τὰ ἱερὰ οὐ γίγνεται ἐπὶ ἀφόδῳ. ἐντεῦθεν κηρύξας τῇ
αὔριον παρεῖναι ἐπὶ τὴν θυσίαν τὸν βουλόμενον, καὶ
μάντις εἴ τις εἴη, παραγγείλας παρεῖναι ὡς συν-
θεασόμενον τὰ ἱερά, ἔθυε· καὶ ἐνταῦθα παρῆσαν πολ-
16 λοί. θυομένῳ δὲ πάλιν εἰς τρὶς ἐπὶ τῇ ἀφόδῳ οὐκ
ἐγίγνετο τὰ ἱερά. ἐκ τούτου χαλεπῶς εἶχον οἱ στρα-
τιῶται· καὶ γὰρ τὰ ἐπιτήδεια ἐπέλιπεν ἃ ἔχοντες
ἦλθον, καὶ ἀγορὰ οὐδεμία πω παρῆν.

17 Ἐκ τούτου συνελθόντων εἶπε πάλιν Ξενοφῶν· Ὦ
ἄνδρες, ἐπὶ μὲν τῇ πορείᾳ, ὡς ὁρᾶτε, τὰ ἱερὰ οὔπω
γίγνεται· τῶν δ᾽ ἐπιτηδείων ὁρῶ ὑμᾶς δεομένους·
ἀνάγκη οὖν μοι δοκεῖ εἶναι θύεσθαι περὶ αὐτοῦ τούτου.
18 ἀναστὰς δέ τις εἶπε· Καὶ εἰκότως ἄρα ἡμῖν οὐ γίγνεται
τὰ ἱερά· ὡς γὰρ ἐγὼ ἀπὸ τοῦ αὐτομάτου ἐχθὲς ἥκοντος
πλοίου ἤκουσά τινος, Κλέανδρος[7] ὁ ἐκ Βυζαντίου
19 ἁρμοστὴς μέλλει ἥξειν πλοῖα καὶ τριήρεις ἔχων. ἐκ
τούτου δὲ ἀναμένειν μὲν πᾶσιν ἐδόκει· ἐπὶ δὲ τὰ
ἐπιτήδεια ἀνάγκη ἦν ἐξιέναι. καὶ ἐπὶ τούτῳ πάλιν

---

[7] Before Κλέανδρος the MSS. have ὅτι, which Mar. brackets,
following Stephanus: Gem. emends to ὅ γε: Hude/Peters omit.
The ὁ that follows is the addition of Schaefer.

[27] Cf. V. vi. 18, 34.

Silanus the Ambraciot had by this time stolen away,[27] on a vessel which he hired at Heracleia. When they sacrificed, however, with a view to their departure, the victims would not prove favourable, and they accordingly ceased their offerings for that day. Now some people had the effrontery to say that Xenophon, in his desire to found a city at this spot, had induced the soothsayer to declare that the sacrifices were not favourable for departure. Consequently he made public proclamation that on the morrow any one who so chose might be present at the sacrifice, and if a man were a soothsayer, he sent him word to be at hand to participate in the inspection of the victims; so he made the offering in the immediate presence of many witnesses. But though he sacrificed a second and a third time with a view to departure, the victims would not prove favourable. At that the soldiers were angry, for the provisions they brought with them had given out and there was not yet any market at hand.

Therefore they held a meeting and Xenophon addressed them again. "Soldiers," he said, "as for setting out upon our journey, the sacrifices, as you see, do not yet prove favourable for that; but I am aware that you are in need of provisions; hence it seems to me that we must sacrifice in regard to this latter point alone." Then some one rose and said: "There appears to be good reason why our sacrifices are not favourable; for as I learned from a vessel that happened to arrive here yesterday, Cleander, the Lacedaemonian governor at Byzantium, is to come here with merchant vessels and men-of-war." At that news all deemed it best to stay, but it was still necessary to go out after provisions. With this object in view Xenophon again sacrificed, going as far as three offerings, and the

505

ἐθύετο εἰς τρίς, καὶ οὐκ ἐγίγνετο τὰ ἱερά. καὶ ἤδη καὶ
ἐπὶ σκηνὴν ἰόντες τὴν Ξενοφῶντος ἔλεγον ὅτι οὐκ
ἔχοιεν τὰ ἐπιτήδεια. ὁ δ᾽ οὐκ ἂν ἔφη ἐξαγαγεῖν μὴ
γιγνομένων τῶν ἱερῶν.

20   Καὶ πάλιν τῇ ὑστεραίᾳ ἐθύετο, καὶ σχεδόν τι πᾶσα
ἡ στρατιὰ διὰ τὸ μέλειν ἅπασιν ἐκυκλοῦντο περὶ τὰ
ἱερά· τὰ δὲ θύματα ἐπελελοίπει. οἱ δὲ στρατηγοὶ
21   ἐξῆγον μὲν οὔ, συνεκάλεσαν δέ. εἶπεν οὖν Ξενοφῶν·
Ἴσως οἱ πολέμιοι συνειλεγμένοι εἰσὶ καὶ ἀνάγκη
μάχεσθαι· εἰ οὖν καταλιπόντες τὰ σκεύη ἐν τῷ ἐρυμνῷ
χωρίῳ ὡς εἰς μάχην παρεσκευασμένοι ἴοιμεν, ἴσως ἂν
22   τὰ ἱερὰ μᾶλλον προχωροίη ἡμῖν. ἀκούσαντες δ᾽ οἱ
στρατιῶται ἀνέκραγον ὡς οὐδὲν δέον εἰς τὸ χωρίον
ἄγειν, ἀλλὰ θύεσθαι ὡς τάχιστα. καὶ πρόβατα μὲν
οὐκέτι ἦν, βοῦς δὲ ὑπὸ ἁμάξης πριάμενοι ἐθύοντο· καὶ
Ξενοφῶν Κλεάνορος ἐδεήθη τοῦ Ἀρκάδος προθυμεῖσθαι, εἴ τι ἐν τούτῳ εἴη. ἀλλ᾽ οὐδ᾽ ὣς ἐγένοντο.

23   Νέων δὲ ἦν μὲν στρατηγὸς κατὰ τὸ Χειρισόφου
μέρος, ἐπεὶ δὲ ἑώρα τοὺς ἀνθρώπους ὡς εἶχον δεινῶς
τῇ ἐνδείᾳ, βουλόμενος αὐτοῖς χαρίζεσθαι, εὑρών τινα
ἄνθρωπον Ἡρακλεώτην, ὃς ἔφη κώμας ἐγγὺς εἰδέναι
ὅθεν εἴη λαβεῖν τὰ ἐπιτήδεια, ἐκήρυξε τὸν βουλόμενον
ἰέναι ἐπὶ τὰ ἐπιτήδεια, ὡς ἡγεμόνος ἐσομένου. ἐξέρ-
χονται δὴ σὺν δορατίοις καὶ ἀσκοῖς καὶ θυλάκοις καὶ
24   ἄλλοις ἀγγείοις εἰς δισχιλίους ἀνθρώπους. ἐπειδὴ δὲ

---

[28] *i.e.* the headland described in §§3 ff. above.

[29] One of the generals.

victims continued unfavourable. By this time people were even coming to Xenophon's tent and declaring that they had no provisions, but he said that he would not lead forth unless the sacrifices turned out favourable.

On the next day he undertook to sacrifice again, and pretty nearly the entire army—for it was a matter of concern to every man—gathered about the place of sacrifice; but the victims had failed. Then the generals, while refusing to lead the men forth, called them together in assembly; and Xenophon said: "It may be that the enemy are gathered together and that we must fight; if, then, we should leave our baggage in the strong place[28] and set out prepared for battle, perhaps our sacrifices would be more successful." Upon hearing this, however, the soldiers cried out that it was not at all necessary to enter the place, but, rather, to offer sacrifice with all speed. Now they no longer had any sheep, but they bought oxen that were yoked to a wagon and proceeded to sacrifice; and Xenophon requested Cleanor[29] the Arcadian to give special attention to see if there was anything auspicious in this offering. But not even so did the omens prove favourable.

Now Neon was general in place of Cheirisophus, and when he saw in what a terrible condition the soldiers were from want, he was desirous of doing them a kindness; so having found a certain Heracleot who claimed to know of villages near at hand from which it was possible to get provisions, he made proclamation that all who so wished were to go after provisions and that he would be their leader. There set out accordingly, with poles,[30] wine-skins, bags, and other vessels, about two thousand men. But

[30] *i.e.* for carrying the booty.

ἦσαν ἐν ταῖς κώμαις καὶ διεσπείροντο ὡς ἐπὶ τὸ
λαμβάνειν, ἐπιπίπτουσιν αὐτοῖς οἱ Φαρναβάζου ἱππεῖς πρῶτοι· βεβοηθηκότες γὰρ ἦσαν τοῖς Βιθυνοῖς,
βουλόμενοι σὺν τοῖς Βιθυνοῖς, εἰ δύναιντο, ἀποκωλῦ-
σαι τοὺς Ἕλληνας μὴ ἐλθεῖν εἰς τὴν Φρυγίαν· οὗτοι
οἱ ἱππεῖς ἀποκτείνουσι τῶν ἀνδρῶν οὐ μεῖον πεντα-
25 κοσίους· οἱ δὲ λοιποὶ ἐπὶ τὸ ὄρος ἀνέφυγον. ἐκ τούτου
ἀπαγγέλλει τις ταῦτα τῶν ἀποπεφευγότων εἰς τὸ
στρατόπεδον. καὶ ὁ Ξενοφῶν, ἐπεὶ οὐκ ἐγεγένητο τὰ
ἱερὰ ταύτῃ τῇ ἡμέρᾳ, λαβὼν βοῦν ὑπὸ ἁμάξης, οὐ
γὰρ ἦν ἄλλα ἱερεῖα, σφαγιασάμενος ἐβοήθει καὶ οἱ
26 ἄλλοι οἱ μέχρι τριάκοντα ἐτῶν ἅπαντες. καὶ ἀναλαβόντες τοὺς λοιποὺς ἄνδρας εἰς τὸ στρατόπεδον
ἀφικνοῦνται, καὶ ἤδη μὲν ἀμφὶ ἡλίου δυσμὰς ἦν καὶ
οἱ Ἕλληνες μάλ' ἀθύμως ἔχοντες ἐδειπνοποιοῦντο, καὶ
ἐξαπίνης διὰ τῶν λασίων τῶν Βιθυνῶν τινες ἐπιγενό-
μενοι τοῖς προφύλαξι τοὺς μὲν κατέκανον τοὺς δὲ
27 ἐδίωξαν μέχρι εἰς τὸ στρατόπεδον. καὶ κραυγῆς γενομένης εἰς τὰ ὅπλα πάντες ἔδραμον οἱ Ἕλληνες· καὶ
διώκειν μὲν καὶ κινεῖν τὸ στρατόπεδον νυκτὸς οὐκ
ἀσφαλὲς ἐδόκει εἶναι· δασέα γὰρ ἦν τὰ χωρία· ἐν δε
τοῖς ὅπλοις ἐνυκτέρευον φυλαττόμενοι ἱκανοῖς φύλαξι.

V. Τὴν μὲν νύκτα οὕτω διήγαγον· ἅμα δὲ τῇ ἡμέρᾳ
οἱ στρατηγοὶ εἰς τὸ ἐρυμνὸν χωρίον ἡγοῦντο· οἱ δὲ
εἵποντο ἀναλαβόντες τὰ ὅπλα καὶ τὰ σκεύη. πρὶν δὲ
ἀρίστου ὥραν εἶναι ἀπετάφρευσαν ᾗ ἡ εἴσοδος ἦν εἰς

when they had reached the villages and were scattering here and there for the purpose of securing plunder, they were attacked first of all by the horsemen of Pharnabazus;[31] for they had come to the aid of the Bithynians, desiring in company with the Bithynians to prevent the Greeks, if they could, from entering Phrygia; these horsemen killed no fewer than five hundred of the soldiers, the rest fleeing for refuge to the heights. After this one of the men who escaped brought back word to the camp of what had happened. And Xenophon, inasmuch as the sacrifices had not proved favourable on that day, took a bullock that was yoked to a wagon—for there were no other sacrificial animals—offered it up, and set out to the rescue, as did all the rest who were under thirty years of age, to the last man. And they picked up the survivors and returned to the camp. By this time it was about sunset, and the Greeks were making preparations for dinner in a state of great despondency when suddenly through the thickets some of the Bithynians burst upon the outposts, killing some of them and pursuing the rest up to the camp. An outcry was raised, and all the Greeks ran to their arms; still, it did not seem safe to undertake a pursuit or to move the camp during the night, seeing that the region was thickly overgrown; so they spent the night under arms, keeping plenty of sentinels on watch.

V. In this way they got through the night, but at daybreak the generals led the way to the strong place and the men followed, taking up their arms and baggage. Before breakfast time came, they proceeded to dig a trench across the way of approach[32] to the place, and they backed it along

31 See V. vi. 24.   32 *i.e.* the isthmus mentioned in iv. 3.

τὸ χωρίον, καὶ ἀπεσταύρωσαν ἅπαν, καταλιπόντες
τρεῖς πύλας. καὶ πλοῖον ἐξ Ἡρακλείας ἦκεν ἄλφιτα
ἄγον καὶ ἱερεῖα καὶ οἶνον.

2   Πρῲ δ' ἀναστὰς Ξενοφῶν ἐθύετο ἐπ' ἐξόδῳ, καὶ
γίγνεται τὰ ἱερὰ ἐπὶ τοῦ πρώτου ἱερείου. καὶ ἤδη τέλος
ἐχόντων τῶν ἱερῶν ὁρᾷ ἀετὸν αἴσιον ὁ μάντις Ἀρηξίων
3 Παρράσιος, καὶ ἡγεῖσθαι κελεύει τὸν Ξενοφῶντα. καὶ
διαβάντες τὴν τάφρον τὰ ὅπλα τίθενται, καὶ ἐκήρυξαν
ἀριστήσαντας ἐξιέναι τοὺς στρατιώτας σὺν τοῖς ὅπλοις, τὸν δὲ ὄχλον καὶ τὰ ἀνδράποδα αὐτοῦ καταλι-
4 πεῖν. οἱ μὲν δὴ ἄλλοι πάντες ἐξῇσαν, Νέων δὲ οὔ·
ἐδόκει γὰρ κάλλιστον εἶναι τοῦτον φύλακα καταλιπεῖν
τῶν ἐπὶ στρατοπέδου. ἐπεὶ δ' οἱ λοχαγοὶ καὶ οἱ στρατιῶται ἀπέλειπον αὐτόν, αἰσχυνόμενοι μὴ ἐφέπεσθαι
τῶν ἄλλων ἐξιόντων, κατέλιπον αὐτοῦ τοὺς ὑπὲρ πέντε
καὶ τετταράκοντα ἔτη. καὶ οὗτοι μὲν ἔμενον, οἱ δ'
5 ἄλλοι ἐπορεύοντο. πρὶν δὲ πεντεκαίδεκα στάδια διεληλυθέναι ἐνέτυχον ἤδη νεκροῖς· καὶ τὴν οὐρὰν τοῦ
κέρατος ποιησάμενοι κατὰ τοὺς πρώτους φανέντας
νεκροὺς ἔθαπτον πάντας ὁπόσους ἐπελάμβανε τὸ κέ-
6 ρας. ἐπεὶ δὲ τοὺς πρώτους ἔθαψαν, προαγαγόντες καὶ
τὴν οὐρὰν αὖθις ποιησάμενοι κατὰ τοὺς πρώτους τῶν
ἀτάφων ἔθαπτον τὸν αὐτὸν τρόπον ὁπόσους ἐπελάμ-
βανεν ἡ στρατιά. ἐπεὶ δὲ εἰς τὴν ὁδὸν ἧκον τὴν ἐκ
τῶν κωμῶν, ἔνθα ἔκειντο ἀθρόοι, συνενεγκόντες αὐτοὺς ἔθαψαν.

7   Ἤδη δὲ πέρα μεσούσης τῆς ἡμέρας προαγαγόντες
τὸ στράτευμα ἔξω τῶν κωμῶν ἐλάμβανον τὰ ἐπιτήδεια

its entire length with a palisade, leaving three gates. And now a vessel arrived from Heracleia, bringing barley meal, sacrificial victims, and wine.

Xenophon arose early and sacrificed with a view to an expedition, and with the first offering the omens turned out favourable. Furthermore, just as the rites were nearing the end, the soothsayer, Arexion the Parrhasian, caught sight of an eagle in an auspicious quarter, and bade Xenophon lead on. So they crossed the trench and grounded arms; then they made proclamation that after taking breakfast the troops were to march out under arms, while the camp-followers and captives were to be left behind where they were. All the rest, then, proceeded to set forth, save only Neon; for it seemed best to leave him behind to keep guard over what was in the camp. But when his captains and soldiers began to abandon him, being ashamed not to follow along when the others were setting out, the generals left behind at the camp everybody who was over forty-five years of age. So these remained and the rest took up the march. Before they had gone fifteen stadia they began to meet with dead bodies; and marching on until they had brought the rear of their column to a point opposite the first bodies which appeared, they proceeded to bury all that the column covered. As soon as they had buried this first group, they marched forward and again brought the rear of the column into line with the first of the bodies which lay farther on, and then in the same way they buried all that the army covered. When, however, they had reached the road leading out of the villages, where the dead lay thick, they gathered them all together for burial.

It was now past midday, and, having led the army forward, they were engaged in taking provisions from the

ὅ τι τις ὁρῴη ἐντὸς τῆς φάλαγγος, καὶ ἐξαίφνης ὁρῶσι
τοὺς πολεμίους ὑπερβάλλοντας κατὰ λόφους τινὰς ἐκ
τοῦ ἐναντίου, τεταγμένους ἐπὶ φάλαγγος ἱππέας τε
πολλοὺς καὶ πεζούς· καὶ γὰρ Σπιθριδάτης καὶ Ῥα-
θίνης ἧκον παρὰ Φαρναβάζου ἔχοντες τὴν δύναμιν.

8 ἐπεὶ δὲ κατεῖδον τοὺς Ἕλληνας οἱ πολέμιοι, ἔστησαν
ἀπέχοντες αὐτῶν ὅσον πεντεκαίδεκα σταδίους. ἐκ τούτου εὐθὺς ὁ Ἀρηξίων ὁ μάντις τῶν Ἑλλήνων σφαγιά-
ζεται, καὶ ἐγένετο ἐπὶ τοῦ πρώτου καλὰ τὸ σφάγια.

9 ἔνθα δὴ Ξενοφῶν λέγει· Δοκεῖ μοι, ὦ ἄνδρες στρατηγοί, ἐπιτάξασθαι τῇ φάλαγγι λόχους φύλακας ἵνα ἤν
που δέῃ ὦσιν οἱ ἐπιβοηθήσοντες τῇ φάλαγγι καὶ οἱ
πολέμιοι τεταραγμένοι ἐμπίπτωσιν εἰς τεταγμένους

10 καὶ ἀκεραίους. συνεδόκει ταῦτα πᾶσιν. Ὑμεῖς μὲν
τοίνυν, ἔφη, προηγεῖσθε τὴν πρὸς τοὺς ἐναντίους, ὡς
μὴ ἑστήκωμεν, ἐπεὶ ὤφθημεν καὶ εἴδομεν τοὺς πολε-
μίους· ἐγὼ δὲ ἥξω τοὺς τελευταίους λόχους καταχω-

11 ρίσας ᾗπερ ὑμῖν δοκεῖ. ἐκ τούτου οἱ μὲν ἡσύχως
προῆγον, ὁ δὲ τρεῖς ἀφελὼν τὰς τελευταίας τάξεις ἀνὰ
διακοσίους ἄνδρας τὴν μὲν ἐπὶ τὸ δεξιὸν ἐπέτρεψεν
ἐφέπεσθαι ἀπολιπόντας ὡς πλέθρον· Σαμόλας Ἀχαιὸς
ταύτης ἦρχε τῆς τάξεως· τὴν δ' ἐπὶ τῷ μέσῳ ἐχώρισεν
ἕπεσθαι· Πυρρίας Ἀρκὰς ταύτης ἦρχε τῆς τάξεως· τὴν
δὲ μίαν ἐπὶ τῷ εὐωνύμῳ· Φρασίας Ἀθηναῖος ταύτῃ
ἐφειστήκει.

---

33 Cf. *Hell*. III. iv. 10 ff., IV. i. 1 ff.

villages—anything there was to be seen within the limits of their line—when suddenly they caught sight of the enemy passing over some hills which lay opposite them, his force consisting of horsemen in large numbers and foot soldiers, all in battle formation; in fact, it was Spithridates and Rhathines,[33] who had been sent out with their army by Pharnabazus. As soon as the enemy sighted the Greeks, they came to a halt, at a distance from the Greeks of about fifteen stadia. Hereupon Arexion, the soothsayer of the Greeks, immediately offered sacrifice, and at the first victim the omens proved favourable. Then Xenophon said: "It seems to me, fellow generals, that we should station reserve companies behind our phalanx, so that we may have men to come to the aid of the phalanx if aid is needed at any point, and that the enemy, after they have fallen into disorder, may come upon troops that are in good order and fresh." All shared this opinion. "Well, then," said Xenophon, "you lead the way toward our adversaries, in order that we may not be standing still now that we have been seen by the enemy and have seen them; and I will come along after arranging the hindmost companies in the way you have decided upon." So while the others led on quietly, he detached the three hindmost battalions, consisting of two hundred men each, and turned the first one to the right with orders to follow after the phalanx at a distance of about a plethrum; this battalion was commanded by Samolas the Achaean; the second battalion he posted at the centre, to follow on in the same way; this one was under the command of Pyrrhias the Arcadian; and the last one he stationed upon the left, Phrasias the Athenian being in command of it.

12   Προϊόντες δέ, ἐπεὶ ἐγένοντο οἱ ἡγούμενοι ἐπὶ νάπει
μεγάλῳ καὶ δυσπόρῳ, ἔστησαν ἀγνοοῦντες εἰ δια-
βατέον εἴη τὸ νάπος. καὶ παρεγγυῶσι στρατηγοὺς καὶ
13   λοχαγοὺς παριέναι ἐπὶ τὸ ἡγούμενον. καὶ ὁ Ξενοφῶν
θαυμάσας ὅ τι τὸ ἴσχον εἴη τὴν πορείαν καὶ ταχὺ
ἀκούων τὴν παρεγγύην, ἐλαύνει ᾗ τάχιστα. ἐπεὶ δὲ
συνῆλθον, λέγει Σοφαίνετος πρεσβύτατος ὢν τῶν
στρατηγῶν ὅτι οὐκ ἄξιον εἴη διαβαίνειν τοιοῦτον ὂν
τὸ νάπος.

14   Καὶ ὁ Ξενοφῶν σπουδῇ ὑπολαβὼν ἔλεξεν· Ἀλλ'
ἴστε μέν με, ὦ ἄνδρες, οὐδένα πω κίνδυνον προξενή-
σαντα ὑμῖν ἐθελούσιον· οὐ γὰρ δόξης ὁρῶ δεομένους
ὑμᾶς εἰς ἀνδρειότητα, ἀλλὰ σωτηρίας. νῦν δὲ οὕτως
15   ἔχει· ἀμαχεὶ μὲν ἐνθένδε οὐκ ἔστιν ἀπελθεῖν· ἢν γὰρ
μὴ ἡμεῖς ἴωμεν ἐπὶ τοὺς πολεμίους, οὗτοι ἡμῖν ὁπόταν
16   ἀπίωμεν ἕψονται καὶ ἐπιπεσοῦνται. ὁρᾶτε δὴ πότερον
κρεῖττον ἰέναι ἐπὶ τοὺς ἄνδρας προβαλλομένους τὰ
ὅπλα ἢ μεταβαλλομένους ὄπισθεν ἡμῶν ἐπιόντας τοὺς
17   πολεμίους θεᾶσθαι. ἴστε γε μέντοι ὅτι τὸ μὲν ἀπιέναι
ἀπὸ πολεμίων οὐδενὶ καλῷ ἔοικε, τὸ δὲ ἐφέπεσθαι καὶ
τοῖς κακίοσι θάρρος ἐμποιεῖ. ἐγὼ γοῦν ἥδιον ἂν σὺν
ἡμίσεσιν ἐπιοίην ἢ σὺν διπλασίοις ἀποχωροίην. καὶ
τούτους οἶδ' ὅτι ἐπιόντων μὲν ἡμῶν οὐδ' ὑμεῖς ἐλπίζετε
δέξασθαι ἡμᾶς, ἀπιόντων δὲ πάντες ἐπιστάμεθα ὅτι
18   τολμήσουσιν ἐφέπεσθαι. τὸ δὲ διαβάντας ὄπισθεν
νάπος χαλεπὸν ποιήσασθαι μέλλοντας μάχεσθαι ἆρ'
οὐχὶ καὶ ἁρπάσαι ἄξιον; τοῖς μὲν γὰρ πολεμίοις ἔγωγε

Now when, as they advanced, the men who were in the lead reached a large ravine, difficult to pass, they halted, in doubt as to whether they ought to cross the ravine; and they passed along word for generals and captains to come up to the front. Then Xenophon, wondering what it was that was holding up the march and speedily hearing the summons, rode forward in all haste. As soon as the officers had come together, Sophaenetus, who was the eldest of the generals, said that it was not worth attempting to cross the ravine, being so impassible.

Xenophon rejoined, with much earnestness: "Well, gentlemen, you know that I have never yet introduced you to any danger that was a matter of choice; for as I see the situation, you do not stand in need of reputation for bravery, but of a safe return. But the conditions at this moment are these: there is no possibility of our getting away from here without a battle; for if we do not advance upon the enemy ourselves, they will follow us when we undertake to retire and fall upon us. Consider, then, whether it is better to go forward against these men with arms advanced, or with arms reversed to behold the enemy coming upon us from behind. Yet you know at the very least that to retire before an enemy is not fitting for any man of honour, while to be in pursuit creates courage even in cowards. For my part, at any rate, I should rather advance to the attack with half as many men than to retreat with twice as many. And as to those troops yonder, I know that if we advance upon them, you do not yourselves expect them to await our attack, while if we retire, we all know that they will have the courage to pursue us. Again, to cross a difficult ravine and get it in your rear when you are about to fight, is not that an opportunity really worth seizing? For it is to the enemy

βουλοίμην ἂν εὔπορα πάντα φαίνεσθαι ὥστε ἀπο-
χωρεῖν· ἡμᾶς δὲ καὶ ἀπὸ τοῦ χωρίου δεῖ διδάσκεσθαι

19 ὅτι οὐκ ἔστι μὴ νικῶσι σωτηρία. θαυμάζω δ' ἔγωγε
καὶ τὸ νάπος τοῦτο εἴ τις μᾶλλον φοβερὸν νομίζει
εἶναι τῶν ἄλλων ὧν διαπεπορεύμεθα χωρίων. πῶς γὰρ
δὴ διαβατὸν τὸ πεδίον, εἰ μὴ νικήσομεν τοὺς ἱππέας;
πῶς δὲ ἃ διεληλύθαμεν ὄρη, ἢν πελτασταὶ τοσοίδε

20 ἐφέπωνται; ἢν δὲ δὴ καὶ σωθῶμεν ἐπὶ θάλατταν,
πόσον τι νάπος ὁ Πόντος; ἔνθα οὔτε πλοῖα ἔστι τὰ
ἀπάξοντα οὔτε σῖτος ᾧ θρεψόμεθα μένοντες, δεήσει
δέ, ἢν θᾶττον ἐκεῖ γενώμεθα, θᾶττον πάλιν ἐξιέναι ἐπὶ

21 τὰ ἐπιτήδεια. οὐκοῦν νῦν κρεῖττον ἠριστηκότας μάχεσθαι ἢ αὔριον ἀναρίστους. ἄνδρες, τά τε ἱερὰ ἡμῖν
καλὰ οἵ τε οἰωνοὶ αἴσιοι τά τε σφάγια κάλλιστα·
ἴωμεν ἐπὶ τοὺς ἄνδρας. οὐ δεῖ ἔτι τούτους, ἐπεὶ ἡμᾶς
πάντως εἶδον, ἡδέως δειπνῆσαι οὐδ' ὅπου ἂν ἐθέλωσι
σκηνῆσαι.

22 Ἐντεῦθεν οἱ λοχαγοὶ ἡγεῖσθαι ἐκέλευον, καὶ οὐδεὶς
ἀντέλεγε. καὶ ὃς ἡγεῖτο, παραγγείλας διαβαίνειν ᾗ
ἕκαστος ἐτύγχανε τοῦ νάπους ὤν· θᾶττον γὰρ ἀθρόον
ἐδόκει ἂν οὕτω πέραν γενέσθαι τὸ στράτευμα ἢ εἰ
κατὰ τὴν γέφυραν ἢ ἐπὶ τῷ νάπει ἦν ἐξεμηρύοντο.

23 ἐπεὶ δὲ διέβησαν, παριὼν παρὰ τὴν φάλαγγα ἔλεγεν·
Ἄνδρες, ἀναμιμνήσκεσθε ὅσας δὴ μάχας σὺν τοῖς
θεοῖς ὁμόσε ἰόντες νενικήκατε καὶ οἷα πάσχουσιν οἱ
πολεμίους φεύγοντες, καὶ τοῦτο ἐννοήσατε ὅτι ἐπὶ ταῖς

that I should myself wish to have all roads seem easy—for
their retreat; as for ourselves, we ought to learn from the
very ground before us that there is no safety for us except
in victory. I do wonder, however, that any one regards this
particular ravine as more dreadful than the rest of the
country we have just marched through. For how is that
plain to be recrossed unless we are victorious over the
enemy's horsemen? how the mountains which we have
passed through, if such a throng of peltasts are to be following at our heels? Again, if we do reach the sea in safety,
what a great ravine, one may say, is the Euxine, where we
have neither ships to take us away nor food to subsist upon
if we remain, while the sooner we reach there, the sooner
we shall have to be off again in quest of provisions. Well,
then, it is better to fight today, with our breakfast already
eaten, than to-morrow breakfastless. Gentlemen, our
sacrificial victims were favourable, the bird omens auspicious, the omens of the sacrifice most favourable; let us
advance upon the enemy. These fellows, now that they
have seen us at all, must not again get a pleasant dinner or
encamp wherever they please."

After that the captains bade him lead on, and no one
spoke in opposition. So he led the way, after giving orders
that every man should cross at whatever point along the
ravine he chanced to be; for it seemed that in this way the
army would get together on the further side more quickly
than if they marched in file along the bridge which was
over the ravine. When they had crossed, he went along the
lines and said: "Soldiers, remember how many battles you
have won, with the help of the gods, by coming to close
quarters, remember what a fate they suffer who flee from
the enemy, and bethink you of this, that we are at the doors

517

24 θύραις τῆς Ἑλλάδος ἐσμέν. ἀλλ᾽ ἔπεσθε ἡγεμόνι τῷ
Ἡρακλεῖ καὶ ἀλλήλους παρακαλεῖτε ὀνομαστί. ἡδύ
τοι ἀνδρεῖόν τι καὶ καλὸν νῦν εἰπόντα καὶ ποιήσαντα
μνήμην ἐν οἷς ἐθέλει παρέχειν ἑαυτοῦ.

25 Ταῦτα παρελαύνων ἔλεγε καὶ ἅμα ὑφηγεῖτο ἐπὶ
φάλαγγος, καὶ τοὺς πελταστὰς ἑκατέρωθεν ποιησάμενοι ἐπορεύοντο ἐπὶ τοὺς πολεμίους. παρήγγελτο δὲ τὰ
μὲν δόρατα ἐπὶ τὸν δεξιὸν ὦμον ἔχειν, ἕως σημαίνοι
τῇ σάλπιγγι· ἔπειτα δὲ εἰς προσβολὴν καθέντας ἕπεσθαι βάδην καὶ μηδένα δρόμῳ διώκειν. ἐκ τούτου
σύνθημα παρῄει Ζεὺς σωτήρ, Ἡρακλῆς ἡγεμών. οἱ δὲ
πολέμιοι ὑπέμενον, νομίζοντες καλὸν ἔχειν τὸ χωρίον.

26 ἐπεὶ δ᾽ ἐπλησίαζον, ἀλαλάξαντες οἱ Ἕλληνες πελτασταὶ ἔθεον ἐπὶ τοὺς πολεμίους πρίν τινα κελεύειν· οἱ
δὲ πολέμιοι ἀντίοι ὥρμησαν, οἵ θ᾽ ἱππεῖς καὶ τὸ
στῖφος τῶν Βιθυνῶν· καὶ τρέπονται τοὺς πελταστάς.

27 ἀλλ᾽ ἐπεὶ ὑπηντίαζεν ἡ φάλαγξ τῶν ὁπλιτῶν ταχὺ
πορευομένη καὶ ἅμα ἡ σάλπιγξ ἐφθέγξατο καὶ ἐπαιάνιζον καὶ μετὰ ταῦτα ἠλάλαζον καὶ ἅμα τὰ δόρατα
καθίεσαν, ἐνταῦθα οὐκέτι ἐδέξαντο οἱ πολέμιοι, ἀλλὰ

28 ἔφευγον. καὶ Τιμασίων μὲν ἔχων τοὺς ἱππέας ἐφείπετο, καὶ ἀπεκτίννυσαν ὅσουσπερ ἐδύναντο ὡς ὀλίγοι
ὄντες. τῶν δὲ πολεμίων τὸ μὲν εὐώνυμον εὐθὺς δι-
εσπάρη, καθ᾽ ὃ οἱ Ἕλληνες ἱππεῖς ἦσαν, τὸ δὲ δεξιὸν

29 ἅτε οὐ σφόδρα διωκόμενον ἐπὶ λόφου συνέστη. ἐπεὶ
δὲ εἶδον οἱ Ἕλληνες ὑπομένοντας αὐτούς, ἐδόκει

of Greece. Follow Heracles the Leader and summon one another on, calling each man by name. It will surely be sweet, through some manly and noble thing which one may say or do today, to keep himself in remembrance among those whom he wishes to remember him."

Thus he spoke as he rode along, while at the same time he began to lead the troops on slowly in line of battle; and after they had got the peltasts into position on either flank, they took up the march against the enemy. The orders had been to keep their spears on the right shoulder until a signal should be given with the trumpet; then, lowering them for the attack, to follow on slowly, nobody to break into a run. And now the watchword was passed along, "Zeus Saviour, Heracles Leader." Meanwhile the enemy were standing their ground, thinking that the position they held was a good one. When the Greeks were drawing near, the peltasts raised the battle-cry and proceeded to charge upon the enemy without waiting for any order; and the enemy rushed forward to meet them, both the horsemen and the mass of the Bithynians, and they put the peltasts to rout. But when the phalanx of the hoplites kept moving on to meet them, marching rapidly, and at the same time the trumpet sounded, and they struck up the paean and after that raised the battle-cry, and at the same moment couched their spears, then the enemy no longer awaited the attack, but took to flight. Timasion and the cavalry pursued, and killed as many as they could, considering their own small numbers. Now the left wing of the enemy, opposite which the Greek cavalry were stationed, was dispersed at once, but the right, since it was not vigorously pursued, got together upon a hill. As soon as the Greeks saw that they were standing their ground there,

ῥᾷστόν τε καὶ ἀκινδυνότατον εἶναι ἰέναι ἤδη ἐπ᾽
αὐτούς. παιανίσαντες οὖν εὐθὺς ἐπέκειντο· οἱ δ᾽ οὐχ
ὑπέμειναν. καὶ ἐνταῦθα οἱ πελτασταὶ ἐδίωκον μέχρι
τὸ δεξιὸν διεσπάρη· ἀπέθανον δὲ ὀλίγοι· τὸ γὰρ ἱπ-
30 πικὸν φόβον παρεῖχε τὸ τῶν πολεμίων πολὺ ὄν. ἐπεὶ
δὲ εἶδον οἱ Ἕλληνες τό τε Φαρναβάζου ἱππικὸν ἔτι
συνεστηκὸς καὶ τοὺς Βιθυνοὺς ἱππέας πρὸς τοῦτο
συναθροιζομένους καὶ ἀπὸ λόφου τινὸς καταθεωμέ-
νους τὰ γιγνόμενα, ἀπειρήκεσαν μέν, ὅμως δὲ ἐδόκει
καὶ ἐπὶ τούτους ἰτέον εἶναι οὕτως ὅπως δύναιντο, ὡς
μὴ τεθαρρηκότες ἀναπαύσαιντο. συνταξάμενοι δὴ
31 πορεύονται. ἐντεῦθεν οἱ πολέμιοι ἱππεῖς φεύγουσι
κατὰ τοῦ πρανοῦς ὁμοίως ὥσπερ ὑπὸ ἱππέων διωκό-
μενοι· νάπος γὰρ αὐτοὺς ὑπεδέχετο, ὃ οὐκ ᾔδεσαν οἱ
Ἕλληνες, ἀλλὰ προαπετράποντο διώκοντες· ὀψὲ γὰρ
32 ἦν. ἐπανελθόντες δὲ ἔνθα ἡ πρώτη συμβολὴ ἐγένετο,
στησάμενοι τρόπαιον ἀπῇσαν ἐπὶ θάλατταν περὶ
ἡλίου δυσμάς· στάδιοι δ᾽ ἦσαν ὡς ἑξήκοντα ἐπὶ τὸ
στρατόπεδον.

VI. Ἐντεῦθεν οἱ μὲν πολέμιοι εἶχον ἀμφὶ τὰ αὑτῶν
καὶ ἀπήγοντο καὶ τοὺς οἰκέτας καὶ τὰ χρήματα ὅποι
ἐδύναντο προσωτάτω· οἱ δὲ Ἕλληνες ἀνέμενον μὲν
Κλέανδρον καὶ τὰς τριήρεις καὶ τὰ πλοῖα ὡς ἥξοντα,
ἐξιόντες δ᾽ ἑκάστης ἡμέρας σὺν τοῖς ὑποζυγίοις καὶ
τοῖς ἀνδραπόδοις ἐφέροντο ἀδεῶς πυροὺς καὶ κριθάς,

---

[34] A man pursued by horsemen takes to rough country, where

they deemed it the easiest and safest course to charge upon them immediately. They accordingly struck up the paean and moved upon them at once; and they stood no longer. Thereupon the peltasts pursued until the right wing was dispersed; but few of the enemy, however, were killed, for his cavalry, numerous as they were, inspired fear. But when the Greeks saw the cavalry of Pharnabazus standing with ranks still unbroken, and the Bithynian horsemen gathering together to join this force and looking down from a hill at what was going on, although they were tired they nevertheless thought that they must make as stout an attack as they could upon these troops also, so that they should not be able to regain courage and get rested. Accordingly, they formed their lines and set forth. Thereupon the enemy's horsemen fled down the slope just as if they were being pursued by horsemen;[34] for a ravine was waiting to receive them, although the Greeks were not aware of the fact and hence turned aside from their pursuit before reaching it; for it was now late in the day. So after returning to the spot where the first encounter took place and erecting a trophy, they set out on their way back to the sea at about sunset; and the distance to the camp was about sixty stadia.

VI. After this the enemy occupied themselves with their own concerns, especially removing their slaves and property to the remotest point they could; meanwhile the Greeks were waiting for Cleander and the triremes and ships which were, presumably, coming, but every day they set forth with their baggage animals and slaves and fear-

horsemen are helpless. In the present case, therefore, the hostile horsemen did precisely the wrong thing, and would probably have suffered severe losses if the Greeks had continued their pursuit.

οἶνον, ὄσπρια, μελίνας, σῦκα· πάντα γὰρ ἀγαθὰ εἶχεν
2 ἡ χώρα πλὴν ἐλαίου. καὶ ὁπότε μὲν καταμένοι τὸ
στράτευμα ἀναπαυόμενον, ἐξῆν ἐπὶ λείαν ἰέναι, καὶ
ἐλάμβανον οἱ ἐξιόντες· ὁπότε δὲ ἐξίοι πᾶν τὸ στράτευμα, εἴ τις χωρὶς ἀπελθὼν λάβοι τι, δημόσιον ἔδο-
3 ξεν εἶναι. ἤδη δὲ ἦν πολλὴ πάντων ἀφθονία· καὶ γὰρ
ἀγοραὶ πάντοθεν ἀφικνοῦντο ἐκ τῶν Ἑλληνίδων
πόλεων καὶ οἱ παραπλέοντες ἄσμενοι κατεῖχον,
4 ἀκούοντες ὡς οἰκίζοιτο πόλις καὶ λιμὴν εἴη. ἔπεμπον
δὲ καὶ οἱ πολέμιοι ἤδη οἱ πλησίον οἰκοῦντες πρὸς
Ξενοφῶντα, ἀκούοντες ὅτι οὗτος πολίζει τὸ χωρίον,
ἐρωτῶντες ὅ τι δέοι ποιοῦντας φίλους εἶναι. ὁ δ᾽
ἐπεδείκνυεν αὐτοὺς τοῖς στρατιώταις.

5 Κἂν ἐν τούτῳ Κλέανδρος ἀφικνεῖται δύο τριήρεις
ἔχων, πλοῖον δ᾽ οὐδέν. ἐτύγχανε δὲ τὸ στράτευμα ἔξω
ὂν ὅτε ἀφίκετο καὶ ἐπὶ λείαν τινὲς οἰχόμενοι ἄλλοι
⟨ἄλλῃ⟩[8] εἰς τὸ ὄρος εἰλήφεσαν πρόβατα πολλά·
ὀκνοῦντες δὲ μὴ ἀφαιρεθεῖεν τῷ Δεξίππῳ λέγουσιν,
ὃς ἀπέδρα τὴν πεντηκόντορον ἔχων ἐκ Τραπεζοῦντος,
καὶ κελεύουσι διασώσαντα αὐτοῖς τὰ πρόβατα τὰ μὲν
6 αὐτὸν λαβεῖν, τὰ δὲ σφίσιν ἀποδοῦναι. εὐθὺς δ᾽ ἐκεῖνος ἀπελαύνει τοὺς περιεστῶτας τῶν στρατιωτῶν καὶ
λέγοντας ὅτι δημόσια εἴη, καὶ τῷ Κλεάνδρῳ εὐθὺς

---

[8] ἄλλοι MSS., Mar., Hude/Peters: ἄλλοσε Gem., following
Bornemann: ἄλλῃ added by Schneider.

---

[35] In accordance with the above-mentioned (§2) decree.

lessly carried off wheat and barley, wine, beans, millet, and figs; for the country had all manner of good things, except olive oil. Whenever the army remained in camp and rested, individuals were permitted to go out after plunder, and in that case kept what they got; but whenever the entire army set out, if an individual went off by himself and got anything, it was decreed to be public property. And by this time there was a great abundance of everything, for market products came in from the Greek cities on all sides, and people coasting past were glad to put in, since they heard that a city was being founded and that there was a harbour. Even the hostile peoples who dwelt near by began now to send envoys to Xenophon—for they heard that he was the man who was making a city of the place—to ask what they must do in order to be his friends; and Xenophon would always show these envoys to the soldiers.

Meanwhile Cleander arrived with two triremes, but not a single merchant ship. It so chanced that the army was out foraging when he arrived, while certain individuals had gone in quest of plunder to different places in the mountains and had secured a large number of sheep; so fearing that they might be deprived of them,[35] they told their story to Dexippus, the man who slipped away from Trapezus with the fifty-oared warship,[36] and urged him to save their sheep for them, with the understanding that he was to get some of the sheep himself and give the rest back to them. So he immediately proceeded to drive away the soldiers who were standing about and declaring that the animals were public property, and then he went straightway and

[36] See V. i. 15, VI. i. 32. Dexippus had manifestly accompanied Cleander to Calpe Harbour.

ἐλθὼν λέγε ὅτι ἁρπάζειν ἐπιχειροῦσιν. ὁ δὲ κελεύει
7 τὸν ἁρπάζοντα ἄγειν πρὸς αὑτόν. καὶ ὁ μὲν λαβὼν
ἄγει τινά· περιτυχὼν δ' Ἀγασίας ἀφαιρεῖται· καὶ γὰρ
ἦν αὐτῷ ὁ ἀγόμενος λοχίτης. οἱ δ' ἄλλοι οἱ παρόντες
τῶν στρατιωτῶν ἐπιχειροῦσι βάλλειν τὸν Δέξιππον,
ἀνακαλοῦντες τὸν προδότην. ἔδεισαν δὲ καὶ τῶν τρι-
ηριτῶν πολλοὶ καὶ ἔφευγον εἰς τὴν θάλατταν, καὶ
8 Κλέανδρος δ' ἔφευγε. Ξενοφῶν δὲ καὶ οἱ ἄλλοι στρατηγοὶ κατεκώλυόν τε καὶ τῷ Κλεάνδρῳ ἔλεγον ὅτι
οὐδὲν εἴη πρᾶγμα, ἀλλὰ τὸ δόγμα αἴτιον εἴη τοῦ
9 στρατεύματος ταῦτα γενέσθαι. ὁ δὲ Κλέανδρος ὑπὸ
τοῦ Δεξίππου τε ἀνερεθιζόμενος καὶ αὐτὸς ἀχθεσθεὶς
ὅτι ἐφοβήθη, ἀποπλευσεῖσθαι ἔφη καὶ κηρύξειν
μηδεμίαν πόλιν δέχεσθαι αὐτούς, ὡς πολεμίους. ἦρ-
χον δὲ τότε πάντων τῶν Ἑλλήνων οἱ Λακεδαιμόνιοι.
10 ἐνταῦθα πονηρὸν ἐδόκει τὸ πρᾶγμα εἶναι τοῖς Ἕλλησιν, καὶ ἐδέοντο μὴ ποιεῖν ταῦτα. ὁ δ' οὐκ ἂν ἄλλως
ἔφη γενέσθαι, εἰ μή τις ἐκδώσει τὸν ἄρξαντα βάλλειν
11 καὶ τὸν ἀφελόμενον. ἦν δὲ ὃν ἐξήτει Ἀγασίας διὰ
τέλους φίλος τῷ Ξενοφῶντι· ἐξ οὗ καὶ διέβαλλεν αὐτὸν
ὁ Δέξιππος.

Καὶ ἐντεῦθεν ἐπειδὴ ἀπορία ἦν, συνήγαγον τὸ
στράτευμα οἱ ἄρχοντες· καὶ ἔνιοι μὲν αὐτῶν παρ'
ὀλίγον ἐποιοῦντο τὸν Κλέανδρον, τῷ δὲ Ξενοφῶντι οὐκ
12 ἐδόκει φαῦλον εἶναι, ἀλλ' ἀναστὰς ἔλεξεν· Ὦ ἄνδρες

told Cleander that they were attempting robbery. Cleander directed him to bring the robber before him. So he seized a man and was taking him to Cleander, but Agasias, happening to meet them, rescued the man, for he was one of his company. Then the other soldiers who were present set about stoning Dexippus, calling him "The traitor." And many of the sailors from the triremes got frightened and began to flee toward the sea, and Cleander also fled. Xenophon, however, and the other generals tried to hold them back, and told Cleander that nothing was the matter, but that the resolution of the army was the reason for this incident taking place. But Cleander, goaded on by Dexippus and angered on his own account also because he had been frightened, declared that he would sail away and issue a proclamation forbidding any city to receive them, on the ground that they were enemies. And at this time the Lacedaemonians[37] held the hegemony over all the Greeks. Upon this the affair seemed to the Greeks a bad business, and they begged Cleander not to carry out his intention. He replied that no other course would be taken unless they should deliver up the man who began the stoning and the one who rescued Dexippus' prisoner. Now Agasias, whom he thus demanded, had been a friend of Xenophon's all through—which was the very reason why Dexippus was slandering him.

After that the commanders, perplexed as they were, called a meeting of the army; and while some of them made light of Cleander, Xenophon thought that it was no trifling matter, and he arose and said: "Fellow soldiers, it seems

---

[37] Cleander was Lacedaemonian harmost, or governor, of Byzantium (ii. 13).

στρατιῶται, ἐμοὶ δὲ οὐ φαῦλον δοκεῖ εἶναι τὸ πρᾶγμα,
εἰ ἡμῖν οὕτως ἔχων τὴν γνώμην Κλέανδρος ἄπεισιν
ὥσπερ λέγει. εἰσὶ μὲν γὰρ ἤδη ἐγγὺς αἱ Ἑλληνίδες
πόλεις· τῆς δὲ Ἑλλάδος Λακεδαιμόνιοι προεστήκασιν·
ἱκανοὶ δέ εἰσι καὶ εἷς ἕκαστος Λακεδαιμονίων ἐν ταῖς
13 πόλεσιν ὅ τι βούλονται διαπράττεσθαι. εἰ οὖν οὗτος
πρῶτον μὲν ἡμᾶς Βυζαντίου ἀποκλείσει, ἔπειτα δὲ τοῖς
ἄλλοις ἁρμοσταῖς παραγγελεῖ εἰς τὰς πόλεις μὴ
δέχεσθαι ὡς ἀπιστοῦντας Λακεδαιμονίοις καὶ ἀνόμους
ὄντας, ἔτι δὲ πρὸς Ἀναξίβιον τὸν ναύαρχον οὗτος ὁ
λόγος περὶ ἡμῶν ἥξει, χαλεπὸν ἔσται καὶ μένειν καὶ
ἀποπλεῖν· καὶ γὰρ ἐν τῇ γῇ ἄρχουσι Λακεδαιμόνιοι
14 καὶ ἐν τῇ θαλάττῃ τὸν νῦν χρόνον. οὔκουν δεῖ οὔτε
ἑνὸς ἀνδρὸς ἕνεκα οὔτε δυοῖν ἡμᾶς τοὺς ἄλλους τῆς
Ἑλλάδος ἀπέχεσθαι, ἀλλὰ πειστέον ὅ τι ἂν κελεύωσι·
καὶ γὰρ αἱ πόλεις ἡμῶν ὅθεν ἐσμὲν πείθονται αὐτοῖς.
15 ἐγὼ μὲν οὖν, καὶ γὰρ ἀκούω Δέξιππον λέγειν πρὸς
Κλέανδρον ὡς οὐκ ἂν ἐποίησεν Ἀγασίας ταῦτα, εἰ μὴ
ἐγὼ αὐτὸν ἐκέλευσα, ἐγὼ μὲν οὖν ἀπολύω καὶ ὑμᾶς
τῆς αἰτίας καὶ Ἀγασίαν, ἂν αὐτὸς Ἀγασίας φήσῃ ἐμέ
τι τούτων αἴτιον εἶναι, καὶ καταδικάζω ἐμαυτοῦ, εἰ ἐγὼ
πετροβολίας ἢ ἄλλου τινὸς βιαίου ἐξάρχω, τῆς
16 ἐσχάτης δίκης ἄξιος εἶναι, καὶ ὑφέξω τὴν δίκην. φημὶ
δὲ καὶ εἴ τινα ἄλλον αἰτιᾶται, χρῆναι ἑαυτὸν παρασχεῖν Κλεάνδρῳ κρῖναι· οὕτω γὰρ ἂν ὑμεῖς ἀπολελυ-
μένοι τῆς αἰτίας εἴητε. ὡς δὲ νῦν ἔχει, χαλεπὸν εἰ
οἰόμενοι ἐν τῇ Ἑλλάδι καὶ ἐπαίνου καὶ τιμῆς τεύξε-

to me it is no trifling matter if Cleander is to go away
with such an intention toward us as he has expressed. For
the Greek cities are now close by, the Lacedaemonians
stand as the leaders of Greece, and they are able, indeed,
any single Lacedaemonian is able, to accomplish in the
cities what he pleases. If this man shall begin by shutting us
out of Byzantium, and then shall send word to the other
governors not to receive us into their cities, on the ground
that we are disobedient to the Lacedaemonians and law-
less, and if, further, this report about us shall reach
Anaxibius,[38] the Lacedaemonian admiral, it will be difficult
for us either to remain or to sail away; for at present the
Lacedaemonians are supreme both on land and sea. Now
the rest of us must not be kept away from Greece for the
sake of one or two men, but we must obey whatever order
the Lacedaemonians may give us; for the cities from which
we come likewise obey them. For my own part, therefore—for I hear that Dexippus is saying to Cleander that
Agasias would not have done what he did if I had not given
him the order—for my own part, I say, I relieve both you
and Agasias of the accusation if Agasias himself shall say
that I was in any way responsible for this occurrence, and
I pass judgment against myself, if I have taken the lead in
stone-throwing or any other sort of violence, that I deserve
to suffer the uttermost penalty, and I shall submit to the
penalty. And I maintain also that if he holds any one else
responsible, that man ought to put himself in Cleander's
hands for trial; for in that way you would stand relieved of
the accusation. But as matters are now, it will be hard if we
who expected to obtain both praise and honour in Greece,

[38] See V. i. 4 and note thereon.

σθαι ἀντὶ δὲ τούτων οὐδ' ὅμοιοι τοῖς ἄλλοις ἐσόμεθα,
ἀλλ' εἰρξόμεθα ἐκ τῶν Ἑλληνίδων πόλεων.

17   Μετὰ ταῦτα ἀναστὰς εἶπεν Ἀγασίας· Ἐγώ, ὦ
ἄνδρες, ὄμνυμι θεοὺς καὶ θεὰς ἦ μὴν μήτε με Ξενοφῶντα κελεῦσαι ἀφελέσθαι τὸν ἄνδρα μήτε ἄλλον
ὑμῶν μηδένα· ἰδόντι δέ μοι ἄνδρα ἀγαθὸν ἀγόμενον
τῶν ἐμῶν λοχιτῶν ὑπὸ Δεξίππου, ὃν ὑμεῖς ἐπίστασθε
ὑμᾶς προδόντα, δεινὸν ἔδοξεν εἶναι· καὶ ἀφειλόμην,
18   ὁμολογῶ. καὶ ὑμεῖς μὲν μὴ ἐκδῶτέ με· ἐγὼ δὲ ἐμαυτόν,
ὥσπερ Ξενοφῶν λέγει, παρασχήσω κρινοῦντι Κλεάνδρῳ ὅ τι ἂν βούληται ποιῆσαι· τούτου ἔνεκα μήτε
πολεμεῖτε Λακεδαιμονίοις σῴζεσθέ τε ἀσφαλῶς ὅποι
θέλει ἕκαστος. συμπέμψατε μέντοι μοι ὑμῶν αὐτῶν
ἑλόμενοι πρὸς Κλέανδρον οἵτινες, ἄν τι ἐγὼ παρα-
λίπω, καὶ λέξουσιν ὑπὲρ ἐμοῦ καὶ πράξουσιν.

19   Ἐκ τούτου ἔδωκεν ἡ στρατιὰ οὕστινας βούλοιτο
προελόμενον ἰέναι. ὁ δὲ προείλετο τοὺς στρατηγούς.
μετὰ ταῦτα ἐπορεύοντο πρὸς Κλέανδρον Ἀγασίας καὶ
οἱ στρατηγοὶ καὶ ὁ ἀφαιρεθεὶς ἀνὴρ ὑπὸ Ἀγασίου.
20   καὶ ἔλεγον οἱ στρατηγοί· Ἔπεμψεν ἡμᾶς ἡ στρατιὰ
πρὸς σέ, ὦ Κλέανδρε, καὶ κελεύουσί σε, εἴτε πάντας
αἰτιᾷ, κρίναντα σὲ αὐτὸν χρῆσθαι ὅ τι ἂν βούλῃ, εἴτε
ἕνα τινὰ ἢ δύο καὶ πλείους αἰτιᾷ, τούτους ἀξιοῦσι
παρασχεῖν σοι ἑαυτοὺς εἰς κρίσιν. εἴτε οὖν ἡμῶν τινα
αἰτιᾷ, πάρεσμέν σοι ἡμεῖς· εἴτε δὲ ἄλλον τινά, φρά-
σον· οὐδεὶς γὰρ ἀπέσται ὅστις ἂν ἡμῖν ἐθελήσῃ πείθε-
21   σθαι. μετὰ ταῦτα παρελθὼν ὁ Ἀγασίας εἶπεν· Ἐγώ
εἰμι, ὦ Κλέανδρε, ὁ ἀφελόμενος Δεξίππου ἄγοντος

shall find instead that we are not even on an equality with the rest of the Greeks, but are shut out from their cities."

After this Agasias rose and said: "'Soldiers, I swear by the gods and goddesses that in very truth neither Xenophon nor any one else among you directed me to rescue the man; but when I saw a good man of my own company being led off by Dexippus, the one who betrayed you, as you know for yourselves, it seemed to me an outrage; and I rescued him, I admit it. Now do not you deliver me up; but I will myself, as Xenophon proposes, put myself in Cleander's hands, so that he may try me and do with me whatever he may choose; do not for this cause make war upon the Lacedaemonians, but rather accomplish a safe return, each of you to the place where he wishes to go. I beg you, however, to choose some of your own number and send them with me to Cleander, so that if I pass over anything, they may speak, and act too, on my behalf.''

Thereupon the army empowered him to choose whomever he wished and take them with him, and he chose the generals. After this Agasias set off to Cleander, and with him the generals and the man he had rescued. And the generals said: "We have been sent to you, Cleander, by the army, and they ask you, in case you accuse them all, to bring them to trial yourself and deal with them as you please; or in case you accuse some one individual, or two or more, they demand of these men that they put themselves in your hands for trial. Therefore if you have any charge against any one of us, we are now here before you; if you have any charge against any one else, tell us; for no one who is ready to yield obedience to us will fail to present himself before you. After this Agasias came forward and said: "I am the person, Cleander, who rescued this man here from

22 τοῦτον τὸν ἄνδρα καὶ παίειν κελεύσας Δέξιππον. τοῦτον μὲν γὰρ οἶδα ἄνδρα ἀγαθὸν ὄντα, Δέξιππον δὲ οἶδα αἱρεθέντα ὑπὸ τῆς στρατιᾶς ἄρχειν τῆς πεντηκοντόρου ἧς ᾐτησάμεθα παρὰ Τραπεζουντίων ἐφ' ᾧτε πλοῖα συλλέγειν ὡς σῳζοίμεθα, καὶ ἀποδράντα Δέξιππον καὶ προδόντα τοὺς στρατιώτας μεθ' ὧν

23 ἐσώθη. καὶ τούς τε Τραπεζουντίους ἀπεστερήκαμεν τὴν πεντηκόντορον καὶ κακοὶ δοκοῦμεν εἶναι διὰ τοῦτον, αὐτοί τε τὸ ἐπὶ τούτῳ ἀπολώλαμεν. ἤκουε γάρ, ὥσπερ ἡμεῖς, ὡς ἄπορον εἴη πεζῇ ἀπιόντας τοὺς ποταμούς τε διαβῆναι καὶ σωθῆναι εἰς τὴν Ἑλλάδα.

24 τοῦτον οὖν τοιοῦτον ὄντα ἀφειλόμην. εἰ δὲ σὺ ἦγες ἢ ἄλλος τις τῶν παρὰ σοῦ, καὶ μὴ τῶν παρ' ἡμῶν ἀποδράντων, εὖ ἴσθι ὅτι οὐδὲν ἂν τούτων ἐποίησα. νόμιζε δ', ἐὰν ἐμὲ νῦν ἀποκτείνῃς, δι' ἄνδρα δειλόν τε καὶ πονηρὸν ἄνδρα ἀγαθὸν ἀποκτενῶν.

25 Ἀκούσας ταῦτα ὁ Κλέανδρος εἶπεν ὅτι Δέξιππον μὲν οὐκ ἐπαινοίη, εἰ ταῦτα πεποιηκὼς εἴη· οὐ μέντοι ἔφη νομίζειν οὐδ' εἰ παμπόνηρος ἦν Δέξιππος βίᾳ χρῆναι πάσχειν αὐτόν, ἀλλὰ κριθέντα, ὥσπερ καὶ

26 ὑμεῖς νῦν ἀξιοῦτε, τῆς δίκης λαχεῖν. νῦν μὲν οὖν ἄπιτε καταλιπόντες τόνδε τὸν ἄνδρα· ὅταν δ' ἐγὼ κελεύσω, πάρεστε πρὸς τὴν κρίσιν. αἰτιῶμαι δὲ οὔτε τὴν στρατιὰν οὔτε ἄλλον οὐδένα ἔτι, ἐπεὶ γε οὗτος αὐτὸς ὁμολο-

Dexippus when he was leading him off, and who gave the
order to strike Dexippus. For I know that this soldier here
is a good man, and I know also that Dexippus was chosen
by the army to be commander of the fifty-oared warship
which we begged for and obtained from the Trapezuntians
on the understanding that with it we were to collect vessels
whereon we might return in safety, and that this Dexippus
slipped away from us, and betrayed the soldiers in whose
company he had gained deliverance. So we have robbed
the Trapezuntians of their warship and are rascals in their
estimation, all on account of this Dexippus; indeed, we
have lost our very lives, so far as lay in this fellow's power;
for he heard, just as we did, that it was impossible, returning by land, to cross the rivers and reach Greece in safety.
It was from that sort of a fellow, then, that I rescued his
prisoner. Had it been you who were leading him off, or
any one of your men, and not one of our runaways, be
well assured that I should have done nothing of this kind.
And believe that if you now put me to death, you will be
putting to death a good man for the sake of a coward and
a scoundrel."

Upon hearing these words Cleander said that he had no
commendation for Dexippus if he had behaved in this way,
but that he nevertheless thought that even if Dexippus
were an utter scoundrel, he ought not to have suffered
violence; "rather," he continued, "he should first have had
a trial, just as you are yourselves asking in the present case,
and should then have received his punishment. For the
moment, therefore, go away, leaving this man here with
me, and when I issue the order, be present for the trial.
And I bring no charge either against the army or any other
person now that this man himself admits that he rescued

27 γεῖ ἀφελέσθαι τὸν ἄνδρα. ὁ δὲ ἀφαιρεθεὶς εἶπεν· Ἐγώ,
ὦ Κλέανδρε, εἰ καὶ οἴει με ἀδικοῦντά τι ἄγεσθαι, οὔτε
ἔπαιον οὐδένα οὔτε ἔβαλλον, ἀλλ᾽ εἶπον ὅτι δημόσια
εἴη τὰ πρόβατα· ἦν γὰρ τῶν στρατιωτῶν δόγμα, εἴ
τις ὁπότε ἡ στρατιὰ ἐξίοι ἰδίᾳ λήζοιτο, δημόσια εἶναι
28 τὰ ληφθέντα. ταῦτα εἶπον· καὶ ἐκ τούτου με λαβὼν
οὗτος ἦγεν, ἵνα μὴ φθέγγοιτο μηδείς, ἀλλ᾽ αὐτὸς
λαβὼν τὸ μέρος διασώσειε τοῖς λῃσταῖς παρὰ τὴν
ῥήτραν τὰ χρήματα. πρὸς ταῦτα ὁ Κλέανδρος εἶπεν·
Ἐπεὶ τοίνυν τορὸς⁹ εἶ, κατάμενε, ἵνα καὶ περὶ σοῦ
βουλευσώμεθα.

29 Ἐκ τούτου οἱ μὲν ἀμφὶ Κλέανδρον ἠρίστων· τὴν δὲ
στρατιὰν συνήγαγε Ξενοφῶν καὶ συνεβούλευε πέμψαι ἄνδρας πρὸς Κλέανδρον παραιτησομένους περὶ
30 τῶν ἀνδρῶν. ἐκ τούτου ἔδοξεν αὐτοῖς πέμψαντας στρατηγοὺς καὶ λοχαγοὺς καὶ Δρακόντιον τὸν Σπαρτιάτην
καὶ τῶν ἄλλων οἳ ἐδόκουν ἐπιτήδειοι εἶναι δεῖσθαι
Κλεάνδρου κατὰ πάντα τρόπον ἀφεῖναι τὼ ἄνδρε.
31 ἐλθὼν οὖν ὁ Ξενοφῶν λέγει· Ἔχεις μέν, ὦ Κλέανδρε,
τοὺς ἄνδρας, καὶ ἡ στρατιά σοι ἐφεῖτο ὅ τι ἐβούλου
ποιῆσαι καὶ περὶ τούτων καὶ περὶ αὑτῶν ἁπάντων. νῦν
δέ σε αἰτοῦνται καὶ δέονται δοῦναι σφίσι τὼ ἄνδρε
καὶ μὴ κατακαίνειν· πολλὰ γὰρ ἐν τῷ ἔμπροσθεν
32 χρόνῳ περὶ τὴν στρατιὰν ἐμοχθησάτην. ταῦτα δὲ σοῦ
τυχόντες ὑπισχνοῦνταί σοι ἀντὶ τούτων, ἢν βούλῃ

⁹ τορὸς: the reading of some MSS., defended by Schenkl, and
adopted by Hude/Peters. Cf. *Lac.* II. 11.

the prisoner." Then the one who had been rescued said: "For myself, Cleander, in case you really imagine that I was being led off for some wrong doing, I neither struck nor stoned anybody but merely said that the sheep were public property. For a resolution had been passed by the soldiers that if any one should do any plundering on his own account when the entire army went out, what he secured was to be public property. That was what I said, and thereupon this fellow seized me and proceeded to lead me off, in order that nobody might utter a word, but that he might save the booty for the plunderers in violation of the ordinance—and get his own share out of it." In reply to this Cleander said: "Well, since in fact you are knowledgeable in the matter, stay behind, so that we can take up your case also."

After that Cleander and his party proceeded to breakfast; and Xenophon called a meeting of the army and advised the sending of a delegation to Cleander to intercede for the men. Thereupon the troops resolved to send the generals and captains, Dracontius the Spartan, and such others as seemed fitted for the mission, and to request Cleander by all means to release the two men. So Xenophon came before him and said: "You have the men, Cleander, and the army has bid you to do what you pleased both with these men and with their entire body. But now they beg and entreat you to give them the two men, and not to put them to death; for many are the labours these two have performed for the army in the past. Should they obtain this favour at your hands, they promise you in return that, if

533

ἡγεῖσθαι αὐτῶν καὶ ἦν οἱ θεοὶ ἵλεῳ ὦσιν, ἐπιδείξειν
σοι καὶ ὡς κόσμιοί εἰσι καὶ ὡς ἱκανοὶ τῷ ἄρχοντι
πειθόμενοι τοὺς πολεμίους σὺν τοῖς θεοῖς μὴ φοβεῖ-
33 σθαι. δέονται δέ σου καὶ τοῦτο, παραγενόμενον καὶ
ἄρξαντα ἑαυτῶν πεῖραν λαβεῖν καὶ Δεξίππου καὶ
σφῶν τῶν ἄλλων οἷος ἕκαστός ἐστι, καὶ τὴν ἀξίαν
34 ἑκάστοις νεῖμαι. ἀκούσας ταῦτα ὁ Κλέανδρος, Ἀλλὰ
ναὶ τὼ σιώ, ἔφη, ταχύ τοι ὑμῖν ἀποκρινοῦμαι. καὶ τώ
τε ἄνδρε ὑμῖν δίδωμι καὶ αὐτὸς παρέσομαι· καὶ ἦν οἱ
θεοὶ παραδιδῶσιν ἐξηγήσομαι εἰς τὴν Ἑλλάδα. καὶ
πολὺ οἱ λόγοι οὗτοι ἀντίοι εἰσὶν ἢ οὓς ἐγὼ περὶ ὑμῶν
ἐνίων ἤκουον ὡς τὸ στράτευμα ἀφίστατε ἀπὸ Λακεδαιμονίων.

35   Ἐκ τούτου οἱ μὲν ἐπαινοῦντες ἀπῆλθον, ἔχοντες τὼ
ἄνδρε· Κλέανδρος δὲ ἐθύετο ἐπὶ τῇ πορείᾳ καὶ συνῆν
Ξενοφῶντι φιλικῶς καὶ ξενίαν συνεβάλοντο. ἐπεὶ δὲ
καὶ ἑώρα αὐτοὺς τὸ παραγγελλόμενον εὐτάκτως ποιοῦντας, καὶ μᾶλλον ἔτι ἐπεθύμει ἡγεμὼν γενέσθαι
36 αὐτῶν. ἐπεὶ μέντοι θυομένῳ αὐτῷ ἐπὶ τρεῖς ἡμέρας οὐκ
ἐγίγνετο τὰ ἱερά, συγκαλέσας τοὺς στρατηγοὺς εἶπεν·
Ἐμοὶ μὲν οὐ τελέθει τὰ ἱερὰ ἐξάγειν· ὑμεῖς μέντοι μὴ
ἀθυμεῖτε τούτου ἕνεκα· ὑμῖν μὲν γάρ, ὡς ἔοικε, δέδοται
ἐκκομίσαι τοὺς ἄνδρας. ἀλλὰ πορεύεσθε. ἡμεῖς δὲ

---

[39] Castor and Pollux, the Dioskouroi, who were important in
the religious and political life of the Lacedaemonians. σιώ is Spartan (Doric) for θεώ.

you wish to be their leader and if the gods are propitious, they will show you not only that they are orderly, but that they are able, with the help of the gods, while yielding obedience to their commander, to feel no fear of the enemy. They make this further request of you, that when you have joined them and assumed command of them, you make trial both of Dexippus and of the rest of them to see how the two sorts of men compare, and then give to each his deserts." Upon hearing these words Cleander replied: "Well, by the twin gods,[39] my answer to you all will be speedy indeed. I give you the two men and I will myself join you, and if the gods so grant, I will lead you to Greece. These words of yours are decidedly the opposite of what I have been hearing about you from some people, namely, that you were trying to make the army disloyal to the Lacedaemonians."

After this they thanked him and departed, taking the two men with them; and Cleander undertook sacrifices with a view to the journey and associated amicably with Xenophon, so that the two men struck up a friendship. Furthermore, when Cleander came to see for himself that the troops carried out their orders with good discipline, he was more than ever eager to become their commander. When, however, although he continued his sacrifices over three days, the victims would not prove favourable, he called a meeting of the generals and said: "The victims do not prove favourable to me as the man to lead you onward; but it is not for you to be despondent on that account; to you, as it seems, is given the office of delivering these soldiers. To the road, then! For our part, we shall give you,

ὑμᾶς, ἐπειδὰν ἐκεῖσε ἥκητε, δεξόμεθα ὡς ἂν δυνώμεθα κάλλιστα.

37 Ἐκ τούτου ἔδοξε τοῖς στρατιώταις δοῦναι αὐτῷ τὰ δημόσια πρόβατα· ὁ δὲ δεξάμενος πάλιν αὐτοῖς ἀπέδωκε. καὶ οὗτος μὲν ἀπέπλει. οἱ δὲ στρατιῶται διαθέμενοι τὸν σῖτον ὃν ἦσαν συγκεκομισμένοι καὶ τἆλλα ἃ εἰλήφεσαν ἐξεπορεύοντο διὰ τῶν Βιθυνῶν.

38 ἐπεὶ δὲ οὐδενὶ ἐνέτυχον πορευόμενοι τὴν ὀρθὴν ὁδόν, ὥστε ἔχοντές τι εἰς τὴν φιλίαν ἐλθεῖν, ἔδοξεν αὐτοῖς τοὔμπαλιν ὑποστρέψαντας ἐλθεῖν μίαν ἡμέραν καὶ νύκτα. τοῦτο δὲ ποιήσαντες ἔλαβον πολλὰ καὶ ἀνδράποδα καὶ πρόβατα· καὶ ἀφίκοντο ἑκταῖοι εἰς Χρυσόπολιν τῆς Καλχηδονίας, καὶ ἐκεῖ ἔμειναν ἡμέρας ἑπτὰ λαφυροπωλοῦντες.

when you have reached your journey's end, as splendid a reception as we can."

Thereupon the soldiers voted to present to him the sheep that were public property, and he accepted them, but gave them back again to the troops. Then he sailed away. And the soldiers, after selling the corn they had gathered together and the other booty they had secured, set out on their march through the country of the Bithynians. But when in following the direct road they failed to find any booty, to enable them to reach friendly territory with a little something in hand, they resolved to turn about and take the opposite direction for one day and night. By so doing they secured slaves and sheep in abundance; and on the sixth day they arrived at Chrysopolis, in Calchedonia, where they remained for seven days, selling their spoils.

Z

2   I.[1] Ἐκ τούτου δὲ Φαρνάβαζος φοβούμενος τὸ στράτευμα μὴ ἐπὶ τὴν αὐτοῦ χώραν στρατεύηται, πέμψας
πρὸς Ἀναξίβιον τὸν ναύαρχον—ὁ δ᾽ ἔτυχεν ἐν Βυζαντίῳ ὤν—ἐδεῖτο διαβιβάσαι τὸ στράτευμα ἐκ τῆς
Ἀσίας, καὶ ὑπισχνεῖτο πάντα ποιήσειν αὐτῷ ὅσα
3   δέοιτο. καὶ ὁ Ἀναξίβιος μετεπέμψατο τοὺς στρατηγοὺς καὶ λοχαγοὺς εἰς Βυζάντιον, καὶ ὑπισχνεῖτο, εἰ
4   διαβαῖεν, μισθοφορὰν ἔσεσθαι τοῖς στρατιώταις. οἱ
μὲν δὴ ἄλλοι ἔφασαν βουλευσάμενοι ἀπαγγελεῖν,
Ξενοφῶν δὲ εἶπεν αὐτῷ ὅτι ἀπαλλάξοιτο ἤδη ἀπὸ τῆς
στρατιᾶς καὶ βούλοιτο ἀποπλεῖν. ὁ δὲ Ἀναξίβιος
ἐκέλευσεν αὐτὸν συνδιαβάντα ἔπειτα οὕτως ἀπαλλάττεσθαι. ἔφη οὖν ταῦτα ποιήσειν.
5   Σεύθης δὲ ὁ Θρᾷξ πέμπει Μηδοσάδην καὶ κελεύει

---

[1] The summary prefixed to Book VII (see note on II. i. 1) reads:
Ὅσα μὲν δὴ ἐν τῇ ἀναβάσει τῇ μετὰ Κύρου ἔπραξαν οἱ
Ἕλληνες μέχρι τῆς μάχης, καὶ ὅσα ἐπεὶ Κῦρος ἐτελεύτησεν
ἐν τῇ πορείᾳ μέχρι εἰς τὸν Πόντον ἀφίκοντο, καὶ ὅσα ἐκ τοῦ
Πόντου πεζῇ ἐξιόντες καὶ ἐκπλέοντες ἐποίουν μέχρι ἔξω τοῦ
στόματος ἐγένοντο ἐν Χρυσοπόλει τῆς Ἀσίας, ἐν τῷ πρόσθεν λόγῳ δεδήλωται.

BOOK VII

I.[1] After this Pharnabazus, in fear that the Greek army might carry on a campaign against his own land, sent to Anaxibius, the admiral, who chanced to be at Byzantium, and asked him to carry the army across[2] out of Asia, promising to do everything for him that he might require. Anaxibius accordingly summoned the generals and captains to Byzantium, and gave them promises that if they crossed over, the soldiers would have regular pay. The rest of the officers replied that they would consider the matter and report back to him, but Xenophon told him that he intended to part company with the army at once, and wanted to sail home. Anaxibius, however, bade him cross over with the others, and leave them only after that. Xenophon said, therefore, that he would do so.

And now Seuthes the Thracian[3] sent Medosades to

---

[1] Summary (see note to text): The preceding narrative has described all that the Greeks did on their upward march with Cyrus until the time of the battle, all that took place after the death of Cyrus on their journey to the Euxine Sea, and the whole course of their doings while they were travelling on, by land and water, from the Euxine, until they got beyond its mouth, arriving at Chrysopolis, in Asia.

[2] The Bosporus. Chrysopolis was directly opposite Byzantium.

[3] On Seuthes, see below ii. 34 and note.

Ξενοφῶντα συμπροθυμεῖσθαι ὅπως διαβῇ τὸ στράτευμα, καὶ ἔφη αὐτῷ ταῦτα συμπροθυμηθέντι ὅτι οὐ
6 μεταμελήσει. ὁ δ' εἶπεν· Ἀλλὰ τὸ μὲν στράτευμα
διαβήσεται· τούτου ἕνεκα μηδὲν τελείτω μήτε ἐμοὶ
μήτε ἄλλῳ μηδενί· ἐπειδὰν δὲ διαβῇ, ἐγὼ μὲν ἀπαλλά-
ξομαι, πρὸς δὲ τοὺς διαμένοντας καὶ ἐπικαιρίους ὄντας
προσφερέσθω ὡς ἂν αὐτῷ δοκῇ.

7   Ἐκ τούτου διαβαίνουσι πάντες εἰς τὸ Βυζάντιον οἱ
στρατιῶται. καὶ μισθὸν μὲν οὐκ ἐδίδου ὁ Ἀναξίβιος,
ἐκήρυξε δὲ λαβόντας τὰ ὅπλα καὶ τὰ σκεύη τοὺς
στρατιώτας ἐξιέναι, ὡς ἀποπέμψων τε ἅμα καὶ ἀριθμὸν ποιήσων. ἐνταῦθα οἱ στρατιῶται ἤχθοντο, ὅτι οὐκ
εἶχον ἀργύριον ἐπισιτίζεσθαι εἰς τὴν πορείαν, καὶ
8 ὀκνηρῶς συνεσκευάζοντο. καὶ ὁ Ξενοφῶν Κλεάνδρῳ
τῷ ἁρμοστῇ ξένος γεγενημένος προσελθὼν ἠσπάζετο
αὐτὸν ὡς ἀποπλευσούμενος ἤδη. ὁ δὲ αὐτῷ λέγει· Μὴ
ποιήσῃς ταῦτα· εἰ δὲ μή, ἔφη, αἰτίαν ἕξεις, ἐπεὶ καὶ
νῦν τινές ἤδη σὲ αἰτιῶνται ὅτι οὐ ταχὺ ἐξέρπει τὸ
9 στράτευμα. ὁ δ' εἶπεν· Ἀλλ' αἴτιος μὲν ἔγωγε οὐκ εἰμὶ
τούτου, οἱ δὲ στρατιῶται αὐτοὶ ἐπισιτισμοῦ δεόμενοι
10 διὰ τοῦτο ἀθυμοῦσι πρὸς τὴν ἔξοδον. Ἀλλ' ὅμως, ἔφη,
ἐγώ σοι συμβουλεύω ἐξελθεῖν μὲν ὡς πορευσόμενον,
ἐπειδὰν δ' ἔξω γένηται τὸ στράτευμα, τότε ἀπαλλάττεσθαι. Ταῦτα τοίνυν, ἔφη ὁ Ξενοφῶν, ἐλθόντες
πρὸς Ἀναξίβιον διαπραξόμεθα. οὕτως ἐλθόντες ἔλε-
11 γον ταῦτα. ὁ δὲ ἐκέλευεν οὕτω ποιεῖν καὶ ἐξιέναι τὴν

Xenophon and urged him to help him to bring the army across, adding that if he did render such assistance, he would not be sorry for it. Xenophon replied: "Why, the army is going to cross over; so far as that is concerned, let not Seuthes pay anything either to me or to any one else; but as soon as it has crossed, when I myself am to leave the army, let him deal with those who stay on and are in authority, in any way that may seem to him best."

After this all the soldiers crossed over to Byzantium. And Anaxibius would not give them pay, but made proclamation that the troops were to take their arms and their baggage and go forth from the city, saying that he was going to send them back home and at the same time to make an enumeration of them. At that the soldiers were angry, for they had no money with which to procure provisions for the journey, and they set about packing up with reluctance. Xenophon meanwhile, since he had become a friend of Cleander, the governor, called to take leave of him, saying that he was to sail home at once. And Cleander said to him: "Do not do so; if you do," said he, "you will be blamed, for even now certain people are laying it to your charge that the army is slow about moving away." Xenophon replied. "Why, I am not responsible for that; it is rather that the soldiers lack food supplies and on that account are depressed about their going away." "Nevertheless," said Cleander, "I advise you to go forth from the city as though you were planning to make a journey, and to leave them only when the army has got outside." "Well, then," said Xenophon, "we will go to Anaxibius and negotiate about this matter." So they went and put the question before him. His orders were, that Xenophon was to follow the course proposed and that the troops were to pack up and leave the

ταχίστην συσκευασαμένους, καὶ προσανεῖπεν, ὃς ἂν
μὴ παρῇ εἰς τὴν ἐξέτασιν καὶ εἰς τὸν ἀριθμόν, ὅτι
αὐτὸς αὑτὸν αἰτιάσεται.

12 Ἐντεῦθεν ἐξῆσαν οἵ τε στρατηγοὶ πρῶτοι καὶ οἱ
ἄλλοι. καὶ ἄρδην πάντες πλὴν ὀλίγων ἔξω ἦσαν, καὶ
Ἐτεόνικος εἱστήκει παρὰ τὰς πύλας ὡς ὁπότε ἔξω
γένοιντο πάντες συγκλείσων τὰς πύλας καὶ τὸν μο-
13 χλὸν ἐμβαλῶν. ὁ δὲ Ἀναξίβιος συγκαλέσας τοὺς
στρατηγοὺς καὶ τοὺς λοχαγοὺς ἔλεγεν· Τὰ μὲν ἐπιτήδεια, ἔφη, λαμβάνετε ἐκ τῶν Θρᾳκίων κωμῶν· εἰσὶ
δὲ αὐτόθι πολλαὶ κριθαὶ καὶ πυροὶ καὶ τἆλλα ἐπιτή-
δεια· λαβόντες δὲ πορεύεσθε εἰς Χερρόνησον, ἐκεῖ δὲ
14 Κυνίσκος ὑμῖν μισθοδοτήσει. ἐπακούσαντες δέ τινες
τῶν στρατιωτῶν ταῦτα, ἢ καὶ τῶν λοχαγῶν τις διαγ-
γέλλει εἰς τὸ στράτευμα. καὶ οἱ μὲν στρατηγοὶ
ἐπυνθάνοντο περὶ τοῦ Σεύθου πότερα πολέμιος εἴη ἢ
φίλος, καὶ πότερα διὰ τοῦ ἱεροῦ ὄρους δέοι πορεύεσθαι
15 ἢ κύκλῳ διὰ μέσης τῆς Θρᾴκης. ἐν ᾧ δὲ ταῦτα
διελέγοντο οἱ στρατιῶται ἀναρπάσαντες τὰ ὅπλα
θέουσι δρόμῳ πρὸς τὰς πύλας, ὡς πάλιν εἰς τὸ τεῖχος
εἰσιόντες. ὁ δὲ Ἐτεόνικος καὶ οἱ σὺν αὐτῷ ὡς εἶδον
προσθέοντας τοὺς ὁπλίτας, συγκλείουσι τὰς πύλας
16 καὶ τὸν μοχλὸν ἐμβάλλουσιν. οἱ δὲ στρατιῶται ἔκοπτον τὰς πύλας καὶ ἔλεγον ὅτι ἀδικώτατα πάσχοιεν

---

[4] A Lacedaemonian officer who figures rather prominently in
the story of the Peloponnesian war (*Hell.* I. i. 32, vi. 26, etc.); now
apparently an aide to Anaxibius.

city with all speed; and he further declared that any one who was not present for the review and the enumeration would have himself to blame for the consequences.

After that the army proceeded to march forth from the city, the generals at the head and then the rest. And now the entire body with the exception of a few men were outside, and Eteonicus[4] was standing by the gates ready, as soon as the last man got out, to close the gates and thrust in the crossbar. Then Anaxibius called together the generals and captains and said: "Get your provisions from the Thracian villages; there is an abundance there of barley and wheat and other supplies; when you have got them, proceed to the Chersonese, and there Cyniscus[5] will take you into his pay." And some of the soldiers, overhearing these words, or perhaps one of the captains, proceeded to spread the report of them through the army. Meanwhile the generals were inquiring about Seuthes, whether he was hostile or friendly, and whether they were to march by way of the Sacred Mountain[6] or go round through the middle of Thrace. While they were talking over these matters, the soldiers caught up their arms and rushed at full speed toward the gates, intending to get back inside the city wall. But when Eteonicus and his men saw the hoplites running towards them, they shut the gates and thrust in the bar. The soldiers, however, set to hammering at the gates, and said that they were most unjustly treated in

---

[5] A Lacedaemonian general engaged in war with the Thracians.   [6] On the northern coast of the Propontis. Their destination was the Gallipoli peninsula, and the alternative routes are a short but difficult one or a long, easy one.

ἐκβαλλόμενοι εἰς τοὺς πολεμίους· κατασχίσειν τε τὰς
17 πύλας ἔφασαν, εἰ μὴ ἑκόντες ἀνοίξουσιν. ἄλλοι δὲ
ἔθεον ἐπὶ θάλατταν καὶ παρὰ τὴν χηλὴν τοῦ τείχους
ὑπερβαίνουσιν εἰς τὴν πόλιν, ἄλλοι δὲ οἳ ἐτύγχανον
ἔνδον ὄντες τῶν στρατιωτῶν, ὡς ὁρῶσι τὰ ἐπὶ ταῖς
πύλαις πράγματα, διακόψαντες ταῖς ἀξίναις τὰ κλεῖ-
θρα ἀναπετανννύασι τὰς πύλας, οἱ δ' εἰσπίπτουσιν.
18 Ὁ δὲ Ξενοφῶν ὡς εἶδε τὰ γιγνόμενα, δείσας μὴ
ἐφ' ἁρπαγὴν τράποιτο τὸ στράτευμα καὶ ἀνήκεστα
κακὰ γένοιτο τῇ πόλει καὶ αὑτῷ καὶ τοῖς στρατιώταις,
ἔθει καὶ συνεισπίπτει εἴσω τῶν πυλῶν σὺν τῷ ὄχλῳ.
19 οἱ δὲ Βυζάντιοι ὡς εἶδον τὸ στράτευμα βίᾳ εἰσπῖπτον,
φεύγουσιν ἐκ τῆς ἀγορᾶς, οἱ μὲν εἰς τὰ πλοῖα, οἱ δὲ
οἴκαδε, ὅσοι δὲ ἔνδον ἐτύγχανον ὄντες, ἔξω, οἱ δὲ
καθεῖλκον τὰς τριήρεις, ὡς ἐν ταῖς τριήρεσι σῴζοιντο,
πάντες δὲ ᾤοντο ἀπολωλέναι, ὡς ἑαλωκυίας τῆς
20 πόλεως. ὁ δὲ Ἐτεόνικος εἰς τὴν ἄκραν ἀποφεύγει. ὁ
δὲ Ἀναξίβιος καταδραμὼν ἐπὶ θάλατταν ἐν ἁλιευτικῷ
πλοίῳ περιέπλει εἰς τὴν ἀκρόπολιν, καὶ εὐθὺς μεταπέμπεται ἐκ Καλχηδόνος φρουρούς· οὐ γὰρ ἱκανοὶ
ἐδόκουν εἶναι οἱ ἐν τῇ ἀκροπόλει σχεῖν τοὺς ἄνδρας.
21 Οἱ δὲ στρατιῶται ὡς εἶδον Ξενοφῶντα, προσπί-
πτουσι πολλοὶ αὐτῷ καὶ λέγουσι· Νῦν σοι ἔξεστιν, ὦ
Ξενοφῶν, ἀνδρὶ γενέσθαι. ἔχεις πόλιν, ἔχεις τριήρεις,
ἔχεις χρήματα, ἔχεις ἄνδρας τοσούτους. νῦν ἄν, εἰ

being cast out and left at the mercy of the enemy; and they declared that they would break through the gates if the keepers did not open them of their own accord. Meanwhile others ran down to the shore, made their way along the breakwater, and thus scaled the wall into the city, while still others, who chanced to be within the walls, seeing what was going on at the gates, cut through the bar with their axes and threw the gates open, whereupon the rest rushed in.

When Xenophon saw what was taking place, being seized with fear lest the army might fall to plundering and irreparable harm might be done to the city, to himself, and to the soldiers, he ran and rushed through the gates along with the rest of the throng. As for the Byzantines, no sooner did they see the army bursting in by force than they fled from the marketplace, some to their boats and others to their homes, while all who chanced to be indoors ran out, and some took to launching the ships-of-war in order to seek safety in them—all alike imagining that they were lost and the city captured. Eteonicus made his escape to the citadel. Anaxibius ran down to the shore, sailed round in a fishing boat to the citadel, and immediately summoned the garrison from Calchedon; for the force in the citadel did not seem adequate to bring the Greek troops under control.

As soon as the soldiers saw Xenophon, many of them rushed towards him and said: "Now is your opportunity, Xenophon, to prove yourself a man. You have a city, you have triremes, you have money, you have this great number of men.[7] Now, should you so wish, you would render us a

[7] Cf. Xen.'s thoughts at Cotyora, V. vi. 15.

βούλοιο, σύ τε ἡμᾶς ὀνήσαις καὶ ἡμεῖς σὲ μέγαν
22 ποιήσαιμεν. ὁ δ᾽ ἀπεκρίνατο, βουλόμενος αὐτοὺς κατ-
ηρεμίσαι.[2] Ἀλλ᾽ εὖ γε λέγετε καὶ ποιήσω ταῦτα· εἰ δὲ
τούτων ἐπιθυμεῖτε, θέσθε τὰ ὅπλα ἐν τάξει ὡς τάχιστα. καὶ αὐτός τε παρηγγύα ταῦτα καὶ τοὺς ἄλλους
23 ἐκέλευε παρεγγυᾶν τίθεσθαι τὰ ὅπλα. οἱ δὲ αὐτοὶ ὑφ᾽
ἑαυτῶν ταττόμενοι οἵ τε ὁπλῖται ἐν ὀλίγῳ χρόνῳ εἰς
ὀκτὼ ἐγένοντο καὶ οἱ πελτασταὶ ἐπὶ τὸ κέρας ἑκάτερον
24 παρεδεδραμήκεσαν. τὸ δὲ χωρίον οἷον κάλλιστον ἐκ-
τάξασθαί ἐστι τὸ Θρᾴκιον καλούμενον, ἔρημον οἰκιῶν
καὶ πεδινόν. ἐπεὶ δὲ ἔκειτο τὰ ὅπλα καὶ κατηρε-
μίσθησαν, συγκαλεῖ ὁ Ξενοφῶν τὴν στρατιὰν καὶ
25 λέγει τάδε. Ὅτι μὲν ὀργίζεσθε, ὦ ἄνδρες στρατιῶται,
καὶ νομίζετε δεινὰ πάσχειν ἐξαπατώμενοι οὐ θαυμάζω.
ἢν δὲ τῷ θυμῷ χαριζώμεθα καὶ Λακεδαιμονίους τε
τοὺς παρόντας τῆς ἐξαπάτης τιμωρησώμεθα καὶ τὴν
πόλιν τὴν οὐδὲν αἰτίαν διαρπάσωμεν, ἐνθυμήθητε ἃ
26 ἔσται ἐντεῦθεν. πολέμιοι μὲν ἐσόμεθα ἀποδεδειγμένοι
Λακεδαιμονίοις τε καὶ τοῖς συμμάχοις. οἷος δ᾽ ὁ πόλεμος ἂν γένοιτο εἰκάζειν δὴ πάρεστιν, ἑορακότας καὶ
27 ἀναμνησθέντας τὰ νῦν δὴ γεγενημένα. ἡμεῖς γὰρ οἱ
Ἀθηναῖοι ἤλθομεν εἰς τὸν πόλεμον τὸν πρὸς Λακεδαιμονίους καὶ τοὺς συμμάχους ἔχοντες τριήρεις τὰς
μὲν ἐν θαλάττῃ τὰς δ᾽ ἐν τοῖς νεωρίοις οὐκ ἐλάττους
τριακοσίων, ὑπαρχόντων δὲ πολλῶν χρημάτων ἐν τῇ

---

[2] βουλόμενος . . . κατηρείμσαι stands in the MSS. after ὡς
τάχιστα: transposed by Schenkl, whom Gem. and Peters follow.

service and we should make you great." He replied, desiring to quiet them down: "Your advice is certainly good, and I shall do as you say; but if this is what you long for, ground your arms in line of battle with all speed." Then he proceeded to pass along this order himself and bade the others send it on—to ground their arms in battle line. The men acted as their own marshals, and within a short time the hoplites had fallen into line eight deep and the peltasts had got into position on either wing. The place where they were, indeed, is a most excellent one for drawing out a line of troops, being the so-called Thracian Square,[8] which is free of houses and level. As soon as their arms were grounded and they had quieted down, Xenophon called the troops together and spoke as follows: "That you are angry, fellow soldiers, and believe you are outrageously treated in being so deceived, I do not wonder. But if we indulge our anger, by taking vengeance for this deception upon the Lacedaemonians who are here and by sacking the city which is in no way to blame, consider the results that will follow. We shall be declared to be at war with the Lacedaemonians and their allies. And what sort of a war that would prove to be one may at least conjecture by having seen and by recalling to mind the events which have quite lately taken place. We Athenians, remember, entered upon our war against the Lacedaemonians and their allies with no fewer than three hundred triremes, some afloat and others in the dockyards, with an abundance of treasure

[8] Cf. Cassius Dio LXXIV. xiv. 5 (Boissevain).

πόλει καὶ προσόδου οὔσης κατ᾽ ἐνιαυτὸν ἀπό τε τῶν
ἐνδήμων καὶ ἐκ τῆς ὑπερορίας οὐ μεῖον χιλίων ταλάν-
των· ἄρχοντες δὲ τῶν νήσων ἁπασῶν καὶ ἔν τε τῇ
Ἀσίᾳ πολλὰς ἔχοντες πόλεις καὶ ἐν τῇ Εὐρώπῃ ἄλλας
τε πολλὰς καὶ αὐτὸ τοῦτο τὸ Βυζάντιον, ὅπου νῦν
ἐσμεν, ἔχοντες κατεπολεμήθημεν οὕτως ὡς πάντες
28 ὑμεῖς ἐπίστασθε. νῦν δὲ δὴ τί ἂν οἰόμεθα παθεῖν,
Λακεδαιμονίοις μὲν καὶ τῶν ἀρχαίων συμμάχων ὑπαρχόντων, Ἀθηναίων δὲ καὶ ὅσοι ἐκείνοις τότε ἦσαν
σύμμαχοι πάντων προσγεγενημένων, Τισσαφέρνους
δὲ καὶ τῶν ἐπὶ θαλάττῃ ἄλλων βαρβάρων πάντων
πολεμίων ἡμῖν ὄντων, πολεμιωτάτου δὲ αὐτοῦ τοῦ ἄνω
βασιλέως, ὃν ἤλθομεν ἀφαιρησόμενοί τε τὴν ἀρχὴν
καὶ ἀποκτενοῦντες, εἰ δυναίμεθα; τούτων δὴ πάντων
ὁμοῦ ὄντων ἔστι τις οὕτως ἄφρων ὅστις οἴεται ἂν ἡμᾶς
29 περιγενέσθαι; μὴ πρὸς θεῶν μαινώμεθα μηδ᾽ αἰσχρῶς
ἀπολώμεθα πολέμιοι ὄντες καὶ ταῖς πατρίσι καὶ τοῖς
ἡμετέροις αὐτῶν φίλοις τε καὶ οἰκείοις. ἐν γὰρ ταῖς
πόλεσίν εἰσι πάντες ταῖς ἐφ᾽ ἡμᾶς στρατευσομέναις,
καὶ δικαίως, εἰ βάρβαρον μὲν πόλιν οὐδεμίαν ἠθελή-
σαμεν κατασχεῖν, καὶ ταῦτα κρατοῦντες, Ἑλληνίδα δὲ
εἰς ἣν πρώτην ἤλθομεν πόλιν, ταύτην ἐξαλαπάξομεν.
30 ἐγὼ μὲν τοίνυν εὔχομαι πρὶν ταῦτα ἐπιδεῖν ὑφ᾽ ὑμῶν
γενόμενα μυρίας ἐμέ γε κατὰ τῆς γῆς ὀργυιὰς γενέσθαι. καὶ ὑμῖν δὲ συμβουλεύω Ἕλληνας ὄντας τοῖς
τῶν Ἑλλήνων προεστηκόσι πειθομένους πειρᾶσθαι
τῶν δικαίων τυγχάνειν. ἐὰν δὲ μὴ δύνησθε ταῦτα,
ἡμᾶς δεῖ ἀδικουμένους τῆς γοῦν Ἑλλάδος μὴ στέρε-

already at hand in our city, and with a yearly revenue, accruing at home or coming in from our foreign possessions, of not less than a thousand talents;[9] we ruled over all the islands, we possessed many cities in Asia, in Europe we possessed among many others this very city of Byzantium also, where we now are—and we were vanquished, in the way that all of you remember. What fate, then, may you and I expect to suffer now, when the Lacedaemonians still have their old allies, when the Athenians and all who at that time were allied with them have been added to the number, when Tissaphernes and all the rest of the barbarians on the coast are hostile to us, and most hostile of all the King himself, up in the interior, the man whom we came to deprive of his empire, and to kill if we could? With all these banded together against us, is there any man so witless as to suppose that we should come off victorious? In the name of the gods let us not be mad, nor let us perish disgracefully as enemies both to our native states and to our own friends and kinsmen. For all of them are in the cities which will take the field against us, and will do so justly if we, after refraining from the seizure of any barbarian city, conquerors though we were, are to take the first Greek city we have come to and pillage that. For my part, therefore, I pray that sooner than live to behold this deed wrought by you, I may be laid ten thousand fathoms underground. And to you my advice is, that being Greeks you endeavour to obtain your just rights by obedience to the leaders of the Greeks. If you are unable to accomplish this, we must not at any rate, even though wronged, be deprived of our return to Greece. And now it is my opinion that we

[9] Cf. Thuc. II. xiii. 3, Gomme, *Hist. Comm. Thuc.* (Oxford, 1956) II, 19.

31 σθαι. καὶ νῦν μοι δοκεῖ πέμψαντας Ἀναξιβίῳ εἰπεῖν
ὅτι ἡμεῖς οὐδὲν βίαιον ποιήσοντες παρεληλύθαμεν εἰς
τὴν πόλιν, ἀλλ' ἢν μὲν δυνώμεθα παρ' ὑμῶν ἀγαθόν
τι εὑρίσκεσθαι, εἰ δὲ μή, ἀλλὰ δηλώσοντες ὅτι οὐκ
ἐξαπατώμενοι ἀλλὰ πειθόμενοι ἐξερχόμεθα.

32   Ταῦτα ἔδοξε, καὶ πέμπουσιν Ἱερώνυμόν τε Ἠλεῖον
ἐροῦντα ταῦτα καὶ Εὐρύλοχον Λουσιέα³ καὶ Φιλήσιον
Ἀχαιόν. οἱ μὲν ταῦτα ᾤχοντο ἐροῦντες.

33   Ἔτι δὲ καθημένων τῶν στρατιωτῶν προσέρχεται
Κοιρατάδας Θηβαῖος, ὃς οὐ φεύγων τὴν Ἑλλάδα
περιῄει ἀλλὰ στρατηγιῶν καὶ ἐπαγγελλόμενος, εἴ τις
ἢ πόλις ἢ ἔθνος στρατηγοῦ δέοιτο· καὶ τότε προσελθὼν ἔλεγεν ὅτι ἕτοιμος εἴη ἡγεῖσθαι αὐτοῖς εἰς τὸ
Δέλτα καλούμενον τῆς Θρᾴκης, ἔνθα πολλὰ καὶ ἀγαθὰ λήψοιντο· ἔστε δ' ἂν μόλωσιν, εἰς ἀφθονίαν παρ-

34 έξειν ἔφη καὶ σῖτα καὶ ποτά. ἀκούουσι ταῦτα τοῖς
στρατιώταις καὶ τὰ παρὰ Ἀναξιβίου ἅμα ἐπαγγελλό-
μενα—ἀπεκρίνατο γὰρ ὅτι πειθομένοις αὐτοῖς οὐ
μεταμελήσει, ἀλλὰ τοῖς τε οἴκοι τέλεσι ταῦτα ἀπαγ-
γελεῖ καὶ αὐτὸς βουλεύσοιτο περὶ αὐτῶν ὅ τι δύναιτο

35 ἀγαθόν—ἐκ τούτου οἱ στρατιῶται τόν τε Κοιρατάδαν
δέχονται στρατηγὸν καὶ ἔξω τοῦ τείχους ἀπῆλθον. ὁ
δὲ Κοιρατάδας συντίθεται αὐτοῖς εἰς τὴν ὑστεραίαν
παρέσεσθαι ἐπὶ τὸ στράτευμα ἔχων καὶ ἱερεῖα καὶ

36 μάντιν καὶ σῖτα καὶ ποτὰ τῇ στρατιᾷ. ἐπεὶ δὲ ἐξῆλθον,

---

³ Λουσιέα reading of one MS., Peters: Ἀρκάδα the other
MSS., Gem., Hude, Mar.

should send messengers to Anaxibius and say to him: 'We have not made our way into the city to do any violence, but to obtain some good thing from you if we can, or if that is not possible, at least to show that we go forth, not because we are deceived, but because we are obedient.'"

This course was resolved upon, and they sent Hieronymus the Elean, Eurylochus the Lusian, and Philesius the Achaean to bear this message. So they departed to perform their mission.

While the soldiers were still in session Coeratadas the Theban came in, a man who was going up and down Greece, not in exile, but because he was afflicted with a desire to be a general, and he was offering his services to any city or people that might be wanting a general; so at this time he came to the troops and said that he was ready to lead them to the Delta,[10] as it is called, of Thrace, where they could get plenty of good things; and until they should reach there, he said he would supply them with food and drink in abundance. When the soldiers heard this proposal and the word that came back at the same time from Anaxibius—his reply was, that if they were obedient they would not be sorry for it, but that he would report the matter to his government at home and would himself devise whatever good counsel he could in their case—they thereupon accepted Coeratadas as general and withdrew outside the walls. And Coeratadas made an agreement with them that he would join the army the next day with sacrificial victims and a soothsayer, as well as food and drink for the troops. Meanwhile, as soon as they had gone forth from

[10] Probably the triangular peninsula lying between the Euxine, the Bosporus, and the Propontis.

ὁ Ἀναξίβιος ἔκλεισέ τε τὰς πύλας καὶ ἐκήρυξεν ὅστις
37 ἂν ἁλῷ ἔνδον ὢν τῶν στρατιωτῶν ὅτι πεπράσεται. τῇ
δ᾽ ὑστεραίᾳ Κοιρατάδας μὲν ἔχων τὰ ἱερεῖα καὶ τὸν
μάντιν ἧκε καὶ ἄλφιτα φέροντες εἵποντο αὐτῷ εἴκοσιν
ἄνδρες καὶ οἶνον ἄλλοι εἴκοσι καὶ ἐλαῶν τρεῖς καὶ
σκορόδων ἀνὴρ ὅσον ἐδύνατο μέγιστον φορτίον καὶ
ἄλλος κρομμύων. ταῦτα δὲ καταθέμενος ὡς ἐπὶ
δάσμευσιν ἐθύετο.

38   Ξενοφῶν δὲ μεταπεμψάμενος Κλέανδρον ἐκέλευέν
οἱ διαπρᾶξαι ὅπως εἰς τὸ τεῖχος εἰσέλθοι καὶ ἀποπλεύ-
39 σαι ἐκ Βυζαντίου. ἐλθὼν δ᾽ ὁ Κλέανδρος, Μάλα μόλις,
ἔφη, διαπραξάμενος ἥκω· λέγειν γὰρ Ἀναξίβιον ὅτι
οὐκ ἐπιτήδειον εἴη τοὺς μὲν στρατιώτας πλησίον εἶναι
τοῦ τείχους, Ξενοφῶντα δὲ ἔνδον· τοὺς Βυζαντίους δὲ
στασιάζειν καὶ πονηροὺς εἶναι πρὸς ἀλλήλους· ὅμως
δὲ εἰσιέναι, ἔφη, ἐκέλευεν, εἰ μέλλοις σὺν αὐτῷ ἐκ-
40 πλεῖν. ὁ μὲν δὴ Ξενοφῶν ἀσπασάμενος τοὺς στρατιώτας εἴσω τοῦ τείχους ἀπῄει σὺν Κλεάνδρῳ. ὁ δὲ
Κοιρατάδας τῇ μὲν πρώτῃ ἡμέρᾳ οὐκ ἐκαλλιέρει οὐδὲ
διεμέτρησεν οὐδὲν τοῖς στρατιώταις· τῇ δ᾽ ὑστεραίᾳ
τὰ μὲν ἱερεῖα εἱστήκει παρὰ τὸν βωμὸν καὶ Κοιρατάδας ἐστεφανωμένος ὡς θύσων· προσελθὼν δὲ
Τιμασίων ὁ Δαρδανεὺς καὶ Νέων ὁ Ἀσιναῖος καὶ
Κλεάνωρ ὁ Ὀρχομένιος ἔλεγον Κοιρατάδᾳ μὴ θύειν,
ὡς οὐχ ἡγησόμενον τῇ στρατιᾷ, εἰ μὴ δώσει τὰ
41 ἐπιτήδεια. ὁ δὲ κελεύει διαμετρεῖσθαι. ἐπεὶ δὲ πολλῶν
ἐνέδει αὐτῷ ὥστε ἡμέρας σῖτον ἑκάστῳ γενέσθαι τῶν
στρατιωτῶν, ἀναλαβὼν τὰ ἱερεῖα ἀπῄει καὶ τὴν στρα-

the city, Anaxibius closed the gates and made proclamation
that any soldier who might be caught inside the city would
be sold as a slave. On the next day Coeratadas arrived with
his sacrificial victims and his soothsayer, and there followed him twenty men loaded with barley-meal, another
twenty with wine, three with olives, another man with as
big a load of garlic as he could carry, and another with
onions. After setting down all these things, as though for
distribution, he proceeded to sacrifice.

And now Xenophon sent for Cleander and bid him to
make arrangements so that he could enter within the wall
and thus sail homeward from Byzantium. When Cleander
returned, he said "it was only with very great difficulty that
I accomplished the arrangement and have come; for
Anaxibius said it was not well to have the soldiers close by
the wall and Xenophon within it; the Byzantines, moreover, were in a factious state and hostile to one another.
Nevertheless," Cleander continued, "he bade you come in
if you are intending to sail away with him." Xenophon
accordingly took his leave of the soldiers and went back
within the wall in company with Cleander. As for Coeratadas, on the first day he could not get good omens from
his sacrifices nor did he serve out any rations at all to the
troops; on the following day the victims were standing beside the altar and Coeratadas had on his chaplet, ready for
the sacrifice, when Timasion the Dardanian, Neon the Asinaean, and Cleanor the Orchomenian came up and told
him not to make the offering, for he was not to be leader
of the army unless he should give them provisions. So he
ordered rations to be served out. When it proved, however,
that his supply fell far short of amounting to a day's food
for each of the soldiers, he took his victims and went away,

553

XENOPHON

τηγίαν ἀπειπών.

II. Νέων δὲ ὁ Ἀσιναῖος καὶ Φρυνίσκος ὁ Ἀχαιὸς
καὶ Φιλήσιος ὁ Ἀχαιὸς καὶ Ξανθικλῆς ὁ Ἀχαιὸς καὶ
Τιμασίων ὁ Δαρδανεὺς ἐπέμενον ἐπὶ τῇ στρατιᾷ, καὶ
εἰς κώμας τῶν Θρᾳκῶν προελθόντες τὰς κατὰ Βυζάν-
2 τιον ἐστρατοπεδεύοντο. καὶ οἱ στρατηγοὶ ἐστασίαζον,
Κλεάνωρ μὲν καὶ Φρυνίσκος πρὸς Σεύθην βουλόμενοι
ἄγειν· ἔπειθε γὰρ αὐτούς, καὶ ἔδωκε τῷ μὲν ἵππον, τῷ
δὲ γυναῖκα· Νέων δὲ εἰς Χερρόνησον, οἰόμενος, εἰ ὑπὸ
Λακεδαιμονίοις γένοιτο, παντὸς ἂν προεστάναι τοῦ
στρατεύματος· Τιμασίων δὲ προυθυμεῖτο πέραν εἰς
τὴν Ἀσίαν πάλιν διαβῆναι, οἰόμενος ἂν οἴκαδε κατελ-
3 θεῖν· καὶ οἱ στρατιῶται ταὐτὰ ἐβούλοντο. διατριβομέ-
νου δὲ τοῦ χρόνου πολλοὶ τῶν στρατιωτῶν, οἱ μὲν τὰ
ὅπλα ἀποδιδόμενοι κατὰ τοὺς χώρους ἀπέπλεον ὡς
ἐδύναντο, οἱ δὲ καὶ εἰς τὰς πόλεις κατεμείγνυντο.
4 Ἀναξίβιος δ᾽ ἔχαιρε ταῦτα ἀκούων, διαφθειρόμενον τὸ
στράτευμα· τούτων γὰρ γιγνομένων ᾤετο μάλιστα
χαρίζεσθαι Φαρναβάζῳ.

5 Ἀποπλέοντι δὲ Ἀναξιβίῳ ἐκ Βυζαντίου συναντᾷ
Ἀρίσταρχος ἐν Κυζίκῳ διάδοχος Κλεάνδρῳ Βυζαντίου
ἁρμοστής· ἐλέγετο δὲ ὅτι καὶ ναύαρχος διάδοχος
6 Πῶλος ὅσον οὐ παρείη ἤδη εἰς Ἑλλήσποντον. καὶ ὁ
Ἀναξίβιος τῷ μὲν Ἀριστάρχῳ ἐπιστέλλει ὁπόσους ἂν
εὕρῃ ἐν Βυζαντίῳ τῶν Κύρου στρατιωτῶν ὑπολελειμ-

---

[11] Cf. i. 13 and note thereon.   [12] *i.e.* since he was the only
Lacedaemonian among the generals.

renouncing his generalship.

II. There now remained in command of the army Neon the Asinaean, Phryniscus the Achaean, Philesius the Achaean, Xanthicles the Achaean, and Timasion the Dardanian, and they proceeded to some villages of the Thracians which were near Byzantium and there encamped. Now the generals were at variance in their views : Cleanor and Phryniscus wanted to lead the army to Seuthes, for he had been trying to persuade them to this course and had given one of them a horse and the other a woman; Neon wanted to go to the Chersonese,[11] thinking that if the troops should fall under the control of the Lacedaemonians, he would be leader of the entire army;[12] and Timasion was eager to cross back again to Asia, for he thought that in this way he could accomplish his return home.[13] As for the troops, to return home was what they also desired. As time wore on, however, many of the soldiers either sold their arms up and down the country and set sail for home in any way they could, or else mingled with the people of the neighbouring Greek cities. And Anaxibius was glad to hear the news that the army was breaking up; for he thought that if this process went on, Pharnabazus would be very greatly pleased.

While Anaxibius was on his homeward voyage from Byzantium, he was met at Cyzicus by Aristarchus, Cleander's successor as governor of Byzantium; and it was reported that his own successor as admiral, Polus, had by this time all but reached the Hellespont. Anaxibius, then, charged Aristarchus to sell as slaves all the soldiers of Cyrus' army that he might find left behind at Byzantium.

[13] Cf. V. vi. 23.

μένους ἀποδόσθαι· ὁ δὲ Κλέανδρος οὐδένα ἐπεπράκει,
ἀλλὰ καὶ τοὺς κάμνοντας ἐθεράπευεν οἰκτίρων καὶ
ἀναγκάζων οἰκίᾳ δέχεσθαι· Ἀρίσταρχος δ' ἐπεὶ ἦλθε

7 τάχιστα, οὐκ ἐλάττους τετρακοσίων ἀπέδοτο. Ἀναξίβιος δὲ παραπλεύσας εἰς Πάριον πέμπει παρὰ Φαρνάβαζον κατὰ τὰ συγκείμενα. ὁ δ' ἐπεὶ ᾔσθετο Ἀρίσταρ-
χόν τε ἥκοντα εἰς Βυζάντιον ἁρμοστὴν καὶ Ἀναξίβιον
οὐκέτι ναυαρχοῦντα, Ἀναξιβίου μὲν ἠμέλησε, πρὸς
Ἀρίσταρχον δὲ διεπράττετο τὰ αὐτὰ περὶ τοῦ Κύρου
στρατεύματος ἅπερ καὶ πρὸς Ἀναξίβιον.

8   Ἐκ τούτου ὁ Ἀναξίβιος καλέσας Ξενοφῶντα κελεύει πάσῃ τέχνῃ καὶ μηχανῇ πλεῦσαι ἐπὶ τὸ στράτευμα
ὡς τάχιστα, καὶ συνέχειν τε αὐτὸ καὶ συναθροίζειν
τῶν διεσπαρμένων ὡς ἂν πλείστους δύνηται, καὶ
παραγαγόντα εἰς τὴν Πέρινθον διαβιβάζειν εἰς τὴν
Ἀσίαν ὅτι τάχιστα· καὶ δίδωσιν αὐτῷ τριακόντορον
καὶ ἐπιστολὴν καὶ ἄνδρα συμπέμπει κελεύσοντα τοὺς
Περινθίους ὡς τάχιστα Ξενοφῶντα προπέμψαι τοῖς

9   ἵπποις ἐπὶ τὸ στράτευμα. καὶ ὁ μὲν Ξενοφῶν δια-
πλεύσας ἀφικνεῖται ἐπὶ τὸ στράτευμα· οἱ δὲ στρατιῶται ἐδέξαντο ἡδέως καὶ εὐθὺς εἵποντο ἄσμενοι ὡς
διαβησόμενοι ἐκ τῆς Θρᾴκης εἰς τὴν Ἀσίαν.

10   Ὁ δὲ Σεύθης ἀκούσας ἥκοντα πάλιν πέμψας πρὸς
αὐτὸν κατὰ θάλατταν Μηδοσάδην ἐδεῖτο τὴν στρατιὰν ἄγειν πρὸς ἑαυτόν, ὑπισχνούμενος αὐτῷ ὅ τι ᾤετο

---

14 Cf. i. 2.   15 Who was manifestly making the voyage with
him. cf. i. 39 above.

As for Cleander, he had not sold one of them, but had even been caring for their sick out of pity and compelling the Byzantines to receive them in their houses; but the moment Aristarchus arrived he sold no fewer than four hundred. When Anaxibius had coasted along to Parium, he sent to Pharnabazus, according to the terms of their agreement.[14] As soon as Pharnabazus learned, however, that Aristarchus had come to Byzantium as governor and that Anaxibius was no longer admiral, he paid no heed to Anaxibius, but set about making the same arrangement with Aristarchus in regard to Cyrus' army as he had also had with Anaxibius.

Thereupon Anaxibius summoned Xenophon[15] and urged him by all manner of means to set sail as quickly as possible and join the army, and not only to keep it together, but likewise to collect the greatest number he could of those who had become scattered from the main body, and then, after leading the entire force along the coast to Perinthus,[16] to take it across to Asia with all speed; he also gave him a thirty-oared warship and a letter, and sent with him a man who was to order the Perinthians to furnish Xenophon with horses and speed him on his way to the army as rapidly as possible. So Xenophon sailed across to Perinthus and then made his way to the army; and the soldiers received him with pleasure, and were glad to follow his lead at once, with the idea of crossing over from Thrace to Asia.

Meanwhile Seuthes,[17] upon hearing of Xenophon's arrival, sent Medosades to him again by sea, and begged him to bring the army to him, offering any promise whereby he

16 On the European shore of the Propontis.
17 See below, n. to §34.

λέγων πείσειν. ὁ δ' ἀπεκρίνατο ὅτι οὐδὲν οἷόν τε εἴη
11 τούτων γενέσθαι. καὶ ὁ μὲν ταῦτα ἀκούσας ᾤχετο. οἱ
δὲ Ἕλληνες ἐπεὶ ἀφίκοντο εἰς Πέρινθον, Νέων μὲν
ἀποσπάσας ἐστρατοπεδεύσατο χωρὶς ἔχων ὡς ὀκτακοσίους ἀνθρώπους· τὸ δ' ἄλλο στράτευμα πᾶν ἐν τῷ
αὐτῷ παρὰ τὸ τεῖχος τὸ Περινθίων ἦν.

12 Μετὰ ταῦτα Ξενοφῶν μὲν ἔπραττε περὶ πλοίων,
ὅπως ὅτι τάχιστα διαβαῖεν. ἐν δὲ τούτῳ ἀφικόμενος
Ἀρίσταρχος ὁ ἐκ Βυζαντίου ἁρμοστής, ἔχων δύο τριήρεις, πεπεισμένος ὑπὸ Φαρναβάζου τοῖς τε ναυκλή-
ροις ἀπεῖπε μὴ διάγειν ἐλθών τε ἐπὶ τὸ στράτευμα
τοῖς στρατιώταις εἶπε μὴ περαιοῦσθαι εἰς τὴν Ἀσίαν.

13 ὁ δὲ Ξενοφῶν ἔλεγεν ὅτι Ἀναξίβιος ἐκέλευσε καὶ ἐμὲ
πρὸς τοῦτο ἔπεμψεν ἐνθάδε. πάλιν δ' Ἀρίσταρχος
ἔλεξεν· Ἀναξίβιος μὲν τοίνυν οὐκέτι ναύαρχος, ἐγὼ δὲ
τῇδε ἁρμοστής· εἰ δέ τινα ὑμῶν λήψομαι ἐν τῇ
θαλάττῃ, καταδύσω. ταῦτ' εἰπὼν ᾤχετο εἰς τὸ τεῖχος.
τῇ δ' ὑστεραίᾳ μεταπέμπεται τοὺς στρατηγοὺς καὶ
14 λοχαγοὺς τοῦ στρατεύματος. ἤδη δὲ ὄντων πρὸς τῷ
τείχει ἐξαγγέλλει τις τῷ Ξενοφῶντι ὅτι εἰ εἴσεισι,
συλληφθήσεται καὶ ἢ αὐτοῦ τι πείσεται ἢ καὶ Φαρναβάζῳ παραδοθήσεται. ὁ δὲ ἀκούσας ταῦτα τοὺς μὲν
προπέμπεται, αὐτὸς δὲ εἶπεν ὅτι θῦσαί τι βούλοιτο.
15 καὶ ἀπελθὼν ἐθύετο εἰ παρεῖεν αὐτῷ οἱ θεοὶ πειρᾶσθαι
πρὸς Σεύθην ἄγειν τὸ στράτευμα. ἑώρα γὰρ οὔτε
διαβαίνειν ἀσφαλὲς ὂν τριήρεις ἔχοντος τοῦ κωλύσον-

imagined he could persuade him. Xenophon replied that it was not possible for anything of this sort to come to pass, and upon receiving this answer Medosades departed. As for the Greeks, when they reached Perinthus, Neon with about eight hundred men parted company with the others and took up a separate camp; but all the rest of the army were together in the same place, beside the wall of the Perinthians.

After this Xenophon proceeded to negotiate for ships, in order that they might cross over with all possible speed. But meantime Aristarchus, the governor at Byzantium, arrived with two triremes and, having been persuaded to this course by Pharnabazus, not only forbade the shipmasters to carry the army across, but came to the camp and told the soldiers not to pass over into Asia. Xenophon replied, "Anaxibius so ordered, and sent me here for that purpose." And Aristarchus retorted, "Anaxibius, mark you, is no longer admiral, and I am governor here; if I catch any one of you on the sea, I will sink him." With these words he departed within the walls of Perinthus. On the next day he sent for the generals and captains of the army. When they were already near the wall, some one brought word to Xenophon that if he went in he would be seized, and would either meet some ill fate then and there or else be delivered over to Pharnabazus. Upon hearing this he sent the rest on ahead, telling them that he was desirous himself of offering a certain sacrifice. Then he went back and sacrificed to learn whether the gods permitted of his endeavouring to take the army to Seuthes. For he saw that it was not safe for them to try to cross over to Asia when the man who intended to prevent their passage possessed triremes; on the other hand, it was not his desire that the

τος, οὔτ᾽ ἐπὶ Χερρόνησον ἐλθὼν κατακλεισθῆναι
ἐβούλετο καὶ τὸ στράτευμα ἐν πολλῇ σπάνει πάντων
γενέσθαι ἔνθα πείθεσθαι μὲν ἀνάγκῃ τῷ ἐκεῖ ἁρμοστῇ, τῶν δ᾽ ἐπιτηδείων οὐδὲν ἔμελλεν ἕξειν τὸ στράτευμα.

16   Καὶ ὁ μὲν ἀμφὶ ταῦτ᾽ εἶχεν· οἱ δὲ στρατηγοὶ καὶ
[οἱ] λοχαγοὶ ἥκοντες παρὰ τοῦ Ἀριστάρχου ἀπήγγελλον ὅτι νῦν μὲν ἀπιέναι σφᾶς κελεύοι, τῆς δείλης δὲ
17   ἥκειν· ἔνθα καὶ δήλη μᾶλλον ἐδόκει ἡ ἐπιβουλή. ὁ οὖν
Ξενοφῶν, ἐπεὶ ἐδόκει τὰ ἱερὰ καλὰ εἶναι αὐτῷ καὶ τῷ
στρατεύματι ἀσφαλῶς πρὸς Σεύθην ἰέναι, παραλαβὼν
Πολυκράτη τὸν Ἀθηναῖον λοχαγὸν καὶ παρὰ τῶν
στρατηγῶν ἑκάστου ἄνδρα—πλὴν παρὰ Νέωνος—ᾧ
ἕκαστος ἐπίστευεν ᾤχετο τῆς νυκτὸς ἐπὶ τὸ Σεύθου
18   στράτευμα ἑξήκοντα στάδια. ἐπεὶ δ᾽ ἐγγὺς ἦσαν
αὐτοῦ, ἐπιτυγχάνει πυροῖς ἐρήμοις. καὶ τὸ μὲν πρῶτον
ᾤετο μετακεχωρηκέναι ποι τὸν Σεύθην· ἐπεὶ δὲ θορύβου τε ᾔσθετο καὶ σημαινόντων ἀλλήλοις τῶν περὶ
Σεύθην, κατέμαθεν ὅτι τούτου ἕνεκα τὰ πυρὰ κεκαυ-
μένα εἴη τῷ Σεύθῃ πρὸ τῶν νυκτοφυλάκων, ὅπως οἱ
μὲν φύλακες μὴ ὁρῷντο ἐν τῷ σκότει ὄντες μήτε
ὁπόσοι μήτε ὅπου εἶεν, οἱ δὲ προσιόντες μὴ λανθά-
νοιεν, ἀλλὰ διὰ τὸ φῶς καταφανεῖς εἶεν.

19   Ἐπεὶ δὲ ᾔσθετο, προπέμπει τὸν ἑρμηνέα ὃν ἐτύγχανεν ἔχων, καὶ εἰπεῖν κελεύει Σεύθῃ ὅτι Ξενοφῶν
πάρεστι βουλόμενος συγγενέσθαι αὐτῷ. οἱ δὲ ἤροντο
20   εἰ ὁ Ἀθηναῖος ὁ ἀπὸ τοῦ στρατεύματος. ἐπειδὴ δὲ ἔφη
οὗτος εἶναι, ἀναπηδήσαντες ἐδίωκον· καὶ ὀλίγον ὕστε-

army should go to the Chersonese and find itself shut up and in sore need of everything in a place where it would be necessary to obey the resident governor and where the army would not obtain anything in the way of provisions.

While Xenophon was occupied with his sacrificing, the generals and captains returned from their visit to Aristarchus with word that he directed them to go away for the present, but to come back during the afternoon; at that report the design against Xenophon seemed to be even more manifest. Since, therefore, the sacrifices appeared to be favourable, portending that he and the army might go to Seuthes in safety, Xenophon took Polycrates, the Athenian captain, and from each of the generals except Neon a man in whom each had confidence, and set off by night to visit Seuthes' army, sixty stadia away. When they had got near it, he came upon watch-fires with no one about them. And at first he supposed that Seuthes had shifted his camp to some other place; but when he became aware of a general uproar and heard Seuthes' followers signalling to one another, he comprehended that the reason Seuthes had his watch-fires kindled in front of the pickets was in order that the pickets might remain unseen, in the darkness as they were, so that no one could tell either how many they were or where they were, while on the other hand people who were approaching could not escape notice, but would be visible in the light of the fires.

When he did see pickets, he sent forward the interpreter he chanced to have and bade them tell Seuthes that Xenophon had come and desired to meet with him. They asked whether he was the Athenian, the one from the army, and when Xenophon made reply that he was the man, they leaped up and hastened off; and a little afterwards about

ρον παρῆσαν πελτασταὶ ὅσον διακόσιοι, καὶ παραλαβόντες Ξενοφῶντα καὶ τοὺς σὺν αὐτῷ ἦγον πρὸς
21 Σεύθην. ὁ δ᾽ ἦν ἐν τύρσει μάλα φυλαττόμενος, καὶ
ἵπποι περὶ αὐτὴν κύκλῳ ἐγκεχαλινωμένοι· διὰ γὰρ τὸν
φόβον τὰς μὲν ἡμέρας ἐχίλου τοὺς ἵππους, τὰς δὲ
22 νύκτας ἐγκεχαλινωμένοις ἐφυλάττετο. ἐλέγετο γὰρ καὶ
πρόσθεν Τήρης ὁ τούτου πρόγονος ἐν ταύτῃ τῇ χώρᾳ
πολὺ ἔχων στράτευμα ὑπὸ τούτων τῶν ἀνδρῶν πολλοὺς ἀπολέσαι καὶ τὰ σκευοφόρα ἀφαιρεθῆναι· ἦσαν
δ᾽ οὗτοι Θυνοί, πάντων λεγόμενοι εἶναι μάλιστα νυκτὸς πολεμικώτατοι.

23 Ἐπεὶ δ᾽ ἐγγὺς ἦσαν, ἐκέλευσεν εἰσελθεῖν Ξενοφῶντα ἔχοντα δύο οὓς βούλοιτο. ἐπειδὴ δ᾽ ἔνδον ἦσαν,
ἠσπάζοντο μὲν πρῶτον ἀλλήλους καὶ κατὰ τὸν Θρᾴκιον νόμον κέρατα οἴνου προύπινον· παρῆν δὲ καὶ
Μηδοσάδης τῷ Σεύθῃ, ὅσπερ ἐπρέσβευεν αὐτῷ πάν-
24 τοσε. ἔπειτα δὲ Ξενοφῶν ἤρχετο λέγειν· Ἔπεμψας
πρὸς ἐμέ, ὦ Σεύθη, εἰς Καλχηδόνα πρῶτον Μηδοσάδην τουτονί, δεόμενός μου συμπροθυμηθῆναι διαβῆναι τὸ στράτευμα ἐκ τῆς Ἀσίας, καὶ ὑπισχνούμενός
μοι, εἰ ταῦτα πράξαιμι, εὖ ποιήσειν, ὡς ἔφη Μηδοσά-
25 δης οὗτος. ταῦτα εἰπὼν ἐπήρετο τὸν Μηδοσάδην εἰ
ἀληθῆ ταῦτ᾽ εἶπεν.[4] ὁ δ᾽ ἔφη. Αὖθις ἦλθε Μηδοσάδης
οὗτος ἐπεὶ ἐγὼ διέβην πάλιν ἐπὶ τὸ στράτευμα ἐκ
Παρίου, ὑπισχνούμενος, εἰ ἄγοιμι τὸ στράτευμα πρὸς

---

[4] One MS. reads here ταῦτ᾽ εἴη.

two hundred peltasts appeared, took Xenophon and his party, and proceeded to conduct them to Seuthes. He was in a tower and well guarded, and all around the tower were horses ready bridled; for out of fear he gave his horses their fodder by day, and by night kept them ready bridled to guard himself with. For there was a story that in time gone by Teres,[18] an ancestor of Seuthes, being in this region with a large army, lost many of his troops and was robbed of his baggage train at the hands of the people of this neighbourhood; they were the Thynians, and were said to be the most warlike of all men, especially by night.

When the Greek party had drawn near, Seuthes directed Xenophon to come in, with any two men he might choose to bring with him. As soon as they were inside, they first greeted one another and drank to each other's health after the Thracian fashion in horns of wine; and Seuthes had Medosades present also, the same man who went everywhere as his envoy.[19] After that Xenophon began the speaking: "You sent to me, Seuthes, first at Calchedon, this man Medosades, with the request that I make every effort on your behalf to bring the army across from Asia, and with the promise that if I should do this, you would treat me well—as Medosades here declared." After saying this, he asked Medosades whether this statement of the matter was a true one. He replied that it was. "Medosades here came to me a second time after I had crossed over from Parium to rejoin the army and promised that if I should bring the army to you, you would not only treat me in all ways as

18 Teres or Tereus: founder of the Odrysian Kingdom (first half of 5th century); cf. Thuc. II. 29.

19 See i. 5, and §10 above.

σέ, τἆλλα τέ σε φίλῳ μοι χρήσεσθαι καὶ ἀδελφῷ καὶ
τὰ ἐπὶ θαλάττῃ μοι χωρία ὧν σὺ κρατεῖς ἔσεσθαι

26 παρὰ σοῦ. ἐπὶ τούτοις πάλιν ἤρετο τὸν Μηδοσάδην εἰ
ἔλεγε ταῦτα. ὁ δὲ συνέφη καὶ ταῦτα. Ἴθι νυν, ἔφη,
ἀφήγησαι τούτῳ τί σοι ἀπεκρινάμην ἐν Καλχηδόνι

27 πρῶτον. Ἀπεκρίνω ὅτι τὸ στράτευμα διαβήσοιτο εἰς
Βυζάντιον καὶ οὐδὲν τούτου ἕνεκα δέοι τελεῖν οὔτε σοὶ
οὔτε ἄλλῳ· αὐτὸς δὲ ἐπεὶ διαβαίης, ἀπιέναι ἔφησθα·

28 καὶ ἐγένετο οὕτως ὥσπερ σὺ ἔλεγες. Τί γὰρ ἔλεγον,
ἔφη, ὅτε κατὰ Σηλυμβρίαν ἀφίκου; Οὐκ ἔφησθα οἷόν
τε εἶναι, ἀλλ᾿ εἰς Πέρινθον ἐλθόντας διαβαίνειν εἰς

29 τὴν Ἀσίαν. Νῦν τοίνυν, ἔφη ὁ Ξενοφῶν, πάρειμι καὶ
ἐγὼ καὶ οὗτος Φρυνίσκος εἷς τῶν στρατηγῶν καὶ
Πολυκράτης οὗτος εἷς τῶν λοχαγῶν, καὶ ἔξω εἰσὶν
ἀπὸ τῶν στρατηγῶν ὁ πιστότατος ἑκάστῳ πλὴν

30 Νέωνος τοῦ Λακωνικοῦ. εἰ οὖν βούλει πιστοτέραν
εἶναι τὴν πρᾶξιν, καὶ ἐκείνους κάλεσαι. τὰ δὲ ὅπλα
σὺ ἐλθὼν εἰπέ, ὦ Πολύκρατες, ὅτι ἐγὼ κελεύω καταλιπεῖν, καὶ αὐτὸς ἐκεῖ καταλιπὼν τὴν μάχαιραν εἴσιθι.

31 Ἀκούσας ταῦτα ὁ Σεύθης εἶπεν ὅτι οὐδενὶ ἂν ἀπι-
στήσειεν Ἀθηναίων· καὶ γὰρ ὅτι συγγενεῖς εἶεν εἰδέναι καὶ φίλους εὔνους ἔφη νομίζειν. μετὰ ταῦτα δ᾿ ἐπεὶ
εἰσῆλθον οὓς ἔδει, πρῶτον Ξενοφῶν ἐπήρετο Σεύθην
ὅ τι δέοιτο χρῆσθαι τῇ στρατιᾷ. ὁ δὲ εἶπεν ὧδε.

---

[20] According to tradition, through the marriage of the Thracian Tereus (or Teres cf. §22 above) with Procne, daughter of the
Athenian king Pandion.

a friend and a brother, but in particular would give me the places on the sea of which you hold possession." Hereupon he again asked Medosades whether this was what he said, and he again agreed that it was. "Come, now," Xenophon went on, "tell Seuthes what answer I made you that first time at Calchedon." "You answered that the army was going to cross over to Byzantium and there was no need, so far as that was concerned, of paying anything to you or any one else; you also stated that when you had got across, you were yourself to leave the army; and it turned out just as you said." "What then did I say," Xenophon asked, "at the time when you came to me near Selymbria?" "You said that the project was not possible, but that you were going to Perinthus and intended to cross over from there to Asia." "Well, then," said Xenophon, "at this moment I am here myself, along with Phryniscus here, one of the generals, and Polycrates yonder, one of the captains, and outside are representatives of the other generals except Neon the Laconian, in each case the man most trusted by each general. If you wish, therefore, to have the transaction better safeguarded, call them in also. Go and say to them, Polycrates, that I direct them to leave their arms behind, and do you yourself leave your sabre out there before coming back again."

Upon hearing these words Seuthes said that he should not distrust any one who was an Athenian; for he knew, he said, that the Athenians were kinsmen[20] of his, and he believed they were loyal friends. After this, when those who were to be present had come in, Xenophon began by asking Seuthes what use he wanted to make of the army. Then Seuthes spoke as follows: "Maesades was my father,

XENOPHON

32 Μαισάδης ἦν μοι πατήρ, ἐκείνου δὲ ἦν ἀρχὴ Μελαν-
δῖται καὶ Θυνοὶ καὶ Τρανίψαι. ἐκ ταύτης οὖν τῆς
χώρας, ἐπεὶ τὰ Ὀδρυσῶν πράγματα ἐνόσησεν, ἐκπε-
σὼν ὁ πατὴρ αὐτὸς μὲν ἀποθνήσκει νόσῳ, ἐγὼ δ᾽
ἐξετράφην ὀρφανὸς παρὰ Μηδόκῳ τῷ νῦν βασιλεῖ.
33 ἐπεὶ δὲ νεανίσκος ἐγενόμην, οὐκ ἐδυνάμην ζῆν εἰς
ἀλλοτρίαν τράπεζαν ἀποβλέπων· καὶ ἐκαθεζόμην ἐν-
δίφριος αὐτῷ ἱκέτης δοῦναί μοι ὁπόσους δυνατὸς εἴη
ἄνδρας, ὅπως καὶ τοὺς ἐκβαλόντας ἡμᾶς εἴ τι δυναίμην κακὸν ποιοίην καὶ ζῴην μὴ εἰς τὴν ἐκείνου
34 τράπεζαν ἀποβλέπων. ἐκ τούτου μοι δίδωσι τοὺς
ἄνδρας καὶ τοὺς ἵππους οὓς ὑμεῖς ὄψεσθε ἐπειδὰν
ἡμέρα γένηται. καὶ νῦν ἐγὼ ζῶ τούτους ἔχων, ληζό-
μενος τὴν ἐμαυτοῦ πατρῴαν χώραν. εἰ δέ μοι ὑμεῖς
παραγένοισθε, οἶμαι ἂν σὺν τοῖς θεοῖς ῥᾳδίως ἀπολαβεῖν τὴν ἀρχήν. ταῦτ᾽ ἐστὶν ἃ ἐγὼ ὑμῶν δέομαι.
35 Τί ἂν οὖν, ἔφη ὁ Ξενοφῶν, σὺ δύναιο, εἰ ἔλθοιμεν,
τῇ τε στρατιᾷ διδόναι καὶ τοῖς λοχαγοῖς καὶ τοῖς
36 στρατηγοῖς; λέξον, ἵνα οὗτοι ἀπαγγέλλωσιν. ὁ δ᾽
ὑπέσχετο τῷ μὲν στρατιώτῃ κυζικηνόν, τῷ δὲ λοχαγῷ
διμοιρίαν, τῷ δὲ στρατηγῷ τετραμοιρίαν, καὶ γῆν
ὁπόσην ἂν βούλωνται καὶ ζεύγη καὶ χωρίον ἐπὶ θα-
37 λάττῃ τετειχισμένον. Ἐὰν δέ, ἔφη ὁ Ξενοφῶν, ταῦτα
πειρώμενοι μὴ διαπράξωμεν, ἀλλά τις φόβος ὑπὸ
Λακεδαιμονίων ᾖ, δέξῃ εἰς τὴν σεαυτοῦ, ἐάν τις ἀπ-

---

[21] Seuthes was trying in fact to establish an independent kingdom. See Z. Archibald, *CAH*[2] VI, 458.

and his realm embraced the Melanditae, the Thynians, and the Tranipsae. Now when the affairs of the Odrysians fell into a bad state, my father was driven out of this country, and thereafter sickened and died, while I, the son, was brought up as an orphan at the court of Medocus, the present king. When I became a young man, however, I could not endure to live with my eyes turned toward another's table; so I sat myself down on the same seat with Medocus as a suppliant and besought him to give me as many men as he could, in order that I might inflict whatever harm I could upon those who drove us out, and might live without turning my eyes toward his table. Thereupon he gave me the men and the horses that you will see for yourselves as soon as day has come. And now I live with them, plundering my own ancestral land. But if you should join me, I think that with the aid of the gods I could easily recover my realm. It is this that I ask from you."[21]

"What, then," said Xenophon, "should you be able, in case we came, to give to the rank and file, to the captains, and to the generals? Tell us, so that these men here may carry back word." And Seuthes promised to give to each soldier a Cyzicene,[22] to the captains twice as much, and to the generals four times as much; furthermore, as much land as they might wish, yokes of oxen, and a fortified place upon the seacoast. "But," said Xenophon, "if we make this attempt[23] and do not succeed, because of some intimidation on the part of the Lacedaemonians, will you receive into your country any one who may wish to leave the army

[22] *i.e.* per month. For the Cyzicene, see note on V. vi. 23.
[23] *i.e.* to persuade the troops to take service under Seuthes. See below.

38 ἰέναι βούληται παρὰ σέ; ὁ δ' εἶπε· Καὶ ἀδελφούς γε
ποιήσομαι καὶ ἐνδιφρίους καὶ κοινωνοὺς ἁπάντων ὧν
ἂν δυνώμεθα κτήσασθαι. σοὶ δέ, ὦ Ξενοφῶν, καὶ
θυγατέρα δώσω καὶ εἴ τις σοὶ ἔστι θυγάτηρ, ὠνήσο-
μαι Θρακίῳ νόμῳ, καὶ Βισάνθην οἴκησιν δώσω, ὅπερ
ἐμοὶ κάλλιστον χωρίον ἐστὶ τῶν ἐπὶ θαλάττῃ.

III. Ἀκούσαντες ταῦτα καὶ δεξιὰς δόντες καὶ
λαβόντες ἀπήλαυνον· καὶ πρὸ ἡμέρας ἐγένοντο ἐπὶ
στρατοπέδῳ καὶ ἀπήγγειλαν ἕκαστοι τοῖς πέμψασιν.
2 ἐπεὶ δὲ ἡμέρα ἐγένετο, ὁ μὲν Ἀρίσταρχος πάλιν ἐκάλει
τοὺς στρατηγοὺς καὶ λοχαγούς· τοῖς δ' ἔδοξε τὴν μὲν
πρὸς Ἀρίσταρχον ὁδὸν ἐᾶσαι, τὸ δὲ στράτευμα
συγκαλέσαι. καὶ συνῆλθον πάντες πλὴν οἱ Νέωνος·
3 οὗτοι δὲ ἀπεῖχον ὡς δέκα στάδια. ἐπεὶ δὲ συνῆλθον,
ἀναστὰς Ξενοφῶν εἶπε τάδε. Ἄνδρες, διαπλεῖν μὲν
ἔνθα βουλόμεθα Ἀρίσταρχος ὅδε τριήρεις ἔχων κω-
λύει· ὥστε εἰς πλοῖα οὐκ ἀσφαλὲς ἐμβαίνειν· οὗτος δὲ
αὐτὸς κελεύει εἰς Χερρόνησον βίᾳ διὰ τοῦ ἱεροῦ ὄρους
πορεύεσθαι· ἢν δὲ κρατήσαντες τούτου ἐκεῖσε ἔλθωμεν, οὔτε πωλήσειν ἔτι ὑμᾶς φησιν ὥσπερ ἐν Βυζαντίῳ, οὔτε ἐξαπατήσεσθαι ἔτι ὑμᾶς, ἀλλὰ λήψεσθαι
μισθόν, οὔτε περιόψεσθαι ἔτι ὥσπερ νυνὶ ἐνδεομένους
4 τῶν ἐπιτηδείων. οὗτος μὲν ταῦτα λέγει· Σεύθης δέ
φησιν, ἂν πρὸς ἐκεῖνον ἴητε, εὖ ποιήσειν ὑμᾶς. νῦν
οὖν σκέψασθε πότερον ἐνθάδε μένοντες τοῦτο βου-

---

24 On Thracian marriage cf. Hdt. V. vi. 1. A daughter of marriageable age would make Xen. over 30; cf. Intro. and III. i. 25; but

and come to you? " And he replied: "Nay, more than that, I will make you my brothers, table-companions, sharers to the uttermost in all that we may find ourselves able to acquire. And to you, Xenophon, I will also give my daughter, and if you have a daughter, I will buy her after the Thracian fashion;[24] and I will give you for a residence Bisanthe, the very fairest of all the places I have upon the seacoast."

III. After hearing these words and giving and receiving pledges they rode away, and before daybreak they arrived at the camp and made their report, each one to those who had sent him. When day came, Aristarchus again summoned the generals and captains; but they resolved to disregard the summons of Aristarchus and instead to call a meeting of the army. And all the troops gathered except Neon's men, who were encamped about ten stadia away. When they had gathered, Xenophon arose and spoke as follows: "Soldiers, as for sailing across to the place where we wish to go, this man Aristarchus with his triremes prevents our doing that; the result is, that it is not safe for us to embark upon boats; but this same Aristarchus directs us to force our way to the Chersonese, through the Sacred Mountain;[25] and if we make ourselves masters of the mountain and get to the Chersonese, he says that he will not sell you any more, as he did at Byzantium, that you will not be cheated any more but will receive pay, and that he will not shut his eyes any more, as he does now, to your being in want of provisions. So much for what Aristarchus says; but Seuthes says that if you come to him, he will treat you well. Now, therefore, make up your minds whether you

cf., too, vi.34.   [25] Cf. i. 13, and note thereon.

5 λεύσεσθε ἢ εἰς τὰ ἐπιτήδεια ἐπανελθόντες. ἐμοὶ μὲν
οὖν δοκεῖ, ἐπεὶ ἐνθάδε οὔτε ἀργύριον ἔχομεν ὥστε
ἀγοράζειν οὔτε ἄνευ ἀργυρίου ἐῶσι λαμβάνειν τὰ
ἐπιτήδεια, ἐπανελθόντας εἰς τὰς κώμας ὅθεν οἱ ἥττους
ἐῶσι λαμβάνειν, ἐκεῖ ἔχοντας τὰ ἐπιτήδεια ἀκούοντας
ὅ τι τις ὑμῶν δεῖται, αἱρεῖσθαι ὅ τι ἂν ὑμῖν δοκῇ
6 κράτιστον εἶναι. καὶ ὅτῳ, ἔφη, ταῦτα δοκεῖ, ἀράτω τὴν
χεῖρα. ἀνέτειναν ἅπαντες. Ἀπιόντες τοίνυν, ἔφη, συ-
σκευάζεσθε, καὶ ἐπειδὰν παραγγέλλῃ τις, ἕπεσθε τῷ
ἡγουμένῳ.

7 Μετὰ ταῦτα Ξενοφῶν μὲν ἡγεῖτο, οἱ δ᾽ εἵποντο.
Νέων δὲ καὶ παρ᾽ Ἀριστάρχου ἄλλοι ἔπειθον ἀπο-
τρέπεσθαι· οἱ δ᾽ οὐχ ὑπήκουον. ἐπεὶ δ᾽ ὅσον τριάκοντα
σταδίους προεληλύθεσαν, ἀπαντᾷ Σεύθης. καὶ ὁ Ξενοφῶν ἰδὼν αὐτὸν προσελάσαι ἐκέλευσεν, ὅπως ὅτι
πλείστων ἀκουόντων εἴποι αὐτῷ ἃ ἐδόκει συμφέρειν.
8 ἐπεὶ δὲ προσῆλθεν, εἶπε Ξενοφῶν· Ἡμεῖς πορευόμεθα
ὅπου μέλλει ἕξειν τὸ στράτευμα τροφήν· ἐκεῖ δ᾽
ἀκούοντες καὶ σοῦ καὶ τῶν τοῦ Λακωνικοῦ αἱρησόμεθα
ἃ ἂν κράτιστα δοκῇ εἶναι. ἢν οὖν ἡμῖν ἡγήσῃ ὅπου
πλεῖστά ἐστιν ἐπιτήδεια, ὑπὸ σοῦ νομιοῦμεν ξενίζε-
9 σθαι. καὶ ὁ Σεύθης εἶπεν· Ἀλλὰ οἶδα κώμας πολλὰς
ἀθρόας καὶ πάντα ἐχούσας τὰ ἐπιτήδεια ἀπεχούσας
10 ἡμῶν ὅσον διελθόντες ἂν ἡδέως ἀριστῴητε. Ἡγοῦ
τοίνυν, ἔφη ὁ Ξενοφῶν. ἐπεὶ δ᾽ ἀφίκοντο εἰς αὐτὰς τῆς

---

[26] Aristarchus.

will consider this question here and now or after you have set forth in quest of provisions. My own opinion is, seeing that here we neither have money with which to buy provisions nor do they permit us to take them without money, that you, having set forth to the villages from which they permit you to take, since their inhabitants are weaker than yourselves, and that there, possessed of provisions and hearing what the service is that one wants you for, you should choose whatever course may seem best to you. Whoever," he said, "holds this opinion, let him raise his hand." Every hand was raised. "Go away, then," Xenophon continued, "and pack up, and when the word is given, follow the van."

After this Xenophon led the way and the troops followed. Neon, indeed, and others from Aristarchus tried to persuade them to turn back, but they would not listen to them. When they had advanced as much as thirty stades, Seuthes met them. And Xenophon, catching sight of him, bade him ride up to the troops, in order that he might tell him within hearing of the greatest possible number what they had decided upon as advantageous. When he had come up, Xenophon said: "We are on our way to a place where the army will be able to get food; there we shall listen both to you and to the Laconian's[26] messengers, and make whatever choice may seem to be best. If, then, you will guide us to a spot where there are provisions in greatest abundance, we shall think we are being hospitably entertained by you." And Seuthes replied: "Why, I know a large number of villages, close together and containing all sorts of provisions, that are just far enough away from us so that, when you have covered the distance, you would enjoy your breakfast." "Lead on, then," said Xenophon.

δείλης, συνῆλθον οἱ στρατιῶται, καὶ εἶπε Σεύθης
τοιάδε. Ἐγώ, ὦ ἄνδρες, δέομαι ὑμῶν στρατεύεσθαι
σὺν ἐμοί, καὶ ὑπισχνοῦμαι ὑμῖν δώσειν τοῖς στρατιώταις κυζικηνόν, λοχαγοῖς δὲ καὶ στρατηγοῖς τὰ
νομιζόμενα· ἔξω δὲ τούτων τὸν ἄξιον τιμήσω. σῖτα δὲ
καὶ ποτὰ ὥσπερ καὶ νῦν ἐκ τῆς χώρας λαμβάνοντες
ἕξετε· ὁπόσα δ᾽ ἂν ἁλίσκηται ἀξιώσω αὐτὸς ἔχειν, ἵνα
11 ταῦτα διατιθέμενος ὑμῖν τὸν μισθὸν ἐκπορίζω. καὶ τὰ
μὲν φεύγοντα καὶ ἀποδιδράσκοντα ἡμεῖς ἱκανοὶ ἐσόμεθα διώκειν καὶ μαστεύειν· ἂν δέ τις ἀνθίστηται, σὺν
12 ὑμῖν πειρασόμεθα χειροῦσθαι. ἐπήρετο ὁ Ξενοφῶν·
Πόσον δὲ ἀπὸ θαλάττης ἀξιώσεις συνέπεσθαί σοι τὸ
στράτευμα; ὁ δ᾽ ἀπεκρίνατο· Οὐδαμῇ πλέον ἑπτὰ
ἡμερῶν, μεῖον δὲ πολλαχῇ.

13   Μετὰ ταῦτα ἐδίδοτο λέγειν τῷ βουλομένῳ· καὶ
ἔλεγον πολλοὶ κατὰ ταὐτὰ ὅτι παντὸς ἄξια λέγει
Σεύθης· χειμὼν γὰρ εἴη καὶ οὔτε οἴκαδε ἀποπλεῖν τῷ
τοῦτο βουλομένῳ δυνατὸν εἴη, διαγενέσθαι τε ἐν φιλίᾳ
οὐχ οἷόν τ᾽ εἴη⁵ εἰ δέοι ὠνουμένους ζῆν, ἐν δὲ τῇ
πολεμίᾳ διατρίβειν καὶ τρέφεσθαι ἀσφαλέστερον
μετὰ Σεύθου ἢ μόνους.⁶ ὄντων δ᾽ ἀγαθῶν τοσούτων, εἰ
14 μισθὸν προσλήψοιντο, εὕρημα ἐδόκει εἶναι. ἐπὶ τούτοις εἶπεν ὁ Ξενοφῶν· Εἴ τις ἀντιλέγει, λεγέτω· εἰ δὲ
μή, ἐπιψηφιζέσθω ταῦτα. ἐπεὶ δὲ οὐδεὶς ἀντέλεγεν,

---

⁵ οἷόν τ᾽ εἴη one MS.: τε ἦ (ἦν) other MSS.
⁶ μόνους. ὄντων ἀγαθῶν τοσούτων, εἰ Gem., Peters, following Cobet: μόνους, ὄντων ἀγαθῶν τοσούτων. εἰ δὲ MSS., Mar.,
Hude.

When they had reached the villages, in the afternoon, the soldiers gathered together and Seuthes spoke as follows: "I ask you, soldiers, to take the field with me, and I promise to give to you who are in the ranks a Cyzicene and to the captains and generals the customary pay; besides this, I shall honour the man who deserves it. Food and drink you will obtain, just as today, by taking from the country; but whatever may be captured I shall expect to retain for myself, so that by selling it I may provide you your pay. All that flees and hides we shall ourselves be able to pursue and seek out; but if any one offers resistance, with your help we shall try to subdue him." Xenophon asked, "And how far from the seacoast shall you expect the army to follow you?" He replied, "Nowhere more than a seven days' journey, and in many places less."

After this the opportunity to speak was offered to any one who desired it; and many spoke to the same effect, saying that Seuthes' proposals were most valuable; for the season was winter, and it was impossible to sail back home, if that was what one wished, and impossible also to get along in a friendly country if they had to maintain themselves by purchasing; on the other hand, to spend their time and get their maintenance in a hostile country was a safer proceeding in Seuthes' company than if they were alone. And if, above and beyond such important advantages, they were also to receive pay, they counted it an unexpected windfall. After that Xenophon said: "If any one holds a contrary opinion, let him speak; if not, I will put this question to vote." And as no one spoke in opposition,

ἐπεψήφισε, καὶ ἔδοξε ταῦτα. εὐθὺς δὲ Σεύθη εἶπεν, ὅτι
συστρατεύσοιντο αὐτῷ.

15 Μετὰ τοῦτο οἱ μὲν ἄλλοι κατὰ τάξεις ἐσκήνησαν,
στρατηγοὺς δὲ καὶ λοχαγοὺς ἐπὶ δεῖπνον Σεύθης ἐκά-
16 λεσε, πλησίον κώμην ἔχων. ἐπεὶ δ᾽ ἐπὶ θύραις ἦσαν
ὡς ἐπὶ δεῖπνον παριόντες, ἦν τις Ἡρακλείδης Μαρω-
νίτης· οὗτος προσιὼν ἑνὶ ἑκάστῳ οὕστινας ᾤετο ἔχειν
τι δοῦναι Σεύθῃ, πρῶτον μὲν πρὸς Παριανούς τινας,
οἳ παρῆσαν φιλίαν διαπραξόμενοι πρὸς Μήδοκον τὸν
Ὀδρυσῶν βασιλέα καὶ δῶρα ἄγοντες αὐτῷ τε καὶ τῇ
γυναικί, ἔλεγεν ὅτι Μήδοκος μὲν ἄνω εἴη δώδεκα
ἡμερῶν ἀπὸ θαλάττης ὁδόν, Σεύθης δ᾽ ἐπεὶ τὸ στράτευμα τοῦτο εἴληφεν, ἄρχων ἔσοιτο ἐπὶ θαλάττῃ.
17 γείτων οὖν ὢν ἱκανώτατος ἔσται ὑμᾶς καὶ εὖ καὶ κακῶς
ποιεῖν. ἢν οὖν σωφρονῆτε, τούτῳ δώσετε ὅ τι ἄγετε·
καὶ ἄμεινον ὑμῖν διακείσεται ἢ ἐὰν Μηδόκῳ τῷ πρόσω
18 οἰκοῦντι διδῶτε. τούτους μὲν οὖν οὕτως ἔπειθεν. αὖθις
δὲ Τιμασίωνι τῷ Δαρδανεῖ προσελθών, ἐπεὶ ἤκουσεν
αὐτῷ εἶναι καὶ ἐκπώματα καὶ τάπιδας βαρβαρικάς,
ἔλεγεν ὅτι νομίζοιτο ὁπότε ἐπὶ δεῖπνον καλέσαι Σεύθης δωρεῖσθαι αὐτῷ τοὺς κληθέντας. οὗτος δ᾽ ἢν
μέγας ἐνθάδε γένηται, ἱκανὸς ἔσται σε καὶ οἴκαδε
καταγαγεῖν καὶ ἐνθάδε πλούσιον ποιῆσαι. τοιαῦτα
19 προυμνᾶτο ἑκάστῳ προσιών. προσελθὼν δὲ καὶ Ξενο-

---

[27] A Greek city in Thrace.
[28] Through the mediation of Seuthes; cf. ii. 32–4.

he put the matter to vote, and this plan was decided upon. So he told Seuthes at once that they would take service with him.

After this the troops went into camp by divisions, but the generals and captains were invited to dinner by Seuthes in a village he was occupying near by. When they had reached his doors and were about to go in to dinner, there stood a certain Heracleides, of Maroneia;[27] this fellow came up to each single one of the guests who, as he imagined, were able to make a present to Seuthes, first of all to some people of Parium who had come to arrange[28] a friendship with Medocus, the king of the Odrysians, and brought gifts with them for him and his wife; to them Heracleides said that Medocus was a twelve days' journey inland from the sea, while Seuthes, now that he had got this army, would be master upon the coast. "He, therefore," Heracleides went on, "being your neighbour, will be best able to do you good or harm. Hence if you are wise, you will present to him what you bring with you; and it will be better for you than if you make your gifts to Medocus, who dwells far away." It was in this way that he tried to persuade these people. Next he came up to Timasion the Dardanian—for he heard that he had some Persian drinking cups and carpets—and said that it was customary when Seuthes invited people to dinner, for those who were thus invited to give him presents. "And," he continued, "in case this Seuthes becomes a great man in this region, he will be able either to restore you to your home[29] or to make you rich here." Such were the solicitations he used as he went to one man after another. He came up to Xenophon also,

[29] Timasion was an exile (V. vi. 23.)

φῶντι ἔλεγε· Σὺ καὶ πόλεως μεγίστης εἶ καὶ παρὰ
Σεύθῃ τὸ σὸν ὄνομα μέγιστόν ἐστι, καὶ ἐν τῇδε τῇ
χώρᾳ ἴσως ἀξιώσεις καὶ τείχη λαμβάνειν, ὥσπερ καὶ
ἄλλοι τῶν ὑμετέρων ἔλαβον, καὶ χώραν· ἄξιον οὖν σοι
20 καὶ μεγαλοπρεπέστατα τιμῆσαι Σεύθην. εὔνους δέ σοι
ὢν παραινῶ· εὖ οἶδα γὰρ ὅτι ὅσῳ ἂν μείζω τούτῳ
δωρήσῃ, τοσούτῳ μείζω ὑπὸ τούτου ἀγαθὰ πείσει.
ἀκούων ταῦτα ὁ Ξενοφῶν ἠπόρει· οὐ γὰρ διεβεβήκει
ἔχων ἐκ Παρίου εἰ μὴ παῖδα καὶ ὅσον ἐφόδιον.

21 Ἐπεὶ δὲ εἰσῆλθον ἐπὶ τὸ δεῖπνον τῶν τε Θρᾳκῶν οἱ
κράτιστοι τῶν παρόντων καὶ οἱ στρατηγοὶ καὶ οἱ
λοχαγοὶ τῶν Ἑλλήνων καὶ εἴ τις πρεσβεία παρῆν ἀπὸ
πόλεως, τὸ δεῖπνον μὲν ἦν καθημένοις κύκλῳ· ἔπειτα
δὲ τρίποδες εἰσηνέχθησαν πᾶσιν· οὗτοι δ᾽ ἦσαν ὅσον
εἴκοσι κρεῶν μεστοὶ νενεμημένων, καὶ ἄρτοι ζυμῖται
μεγάλοι προσπεπερονημένοι ἦσαν πρὸς τοῖς κρέασι.
22 μάλιστα δ᾽ αἱ τράπεζαι κατὰ τοὺς ξένους ἀεὶ ἐτίθεντο·
νόμος γὰρ ἦν. καὶ πρῶτος τοῦτο ἐποίει Σεύθης·
ἀνελόμενος τοὺς παρακειμένους ἄρτους διέκλα κατὰ
μικρὸν καὶ διερρίπτει οἷς αὐτῷ ἐδόκει, καὶ τὰ κρέα
ὡσαύτως, ὅσον μόνον γεύσασθαι ἑαυτῷ καταλιπών.
23 καὶ οἱ ἄλλοι δὲ κατὰ ταὐτὰ ἐποίουν καθ᾽ οὓς αἱ
τράπεζαι ἔκειντο. Ἀρκὰς δέ τις Ἀρύστας ὄνομα, φα-
γεῖν δεινός, τὸ μὲν διαρριπτεῖν εἴα χαίρειν, λαβὼν δὲ
εἰς τὴν χεῖρα ὅσον τριχοίνικον ἄρτον καὶ κρέα θέμενος

---

30 Especially Alcibiades (*Hell* I. v. 17; Nepos, *Alc.* VII. 4).

and said to him: " You are a citizen of a very great state and your name is a very great one with Seuthes; perhaps you will expect to obtain fortresses in this land, as others among your countrymen have done,[30] and territory; it is proper, therefore, for you to honour Seuthes in the most magnificent way. It is out of good-will to you that I give this advice for I am quite sure that the greater the gifts you bestow upon this man, the greater the favours that you will receive at his hands." Upon hearing this Xenophon was dismayed; for he had come across from Parium with nothing but a slave and money enough for his travelling expenses.

When they had come in for the dinner—the noblest of the Thracians who were present, the generals and the captains of the Greeks, and whatever embassy from any state was there—the dinner was served with the guests seated in a circle; then three-legged tables were brought in for the whole company; these were about twenty in number, full of meat, cut up into pieces, and there were great loaves of leavened bread fastened with skewers to the pieces of meat. The tables were placed especially opposite the strangers in each case; for it was customary among the Thracians. And then Seuthes was the first to do the following: picking up the loaves which were laid out, he would break them into small pieces, and throw the pieces around to whomever he pleased, following the same fashion with the meat also, and leaving himself only enough for a mere taste. Then the others also who had tables placed opposite them, set about doing the same thing. But a certain Arcadian named Arystas, a terrible eater, would have none of this throwing about, but took in his hand a loaf as big as a three-quart measure, put some pieces of meat upon his

24 ἐπὶ τὰ γόνατα ἐδείπνει. κέρατα δὲ οἴνου περιέφερον,
καὶ πάντες ἐδέχοντο· ὁ δ' Ἀρύστας, ἐπεὶ παρ' αὐτὸν
φέρων τὸ κέρας ὁ οἰνοχόος ἧκεν, εἶπεν ἰδὼν τὸν
Ξενοφῶντα οὐκέτι δειπνοῦντα, Ἐκείνῳ, ἔφη, δός· σχο-
25 λάζει γὰρ ἤδη, ἐγὼ δὲ οὔπω. ἀκούσας Σεύθης τὴν
φωνὴν ἠρώτα τὸν οἰνοχόον τί λέγει. ὁ δὲ οἰνοχόος
εἶπεν· ἑλληνίζειν γὰρ ἠπίστατο. ἐνταῦθα μὲν δὴ γέλως
ἐγένετο.

26   Ἐπειδὴ δὲ προυχώρει ὁ πότος, εἰσῆλθεν ἀνὴρ Θρᾷξ
ἵππον ἔχων λευκόν, καὶ λαβὼν κέρας μεστὸν εἶπε·
Προπίνω σοι, ὦ Σεύθη, καὶ τὸν ἵππον τοῦτον δωροῦ-
μαι, ἐφ' οὗ καὶ διώκων ὃν ἂν ἐθέλῃς αἱρήσεις καὶ
27 ἀποχωρῶν οὐ μὴ δείσῃς τὸν πολέμιον. ἄλλος παῖδα
εἰσαγαγὼν οὕτως ἐδωρήσατο προπίνων, καὶ ἄλλος
ἱμάτια τῇ γυναικί. καὶ Τιμασίων προπίνων ἐδωρήσατο
φιάλην τε ἀργυρᾶν καὶ τάπιδα ἀξίαν δέκα μνῶν.
28 Γνήσιππος δέ τις Ἀθηναῖος ἀναστὰς εἶπεν ὅτι ἀρ-
χαῖος εἴη νόμος κάλλιστος τοὺς μὲν ἔχοντας διδόναι
τῷ βασιλεῖ τιμῆς ἕνεκα, τοῖς δὲ μὴ ἔχουσι διδόναι
τὸν βασιλέα, ἵνα καὶ ἐγώ, ἔφη, ἔχω σοι δωρεῖσθαι καὶ
29 τιμᾶν. ὁ δὲ Ξενοφῶν ἠπορεῖτο τί ποιήσει· καὶ γὰρ
ἐτύγχανεν ὡς τιμώμενος ἐν τῷ πλησιαιτάτῳ δίφρῳ
Σεύθῃ καθήμενος. ὁ δὲ Ἡρακλείδης ἐκέλευεν αὐτῷ τὸ
κέρας ὀρέξαι τὸν οἰνοχόον. ὁ δὲ Ξενοφῶν, ἤδη γὰρ
ὑποπεπωκὼς ἐτύγχανεν, ἀνέστη θαρραλέως δεξάμενος
30 τὸ κέρας καὶ εἶπεν· Ἐγὼ δέ σοι, ὦ Σεύθη, δίδωμι

knees, and proceeded to dine. They carried round horns of wine, and all took them; but Arystas, when the cupbearer came and brought him his horn, said to the man, after observing that Xenophon had finished his dinner, "Give it to him; for he's already at leisure, but I'm not as yet." When Seuthes heard the sound of his voice, he asked the cupbearer what he was saying. And the cupbearer, who understood Greek, told him. So then there was an outburst of laughter.

When the drinking was well under way, there came in a Thracian with a white horse, and taking a full horn he said: "I drink your health, Seuthes, and present to you this horse; on his back pursuing you shall catch whomever you choose, and retreating you shall not fear the enemy." Another brought in a boy and presented him in the same way, with a toast of health to Seuthes, while another presented clothes for his wife. Timasion also drank his health and presented to him a silver bowl and a carpet worth ten minas.[31] Then one Gnesippus, an Athenian, rose and said that it was an ancient and most excellent custom that those who had possessions should give to the king for honour's sake, and that to those who had nought the king should give, "that so," he continued, "I too may be able to bestow gifts upon you and do you honour." As for Xenophon, he was at a loss to know what he should do; for he chanced, as one held in honour, to be seated on the stool nearest to Seuthes. And Heracleides directed the cupbearer to proffer him the horn. Then Xenophon, who already as it happened had been drinking a little, arose courageously after taking the horn and said: "And I, Seuthes, give you myself

---

[31] Cf. above §18; extremely valuable objects.

XENOPHON

ἐμαυτὸν καὶ τοὺς ἐμοὺς τούτους ἑταίρους φίλους εἶναι
πιστούς, καὶ οὐδένα ἄκοντα, ἀλλὰ πάντας μᾶλλον ἔτι
31 ἐμοῦ σοι βουλομένους φίλους εἶναι. καὶ νῦν πάρεισιν
οὐδέν σε προσαιτοῦντες, ἀλλὰ καὶ προϊέμενοι καὶ
πονεῖν ὑπὲρ σοῦ καὶ προκινδυνεύειν ἐθέλοντες· μεθ'
ὧν, ἂν οἱ θεοὶ θέλωσι, πολλὴν χώραν τὴν μὲν ἀπο-
λήψει πατρῴαν οὖσαν, τὴν δὲ κτήσει, πολλοὺς δὲ
ἵππους, πολλοὺς δὲ ἄνδρας καὶ γυναῖκας καλὰς κτήσει, οὓς οὐ λῄζεσθαί σε δεήσει, ἀλλ' αὐτοὶ φέροντες
32 παρέσονται πρὸς σὲ δῶρα. ἀναστὰς ὁ Σεύθης συν-
εξέπιε καὶ συγκατεσκεδάσατο μετ' αὐτοῦ τὸ κέρας.
μετὰ ταῦτα εἰσῆλθον κέρασί τε οἵοις σημαίνουσιν
αὐλοῦντες καὶ σάλπιγξιν ὠμοβοΐναις ῥυθμούς τε καὶ
33 οἷον μαγάδι σαλπίζοντες. καὶ αὐτὸς Σεύθης ἀναστὰς
ἀνέκραγέ τε πολεμικὸν καὶ ἐξήλατο ὥσπερ βέλος
φυλαττόμενος μάλα ἐλαφρῶς. εἰσῆσαν δὲ καὶ γελωτο-
ποιοί.
34 Ὡς δ' ἦν ἥλιος ἐπὶ δυσμαῖς, ἀνέστησαν οἱ Ἕλληνες καὶ εἶπον ὅτι ὥρα νυκτοφύλακας καθιστάναι καὶ
σύνθημα παραδιδόναι. καὶ Σεύθην ἐκέλευον παραγγεῖλαι ὅπως εἰς τὰ Ἑλληνικὰ στρατόπεδα μηδεὶς τῶν
Θρᾳκῶν εἴσεισι νυκτός· οἵ τε γὰρ πολέμιοι Θρᾷκες
35 ἡμῖν καὶ ὑμεῖς οἱ φίλοι. ὡς δ' ἐξῆσαν, συνανέστη ὁ

---

32 The reference is to the Thracian custom, known to us
through the Suda (sv κατασκεδάζειν), of sprinkling the last drops

580

and these my comrades to be your faithful friends; and not one of them do I give against his will, but all are even more desirous than I of being your friends. And now they are here, asking you for nothing more, but rather putting themselves in your hands and willing to endure toil and danger on your behalf. With them, if the gods so will, you will acquire great territory, recovering all that belonged to your fathers and gaining yet more, and you will acquire many horses, and many men and fair women; and these things you will not need to take as plunder, but my comrades of their own accord shall bring them before you as gifts." Up rose Seuthes, drained the horn with Xenophon, and joined him in sprinkling the last drops.[32] After this there came in musicians blowing upon horns such as they use in giving signals, and playing upon trumpets of raw ox-hide not only measured notes, but music like that of a harp.[33] And Seuthes himself got up, raised a war-cry, and sprang aside very nimbly, as though avoiding a missile. There entered also a company of buffoons.

When the sun was about setting, the Greeks arose and said that it was time to post sentinels and give out the watchword. They also urged Seuthes to issue an order that none of the Thracians were to enter the Greek camp by night; "for," they said, "our enemies are Thracians and our friends are yourselves."[34] As the Greeks were setting forth, Seuthes arose with them, not in the least like a drunken

that remained in the drinking horn upon one's fellow guests. Cf. Plato, *Lg.* 637e.

[33] The *magadis* was a Thracian harp; cf. Duris, *FGH* 76 F 28.

[34] *viz.* Thracians also; in other words, the Greeks could not tell whether an individual Thracian was friend or foe.

Σεύθης οὐδέν τι μεθύοντι ἐοικώς. ἐξελθὼν δ᾽ εἶπεν
αὐτοὺς τοὺς στρατηγοὺς ἀποκαλέσας· Ὦ ἄνδρες, οἱ
πολέμιοι ἡμῶν οὐκ ἴσασί πω τὴν ἡμετέραν συμ-
μαχίαν· ἢν οὖν ἔλθωμεν ἐπ᾽ αὐτοὺς πρὶν φυλάξασθαι
ὥστε μὴ ληφθῆναι ἢ παρασκευάσασθαι ὥστε ἀμύνα-
σθαι, μάλιστα ἂν λάβοιμεν καὶ ἀνθρώπους καὶ χρή-
36 ματα. συνεπήνουν ταῦτα οἱ στρατηγοὶ καὶ ἡγεῖσθαι
ἐκέλευον. ὁ δ᾽ εἶπε· Παρασκευασάμενοι ἀναμένετε· ἐγὼ
δὲ ὁπόταν καιρὸς ᾖ ἥξω παρ᾽ ὑμᾶς, καὶ τοὺς πελταστὰς καὶ ὑμᾶς ἀναλαβὼν ἡγήσομαι σὺν τοῖς ἵπ-
37 ποις.[7] καὶ ὁ Ξενοφῶν εἶπε· Σκέψαι τοίνυν, εἴπερ νυκτὸς
πορευσόμεθα, εἰ ὁ Ἑλληνικὸς νόμος κάλλιον ἔχει· μεθ᾽
ἡμέραν μὲν γὰρ ἐν ταῖς πορείαις ἡγεῖται τοῦ στρατεύματος ὁποῖον ἂν ἀεὶ πρὸς τὴν χώραν συμφέρῃ, ἐάν
τε ὁπλιτικὸν ἐάν τε πελταστικὸν ἐάν τε ἱππικόν·
νύκτωρ δὲ νόμος τοῖς Ἕλλησιν ἡγεῖσθαί ἐστι τὸ
38 βραδύτατον· οὕτω γὰρ ἥκιστα διασπᾶται τὰ στρατεύματα καὶ ἥκιστα λανθάνουσιν ἀποδιδράσκοντες
ἀλλήλους· οἱ δὲ διασπασθέντες πολλάκις καὶ περι-
πίπτουσιν ἀλλήλοις καὶ ἀγνοοῦντες κακῶς ποιοῦσι
39 καὶ πάσχουσιν. εἶπεν οὖν Σεύθης· Ὀρθῶς τε λέγετε
καὶ ἐγὼ τῷ νόμῳ τῷ ὑμετέρῳ πείσομαι. καὶ ὑμῖν μὲν
ἡγεμόνας δώσω τῶν πρεσβυτάτων τοὺς ἐμπειροτάτους
τῆς χώρας, αὐτὸς δ᾽ ἐφέψομαι τελευταῖος τοὺς ἵππους
ἔχων· ταχὺ γὰρ πρῶτος, ἂν δέῃ, παρέσομαι. σύνθημα

---

[7] ἵπποις Gem., Hude/Peters, following Hirschig: θεοῖς MSS.,
Mar.

man. And after coming out he called the generals aside by themselves and said: "Gentlemen, our enemies do not yet know of our alliance; therefore if we go against them before they have got on guard against being captured or have made preparations to defend themselves, we should most surely get both captives and property." The generals agreed in approving this plan, and bade him lead on. And he said: "Get yourselves ready and wait; and when the proper time comes, I will return to you and, picking up my peltasts and yourselves, will lead the way with my horsemen." And Xenophon said: "Well, now, consider this point, whether, if we are to make a night march, the Greek practice is not the better: in our marches by day, you know, that part of the army takes the lead which is suited to the nature of the ground in each case, whether it be hoplites or peltasts or cavalry; but by night it is the practice of the Greeks that the slowest arm should lead the way; for thus the various parts of the army are least likely to become separated, and men are least likely to drop away from one another without knowing it; and it often happens that scattered divisions fall in with one another and in their ignorance inflict and suffer harm." Then Seuthes replied: "You are right, and I will adopt your practice. I will give you guides[35] from among the oldest men, who know the country best, and I myself will bring up the rear with my horsemen; for I can speedily reach the front if need be." Then

[35] Which are necessary now that the Greeks, whose hoplites form "the slowest arm," are to lead the way.

583

δ' εἶπον Ἀθηναίαν κατὰ τὴν συγγένειαν. ταῦτα εἰπόντες ἀνεπαύοντο.

40 Ἡνίκα δ' ἦν ἀμφὶ μέσας νύκτας, παρῆν Σεύθης
ἔχων τοὺς ἱππέας τεθωρακισμένους καὶ τοὺς πελταστὰς σὺν τοῖς ὅπλοις. καὶ ἐπεὶ παρέδωκε τοὺς ἡγεμόνας, οἱ μὲν ὁπλῖται ἡγοῦντο, οἱ δὲ πελτασταὶ
41 εἵποντο, οἱ δ' ἱππεῖς ὠπισθοφυλάκουν. ἐπεὶ δ' ἡμέρα
ἦν, ὁ Σεύθης παρήλαυνεν εἰς τὸ πρόσθεν καὶ ἐπήνεσε
τὸν Ἑλληνικὸν νόμον. πολλάκις γὰρ ἔφη νύκτωρ
αὐτὸς καὶ σὺν ὀλίγοις πορευόμενος ἀποσπασθῆναι
σὺν τοῖς ἵπποις ἀπὸ τῶν πεζῶν· νῦν δ' ὥσπερ δεῖ
ἀθρόοι πάντες ἅμα τῇ ἡμέρᾳ φαινόμεθα. ἀλλὰ ὑμεῖς
μὲν περιμένετε αὐτοῦ καὶ ἀναπαύσασθε, ἐγὼ δὲ
σκεψάμενός τι ἥξω. ταῦτ' εἰπὼν ἤλαυνε δι' ὄρους ὁδόν
42 τινα λαβών. ἐπεὶ δ' ἀφίκετο εἰς χιόνα πολλήν, ἐσκέ-
ψατο εἰ εἴη ἴχνη ἀνθρώπων ἢ πρόσω ἡγούμενα ἢ
ἐναντία. ἐπεὶ δὲ ἀτριβῆ ἑώρα τὴν ὁδόν, ἧκε ταχὺ πάλιν
43 καὶ ἔλεγεν· Ἄνδρες, καλῶς ἔσται, ἢν θεὸς θέλῃ· τοὺς
γὰρ ἀνθρώπους λήσομεν ἐπιπεσόντες. ἀλλ' ἐγὼ μὲν
ἡγήσομαι τοῖς ἵπποις, ὅπως ἄν τινα ἴδωμεν, μὴ δια-
φυγὼν σημήνῃ τοῖς πολεμίοις· ὑμεῖς δ' ἔπεσθε· κἂν
λειφθῆτε, τῷ στίβῳ τῶν ἵππων ἔπεσθε. ὑπερβάντες δὲ
τὰ ὄρη ἥξομεν εἰς κώμας πολλάς τε καὶ εὐδαίμονας.
44 Ἡνίκα δ' ἦν μέσον ἡμέρας, ἤδη τε ἦν ἐπὶ τοῖς
ἄκροις καὶ κατιδὼν τὰς κώμας ἧκεν ἐλαύνων πρὸς τοὺς
ὁπλίτας καὶ ἔλεγεν· Ἀφήσω ἤδη καταθεῖν τοὺς μὲν

---

[36] Cf. ii. 31.

they gave out "Athena" as the watchword, on account of their kinship.[36] After this conference they went to rest.

When it was about midnight, Seuthes was at hand with his horsemen armed with breast-plates and his peltasts equipped with their arms. And as soon as he had given over their guides to the Greeks, the hoplites took the lead, the peltasts followed, and the horsemen brought up the rear. When day came, Seuthes rode along to the front and expressed his approval of the Greek practice. For many times, he said, while marching by night with even a small force he himself, along with his cavalry, had got separated from his infantry; "but now," he continued, "we find ourselves at daybreak all together, just as we should be. But do you wait where you are and take a rest, and I will return after I have looked around a little." With these words he rode off along a mountain side, following a kind of road. When he had reached a place where there was deep snow, he looked about to see whether there were human footprints, either leading onward or back. As soon as he saw that the road was untrodden, he quickly returned and said: "All will be well, gentlemen, if god will; for we shall fall upon these people before they know it. Now I will lead the way with the cavalry, so that if we catch sight of any one, he may not slip through our fingers and give word to the enemy; and do you follow after me, and in case you get left behind, keep to the trail of the horses. Once we have crossed over the mountains, we shall come to many prosperous villages."

By the time it was midday he was already upon the heights, and catching sight of the villages below he came riding up to the hoplites and said: "Now I am going to let

585

ἱππέας εἰς τὸ πεδίον, τοὺς δὲ πελταστὰς ἐπὶ τὰς
κώμας. ἀλλ᾽ ἕπεσθε ὡς ἂν δύνησθε τάχιστα, ὅπως ἐάν
45 τις ὑφιστῆται, ἀλέξησθε. ἀκούσας ταῦτα ὁ Ξενοφῶν
κατέβη ἀπὸ τοῦ ἵππου. καὶ ὃς ἤρετο· Τί καταβαίνεις,
ἐπεὶ σπεύδειν δεῖ; Οἶδα, ἔφη, ὅτι οὐκ ἐμοῦ μόνου δέει·
οἱ δὲ ὁπλῖται θᾶττον δραμοῦνται καὶ ἥδιον, ἐὰν καὶ
46 ἐγὼ πεζὸς ἡγῶμαι. μετὰ ταῦτα ᾤχετο, καὶ Τιμασίων
μετ᾽ αὐτοῦ ἔχων ἱππέας ὡς τετταράκοντα τῶν Ἑλλήνων. Ξενοφῶν δὲ παρηγγύησε τοὺς εἰς τριάκοντα ἔτη
παριέναι ἀπὸ τῶν λόχων εὐζώνους. καὶ αὐτὸς μὲν
ἐτρόχαζε τούτους ἔχων, Κλεάνωρ δ᾽ ἡγεῖτο τῶν ἄλλων.
47 ἐπεὶ δ᾽ ἐν ταῖς κώμαις ἦσαν, Σεύθης ἔχων ὅσον τριάκοντα ἱππέας προσελάσας εἶπε· Τάδε δή, ὦ Ξενοφῶν,
ἃ σὺ ἔλεγες· ἔχονται οἱ ἄνθρωποι· ἀλλὰ γὰρ ἔρημοι
οἱ ἱππεῖς οἴχονταί μοι ἄλλος ἀλλαχῇ διώκων, καὶ
δέδοικα μὴ συστάντες ἁθρόοι που κακόν τι ἐργά-
σωνται οἱ πολέμιοι. δεῖ δὲ καὶ ἐν ταῖς κώμαις κατα-
48 μένειν τινὰς ἡμῶν· μεσταὶ γάρ εἰσιν ἀνθρώπων. Ἀλλ᾽
ἐγὼ μέν, ἔφη ὁ Ξενοφῶν, σὺν οἷς ἔχω τὰ ἄκρα
καταλήψομαι· σὺ δὲ Κλεάνορα κέλευε διὰ τοῦ πεδίου
παρατεῖναι τὴν φάλαγγα παρὰ τὰς κώμας. ἐπεὶ δὲ
ταῦτα ἐποίησαν, συνηλίσθησαν ἀνδράποδα μὲν ὡς
χίλια, βόες δὲ δισχίλιοι, καὶ ἄλλα πρόβατα μύρια.
τότε μὲν δὴ αὐτοῦ ηὐλίσθησαν.

---

[37] See §§37, 38 above. Seuthes has again (cf. §41) gone ahead

the horsemen charge down to the plain on the run, and to send the peltasts against the villages. Do you, then, follow as fast as you can, so that if any resistance is offered, you may meet it." Upon hearing these words Xenophon dismounted from his horse. And Seuthes asked: "Why do you dismount, for there is need of haste?" "I know," Xenophon replied, "that I am not the only one you need; and the hoplites will run faster and more cheerfully if I also am on foot leading the way." After this Seuthes went off, and with him Timasion at the head of about forty horsemen of the Greeks. Then Xenophon gave orders that the active men up to thirty years of age should move up from their several companies to the front. So he himself ran along with them, while Cleanor led the rest. When they had reached the villages, Seuthes with about thirty horsemen rode up to him and said: "Here's the very thing, Xenophon, that you were saying;[37] these fellows are caught, but unhappily my horsemen have gone off unsupported, scattering in their pursuit here and there, and I fear that the enemy may get together somewhere in a body and work some harm. On the other hand, some of us also must remain in the villages, for they are full of people." "Well," Xenophon replied, "I myself with the troops I have will seize the heights, and do you direct Cleanor to extend his line through the plain alongside the villages." When they had done these things, there were gathered together captives to the number of about a thousand, two thousand cattle, and ten thousand smaller animals besides. Then they bivouacked where they were.

with his fastest arm (his cavalry), and now appreciates the danger of having them unsupported (cf. ἔρημοι below) by infantry.

587

IV. Τῇ δ' ὑστεραίᾳ κατακαύσας ὁ Σεύθης τὰς κώμας παντελῶς καὶ οἰκίαν οὐδεμίαν λιπών, ὅπως φόβον ἐνθείη καὶ τοῖς ἄλλοις οἷα πείσονται, ἂν μὴ
2 πείθωνται, ἀπήει πάλιν. καὶ τὴν μὲν λείαν ἀπέπεμψε διατίθεσθαι Ἡρακλείδην εἰς Πέρινθον, ὅπως ἂν μισθὸς γένοιτο τοῖς στρατιώταις· αὐτὸς δὲ καὶ οἱ Ἕλληνες ἐστρατοπεδεύοντο ἀνὰ τὸ Θυνῶν πεδίον· οἱ δ'
3 ἐκλιπόντες ἔφευγον εἰς τὰ ὄρη. ἦν δὲ χιὼν πολλὴ καὶ ψῦχος οὕτως ὥστε τὸ ὕδωρ ὃ ἐφέροντο ἐπὶ δεῖπνον ἐπήγνυτο καὶ ὁ οἶνος ὁ ἐν τοῖς ἀγγείοις, καὶ τῶν
4 Ἑλλήνων πολλῶν καὶ ῥῖνες ἀπεκαίοντο καὶ ὦτα. καὶ τότε δῆλον ἐγένετο οὗ ἕνεκα οἱ Θρᾷκες τὰς ἀλωπεκίδας ἐπὶ ταῖς κεφαλαῖς φοροῦσι καὶ τοῖς ὠσί, καὶ χιτῶνας οὐ μόνον περὶ τοῖς στέρνοις ἀλλὰ καὶ περὶ τοῖς μηροῖς, καὶ ζειρὰς μέχρι τῶν ποδῶν ἐπὶ τῶν
5 ἵππων ἔχουσιν, ἀλλ' οὐ χλαμύδας. ἀφιεὶς δὲ τῶν αἰχμαλώτων ὁ Σεύθης εἰς τὰ ὄρη ἔλεγεν ὅτι εἰ μὴ καταβήσονται οἰκήσοντες καὶ πείσονται, ὅτι κατακαύσει καὶ τούτων τὰς κώμας καὶ τὸν σῖτον, καὶ ἀπολοῦνται τῷ λιμῷ. ἐκ τούτου κατέβαινον καὶ γυναῖκες καὶ παῖδες καὶ πρεσβύτεροι· οἱ δὲ νεώτεροι ἐν
6 ταῖς ὑπὸ τὸ ὄρος κώμαις ηὐλίζοντο. καὶ ὁ Σεύθης καταμαθὼν ἐκέλευσε τὸν Ξενοφῶντα τῶν ὁπλιτῶν τοὺς νεωτάτους λαβόντα συνεπισπέσθαι. καὶ ἀναστάντες τῆς νυκτὸς ἅμα τῇ ἡμέρᾳ παρῆσαν εἰς τὰς κώμας. καὶ οἱ μὲν πλεῖστοι ἐξέφυγον· πλησίον γὰρ ἦν τὸ ὄρος· ὅσους δὲ κατέλαβον κατηκόντισεν ἀφειδῶς Σεύθης.

7 Ἐπισθένης δ' ἦν τις Ὀλύνθιος παιδεραστής, ὃς

IV. On the following day, after Seuthes had burned up the villages completely and left not a single house, in order that he might inspire the rest of his enemies also with fear of the sort of fate they would suffer if they did not yield him obedience, he went back again. Then he dispatched Heracleides to Perinthus to sell the booty, so that he might get money to pay the soldiers with; while he himself and the Greeks encamped on the plain of the Thynians, the inhabitants abandoned their homes and were fleeing to the mountains. There was deep snow on the plain, and it was so cold that the water which they carried in for dinner and the wine in the jars would freeze, and many of the Greeks had their noses and ears frost-bitten. Then it became clear why the Thracians wear fox-skin caps on their heads and over their ears, and tunics not merely about their chests, but also round their thighs, and why, when on horseback, they wear long cloaks reaching to their feet instead of mantles. And now Seuthes allowed some of his captives to go off to the mountains with word that if the Thynians did not come down to the plain to live and did not yield him obedience, he would burn up their villages also and their grain, and they would perish with hunger. Thereupon the women, children, and older men did come down, but the younger men bivouacked in the villages under the mountain. And Seuthes, upon learning of this, ordered Xenophon to take the youngest of the hoplites and follow him. So they arose during the night, and at daybreak reached the villages. Now most of the villagers made their escape, for the mountain was close at hand; but all that they did capture, Seuthes shot down unsparingly.

There was a certain Episthenes of Olynthus who was a

ἰδὼν παῖδα καλὸν ἡβάσκοντα ἄρτι πέλτην ἔχοντα
μέλλοντα ἀποθνήσκειν, προσδραμὼν Ξενοφῶντα ἱκέ-
8 τευε βοηθῆσαι παιδὶ καλῷ. καὶ ὃς προσελθὼν τῷ
Σεύθῃ δεῖται μὴ ἀποκτεῖναι τὸν παῖδα, καὶ τοῦ Ἐπι-
σθένους διηγεῖται τὸν τρόπον, καὶ ὅτι λόχον ποτὲ
συνελέξατο σκοπῶν οὐδὲν ἄλλο ἢ εἴ τινες εἶεν καλοί,
9 καὶ μετὰ τούτων ἦν ἀνὴρ ἀγαθός. ὁ δὲ Σεύθης ἤρετο·
Ἦ καὶ ἐθέλοις ἄν, ὦ Ἐπίσθενες, ὑπὲρ τούτου ἀποθανεῖν; ὁ δ' ἐπανατείνας τὸν τράχηλον, Παῖε, ἔφη, εἰ
10 κελεύει ὁ παῖς καὶ μέλλει χάριν εἰδέναι. ἐπήρετο ὁ
Σεύθης τὸν παῖδα εἰ παίσειεν αὐτὸν ἀντ' ἐκείνου. οὐκ
εἴα ὁ παῖς, ἀλλ' ἱκέτευε μηδέτερον κατακαίνειν. ἐνταῦθα ὁ Ἐπισθένης περιλαβὼν τὸν παῖδα εἶπεν· Ὥρα
11 σοι, ὦ Σεύθη, περὶ τοῦδέ μοι διαμάχεσθαι· οὐ γὰρ
μεθήσω τὸν παῖδα. ὁ δὲ Σεύθης γελῶν ταῦτα μὲν εἴα·
ἔδοξε δὲ αὐτῷ αὐτοῦ αὐλισθῆναι, ἵνα μηδ' ἐκ τούτων
τῶν κωμῶν οἱ ἐπὶ τοῦ ὄρους τρέφοιντο. καὶ αὐτὸς μὲν
ἐν τῷ πεδίῳ ὑποκαταβὰς ἐσκήνου, ὁ δὲ Ξενοφῶν ἔχων
τοὺς ἐπιλέκτους ἐν τῇ ὑπὸ τὸ ὄρος ἀνωτάτω κώμῃ, καὶ
οἱ ἄλλοι Ἕλληνες ἐν τοῖς ὀρεινοῖς καλουμένοις Θραξὶ
πλησίον κατεσκήνησαν.

12 Ἐκ τούτου ἡμέραι τ' οὐ πολλαὶ διετρίβοντο καὶ οἱ
ἐκ τοῦ ὄρους Θρᾷκες καταβαίνοντες πρὸς τὸν Σεύθην
περὶ σπονδῶν καὶ ὁμήρων διεπράττοντο. καὶ ὁ Ξενοφῶν ἐλθὼν ἔλεγε τῷ Σεύθῃ ὅτι ἐν πονηροῖς τόποις

---

[38] Supplies from the villages in the plain having already been
cut off (§5).

lover of boys, and upon seeing a handsome boy, just in the bloom of youth and carrying a light shield, on the point of being put to death, he ran up to Xenophon and besought him to come to the rescue of a handsome lad. So Xenophon went to Seuthes and begged him not to kill the boy, telling him of Episthenes' turn of mind, how he had once assembled a battalion with an eye to nothing else save the question whether a man was handsome, and that with this battalion he proved himself a brave man. And Seuthes asked: "Would you even be willing, Episthenes, to die for this boy's sake?" Then Episthenes stretched out his neck and said, "Strike, if the lad bids you and will be grateful." Seuthes asked the boy whether he should strike Episthenes in his stead. The boy forbade it, and besought him not to slay either. Thereupon Episthenes threw his arms around the boy and said: "It is time, Seuthes, for you to fight it out with me for this boy; for I shall not give him up." And Seuthes laughed and let the matter go. He resolved, however, to establish a camp where they were, in order that the people on the mountain should not be supplied with food from these villages, either.[38] So he himself went quietly down the mountain and encamped upon the plain, while Xenophon with his picked men took quarters in the uppermost village below the summit and the rest of the Greeks close by, among the so-called "mountain" Thracians.

Not many days had passed after this when the Thracians on the mountain came down and entered into negotiations with Seuthes in regard to a truce and hostages. And Xenophon came and told Seuthes that his men were in bad

σκηνοῖεν καὶ πλησίον εἶεν οἱ πολέμιοι· ἥδιόν τ' ἂν
ἔξω αὐλίζεσθαι ἔφη ἐν ἐχυροῖς χωρίοις μᾶλλον ἢ ἐν
τοῖς στεγνοῖς, ὥστε ἀπολέσθαι. ὁ δὲ θαρρεῖν ἐκέλευε

13 καὶ ἔδειξεν ὁμήρους παρόντας αὐτῶν. ἐδέοντο δὲ καὶ
αὐτοῦ Ξενοφῶντος καταβαίνοντές τινες τῶν ἐκ τοῦ
ὄρους συμπρᾶξαι σφίσι τὰς σπονδάς. ὁ δ' ὡμολόγει
καὶ θαρρεῖν ἐκέλευε καὶ ἠγγυᾶτο μηδὲν αὐτοὺς κακὸν
πείσεσθαι πειθομένους Σεύθῃ. οἱ δ' ἄρα ταῦτ' ἔλεγον
κατασκοπῆς ἕνεκα.

14   Ταῦτα μὲν τῆς ἡμέρας ἐγένετο· εἰς δὲ τὴν ἐπιοῦσαν
νύκτα ἐπιτίθενται ἐλθόντες ἐκ τοῦ ὄρους οἱ Θυνοί. καὶ
ἡγεμὼν μὲν ἦν ὁ δεσπότης ἑκάστης τῆς οἰκίας· χαλεπὸν γὰρ ἦν ἄλλως τὰς οἰκίας σκότους ὄντος
ἀνευρίσκειν ἐν ταῖς κώμαις· καὶ γὰρ αἱ οἰκίαι κύκλῳ
περιεσταύρωντο μεγάλοις σταυροῖς τῶν προβάτων

15 ἕνεκα. ἐπεὶ δ' ἐγένοντο κατὰ τὰς θύρας ἑκάστου τοῦ
οἰκήματος, οἱ μὲν εἰσηκόντιζον, οἱ δὲ τοῖς σκυτάλοις
ἔβαλλον, ἃ ἔχειν ἔφασαν ὡς ἀποκόψοντες τῶν δορά-
των τὰς λόγχας, οἱ δ' ἐνεπίμπρασαν, καὶ Ξενοφῶντα
ὀνομαστὶ καλοῦντες ἐξιόντα ἐκέλευον ἀποθνήσκειν, ἢ

16 αὐτοῦ ἔφασαν κατακαυθήσεσθαι αὐτόν. καὶ ἤδη τε
διὰ τοῦ ὀρόφου ἐφαίνετο πῦρ, καὶ ἐντεθωρακισμένοι οἱ
περὶ τὸν Ξενοφῶντα ἔνδον ἦσαν ἀσπίδας καὶ μαχαίρας καὶ κράνη ἔχοντες, καὶ Σιλανὸς Μακίστιος ἐτῶν
ὡς ὀκτωκαίδεκα σημαίνει τῇ σάλπιγγι· καὶ εὐθὺς
ἐκπηδῶσιν ἐσπασμένοι τὰ ξίφη καὶ οἱ ἐκ τῶν ἄλλων

quarters and the enemy were close at hand; he would be better pleased, he said, to bivouac in the open in a strong position than to be in the houses and run the risk of being destroyed. But Seuthes bade him have no fear and showed him hostages that had come from the enemy. Meanwhile some of the people on the mountain came down and actually requested Xenophon himself to help them obtain the truce. He agreed to do so, told them to have no fear, and gave them his word that they would suffer no harm if they were obedient to Seuthes. But they, as it proved, were talking about this matter merely in order to spy out the situation.

All this happened during the day, but in the night that followed the Thynians issued from the mountain and made an attack. And the master of each separate house acted as guide to that house; for in the darkness it would have been difficult to find the houses in these villages in any other way; for each house was surrounded by a paling, made of great stakes, to keep in the cattle. When they had reached the doors of a particular house, some would throw in javelins, others would lay on with their clubs, which they carried, so it was said, to knock off the heads of hostile spears, and still others would be setting the house on fire meanwhile calling Xenophon by name and bidding him come out and be killed, or else, they said, he would be burned up then and there. And now fire was already showing through the roof, and Xenophon and his men inside the house had equipped themselves with breastplates and were furnished with shields and swords and helmets, when Silanus the Macistian, a lad of about eighteen years, gave a signal with the trumpet; and on the instant they leaped forth with swords drawn, and so did the Greeks from the

17 σκηνωμάτων. οἱ δὲ Θρᾷκες φεύγουσιν, ὥσπερ δὴ τρόπος ἦν αὐτοῖς, ὄπισθεν περιβαλλόμενοι τὰς πέλτας·
καὶ αὐτῶν ὑπεραλλομένων τοὺς σταυροὺς ἐλήφθησάν
τινες κρεμασθέντες ἐνεχομένων τῶν πελτῶν τοῖς σταυ-
ροῖς· οἱ δὲ καὶ ἀπέθανον διαμαρτόντες τῶν ἐξόδων· οἱ
18 δὲ Ἕλληνες ἐδίωκον ἔξω τῆς κώμης. τῶν δὲ Θυνῶν
ὑποστραφέντες τινὲς ἐν τῷ σκότει τοὺς παρατρέχον-
τας παρ᾽ οἰκίαν καιομένην ἠκόντιζον εἰς τὸ φῶς ἐκ τοῦ
σκότους· καὶ ἔτρωσαν Ἱερώνυμόν τε Εὐοδέα[8] λοχαγὸν
καὶ Θεογένην Λοκρὸν λοχαγόν· ἀπέθανε δὲ οὐδείς·
19 κατεκαύθη μέντοι καὶ ἐσθής τινων καὶ σκεύη. Σεύθης
δὲ ἧκε βοηθῶν σὺν ἑπτὰ ἱππεῦσι τοῖς πρώτοις καὶ τὸν
σαλπικτὴν ἔχων τὸν Θρᾴκιον. καὶ ἐπείπερ ᾔσθετο,
ὅσονπερ χρόνον ἐβοήθει, τοσοῦτον καὶ τὸ κέρας
ἐφθέγγετο αὐτῷ· ὥστε καὶ τοῦτο φόβον συμπαρέσχε
τοῖς πολεμίοις. ἐπεὶ δ᾽ ἦλθεν, ἐδεξιοῦτό τε καὶ ἔλεγεν
ὅτι οἴοιτο τεθνεῶτας πολλοὺς εὑρήσειν.

20 Ἐκ τούτου ὁ Ξενοφῶν δεῖται τοὺς ὁμήρους τε αὐτῷ
παραδοῦναι καὶ ἐπὶ τὸ ὄρος, εἰ βούλεται, συστρα-
21 τεύεσθαι· εἰ δὲ μή, αὐτὸν ἐᾶσαι. τῇ οὖν ὑστεραίᾳ
παραδίδωσιν ὁ Σεύθης τοὺς ὁμήρους, πρεσβυτέρους
ἄνδρας ἤδη, τοὺς κρατίστους, ὡς ἔφασαν, τῶν ὀρει-
νῶν, καὶ αὐτὸς ἔρχεται σὺν τῇ δυνάμει. ἤδη δὲ εἶχε
καὶ τριπλασίαν δύναμιν ὁ Σεύθης· ἐκ γὰρ τῶν Ὀδρυσῶν ἀκούοντες ἃ πράττοι ὁ Σεύθης πολλοὶ κατέβαινον

---

[8] Εὐοδέα Hude/Peters: καὶ Εὐοδέα MSS. (Mar. doubts):
Ἐπιταλιέα Schenkl: Εὐβοέα Gem., following Ullrich.

other houses. Then the Thracians took to flight, swinging their shields around behind them, as was their custom; and some of them who tried to jump over the palings were captured hanging in the air, with their shields caught in the stakes, while others missed entirely the ways that led out and were killed; and the Greeks continued the pursuit till they were outside the village. Some of the Thynians, however, turned about in the darkness and hurled javelins at men who were running along past a burning house, throwing out of the darkness toward the light; and they wounded Hieronymus the Euodian, a captain, and Theogenes the Locrian, also a captain; no one, however, was killed, but some men had clothes and baggage burned up. Meanwhile, Seuthes came to their aid with seven horsemen of his front line and his Thracian trumpeter. And from the instant he learned of the trouble, through all the time that he was hurrying to the rescue, every moment his horn was kept sounding; the result was, that this also helped to inspire fear in the enemy. When he did arrive, he clasped their hands and said that he had supposed he should find many of them slain.

After this Xenophon asked Seuthes to give over the hostages to him and to join him on an expedition to the mountain, if he so pleased; otherwise, to let him go by himself. On the next day, accordingly, Seuthes gave over the hostages—men already elderly and the most powerful, so it was said, of the mountaineers—and came himself with his troops. Now by this time Seuthes had a force quite three times as large as before; for many of the Odrysians, hearing what success Seuthes was enjoying, came down

22 συστρατευσόμενοι. οἱ δὲ Θυνοὶ ἐπεὶ εἶδον ἀπὸ τοῦ
ὄρους πολλοὺς μὲν ὁπλίτας, πολλοὺς δὲ πελταστάς,
πολλοὺς δὲ ἱππέας, καταβάντες ἱκέτευον σπείσασθαι,
καὶ πάντα ὡμολόγουν ποιήσειν καὶ τὰ πιστὰ λαμ-
23 βάνειν ἐκέλευον. ὁ δὲ Σεύθης καλέσας τὸν Ξενοφῶντα
ἐπεδείκνυεν ἃ λέγοιεν, καὶ οὐκ ἂν ἔφη σπείσασθαι, εἰ
Ξενοφῶν βούλοιτο τιμωρήσασθαι αὐτοὺς τῆς ἐπι-
24 θέσεως. ὁ δ᾽ εἶπεν· Ἀλλ᾽ ἔγωγε ἱκανὴν νομίζω καὶ νῦν
δίκην ἔχειν, εἰ οὗτοι δοῦλοι ἔσονται ἀντ᾽ ἐλευθέρων.
συμβουλεύειν μέντοι ἔφη αὐτῷ τὸ λοιπὸν ὁμήρους
λαμβάνειν τοὺς δυνατωτάτους κακόν τι ποιεῖν, τοὺς
δὲ γέροντας οἴκοι ἐᾶν. οἱ μὲν οὖν ταύτῃ πάντες δὴ
προσωμολόγουν.

V. Ὑπερβάλλουσι δὲ πρὸς τοὺς ὑπὲρ Βυζαντίου
Θρᾷκας εἰς τὸ Δέλτα καλούμενον· αὕτη δ᾽ ἦν οὐκέτι
2 ἀρχὴ Μαισάδου, ἀλλὰ Τήρους τοῦ Ὀδρύσου. καὶ ὁ
Ἡρακλείδης ἐνταῦθα ἔχων τὴν τιμὴν τῆς λείας παρῆν.
καὶ Σεύθης ἐξαγαγὼν ζεύγη ἡμιονικὰ τρία, οὐ γὰρ ἦν
πλείω, τὰ δ᾽ ἄλλα βοεικά, καλέσας Ξενοφῶντα ἐκέλευε
λαβεῖν, τὰ δὲ ἄλλα διανεῖμαι τοῖς στρατηγοῖς καὶ
3 λοχαγοῖς. Ξενοφῶν δὲ τάδ᾽ εἶπεν· Ἐμοὶ τοίνυν ἀρκεῖ
καὶ αὖθις λαβεῖν· τούτοις δὲ τοῖς στρατηγοῖς δωροῦ
4 οἳ σὺν ἐμοὶ ἠκολούθησαν καὶ λοχαγοῖς. καὶ τῶν
ζευγῶν λαμβάνει ἐν μὲν Τιμασίων ὁ Δαρδανεύς, ἐν δὲ
Κλεάνωρ ὁ Ὀρχομένιος, ἐν δὲ Φρυνίσκος ὁ Ἀχαιός·
τὰ δὲ βοεικὰ ζεύγη τοῖς λοχαγοῖς κατεμερίσθη. τὸν

from the upper country to take service with him. And when the Thynians saw from their mountain masses of hoplites, masses of peltasts, and troops of horsemen, they descended and besought him to grant them a truce, agreeing to do anything and everything and urging him to receive their pledges. Thereupon Seuthes summoned Xenophon, disclosed to him the proposals they were making, and said that he should not grant them a truce if Xenophon wanted to punish them for their attack. And Xenophon said: "Why, for my part I think I have abundant satisfaction as it is, if these people are to be slaves instead of free men." He added, however, that he advised Seuthes to take as hostages in the future those who were most capable of doing harm and to leave the old men at home. Thus it was that all the people in this region surrendered.

V. And now they crossed over to the country of the Thracians above Byzantium, in the so-called Delta;[39] this was beyond the domain of Maesades, being the land of Teres the Odrysian. There Heracleides presented himself, with the proceeds from the sale of the booty. And Seuthes, leading forth three pairs of mules—for there were no more than three—and the yokes of oxen besides, called Xenophon and bade him take for himself and then distribute the rest among the generals and captains. Xenophon replied as follows: "Well, for my part I am content to get something at a later time; give rather to these generals and captains who have followed with me." So one of the mule teams was given to Timasion the Dardanian, one to Cleanor the Orchomenian, and one to Phryniscus the Achaean, while the yokes of oxen were distributed among

39 See on i. 33.

δὲ μισθὸν ἀποδίδωσιν ἐξεληλυθότος ἤδη τοῦ μηνὸς
εἴκοσι μόνον ἡμερῶν· ὁ γὰρ Ἡρακλείδης ἔλεγεν ὅτι
5 οὐ πλέον ἐμπολήσαι. ὁ οὖν Ξενοφῶν ἀχθεσθεὶς εἶπεν
ἐπομόσας· Δοκεῖς μοι, ὦ Ἡρακλείδη, οὐχ ὡς δεῖ
κήδεσθαι Σεύθου· εἰ γὰρ ἐκήδου, ἧκες ἂν φέρων πλήρη
τὸν μισθὸν καὶ προσδανεισάμενος, εἰ μή γ' ἄλλως
ἐδύνω, καὶ ἀποδόμενος τὰ ἑαυτοῦ ἱμάτια.

6 Ἐντεῦθεν ὁ Ἡρακλείδης ἠχθέσθη τε καὶ ἔδεισε μὴ
ἐκ τῆς Σεύθου φιλίας ἐκβληθείη, καὶ ὅ τι ἐδύνατο ἀπὸ
ταύτης τῆς ἡμέρας Ξενοφῶντα διέβαλλε πρὸς Σεύθην.
7 οἱ μὲν δὴ στρατιῶται Ξενοφῶντι ἐνεκάλουν ὅτι οὐκ
εἶχον τὸν μισθόν· Σεύθης δὲ ἤχθετο αὐτῷ ὅτι ἐντόνως
8 τοῖς στρατιώταις ἀπῄτει τὸν μισθόν. καὶ τέως μὲν ἀεὶ
ἐμέμνητο ὡς, ἐπειδὰν ἐπὶ θάλατταν ἀπέλθῃ, παρα-
δώσει αὐτῷ Βισάνθην καὶ Γάνον καὶ Νέον τεῖχος· ἀπὸ
δὲ τούτου τοῦ χρόνου οὐδενὸς ἔτι τούτων ἐμέμνητο. ὁ
μὲν γὰρ Ἡρακλείδης καὶ τοῦτο διεβεβλήκει ὡς οὐκ
ἀσφαλὲς εἴη τείχη παραδιδόναι ἀνδρὶ δύναμιν ἔχοντι.
9 Ἐκ τούτου ὁ μὲν Ξενοφῶν ἐβουλεύετο τί χρὴ ποιεῖν
περὶ τοῦ ἔτι ἄνω στρατεύεσθαι· ὁ δ' Ἡρακλείδης
εἰσαγαγὼν τοὺς ἄλλους στρατηγοὺς πρὸς Σεύθην
λέγειν τε ἐκέλευεν αὐτοὺς ὅτι οὐδὲν ἂν ἧττον σφεῖς
ἀγάγοιεν τὴν στρατιὰν ἢ Ξενοφῶν, τόν τε μισθὸν
ὑπισχνεῖτο αὐτοῖς ἐντὸς ὀλίγων ἡμερῶν ἔκπλεων
παρέσεσθαι δυοῖν μηνοῖν, καὶ συστρατεύεσθαι ἐκέ-

---

[40] Note the list Nepos gives of Alcibiades' forts: Ornos (=
Ganos?), Bizanthen, Neontichos (*Alc*. VII. 4).

the captains. Seuthes also paid over the wages of the troops, but for twenty days only of the month that had now passed; for Heracleides said that he had not obtained any more than that from his sale. Xenophon was angered at this, and said to him with an oath: "It seems to me, Heracleides, that you are not caring for Seuthes' interest as you should; for if you were, you would have brought back with you our wages in full, even if you had to borrow something, in case you could not do it in any other way, or to sell your own clothes."

This made Heracleides not only angry, but fearful that he might be banished from the favour of Seuthes, and from that day he slandered Xenophon before Seuthes to the best of his ability. As for the soldiers, they held Xenophon to blame for their not having received their pay; and Seuthes, on the other hand, was angry with him because he was insistent in demanding their pay for the soldiers. Hitherto, he had continually been mentioning the fact that upon his return to the coast he was going to give Xenophon Bisanthe and Ganos and Neonteichos,[40] but from this time he did not allude to a single one of these places again. For Heracleides had put in this slanderous suggestion with the rest, that it was not safe to be giving over fortresses to a man who had a force of troops.

Hereupon Xenophon began to consider what it was best to do about continuing the march still farther inland; Heracleides, on the other hand, took the rest of the generals in to visit Seuthes and bade them say that they could lead the army just as well as Xenophon, while at the same time he promised them that within a few days they would have their pay in full for two months and urged them to continue

599

XENOPHON

10 λευε. καὶ ὁ Τιμασίων εἶπεν· Ἐγὼ μὲν τοίνυν οὐδ' ἂν
πέντε μηνῶν μισθὸς μέλλῃ εἶναι στρατευσαίμην ἂν
ἄνευ Ξενοφῶντος. καὶ ὁ Φρυνίσκος καὶ ὁ Κλεάνωρ

11 συνωμολόγουν τῷ Τιμασίωνι. ἐντεῦθεν ὁ Σεύθης ἐλοι-
δόρει τὸν Ἡρακλείδην ὅτι οὐ παρεκάλει καὶ Ξενοφῶντα. ἐκ δὲ τούτου παρακαλοῦσιν αὐτὸν μόνον. ὁ δὲ
γνοὺς τοῦ Ἡρακλείδου τὴν πανουργίαν ὅτι βούλοιτο
αὐτὸν διαβάλλειν πρὸς τοὺς ἄλλους στρατηγούς, παρέρχεται λαβὼν τούς τε στρατηγοὺς πάντας καὶ τοὺς

12 λοχαγούς. καὶ ἐπεὶ πάντες ἐπείσθησαν, συνεστρα-
τεύοντο καὶ ἀφικνοῦνται ἐν δεξιᾷ ἔχοντες τὸν Πόντον
διὰ τῶν Μελινοφάγων καλουμένων Θρᾳκῶν εἰς τὸν
Σαλμυδησσόν. ἔνθα τῶν εἰς τὸν Πόντον πλεουσῶν
νεῶν πολλαὶ ὀκέλλουσι καὶ ἐκπίπτουσι· τέναγος γάρ

13 ἐστιν ἐπὶ πάμπολυ τῆς θαλάττης. καὶ οἱ Θρᾷκες οἱ
κατὰ ταῦτα οἰκοῦντες στήλας ὁρισάμενοι τὰ καθ'
αὑτοὺς ἐκπίπτοντα ἕκαστοι λῄζονται· τέως δὲ ἔλεγον
πρὶν ὁρίσασθαι ἁρπάζοντας πολλοὺς ὑπ' ἀλλήλων

14 ἀποθνήσκειν. ἐνταῦθα ηὑρίσκοντο πολλαὶ μὲν κλῖναι,
πολλὰ δὲ κιβώτια, πολλαὶ δὲ βίβλοι γεγραμμέναι,[9]
καὶ τἆλλα πολλὰ ὅσα ἐν ξυλίνοις τεύχεσι ναύκληροι
ἄγουσιν. ἐντεῦθεν ταῦτα καταστρεψάμενοι ἀπῇσαν

15 πάλιν. ἔνθα δὴ Σεύθης εἶχε στράτευμα ἤδη πλέον τοῦ
Ἑλληνικοῦ· ἔκ τε γὰρ Ὀδρυσῶν πολὺ ἔτι πλείους

---

[9] γεγραμμέναι om. some MSS.; Hude/Peters doubt, Mar. accepts.

the campaign with Seuthes. And Timasion said: "Well, so far as I am concerned, I shall undertake no campaign without Xenophon even if there is going to be five months' pay." And Phryniscus and Cleanor agreed with Timasion. Thereupon Seuthes fell to abusing Heracleides because he had not invited Xenophon in also. The upshot of this was, that they invited Xenophon by himself. And he, comprehending the rascality of Heracleides, in wanting to make him an object of suspicion to the other generals, brought with him when he came all the generals and the captains. When all of them had been prevailed upon, they continued the march with Seuthes, and, keeping the Pontus upon the right through the country of the millet-eating Thracians, as they are called, arrived at Salmydessus. Here many vessels sailing to the Pontus run aground and are wrecked; for there are shoals that extend far and wide.[41] And the Thracians who dwell on this coast have boundary stones set up and each group of them plunder the ships that are wrecked within their own limits; but in earlier days, before they fixed the boundaries, it was said that in the course of their plundering many of them used to be killed by one another. Here there were found great numbers of beds and boxes, quantities of written books,[42] and an abundance of all the other articles that shipowners carry in wooden chests. After subduing the country in this neighbourbood they set out upon their return. By that time Seuthes had an army larger than the Greek army; for more and still more of the Odrysians had come down from the interior, and the

[41] Hipponax 115 West (Archilochus?); [Aes.] *PV* 725 ff.

[42] Written as opposed to blank rolls; suggests works were articles of trade. Reynolds & Wilson, *Scribes and Scholars* 3rd ed. (Oxford, 1991) 244.

XENOPHON

κατεβεβήκεσαν καὶ οἱ ἀεὶ πειθόμενοι συνεστρατεύ-
οντο. κατηυλίσθησαν δ' ἐν τῷ πεδίῳ ὑπὲρ Σηλυμβρίας
ὅσον τριάκοντα σταδίους ἀπέχοντες τῆς θαλάττης.
16 καὶ μισθὸς μὲν οὐδείς πω ἐφαίνετο· πρὸς δὲ τὸν
Ξενοφῶντα οἵ τε στρατιῶται παγχαλέπως εἶχον ὅ τε
Σεύθης οὐκέτι οἰκείως διέκειτο, ἀλλ' ὁπότε συγγενέσθαι αὐτῷ βουλόμενος ἔλθοι, πολλαὶ ἤδη ἀσχολίαι
ἐφαίνοντο.

VI. Ἐν τούτῳ τῷ χρόνῳ σχεδὸν ἤδη δύο μηνῶν
ὄντων ἀφικνεῖται Χαρμῖνός τε ὁ Λάκων καὶ Πολύνικος
παρὰ Θίβρωνος, καὶ λέγουσιν ὅτι Λακεδαιμονίοις
δοκεῖ στρατεύεσθαι ὡς ἐπὶ Τισσαφέρνη, καὶ Θίβρων
ἐκπέπλευκεν ὡς πολεμήσων, καὶ δεῖται ταύτης τῆς
στρατιᾶς καὶ λέγει ὅτι δαρεικὸς ἑκάστῳ ἔσται μισθὸς
τοῦ μηνός, καὶ τοῖς λοχαγοῖς διμοιρία, τοῖς δὲ στρατηγοῖς τετραμοιρία.

2 Ἐπεὶ δ' ἦλθον οἱ Λακεδαιμόνιοι, εὐθὺς ὁ Ἡρακλείδης πυθόμενος ὅτι ἐπὶ τὸ στράτευμα ἥκουσι λέγει
τῷ Σεύθῃ ὅτι κάλλιστόν τι γεγένηται· οἱ μὲν γὰρ
Λακεδαιμόνιοι δέονται τοῦ στρατεύματος, σὺ δὲ οὐκέτι
δέει· ἀποδιδοὺς δὲ τὸ στράτευμα χαριῇ αὐτοῖς, σὲ δὲ
οὐκέτι ἀπαιτήσουσι τὸν μισθόν, ἀλλ' ἀπαλλάξονται
3 ἐκ τῆς χώρας. ἀκούσας ταῦτα ὁ Σεύθης κελεύει παρ-
άγειν· καὶ ἐπεὶ εἶπον ὅτι ἐπὶ τὸ στράτευμα ἥκουσιν,
λέγει ὅτι τὸ στράτευμα ἀποδίδωσι, φίλος τε καὶ σύμ-
μαχος εἶναι βούλεται, καλεῖ τε αὐτοὺς ἐπὶ ξένια· καὶ
ἐξένιζε μεγαλοπρεπῶς. Ξενοφῶντα δὲ οὐκ ἐκάλει, οὐδὲ

peoples that from time to time were reduced to obedience would join in the campaign. And they went into camp on the plain above Selymbria, at a distance of about thirty stadia from the coast. As for pay, there was none to be seen as yet; and not only did the soldiers entertain very hard feelings toward Xenophon, but Seuthes no longer felt kindly toward him, and whenever Xenophon came and wanted to have a meeting with him, it would straightway be found that he had engagements in abundance.

VI. At this time, when nearly two months had already passed, Charminus the Laconian and Polynicus arrived on a mission from Thibron: they said that the Lacedaemonians had resolved to undertake a campaign against Tissaphernes, that Thibron had set sail to wage the war, and that he wanted this army; also that he said the pay would be a daric per month for every man, twice as much for the captains, and four times as much for the generals.[43]

When the Lacedaemonians arrived, on the instant Heracleides learned that they had come to get the army, and told Seuthes that a most fortunate thing had happened: "The Lacedaemonians want the army, and you no longer want it; by giving up the army you will be doing them a favour, while, on your side, the troops will not go on demanding their pay from you, but will soon be quitting the country." Upon hearing these words Seuthes directed him to introduce the envoys; and when they told him that they had come after the army, he replied that he would deliver it up and that he desired to be their friend and ally; he also invited them to dinner, and entertained them magnificently. Xenophon, however, he did not invite, nor

43 Cf. ii. 36, vi. 7; *Hell.* III. i. 4.

4 τῶν ἄλλων στρατηγῶν οὐδένα. ἐρωτώντων δὲ τῶν
Λακεδαιμονίων τίς ἀνὴρ εἴη Ξενοφῶν ἀπεκρίνατο ὅτι
τὰ μὲν ἄλλα εἴη οὐ κακός, φιλοστρατιώτης δέ· καὶ διὰ
τοῦτο χεῖρόν ἐστιν αὐτῷ. καὶ οἳ εἶπον· Ἀλλ᾽ ἦ
δημαγωγεῖ ὁ ἀνὴρ τοὺς ἄνδρας; καὶ ὁ Ἡρακλείδης,
5 Πάνυ μὲν οὖν, ἔφη. Ἆρ᾽ οὖν, ἔφασαν, μὴ καὶ ἡμῖν
ἐναντιώσεται τῆς ἀπαγωγῆς; Ἀλλ᾽ ἢν ὑμεῖς, ἔφη ὁ
Ἡρακλείδης, συλλέξαντες αὐτοὺς ὑπόσχησθε τὸν
μισθόν, ὀλίγον ἐκείνῳ προσσχόντες ἀποδραμοῦνται
6 σὺν ὑμῖν. Πῶς οὖν ἄν, ἔφασαν, ἡμῖν συλλεγεῖεν;
Αὔριον ὑμᾶς, ἔφη ὁ Ἡρακλείδης, πρῲ ἄξομεν πρὸς
αὐτούς· καὶ οἶδα, ἔφη, ὅτι ἐπειδὰν ὑμᾶς ἴδωσιν, ἄσμενοι συνδραμοῦνται. αὕτη μὲν ἡ ἡμέρα οὕτως ἔληξεν.
7 Τῇ δ᾽ ὑστεραίᾳ ἄγουσιν ἐπὶ τὸ στράτευμα τοὺς
Λάκωνας Σεύθης τε καὶ Ἡρακλείδης, καὶ συλλέγεται
ἡ στρατιά. τὼ δὲ Λάκωνε ἐλεγέτην ὅτι Λακεδαιμονίοις
δοκεῖ πολεμεῖν Τισσαφέρνει τῷ ὑμᾶς ἀδικήσαντι· ἢν
οὖν ἴητε σὺν ἡμῖν, τόν τε ἐχθρὸν τιμωρήσεσθε καὶ
δαρεικὸν ἕκαστος οἴσει τοῦ μηνὸς ὑμῶν, λοχαγὸς δὲ
8 τὸ διπλοῦν, στρατηγὸς δὲ τὸ τετραπλοῦν. καὶ οἱ στρατιῶται ἄσμενοί τε ἤκουσαν καὶ εὐθὺς ἀνίσταταί τις
τῶν Ἀρκάδων τοῦ Ξενοφῶντος κατηγορήσων. παρῆν
δὲ καὶ Σεύθης βουλόμενος εἰδέναι τί πραχθήσεται, καὶ
9 ἐν ἐπηκόῳ εἱστήκει ἔχων ἑρμηνέα· συνίει δὲ καὶ αὐτὸς
ἑλληνιστὶ τὰ πλεῖστα. ἔνθα δὴ λέγει ὁ Ἀρκάς· Ἀλλ᾽

---

44 The first clear use of 'demagogue' in a derogatory sense: see

any one of the other generals. When the Lacedaemonians asked what sort of a man Xenophon was, he replied that he was not a bad fellow on the whole, but he was a friend of the soldiers, and on that account things went the worse for him. And they said: "He plays the demagogue, you mean, with the men?"[44] "Exactly that," said Heracleides. "Well," said they, "he won't go so far, will he, as to oppose us in the matter of taking away the army?" "Why," said Heracleides, "if you gather the men together and promise them their pay, they will hurry after you, paying scant heed to him." "How, then," they said, "could we get them together?" "Tomorrow morning," Heracleides replied, "we will take you to them; and I know," he continued, "that as soon as they catch sight of you, they will hurry together with all eagerness." So ended this day.

The next day Seuthes and Heracleides conducted the Laconians to the army, and the troops gathered together. And the two Laconians said: "The Lacedaemonians have resolved to make war upon Tissaphernes, the man who wronged you; so if you will come with us, you will punish your enemy and, besides, each one of you will receive a daric a month, each captain twofold, and each general fourfold." The soldiers were delighted to hear these words, and straightway one of the Arcadians got up to accuse Xenophon. Now Seuthes also was present, for he wanted to know what would be done, and was standing within hearing distance along with an interpreter, although he could really understand for himself most of what was said in Greek. Thereupon this Arcadian said: "For our part,

W. R. Connor, *The New Politicians of Fifth-Century Athens* (Princeton, 1971) 110 n. 34.

ἡμεῖς μέν, ὦ Λακεδαιμόνιοι, καὶ πάλαι ἂν ἦμεν παρ'
ὑμῖν, εἰ μὴ Ξενοφῶν ἡμᾶς δεῦρο πείσας ἀπήγαγεν,
ἔνθα δὴ ἡμεῖς μὲν τὸν δεινὸν χειμῶνα στρατευόμενοι
καὶ νύκτα καὶ ἡμέραν οὐδὲν πεπαύμεθα· ὁ δὲ τοὺς
ἡμετέρους πόνους ἔχει· καὶ Σεύθης ἐκεῖνον μὲν ἰδίᾳ
10 πεπλούτικεν, ἡμᾶς δὲ ἀποστερεῖ τὸν μισθόν· ὥστε ἐγὼ
μὲν εἰ τοῦτον ἴδοιμι καταλευσθέντα καὶ δόντα δίκην
ὧν ἡμᾶς περιεῖλκε, καὶ τὸν μισθὸν ἄν μοι δοκῶ ἔχειν
καὶ οὐδὲν ἐπὶ τοῖς πεπονημένοις ἄχθεσθαι. μετὰ
τούτου ἄλλος ἀνέστη ὁμοίως καὶ ἄλλος. ἐκ δὲ τούτου
Ξενοφῶν ἔλεξεν ὧδε.

11 Ἀλλὰ πάντα μὲν ἄρα ἄνθρωπον ὄντα προσδοκᾶν
δεῖ, ὁπότε γε καὶ ἐγὼ νῦν ὑφ' ὑμῶν αἰτίας ἔχω ἐν ᾧ
πλείστην προθυμίαν ἐμαυτῷ γε δή μοι δοκῶ συν-
ειδέναι περὶ ὑμᾶς παρεσχημένος. ἀπετραπόμην μέν
γε ἤδη οἴκαδε ὡρμημένος, οὐ μὰ τὸν Δία οὔτοι πυν-
θανόμενος ὑμᾶς εὖ πράττειν, ἀλλὰ μᾶλλον ἀκούων ἐν
12 ἀπόροις εἶναι, ὡς ὠφελήσων εἴ τι δυναίμην. ἐπεὶ δὲ
ἦλθον, Σεύθου τουτουὶ πολλοὺς ἀγγέλους πρὸς ἐμὲ
πέμποντος καὶ πολλὰ ὑπισχνουμένου μοι, εἰ πείσαιμι
ὑμᾶς πρὸς αὐτὸν ἐλθεῖν, τοῦτο μὲν οὐκ ἐπεχείρησα
ποιεῖν, ὡς αὐτοὶ ὑμεῖς ἐπίστασθε. ἦγον δὲ ὅθεν ᾤμην
τάχιστ' ἂν ὑμᾶς εἰς τὴν Ἀσίαν διαβῆναι. ταῦτα γὰρ
καὶ βέλτιστα ἐνόμιζον ὑμῖν εἶναι καὶ ὑμᾶς ᾔδειν
13 βουλομένους. ἐπεὶ δ' Ἀρίσταρχος ἐλθὼν σὺν τριήρε-
σιν ἐκώλυσε διαπλεῖν ἡμᾶς, ἐκ τούτου, ὅπερ εἰκὸς
δήπου ἦν, συνέλεξα ὑμᾶς, ὅπως βουλευσαίμεθα ὅ τι
14 χρὴ ποιεῖν. οὐκοῦν ὑμεῖς ἀκούοντες μὲν Ἀριστάρχου

Lacedaemonians, we should have been with you a long time ago if Xenophon had not talked us over and led us off to this region, where we have never ceased campaigning, by night or day, through an awful winter, while he gets the fruits of our toils; for Seuthes has enriched him personally while he defrauds us of our pay; so for myself, if I could see this fellow stoned to death as punishment for having dragged us about as he has done, I should consider that I had my pay and should feel no anger over the toils I have endured." After this speaker another arose and talked in the same way, and then another. After that Xenophon spoke as follows:

"Well, it is true, after all, that a human being must expect anything and everything, seeing that I now find myself blamed by you in a matter where I am conscious—at least, in my own opinion—of having shown the utmost zeal in your behalf. I turned back after I had already set out for home, not—Heaven knows it was not—because I learned that you were prospering, but rather because I heard that you were in difficulties; and I turned back to help you in any way I could. When I had arrived, although Seuthes here sent many messengers to me and made me many promises if only I would persuade you to come to him, I did not try to do that, as you know for yourselves. Instead, I led you to a place from which I thought you could most speedily cross over to Asia; for I believed that this course was the best one for you and I knew it was the one you desired. But when Aristarchus came with his triremes and prevented our sailing across, at that moment—and surely it was exactly the proper step—I gathered you together so that we might consider what we should better do. So you with your own ears heard Aristar-

ἐπιτάττοντος ὑμῖν εἰς Χερρόνησον πορεύεσθαι,
ἀκούοντες δὲ Σεύθου πείθοντος αὐτῷ συστρατεύεσθαι,
πάντες μὲν ἐλέγετε σὺν Σεύθῃ ἰέναι, πάντες δ᾽
ἐψηφίσασθε ταῦτα. τί οὖν ἐγὼ ἐνταῦθα ἠδίκησα
15 ἀγαγὼν ὑμᾶς ἔνθα πᾶσιν ὑμῖν ἐδόκει; ἐπεί γε μὴν
ψεύδεσθαι ἤρξατο Σεύθης περὶ τοῦ μισθοῦ, εἰ μὲν
ἐπαινῶ αὐτόν, δικαίως ἄν με καὶ αἰτιῷσθε καὶ μισοῖτε·
εἰ δὲ πρόσθεν αὐτῷ πάντων μάλιστα φίλος ὢν νῦν
πάντων διαφορώτατός εἰμι, πῶς ἂν ἔτι δικαίως ὑμᾶς
αἱρούμενος ἀντὶ Σεύθου ὑφ᾽ ὑμῶν αἰτίαν ἔχοιμι περὶ
ὧν πρὸς τοῦτον διαφέρομαι;

16 Ἀλλ᾽ εἴποιτ᾽ ἂν ὅτι ἔξεστι καὶ τὰ ὑμέτερα ἔχοντα
παρὰ Σεύθου τεχνάζειν. οὐκοῦν δῆλον τοῦτό γέ ἐστιν,
εἴπερ ἐμοὶ ἐτέλει τι Σεύθης, οὐχ οὕτως ἐτέλει δήπου
ὡς ὧν τε ἐμοὶ δοίη στέροιτο καὶ ἄλλα ὑμῖν ἀπο-
τείσειεν, ἀλλ᾽ οἶμαι, εἰ ἐδίδου, ἐπὶ τούτῳ ἂν ἐδίδου
17 ὅπως ἐμοὶ δοὺς μεῖον μὴ ἀποδοίη ὑμῖν τὸ πλέον. εἰ
τοίνυν οὕτως ἔχειν οἴεσθε, ἔξεστιν ὑμῖν αὐτίκα μάλα
ματαίαν ταύτην τὴν πρᾶξιν ἀμφοτέροις ἡμῖν ποιῆσαι,
ἐὰν πράττητε αὐτὸν τὰ χρήματα. δῆλον γὰρ ὅτι Σεύθης, εἰ ἔχω τι παρ᾽ αὐτοῦ, ἀπαιτήσει με, καὶ ἀπαιτήσει
μέντοι δικαίως, ἐὰν μὴ βεβαιῶ τὴν πρᾶξιν αὐτῷ ἐφ᾽ ᾗ
18 ἐδωροδόκουν. ἀλλὰ πολλοῦ μοι δοκῶ δεῖν τὰ ὑμέτερα ἔχειν· ὀμνύω γὰρ ὑμῖν θεοὺς ἅπαντας καὶ πάσας

chus direct you to march to the Chersonese and you heard
Seuthes urge you to take the field with him, and then every
man of you spoke in favour of going with Seuthes and every
man of you voted to do so. What wrong, therefore, did I
do in that matter, when I led you to the place where you
had all decided to go? When Seuthes began to play false
with you in the matter of your pay, if I am his supporter in
that, it would be just for you to blame me and hate me; but
if the truth is that I, who before that was the most friendly
to him of us all, am now most of all at variance with him,
how can it be just in this case that, when I sided with you
rather than with Seuthes, I should be blamed by you about
the things in which I am at variance with him?

"But it is possible, you might say, that I really have
received from Seuthes the money that belongs to you, and
am only tricking you. Then this at least is clear: if Seuthes
was in fact paying anything to me, he surely was not paying
it with the understanding that he was both to lose whatever
he gave me and at the same time was to pay other sums to
you, but rather, I presume, if he were giving me anything,
he would be giving it with this understanding, that by giving a smaller sum to me he would escape paying over the
larger to you. Now if you imagine that this is the case, it is
within your power upon the instant to make this transaction a vain one for us both by exacting your money from
him. For it is clear that, if I have received anything from
Seuthes, he will demand it back from me, and, moreover,
he will demand it back with justice if I am failing to fulfil
for him the undertaking for which I was accepting his gifts.
But it is far from being true, in my opinion, that I have
received what belongs to you; for I swear to you by all the
gods and goddesses that I have not even received what

609

μηδ' ἃ ἐμοὶ ἰδίᾳ ὑπέσχετο Σεύθης ἔχειν· πάρεστι δὲ
19 καὶ αὐτὸς καὶ ἀκούων σύνοιδέ μοι εἰ ἐπιορκῶ· ἵνα δὲ
μᾶλλον θαυμάσητε, συνεπόμνυμι μηδὲ ἃ οἱ ἄλλοι
στρατηγοὶ ἔλαβον εἰληφέναι, μὴ τοίνυν μηδὲ ὅσα τῶν
λοχαγῶν ἔνιοι.

20 Καὶ τί δὴ ταῦτ' ἐποίουν; ᾤμην, ὦ ἄνδρες, ὅσῳ
μᾶλλον συμφέροιμι τούτῳ τὴν τότε πενίαν, τοσούτῳ
μᾶλλον αὐτὸν φίλον μοι ἔσεσθαι, ὁπότε δυνασθείη.
ἐγὼ δὲ ἅμα τε αὐτὸν ὁρῶ εὖ πράττοντα καὶ γιγνώσκω
21 δὴ αὐτοῦ τὴν γνώμην. εἴποι δή τις ἄν, οὔκουν αἰσχύνει
οὕτω μώρως ἐξαπατώμενος; ναὶ μὰ Δία ᾐσχυνόμην
μεντἄν, εἰ ὑπὸ πολεμίου γε ὄντος ἐξηπατήθην· φίλῳ
δὲ ὄντι ἐξαπατᾶν αἴσχιόν μοι δοκεῖ εἶναι ἢ ἐξα-
22 πατᾶσθαι. ἐπεὶ εἴ γε πρὸς φίλους ἐστὶ φυλακή, πᾶσαν
οἶδα ἡμᾶς φυλαξαμένους ὡς μὴ παρασχεῖν τούτῳ
πρόφασιν δικαίαν μὴ ἀποδιδόναι ἡμῖν ἃ ὑπέσχετο·
οὔτε γὰρ ἠδικήσαμεν τοῦτον οὐδὲν οὔτε κατεβλα-
κεύσαμεν τὰ τούτου οὐδὲ μὴν κατεδειλιάσαμεν οὐδὲν
ἐφ' ὅ τι ἡμᾶς οὗτος παρεκάλεσεν.

23 Ἀλλά, φαίητε ἄν, ἔδει τὰ ἐνέχυρα τότε λαβεῖν, ὡς
μηδ' εἰ ἐβούλετο ἐδύνατο ἐξαπατᾶν. πρὸς ταῦτα δὴ
ἀκούσατε ἃ ἐγὼ οὐκ ἄν ποτε εἶπον τούτου ἐναντίον, εἰ
μή μοι παντάπασιν ἀγνώμονες ἐδοκεῖτε εἶναι ἢ λίαν
24 εἰς ἐμὲ ἀχάριστοι. ἀναμνήσθητε γὰρ ἐν ποίοις τισὶ
πράγμασιν ὄντες ἐτυγχάνετε, ἐξ ὧν ὑμᾶς ἐγὼ ἀνήγα-

Seuthes promised to me for my own services; he is present here himself, and as he listens he knows as well as I do whether I am swearing falsely; furthermore, to make your wonder the greater, I swear besides that I have not even received what the other generals have received—nay, not even so much as some of the captains.

"And why, then, did I follow this course? I supposed, soldiers, that the more I helped this man to bear the poverty in which he then was, the more he would be my friend when he should have gained power. But in fact I no sooner see him enjoying prosperity than I recognize his true character. One might say, 'Are you not ashamed of being so stupidly deceived?' I certainly should be ashamed, by Zeus, if I had been deceived by one who was an enemy; but for one who is a friend, to deceive seems to me more shameful than to be deceived.[45] For if there is such a thing as precaution toward friends, I know that we took every precaution not to afford this man a just pretext for not paying us what he had promised; for we neither did this man any wrong, nor did we mismanage his affairs, nor yet did we shrink like cowards from any service to which he summoned us.

"But, you might say, sureties ought to have been taken at the time, so that he could not have deceived us even if he had wanted to do so. In reply to that, listen to words which I never should have spoken in this man's presence if you had not seemed to me utterly senseless—or at least exceedingly thankless toward me. Recollect in what sort of troubles you then found yourselves, troubles out of which

[45] Contrast *Mem.* IV. ii. 27. Closer to this remark is the defence of Socrates at *Mem.* I. ii; cf. also Plato, *Smp.* 185a–b.

γον πρὸς Σεύθην. οὐκ εἰς μὲν Πέρινθον, εἰ προσῆτε
τῇ πόλει,[10] Ἀρίσταρχος ὑμᾶς ὁ Λακεδαιμόνιος οὐκ εἴα
εἰσιέναι ἀποκλείσας τὰς πύλας; ὑπαίθριοι δ᾽ ἔξω
ἐστρατοπεδεύετε, μέσος δὲ χειμὼν ἦν, ἀγορᾷ δὲ
ἐχρῆσθε σπάνια μὲν ὁρῶντες τὰ ὤνια, σπάνια δ᾽
25 ἔχοντες ὅτων ὠνήσεσθε· ἀνάγκη δὲ ἦν μένειν ἐπὶ
Θρᾴκης, τριήρεις γὰρ ἐφορμοῦσαι ἐκώλυον διαπλεῖν·
εἰ δὲ μένοι τις, ἐν πολεμίᾳ εἶναι, ἔνθα πολλοὶ μὲν
26 ἱππεῖς ἦσαν ἐναντίοι, πολλοὶ δὲ πελτασταί, ἡμῖν δὲ
ὁπλιτικὸν μὲν ἦν ᾧ ἀθρόοι μὲν ἰόντες ἐπὶ τὰς κώμας
ἴσως ἂν ἐδυνάμεθα σῖτον λαμβάνειν οὐδέν τι ἄφθο-
νον, ὅτῳ δὲ διώκοντες ἂν ἢ ἀνδράποδα ἢ πρόβατα
κατελαμβάνομεν οὐκ ἦν ἡμῖν· οὔτε γὰρ ἱππικὸν οὔτε
πελταστικὸν ἔτι ἐγὼ συνεστηκὸς κατέλαβον παρ᾽
ὑμῖν.

27 Εἰ οὖν ἐν τοιαύτῃ ἀνάγκῃ ὄντων ὑμῶν μηδ᾽ ὀντι-
ναοῦν μισθὸν προσαιτήσας Σεύθην σύμμαχον ὑμῖν
προσέλαβον, ἔχοντα καὶ ἱππέας καὶ πελταστὰς ὧν
ὑμεῖς προσεδεῖσθε, ἦ κακῶς ἂν ἐδόκουν ὑμῖν βε-
28 βουλεῦσθαι πρὸ ὑμῶν; τούτων γὰρ δήπου κοινωνή-
σαντες καὶ σῖτον ἀφθονώτερον ἐν ταῖς κώμαις ηὑρί-
σκετε διὰ τὸ ἀναγκάζεσθαι τοὺς Θρᾷκας κατὰ
σπουδὴν μᾶλλον φεύγειν, καὶ προβάτων καὶ ἀνδρα-

---

[10] τῇ πόλει some MSS., followed by Hude/Peters: other MSS.
have πόλιν, which Mar. brackets, while Gem. adds τὴν.

---

[46] *i.e.* upon his return to the army. Divisions of cavalry and
peltasts had existed during the retreat, and it would seem from

I delivered you when I brought you to Seuthes. Did not the Lacedaemonian Aristarchus prevent you from entering Perinthus by shutting the gates, whenever you drew near the city? So you encamped outside, under the sky, though it was midwinter, and you got your provisions by purchase at a market, though scanty were the supplies you saw offered for sale and scanty the means you had with which to buy; yet you were compelled to remain upon the Thracian coast, for over against you lay triremes that prevented your crossing to Asia; and remaining there, you were of necessity in a hostile country, where there were many horsemen opposed to you and many peltasts; as for ourselves, we had a force of hoplites to be sure, with which, in case we went in a body against the villages, we might perhaps have been able to obtain food, though by no means an abundant supply, but any force with which we could have pursued and captured either slaves or cattle we had not; for I had found[46] no division either of cavalry or of peltasts in existence any longer among you.

"Now when you were in such straits, if I had obtained for you, without demanding into the bargain any pay whatsoever, simply an alliance with Seuthes, who possessed both the cavalry and the peltasts that you were in need of, would you have thought that I had carried through a bad plan on your behalf? For you remember, I imagine, that when you had joined forces with these troops, you not only found food in greater abundance in the villages, for the reason that the Thracians were compelled to flee in greater haste, but you also got a larger share of cattle and captives.

the present passage that they were not broken up till after Xenophon set sail for Greece (ii. 5, 8).

29 πόδων μᾶλλον μετέσχετε. καὶ πολέμιον οὐκέτι οὐδένα
ἑωρῶμεν ἐπειδὴ τὸ ἱππικὸν ἡμῖν προσεγένετο· τέως
δὲ θαρραλέως ἡμῖν ἐφείποντο οἱ πολέμιοι καὶ ἱππικῷ
καὶ πελταστικῷ κωλύοντες μηδαμῇ κατ' ὀλίγους ἀποσκεδαννυμένους τὰ ἐπιτήδεια ἀφθονώτερα ἡμᾶς
30 πορίζεσθαι. εἰ δὲ δὴ ὁ συμπαρέχων ὑμῖν ταύτην τὴν
ἀσφάλειαν μὴ πάνυ πολὺν μισθὸν προσετέλει τῆς
ἀσφαλείας, τοῦτο δὴ τὸ πάθημα τὸ σχέτλιον καὶ διὰ
τοῦτο οὐδαμῇ οἴεσθε χρῆναι ζῶντα ἐμὲ ἀνεῖναι;

31   Νῦν δὲ δὴ πῶς ἀπέρχεσθε; οὐ διαχειμάσαντες μὲν
ἐν ἀφθόνοις τοῖς ἐπιτηδείοις, περιττὸν δ' ἔχοντες τοῦτο
εἴ τι ἐλάβετε παρὰ Σεύθου; τὰ γὰρ τῶν πολεμίων
ἐδαπανᾶτε. καὶ ταῦτα πράττοντες οὔτε ἄνδρας ἐπείδετε
32 ὑμῶν αὐτῶν ἀποθανόντας οὔτε ζῶντας ἀπεβάλετε. εἰ
δέ τι καλὸν πρὸς τοὺς ἐν τῇ Ἀσίᾳ βαρβάρους
ἐπέπρακτο ὑμῖν, οὐ καὶ ἐκεῖνο σῶν ἔχετε καὶ πρὸς
ἐκείνοις νῦν ἄλλην εὔκλειαν προσειλήφατε καὶ τοὺς
ἐν τῇ Εὐρώπῃ Θρᾷκας ἐφ' οὓς ἐστρατεύσασθε κρατήσαντες; ἐγὼ μὲν ὑμᾶς φημι δικαίως ἂν ὧν ἐμοὶ χαλε-
παίνετε τούτων τοῖς θεοῖς χάριν εἰδέναι ὡς ἀγαθῶν.

33   Καὶ τὰ μὲν δὴ ὑμέτερα τοιαῦτα. ἄγετε δὴ πρὸς θεῶν
καὶ τὰ ἐμὰ σκέψασθε ὡς ἔχει. ἐγὼ γὰρ ὅτε μὲν
πρότερον ἀπῇα οἴκαδε, ἔχων μὲν ἔπαινον πολὺν πρὸς
ὑμῶν ἀπεπορευόμην, ἔχων δὲ δι' ὑμᾶς καὶ ὑπὸ τῶν
ἄλλων Ἑλλήνων εὔκλειαν. ἐπιστευόμην δὲ ὑπὸ Λακε-
δαιμονίων· οὐ γὰρ ἄν με ἔπεμπον πάλιν πρὸς ὑμᾶς.

In fact, we never saw the face of an enemy again after the cavalry had joined us, whereas up to that time the enemy had been following boldly at our heels with horsemen and peltasts and had prevented us from scattering in any direction in small parties and thus securing a greater abundance of provisions. And if, then, the man who aided in providing you this security did not give you, besides, very generous pay for your security, is that a misfortune, a terrible one, and do you think that on that account you cannot possibly let me go alive?

"As matters stand now, what is your situation in departing from here? Have you not passed the winter amid an abundance of provisions, and, whatever you have received from Seuthes, is it not really so much clear gain? For it was the enemy's possessions that you have been consuming. And while enjoying such fortune, you have not had to see any of your number slain nor have you lost any men alive. And if any glorious deed was earlier performed by you against the barbarians in Asia, have you not at the same time kept that secure and likewise gained other glory besides in the present, by vanquishing, in addition, the Thracians in Europe against whom you took the field? For my part, I assert that for the very acts on account of which you now feel angry toward me, you should, in all justice, feel grateful to the gods, counting them as blessings.

"So much, then, for your situation. And now, in the name of the gods, come, and consider how the case stands with me. At the time when I first set out to return home, I possessed, as I departed, abundant praise in your eyes, and I also possessed, through you, fair fame in the eyes of the Greeks at large. And I was trusted by the Lacedaemonians, for otherwise they would not have sent me back to you

615

34 νῦν δὲ ἀπέρχομαι πρὸς μὲν Λακεδαιμονίους ὑφ' ὑμῶν
διαβεβλημένος, Σεύθῃ δὲ ἀπηχθημένος ὑπὲρ ὑμῶν, ὃν
ἤλπιζον εὖ ποιήσας μεθ' ὑμῶν ἀποστροφὴν καὶ ἐμοὶ
35 καλὴν καὶ παισίν, εἰ γένοιντο, καταθήσεσθαι. ὑμεῖς
δ', ὑπὲρ ὧν ἐγὼ ἀπήχθημαί τε πλεῖστα καὶ ταῦτα πολὺ
κρείττοσιν ἐμαυτοῦ, πραγματευόμενός τε οὐδὲ νῦν πω
πέπαυμαι ὅ τι δύναμαι ἀγαθὸν [ὑμῖν], τοιαύτην ἔχετε
γνώμην περὶ ἐμοῦ.

36 Ἀλλ' ἔχετε μέν με οὔτε φεύγοντα λαβόντες οὔτε
ἀποδιδράσκοντα· ἢν δὲ ποιήσητε ἃ λέγετε, ἴστε ὅτι
ἄνδρα κατακεκονότες ἔσεσθε πολλὰ μὲν δὴ πρὸ ὑμῶν
ἀγρυπνήσαντα, πολλὰ δὲ σὺν ὑμῖν πονήσαντα καὶ
κινδυνεύσαντα καὶ ἐν τῷ μέρει καὶ παρὰ τὸ μέρος,
θεῶν δ' ἵλεων ὄντων καὶ τρόπαια βαρβάρων πολλὰ
δὴ σὺν ὑμῖν στησάμενον, ὅπως δέ γε μηδενὶ τῶν
Ἑλλήνων πολέμιοι γένησθε, πᾶν ὅσον ἐγὼ ἐδυνάμην
37 πρὸς ὑμᾶς διατεινάμενον. καὶ γὰρ νῦν ὑμῖν ἔξεστιν
ἀνεπιλήπτως πορεύεσθαι ὅπῃ ἂν ἔλησθε καὶ κατὰ γῆν
καὶ κατὰ θάλατταν. ὑμεῖς δέ, ὅτε πολλὴ ὑμῖν εὐπορία
φαίνεται, καὶ πλεῖτε ἔνθα δὴ ἐπεθυμεῖτε πάλαι, δέονται δὲ ὑμῶν οἱ τὸ μέγιστον δυνάμενοι, μισθὸς δὲ
φαίνεται, ἡγεμόνες δὲ ἥκουσι Λακεδαιμόνιοι οἱ κράτιστοι νομιζόμενοι εἶναι, νῦν δὴ καιρὸς ὑμῖν δοκεῖ εἶναι
38 ὡς τάχιστα ἐμὲ κατακανεῖν; οὐ μὴν ὅτε γε ἐν τοῖς
ἀπόροις ἦμεν, ὦ πάντων μνημονικώτατοι, ἀλλὰ καὶ
πατέρα ἐμὲ ἐκαλεῖτε καὶ ἀεὶ ὡς εὐεργέτου μεμνῆσθαι

again. Now, on the other hand, I am going away traduced by you before the Lacedaemonians and hated on your account by Seuthes, the man through whom I hoped to secure, by rendering him good service with your help, a fair place of refuge for myself and my children, in case children should ever be born to me. And you, for whose sake I have incurred most hatred, and the hatred of men far stronger than I am, for whose sake I have not even to this moment ceased striving to accomplish whatever good I may, hold such an opinion of me as this!

"You hold me in your power, then, and not as a captive that you have taken in flight or as a runaway slave; and if you do what you are proposing, be sure that you will have slain a man who has passed many sleepless nights for your sake, who has endured many toils and dangers with you, both when it was his duty and when it was not, who has also, by the graciousness of the gods, set up with you many trophies of victory over the barbarians and who, in order to prevent your becoming enemies to any one among the Greeks, has exerted himself to the very utmost of his power in opposition to you. In fact, you are now free to journey in security wherever you may choose, whether by land or by sea. And you, at the moment when such abundant freedom is evident for you, when you are sailing to the very place where you have long been eager to go and the mightiest are suing for your aid, when pay is within sight and the Lacedaemonians, who are deemed the most powerful leaders, have come to lead you—do you, I say, think that now is the proper time to put me to death with all speed? It was not so, surely, in the days when we were in straits, O you who remember better than all other men; nay, then you called me 'father,' and you promised to keep me for

617

ὑπισχνεῖσθε. οὐ μέντοι ἀγνώμονες οὐδὲ οὗτοί εἰσιν οἱ
νῦν ἥκον ἐφ᾽ ὑμᾶς· ὥστε, ὡς ἐγὼ οἶμαι, οὐδὲ τούτοις
δοκεῖτε βελτίονες εἶναι τοιοῦτοι ὄντες περὶ ἐμέ. ταῦτ᾽
εἰπὼν ἐπαύσατο.

39   Χαρμῖνος δὲ ὁ Λακεδαιμόνιος ἀναστὰς εἶπεν·
Ἀλλὰ μὰ τὼ σιώ, ὦ ἄνδρες,[11] ἐμοὶ μέντοι οὐ δικαίως
δοκεῖτε τῷ ἀνδρὶ τούτῳ χαλεπαίνειν· ἔχω γὰρ καὶ
αὐτὸς αὐτῷ μαρτυρῆσαι. Σεύθης γὰρ ἐρωτῶντος ἐμοῦ
καὶ Πολυνίκου περὶ Ξενοφῶντος τίς ἀνὴρ εἴη, ἄλλο
μὲν οὐδὲν εἶχε μέμψασθαι, ἄγαν δὲ φιλοστρατιώτην
ἔφη αὐτὸν εἶναι· διὸ καὶ χεῖρον αὐτῷ εἶναι πρὸς ἡμῶν
40   τε τῶν Λακεδαιμονίων καὶ πρὸς αὐτοῦ. ἀναστὰς ἐπὶ
τούτῳ Εὐρύλοχος Λουσιάτης εἶπε· Καὶ δοκεῖ γέ μοι,
ἄνδρες Λακεδαιμόνιοι, τοῦτο ὑμᾶς πρῶτον ἡμῶν στρα-
τηγῆσαι, παρὰ Σεύθου ἡμῖν τὸν μισθὸν ἀναπρᾶξαι ἢ
ἑκόντος ἢ ἄκοντος, καὶ μὴ πρότερον ἡμᾶς ἀπαγαγεῖν.
41   Πολυκράτης δὲ Ἀθηναῖος εἶπεν ἐνετὸς ὑπὸ Ξενοφῶν-
τος· Ὁρῶ γε μήν, ἔφη, ὦ ἄνδρες, καὶ Ἡρακλείδην
ἐνταῦθα παρόντα, ὃς παραλαβὼν τὰ χρήματα ἃ ἡμεῖς
ἐπονήσαμεν, ταῦτα ἀποδόμενος οὔτε Σεύθῃ ἀπέδωκεν
οὔτε ἡμῖν τὰ γιγνόμενα, ἀλλ᾽ αὐτὸς κλέψας πέπαται.
ἢν οὖν σωφρονῶμεν, ἑξόμεθα αὐτοῦ· οὐ γὰρ δὴ οὗτός
γε, ἔφη, Θρᾷξ ἐστιν, ἀλλ᾽ Ἕλλην ὢν Ἕλληνας ἀδικεῖ.
42   Ταῦτα ἀκούσας ὁ Ἡρακλείδης μάλα ἐξεπλάγη· καὶ
προσελθὼν τῷ Σεύθῃ λέγει· Ἡμεῖς ἢν σωφρονῶμεν,

____

11 Ἀλλὰ μὰ τὼ σιώ, ὦ ἄνδρες, one MS., followed by Cas-
tiglione, Peters: ἀλλ᾽ οὐ τὼ σιώ most MSS., Hude.

ever in memory as a benefactor! Not by any means, however, are these men, who have now come after you, wanting in judgment; therefore, I imagine, they also think none the better of you for behaving in this manner towards me." With these words he ceased speaking.

Then Charminus the Lacedaemonian arose and said: "Well, by the twin gods,[47] men, I, at any rate, think you are unjust in being angry with this man; for I can bear witness for him myself. When I and Polynicus asked Seuthes about Xenophon, to learn what sort of a man he was, Seuthes had no fault to find with him save that, as he said, he was 'too great a friend of the soldiers,' and on that account, he added, things went the worse for him, both so far as we the Lacedaemonians were concerned and on his own account." After him Eurylochus of Lusi rose and said: "Yes, and I believe, men of Lacedaemon, that you first of all ought to assume leadership over us in this enterprise exacting our pay from Seuthes whether he will or no, and that you should not take us away till that is done." And Polycrates the Athenian said, at the instigation of Xenophon: "Look you, fellow soldiers, I see Heracleides also present here, the man who took in charge the property which we had won by our toil, and then sold it, and did not pay over the proceeds either to Seuthes or to us, but stole the money, and is keeping it for himself. If we are wise, therefore, we shall lay hold of him; for this fellow," said he, "is no Thracian, but a Greek, and yet he is wronging Greeks."

Upon hearing these words Heracleides was exceedingly terrified; and going up to Seuthes, he said: "And if we are

47 Cf. above, VI. vi. 34 and note.

ἄπιμεν ἐντεῦθεν ἐκ τῆς τούτων ἐπικρατείας. καὶ ἀναβάντες ἐπὶ τοὺς ἵππους ᾤχοντο ἀπελαύνοντες εἰς τὸ
43 ἑαυτῶν στρατόπεδον. καὶ ἐντεῦθεν Σεύθης πέμπει
Ἀβροζέλμην τὸν ἑαυτοῦ ἑρμηνέα πρὸς Ξενοφῶντα καὶ
κελεύει αὐτὸν καταμεῖναι παρ' ἑαυτῷ ἔχοντα χιλίους
ὁπλίτας, καὶ ὑπισχνεῖται αὐτῷ ἀποδώσειν τά τε χωρία
τὰ ἐπὶ θαλάττῃ καὶ τὰ ἄλλα ἃ ὑπέσχετο. καὶ ἐν
ἀπορρήτῳ ποιησάμενος λέγει ὅτι ἀκήκοε Πολυνίκου
ὡς εἰ ὑποχείριος ἔσται Λακεδαιμονίοις, σαφῶς ἀπο-
44 θανοῖτο ὑπὸ Θίβρωνος. ἐπέστελλον δὲ ταῦτα καὶ
ἄλλοι πολλοὶ τῷ Ξενοφῶντι ὡς διαβεβλημένος εἴη καὶ
φυλάττεσθαι δέοι. ὁ δὲ ἀκούων ταῦτα δύο ἱερεῖα
λαβὼν ἐθύετο τῷ Διὶ τῷ βασιλεῖ πότερά οἱ λῷον καὶ
ἄμεινον εἴη μένειν παρὰ Σεύθῃ ἐφ' οἷς Σεύθης λέγει ἢ
ἀπιέναι σὺν τῷ στρατεύματι. ἀναιρεῖ αὐτῷ ἀπιέναι.

VII. Ἐντεῦθεν Σεύθης μὲν ἀπεστρατοπεδεύσατο
προσωτέρω· οἱ δὲ Ἕλληνες ἐσκήνησαν εἰς κώμας ὅθεν
ἔμελλον πλεῖστα ἐπισιτισάμενοι ἐπὶ θάλατταν ἥξειν.
αἱ δὲ κῶμαι αὗται ἦσαν δεδομέναι ὑπὸ Σεύθου Μηδο-
2 σάδῃ. ὁρῶν οὖν ὁ Μηδοσάδης δαπανώμενα τὰ ἐν ταῖς
κώμαις ὑπὸ τῶν Ἑλλήνων χαλεπῶς ἔφερε· καὶ λαβὼν
ἄνδρα Ὀδρύσην δυνατώτατον τῶν ἄνωθεν καταβεβη-
κότων καὶ ἱππέας ὅσον τριάκοντα ἔρχεται καὶ προκα-
λεῖται Ξενοφῶντα ἐκ τοῦ Ἑλληνικοῦ στρατεύματος.
καὶ ὃς λαβών τινας τῶν λοχαγῶν καὶ ἄλλους τῶν

---

48 A Persian, to judge by his name, who spoke Greek, as well
as Thracian.   49 See iv. 21, v. 15.

wise, we shall go away from here and get out of the power of these fellows." So they mounted their horses and went riding off to their own camp. And after that Seuthes sent Abrozelmes, his interpreter,[48] to Xenophon and urged him to stay behind with him with a force of a thousand hoplites, promising that he would deliver over to him not only the fortresses upon the coast, but also the other things which he had promised. He likewise said, making a great secret of it, that he had heard from Polynicus that if Xenophon should fall into the hands of the Lacedaemonians, he would certainly be put to death by Thibron. Many other people also sent Xenophon this message, saying that he had been traduced and would better be on his guard. And he, hearing these reports, took two victims and proceeded to offer sacrifice to Zeus the King, to learn whether it was better and more profitable for him to remain with Seuthes on the conditions that Seuthes proposed, or to depart with the army. The god directed him to depart.

VII. After that Seuthes encamped at a greater distance away, while the Greeks took up quarters in villages from which they could secure provisions in greatest abundance before their journey to the coast. Now these villages had been given by Seuthes to Medosades. When, therefore, Medosades saw that the supplies in the villages were being used up by the Greeks, he was angry; and taking with him an Odrysian who was exceedingly powerful, from among those who had come down from the interior,[49] and likewise about thirty horsemen, he came and summoned Xenophon forth from the Greek camp. So Xenophon took certain of the captains as well as others who were fit men for the

3 ἐπιτηδείων προσέρχεται. ἔνθα δὴ λέγει Μηδοσάδης·
Ἀδικεῖτε, ὦ Ξενοφῶν, τὰς ἡμετέρας κώμας πορθοῦντες. προλέγομεν οὖν ὑμῖν, ἐγώ τε ὑπὲρ Σεύθου καὶ ὅδε
ἀνὴρ παρὰ Μηδόκου ἥκων τοῦ ἄνω βασιλέως, ἀπιέναι
ἐκ τῆς χώρας· εἰ δὲ μή, οὐκ ἐπιτρέψομεν ὑμῖν, ἀλλ᾽ ἐὰν
ποιῆτε κακῶς τὴν ἡμετέραν χώραν, ὡς πολεμίους
ἀλεξόμεθα.

4 Ὁ δὲ Ξενοφῶν ἀκούσας ταῦτα εἶπεν· Ἀλλὰ σοὶ μὲν
τοιαῦτα λέγοντι καὶ ἀποκρίνασθαι χαλεπόν· τοῦδε δ᾽
ἕνεκα τοῦ νεανίσκου λέξω, ἵν᾽ εἰδῇ οἷοί τε ὑμεῖς ἐστε
5 καὶ οἷοι ἡμεῖς, ἡμεῖς, μὲν γάρ, ἔφη, πρὶν ὑμῖν φίλοι
γενέσθαι ἐπορευόμεθα διὰ ταύτης τῆς χώρας ὅπῃ
6 ἐβουλόμεθα. ἢν μὲν ἐθέλοιμεν πορθοῦντες, ἢν δ᾽
ἐθέλοιμεν καίοντες, καὶ σὺ ὁπότε πρὸς ἡμᾶς ἔλθοις
πρεσβεύων, ηὐλίζου παρ᾽ ἡμῖν οὐδένα φοβούμενος
τῶν πολεμίων· ὑμεῖς δὲ οὐκ ᾖτε εἰς τήνδε τὴν χώραν, ἢ
εἴ ποτε ἔλθοιτε, ὡς ἐν κρειττόνων χώρᾳ ηὐλίζεσθε
7 ἐγκεχαλινωμένοις τοῖς ἵπποις. ἐπεὶ δὲ ἡμῖν φίλοι
ἐγένεσθε καὶ δι᾽ ἡμᾶς σὺν θεοῖς ἔχετε τήνδε τὴν
χώραν, νῦν δὴ ἐξελαύνετε ἡμᾶς ἐκ τῆσδε τῆς χώρας
ἣν παρ᾽ ἡμῶν ἐχόντων κατὰ κράτος παρελάβετε· ὡς
γὰρ αὐτὸς οἶσθα, οἵ γε πολέμιοι οὐχ ἱκανοὶ ἦσαν
8 ἡμᾶς ἐξελαύνειν. καὶ οὐχ ὅπως δῶρα δοὺς καὶ εὖ
ποιήσας ἀνθ᾽ ὧν εὖ ἔπαθες ἀξιοῖς ἡμᾶς ἀποπέμψα-
σθαι, ἀλλ᾽ ἀποπορευομένους ἡμᾶς οὐδ᾽ ἐναυλισθῆναι

---

[50] Cf. above, ii. 21.

purpose, and came to meet him. Then Medosades said: "You Greeks are committing a wrong, Xenophon, in plundering our villages. Therefore we give you public warning, I on behalf of Seuthes, and this man who has come from Medocus, who is king in the interior, to depart from the country; and if you fail to depart, we shall not leave you a free hand, but in case you continue to do harm to our territory, we shall defend ourselves against you as against enemies."

Upon hearing these words Xenophon said: "As for you, when you say such things as these it is painful even to give you an answer; yet for the sake of this young man here I will speak, that he may know what sort of people you are and what we are. For we," he went on, "before we became friends of yours, marched wherever we chose through this country, plundering where we wished and burning where we wished, and whenever you came to us as envoy, you used to bivouac with us without fear of any enemy; your people, on the other hand, never came into this country, or if at any time you did come, you would bivouac as in the land of men stronger than yourselves, keeping your horses all bridled.[50] But after you had once become friends of ours and now through us, with the aid of the gods, enjoy possession of this land, you seek to drive us forth, out of this land that you received from us, who held it by right of strength; for as you know yourself, the enemy, for their part, were not able to drive us out. And yet, so far from deeming it proper to speed us on our way after bestowing gifts upon us and doing us kindnesses in return for the benefits you have received at our hands, you will not, so far as you have the power to prevent it, allow us at the moment of our departure even to bivouac in the country. And in -

9 ὅσον δύνασαι ἐπιτρέπεις. καὶ ταῦτα λέγων οὔτε θεοὺς
αἰσχύνει οὔτε τόνδε τὸν ἄνδρα, ὃς νῦν μέν σε ὁρᾷ
πλουτοῦντα, πρὶν δὲ ἡμῖν φίλον γενέσθαι ἀπὸ λη-
10 στείας τὸν βίον ἔχοντα, ὡς αὐτὸς ἔφησθα. ἀτὰρ τί
καὶ πρὸς ἐμὲ λέγεις ταῦτα; ἔφη· οὐ γὰρ ἔγωγ' ἔτι
ἄρχω, ἀλλὰ Λακεδαιμόνιοι, οἷς ὑμεῖς παρεδώκατε τὸ
στράτευμα ἀπαγαγεῖν οὐδὲ ἐμὲ παρακαλέσαντες, ὦ
θαυμαστότατοι, ὅπως ὥσπερ ἀπηχθανόμην αὐτοῖς ὅτε
πρὸς ὑμᾶς ἦγον, οὕτω καὶ χαρισαίμην νῦν ἀποδιδούς.

11 Ἐπεὶ ταῦτα ἤκουσεν ὁ Ὀδρύσης, εἶπεν· Ἐγὼ μέν,
ὦ Μηδόσαδες, κατὰ τῆς γῆς καταδύομαι ὑπὸ τῆς
αἰσχύνης ἀκούων ταῦτα. καὶ εἰ μὲν πρόσθεν ἠπιστά-
μην, οὐδ' ἂν συνηκολούθησά σοι· καὶ νῦν ἄπειμι. οὐδὲ
γὰρ ἂν Μήδοκός με ὁ βασιλεὺς ἐπαινοίη, εἰ ἐξελαύ-
12 νοιμι τοὺς εὐεργέτας. ταῦτ' εἰπὼν ἀναβὰς ἐπὶ τὸν
ἵππον ἀπήλαυνε καὶ σὺν αὐτῷ οἱ ἄλλοι ἱππεῖς πλὴν
τεττάρων ἢ πέντε. ὁ δὲ Μηδοσάδης, ἐλύπει γὰρ αὐτὸν
ἡ χώρα πορθουμένη, ἐκέλευε τὸν Ξενοφῶντα καλέσαι
13 τὼ Λακεδαιμονίω. καὶ ὃς λαβὼν τοὺς ἐπιτηδειοτάτους
προσῆλθε τῷ Χαρμίνῳ καὶ τῷ Πολυνίκῳ καὶ ἔλεξεν
ὅτι καλεῖ αὐτοὺς Μηδοσάδης προερῶν ἅπερ αὐτῷ,
14 ἀπιέναι ἐκ τῆς χώρας. οἶμαι ἂν οὖν, ἔφη, ὑμᾶς ἀπολαβεῖν τῇ στρατιᾷ τὸν ὀφειλόμενον μισθόν, εἰ εἴποιτε
ὅτι δεδέηται ὑμῶν ἡ στρατιὰ συναναπρᾶξαι τὸν μισθὸν ἢ παρ' ἑκόντος ἢ παρ' ἄκοντος Σεύθου, καὶ ὅτι
τούτων τυχόντες προθύμως ἂν συνέπεσθαι ὑμῖν φασι·
καὶ ὅτι δίκαια ὑμῖν δοκοῦσι λέγειν· καὶ ὅτι ὑπέσχεσθε

uttering these words you are not ashamed either before the gods or before this Odrysian, who now sees you possessed of riches, whereas before you became our friend you got your living, as you said yourself, from pillaging. But really, why do you," he added, "address these words to me? For I am no longer in command, but rather the Lacedaemonians; and it was to them that you yourselves delivered over the army to be led away, and that, you most ill-mannered of men, without even inviting me to be present, so that even as I had incurred their hatred at the time when I led the army to you, so I might now win their favour by giving it back."

When the Odrysian heard this, he said: "As for me, Medosades, I sink beneath the earth for shame at this which I hear. If I had understood the matter before, I should not even have accompanied you; and now I am going back. For Medocus, the king, would never commend me if I should drive forth his benefactors." With these words he mounted his horse and rode away, and with him went the horsemen also, except four or five. But Medosades, still distressed by the plundering of the country, urged Xenophon to summon the two Lacedaemonians. And Xenophon, taking with him the best men he had, went to Charminus and Polynicus and said that Medosades was summoning them in order to give them the same warning as he had already given him—to depart from the country. "I should think, therefore," he continued, "that you might recover for the army the pay that is due if you should say that the army has requested you to aid them in exacting their pay from Seuthes whether he will or no, and that the troops say that they would follow you eagerly in case they should obtain it; also, that their words seem to you just,

625

αὐτοῖς τότε ἀπιέναι ὅταν τὰ δίκαια ἔχωσιν οἱ στρατιῶται.

15 Ἀκούσαντες οἱ Λάκωνες ταῦτα ἔφασαν ἐρεῖν καὶ ἄλλα ὁποῖα ἂν δύνωνται κράτιστα· καὶ εὐθὺς ἐπορεύοντο ἔχοντες πάντας τοὺς ἐπικαιρίους. ἐλθόντων δὲ ἔλεξε Χαρμῖνος· Εἰ μὲν σύ τι ἔχεις, ὦ Μηδόσαδες,
16 πρὸς ἡμᾶς λέγειν, εἰ δὲ μή, ἡμεῖς πρὸς σὲ ἔχομεν. ὁ δὲ Μηδοσάδης μάλα δὴ ὑφειμένως· Ἀλλ᾽ ἐγὼ μὲν λέγω, ἔφη, καὶ Σεύθης ταὐτά, ὅτι ἀξιοῦμεν τοὺς φίλους ἡμῖν γεγενημένους μὴ κακῶς πάσχειν ὑφ᾽ ὑμῶν. ὅ τι γὰρ ἂν τούτους κακῶς ποιῆτε ἡμᾶς ἤδη
17 ποιεῖτε· ἡμέτεροι γάρ εἰσιν. Ἡμεῖς τοίνυν, ἔφασαν οἱ Λάκωνες, ἀπίοιμεν ἂν ὁπότε τὸν μισθὸν ἔχοιεν οἱ ταῦτα ὑμῖν καταπράξαντες· εἰ δὲ μή, ἐρχόμεθα μὲν καὶ νῦν βοηθήσοντες τούτοις καὶ τιμωρησόμενοι ἄνδρας οἳ τούτους παρὰ τοὺς ὅρκους ἠδίκησαν. ἢν δὲ δὴ καὶ ὑμεῖς τοιοῦτοι ἦτε, ἐνθένδε ἀρξόμεθα τὰ δίκαια
18 λαμβάνειν. ὁ δὲ Ξενοφῶν εἶπεν· Ἐθέλοιτε δ᾽ ἂν τούτοις, ὦ Μηδόσαδες, ἐπιτρέψαι, ἐπειδὴ φίλους φατὲ εἶναι ὑμῖν, ἐν ὧν τῇ χώρᾳ ἐσμέν, ὁπότερ᾽ ἂν ψηφίσωνται, εἴθ᾽ ὑμᾶς προσήκει[12] ἐκ τῆς χώρας ἀπιέναι εἴτε
19 ἡμᾶς; ὁ δὲ ταῦτα μὲν οὐκ ἔφη· ἐκέλευε δὲ μάλιστα μὲν αὐτὼ τὼ Λάκωνε ἐλθεῖν παρὰ Σεύθην περὶ τοῦ μισθοῦ, καὶ οἴεσθαι ἂν Σεύθην πεῖσαι· εἰ δὲ μή, Ξενοφῶντα σὺν αὐτῷ πέμπειν, καὶ συμπράξειν ὑπισχνεῖτο. ἐδεῖτο δὲ τὰς κώμας μὴ καίειν.

[12] προσήκει Gem., Hude/Peters, following Poppo: προσῆκεν MSS., Mar.

and that you promised them not to depart until the soldiers should obtain their rights."

When they had heard him, the Laconians replied that they would make such statements, adding others as forceful as they could make them; and straightway they set forth, taking with them all the important men of the army. Upon their arrival Charminus said: "If you have anything to say to us, Medosades, say it; if not, we have something to say to you." And Medosades replied, very submissively: "I say and Seuthes also says the same, that we ask that those who have become friends of ours should not suffer harm at your hands; for whatever harm you may do to them, you are then and there doing to us; for they are ours." "As for ourselves, then," said the Laconians, "we shall depart whenever the men who obtained these possessions for you, have received their pay; failing that, we intend here and now to lend them our assistance and to punish the men who, in violation of their oaths, have done them wrong. And if you belong to that number, it is with you that we shall begin in obtaining their rights." Then Xenophon said: "Would you be willing, Medosades, to leave the question to these people (since you say that they are your friends) in whose country we are, to vote, one way or the other, whether it is proper for you or ourselves to depart from their country?" Medosades said no to that; but he urged, as his preference, that the two Laconians should go to Seuthes themselves about the pay, and said that he thought they might persuade Seuthes; or if they would not consent to go, he asked them to send Xenophon along with himself, and promised to support him. And he begged them not to burn the villages.

20 Ἐντεῦθεν πέμπουσι Ξενοφῶντα καὶ σὺν αὐτῷ οἳ
ἐδόκουν ἐπιτηδειότατοι εἶναι. ὁ δὲ ἐλθὼν λέγει πρὸς

21 τὸν Σεύθην· Οὐδὲν ἀπαιτήσων, ὦ Σεύθη, πάρειμί σε,
ἀλλὰ διδάξων, ἢν δύνωμαι, ὡς οὐ δικαίως μοι
ἠχθέσθης ὅτι ὑπὲρ τῶν στρατιωτῶν ἀπῄτουν σε ἃ
ὑπέσχου αὐτοῖς προθύμως· σοὶ γὰρ ἔγωγε οὐχ ἧττον
ἐνόμιζον εἶναι σύμφορον ἀποδοῦναι ἢ ἐκείνοις ἀπολα-

22 βεῖν. πρῶτον μὲν γὰρ οἶδα μετὰ τοὺς θεοὺς εἰς τὸ
φανερόν σε τούτους καταστήσαντας, ἐπεί γε βασιλέα
σε ἐποίησαν πολλῆς χώρας καὶ πολλῶν ἀνθρώπων·
ὥστε οὐχ οἷόν τέ σοι λανθάνειν οὔτε ἤν τι καλὸν οὔτε

23 ἤν τι αἰσχρὸν ποιήσῃς. τοιούτῳ δὲ ὄντι ἀνδρὶ μέγα
μέν μοι δοκεῖ εἶναι μὴ δοκεῖν ἀχαρίστως ἀποπέμψα-
σθαι ἄνδρας εὐεργέτας, μέγα δὲ εὖ ἀκούειν ὑπὸ ἑξα-
κισχιλίων ἀνθρώπων, τὸ δὲ μέγιστον μηδαμῶς ἄπι-

24 στον σαυτὸν καταστῆσαι ὅ τι λέγοις. ὁρῶ γὰρ τῶν
μὲν ἀπίστων ματαίους καὶ ἀδυνάτους καὶ ἀτίμους τοὺς
λόγους πλανωμένους· οἳ δ' ἂν φανεροὶ ὦσιν ἀλήθειαν
ἀσκοῦντες, τούτων οἱ λόγοι, ἤν τι δέωνται, οὐδὲν μεῖον
δύνανται ἀνύσασθαι ἢ ἄλλων ἡ βία· ἤν τέ τινας
σωφρονίζειν βούλωνται, γιγνώσκω τὰς τούτων ἀπει-
λὰς οὐχ ἧττον σωφρονιζούσας ἢ ἄλλων τὸ ἤδη κολά-
ζειν· ἤν τέ τῳ τι ὑπισχνῶνται οἱ τοιοῦτοι ἄνδρες, οὐδὲν
μείω διαπράττονται ἢ ἄλλοι παραχρῆμα διδόντες.

---

[51] Cf. the enumeration of the "Ten Thousand" in V. iii. 3, and
see especially ii. 3–4 and 6.

Thereupon they sent Xenophon, and with him the men who seemed to be fittest. When he had come, he said to Seuthes: " I am here, Seuthes, not to present you any demand, but to show you, if I can, that you were wrong in getting angry with me because in the name of the soldiers I zealously demanded from you what you had promised them; for I believed that it was no less to your advantage to pay them than it was to theirs to get their pay. For, in the first place, I know that next to the gods it was these men who set you in a conspicuous position, since they made you king over a large territory and many people; hence it is not possible for you to escape notice, whether you perform an honourable deed or a base one. Now it seems to me an important thing that a man in such a place should not be thought to have dismissed benefactors without gratitude, an important thing also to be well spoken of by six thousand men,[51] but most important of all that you should by no means set yourself down as untrustworthy in whatever you say. For I see that the words of untrustworthy men wander here and there without result, without power, and without honour; but if men are seen to practise truth, their words, if they desire anything, have power to accomplish no less than force in the hands of other men; and if they wish to bring one to reason, I perceive that their threats can do this no less than present chastisement applied by others; and if such men make a promise to any one, they accomplish no less than others do by an immediate gift.[52]

[52] Contrast this characterization with the virtues of Cyrus, I. ix.

25 Ἀναμνήσθητι δὲ καὶ σὺ τί προτελέσας ἡμῖν συμμάχους ἡμᾶς ἔλαβες. οἶσθ᾽ ὅτι οὐδέν· ἀλλὰ πιστευθεὶς
ἀληθεύσειν ἃ ἔλεγες ἐπῆρας τοσούτους ἀνθρώπους
συστρατεύεσθαί τε καὶ κατεργάσασθαί σοι ἀρχὴν οὐ
τριάκοντα μόνον ἀξίαν ταλάντων, ὅσα οἴονται δεῖν
26 οὗτοι νῦν ἀπολαβεῖν, ἀλλὰ πολλαπλασίων. οὐκοῦν
τοῦτο μὲν πρῶτον τὸ πιστεύεσθαί σε, τὸ καὶ τὴν
βασιλείαν σοι κατεργασάμενον, τούτων τῶν χρημάτων ὑπὸ σοῦ πιπράσκεται.

27 Ἴθι δὴ ἀναμνήσθητι πῶς μέγα ἡγοῦ τότε κατα-
πρᾶξαι ἃ νῦν καταστρεψάμενος ἔχεις. ἐγὼ μὲν εὖ οἶδ᾽
ὅτι ηὔξω ἂν τὰ νῦν πεπραγμένα μᾶλλόν σοι κατα-
πραχθῆναι ἢ πολλαπλάσια τούτων τῶν χρημάτων
28 γενέσθαι. ἐμοὶ τοίνυν μεῖζον βλάβος καὶ αἴσχιον
δοκεῖ εἶναι τὸ ταῦτα νῦν μὴ κατασχεῖν ἢ τότε μὴ
λαβεῖν, ὅσῳπερ χαλεπώτερον ἐκ πλουσίου πένητα
γενέσθαι ἢ ἀρχὴν μὴ πλουτῆσαι, καὶ ὅσῳ λυπη-
ρότερον ἐκ βασιλέως ἰδιώτην φανῆναι ἢ ἀρχὴν μὴ
29 βασιλεῦσαι. οὐκοῦν ἐπίστασαι μὲν ὅτι οἱ νῦν σοι
ὑπήκοοι γενόμενοι οὐ φιλίᾳ τῇ σῇ ἐπείσθησαν ὑπὸ
σοῦ ἄρχεσθαι ἀλλ᾽ ἀνάγκῃ, καὶ ὅτι ἐπιχειροῖεν ἂν
πάλιν ἐλεύθεροι γίγνεσθαι, εἰ μή τις αὐτοὺς φόβος
30 κατέχοι. ποτέρως οὖν οἴει μᾶλλον ἂν φοβεῖσθαί τε
αὐτοὺς καὶ σωφρονεῖν τὰ πρὸς σέ, εἰ ὁρῷέν σοι τοὺς
στρατιώτας οὕτω διακειμένους ὡς νῦν τε μένοντας ἄν,
εἰ σὺ κελεύοις, αὖθίς τ᾽ ἂν ταχὺ ἐλθόντας, εἰ δέοι,
ἄλλους τε τούτων περὶ σοῦ ἀκούοντας πολλὰ ἀγαθὰ

"Recall for yourself what amount you paid to us in advance in order to obtain us as allies. You know that it was nothing; but because you were trusted to carry out truthfully whatever you said, you induced that great body of men to take the field with you and to gain for you a realm worth not merely thirty talents, the sum which these men think they ought now to recover, but many times as much. First of all, then, your trustworthiness, the very thing which gained your kingdom for you, is being sold by you for this sum.

"Come, now, recall how great a thing you then deemed it to achieve the conquests which you now have achieved. For my part, I am sure you would have prayed that the deeds now done might be accomplished for you rather than that many times that amount of money might fall to your lot. Now I count it greater hurt and shame not to hold these possessions firmly now than not to have gained them then, by so much as it is a harder fate to become poor after being rich than not to become rich at all, and by so much as it is more painful to be found a subject after being a king than not to become king at all. You understand, then, that those who have now become your subjects were not persuaded to live under your rule out of affection for you, but by stress of necessity, and that unless some fear should - restrain them, they would endeavour to become free again. In which of these two cases, therefore, do you think they would feel greater fear and be more moderate in their relations with you: if they should see the soldiers cherishing such feelings toward you that they would stay with you now if you so bade them and would quickly come back to you again if you needed them, and should see also that others, hearing many good things about you from these

ταχὺ ἄν σοι ὁπότε βούλοιο παραγενέσθαι, ἢ εἰ κατα-
δοξάσειαν μήτ᾽ ἂν ἄλλους σοι ἐλθεῖν δι᾽ ἀπιστίαν ἐκ
τῶν νῦν γεγενημένων τούτους τε αὐτοῖς εὐνουστέρους
31 εἶναι ἢ σοί· ἀλλὰ μὴν οὐδὲ πλήθει γε ἡμῶν λειφθέντες
ὑπείξάν σοι, ἀλλὰ προστατῶν ἀπορίᾳ. οὐκοῦν νῦν καὶ
τοῦτο κίνδυνος μὴ λάβωσι προστάτας αὑτῶν τινας
τούτων οἳ νομίζουσιν ὑπὸ σοῦ ἀδικεῖσθαι. ἢ καὶ
τούτων κρείττονας τοὺς Λακεδαιμονίους, ἐὰν οἱ μὲν
στρατιῶται ὑπισχνῶνται προθυμότερον αὐτοῖς συ-
στρατεύσεσθαι, ἂν τὰ παρὰ σοῦ νῦν ἀναπράξωσιν, οἱ
δὲ Λακεδαιμόνιοι διὰ τὸ δεῖσθαι τῆς στρατιᾶς συν-
32 αινέσωσιν αὐτοῖς ταῦτα. ὅτι γε μὴν οἱ νῦν ὑπὸ σοὶ
Θρᾷκες γενόμενοι πολὺ ἂν προθυμότερον ἴοιεν ἐπί σε
ἢ σύν σοι οὐκ ἄδηλον· σοῦ μὲν γὰρ κρατοῦντος
δουλεία ὑπάρχει αὐτοῖς, κρατουμένου δέ σου ἐλευθερία.

33   Εἰ δὲ καὶ τῆς χώρας προνοεῖσθαι ἤδη τι δεῖ ὡς
σῆς οὔσης, ποτέρως ἂν οἴει ἀπαθῆ κακῶν μᾶλλον
αὐτὴν εἶναι, εἰ οὗτοι οἱ στρατιῶται ἀπολαβόντες ἃ
ἐγκαλοῦσιν εἰρήνην καταλιπόντες οἴχοιντο, ἢ εἰ οὗτοί
τε μένοιεν ὡς ἐν πολεμίᾳ σύ τε ἄλλους πειρῷο πλέονας
τούτων ἔχων ἀντιστρατοπεδεύεσθαι δεομένους τῶν
34 ἐπιτηδείων· ἀργύριον δὲ ποτέρως ἂν πλέον ἀναλωθείη,
εἰ τούτοις τὸ ὀφειλόμενον ἀποδοθείη, ἢ εἰ ταῦτά τε
ὀφείλοιντο ἄλλους τε κρείττονας δέοι σε μισθοῦσθαι;

troops, would quickly present themselves to take service with you whenever you wished it—or if they should form the unkind opinion that no other soldiers would come to you, in consequence of a distrust resulting from what has now happened, and that these whom you have are more friendly to them than to you? Again, it was by no means because they fell short of us in numbers that they yielded to you, but because they lacked leaders. Hence there is now danger on this count also, the danger that they may find leaders in some of these soldiers who regard themselves as wronged by you, or else in men who are even stronger than these are—I mean the Lacedaemonians—in case the soldiers promise to render them more zealous service if they now exact what is due from you, and in case the Lacedaemonians, on account of their needing the army, grant them this request. Again, that the Thracians who have now fallen under your sway would far more eagerly go against you than with you, is quite certain; for when you are conqueror their lot is slavery, and when you are conquered it is freedom.

"And if you need henceforth to take some thought for the sake of this land also, seeing that it is yours, in which case do you suppose it would be freer from ills: if these soldiers should recover what they claim and go away leaving a state of peace behind them, or if they should remain as in a hostile country and you should undertake to maintain an opposing camp with other troops, that would have to be more numerous than these and would need provisions? And in which case would more money be spent, if what is owing to these men should be paid over to them, or if this sum should be left owing and you should have to hire other troops stronger than they are? Yes, but Hera-

35 ἀλλὰ γὰρ Ἡρακλείδῃ, ὡς πρὸς ἐμὲ ἐδήλου, πάμπολυ
δοκεῖ τοῦτο τὸ ἀργύριον εἶναι. ἦ μὴν πολύ γέ ἐστιν
ἔλαττον νῦν σοι καὶ λαβεῖν τοῦτο καὶ ἀποδοῦναι ἢ
36 πρὶν ἡμᾶς ἐλθεῖν πρὸς σὲ δέκατον τούτου μέρος. οὐ
γὰρ ὁ ἀριθμός ἐστιν ὁ ὁρίζων τὸ πολὺ καὶ τὸ ὀλίγον,
ἀλλ᾿ ἡ δύναμις τοῦ τε ἀποδιδόντος καὶ τοῦ λαμβάνον-
τος. σοὶ δὲ νῦν ἡ κατ᾿ ἐνιαυτὸν πρόσοδος πλείων ἔσται
ἢ ἔμπροσθεν τὰ παρόντα πάντα ἃ ἐκέκτησο.

37 Ἐγὼ μέν, ὦ Σεύθη, ταῦτα ὡς φίλου ὄντος σου
προυνοούμην, ὅπως σύ τε ἄξιος δοκοίης εἶναι ὧν οἱ
θεοί σοι ἔδωκαν ἀγαθῶν ἐγώ τε μὴ διαφθαρείην ἐν τῇ
38 στρατιᾷ. εὖ γὰρ ἴσθι ὅτι νῦν ἐγὼ οὔτ᾿ ἂν ἐχθρὸν
βουλόμενος κακῶς ποιῆσαι δυνηθείην σὺν ταύτῃ τῇ
στρατιᾷ οὔτ᾿ ἂν εἴ σοι πάλιν βουλοίμην βοηθῆσαι,
ἱκανὸς ἂν γενοίμην· οὕτω γὰρ πρὸς ἐμὲ ἡ στρατιὰ
39 διάκειται. καίτοι αὐτόν σε μάρτυρα σὺν θεοῖς εἰδόσι
ποιοῦμαι ὅτι οὔτε ἔχω παρὰ σοῦ ἐπὶ τοῖς στρατιώταις
οὐδὲν οὔτε ᾔτησα πώποτε εἰς τὸ ἴδιον τὰ ἐκείνων οὔτε
40 ἃ ὑπέσχου μοι ἀπῄτησα· ὄμνυμι δέ σοι μηδὲ ἀποδιδόντος δέξασθαι ἄν, εἰ μὴ καὶ οἱ στρατιῶται ἔμελλον τὰ ἑαυτῶν συναπολαμβάνειν. αἰσχρὸν γὰρ ἦν τὰ
μὲν ἐμὰ διαπεπρᾶχθαι, τὰ δ᾿ ἐκείνων περιιδεῖν ἐμὲ
κακῶς ἔχοντα, ἄλλως τε καὶ τιμώμενον ὑπ᾿ ἐκείνων.
41 καίτοι Ἡρακλείδῃ γε λῆρος πάντα δοκεῖ εἶναι πρὸς
τὸ ἀργύριον ἔχειν ἐκ παντὸς τρόπου· ἐγὼ δέ, ὦ Σεύθη,
οὐδὲν νομίζω ἀνδρὶ ἄλλως τε καὶ ἄρχοντι κάλλιον
εἶναι κτῆμα οὐδὲ λαμπρότερον ἀρετῆς καὶ δικαιο-

cleides thinks, as he used to explain to me, that this sum of money is a very large one. Upon my word it is a far smaller thing now for you to receive or to pay this sum than it would have been before we came to you to receive or to pay a tenth part of it. For it is not the number that determines what is much and what is little, but the capacity of the man who pays and of him who receives. And as for yourself, your yearly income is going to be greater now than all the property you possessed amounted to before.

"For my part, Seuthes, it was out of regard for you as a friend that I urged this course, in order that you might be deemed worthy of the good things which the gods have given to you and that I might not lose credit with the army. For be well assured that at present if I should wish to inflict harm upon a foe, I could not do it with this army, and if I should wish to come to your assistance again, I should not find myself able to do that; such is the feeling of the army toward me. And yet I make your own self my witness, along with the gods, who know, that I have neither received anything from you that was intended for the soldiers, nor have ever asked what was theirs for my private use, nor demanded from you what you had promised me; and I swear to you that even if you had offered to pay what was due to me, I should not have accepted it unless the soldiers also were at the same time to recover what was due to them. For it would have been disgraceful to get my own affairs arranged and for me to ignore theirs in an evil state, especially since I was honoured by them. And yet Heracleides thinks that everything is but nonsense in comparison with possessing money, by every means; but I believe, Seuthes, that no possession is more honourable for a man, especially a commander, or more splendid than valour and justice and

42 σύνης καὶ γενναιότητος. ὁ γὰρ ταῦτα ἔχων πλουτεῖ
μὲν ὄντων φίλων πολλῶν, πλουτεῖ δὲ καὶ ἄλλων βουλομένων γενέσθαι, καὶ εὖ μὲν πράττων ἔχει τοὺς
συνησθησομένους, ἐὰν δέ τι σφαλῇ, οὐ σπανίζει τῶν
βοηθησόντων.

43 Ἀλλὰ γὰρ εἰ μήτε ἐκ τῶν ἐμῶν ἔργων κατέμαθες
ὅτι σοι ἐκ τῆς ψυχῆς φίλος ἦν, μήτε ἐκ τῶν ἐμῶν
λόγων δύνασαι τοῦτο γνῶναι, ἀλλὰ τοὺς τῶν στρατιωτῶν λόγους πάντως κατανόησον· παρῆσθα γὰρ καὶ

44 ἤκουες οὓς ἔλεγον οἱ ψέγειν ἐμὲ βουλόμενοι. κατη-
γόρουν μὲν γάρ μου πρὸς Λακεδαιμονίους ὡς σὲ περὶ
πλείονος ποιοίμην ἢ Λακεδαιμονίους, αὐτοὶ δ᾽ ἐνεκάλουν ἐμοὶ ὡς μᾶλλον μέλοι μοι ὅπως τὰ σὰ καλῶς
ἔχοι ἢ ὅπως τὰ ἑαυτῶν· ἔφασαν δέ με καὶ δῶρα ἔχειν

45 παρὰ σοῦ. καίτοι τὰ δῶρα ταῦτα πότερον οἴει αὐτοὺς
κακόνοιάν τινα ἐνιδόντας μοι πρὸς σὲ αἰτιᾶσθαί με
ἔχειν παρὰ σοῦ ἢ προθυμίαν πολλὴν περὶ σὲ

46 κατανοήσαντας; ἐγὼ μὲν οἶμαι πάντας ἀνθρώπους
νομίζειν εὔνοιαν δεῖν ἀποκεῖσθαι τούτῳ παρ᾽ οὗ ἂν
δῶρά τις λαμβάνῃ. σὺ δὲ πρὶν μὲν ὑπηρετῆσαί τί σοι
ἐμὲ ἐδέξω ἡδέως καὶ ὄμμασι καὶ φωνῇ καὶ ξενίοις καὶ
ὅσα ἔσοιτο ὑπισχνούμενος οὐκ ἐνεπίμπλασο· ἐπεὶ δὲ
κατέπραξας ἃ ἐβούλου καὶ γεγένησαι ὅσον ἐγὼ ἐδυνάμην μέγιστος, νῦν οὕτω με ἄτιμον ὄντα ἐν τοῖς

47 στρατιώταις τολμᾷς περιορᾶν; ἀλλὰ μὴν ὅτι σοι δόξει
ἀποδοῦναι πιστεύω καὶ τὸν χρόνον διδάξειν σε καὶ

generosity.[53] For he who possesses these things is rich because many are his friends, and rich because still others desire to become his friends; if he prospers he has those who will rejoice with him, and if he meets with a mischance he does not lack those who will come to his aid.

"But if you neither learned from my deeds that I was your friend from the bottom of my heart nor are able to perceive this from my words, at any rate give a thought to what the soldiers say; for you were present and heard what those who wished to censure me said. On the one hand they accused me before the Lacedaemonians of regarding you more highly than I did the Lacedaemonians, while on their own account they charged me with being more concerned that your affairs should be well than that their own should be; and they also said that I was receiving gifts from you. And yet, touching these gifts, do you imagine it was because they had observed in me some ill-will toward you that they charged me with having received them from you, or because they perceived in me abundant good-will for you? For my part, I presume that everybody believes he ought to reserve good-will for the man from whom he receives gifts. You, however, before I had rendered you any service, welcomed me with a pleasure which you showed by your eyes, your voice, and your hospitality, and you could not make promises enough about all that should be done for me; yet now that you have accomplished what you desired and have become as great as I could possibly make you, have you now the heart to allow me to be held in such dishonour among the soldiers? But truly I have confidence, not only that time will teach you that you must resolve to

53 Again, compare Cyrus, I. ix.

αὐτόν γέ σε οὐχὶ ἀνέξεσθαι τοὺς σοὶ προεμένους
εὐεργεσίαν ὁρῶντά σοι ἐγκαλοῦντας. δέομαι οὖν σου,
ὅταν ἀποδιδῷς, προθυμεῖσθαι ἐμὲ παρὰ τοῖς στρατιώταις τοιοῦτον ποιῆσαι οἷόνπερ καὶ παρέλαβες.

48 Ἀκούσας ταῦτα ὁ Σεύθης κατηράσατο τῷ αἰτίῳ τοῦ
μὴ πάλαι ἀποδεδόσθαι τὸν μισθόν· καὶ πάντες Ἡρακλείδην τοῦτον ὑπώπτευσαν εἶναι· ἐγὼ γάρ, ἔφη, οὔτε
49 διενοήθην πώποτε ἀποστερῆσαι ἀποδώσω τε. ἐντεῦθεν
πάλιν εἶπεν ὁ Ξενοφῶν· Ἐπεὶ τοίνυν διανοεῖ ἀποδιδόναι, νῦν ἐγώ σου δέομαι δι᾽ ἐμοῦ ἀποδιδόναι, καὶ
μὴ περιιδεῖν με διὰ σὲ ἀνομοίως ἔχοντα ἐν τῇ στρατιᾷ
50 νῦν τε καὶ ὅτε πρὸς σὲ ἀφικόμεθα. ὁ δ᾽ εἶπεν· Ἀλλ᾽
οὔτ᾽ ἐν τοῖς στρατιώταις ἔσει δι᾽ ἐμὲ ἀτιμότερος ἄν τε
μένῃς παρ᾽ ἐμοὶ χιλίους μόνους ὁπλίτας ἔχων, ἐγώ
51 σοι τά τε χωρία ἀποδώσω καὶ τἆλλα ἃ ὑπεσχόμην. ὁ
δὲ πάλιν εἶπε· Ταῦτα μὲν ἔχειν οὕτως οὐχ οἷόν τε·
ἀπόπεμπε δὲ ἡμᾶς. Καὶ μήν, ἔφη ὁ Σεύθης, καὶ ἀσφαλέστερόν γέ σοι οἶδα ὂν παρ᾽ ἐμοὶ μένειν ἢ ἀπιέναι. ὁ
52 δὲ πάλιν εἶπεν· Ἀλλὰ τὴν μὲν σὴν πρόνοιαν ἐπαινῶ·
ἐμοὶ δὲ μένειν οὐχ οἷόν τε· ὅπου δ᾽ ἂν ἐγὼ ἐντιμότερος
53 ὦ, νόμιζε καὶ σοὶ τοῦτο ἀγαθὸν ἔσεσθαι. ἐντεῦθεν
λέγει Σεύθης· Ἀργύριον μὲν οὐκ ἔχω ἀλλ᾽ ἢ μικρόν
τι, καὶ τοῦτό σοι δίδωμι, τάλαντον· βοῦς δὲ ἑξακοσίους καὶ πρόβατα εἰς τετρακισχίλια καὶ ἀνδράποδα
εἰς εἴκοσι καὶ ἑκατόν. ταῦτα λαβὼν καὶ τοὺς τῶν
54 ἀδικησάντων σε ὁμήρους προσλαβὼν ἄπιθι. γελάσας

pay what is due, but also that you will not yourself endure
to see those men who have freely given you good service,
accusing you. I ask you, therefore, when you render payment, to use all zeal to make me just such a man in the eyes
of the soldiers as I was when you made me your friend."

Upon hearing these words Seuthes cursed the man who
was to blame for the fact that the soldiers' wages had not
been paid long ago; and everybody suspected that Heracleides was that man; "for I," said Seuthes, "never intended
to defraud them, and I will pay over the money." Thereupon Xenophon said again: "Then since you intend to
make payment, I now request you to do it through me, and
not to allow me to have, on your account, a different standing with the army now from what I had at the time when
we came to you." And Seuthes replied: "But you will not
be less honoured among the soldiers on my account if you
will stay with me, keeping only a thousand hoplites, and,
besides, I will give over the fortresses to you and the other
things that I promised." And Xenophon answered: "This
plan is not a possible one; so dismiss us." "Yet really," said
Seuthes, "I know that it is also safer for you to stay with me
than to go away." And Xenophon replied: "Well, I thank
you for your solicitude; it is not possible, however, for me
to stay; but wherever I may enjoy greater honour, be sure
that it will be a good thing for you as well as myself."
Thereupon Seuthes said: "As for ready money, I have only
a little, and that I give you, a talent;[54] but I have six hundred
cattle, and sheep to the number of four thousand, and
nearly a hundred and twenty slaves. Take these, and likewise the hostages of the people who wronged you,[55] and

[54] See note on I. vii. 18.   [55] Cf. iv. 12–24.

ὁ Ξενοφῶν εἶπεν· Ἦν οὖν μὴ ἐξικνῆται ταῦτ᾽ εἰς τὸν
μισθόν, τίνος τάλαντον φήσω ἔχειν; ἆρ᾽ οὐκ, ἐπειδὴ
καὶ ἐπικίνδυνόν μοί ἐστιν, ἀπιόντα γε ἄμεινον φυλάττεσθαι πέτρους; ἤκουες δὲ τὰς ἀπειλάς. τότε μὲν δὴ
αὐτοῦ ἔμεινε.

55   Τῇ δ᾽ ὑστεραίᾳ ἀπέδωκέ τε αὐτοῖς ἃ ὑπέσχετο καὶ
τοὺς ἐλῶντας συνέπεμψεν. οἱ δὲ στρατιῶται τέως μὲν
ἔλεγον ὡς ὁ Ξενοφῶν οἴχοιτο ὡς Σεύθην οἰκήσων καὶ
ἃ ὑπέσχετο αὐτῷ ἀποληψόμενος· ἐπεὶ δὲ αὐτὸν ἥκοντα
56   εἶδον, ἤσθησαν καὶ προσέθεον. Ξενοφῶν δ᾽ ἐπεὶ εἶδε
Χαρμῖνόν τε καὶ Πολύνικον, Ταῦτα, ἔφη, καὶ σέσωσται δι᾽ ὑμᾶς τῇ στρατιᾷ καὶ παραδίδωμι αὐτὰ ἐγὼ
ὑμῖν· ὑμεῖς δὲ διαθέμενοι διάδοτε τῇ στρατιᾷ. οἱ μὲν
οὖν παραλαβόντες καὶ λαφυροπώλας καταστήσαντες
57   ἐπώλουν, καὶ πολλὴν εἶχον αἰτίαν. Ξενοφῶν δὲ οὐ
προσῄει, ἀλλὰ φανερὸς ἦν οἴκαδε παρασκευαζόμενος·
οὐ γάρ πω ψῆφος αὐτῷ ἐπῆκτο Ἀθήνησι περὶ φυγῆς.
προσελθόντες δὲ αὐτῷ οἱ ἐπιτήδειοι ἐν τῷ στρατοπέδῳ
ἐδέοντο μὴ ἀπελθεῖν πρὶν ἂν ἀπαγάγοι τὸ στράτευμα
καὶ Θίβρωνι παραδοίη.

VIII. Ἐντεῦθεν διέπλευσαν εἰς Λάμψακον, καὶ
ἀπαντᾷ τῷ Ξενοφῶντι Εὐκλείδης μάντις Φλειάσιος ὁ
Κλεαγόρου υἱὸς τοῦ τὰ ἐντοίχια[13] ἐν Λυκείῳ γεγρα-

---

[13] ἐντοίχια anonymous: ἐνύπνια some MSS.: others ἐνοίκια
(ἐν οἰκία): ἐνώπια Toup. See A. Lippold, RE XI, 556.

---

56 With reference to vi. 10.

go your way." Xenophon laughed and said: "Now supposing all this does not suffice to cover the amount of the pay, whose talent shall I say I have? Would I not better, seeing that it is really a source of danger to me, be on my guard against stones[56] on my way back? For you heard the threats." For the time, then, he remained there at Seuthes' quarters.

On the next day Seuthes delivered over to them what he had promised, and sent men with them to drive the cattle. As for the soldiers, up to this time they had been saying that Xenophon had gone off to Seuthes to dwell with him and to receive what Seuthes had promised him; but when they caught sight of him having arrived, they were delighted, and ran out to meet him. As soon as Xenophon saw Charminus and Polynicus, he said to them: "This property has been saved for the army through you, and to you I turn it over; do you, then, dispose of it and make the distribution to the army." They, accordingly, took it over, appointed booty-vendors, and proceeded to sell it; and they incurred a great deal of blame. As for Xenophon, he would not go near them, but it was plain that he was making preparations for his homeward journey; for not yet had sentence of exile been pronounced against him at Athens.[57] His friends in the camp, however, came to him and begged him not to depart until he should lead the army away and turn it over to Thibron.

VIII. From there they sailed across to Lampsacus, where Xenophon was met by Eucleides, the Phliasian seer, son of the Cleagoras who painted the murals in the Ly-

[57] The precise date of Xenophon's banishment is uncertain. See Intro.

φότος. οὗτος συνήδετο τῷ Ξενοφῶντι ὅτι ἐσέσωστο,
2 καὶ ἠρώτα αὐτὸν πόσον χρυσίον ἔχει. ὁ δ᾽ αὐτῷ
ἐπομόσας εἶπεν ἦ μὴν ἔσεσθαι μηδὲ ἐφόδιον ἱκανὸν
οἴκαδε ἀπιόντι, εἰ μὴ ἀπόδοιτο τὸν ἵππον καὶ ἃ ἀμφ᾽
3 αὐτὸν εἶχεν. ὁ δ᾽ αὐτῷ οὐκ ἐπίστευεν. ἐπεὶ δ᾽ ἔπεμψαν
Λαμψακηνοὶ ξένια τῷ Ξενοφῶντι καὶ ἔθυε τῷ Ἀπόλλωνι, παρεστήσατο τὸν Εὐκλείδην· ἰδὼν δὲ τὰ ἱερὰ
Εὐκλείδης εἶπεν ὅτι πείθοιτο αὐτῷ μὴ εἶναι χρήματα.
Ἀλλ᾽ οἶδα, ἔφη, ὅτι κἂν μέλλῃ ποτὲ ἔσεσθαι, φαίνεταί
τι ἐμπόδιον, ἂν μηδὲν ἄλλο, σὺ σαυτῷ. συνομολόγει
4 ταῦτα ὁ Ξενοφῶν. ὁ δὲ εἶπεν· Ἐμπόδιος γάρ σοι ὁ
Ζεὺς ὁ μειλίχιός ἐστι, καὶ ἐπήρετο εἰ ἤδη θύσειεν,
ὥσπερ οἴκοι, ἔφη, εἰώθειν ἐγὼ ὑμῖν θύεσθαι καὶ
ὁλοκαυτεῖν. ὁ δ᾽ οὐκ ἔφη ἐξ ὅτου ἀπεδήμησε τεθυκέναι
τούτῳ τῷ θεῷ. συνεβούλευσεν οὖν αὐτῷ θύεσθαι καθὰ
5 εἰώθει, καὶ ἔφη συνοίσειν ἐπὶ τὸ βέλτιον. τῇ δὲ
ὑστεραίᾳ Ξενοφῶν προσελθὼν εἰς Ὀφρύνιον ἐθύετο
καὶ ὡλοκαύτει χοίρους τῷ πατρίῳ νόμῳ, καὶ καλ-
6 λιερεῖται. καὶ ταύτῃ τῇ ἡμέρᾳ ἀφικνεῖται Βίτων καὶ
Ναυσικλείδης χρήματα δώσοντες τῷ στρατεύματι καὶ
ξενοῦνταί τε τῷ Ξενοφῶντι, καὶ ἵππον ὃν ἐν Λαμψάκῳ
ἀπέδοτο πεντήκοντα δαρεικῶν, ὑποπτεύοντες αὐτὸν δι᾽
ἔνδειαν πεπρακέναι, ὅτι ἤκουον αὐτὸν ἥδεσθαι τῷ

---

58 The famous gymnasium at Athens. This Eucleides is otherwise unknown.

59 i.e. Zeus in this particular one of his functions, as "the Merciful." cf. vi. 44

ceum.[58] Eucleides congratulated Xenophon upon his safe return, and asked him how much gold he had got. He replied, swearing to the truth of his statement, that he would not have even enough money to pay his travelling expenses on the way home unless he should sell his horse and what he had about his person. And Eucleides would not believe him. But when the Lampsacenes sent gifts of hospitality to Xenophon and he was sacrificing to Apollo, he gave Eucleides a place beside him; and when Eucleides saw the vitals of the victims, he said that he well believed that Xenophon had no money. "But I am sure," he went on, "that even if money should ever be about to come to you, some obstacle always appears—if nothing else, your own self." In this Xenophon agreed with him. Then Eucleides said, "Yes, Zeus the Merciful is an obstacle in your way," and asked whether he had yet sacrificed to him, "just as at home," he continued, "where I was wont to offer the sacrifices for you, and with whole victims." Xenophon replied that not since he left home had he sacrificed to that god.[59] Eucleides, accordingly, advised him to sacrifice just as he used to do, and said that it would be to his advantage. And the next day, upon coming to Ophrynium, Xenophon proceeded to sacrifice, offering whole victims of swine after the custom of his fathers, and he obtained favourable omens. In fact, on that very day Biton and Nausicleides[60] arrived with money to give to the army and were entertained by Xenophon, and they redeemed his horse, which he had sold at Lampsacus for fifty darics—for they suspected that he had sold it for want of money, since they

[60] Apparently officers sent by Thibron.

ἵππῳ, λυσάμενοι ἀπέδοσαν καὶ τὴν τιμὴν οὐκ ἤθελον
ἀπολαβεῖν.

7   Ἐντεῦθεν ἐπορεύοντο διὰ τῆς Τρῳάδος, καὶ ὑπερβάντες τὴν Ἴδην εἰς Ἄντανδρον ἀφικνοῦνται πρῶτον,
εἶτα παρὰ θάλατταν πορευόμενοι τῆς Μυσίας εἰς
8   Θήβης πεδίον. ἐντεῦθεν δι᾽ Ἀτραμυττείου καὶ Κερτω-
νίου ὁδεύσαντες παρ᾽ Ἀταρνέα εἰς Καΐκου πεδίον
ἐλθόντες Πέργαμον καταλαμβάνουσι τῆς Μυσίας.

Ἐνταῦθα δὴ ξενοῦται Ξενοφῶν Ἑλλάδι τῇ Γογγύ-
λου τοῦ Ἐρετριέως γυναικὶ καὶ Γοργίωνος καὶ Γογ-
9   γύλου μητρί. αὕτη δ᾽ αὐτῷ φράζει ὅτι Ἀσιδάτης ἐστὶν
ἐν τῷ πεδίῳ ἀνὴρ Πέρσης· τοῦτον ἔφη αὐτόν, εἰ ἔλθοι
τῆς νυκτὸς σὺν τριακοσίοις ἀνδράσι, λαβεῖν ἂν καὶ
αὐτὸν καὶ γυναῖκα καὶ παῖδας καὶ τὰ χρήματα· εἶναι
δὲ πολλά. ταῦτα δὲ καθηγησομένους ἔπεμψε τόν τε
αὑτῆς ἀνεψιὸν καὶ Δαφναγόραν, ὃν περὶ πλείστου
10   ἐποιεῖτο. ἔχων οὖν ὁ Ξενοφῶν τούτους παρ᾽ ἑαυτῷ
ἐθύετο. καὶ Βασίας ὁ Ἠλεῖος μάντις παρὼν εἶπεν ὅτι
κάλλιστα εἶεν τὰ ἱερὰ αὐτῷ καὶ ὁ ἀνὴρ ἁλώσιμος εἴη.
11   δειπνήσας οὖν ἐπορεύετο τούς τε λοχαγοὺς τοὺς μάλιστα φίλους λαβὼν καὶ ἄλλους[14] πιστοὺς γεγενημένους διὰ παντός, ὅπως εὖ ποιῆσαι αὐτούς. συνεξέρ-
χονται δὲ αὐτῷ καὶ ἄλλοι βιασάμενοι εἰς ἑξακοσίους·
οἱ δὲ λοχαγοὶ ἀπήλαυνον, ἵνα μὴ μεταδοῖεν τὸ μέρος,

[14] ἄλλους inserted by Hug, whom Mar. inclines to follow:
Gem. emends by inserting τε before μάλιστα.

heard he was fond of the horse—gave it back to him, and would not accept from him the price of it.

From there they marched through the Troad and, crossing over Mount Ida, arrived first at Antandrus, and then, proceeding along the coast, reached the plain of Thebe in Mysia. Making their way from there through Adramyttium and Certonium, they travelled by Atarneus and came to the plain of the Caïcus and so reached Pergamum, in Mysia.

Here Xenophon was entertained by Hellas, the wife of Gongylus[61] the Eretrian and mother of Gorgion and Gongylus. She told him that there was a Persian in the plain named Asidates, and said that if he should go by night with three hundred troops, he could capture this man, along with his wife and children and property, of which he had a great deal. And she sent as guides for this enterprise not only her own cousin, but also Daphnagoras, whom she regarded very highly. Xenophon, accordingly, proceeded to sacrifice, keeping these two by his side. And Basias, the Elean seer who was present, said that the omens were extremely favourable for him and that the man was easy to capture. So after dinner he set forth, taking with him the captains who were his closest friends and others who had proved themselves trustworthy throughout, in order that he might do them a good turn. But there joined him still others who forced themselves in, to the number of six hundred; and the captains tried to drive them away, so that they might not have to give them a share in the booty—just

---

[61] Whose ancestor (father?), according to *Hell*. III. i. 6, had been given four cities in this neighbourhood by Xerxes "because he espoused the Persian cause, being the only man among the Eretrians who did so, and was therefore banished." Cf. II. i. 3 and note. See Briant, *Histoire* I, 517.

ὡς ἑτοίμων δὴ χρημάτων.

12 Ἐπεὶ δὲ ἀφίκοντο περὶ μέσας νύκτας, τὰ μὲν πέριξ
ὄντα ἀνδράποδα τῆς τύρσιος καὶ χρήματα τὰ πλεῖστα
ἀπέδρα αὐτοὺς παραμελοῦντας, ὡς τὸν Ἀσιδάτην αὐ-
13 τὸν λάβοιεν καὶ τὰ ἐκείνου. πυργομαχοῦντες δὲ ἐπεὶ
οὐκ ἐδύναντο τὴν τύρσιν ἑλεῖν—ὑψηλὴ γὰρ ἦν καὶ
μεγάλη καὶ προμαχεῶνας καὶ ἄνδρας πολλοὺς καὶ
μαχίμους ἔχουσα—διορύττειν ἐπεχείρησαν τὸν πύρ-
14 γον. ὁ δὲ τοῖχος ἦν ἐπ' ὀκτὼ πλίνθων γηίνων τὸ εὖρος.
ἅμα δὲ τῇ ἡμέρᾳ διωρώρυκτο· καὶ ὡς τὸ πρῶτον
διεφάνη, ἐπάταξεν ἔνδοθεν βουπόρῳ τις ὀβελίσκῳ
διαμπερὲς τὸν μηρὸν τοῦ ἐγγυτάτω· τὸ δὲ λοιπὸν
ἐκτοξεύοντες ἐποίουν μηδὲ παριέναι ἔτι ἀσφαλὲς εἶναι.
15 κεκραγότων δὲ αὐτῶν καὶ πυρσευόντων ἐκβοηθοῦσιν
Ἰταμένης μὲν ἔχων τὴν ἑαυτοῦ δύναμιν, ἐκ Κομανίας
δὲ ὁπλῖται Ἀσσύριοι καὶ Ὑρκάνιοι ἱππεῖς καὶ οὗτοι
βασιλέως μισθοφόροι ὡς ὀγδοήκοντα, καὶ ἄλλοι πελτασταὶ εἰς ὀκτακοσίους, ἄλλοι δ' ἐκ Παρθενίου, ἄλλοι
δ' ἐξ Ἀπολλωνίας καὶ ἐκ τῶν πλησίον χωρίων καὶ
ἱππεῖς.

16 Ἐνταῦθα δὴ ὥρα ἦν σκοπεῖν πῶς ἔσται ἡ ἄφοδος·
καὶ λαβόντες ὅσοι ἦσαν βόες καὶ πρόβατα ἤλαυνον
καὶ ἀνδράποδα ἐντὸς πλαισίου ποιησάμενοι, οὐ τοῖς
χρήμασιν ἔτι προσέχοντες τὸν νοῦν, ἀλλὰ μὴ φυγὴ
εἴη ἡ ἄφοδος, εἰ καταλιπόντες τὰ χρήματα ἀπίοιεν,
καὶ οἵ τε πολέμιοι θρασύτεροι εἶεν καὶ οἱ στρατιῶται
ἀθυμότεροι· νῦν δὲ ἀπῇσαν ὡς περὶ τῶν χρημάτων

as though the property was already in hand.

When they reached the place, about midnight, the slaves that were round about the tower and most of the animals ran away, the Greeks leaving them unheeded in order to capture Asidates himself and his belongings. And when they found themselves unable to take the tower by storm (for it was high and large, and furnished with battlements and a considerable force of warlike defenders), they attempted to dig through the tower-wall. Now the wall had a thickness of eight earthen bricks. At daybreak, however, a breach had been made; and just as soon as the light showed through, some one from within struck with an ox-spit clean through the thigh of the man who was nearest the hole; and from that time on they kept shooting out arrows and so made it unsafe even to pass by the place any more. Then, as the result of their shouting and lighting of beacon fires, there came to their assistance Itamenes with his own force, and from Comania Assyrian hoplites and Hyrcanian horsemen—these also being mercenaries in the service of the King—to the number of eighty, as well as about eight hundred peltasts, and more from Parthenium, and more from Apollonia and from the near-by places, including horsemen.

Then it was time to consider how the retreat was to be effected; so seizing all the cattle and sheep there were, as well as slaves, they got them inside of a hollow square and proceeded to drive them along with them, not because they were any longer giving thought to the matter of booty, but out of fear that the retreat might become a rout if they should go off and leave their booty behind, and that the enemy might become bolder and the soldiers more disheartened; while as it was, they were withdrawing like

647

17 μαχούμενοι. ἐπεὶ δὲ ἑώρα Γογγύλος ὀλίγους μὲν τοὺς
Ἕλληνας, πολλοὺς δὲ τοὺς ἐπικειμένους, ἐξέρχεται
καὶ αὐτὸς βίᾳ τῆς μητρὸς ἔχων τὴν ἑαυτοῦ δύναμιν,
βουλόμενος μετασχεῖν τοῦ ἔργου· συνεβοήθει δὲ καὶ
Προκλῆς ἐξ Ἁλισάρνης καὶ Τευθρανίας ὁ ἀπὸ Δαμα-

18 ράτου. οἱ δὲ περὶ Ξενοφῶντα ἐπεὶ πάνυ ἤδη ἐπιέζοντο
ὑπὸ τῶν τοξευμάτων καὶ σφενδονῶν, πορευόμενοι κύκλῳ, ὅπως τὰ ὅπλα ἔχοιεν πρὸ τῶν τοξευμάτων, μόλις
διαβαίνουσι τὸν Κάρκασον ποταμόν, τετρωμένοι ἐγ-

19 γὺς οἱ ἡμίσεις. ἐνταῦθα δὲ Ἀγασίας ὁ Στυμφάλιος
λοχαγὸς τιτρώσκεται, τὸν πάντα χρόνον μαχόμενος
πρὸς τοὺς πολεμίους. καὶ διασῴζονται ἀνδράποδα ὡς
διακόσια ἔχοντες καὶ πρόβατα ὅσον θύματα.

20 Τῇ δὲ ὑστεραίᾳ θυσάμενος ὁ Ξενοφῶν ἐξάγει
νύκτωρ πᾶν τὸ στράτευμα, ὅπως ὅτι μακροτάτην ἔλθοι
τῆς Λυδίας, εἰς τὸ μὴ διὰ τὸ ἐγγὺς εἶναι φοβεῖσθαι,

21 ἀλλ᾽ ἀφυλακτεῖν. ὁ δὲ Ἀσιδάτης ἀκούσας ὅτι πάλιν
ἐπ᾽ αὐτὸν τεθυμένος εἴη ὁ Ξενοφῶν καὶ παντὶ πῷ
στρατεύματι ἥξοι, ἐξαυλίζεται εἰς κώμας ὑπὸ τὸ Παρ-

22 θένιον πόλισμα ἐχούσας. ἐνταῦθα οἱ περὶ Ξενοφῶντα
συντυγχάνουσιν αὐτῷ καὶ λαμβάνουσιν αὐτὸν καὶ
γυναῖκα καὶ παῖδας καὶ τοὺς ἵππους καὶ πάντα τὰ

23 ὄντα· καὶ οὕτω τὰ πρότερα ἱερὰ ἀπέβη. ἔπειτα πάλιν
ἀφικνοῦνται εἰς Πέργαμον. ἐνταῦθα τὸν θεὸν ἠσπά-
σατο Ξενοφῶν· συνέπραττον γὰρ καὶ οἱ Λάκωνες καὶ
οἱ λοχαγοὶ καὶ οἱ ἄλλοι στρατηγοὶ καὶ οἱ στρατιῶται

men ready to fight for their possessions. But as soon as Gongylus saw that the Greeks were few and those who were attacking them many, he sallied forth himself, in spite of his mother, at the head of his own force, desiring to take part in the action; and Procles[62] also came to the rescue, from Halisarna and Teuthrania, the descendant of Damaratus. And Xenophon and his men, by this time sorely distressed by the arrows and sling-stones, and marching in a curved line in order to keep their shields facing the arrows, succeeded with difficulty in crossing the Carcasus river, almost half of their number wounded. It was here that Agasias, the Stymphalian captain, was wounded, though he continued to fight all the time against the enemy. So they came out of it in safety, with about two hundred slaves and sheep enough for sacrificial victims.

The next day Xenophon offered sacrifice, and then by night led forth the entire army with the intention of making as long a march as possible through Lydia, to the end that Asidates might not be fearful on account of their nearness, but be off his guard. Asidates, however, hearing that Xenophon had sacrificed again with a view to attacking him and that he was to come with the entire army, left his tower and encamped in villages that lay below the town of Parthenium. There Xenophon and his men fell in with him, and they captured him, his wife and children, his horses, and all that he had; and thus the omens of the earlier sacrifice proved true. After that they came back again to Pergamum. And there Xenophon paid his greeting to the god; for the Laconians, the captains, the other generals, and the soldiers joined in arranging matters so that he got the pick

62 Cf. II. i. 3 and note.

ὥστ᾽ ἐξαίρετα λαβεῖν καὶ ἵππους καὶ ζεύγη καὶ τἆλλα·
ὥστε ἱκανὸν εἶναι καὶ ἄλλον ἤδη εὖ ποιεῖν.

24   Ἐν τούτῳ Θίβρων παραγενόμενος παρέλαβε τὸ
στράτευμα καὶ συμμείξας τῷ ἄλλῳ Ἑλληνικῷ ἐπολέμει πρὸς Τισσαφέρνη καὶ Φαρνάβαζον.[15]

[15] The MSS. add the following statistical notes, which, like the
summaries prefixed to the several books (see note on II. i. l), must
have been the contribution of a late editor: Ἄρχοντες δὲ οἵδε
τῆς βασιλέως χώρας ὅσην ἐπήλθομεν. Λυδίας Ἀρτίμας,
Φρυγίας Ἀρτακάμας, Λυκαονίας καὶ Καππαδοκίας Μιθραδάτης, Κιλικίας Συέννεσις, Φοινίκης καὶ Ἀραβίας Δέρνης,
Συρίας καὶ Ἀσσυρίας Βέλεσυς, Βαβυλῶνος Ῥωπάρας, Μηδίας Ἀρβάκας, Φασιανῶν καὶ Ἑσπεριτῶν Τιρίβαζος· Καρδοῦχοι δὲ καὶ Χάλυβες καὶ Χαλδαῖοι καὶ Μάκρωνες καὶ
Κόλχοι καὶ Μοσσύνοικοι καὶ Κοῖτοι καὶ Τιβαρηνοὶ αὐτόνο-
μοι· Παφλαγονίας Κορύλας, Βιθυνῶν Φαρνάβαζος, τῶν
Εὐρώπῃ Θρᾳκῶν Σεύθης.

Ἀριθμὸς συμπάσης τῆς ὁδοῦ τῆς ἀναβάσεως καὶ καταβάσεως σταθμοὶ διακόσιοι δεκαπέντε, παρασάγγαι χίλιοι
ἑκατὸν πεντήκοντα, στάδια τρισμύρια τετρακισχίλια διακόσια πεντήκοντα πέντε. χρόνου πλῆθος τῆς ἀναβάσεως καὶ
καταβάσεως ἐνιαυτὸς καὶ τρεῖς μῆνες.

of horses and teams of oxen and all the rest; the result was, that he was now able even to do a kindness to another.

Meanwhile Thibron arrived and took over the army, and uniting it with the rest of his Greek forces, proceeded to wage war upon Tissaphernes and Pharnabazus.[63]

[63] Statistical notes (see note to text): The governors of all the King's territories that we traversed were as follows: Artimas of Lydia, Artacamas of Phrygia, Mithradates of Lycaonia and Cappadocia, Syennesis of Cilicia, Dernes of Phoenicia and Arabia, Belesys of Syria and Assyria, Rhoparas of Babylon, Arbacas of Media, Tiribazus of the Phasians and Hesperites; then the Carduchians, Chalybians, Chaldaeans, Macronians, Colchians, Mossynoecians, Coetians, and Tibarenians, who were independent; and then Corylas governor of Paphlagonia, Pharnabazus of the Bithynians, and Seuthes of the Thracians in Europe.

The length of the entire journey, upward and downward, was two hundred and fifteen stages, one thousand, one hundred and fifty parasangs, or thirty-four thousand, two hundred and fifty-five stadia; and the length in time, upward and downward, a year and three months.

[This passage is a relatively accurate sketch of Achaemenid administration: cf. A. H. D. Bivar, *Numismatic Chronicle* N.S. 1 (1961) 121–122.]

INDEX

653

INDEX

and Armenia, III.v.15, 17;
IV.i.8–11, iii.1–30, iv.1; v.v.17

Carsus, river between Cilicia
and Syria, I.iv.4

Castolus, town in Lydia, near
Sardis, I.i.2, ix.7

Castru-pedion, town in
Phrygia, I.ii.11

Celaenae, city in Phrygia,
I.ii.7–9

Centrites, river between
Armenia and the country of
the Carduchians, IV.iii.1

Cephisodorus, Athenian,
captain, IV.ii.13, 17

Cephisophon, Athenian,
IV.ii.13

Ceramon-agora, town in
Phrygia, I.ii.10

Cerasus, Greek city on the
Euxine Sea, colony of
Sinope, V.iii.2, iv.1, vii.16, 17,
19, 30

Cerasuntians, v.v.10, vii.13–30

Cerberus, watch-dog of the
lower world, VI.ii.2

Certonus, city in Mysia,
VII.viii.8

Chaldaeans, tribe in Armenia,
IV.iii.4; v.v.17

Chalus, river in Syria, I.iv.9

Chalybians, tribe in Pontus, on
northern frontier of
Armenia, IV.iv.18, v.34, vi.5,
vii.15; v.v.1

Charmande, city in Arabia, on
the Euphrates, I.v.10

Charminus, Lacedaemonian, in

service of Thibron, VII.vi.1,
39, vii.13, 15, 56

Cheirisophus, Lacedaemonian
general, commander of the
Greek vanguard in the
Retreat, I.iv.3; II.i.5, ii.1, v.37;
III.i.45, ii.1, 33, 37, iii.3, 11,
iv.38–43, v.1, 4, 6; IV.vi.6–20,
ii.8, 23, 26, iii.8–27, v.9–34,
vi.1–25, vii.2–8, viii.16;
v.i.3–10, iii.1, 4, vi.36; VI.i.16,
32, ii.6–18, iii.10–15, iv.11, 23

Chersonese, the Acherusian,
peninsula near Heracleia, in
Bithynia, VI.ii.2

Chersonese, the Thracian,
peninsula north of the
Hellespont, I.i.9, iii.4; II.vi.2;
v.vi.25; VII.i.13, ii.2, 15, iii.3,
vi.14

Chian, inh. of Chios, island
west of Lydia, IV.i.28, vi.20

Chrysopolis, city on the
Bosporus, opposite
Byzantium, VI.iii.14, vi.38

Cilicia, province on
south-eastern coast of Asia
Minor, I.ii.20, 21, 23, iv.1, 4,
5; III.i.10

Cilician, I.ii.12–25, iii.14, iv.4

Cleaenetus, captain, v.i.17

Cleagoras, Phliasian, VII.viii.1

Cleander, Lacedaemonian
governor of Byzantium,
VI.ii.13, iv.18, vi.1–35; VII.i.8,
38, 39, 40, ii.5, 6

Cleanor, Orchomenian general,
II.i.10, v.37, 39; III.i.47, ii.4, 8;

656

INDEX

INDEX

INDEX

INDEX

IV.vi.4; (2) river in Colchis, v.vi.36, vii.1, 5, 7, 9

Philesius, Achaean general, III.i.47; v.iii.1, vi.27, viii.1; VII.i.32, ii.1

Phliasian, inh. of Phlius, city in Peloponnesus, VII.viii.1

Philoxenus, Pellenean, v.ii.15

Phocaean, inh. of Phocaea, city in Ionia, I.x.2

Phoenicia, country on eastern coast of Mediterranean Sea, I.iv.5, vii.12

Phoenicians, I.iv.6

Pholoe, mountain between Arcadia and Elis, v.iii.10

Phrasias, Athenian captain, VI.v.11

Phrygia, (1) the Greater, province in central Asia Minor, I.ii.6, 7, 19, ix.7; (2) the Lesser, province in north-western Asia Minor, v.vi.24; VI.iv.24

Phrygians, inh. of Phrygia (1), I.ii.13

Phryniscus, Achaean general, VII.ii.1, 2, 29, v.4, 10

Physcus, river in Assyria, tributary of Tigris, II.iv.25

Pigres, Cyrus' interpreter, I.ii.17, v.7, viii.12

Pisidians, inh. of Pisidia, province in southern Asia Minor, I.i.11, ii.1, 4, ix.14; II.v.13; III.i.9, ii.23

Polus, Lacedaemonian admiral, VII.ii.5

Polycrates, Athenian captain, IV.v.24; v.i.16; VII.ii.17, 29, 30, vi.41

Polynicus, Lacedaemonian in service of Thibron, VII.vi.1, 39, 43, vii.13, 56

Polystratus, Athenian, III.iii.20

Pontus, (1) the Euxine or Black Sea, IV.viii.22; v.i.15, ii.2, vi.16, 20, vii.7, 15; VI.i.16, iv.1, v.20; VII.v.12; (2) the region along the south-eastern coast of the Euxine, v.vi.15, 19, 25; VI.ii.4

Procles, ruler of Teuthrania, II.i.3, ii.1; VII.viii.17

Proxenus, Boeotian general, I.i.11, ii.3, v.14, 16, viii.4, x.5; II.i.10, iv.15, 16, v.31, 37, 38, 41, vi.16; III.i.4, 8, 9, 10, 15, 34, 47; v.iii.5

Psarus, river in Cilicia, I.iv.1

Pylae, fortress on the frontier of Babylonia, I.v.5

Pyramus, river in eastern Asia Minor, I.iv.1

Pyrrhias, Arcadian captain, VI.v.11

Pythagoras, Lacedaemonian admiral, I.iv.2

Rhathines, officer under Pharnabazus, VI.v.7

Rhodians, inh. of Rhodes, island off south-western coast of Asia Minor, III.iii.16, 17, iv.15, 16, v.8

663

INDEX